Handbook of Multicultural Mental Health

Handbook of Multicultural Mental Health

ASSESSMENT AND TREATMENT OF DIVERSE POPULATIONS

Edited by

Israel Cuéllar

Department of Psychology and Anthropology
University of Texas—Pan American
Edinburg, Texas

Freddy A. Paniagua

Department of Psychiatry and Behavioral Sciences
University of Texas Medical Branch
Galveston, Texas

ACADEMIC PRESS

A Harcourt Science and Technology Company

San Diego   San Francisco   New York   Boston   London   Sydney   Tokyo

Academic Press
A Harcourt Science and Technology Company
525 B Street, Suite 1900, San Diego, California 92101-4495, U.S.A.
http://www.academicpress.com

Academic Press
24-28 Oval Road, London NW1 7DX, UK
http://www.hbuk.co.uk/ap/

Library of Congress Catalog Card Number: 99-66278

International Standard Book Number: 0-12-199370-1

PRINTED IN THE UNITED STATES OF AMERICA
00   01   02   03   04   05   EB   9   8   7   6   5   4   3   2   1

Israel Cuéllar dedicates this book to Dr. Ira Iscoe,
retired Professor of Psychology and Education,
Department of Psychology, University of Texas at Austin.

Freddy A. Paniagua dedicates this book to
Dr. Enerio Rodriguez Arias, Professor of Psychology,
Universidad Autōnoma de Santo Domingo, Dominican Republic.

In appreciation for their respective
teaching, inspiration, and invaluable mentorship.

CONTENTS

2 Cultural Models of Health and Illness
Ronald J. Angel and Kristi Williams

3 Acculturation and Mental Health: Ecological Transactional Relations of Adjustment
Israel Cuéllar

4 Gender as Subculture: The First Division of Multicultural Diversity
Genevieve Canales

5 Multicultural Demographic Developments: Current and Future Trends

Uzzer A. Raajpoot

PART II
Methodology

6 Culture and Methodology in Personality Assessment

Richard H. Dana

7 Test Translation and Cultural Equivalence Methodologies for Use with Diverse Populations

Bill R. Arnold and Yolanda E. Matus

PART **III**

Assessment and Treatment

8 Culture-Bound Syndromes, Cultural Variations, and Psychopathology

Freddy A. Paniagua

9 Assessing and Treating Asian Americans: Recent Advances

Sumie Okazaki

10 Mental Health Assessment and Treatment of African Americans: A Multicultural Perspective

Michael L. Lindsey and Israel Cuéllar

11 Assessing and Treating Latinos: Overview of Research

Andrea J. Romero

12 Assessing and Treating American Indians and Alaska Natives

Denise Anne Dillard and Spero M. Manson

13 Multicultural Issues in Treating Clients with HIV/AIDS from the African American, American Indian, Asian, and Hispanic Populations

Freddy A. Paniagua

14 The History, Current Status, and Future of Multicultural Psychotherapy

Richard M. Lee and Manuel Ramirez III

15 Conducting the Cross-Cultural Clinical Interview

Cervando Martinez

16 The Mental Health of Culturally Diverse Elderly: Research and Clinical Issues

Sandra A. Black

17 Race, Ethnicity, and the Epidemiology of Mental Disorders in Adults

Charles E. Holzer III and Sam Copeland

18 Depression and Suicidal Behaviors among Adolescents: The Role of Ethnicity

Robert E. Roberts

19 Culturally Competent Use of the Minnesota Multiphasic Personality Inventory-2 with Minorities

Roberto J. Velásquez, Guadalupe X. Ayala, Sonia A. Mendoza,
Elahe Nezami, Idalia Castillo-Canez, Terry M. Pace, Sandra K. Choney,
Francisco C. Gomez, Jr., and Lauralyn E. Miles

20 Neuropsychological Assessment of Ethnic Minorities: Clinical Issues

Antonio E. Puente and Miguel Perez-Garcia

PART **IV**

Training in Cultural Competence

21 Limitations of the Multicultural Approach to Psychotherapy with Diverse Clients

Charles Negy

22 Responding to the Challenge: Preparing Mental Health Professionals for the New Millennium

George K. Hong, Margaret Garcia, and Marcel Soriano

CONTRIBUTORS

Numbers in parentheses indicate the pages on which the authors' contributions begin.

RONALD J. ANGEL (25), Department of Sociology, University of Texas at Austin, Austin, Texas 78712

BILL R. ARNOLD (121), Department of Psychology and Anthropology, University of Texas—Pan American, Edinburg, Texas 78539

GUADALUPE X. AYALA (389), Joint Doctoral Program in Clinical Psychology, San Diego State University–University of California, San Diego, San Diego, California 92102

SANDRA A. BLACK (325), Center on Aging and Department of Internal Medicine, University of Texas Medical Branch, Galveston, Texas 77555

GENEVIEVE CANALES (63), Department of Hispanic Studies, University of Northern Colorado, Greeley, Colorado 80634

IDALIA CASTILLO-CANEZ (389), Joint Doctoral Program in Clinical Psychology, San Diego State University–University of California, San Diego, San Diego, California 92102

SANDRA K. CHONEY (389), Behavioral Health Services—Muscogee (Creek Nation), Okmulgee, Oklahoma 74447

SAM COPELAND (341), School of Social Work, Stephen F. Austin State University, Nacogdoches, Texas 75961

ISRAEL CUÉLLAR (45, 195), Department of Psychology and Anthropology, University of Texas—Pan American, Edinburg, Texas 78539

RICHARD DANA (97), Regional Research Institute, Portland State University, Portland, Oregon 97201

DENISE ANNE DILLARD (225), Apache Behavioral Health Service, White-river, Arizona 85901

MARGARET GARCIA (455), Division of Administration and Counseling, California State University, Los Angeles, Los Angeles, California 90032

FRANCISCO C. GOMEZ, JR. (389), San Diego, California 92103

CHARLES E. HOLZER III (341), Department of Psychiatry and Behavioral Sciences, University of Texas Medical Branch, Galveston, Texas 77555

GEORGE K. HONG (455), Division of Administration and Counseling, California State University, Los Angeles, Los Angeles, California 90032

RICHARD M. LEE (279), Department of Educational Psychology, University of Texas at Austin, Austin, Texas 78712

MICHAEL L. LINDSEY (195), Nestor Consultants, Inc., Dallas, Texas 75011

SPERO M. MANSON (225), National Center for American Indian and Alaska Native Mental Health Research, Department of Psychiatry, University of Colorado Health Sciences Center, Denver, Colorado 80220

ANTHONY J. MARSELLA (3), Department of Psychology, University of Hawai'i, Honolulu, Hawai'i 96822

CERVANDO MARTINEZ (311), Department of Psychiatry, University of Texas Health Science Center, San Antonio, Texas 78229

YOLANDA E. MATUS (121), Department of Psychology and Anthropology, University of Texas—Pan American, Edinburg, Texas 78539

SONIA A. MENDOZA (389), California School of Professional Psychology, San Diego, California 92121

LAURALYN E. MILES (389), Joint Doctoral Program in Clinical Psychology, San Diego State University–University of California, San Diego, San Diego, California 92102

CHARLES NEGY (439), Department of Psychology, University of Central Florida, Orlando, Florida 32828

ELAHE NEZAMI (389), Institute of Health and Promotion and Disease Prevention Research, University of Southern California, Los Angeles, California 90033

SUMIE OKAZAKI[1] (171), Department of Psychology, University of Wisconsin—Madison, Madison, Wisconsin 53706

[1]Current address: Department of Psychology, University of Illinois at Urbana-Champaign, Champaign, Illinois 60020

TERRY M. PACE (389), Counseling Psychology Program, University of Oklahoma, Norman, Oklahoma 73019

FREDDY A. PANIAGUA (139, 249), Department of Psychiatry and Behavioral Sciences, University of Texas Medical Branch, Galveston, Texas 77555

MIGUEL PEREZ-GARCIA (419), Department of Psychology, Universidad de Granada, Granada, Spain

ANTONIO E. PUENTE (419), Department of Psychology, University of North Carolina at Wilmington, Wilmington, North Carolina 28403

UZZER A. RAAJPOOT (79), Department of Sociology, University of Texas—Pan American, Edinburg, Texas 78539

MANUEL RAMIREZ III (279), Department of Psychology, University of Texas at Austin, Austin, Texas 78712

ROBERT E. ROBERTS (359), Departments of Behavioral Sciences and International and Family Health, School of Public Health, University of Texas, Houston, Texas 77030

ANDREA J. ROMERO (209), Stanford Center for Research in Disease Prevention, Stanford University School of Medicine, Palo Alto, California 94304

MARCEL SORIANO (455), Division of Administration and Counseling, California State University, Los Angeles, Los Angeles, California 90032

ROBERTO VELÁSQUEZ (389), Joint Doctoral Program in Clinical Psychology, San Diego State University–University of California, San Diego, San Diego, California 92102

KRISTI WILLIAMS (25), Department of Sociology, University of Texas, Austin, Austin, Texas 78712

ANN MARIE YAMADA (3), Department of Psychology, University of Hawai'i, Honolulu, Hawai'i 96822

PREFACE

During the last half of the 20th century, researchers placed a great deal of importance on brain–behavior relations. Much knowledge and control were undeniably gained from such efforts, but unfortunately culture, the true roots of much of our behavior, was largely overlooked. This general disregard of cultural factors not only led to false generalizations but blocked understanding of the real forces that motivate and shape our perceptions, attitudes, and actions (Horney, 1937). The aspiration of the editors and contributors of this handbook is to right this wrong and to lay the foundations for a more balanced perspective in the coming century.

What clinicians or students of mental health must know about delivering mental health services to diverse populations is complex and multifaceted, but the essentials are within their grasp. The clinician trained to be competent with persons from different cultures must integrate formalized research-based knowledge about a given cultural group with experiential and practice-based knowledge about that specific cultural group. This handbook follows the same principle; the reader's challenge is to learn as much relevant scientific knowledge as possible and to integrate that knowledge with experiential, practice-based knowledge. The contributors to this handbook have provided multiple methods for depicting and integrating research knowledge with experiential knowledge. Learning relevant skills is a continuous process, and cultural competence, likewise, is an ongoing process—not a state to be achieved. As our knowledge of a domain grows, this knowledge must be integrated with what was previously known. Unfortunately, this process often entails unlearning what was previously learned. This is particularly true when we are learning about diverse groups, as too often our knowledge about a group, even our own group, is based on erroneous and stereotypic information gained from

childhood experiences. It is important to have an open mind when we approach
something new and different.

The handbook is divided into four parts. Part I provides a foundation of
history, theory, and concepts. Models and schemas for understanding the role
of culture with respect to illness and behavior are included. Part II addresses
methodological concerns vital to understanding and interpretating data obtained in cross-cultural clinical practice regardless of whether etic or emic
measures were used in assessment processes. Part III provides essential content
knowledge and research-based clinical knowledge, including unique etiological
factors, prevalence data, symptom patterns and manifestations, cultural illness
ideologies, and treatment considerations for each of the four racially or ethnically diverse populations. Additionally, Part III contains several chapters addressing the effects of ethnocultural factors on the assessment and treatment of
adolescents, adults, elderly, and HIV/AIDS groups. Several chapters in Part III
also focus on how to conduct the cross-cultural interview, how to interpret
the Minnesota Multiphasic Personality Inventory, 2nd ed. (MMPI-2), how to
conduct cross-cultural neuropsychological assessments, and how to identify
cultural influences on *Diagnostic and Statistical Manual of Mental Disorders,* 4th
ed. *(DSM-IV)* diagnostic categories. Part III includes an important chapter on
the essentials of multicultural psychotherapy along with its current status and
future prospects. Part IV addresses training concerns with respect to multiculturalism, undoubtedly a potent force in the behavioral sciences.

In addition to the above explicit knowledge in multicultural assessment and
treatment, some fundamental concepts are implicit in this handbook. One important implicit concept is the concept of *cultural competence:* What is it and
how is it achieved? In these challenging times for practitioners of health and
human services, cultural competence is a means of defending, protecting,
and enhancing professional mental health care practice. Some of the essentials
of cultural competence addressed in this handbook are briefly reviewed here:

1. The employment of an ecological perspective
2. An understanding of the relations of culture and mental health
3. Mastery of knowledge in content areas: knowing about various cultures
4. Practice knowledge and experiential skills
5. Integration of practice knowledge and practice skills

THE EMPLOYMENT OF AN
ECOLOGICAL PERSPECTIVE

To truly appreciate the importance and complexity of culture throughout the
life span, it is necessary to employ an ecological perspective that examines

behavior within the "web of life." The most personal and private thoughts of each individual as well as outwardly expressed behaviors are products of the interaction of genetic and environmental forces. Cultural factors are a significant part of environmental forces, and cultural factors are a significant component of family, community values, meaning, purpose, motivations, and spiritual life. All the chapters, either directly or indirectly, address the importance of an ecological perspective in understanding cultural forces in mental health in diverse populations.

The student of mental health and culture needs to have some understanding of how culture influences behavior, both normal and abnormal. A prerequisite to understanding mental health and mental illness is having some model of how culture influences our perceptions, cognition, belief systems, emotions, values, and behaviors. Chapter 1 introduces through an historical account the shifting prominence assigned to the role of culture in the fields of psychiatry and psychology. It also introduces new conceptual and methodological frameworks that position culture as a major determinant of the onset, expression, course, and outcome of mental disorders.

In the new upgraded models of culture and behavior, individual mental health and societal mental health are seen as inextricably linked. The newer models place culture within an ecological framework, assigning culture a prominent role linked both to the individual and to the context or situation in which behavior occurs and is vitally linked to family, community, socialization processes, educational processes, and social–political and cultural processes. The multiple levels, macro to micro, existing within all communities are ecologically linked. Both the array of problems and the solutions are enormously broadened with the inclusion of culture as a determinant of behavior. As Marsella and Yamada note in Chapter 1, mental health is not only about biology and psychology but also about education, economics, social structure, religion, and politics.

Angel and Williams (Chapter 2) remind us of the importance of culture in forming the backdrop against which all human action has meaning. They emphasize that illness is as much personal and subjective as it is objective and physiological. They also note that emotions and illness are intertwined. Understanding the events and contexts that elicit and label both emotions and illness can be just as important as understanding the physiological aspects of mental health and illness. A culturally informed clinical picture includes an understanding of the relations of cultural, social, psychological, emotional, and cognitive factors as they relate to health and illness.

The behavioral sciences clearly have much to offer in the understanding and treatment of both mental and physical illnesses. The perspectives, paradigms, and models included provide conceptual practical frameworks for relating culture to illness and health.

AN UNDERSTANDING OF THE RELATIONS
OF CULTURE AND MENTAL HEALTH

The research findings reported in this handbook indicate that there is a growing body of knowledge of cultural influences on mental health. Methodological problems have been plentiful and most challenging. Methodological advances are an integral part of the growing body of research on culture. Just as each ore has its own means of extraction, each cultural group requires its own emic-specific tools, measures, and indices if investigators are to fully understand that culture. Methodology is seen as the key to meaningful qualitative and quantitative understanding and interpretation of data with respect to culture.

Research helps build on scientific principles. Research also helps define practice by providing objective data on which to base interventions. The inclusion of cultural data provides meaningful, substantive knowledge upon which to formulate interventions and a treatment plan. Gross errors in diagnosing and grossly inappropriate services and interventions have resulted from cultural and linguistic misunderstandings. Service delivery systems, like the providers of such services, must at times adjust to provide more effectual and efficient services. Ineffectual services and interventions require significant restructuring and improvement to minimze cross-cultural errors. These errors can be minimized when a cultural formulation is incorporated concurrently with the diagnostic and clinical interview. It is imperative that clinicians be trained to recognize culture-specific influences related to assessment and treatment of mental disorders.

Communities are not homogeneous entities. All residents of all communities are cultural beings; that is, they belong to some culture that assists them in conducting economic and other endeavors as they live their lives. The culture that envelops the community provides meaning, education, structure, organization, and purpose. There may be several competing cultures within a community. A given community may be made of numerous cultures and numerous diverse ethnic/cultural population groups.

Many special problems and cultural conflicts emerge from multicultural environments. People use multiple ways to adapt to their environments. When people from different cultures interact, there are a host of possible outcomes with definite implications for adjustment. The modes of acculturation significantly influence psychological adjustment and risk for emotional and mental-health-related problems.

Emotional and psychological problems are closely linked to conflict, as are anxieties and neuroses (historically). Within any culture there are individual quests, such as the quest for affection, security, spirituality, prominence or fame, power, or wealth. Cultures provide vehicles for some and barriers for others in achieving and sustaining growth as each of us traverses the various stages of the life span.

MASTERY OF KNOWLEDGE IN CONTENT AREAS: KNOWING ABOUT VARIOUS CULTURES

An essential consideration in developing cultural competence with individuals from ethnocultural groups different from one's own is knowledge about that group. This is as basic as assessment of the individual to be treated. Knowledge of the cultural identity of the person being treated is essential to the understanding of the "self," the ideologies, including illness and health ideologies, values, needs, motives, and drives of the person being treated. The psychosocial stressors and meanings applied to them are important elements in understanding the psychological life of the person. The more one learns about the history, culture, and current life of a specific ethnocultural group, the better prepared one is to understand and help individuals from that group. Sometimes this is known as cultural awareness. Some critics have stated that cultural awareness is not enough, that more specific knowledge is needed to develop cultural competence. The editors concur. Cultural awareness is essential but not sufficient, and for this reason this handbook has gone far beyond awareness to include multiple domains of cultural competence both explicitly and implicitly. There is never too much to know or a point at which one knows all that is needed to know about any group. It is a continual process of learning, and many of the chapters are richly loaded with sociocultural, historical, and meaningful content knowledge about each of the four major U.S. racial and ethnic groups. Many of the chapters are particularly meaningful because they were contributed by an ethnic minority behavioral scientist writing about his or her own ethnocultural group.

PRACTICE KNOWLEDGE AND PRACTICE SKILLS

In this handbook a loose definition of cross-culture is employed: a cross-cultural setting is one in which a provider and a consumer of mental health services are from two differrent ethnocultural groups. There are providers who deliver cross-cultural services who are not formally trained, via research-based knowledge, but nonetheless have practice experience. As aptly stated by Cervando Martinez in Chapter 15, "One does not learn to conduct a good interview solely by reading about it." Most skills are acquired by studying them, performing them, and observing others performing them. Throughout all the chapters, contributors interject their experiential knowledge with research-based knowledge where possible. Although this handbook cannot provide direct experiential knowledge, it can serve as a resource for reflecting on cross-cultural experiences.

It is common knowledge in the mental health field that each ethnic group has its own special needs. The report of the Four National Panels on Cultural Competence in Managed Care Mental Health Service (Western Interstate Commission for Higher Education, 1997) documents the following: (a) African Americans drop out of services at significantly higher rates than white populations and are more often misdiagnosed; (b) Asian Americans are more likely to drop out after initial contact or terminate prematurely from mental health services; (c) Latinos are adversely affected by undereducation, underemployment, and insufficient access to health care services and tend to underutilize mental health services in comparison to the general population except in crisis situations; (d) American Indians appear to be at higher risk for mental disorders than most other ethnic groups. These types of findings mandate a restructuring of services, a reduction of cultural barriers, and the identification of ethnospecific needs and interventions. The type and quality of interventions most appropriate for specific populations and across settings are not always well established. There is a need for more service and practice research. Practitioners in cross-cultural settings are often pioneers, challenged by the task of providing mental health services to populations for which much practice knowledge is lacking.

INTEGRATION OF PRACTICE KNOWLEDGE AND PRACTICE SKILLS

The last prerequisite for profesional competence in multicultural mental health is that each provider of service integrate research-based knowledge with knowledge gained from practice. Whether interventions are directed toward individuals, groups, or institutions, scientific practices dictate a feedback loop in which practice knowledge is evaluated to modify existing practices where deemed necessary and to modify theory, as well as research, when required. At the individual level this means that service providers change their service to be more consistent with the latest more efficient and effective practices. At the ecological level, this may mean that the basic structure of the culture, such as its institution(s) or its educational and parenting practices, require modification. Socioeconomic status is a particularly potent cultural force in human behavior, including prevalence of disorders, manifestations of illness, health status, physical illness (particularly infectious illnesses), mental illness, and treatment.

Understanding multiculturalism with all its immense ramifications for society at all levels is an implicit objective of this handbook. Multiculturalism as a force in psychology appears to be growing, and its theoretical and professional underpinnings are examined in several chapters. It is clear that a new multicultural worldview is in the making, with profound implications for identity, relations with others, health, illness, and adjustment.

In summary, this handbook is unique in its theoretical and thematic approach in which the role of culture is viewed as central, not peripheral, to mental health and to mental illness. It assigns to culture the potential of influencing the etiology, manifestations, and treatment of mental disorders. This handbook is unique in that it integrates *DSM-IV* cultural conceptualizations, criteria, and formulations. It goes far beyond cultural awareness and provides meaningful knowledge that bears directly on the assessment and treatment of diverse populations. Culture in the context of multicultural assessment and treatment practices is viewed as not just another variable or set of variables, but rather as a multitude of variables that constitute the context for the operation of all other variables. This prominence assigned to culture gives to both the experienced and the beginning mental health provider an array of conceptual tools and knowledge gained from both research and practice for delivering better mental health services for diverse populations.

Our minds are formed from our cultural experiences in interaction with our physiological development. Our perceptions, our values, our beliefs, and our emotions are formed and shaped by the cultures in which we are born and raised. Just as a ball of clay is shaped not only by the hands but also by the mind (in interaction, of course, with our physiology), the mind is shaped by cultural experiences and forces. Unlike the ball of clay, however, the mind has a dynamic quality, thanks to its computer and learning capabilities. As more than one writer has noted, we are each born into a story, but we also can make our own story. The mind thus has the ability to create its own story and to learn from others' stories as well. We are formed by our culture, but we have the potential of changing our culture as well, and in doing so, change ourselves or transcend our culture. No matter how far we take our own story, its roots always remain in our cultural experiences.

REFERENCES

Horney, K. (1937). Cultural and psychological implications of neuroses. In K. Horney, *The neurotic personality of our time* (pp. 13–29). New York: Norton.

Western Interstate Commission for Higher Education (1997, October). *Cultural competence standards in mental health care mental health services for four underserved and/or underrepresented racial/ethnic groups*. Report of the Four National Panels on Cultural Competence in Managed Care Mental Health Services. Boulder, CO: Author.

Israel Cuéllar
Freddy A. Paniagua

PART I

Overview Theory, Models, and Demographics

Culture and Mental Health: An Introduction and Overview of Foundations, Concepts, and Issues

ANTHONY J. MARSELLA
ANN MARIE YAMADA
Department of Psychology
University of Hawai'i
Honolulu, Hawai'i

I. INTRODUCTION

A. OVERVIEW OF FOUNDATIONS

1. Emil Kraepelin—Comparative Psychiatry

In the early years of the twentieth century, Emil Kraepelin (1904), the father of modern Western psychiatry, journeyed from his home in Germany to Asia and North America as part of a worldwide lecture tour. During the course of his travels, Kraepelin experienced difficulties diagnosing some patients. He noted that the patients in these lands failed to express their illness with the prototypical symptoms characteristic of his patients in Germany and Northern Europe. Puzzled by this situation, Kraepelin suggested a new specialty within psychiatry be created—*Vergleichende Psychiatrie* or Comparative Psychiatry—to study cultural differences in psychopathology:

Handbook of Multicultural Mental Health: Assessment and Treatment of Diverse Populations

> The characteristics of a people should find expression in the frequency as well as the
> shaping of the manifestations of mental illness in general; so that comparative psy-
> chiatry shall make it possible to gain valuable insights into the psyche of nations and
> shall in turn also be able to contribute to the understanding of pathological psychic
> processes. (1904, p. 9)

It is ironic that Kraepelin, who was, like many 19th-century psychiatrists, committed to a biological view of mental illness should be among the very first to note the importance of cultural differences in the frequency and expression of disorders. In the interim between Kraepelin's early remarks and present times, the study of cultural differences in psychopathology has progressed under a number of names within psychiatry (e.g., transcultural psychiatry, cultural psychiatry, ethnopsychiatry, cross-cultural psychiatry) and related social sciences (e.g., psychiatric anthropology, culture and psychopathology, culture and mental health) (Marsella, 1993).

2. Culture and Mental Health: The Early Struggle

Within the last few decades, psychiatry and the other mental health professions and sciences (i.e., anthropology, psychology, sociology, public health, and social work) increasingly have acknowledged the critical importance of cultural factors in mental illness. This had led to new conceptual and methodological frameworks that position cultural factors as a major determinant of the onset, expression, course, and outcome of mental disorders. Indeed, for much of the past century, the mental health professions and sciences failed to recognize or acknowledge the importance of cultural factors in psychopathology (e.g., Mezzich, Kleinman, Fabrega, & Parrone, 1996). Indeed, it was often assumed by those in positions of power and influence that mental disorders were universal in their onset, expression, course, and outcome, and that any variations (e.g., culture-specific disorders such as *koro, latah, susto*) were simply minor deviations within a prototypic universal disorder (e.g., Marsella, in press,b).

There were, of course, numerous voices that were raised in opposition to this position. But, these voices were often those of minority group members or clinical scientists who were marginalized and powerless because of their different views. In fact, many Western professionals and scientists who were pioneers in the field of transcultural psychiatry (e.g., Jane Murphy, Eric Wittkower) often tended to minimize the importance of cultural differences in psychopathology even as they studied variations (e.g., J. Murphy, 1976; Wittkower, 1969). To make matters worse, even some non-Western psychiatric pioneers accepted this perspective (e.g., Pow Meng Yap, Adeyo Lambo), owing, in large part, to their training in Western medical schools and residency programs (e.g., Yap, 1951; Leighton et al., 1963). All were part of the culture of Western psychiatry, and even as they studied cultural psychiatry, they were embedded and enmeshed in a professional and scientific worldview and ethic whose assumptions argued in favor of universals and against cultural differences in mental disorders.

The situation was, and still remains today, a perfect example of the unintentional abuses of power that can occur even among persons of goodwill. Although Western medical science considered itself to be objective in its quest for truth, it failed to recognize its own cultural relativity. Western medical science failed to grasp that its assumptions and methods were deeply rooted within Western cultural traditions, and as such, were at best, a limited and restricted perspective on the nature of psychopathology beyond Western cultural borders (e.g., Jenkins, 1998; Kirmayer, 1998; Mezzich, Kleinman, Fabrega, & Parrone, 1996; Lin, Tseng, & Yeh, 1995). Members of non-Western cultures often accepted the conclusions that were rendered without question because they were, after all, coming from professionals and scientists that were from the world's leading economic and political powers—modern technological societies who dominated the world. That this was the case should not be surprising, for it has only been within recent years, as ethnic and racial minorities and non-Western cultural members have become more prominent in number and influence among the mental health professions and sciences, that the bias inherent in much of our prior mental health knowledge and practice has become widely known and criticized (e.g., Chakraborty, 1991; Lin et al., 1995; Misra, 1996).

B. THE "NEW" CULTURE AND MENTAL HEALTH

Today, as we enter a new century, voices that were long silenced because of their powerlessness within the professional and scientific culture are now speaking out with force and energy. A perfect example of this is the inclusion of the section on culture-bound disorders in the *Diagnostic and Statistical Manual of Mental Disorders (4th ed.) (DSM-IV)* (American Psychiatric Association, 1994). This section of *DSM-IV* came to be included only after some ethnic minority psychiatrists (e.g., Glorisa Canino, Juan Mezzich, Frances Lu, Horacio Fabrega) and a new generation of White transcultural psychiatrists (e.g., Laurence Kirmayer, Arthur Kleinman, Ronald Wintrob) expressed the importance of culture for diagnosis, assessment, and treatment. Using knowledge from the social sciences and the "new" transcultural psychiatry (e.g., Mezzich, Kleinman, Fabrega, & Parron, 1996), changes were made in the *DSM-IV*, even as those in power continued to resist some recommendations (e.g., Jenkins, 1998).

A recent issue of the journal *Transcultural Psychiatry* (September 1998, Vol. 35) was devoted to the issue of culture in *DSM-IV*. The various articles provide candid statements about the cultural limitations of the *DSM-IV* and the struggles to reduce the ethnocentricity in the disorder categories. Kirmayer (1998), the editor-in-chief of the journal, captured the dilemma facing those supporting the "new" transcultural psychiatry and those holding traditional medical perspectives, when he wrote the following:

> While cultural psychiatry aims to understand problems in context, diagnosis is essentializing: referring to decontextualized entities whose characteristics can be studied independently of the particulars of a person's life and social circumstances. The entities of the *DSM* implicitly situate human problems within the brain or the psychology of the individual, while many human problems brought to psychiatrists are located in patterns of interaction in families, communities, or wider social spheres. Ultimately, whatever the extent to which we can universalize the categories of the DSM by choosing suitable level of abstraction, diagnosis remains a social practice that must be studied, critiqued, and clarified by cultural analysis. (1998, p. 342)

C. THE NEO-KRAEPELINIAN MOVEMENT

But who were these people in power who rejected evidence of cultural variations? They were those who favored a biological perspective—a medical model—of mental illness. It is no secret that for the past few decades, psychiatry has sought to extricate itself from its Freudian heritage and to re-establish itself as a medical specialty. To accomplish this, it would be necessary to support a medical model of psychopathology, which sought etiological causes within reductionist levels of explanation. Klerman (1978), a staunch supporter of the efforts to establish psychiatry as a medical profession and science (i.e., Neo-Kraepelinian viewpoint) wrote the credo for the new orientation. Some key points in Klerman's credo include the following: (a) psychiatry is a branch of medicine, (b) there is a boundary between the normal and the sick, (c) There are many discrete types of mental illness, (d) the focus of psychiatric physicians should be particularly (directed toward) the biological aspects of mental illness. Blashfield (1984), a psychologist with a jaded but probably accurate view of the unfolding events of the day, referred to these efforts as a "neo-Kraepelinian conspiracy."

Regardless of the terms used to describe the situation, the fact of the matter was that psychiatrists in positions of power and authority were exercising their influence to shape the values and directions of the field. They were doing so because they believed that psychiatry was moving away from its medical roots toward a social science conception of mental illness. Their struggle for identity, purpose, and professional direction was real. Ultimately, those favoring a biomedical orientation for psychiatry won the power positions. This, too, should not be surprising since it has been the norm among the mental health professions and sciences since their emergence in the 19th century, regardless of American psychiatry's ambivalent involvement with psychoanalysis between

1920–1960 (e.g., Foucault, 1967; Rosen, 1968; Zilboorg, 1941/1967). Those in power shape the "conventional" viewpoints, and those that differ remain marginalized until they acquire power or form and alternative perspective. At present, there is no doubt that the biomedical position dominates psychiatry. But, it is also clear that the cultural psychiatry position—and related viewpoints in the social sciences such as psychiatric anthropology and cultural psychology— are acquiring a stronger voice and position.

D. POSTMODERN VIEWS

The emergence of postmodernism and related changes in intellectual thought have taught us in recent years that our realities, including our scientific realities, are all culturally constructed. Knowledge in psychiatry and the social sciences is culturally relative, and as such, it is ethnocentric and biased. What passes for truth is, in fact, a function of who holds the power. Those who are in power (e.g., Western psychiatry) have the "privilege" of determining what is acceptable, and those who are not, are marginalized in their opinion and influence. This is not a pleasant reality for many, but it is an accurate portrayal of the situation. It is difficult for professionals to work within a context that questions the validity of their decisions and that suggests that "truths" may be little more than relativistic assumptions supported by data that are themselves questionable. Yet, it is now evident that many mistakes have been made in the care of the mentally ill. This is especially true for ethnic minority patients and for patients in non-Western countries who have been assessed, diagnosed, and treated by culturally insensitive approaches.

Today, the situation is changing (see Marsella, 1993, for a discussion of the convergence of factors that have contributed to new views) and ethnic minority and non-Western professionals and scientists are speaking against the ethnocentric biases of Western psychiatry and social sciences. Chakraborty (1991), an Asian Indian psychiatrist, writes:

> Even where studies were sensitive, and the aim was to show relative differences caused by culture, the ideas and tools were still derived from a circumscribed area of European thought. This difficulty still continues and, despite modifications, mainstream psychiatry remains rooted in Kraepelin's classic 19th century classification, the essence of which is the description of the two major "mental diseases" seen in mental hospitals in his time—schizophrenia and manic depression. Research is constrained by this view of psychiatry. A central pattern of (western) disorders is identified and taken as the standard by which other (local) patterns are seen as minor variations. Such a construct implies some inadequacy on the part of those patients who fail to reach "standard." Though few people would agree with such statements, there is evidence of biased, value-based, and often racist undercurrents in psychiatry. . . . Psychiatrists in the developing world . . . have accepted a diagnostic framework

developed by western medicine, but which does not seem to take into account the diversity of behavioral patterns they encounter. (p. 1204)

Similarly, Misra (1996), an Asian Indian psychologist, writes:

> The current Western thinking of the science of psychology in its prototypical form, despite being local and indigenous, assumes a global relevance and is treated as a universal mode of generating knowledge. Its dominant voice subscribes to a decontextualized vision with an extraordinary emphasis on individualism, mechanism, and objectivity. This peculiarly Western mode of thinking is fabricated, projected, and institutionalized through representation technologies and scientific rituals and transported on a large scale to the non-Western societies under political-economic domination. As a result, Western psychology tends to maintain an independent stance at cost of ignoring other substantive possibilities from disparate cultural traditions. Mapping reality through Western constructs has offered a pseudounderstanding of the people of alien cultures and has had debilitating effects in terms of misconstruing the special realities of other people and exoticizing or disregarding psychologies that are non-Western. Consequently, when people from other cultures are exposed to Western psychology, they find their identities placed in question and their conceptual repertoires rendered obsolete. (p. 497–498)

E. INDIVIDUALISM AND SCIENTISM

It is time for Western mental health professionals and scientists to reconsider their assumptions, methods, and conclusions within the culturally pluralistic context of our world. The current world population now exceeds six billion people. Of this number, only one billion are of European and North American ancestry. However, because their nations are the dominant economic and political powers, their cultural tradition—their worldview—exercises a disproportionate influence on our approaches to mental health theory and practices. Sloan (1996a) noted the following:

> Psychological theory and practice embody Western cultural assumptions to such an extent that they primarily perform an ideological function. That is, they serve to reproduce and sustain societal *status quo* characterized by economic inequality and other forms of oppression such as sexism and racism. The core operative assumptions that produce this ideological effect both in theory and practice are individualism and scientism. (1996a, p. 39)

Sloan's observations on individualism and scientism address two basic cultural assumptions of Western mental health professionals and scientists: (a) problems reside in individual brains and minds, and thus, individual brains and minds should be locus of treatment and prevention; (b) the world in which we live can be understood objectively through the use of quantitative and empirical data. Both of these assumptions stand in direct opposition to the postmodernist views that currently characterize and inform the study of culture and mental health relationships. These views emphasize the importance of the social context of psychological problems (i.e., powerlessness, poverty, marginalization, inequality) in understanding the etiology and expression of psychopathology. They point out that the individual psyche comes to represent and reflect the struggles and conflicts in our cultural environment and the subjective nature of our knowledge about the world in which we live. This has led to an increased emphasis on qualitative research (e.g., Marsella, Purcell, & Carr, 1999).

F. AMERICAN PSYCHOLOGICAL ASSOCIATION GUIDELINES

In response to the changing context of our times, the American Psychological Association (1992) adopted a set of guidelines for psychologists working with patients from different ethnocultural groups. These guidelines are clear and unambiguous in their assertion that psychologist should refrain from working with people from different ethnocultural traditions if the psychologist has no knowledge, experience, nor training with the group. These guidelines were enacted when it was pointed out that there was a bias in the APA Code of Ethics and that many ethnic minority patients were being inaccurately diagnosed and inappropriately treated (e.g., Pedersen & Marsella, 1982).

G. THE MATURATION OF THE FIELD

It is noteworthy that the study of culture and mental health has greatly matured in recent years, and many publications now provide a substantial theoretical, methodological, and clinical basis for the field. Numerous books have been published on the following:

1. *Disorders* (e.g., depression—Kleinman & Good, 1985; posttraumatic stress disorder (PTSD)—Marsella, Friedman, Gerrity, & Scurfield, 1996; and culture-bound disorders—Simons & Hughes, 1985)
2. *Ethnocultural groups* (e.g., Chinese—Lin et al., 1995)
3. *Risk populations* (e.g., refugees—Marsella, Bornemann, Ekblad, & Orley, 1994)
4. *Issues* (e.g., classification—Mezzich et al., 1996)
5. *Pathological cultural processes* (e.g., modernization—Sloan, 1996b; urbanization—Marsella, 1998b).

In addition, there are a score of readily available general texts (e.g., Al-Issa, 1995; Castillo, 1997; Gaw, 1993; Leff, 1988), and a growing number of specialized research and clinical journals (e.g., *Transcultural Psychiatry; Culture,*

Medicine, and Psychiatry; Cultural Diversity and Ethnic Minority Psychology) that publish rigorous and scholarly articles reflecting the new orientation.

The "new" culture and mental health professional and researcher believes individual and societal mental health are inextricably linked—that we must understand the ecology of mental health. Thus, mental health is not only about biology and psychology, but also about education, economics, social structure, religion, and politics. There can be no mental health where there is powerlessness, because powerlessness breeds despair. There can be no mental health where there is poverty, because poverty breeds hopelessness. There can be no mental health where there is inequality, because inequality breeds anger and resentment. There can be no mental health where there is racism, because racism breeds low self-esteem and self-denigration; and lastly, there can be no mental health where there is cultural disintegration and destruction, because cultural disintegration and destruction breed confusion and conflict.

In brief, the roots of despair, hopelessness, anger, low self-esteem, and confusion reside in the ecological relationships among human biology, psychology, and sociocultural and environmental millieus and contexts. This does not mean our biological (e.g., genetics, neurotransmitters) nature is unimportant. Rather, this view repositions biology as one of many interactive determinants of mental health, and it acknowledges the importance of socioenvironmental demands. The "new" culture and mental health professional and researcher must be skilled and adept at diagnosing and treating individual and sociocultural problems within an ecological framework. This will often require him or her to initiate economic, political, and community actions. Table I presents the emerging array of challenges and possibilities within this ecological framework.

It is clear from Table I that the "new" culture and mental health professional will need to be versed in a broader spectrum of conceptual approaches to diagnosis and treatment. Concern for the ecology of mental health will require training in multicultural, multidisciplinary, and multisectoral areas. It is time, perhaps, for a "new" professional code for culture and mental health clinicians and researchers, a code that affirms that being a culture and mental health professional is a way of life and not simply a job, because the work we do has serious moral and political implications. The following characteristics are offered as a foundation for the "new" culture and mental health:

1. It is a worldview.
2. It is committed to diversity.
3. It is committed to social justice and activism.
4. It is concerned with optimizing communication.
5. It is concerned with empowering individuals, groups, and nations.
6. It is concerned with offering hope, optimism, and opportunity.
7. It is multicultural, multidisciplinary, and multisectoral.
8. It is ecological, historical, interactional, and contextual.

TABLE I Ecological Spectrum of Concerns for the "New" Culture and
Mental Health Professional

	Level of interest		
	Individual level	Cultural level	Sociopolitical level
Sample negative concerns			
	Discontent	Disintegration	Colonization
	Distress	Denial	Exploitation
	Disorder	Dislocation	Domination
	Deviancy	Decline	Oppression
	Disease	Destruction	Persecution
Sample positive concerns			
	Health	Organization	Reconstruction
	Adaptation	Revitalization	Reform
	Competence	Integration	Democracy
	Meaning	Coherence	Justice
	Spirituality	Resilience	Civility

9. It is biopsychosocial.
10. It is revolutionary and progressive.

II. OVERVIEW OF CULTURE AND MENTAL HEALTH QUESTIONS, CONCEPTS, AND ISSUES

A. SOME DEFINING QUESTIONS

Although the topic of culture and mental health is studied in a number of different academic disciplines and professional fields under such names as transcultural psychiatry, cultural psychiatry, ethnopsychiatry, culture and psychopathology, and psychiatric anthropology, the disciplines and professions are guided by a set of common concerns and questions:

1. What is the role of cultural variables in the etiology of mental disorders? How do cultural variables interact with biological, psychological, and environmental variables to influence psychopathology?
2. What are the cultural variations in standards of normality and abnormality?
3. What are the cultural variations in the classification and diagnosis of psychopathology?

4. What are the cultural variations in the rates and distribution of psychopathology according to both indigenous and Western categories of psychopathology?

5. What are the cultural variations in the expression, course, and outcome of psychopathology?

B. Some Important Concepts

1. Ethnocentrism

Ethnocentrism refers to the natural tendency or inclination among all people to view reality from their own cultural experience and perspective. In the course of doing so, the traditions, behaviors, and practices of people from other cultures are often considered inferior, strange, abnormal, and/or deviant. Ethnocentrism becomes a problem in the field of mental health when certain realities regarding the nature and treatment of mental health are imposed on people by those in power without concern for possible bias (Marsella, in press,a).

2. Culture

An older effort at compiling the different definitions of culture (Kluckhohn & Kroeber, 1952) listed more than 150 different definitions. For current purposes, a psycho-behavioral definition of culture used by the senior author for a number of years will be used:

> Shared learned meanings and behaviors that are transmitted from within a social activity context for purposes of promoting individual/societal adjustment, growth, and development. Culture has both *external* (i.e., artifacts, roles, activity contexts, institutions) and *internal* (i.e., values, beliefs, attitudes, activity contexts, patterns of consciousness, personality styles, epistemology) representations. The shared meanings and behaviors are subject to continuous change and modification in response to changing internal and external circumstances.

This definition acknowledges that the meanings and behaviors shaped by culture, in both its external and internal representations, are dynamic and subject to continuous modification and change. Although the impulse is generally toward adaptation and adjustment, it should be noted that cultures can frequently become pathogenic (e.g., Edgerton, 1992) because of the values and cultural constructions of reality they impart. Culture is the lens or template we use in constructing, defining, and interpreting reality. This definition suggests that people from different cultural contexts and traditions will define and experience reality in very different ways. Thus, even mental disorders must vary across cultures because they cannot be separated from cultural experience. Marsella (1982) stated:

> We cannot separate our experience of an event from our sensory and linguistic mediation of it. If these differ, so must the experience differ across cultures. If we define who we are in different ways (i.e., self as object), if we process reality in different ways (i.e., self as process), if we define the very nature of what is real, and what is acceptable, and even what is right and wrong, how can we then expect similarities in something as complex as madness? (1982, p. 363)

3. Ethnocultural Identity

Ethnocultural identity refers to the extent to which an individual endorses and manifests the cultural traditions and practices of a particular group. Clearly, what is important is not a person's ethnicity, but rather, the extent to which they actually are identified with and practice the lifestyle of that group. In groups undergoing acculturation, there can be considerable variation in the extent of ethnocultural identity with a particular cultural tradition. Thus, it is important to determine both a person's ethnicity and their degree of identification with their ethnocultural heritage. Although some individuals may be bicultural, others may be fully acculturated, and still others may maintain a traditional identification.

Ethnocultural identity has emerged as one of the most popular new areas of inquiry in cross-cultural research. It is the "new" independent variable in cross-cultural research, replacing the simple comparison of different ethnic groups. Today, ethnocultural identity is being assessed by a variety of methods including the measurement of similarities in attitudes, values, and behaviors of different groups (e.g., Yamada, Marsella, & Yamada, 1998). In studying cultural aspects of mental disorder, it is important that patients be evaluated for their degree of ethnocultural identification. For example, if we are studying mental illness in Hispanic-Americans, we should first determine the extent of the patients' identification with Hispanic culture. If we use Western standards for assessment and diagnosis, we may create many problems. Yamada et al. (1998) have developed a valid and reliable behavioral scale for the assessment of ethnocultural identification across ethnic groups. The *DSM-IV* (APA, 1994, p. 843) guidelines for the cultural formulation of a case list the cultural identity of the individual as the first criteria to be assessed when conducting a cultural formulation.

C. Cultures as Causative of Psychiatric Disorders

Cultural factors may play an important role in causing psychiatric disorders, via their roles as a stressor, resource/support system, definition and standard of normality/abnormality, and the concepts of self and personhood.

1. Stress and Stressors

A cultural context can be a major stressor by confronting individuals and/or groups with demands that exceed their abilities and resources to cope. A typical example of this is the rapid social change that characterizes contemporary life and the serious problems associated with urbanization and urban lifestyles (Marsella, 1998b) or modernization and change (e.g., Sloan, 1996b). Other culture-related stressors that may play a role in the etiology of mental disorders include racism, acculturation, social change, cultural abuse, and cultural disintegration.

Acculturation is a good example of the kind of stress that may be imposed on an individual or group of people. Acculturation refers to the process that occurs when an individual or group from a given culture is required to adapt and adjust to the cultural worldviews, customs, and traditions of another group. In many instances, the latter culture is a dominant culture in the interaction. Under pressures to conform, comply, and accommodate to the dominant culture's way of life, the acculturating individual or group may find their own cultural worldviews, customs, and traditions are denigrated, devalued, or denied. Thus, the acculturating individual or group may be left without the cultural anchors that defined their identity and meanings. Sometimes, the acculturation pressures are so great that they provoke burdensome and oppressive patterns of uncertainty, anger, resentment, and despair. The ways of life that had guided people for centuries are now devalued or destroyed. Languages and customs are lost, and children caught in the turmoil of change are often caught between the new and old worlds with resulting anomie and alienation. David Stannard's (1992) poignant analysis of the tragic consequences of acculturation for indigenous people in America captures the stresses of acculturation and cultural disintegration. Table II provides a conceptual model of acculturation. As Table II indicates, the acculturation process is complex and can result in a spectrum of outcomes at individual, cultural, and geographic levels. The key factors may be the circumstances of the culture contact process.

2. Resources and Supports

Culture may be implicated in the etiology of mental disorders because of the presence or absence of different resources or supports. Resources and supports include such factors as social support systems, effective communication networks, effective leaders, flexible belief systems, and the socialization of effective personality dispositions (e.g., hardiness, ego strength, sense of coherence) (Marsella & Scheuer, 1993). Consider the power of a belief. In Islamic cultures, the phrase "*Inshallah*" means "If Allah will it" or "It is the will of Allah." This belief is invoked to help explain and accept many life circumstances and diffi-

TABLE II   Acculturation and Mental Health Model[a]

Culture contact variables	Individual levels	Cultural levels	Geocultural levels
Number of cultures	Interpersonal processes	Sociocultural ethos	Urbanization
Diversity of cultures		Social structure	Environment
Culture contact Circumstances (Forced, invited)	Personality processes	Institutions	Ecology
	Cognitive processes	A. Family	Population distribution
		B. Religion	
Extent of culture contact	Sensorimotor processes	C. Education	Disease exposure
		D. Politics	
Culture exposure (Frequency, duration, intensity)	Psychophysiological processes	E. Health	Pollution
		F. Economics	
	Neuroanatomical neurochemical/ processes	Social roles	
Mechanism of culture contact (individual, societal, media)			
Locus of culture contact (e.g., Religion, family, workplace)			

[a] Adapted from Marsella, 1978.

culties. Thus, rather than accepting personal or individual responsibility for failure, a person can instead say "It is the will of Allah." Within the Hindu and Buddhist cultural traditions, the belief in *Kharma,* or cosmic destiny serves a similar function. Although some in the West may consider this fatalism, the positive functions these beliefs serve suggest it should be called "optimistic fatalism." But, in any case, the use of this kind of belief frees the person from assuming personal responsibility. The availability of strong family (extended family) support systems also provides a major resource for mediating the effects of stress and ultimately poor mental health (e.g., Marsella, 1985).

3. Standards of Normality/Abnormality

Culture also may influence the etiology of mental disorders by its standards for normality and abnormality. Problems in defining the limits in these areas can lead to serious problems regarding deviancy and conformity. The main issue here is often the balance between tolerance and suppression. Certain cultures insist on absolute conformity while others tolerate high levels of deviancy (e.g., Edgerton, 1992). These standards both define what is acceptable, and also set tolerance limits that may promote or discourage eccentricity and deviancy. It is essential the mental health professional be alert to cultural variations in normality. More than a half-century ago, Hallowell (1934) wrote that the cross-cultural investigator must have

> An intimate knowledge of the culture as a whole, he must also be aware of the normal range of individual behavior within the cultural pattern and likewise understand what the people themselves consider to be extreme deviations from this norm. In short, he must develop a standard of normality with reference to the culture itself, as a means of controlling an uncritical application of the criteria he brings with him from our civilization. (p. 2)

Hallowell's words have contemporary relevance. But, they also need to be attenuated within the culturally pluralistic context of our modern world. Clearly, a mental health professional must be alert to cultural variations in normality and abnormality; however, they must be able to negotiate the controversial demands that dominant cultural norms place on minority culture members. Killing a young daughter for losing her virginity before marriage in culture A does not mean it must be accepted in culture B. As the Western nations become home to more and more immigrants and refugees from Asian, Middle-Eastern, and Latino nations, there are a growing number of problems that are arising regarding value differences such as polygamy, rituals such as clitorectomy, impulse control behaviors, drug and alcohol use, cult memberships, religious rituals promoting particular kinds of altered states of experience, and various indigenous healing methods that conflict with conventional practices.

4. Defnition of Selfhood and Personhood

Culture helps shape the etiology of mental disorders by socializing particular patterns of selfhood and personhood (e.g., Marsella, 1985; Shweder, 1991). These patterns not only define what is acceptable behavior, but also influence the types of symptoms that may define an illness (e.g., isolation, loneliness, narcissims, dependency, delusions) because of the view of self and person that is promulgated. For example, Geertz (1973), an American cultural anthropologist, and a leader in studies of cultural variations in selfhood wrote the following:

> The Western conception of the person as a bounded, unique, more or less integrated motivational and cognitive universe, a dynamic center of awareness, emotion, judgment, and action, organized into a distinctive whole and set contrastively—both against other such wholes and against social and natural background—is however incorrigible it may seem to us, a rather peculiar idea within the context of the world's cultures. (Geertz, 1973, p. 34)

Marsella (1985) noted that depression in non-Western cultures is often expressed without the associated existential problems found in the West because the non-Western collective or sociocentric identity limits the construction and experience of the disorder to somatic or interpersonal domains. The result is that personal meaninglessness, worthlessness, helplessness, guilt, and suicidal thoughts are reduced or absent.

D. IMPORTANT ISSUES

1. Concepts of Illness and Disease

In his review of concepts of health and illness across cultures, Murdock (1980), an American anthropologist, separated Western views from non-Western views of disease causality. He reported that Western models were based on *naturalistic* views of disease causation including infection, stress, organic deterioration, accidents, and acts of overt human aggression. In contrast, among many non-Western societies, disease models were based on *supernatural* views (i.e., any disease which accounts for impairment of health as a consequence of some intangible force) including (a) theories of mystical causation because of impersonal forces such as fate, ominous sensations, contagion, mystical retribution, (b) theories of animistic causation because of personalized forces such as soul loss and spirit aggression, and (c) theories of magical causation or actions of evil forces including sorcery and witchcraft.

Non-Western notions of disease causality are seldom used by Western professionals, and because of this, non-Western patient compliance is often a problem. The patient's perception of reality is as important as the doctor's perception of reality in bringing about comfort and cure. When professionals ignore the patient's perspective, this may create relationship problems and communication problems. If a patient strongly believes that supernatural causes are responsible for the disorder, then they may conclude that only treatment regimens that acknowledge the supernatural are likely to be useful. Although professionals may not choose to intervene at supernatural levels, they cannot ignore the power these beliefs may have in shaping the etiology, expression, and course and outcome of the disorder. This reality suggests professionals may need to work with culturally relevant healers (e.g., shamans, curanderos, fakirs, dukhas, mudangs) in their efforts to bring about a complete a meaningful cure for members of particular cultural traditions (e.g., Jilek, 1993; Lee & Armstrong, 1995; Marsella & Higginbotham, 1984). Lee and Armstrong (1995) note that alternative healers, such as shamans, provide a different orientation to healing that includes holistic health, alternative realities, and an emphasis on the psychospiritual realm of personality.

2. Epidemiology

Epidemiology refers to the distribution of disorders. Typically, epidemiological studies seek to identify the number of people who have a particular disorder at a specific point in time (i.e., prevalence) and/or the number of people who are likely to develop a disorder in a given time period (i.e., incidence). Cross-cultural epidemiological studies of various psychiatric disorders have been widely reviewed (e.g., DeGirolamo & MacFarlane, 1996; Eaton, 1992; Jablensky, 1992). However, because of variations in case definition and identification, the findings have often been difficult to compare. In addition, because most of the studies have used Western standards of mental disorder, there is an inherent bias in the results. Marsella, Sartorius, Jablensky, and Fenton (1986) recommended criteria to improve cross-cultural epidemiological studies. Marsella et al. (1986) noted that cross-cultural epidemiological studies must do the following:

1. Use relevant ethnographic and anthropological data in designing a study, especially in determining what constitutes a symptom or category;

2. Develop glossaries of terms and definitions for symptoms and categories;

3. Derive symptom patterns and clusters using multivariate techniques rather than relying on simple *a priori* clinical categories;

4. Use similar/comparable case identification and validation methods;

5. Use culturally appropriate measurement methods that include a broad range of indigenous symptoms and signs that can be reliably assessed;

6. Establish frequency, severity, and duration baselines for indigenous and medical symptoms for normal and pathological populations.

Epidemiology is an important research activity because it documents the distribution of disorder, deviancy, and disease. Many critical policy decisions are made on the basis of epidemiological findings. Thus, it is essential that results be accurate. Although disease detection and enumeration for many medical disorders is often straightforward and obvious because of the presence of distinct symptomatology and/or syndromes, criteria for mental disorders and diseases are often far more ambiguous because of individual and cultural influences. It is essential that epidemiological researchers explicitly state the basis of their case-detection definitions and methods, and that they acknowledge the possibility of false positives and false negatives because of cultural bias.

3. Understanding Culture and Symptomatology Relationships

Marsella (1979) stated that researchers have used a variety of research strategies to study the expression of symptomatology across cultures, including the following:

1. Matched diagnosis (i.e., comparing patients from different cultures with similar diagnoses)

2. Matched samples (i.e., comparing patients from different cultures who are similar in age, social class, religion, etc.)

3. International surveys (i.e., profiling symptoms across large samples from many different countries)

4. Culture-specific disorders (i.e., investigating culture-specific patterns of disorders such as *latah, koro, susto, amok*)

5. Multivariate analyses (i.e., generating symptom clusters based on statistical analyses rather than clinical perceptions and experiences)

More recent publications by Kleinman (1988), Fabrega (1993), and Castillo (1997) capture the complex and interactive meanings that symptoms have across cultures. What emerges from their writing is that a symptom is not simply a symptom, but a valuable opportunity for understanding the myriad ways in which culture impacts health and illness. A symptom is a sign and expression of illness, but it is also an insight into the nature of health. A symptom is a communication, an interpretation, and an experience. It is also a signal from patient to self and to others of a changing relationship, a changing role, and a changing set of expectations and demands. In all these instances, whether it is expressed idiomatically or within conventional Western medical terms and contexts, a symptom reveals culture and its influences.

4. Ethnocultural Parameters of Psychopathology

Research indicates that there are ethnocultural variations across many parameters of psychopathology, including perceptions of the causes, nature, onset patterns, symptom expression, disability levels, idioms of distress, course, and outcome. This has been true for even the most severe forms of psychypathology, including *depressive disorders* (e.g., Kleinman & Good, 1985; Manson & Kleinman, 1998), *PTSD* (e.g., Marsella, Friedman, et al., 1996), and *schizophrenic disorders* (e.g., Jablensky et al., 1992).

For example, there is considerable evidence that among many non-Western cultural groups, depressive disorders have wide ethnocultural variations in basic symptom patterns, including an absence of guilt, suicidal tendencies, withdrawal, anger, and negative self-image. It is not that extreme sadness and grief are absent in non-Western cultures, but rather that the situations that elicit them, their perceived meaning and implications, their expressions, and the social response to them varies. In the case of schizophrenic disorders, considered by many to be the most universal of the psychoses in its expression and clinical parameters because of possible neurological dysfunctions, research conducted by the World Health Organization (WHO) (see Jablensky et al., 1992) reports similarities in core symptoms, but also considerable variations in secondary symptoms, the course and outcome of the disorders, and the rates of the disorders. Marsella, Suarez, et al. (1996) identified a number of ethnocultural determinants of schizophrenic disorders. These are listed in Table III.

TABLE III   Some Cultural Determinants of Schizophrenia[a]

1. Cultural concepts of personhood and the related implications of this for individuated versus unindividuated definitions of person-context relations;
2. Cultural concepts regarding the nature and causes of abnormality and normality, health, and well-being;
3. Cultural concepts and practices regarding attitudes toward illness and disease;
4. Cultural concepts and practices regarding breeding patterns and genetic lineages;
5. Cultural concepts regarding prenatal care, birth practices, and postnatal care, especially in such areas as nutrition and disease exposure;
6. Cultural concepts and practices regarding socialization, especially family, community, and religious institutions, structures, and processes;
7. Cultural concepts and practices regarding medical and health care, especially with regard to the number and types of healers, doctors, sick-role statuses, etc.
8. Cultural stressors such as rates of sociotechnical change, sociocultural disintegration, family disintegration, migration, economic development, industrialization, and urbanization;
9. Culturally related patterns of deviance and dysfunction, including the creation of pathological and deviant subcultures;
10. Cultural stressors related to the clarity, conflicts, deprivations, denigrations, and discrepancies associated with particular needs, roles, values, statuses, and identities;
11. Cultural stressors related to sociopolitical factors such as racism, sexism, and ageism and the accompanying marginalization, segmentalization, and underprivileging;
12. Cultural resources and coping patterns including institutional supports, social networks, social supports, and religious beliefs and practices.

[a] Adapted from Marsella, Suarez, et al., 1996.

As Table III indicates, the range of cultural determinants of schizophrenic disorders is broad and the determinants are powerful. Quite aside from biological factors, such as genetics and neurological impairments, cultural factors have a unique potency in shaping the etiology, expression, and course and outcome of schizophrenic disorders. Thus, mental health requires consideration of cultural variables.

5. Culture-Bound Disorders

Culture-bound disorders represent a major area of concern and debate in the study of culture and mental health because their existence calls into question the very foundations on which so much Western psychiatry is based. The *DSM-IV* (American Psychiatric Association, 1994) states the following about culture-bound disorders.

> Culture-bound syndromes are generally limited to specific societies or culture areas and are localized, folk, diagnostic categories that frame coherent meanings for certain repetitive, patterned, and troubling sets of experiences and observations. There

is seldom a one-to-one equivalence of any culture-bound syndrome with a *DSM* diagnostic entity. (APA, *DSM-IV*, 1994, p. 844)

But, if culture-bound syndromes are limited to specific societies or culture areas, who defines what are the criteria for mental illness—American or European psychiatrists? Is it not possible that Western disorders also constitute culture-bound syndromes since they are found primarily in Western cultures? Marsella (in press,b), noted that there are many questions that are still being debated regarding culture-bound disorders, including the following:

1. Should culture-bound disorders be considered neurotic, psychotic, or personality disorders?
2. Should these disorders be considered variants of disorders considered to be "universal" by Western scientists and professionals (e.g., Is *susto* [soul loss] merely a variant of depression?)?
3. Are these disorders variants of a common "hysterical anxiety," "depression," or "psychotic" processes that arise in response to severe tension, stress, and/or fear, and present with specific culture content and expression?
4. Are there taxonomically different kinds of culture-bound syndromes (i.e., anxiety syndromes, depression syndromes, violence/anger syndromes, startle syndromes, dissociation syndromes)?
5. Do some culture-bound disorders have biological origins (e.g., *pibloktoq*—screaming and running naked in the Arctic snow—has been considered to result from calcium and potassium deficiencies because of dietary restrictions; *amok* has been considered to result from febrile disorders and neurological damage)?
6. Are all disorders "culture-bound" disorders since no disorder can escape cultural encoding, shaping, and presentation (e.g., schizophrenia, depression, anxiety disorders)?

It is becoming increasingly clear to culture and mental health professionals that the disorders their patients experience and manifest can never be decontextualized from the cultural milieu in which they were shaped and responded to by others. It is this ecology that gives the disorder its meaning and consequence. Culture-bound disorders provide a useful mirror for Western mental health professionals to examine their fundamental assumptions about the nature, diagnosis, and treatment of mental disorders.

E. ETHNOCULTURAL DIVERSITY

Every time that a culture disappears, the world loses an alternative way of perceiving reality and for living. Mental health professionals and researchers contribute to the demise of cultures and the reduction of diversity when they fail to consider cultural factors in their clinical and research activities. Octavio Paz (1967), the Nobel Prize-winning Mexican poet and essayist, wrote the following:

> What sets worlds in motion is the interplay of differences, their attractions and repulsions. Life is plurality, death is uniformity. By suppressing differences and pecularities, by eliminating different civilizations and cultures, progress weakens life and favors death. The ideal of a single civilization for everyone, implicit in the cult of progress and technique, impoverishes and mutilates us. Every view of the world that becomes extinct, every culture that disappears, diminishes a possibility of life.

The words of Octavio Paz are ample reason to justify our interest, understanding, and concern for culture and mental health as a profession and as a disciplinary specialty. It seems there are many reasons to conclude that within the various mental health professions and sciences, a commitment to a biopsychosocial approach that firmly incorporates cultural considerations and materials is the only basis for accurate and meaningful practice and research.

REFERENCES

Al-Issa, I. (1995). *Handbook of culture and mental illness: An international perspective*. Madison, CT: International Universities Press.

American Psychiatric Association (1994). *Diagnostic and statistical manual of mental disorders. Fourth edition*. Washington, DC: American Psychiatric Press.

American Psychological Association (1992). Guidelines for providers of psychological services to ethnic, linguistic, and culturally diverse populations. *American Psychologist, 48*, 45–48.

Blashfield, R. (1984). *The classification of psychopathology: Neo-Kraepelinian and quantitative approaches*. New York: Plenum.

Castillo, R. (1997). *Culture and mental illness: A client-centered approach*. Pacific Grove, CA: Brooks-Cole.

Chakraborty, A. (1991). Culture, colonialism, and psychiatry. *The Lancet, 337*, 1204–1207.

DiGirolamo, G., & MacFarlane, A. (1996). The epidemiology of PTSD: An international review of the literature. In A. J. Marsella, M. Friedman, E. Gerrity, & R. Scurfield (Eds.) *Ethnocultural aspects of PTSD: Issues, research, and clinical applications* (pp. 33–86). Washington, DC: American Psychological Association Press.

Eaton, W. (1991). Update on the epidemiology of schizophrenia. *Epidemiological reviews, 13*, 320–328.

Edgerton, R. (1992). *Sick societies: Challenging the myth of primitive harmony*. New York: Free Press.

Fabrega, H. (1993). A cultural analysis of human breakdown patterns: An approach to the ontology and epistemology of psychiatric phenomena. *Culture, Medicine, and Psychiatry, 17*, 99–132.

Foucault, M. (1967). *Madness and civilization: A history of insanity in the Age of Reason*. London: Vintage Press.

Gaw, A. (Ed.) (1993). *Culture, ethnicity, and mental illness*. Washington, DC: American Psychiatric Press.

Geertz, C. (1973). *The interpretation of cultures: Selected essays*. New York: Basic Books.

Jablensky, A. (1992). Cross-cultural aspects of schizophrenia. *Triangle: Sandoz Journal of Medical Science, 31*, 163–174.

Jablensky, A., Sartorius, N., Ernberg, Anker, Korten, Cooper, Day, R., & Bertelsen (1992). Schizophrenia: Manifestations incidence, and course in different cultures: A WHO ten country study. *Psychological Medicine, Monograph Supplement #20*, 1–97.

Jenkins, J. (1998). Diagnostic criteria for schizophrenia and related psychotic disorders: Integration and suppression of cultural evidence in *DSM-IV. Transcultural Psychiatry, 35*, 357–376.

Jilek, W. (1993). Traditional medicine relevant to psychiatry. In N. Sartorius, G. DiGirolamo, G. Andrews, G. Allen German, & L. Eisenberg (Eds.). *Treatment of mental disorders: A review of effectiveness* (pp. 341–390). Washington, DC: American Psychiatric Press.

Kirmayer, L. (1998). Editorial: The fate of culture in DSM-IV. *Transcultural Psychiatry, 35*, 339–343.

Kleinman, A. (1988). *The illness narratives: Suffering, healing, and the human condition*. New York, NY: Basic Books.

Kleinman, A., & Good, B. (1985). *Culture and depression*. Berkeley, CA: University of California Press.

Klerman, G. (1978). The evolution of a scientific nosology. In J. Shershow (Ed.) *Schizophrenia: Science and practice*. Cambridge, MA: Harvard University Press.

Kluckholm, C., & Kroeber, A. (1952). *Culture: A critical review of concepts and definitions*. Cambridge, MA: Peabody Museum.

Kraepelin, E. (1904). *Vergleichende psychaitrie. Zentralblatt fur Nervenherlkande und Psychiatrie, 15*, 433–37.

Lee, C., & Armstrong, K. (1995). Indigenous models of mental health intervention: Lessons from traditional healers. In J. Ponterotto, J. Casa, L. Suzuki, & C. Alexander (Eds.). *Handbook of multicultural counseling* (pp. 441–456). Thousand Oaks, CA: Sage Publications.

Leff, J. (1988). *Psychiatry around the globe*. London: Gaskell.

Leighton, A., Lambo, A., Hughes, C., Leighton, D., Murphy, J., & Macklin, D. (1963). *Psychiatric disorder among the Yoruba*. Ithaca, NY: Cornell University Press.

Lin, T., Tseng, W., & Yeh, E. (1995). *Chinese societies and mental health*. New York: Oxford University Press.

Littlewood, R., & Lipsedge, M. (1997). *Aliens and alienists: Ethnic minorities and psychiatry*. London: Routledge.

Manson, S., & Kleinman, A. (1998). DSM-IV, culture, and mood disorders: A critical reflection on recent progress. *Transcultural Psychiatry, 35*, 377–386.

Marsella, A. J. (1978). The modernization of traditional cultures: Consequences for the individual. In D. Hoopes, P. Pedersen, & G. Renwick (Eds.). *Intercultural education, training, and research: The state of the art*. Washington, DC: SIETAR and U.S. Department of State.

Marsella, A. J. (1979). Cross-cultural studies of mental disorders. In A. J. Marsella, R. Tharp, & T. Ciborowski (Eds.) *Perspectives on cross-cultural psychology* (pp. 233–264). New York: Academic Press.

Marsella, A. J. (1982). Culture and mental health: An overview. In Marsella, A. J. & White, G. (Eds.) *Cultural conceptions of mental health and therapy* (pp. 359–388). Boston, MA: G. Reidel/Kluwer.

Marsella, A. J. (1985). Culture, self, and mental disorder. In A. J. Marsella, G. DeVos, & F. Hsu (Eds.) *Culture and self: Asian and Western perspectives* (pp. 281–308). London: Tavistock Press.

Marsella, A. J. (1993). Sociocultural foundations of psychopathology: A pre-1970 historical overview. *Transcultural Psychiatric Research and Review, 30*, 97–142.

Marsella, A. J. (1998). Urbanization, mental health, and social deviancy: An overview of research findings. *American Psychologist, 53*, 624–634.

Marsella, A. J. (in press,a). Culture and psychopathology. In A. Kazdin (Ed.) *The encyclopedia of psychology*. Washington, DC: American Psychological Association Press/Oxford University Press.

Marsella, A. J. (in press,b). Culture bound disorders. In A. Kazdin (Ed.) *The encyclopedia of psychology*. Washington, DC: American Psychological Association Press/Oxford University Press.

Marsella, A. J., Bornemann, T., Ekblad, S., & Orley, J. (1994). *Amidst peril and pain: The mental health and wellbeing of the world's refugees.* Washington, DC: American Psychological Association Press.

Marsella, A. J., Friedman, M., Gerrity, E., & Scurfield, R. (1996). *Ethnocultural aspects of PTSD.* Washington, DC: American Psychological Association Press.

Marsella, A. J., & Higginbotham, H. (1984). Traditional Asian medicine: Applications to psychiatric services. In P. Pedersen, N. Sartorius, & A. Marsella (Eds.). *Mental health services: The cross-cultural context.* (pp. 175–198). Beverly Hills, CA: Sage.

Marsella, A. J., Purcell, I., & Carr, s. (1999). *Qualitative and quantitative research methods in intercultural relations.* Unpublished manuscript.

Marsella, A. J., Sartorius, N., Jablensky, A., & Fenton, R. (1986). Culture and depressive disorders. In A. Kleinman & B. Good (Eds.), *Culture and depression* (pp. 299–324). Berkeley, CA: University of California Press.

Marsella, A. J., & Scheuer, A. (1993). Coping: Definitions, conceptualizations, and issues. *Integrative Psychiatry, 9,* 124–134.

Marsella, A. J., Suarez, E., Leland, T., Morse, H., Digman, B., & Scheuer, A. (1996). *Culture and schizophrenia: An overview of the research and clinical literature.* Unpublished paper. Department of Psychology, University of Hawai'i, Honolulu, Hawai'i.

Mezzich, J., Kleinman, A., Fabrega, H., & Parron, D. (Eds.) (1996). *Culture and psychiatric diagnosis: A DSM-IV perspective.* Washington, DC: American Psychiatric Press.

Misra, G. (1996). Section in Gergen, K., Gulerce, A., Lock, A., & Misra, G. (1996). Psychological science in cultural context. *American Psychologist, 51,* 496–503.

Murdock, G. (1980). *Theories of illness: A world survey.* Pittsburgh, PA: University of Pittsburgh Press.

Murphy, J. (1976). Psychiatric labeling in cross-cultural perspective. *Science, 191,* 1019–1028.

Paz, O. (1967). *The labyrinth of solitude.* London: Penguin Press.

Pedersen, P., & Marsella, A. J. (1982). The ethical crisis in cross-cultural/counseling and psychotherapy. *Professional Psychology, 13,* 492–500.

Rosen, G. (1968). *Madness in society: Chapters in the historical sociology of mental illness.* New York: Harper Torchbooks.

Shweder, R. (1991). *Thinking through cultures: Expeditions in cultural psychology.* Cambridge, MA: Harvard University Press.

Simons, R., & Hughes, C. (Eds.) (1985). *The culture-bound syndromes.* Boston, MA: G. Reidel/Kluwer.

Sloan, T. (1996a). Psychological research methods in developing countries. In S. Carr & J. Schumaker (Eds.) *Psychology and the developing world* (pp. 38–45). New York: Praeger.

Sloan, T. (1996b). *Damaged life: The crisis of the modern psyche.* London: Routledge.

Stannard, D. (1992). *American holocaust:* The conquest of the new world. New York: Oxford University Press.

Wittkower, E. (1969). Perspectives of transcultural psychiatry. *International Journal of Psychiatry, 8,* 811–824.

Yamada, A. M., Marsella, A. J., & Yamada. S. (1998). The development of the Ethnocultural Identity Behavioral Index: Psychometric properties and validation with Asian-American and Pacific islanders. *Asian-American and Pacific Islander Journal of Health, 6,* 35–45.

Yap, P. M. (1951). Mental disease peculiar to certain cultures: A survey of comparative psychiatry. *Journal of Mental Science, 97,* 313–327.

Zilboorg, G. (1967). *A history of medical psychology.* New York: Norton. Original work published 1941.

Cultural Models of Health and Illness

RONALD J. ANGEL
KRISTI WILLIAMS
Department of Sociology
University of Texas at Austin
Austin, Texas

A physician diagnoses disease on the basis of signs and symptoms, and society evaluates and responds to sickness with understanding or condemnation depending on the moral loadings of the behaviors involved. For the individual experiencing symptoms, though, illness remains intensely personal and subjective. No one besides the ill person can feel his or her pain. Ironically, that intensely personal experience reveals the meeting of private and social worlds. The meaning that illness has for the individual, and his or her response to it, are based both on individual psychological factors and the socially based cognitive models concerning pain and suffering, as well as their causes and consequences, that are part of one's cultural tradition. One experiences illness alone, but one does so using cognitive schemas and language that are part of the culture that one inherits from one's progenitors.

The anthropological literature is filled with examples of cultural differences in how individuals categorize and label diseases and symptoms (Gaines, 1992a; Kleinman, 1982; Yoder, 1995). People from different cultures think and talk

Handbook of Multicultural Mental Health: Assessment and Treatment of Diverse Populations

about their suffering using their own idioms of distress. For the scientific observer, the consequence is that he or she simply cannot assume that the illness terms used in standard research protocols that are based on the illness experiences of one culture remain conceptually equivalent in any other (Good, 1993; Marsella, 1987). Although basic pathological processes may be culturally invariant, the subjective experience of illness and its emotional consequences are certainly not.

For researchers, the message is that one cannot study disease in isolation of other aspects of personality, social organization, and culture. Most immediately, understanding the impact of culture on the subjective aspects of illness requires understanding the role of culture in defining the self and threats to the self. Like illness, the self is conceptualized in unique ways by individuals from different cultures (Lock & Scheper-Hughes, 1996). In the West we distinguish between mind and body, but this distinction and our separation of somatic and psychiatric medicine, is only one among many ways of conceiving the person (Kleinman & Kleinman, 1985). Many, if not most, cultures do not conceive of the mind as something independent of the body, and different cultures construe the self in very different ways. In some, individuals perceive themselves as having several selves, and in others, the individual self and the social self are synonymous (Lock & Scheper-Hughes, 1996). This diversity in conceptions of the self is paralleled by differences in how threats to the self are perceived and how these threats influence health.

In this chapter we do not attempt to review the massive literature related to culture and health, especially since there is a large body of work on the impact of culture on emotion and the self that is directly relevant to understanding the subjective aspects of physical and mental illness. There are too many fields and approaches involved in the study of the impact of culture on health and related issues, and one chapter is simply too limited to even superficially summarize what has been done in anthropology, sociology, and psychology with respect to culture, emotions, self-concept, and health. The literature cited in this chapter, as well as several surveys, serve as a good entry point for the general reader (D'Andrade, 1995; D'Andrade & Strauss, 1992; Holland & Quinn, 1987; Sargent & Johnson, 1996; Shweder & LeVine, 1984; Shweder & Sullivan, 1993).

This chapter focuses on the articulation of personal narratives and larger public discourses, including scientific discourses, that relate to health and illness. In it, we situate the study of culture, health, and illness within larger discussions of culture, self, and emotions, and develop a complex conception of culture that goes beyond simple notions of guiding principles, norms, or latent structures. We also develop an active conception of culture in which the narrative structures with which health and illness are perceived and acted upon are the result of purposive action by information-gathering actors who operate within changing, information-rich physical and social environments (Sewell, 1992).

I. CULTURE AND MEANING

Culture lies at the very heart of what it means to be human. Yet the study of culture has become an increasingly sophisticated undertaking that proceeds well outside of the language of everyday discourse, even as its objective is to understand everyday discourse. This situation results from the fact that understanding the role of culture in social and personal life requires that we somehow stand outside of it, and that we observe the social world from a privileged position unaffected by the culturally based cognitive schemas that structure our very perceptions and cognitions. Clearly, that level of objectivity is impossible since our understanding of the social world is inevitably filtered through the parochial worldviews that we inherit, like the language we use to describe it, from the culture into which we were born. Perhaps the greatest utility of the study of cultural influences in human perceptions, emotions, and behavior is that it leads us to realize that pure objectivity is impossible in understanding human life, and that all understanding involves interpretation that is grounded in a specific cultural perspective (Geertz, 1973, 1984). An appreciation of the impact of culture, then, is important both for understanding the motivations and worldviews of social actors, as well as the motivations and worldviews of those who study them.

Clearly, we are not inevitably trapped in only one culture or one way of seeing the world. Many individuals are fluent in several languages and easily navigate between two or more cultures. Anthropology, linguistics, sociology, psychology, culture studies, and cognitive science are all involved in going beyond parochial approaches to the study of human behavior to a fuller understanding of what is common to all human societies. Unfortunately, understanding another's worldview, like learning their language, is not easy, and a superficial understanding can be as misleading as no understanding at all. Gaining insight into what it means to be human in the larger sense, though, means first understanding what is involved in existing as a particular person in a particular society who has been socialized into a particular set of cultural beliefs and practices.

Today culture is increasingly seen to be more than a fixed set of guiding principles or latent structures that mechanically guide aggregate or individual behavior. Rather, culture is recognized as a set of malleable and changing cognitive options, a "tool kit" (Swidler, 1986) from which individuals and groups choose in order to accomplish specific goals (D'Andrade & Strauss, 1992; R. Rosaldo, 1993; Sewell, 1992). This more dynamic and complex view of culture has resulted in a greater appreciation of the deliberate, and often rational, behavior of social actors (Bourdieu, 1990; D'Andrade, 1995; Zarubavel, 1997).

Characterizations of cultural groups as homogeneous in almost any characteristic are increasingly recognized to be little more than caricatures (R. Rosaldo,

1993). Americans of Mexican origin, for example, may share certain cultural features, but Mexican-American culture does little more than provide certain ways of seeing and talking about the world that individuals adopt to varying degrees depending upon their individual agendas. If it serves the purpose of political empowerment, a strong Mexican identity may be useful; if it does not, that identity may erode.

The growing realization of the dynamic character of culture has important implications for the social and behavioral sciences, as well as for our understanding of the subjective aspects of health and illness. Yet even as we begin to appreciate the importance of culture in human emotion and cognition, understanding culture and its role in human behavior has been made more difficult by the almost unimaginable pace of growth in communication technology, as well as by the large-scale migration characteristic of the modern world. Few cultures are isolated any longer, and there is almost no place on the planet into which modern medical knowledge and public health campaigns have not made inroads. The extensive reach of modern medical knowledge, spread often through aggressive educational campaigns, creates situations in which folk beliefs and practices exist alongside biomedically based beliefs and practices (Kelleher & Hillier, 1996; Lane, 1997; Marsella & White, 1982; Pelto & Pelto, 1996; Rubel & Hass, 1996; Vecchiato, 1997; Whiteford, 1997; Young, 1981).

Individuals in all cultures have multiple explanatory options from which to draw, and they are able to shop around for explanations, diagnoses, and treatments for specific sets of symptoms. What is adopted from another explanatory system is often reinterpreted to better conform to local conceptions of the causes and treatment of specific illness (Kleinman, 1980, 1988b; Pelto & Pelto, 1997; Pollock, 1996). For the social scientific observer, this mingling of the cultures of Western biomedicine and what anthropologists term "ethnobiologies" introduces greater complexity into understanding how individuals define, evaluate, and respond to symptoms. In the modern world, many individuals consciously adopt new explanatory systems. A growing number of middle-class Americans, for example, have adopted the practices and associated explanations of the relationship between mind and body and the causes of health and illness taught by traditional Chinese medicine. The villages that scientists study today are increasingly large urban ones, and any specific culture we wish to understand is unlikely to have remained isolated from larger global influences.

Understanding the health beliefs and practices, as well as the illness behavior, of poor urban minority Americans requires more than traditional epidemiology or ethnography. Rather, as we propose at the end of this chapter, what is required is a cultural epidemiology that combines the methodologies, as well as the theoretical insights, of a traditional ethnographic focus on the individual and his or her belief systems, with that of epidemiology and its focus on the social and economic causes of illness (Pelto & Pelto, 1997; Trostle & Sommerfeld, 1996).

II. SOCIAL DIFFERENTIATION AND CULTURE

The growing acceptance of culture as a malleable, changing set of cognitive options is a clear improvement over previous characterizations of culture as a set of prescribed beliefs and practices that all members of the group accept and follow slavishly. What has been less well developed, though, is the close association between culture as a purely symbolic system and social class or social status (Sewell, 1992). In the modern world the domination of one people by another, which is the very definition of colonialism, and the global domination of Western scientific medicine has resulted in a complex situation in which social hierarchies intersect with racial and ethnic differences, resulting not only in variations in health between the rich and the poor, but also inequalities in access to medical care and medical knowledge (Chavez, 1986; Morsy, 1996; Navarro, 1986; Turshen, 1989).

All societies are based on social hierarchies. What differs between nation-states is the degree of disparity in power, wealth, and control over their own lives between the rich and the poor. What also differs is the extent to which these distinctions are based on ethnic or racial group membership. Black South Africans, as well as many black Americans, continue to live in separate worlds than those of their white conationalists. Large fractions of the indigenous populations of many nations, including the Native American population of the United States, occupy the lowest rungs in the social hierarchy, where they suffer the deleterious health consequences of poverty and political powerlessness.

The result is that what we think of as culture, the purely cognitive set of symbols, rules, values, norms, and linguistic tropes that are informed by the internalized frames or schemas with which we interpret that world, is confounded with structured systems of social differentiation. This fact brings what is purely cultural into direct contact with the political and the economic. An understanding of culture, and especially its role in health and illness, must deal with all of these complex interconnections and immediately come to terms with the reality of power differentials between groups, including those based on race and ethnicity, gender, and age.

III. OBJECTIVITY AND SUBJECTIVITY

In science objectivity is the ideal, yet objectivity in the study of culture and its influence is particularly elusive, because we can only view the world from some specific cultural vantage point, and our own culture, like the native language that we speak expertly without necessarily being able to state its rules of grammar, has a taken-for-granted nature to it. We are experts in our own culture, and we navigate its complexity without having to consciously attend to the myriad of implicit and explicit rules that over a lifetime have become an almost unconscious part of our perceptual and behavioral repertory. It is only when we attempt to learn a new language that the full complexity of semantics and grammar becomes manifest, and the elusiveness of the subjective world of other language communities becomes apparent.

The same is true of other aspects of culture, as translation from one complex symbolic system into another requires a deep understanding of each and, even then, the newcomer often remains an outsider. It is important to differentiate, especially for the study of health, between those aspects of culture that are observable by an outsider and the subjective manifestations of culture that represent the private experiences of individuals. Later we will develop this contrast between what can be directly observed and confirmed and that which is personal and inaccessible to anyone but the person who experiences it. Subjective experience is overdetermined, which means that it arises from many different realms simultaneously, and although the language and the cognitive schema through which illness is experienced is influenced in important respects by cultural factors, subjective experience and one's sense of being well or ill are influenced as well by individual psychological and emotional factors. An appreciation of the complexity and difficulty inherent in understanding the subjective worlds of other human beings is necessary if explanations of individual and aggregate behaviors that draw upon "culture" are to do more than beg the question as to what specific influences are at work, or if they are not to mask the influence of power and social class as something more innocuous.

IV. THE ROLE OF CULTURE IN HEALTH AND ILLNESS

Interest in the role of culture in defining health and illness and help-seeking behavior continues to grow because of the framing function that culture serves in forming the backdrop against which all aspects of our lives are interpreted and from which our actions take meaning. Numerous general overviews and critiques of contemporary medical anthropology provide useful insights into the state of both theory and practice in the study of culture and physical and mental health (e.g., Good, 1993; Sargent & Johnson, 1996; Yoder, 1997). These overviews make the point that without an appreciation of the role of culture in human perception (including scientific observation), we run the risk of misinterpreting and misdiagnosing illnesses because of our own ethnocentric biases. Such biases are built into the very diagnostic instruments that we imagine are objective (Good, 1993, 1994; Marsella, 1987).

Contemporary theories of psychopathology focus heavily on the biological or psychological correlates of emotional illness and ignore the contribution of the physical, social, and cultural environment to such disorders as depression (Marsella, 1987). As Anthony Marsella (1987) notes, however, mental and emotional well-being are embedded in a hierarchy of meaning-giving systems that include family and social networks at the interpersonal level, and culture and macro social structures at even higher levels (Marsella, 1987). To focus solely on biological or psychological processes is to ignore the context in which they operate and in which threats to one's sense of self and autonomy are interpreted and in which illness in defined, both by the individual and by society.

Yet, even a basic description of verbal illness categories, local explanatory models, and other cultural knowledge are not sufficient to predict behavior or to fully understand subjective experience (R. Rosaldo 1993; Rubel & Hass, 1996). In order to understand what makes individuals act in response to symptoms and malaise, it is necessary to understand the culturally based schemas that give rise to such explanatory models and illness labels. That meaning comes from multiple and changing sources, and it is negotiated between the individual and the healer (Hunt, Jordan, Irwin, & Browner, 1989). Ultimately, the meaning that symptoms and illness have for individuals is revealed narratively, because descriptions of structure provide only snapshots of dynamic processes.

Although we tend to think of culture as consisting of fundamental identities, typically those associated with one's tribal or national group, individuals can participate in several cultures at the same time, just as one can become fluent in more than one language. Professional groups, formal organizations, clubs, religious denominations, cults, and so on, have their own institutional cultures. Western biomedically based medicine itself represents a culture into which medical students are enculturated (Good, 1994; Pelto & Pelto, 1996). The cross-fertilization of these cultures is one of the most striking aspects of our modern world in which cultural isolation is almost impossible.

Education, including medical education and public health, is a form of enculturation or acculturation (Angel & Thoits, 1987). The fundamental objective of public health campaigns, whether aimed at getting people to practice breast self-examinations or to reduce the amount of fat in their diet in order to reduce their risk of heart disease, is to change people's understanding of how their bodies operate and convince them that they can and should take control of aspects of their own health. Whether changes in diet will, in fact, result in a longer life for any individual is as much an act of faith as the Hopi's belief that by dancing they can bring rain. Modern clinical medicine and epidemiology are as much belief systems as any other, even if a large body of that belief has empirical support. Much else in the canon does not.

To be useful, therefore, our understanding of culture must take into account many other institutions, including economic and political ones, that comprise part of the formal and informal system that gives meaning to the actions of any group, both to themselves and outside observers (Marsella, 1987). It must be understood as the context from which an individual draws social capital and resources and within which he or she interprets the world and acts.

V. SCHEMATA AND COGNITIVE PROCESSES

One very useful way to begin to understand how culture influences individuals' beliefs concerning the preservation of health, the causes of illness, and appropriate courses of action to take in the event of illness is the concept of cognitive schemas (Angel & Thoits, 1987; D'Andrade, 1992, 1995; Langacker, 1987; Singer & Salovey, 1991). Schemas refer to culturally based embedded and hierarchical abstractions concerning both categories and processes (D'Andrade, 1995). Several schemas are involved in recognizing, labeling, and acting on any aspect of reality, in our case, symptoms and illnesses. Schemas can perhaps be best conceived of as stored bodies of lore, knowledge, and experience that we use to make sense out of raw input. Obviously, the concept of schema is only a useful way of characterizing the complexity of human cognitive processing. Schemas do not exist in some specific area of the brain, and they are constantly being revised and altered as we experience new things and learn about the particular aspect of reality to which they refer (Angel & Thoits, 1987).

Schemas concerning health and illness are particularly salient to the study of health and illness because they influence what we label and react to as pathological and how we respond to symptoms and deviations from what we consider normal. They also help influence our perceptions of good health and what we need to do to maintain it (Angel & Thoits, 1987). D'Andrade (1995), a leading cognitive anthropologist, provides a useful example of the importance of understanding illness-based schemas in determining how people make sense of illnesses. D'Andrade has carefully studied American's beliefs about illness. His work began with the traditional anthropological categorization of symptoms and illness in terms of their characteristics. For example, people find it simple to categorize specific illness in terms of such statements as "you can catch ＿＿＿ from other people," or "＿＿＿ is the result of old age," or "＿＿＿ runs in families." In one study, D'Andrade had his college student respondents categorize 30 illnesses in terms of 30 such statements for a total of 900 judgments. By examining the logical connections between these, he was able to reduce the number of meaningful clusters to three: (a) those consisting of illnesses that are serious, fatal, crippling, affect the heart, and are not experienced by everyone, (b) those illnesses that are caused by germs or a lack of resistance, contracted in cold weather, accompanied by a fever, sore throat, or runny nose, and are not crippling or incurable, and (c) diseases that have no cure, run in the family, indicate old age, and are caused by emotions (D'Andrade, 1995, pp. 127–128).

Although these clusters make sense to participants in the culture that produced them, D'Andrade was dissatisfied by the fact that the categorizations themselves provide no information on how they are generated. As a sensitive observer, he came to realize that in order for one to understand how people make judgments about illnesses, one must understand the schemas that give rise to the categorizations. D'Andrade's focus on schemas provides a potentially fruitful way of examining the social and cultural aspects of health and illness. Culture, as it is reflected in our internal schemas, influences how we interpret symptoms, feelings, and behaviors, both our own and those of others. Through its influence on interpretive schemas, it defines what is healthy, acceptable, and normal, and what is ill, deviant, and abnormal. The task for researchers is to discover new and imaginative ways of studying individuals' schemas as they relate to health and illness, and to determine exactly how those schemas are influenced by culture and social class.

Unfortunately, the concept of schema introduces a serious complexity into the study of the cognitive aspects of illness. There is no reason, in fact, to treat schemas as if they are entirely cognitive (D'Andrade, 1995). Cognitions, after all, are closely tied to basic emotions and physiological processes. The complexity introduced into the study of culture and human cognition by the concept of schema makes our task of understanding illness behavior more difficult, but it clearly reflects the real complexity that exists in this world of mingling cultures. The concept of culturally influenced schema is a clear theoretical advancement because it goes beyond the notion of culture as a set of rules or norms that inevitably structure behavior or understanding. Schemas are highly malleable, and individuals can use them or aspects of them as their personal agendas require. It is important, after all, to view the human actor as a culturally embedded, yet autonomous actor who need not be led blindly by aggregate beliefs and practices. Rather, he or she should be understood as someone who can pick and choose from the cultural repertoires with which he or she is presented.

VI. PSYCHE AND SOMA: THE MIND–BODY DISTINCTION IN WESTERN MEDICINE

To be human is to inhabit a body. Yet the notion of inhabiting a body implies that there is some nonmaterial essence that coexists with the body, but that is in some way separate from it. Such an entity can be seen as a soul or a vital force, or perhaps even the "mind." Cultures differ in the extent to which they differentiate between the physical and the nonphysical aspects of the self. In the West, both medical and popular discourse differentiate between the mind and the body, or the psyche and the soma, to use the Greek roots that refer to these aspects of the self (Lock, 1993; Lock & Scheper-Hughes, 1996; Pollock, 1996). The psychological and psychiatric specialties deal with disorders of the mind and emotions, and somatic medicine treats the body and its disorders. What mind actually consist of is a matter of continuing debate, and we will leave the resolution of that debate to philosophers and cognitive scientists. What is of great importance for our purpose, though, is the fact that in the West people differentiate between the mind and the body in how they talk about symptoms. In the United States we feel "stressed" or "depressed" or "anxious," and we attribute nonphysical causes to these feelings. Other cultures do not differentiate between the psychological and the somatic in quite so clear a manner (Angel & Guarnaccia, 1989; Kleinman, 1988b; M. Rosaldo, 1984).

VII. CULTURE, EMOTION, AND HEALTH

The intensely personal and subjective nature of illness leads us to the realization that emotion and illness are closely intertwined. When one is ill, one feels discouraged, anxious, tired, and so on. As critics of extreme mind–body dualism point out, physical illness has immediate emotional correlates, and emotional distress can manifest itself somatically. Those cultural factors, therefore, that influence emotion and self-perception are highly salient in the study of cultural influences on health.

A growing body of anthropological literature is providing convincing evidence that although basic emotions may be the same in different cultures, the events and contexts that elicit them and provide labels for emotions such as anger, shame, and despair can be rather different. Behaviors by others that threaten one's sense of self in a culture like that of the United States in which individuality and personal autonomy are valued may cause anger, whereas similar behavior in a less individualistic Asian culture may not elicit that particular emotion. It would be possible, but also a mistake, to conceive of the schema governing illness perception and behaviors as purely cognitive. The culturally based cognitive aspects of schemas clearly give meaning to symptoms and behaviors, but they also directly elicit such emotions as fear, anxiety, or anger. The emotional aspect of illness, therefore, must be understood in conjunction with its cognitive aspect.

In recent years the study of cultural influences on emotions and self-concept has blossomed (Cousins, 1989; Heine & Lehman, 1995; Holland & Quinn, 1987; Kitayama & Markus, 1994; Markus & Kitayama, 1991; Marsella, DeVos, & Hsu, 1985; Pollock, 1996; Shweder & LeVine, 1984; Shweder & Sullivan, 1993). The core question motivating these investigations is whether or not emotions are culturally universal (Wierzbicka, 1986). The growing consensus, and our own view, is that cognition and emotion are intimately intertwined in specifically contexualized ways. In Michelle Rosaldo's words, "feeling is forever given shape through thought and thought is laden with emotional meaning" (M. Rosaldo, 1984, p. 143.). What elicits anger or fear or insecurity or any other emotion or feeling depends upon what we, as cultural actors, find enraging, frightful, or threatening.

Together the mind and the body make up the "person" whose personal experiences are interpreted and influenced by the social context that defines the local moral order (Fabrega, 1974; Kleinman 1988a, 1986; Kleinman & Good, 1985; Lock, 1993; Pollock, 1996). In Asian societies, in which interdependence is valued over independence, the self is construed much more collectively than in the West, and emotional responses to what are viewed as threats to the self are commensurately different (Heine & Lehman, 1995; Kitayama & Markus, 1994; Kitayama, Markus, Matsumoto, & Norasakkunkit, 1997; Markus & Kitayama, 1991; Scherer, 1997; Suh, Diener, Oishi, & Triandis, 1998). Such culturally based aspects of the self-concept are affected by acculturation and one's degree of identity with a traditional or host culture (Rhee, Uleman, Lee, & Roman, 1995), and, given the changing nature of culture, they are clearly historically and politically situated as well (Schooler, 1996).

A. A CONCEPTUAL MODEL

In order to help make sense of the complexity involved in the association between culture and health, we posit a basic model with two axes around which the literature indicates that individuals and cultures construe illness. In the figure below, an illness definition model, the horizontal axis differentiates between what is publicly observable (objective) and what is entirely private (subjective). This axis allows us to differentiate between those aspects of disease and sickness that are publicly visible or that can be objectively diagnosed and verified, and those that cannot be verified by an external observer. A florid psychotic episode, for example, provides public verification of psychiatric disease, especially when it is combined with a physician's diagnosis. Cancer or heart disease, as clinical entities, can be diagnosed through clinical tests.

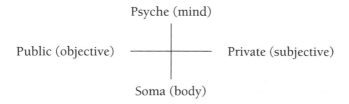

Subjective experience, on the other hand, cannot be objectively verified and remains the privileged domain of the individual. It is, in principle, private, and information that an individual provides concerning his or her internal state must be taken at face value because it cannot be objectively verified. Much mental illness and personal suffering is of this nature; when there are no objective tests that can be employed to verify the existence of pathology, self-reports of subjective states serve as the only markers of illness. When no objective indicators of disease are present, an individual is at risk of being considered a malingerer or hypochondriac.

On the vertical axis of the model we differentiate between the mind (psyche) and the body (soma). As noted, in the West we differentiate between somatic illness and psychiatric illness in medical specializations, as well as in public discourse. As the work we cited earlier makes clear, though, not all cultures differentiate between the mind and the body to this extent. Nor, we would add, does our subjective experience. More traditional cultures typically view the self as holistic and illness as consisting simultaneously of physical, mental, and even social components.

Although there are clearly other dimensions that we could introduce, this model emphasizes two important dimensions that are directly affected by culture. Western biomedicine focuses most heavily in the somatic/objective quadrant and deals with physical diseases with clear biological markers. The softer sciences, including social psychiatry, focus more on the psychic half of the model, especially on the social and cultural influences on disease.

B. SOMATIZATION: AN EXAMPLE

The fact that subjective experience does not differentiate between physical and mental states has important implications for research on culture and health, as well as for clinical practice (Angel & Thoits, 1987; Lock, 1993; Lock & Scheper-Hughes, 1996). Angel and Guarnaccia (1989) illustrate how emotional status and perceptions of physical health are intertwined in a study that used survey responses from a large sample of Mexican Americans and Puerto Ricans in the United States. This study illustrated the fact that standard survey methodologies, which are frequently used to assess physical and emotional status, may confound the two, because individuals do not distinguish between the physical and the emotional in their lived experience.

This work is part of a tradition dating from Zborowski's (1952) classic study in which he found that individuals from different ethnic groups respond to pain differently, and subsequent research that documented a tendency among members of traditional cultures to "somatize," a term used to characterize the tendency to express affective distress or social discord as physical (somatic) illness

(Grau & Padgett, 1988; Katon, Kleinman, & Rosen, 1982a, 1982b). Somatization refers to the presence of physical symptoms for which there is no diagnosable physical pathology (Kirmayer, 1984a, 1984b). In somatization disorder the body serves as a medium for expressing social and emotional distress. The expression of affective distress somatically is common among the old and the poor, who must deal with physical decline, isolation, and poverty (Grau and Padgett, 1988; Kleinman, Good, & Guarnaccia, 1986; Krause & Carr, 1978).

One of the major motivations for the study of the role of affective distress on physical illness is the consistent finding that a large proportion of those seeking general medical services have little organic basis for their symptoms (Grau & Padgett, 1988; Katon et al., 1982a, 1982b). In their study, Angel and Guarnaccia (1989) used the Hispanic Health and Nutrition Examination Survey (H-HANES), a large-scale epidemiological and health survey in which respondents received a physical examination, to compare a physician's overall assessment of an individual's health to the respondent's own assessment. The physician and the respondent independently rated the respondents health as excellent, very good, good, fair, or poor. Angel and Guarnaccia found that respondents who had high scores on a standard depressive affect scale, the Center for Epidemiologic Studies Depression scale (CES-D), rated their health as significantly worse than did the physicians. This association was significantly affected by the language in which the survey was conducted. It appears, then, that rates of physical illness and psychological distress that are found using standard survey instruments are potentially influenced by factors related to culture, language, and level of acculturation (Angel & Thoits, 1987).

Angel and Guarnaccia (1989) also reported large differences between Mexican Americans and Puerto Ricans in levels of affective distress. Although the association between depressive affect and negative assessments of physical health held for both groups, Puerto Ricans reported much higher levels of affective distress and poorer physical health than Mexican Americans. Researchers, in fact, consistently find that Puerto Ricans score higher on standard symptom checklists than any other ethnic group (Dohrenwend, 1966; Haberman, 1976, 1970; Srole et al., 1978). This may, of course, reflect differences in the social desirability of the symptoms in the scales (Dohrenwend, 1966), or it may be a reflection of cultural patterned ways of expressing distress (Haberman, 1976).

With the data available it is not possible to definitively determine why Puerto Ricans score so much higher on scales of affective distress than other groups. Angel and Guarnaccia (1989) speculate, however, that the symptoms included in the scales used in these studies are similar to those that are typical of a condition called *nervios* (nerves) in traditional Puerto Rican and other Hispanic cultures. *Nervios* is a culturally meaningful idiom of distress among Puerto Ricans. Those who have recently arrived from the island, and who are experiencing hardship may well express their distress using this idiom (Angel &

Guarnaccia, 1989; Kleinman et al., 1986; Krause & Carr; 1978). Symptoms of *nervios* include, headaches, trembling, heart palpitations, stomach and appetite disturbances, trouble with concentration, sleep problems, and worrying (Guarnaccia & Farias, 1988). Sufferers are more frequently women than men, and they are disportionately from rural and lower class backgrounds.

Certain evidence suggests that Mexican Americans may also express distress in terms of a similar idiom. A study of schizophrenics by Jenkins (1988) found that Mexican-American families characterized their family member's schizophrenic symptoms as symptoms of *nervios* and that they focused on a series of somatic complaints that tended to destigmatize the illness. Unfortunately, the literature on psychopathology for Mexican Americans provides quite inconsistent findings (Angel & Thoits, 1987). Again, though, the data reveal that the social desirability of symptoms, levels of acculturation, and culturally specific response styles influence responses to survey probes in, as yet, poorly understood ways.

Much research will be necessary to better understand what cultural factors affect the subjective experience of mental and physical illness and its expression. Numerous anthropologists have worked on this problem (Frake, 1961; Gaines, 1992b; Good, 1977; Kleinman, 1986; Kleinman & Kleinman, 1985; Manson, Shore, & Bloom, 1985). The importance of a better understanding has been made clearer by the very cosmopolitan nature of the modern world. In recent years the number of large multinational projects has increased, and it has simply become impossible to ignore local cultural and social class influences on health. Increasingly, even quantitatively oriented researchers are beginning to appreciate the importance of ethnography in epidemiological and health studies (Pelto & Pelto, 1997; Trostle & Sommerfeld, 1996).

VIII. CULTURAL VERSUS PSYCHOLOGICAL DETERMINISM

The literature we have reviewed demonstrates that a growing number of researchers have come to the realization that individual behaviors are motivated by psychological factors that give meaning to actions within specific cultural and social contexts, yet those contexts are fluid and changing. Socialization is far more complex than traditional sociological theories held, and culture does not consist of a set of rigid norms that all members of a particular culture follow blindly. Cultural patterns and messages are, to differing degrees, ambiguous and tentative. They are incompletely internalized, and they compete with other social, cultural, and personal needs (Harkness, Super, & Keefer, 1992). In addition, the meaning of symptoms itself is ambiguous, and diagnoses must be negotiated within what are ill-defined and fluid situations (Kirmayer, 1994).

Much traditional work on culture unfortunately left the impression that cultural patterns are more structured and permanent than they are. A Zapotec Indian in Mexico may recognize various artifacts as part of his culture and he or she may even share in a common conception of the causes, and consequences of some particular illness. To speak of the typical Zapotec, though, or to try to predict how any individual will behave from knowing general cultural patterns related to any area of life is futile. Work by Young (1981) in Mexico shows that practical considerations, such as money and transportation, are as important as, if not more important than, strictly cultural factors in seeking health care. Even during the heyday of classical anthropology, the impact of European material and scientific culture was changing simple tribal life (R. Rosaldo, 1993). Today everyone has a complex set of explanatory systems and behavioral options to choose from when it comes to health and illness. Western biomedicine has extended over the planet since, although it is a discourse like any other, it has proved to be remarkably effective in dealing with disease (Pelto & Pelto, 1997).

The result is that, just as we begin to appreciate the situated and contextualized nature of all human behavior, including that related to health and illness, dealing with those situations and that context has become much more complex. Just as it is incorrect to posit that physical and mental health and illness are purely objective and the same from one cultural and social context to the next, so it would be wrong to adopt a cultural determinist perspective in which all aspects of health and illness are viewed as social or cultural constructions. Clearly, clinical entities exist, and basic human physiological processes are everywhere and always the same. What differs is the context in which those processes are experienced and the ways in which individuals and groups recognize and define physical and mental health and illness. To be useful, a culturally informed approach to illness brings the individual, in his or her full cultural, social, and physical context back into the picture. The utility of an understanding of culture as dynamic, and confounded with other organizational and social class processes, is that it offers a way of understanding how universal physiological and psychological processes are structured by one's physical and social environment and how these together give rise to one's sense of self and well-being.

IX. A NEW CULTURAL PUBLIC HEALTH

Understanding why and how individuals respond to illness, as well as what they do to maintain their health, requires that we go beyond traditional health belief models to a better understanding of both the cognitive and the structural factors that influence action and individual's illness vocabularies (Lane, 1997; Pelto & Pelto, 1997; Vecchiato, 1997; Whiteford, 1997; Yoder, 1997). The overwhelming majority of humanity is moving rapidly into a world characterized by medical pluralism, in which they draw from several health-care systems, including that of modern medicine. Today, public health focuses on urban populations, rather than isolated tribal societies. The factors that affect both the beliefs and behaviors of individuals in such environments include many factors associated with social class and economics. Understanding social structures, and their impact on health, requires an emphasis on both the cognitive aspects of culture and the social and the material resources that individuals have at their disposal (Sewell, 1992).

This new reality calls for the combination of traditional epidemiological methods with ethnographic techniques that are better suited to assessing the terminology that individuals use to talk about disease and the meaning it has for them. Pelto and Pelto (1997) offer several techniques that the researcher can use to efficiently determine what terms individuals use to refer to specific illnesses and symptoms. Often these terms are borrowed from clinical medicine, yet the meaning that these terms have for locals may be very different than the meaning attached to them by medical professionals. Traditional health surveys and epidemiological studies would benefit greatly by such an initial attempt to better understand how people label symptoms and illnesses and what they actually imagine the illness to be.

The traditional approaches discussed earlier involve classifying and rank ordering symptoms to determine which are seen as belonging to the same or similar domains (D'Andrade, 1995; Pelto & Pelto, 1997). These techniques remain valuable, especially when they are combined with more narrative approaches that are aimed at determining the meaning systems (schemas) that give rise to the groupings.

Ultimately, our objective is to understand how and why individuals respond to specific symptoms and illnesses in the way they do. Traditional public health approaches assumed that risky health behavior or noncompliance with health-maintenance regimens was simply the result of ignorance and that this ignorance could be remedied through educational campaigns. Such campaigns, like the antismoking campaign of recent decades, met with less than complete success. Such efforts made it clear that people's behavior is determined by a combination of knowledge, culturally based beliefs about personal risk and the severity of potential outcomes, as well as practical factors like income and the availability of transportation. A new cultural public health will allow us to focus on traditional public health objectives, but to do so with a much better understanding of the complex interaction between knowledge, beliefs, and practical factors that determine behavior and individuals' overall sense of well-being.

REFERENCES

Angel, R., & Guarnaccia, P. J. (1989). Mind, body, and culture: Somatization among Hispanics. *Social Science and Medicine, 28,* 1229–1238.

Angel, R., & Thoits, P. (1987). The impact of culture on the cognitive structure of illness. *Culture, Medicine and Psychiatry, 11,* 465–494.

Bourdieu, P. (1990). *The logic of practice.* Stanford: Stanford University Press.

Chavez, L. R. (1986). Mexican immigration and health care: A political economic perspective. *Human Organization, 45,* 344–352.

Cousins, S. D. (1989). Culture and self-perception in Japan and the United States. *Journal of Personality and Social Psychology, 56,* 124–131.

D'Andrade, R. (1995). *The development of cognitive anthropology.* Cambridge, UK: Cambridge University Press.

D'Andrade, R. (1992). Schemas and motivation. In R. D'Andrade & C. Strauss (Eds.), *Human motives and cultural models* (pp. 23–44). Cambridge, UK: Cambridge University Press.

D'Andrade, R., & Strauss, C. (Eds.) (1992). *Human motives and cultural models.* Cambridge, UK: Cambridge University Press.

Dohrenwend, B. P. (1966). Social status and psychological disorder: An issue of substance and an issue of method. *American Sociological Review, 31,* 14–34.

Fabrega, H., Jr. (1974). *Disease and social behavior: An interdisciplinary perspective.* Cambridge, MA: Massachusetts Institute of Technology.

Frake, C. O. (1961). The diagnosis of disease among the Subanun of Mindanao. *American Anthropologist, 63,* 113–132.

Gaines, A. D. (Ed.) (1992a). *Ethnopsychiatry: The cultural construction of professional and folk psychiatries.* Albany, NY: State University of New York Press.

Gaines, A. D. (1992b). Medical/psychiatric knowledge in France and the United States: Culture and sickness in history and biology. In A. D. Gaines (Ed.), *Ethnopsychiatry: The cultural construction of professional and folk psychiatries* (pp. 171–201). Albany, NY: State University of New York Press.

Geertz, C. (1984). From the native's point of view: On the nature of anthropological understanding. In R. A. Shweder & R. A. LeVine (Eds.), *Culture theory: Essays on mind, self, and emotion* (pp. 123–136). Cambridge, UK: Cambridge University Press.

Geertz, C. (1973). *The interpretation of cultures.* New York: Basic Books.

Good, B. J. (1994). *Medicine, rationality, and experience: An anthropological perspective.* Cambridge, UK: Cambridge University Press.

Good, B. J. (1993). Culture, diagnosis and comorbidity. *Culture, Medicine and Psychiatry, 16,* 427–446.

Good, B. J. (1977). The heart of what's the matter: The semantics of illness in Iran. *Culture, Medicine and Psychiatry, 1,* 25–58.

Grau, L., & Padgett, D. (1988). Somatic depression among the elderly: A sociocultural perspective. *International Journal of Geriatric Psychiatry, 3,* 201–207.

Guarnaccia, P., & Farias, P. (1988). The social meanings of *nervios:* A case study of a central American woman. *Social Science and Medicine, 26,* 1223–1231.

Haberman, P. W. (1976). Psychiatric symptoms among Puerto Ricans in Puerto Rico and New York City. *Ethnicity, 3,* 133–144.

Haberman, P. W. (1970). Ethnic differences in psychiatric symptoms reported in community surveys. *Public Health Reports, 85,* 495–502.

Harkness, S., Super, C. M., & Keefer, C. H. (1992). Learning to be an American parent: How cultural models gain directive force. In R. G. D'Andrade & C. Strauss (Eds.), *Human motives and cultural models* (pp. 163–178). Cambridge, UK: Cambridge University Press.

Heine, S. J., & Lehman, D. R. (1995). Cultural variation in unrealistic optimism: Does the West feel more invulnerable than the East? *Journal of Personality and Social Psychology, 68,* 595–607.

Holland, D., & Quinn, N. (Eds.) (1987). *Cultural models in language and thought.* Cambridge, UK: Cambridge University Press.

Hunt, L. M., Jordan, B., Irwin, S., & Browner, C. H. (1989). Compliance and the patient's perspective. *Culture, Medicine and Psychiatry, 13,* 315–334.

Jenkins, J. H. (1988). Ethnopsychiatric interpretations of schizophrenic illness: The problem of *nervios* within Mexican-American families. *Culture, Medicine and Psychiatry, 12,* 301–329.

Katon, W., Kleinman, A., & Rosen, G. (1982a). Depression and somatization: A review, part I. *American Journal of Medicine, 72,* 127–135.

Katon, W., Kleinman, A., & Rosen, G. (1982b). Depression and somatization: A review, part II. *American Journal of Medicine, 72,* 241–247.

Kelleher, D., & Hillier, S. (Eds.) (1996). *Researching cultural differences in health.* London: Routledge.

Kirmayer, L. J. (1994). Improvisation and authority in illness meaning. *Culture, Medicine and Psychiatry, 18,* 183–214.

Kirmayer, L. J. (1984a). Culture, affect and somatization, part I. *Transcultural Psychiatric Research Review, 21,* 159–188.

Kirmayer, L. J. (1984b). Culture, affect and somatization, part II. *Transcultural Psychiatric Research Review, 21,* 237–262.

Kitayama, S., & Markus, H. R. (Eds.) (1994). *Emotion and culture: Empirical studies of mutual influence.* Washington, DC: American Psychological Association.

Kitayama, S., Markus, H. R., Matsumoto, H., & Norasakkunkit, V. (1997). Individual and collective processes in the construction of the self: Self-enhancement in the United States and self-criticism in Japan. *Journal of Personality and Social Psychology, 72,* 1245–1267.

Kleinman, A. (1988a). *The illness narratives: Suffering, healing, and the human condition.* New York: Basic Books.

Kleinman, A. (1988b). *Rethinking psychiatry.* New York: The Free Press.

Kleinman, A. (1986). *Social origins of distress and disease: Depression, neurasthenia, and pain in modern China.* New Haven, CT: Yale University Press.

Kleinman, A. (1982). Neurasthenia and depression: A study of somatization and culture in China. *Culture, Medicine and Psychiatry, 6,* 117–190.

Kleinman, A. (1980). *Patients and healers in the context of culture: An exploration of the borderland between anthropology, medicine, and psychiatry.* Berkeley: University of California Press.

Kleinman, A., & Good, B. (Eds.) (1985). *Culture and depression: Studies in the anthropology and cross-cultural psychiatry of affect and disorder.* Berkeley: University of California Press.

Kleinman, A., & Kleinman, J. (1985). Somatization: The interconnections in Chinese society among culture, depressive experiences, and the meanings of pain. In A. Kleinman & B. Good (Eds.), *Culture and depression* (pp. 429–490). Berkeley: University of California Press.

Kleinman, A. Good, B., & Guarnaccia, P. J. (1986). *Critical review of selected cross cultural literature on depression and anxiety disorders.* Final report under a contract with the National Institute of Mental Health (PLO No. 85M029642401D).

Krause, N., & Carr, L. G. (1978). The effects of response bias in the survey assessment of the mental health of Puerto Rican migrants. *Social Psychiatry, 13,* 167–173.

Lane, S. D. (1997). Television minidramas: Social marketing and evaluation in Egypt. *Medical Anthropology Quarterly, 11,* 164–182.

Langacker, R. (1987). *Foundations of cognitive grammar* (Vol. 1. Theoretical perspectives). Stanford: Stanford University Press.

Lock, M. M. (1993). *Encounters with aging: Mythologies of menopause in Japan and North America.* Berkeley: University of California Press.

Lock, M., & Scheper-Hughes, N. (1996). A critical-interpretive approach in medical anthropology: Rituals and routines of discipline and dissent. In C. F. Sargent & T. M. Johnson (Eds.), *Medical anthropology: Contemporary theory and method* (rev. ed.) (pp. 41–70). Westport, CT: Praeger.

Manson, S. M., Shore, J. H., & Bloom, J. D. (1985). The depressive experience in American Indian communities: A challenge for psychiatric theory and diagnosis. In A. Kleinman & B. Good (Eds.), *Culture and depression* (pp. 331–368). Berkeley: University of California Press.

Markus, H. R., & Kitayama, S. (1991). Culture and the self: Implications for cognition, emotion, and motivation. *Psychological Review, 98,* 224–253.

Marsella, A. J. (1987). The measurement of depressive experience and disorder across cultures. In A. J. Marsella, R. M. A.

Marsella, A. J., DeVos, G., & Hsu, F. L. K. (Eds.) (1985). *Culture and self: Asian and Western perspectives.* New York: Tavistock Publications.

Marsella, A. J., & White, G. M. (Eds.) (1982). *Cultural conceptions of mental health and therapy.* Boston: D. Reidel.

Morsy, S. A. (1996). Political economy in medical anthropology. In C. F. Sargent & T. M. Johnson (Eds.), *Medical anthropology: contemporary theory and method* (rev. ed.) (pp. 21–40). Westport, CT: Praeger.

Navarro, V. (1986). *Crisis, health and medicine: A social critique.* London: Tavistock.

Pelto, P. J. & Pelto, G. H. (1997). Studying knowledge, culture, and behavior in applied medical anthropology. *Medical Anthropology Quarterly, 11,* 147–163.

Pelto, P. J., & Pelto, G. H. (1996). Research designs in medical anthropology. In C. F. Sargent & T. M. Johnson (Eds.), *Medical anthropology: Contemporary theory and method* (rev. ed.) (pp. 293–324). Westport, Ct: Praeger.

Pollock, D. (1996). Personhood and illness among the Kulina. *Medical Anthropology Quarterly, 10,* 319–341.

Rhee, E., Uleman, J. S., Lee, H. K., & Roman, R. J. (1995). Spontaneous self-descriptions and ethnic identities in individualistic and collectivist cultures. *Journal of Personality and Social Psychology, 69,* 142–152.

Rosaldo, M. (1984). Toward an anthropology of self and feeling. In R. A. Shweder & R. A. LeVine (Eds.), *Culture theory: Essays on mind, self, and emotion* (pp. 137–157). Cambridge, UK: Cambridge University Press.

Rosaldo, R. (1993). *Culture and truth: The remaking of social analysis.* Boston: Beacon.

Rubel, A. J., & Hass, M. R. (1996). Ethnomedicine. In C. F. Sargent & T. M. Johnson (Eds.), *Medical anthropology: contemporary theory and method* (rev. ed.) (pp. 113–130). Westport, CT: Praeger.

Sargent, C. F., & Johnson, T. M. (Eds.) (1996). *Medical anthropology: Contemporary theory and method* (rev. ed.). Westport, CT: Praeger.

Scherer, K. R. (1997). The role of culture in emotion-antecedent appraisal. *Journal of Personality and Social Psychology, 73,* 902–922.

Sewell, W. H., Jr. (1992). A theory of structure: Duality, agency, and transformation. *American Journal of Sociology, 98,* 1–29.

Schooler, C. (1996). Cultural and social-structural explanations of cross-national psychological differences. *Annual Review of Sociology, 22,* 323–349.

Shweder, R. A., & LeVine, R. A. (Eds.) (1984). *Culture theory: Essays on mind, self, and emotion.* Cambridge, UK: Cambridge University Press.

Shweder, R. A., & Sullivan, M. A. (1993). Cultural psychology: Who needs it? *Annual Review of Psychology, 44,* 497–523.

Singer, J., & Salovey, P. (1991). Organized knowledge structures and personality. In M. Horowitz (Ed.), *Person schemas and maladaptive interpersonal patterns* (pp. 33–79). Chicago: University of Chicago Press.

Srole, L. Langner, T. S., Michael, S. T., Kirkpatrick, P. O., Marvin, K., & Rennie, T. A. C. (1978). *Mental health in the metropolis: The midtown Manhattan study.* New York: McGraw-Hill.

Suh, E., Diener, E., Oishi, S., & Triandis, H. C. (1998). The shifting basis of life satisfaction judgments across cultures: Emotions versus norms. *Journal of Personality and Social Psychology, 74,* 482–493.

Swidler, A. (1986). Culture in action: Symbols and strategies. *American Sociological Review, 51,* 273–286.

Trostle, J. A., & Sommerfeld, J. (1996). Medical anthropology and epidemiology. *Annual Review of Anthropology, 25,* 253–274.

Turshen, M. (1989). *The politics of public health.* New Brunswick, NJ: Rutgers University Press.

Vecchiato, N. L. (1997). Sociocultural aspects of tuberculosis control in Ethiopia. *Medical Anthropology Quarterly, 11,* 183–201.

Wierzbicka, A. (1986). Human emotions: Universal or culture-specific? *American Anthropologist, 88,* 584–594.

Whiteford, L. M. (1997). The ethnoecology of dengue fever. *Medical Anthropology Quarterly, 11,* 202–223.

Yoder, P. S. (1997). Negotiating relevance: Belief, knowledge, and practice in international health projects. *Medical Anthropology Quarterly, 11,* 131–146.

Yoder, P. S. (1995). Ethnomedical knowledge of diarrheal disorders in Lubumbashi Swahili. *Medical Anthropology, 16,* 211–247.

Young, J. C. (1981). *Medical choice in a Mexican village.* New Brunswick, NJ: Rutgers University Press.

Zarubavel, E. (1997). *Social mindscapes: An invitation to cognitive sociology.* Cambridge, MA: Harvard University Press.

Zborowski, M. (1952). Cultural components of responses to pain. *Journal of Social Issues, 8,* 16–30.

CHAPTER 3

Acculturation and Mental Health: Ecological Transactional Relations of Adjustment

ISRAEL CUÉLLAR

Department of Psychology and Anthropology
University of Texas—Pan American
Edinburg, Texas

I. INTRODUCTION

This chapter provides an ecological perspective to the role of culture and behavior. A multilevel systems perspective is applied consistent with Bronfenbrenner's Ecological Systems Theory (1989). It is essential to eliminate from the mind the notion that culture is a singular variable. A "big perspective" is required to understand culture in its entirety (C. Cheney, personal communication, June, 1973). This chapter aims to maintain that perspective in understanding psychological adjustment, particularly with respect to the interactions of health, illness, and behavior.

Charles Darwin is credited for modern ecological theory (Hawley, 1950). Ecological concepts initially formulated by Darwin (1963) maintain that all life has its province and is related to others in a 'web of life' in which each struggles for existence. This struggle constitutes an adjustment to other organisms and their way of life. The adjustment process is a competitive struggle for existence, referring to relations among organisms, including cooperation and mutual aid that develops among organisms in the struggle to adjust (Hawley, 1950). No other organism is believed to have advanced their culture as rapidly as man from a rudimentary state to its current, modern, highly sophisticated complexity. Mankind's superior culture-building skills are believed to be critical to past and future capabilities and capacities to adjust. An ecological perspective thus provides the environment and culture imminent roles with respect to humankind's struggle for adjustment.

Human culture is as varied as there are human communities on earth. There is much truth in the analogy that water is to fish as culture is to a person. Culture, as emphasized throughout this handbook, is a highly potent variable; it provides people a means of communication, a sense of belonging, meaningful systems of beliefs, views of self and others, means of commerce, among many other vastly important influences on the essentials of living and procreation. What happens when distinct cultures come into contact with one another? Some of the world's great meccas are cities where major cultures come into contact, but these places also have some of the most long-lasting conflicts between communities. Cultures come into contact in many ways and in all places, and that acculturation, the process in which cultures and people change as a function of culture contact, is a common phenomenon. It used to be true that first-hand contact was required for acculturation changes to take place. In today's advanced technological, satellite-internet age, acculturation changes occur via electronic media and satellite devices without any "first-hand" contact having occurred. In every culture, although more in some than others, gender subcultures represent a common, initial, and continuous experience of acculturation. This is because each person has a gender identity formulated in part from experiences and knowledge about both genders (see Canales, chapter 4, this volume, for further discussion of gender as a subculture).

Along with the postindustrial technological revolution of the 20th century, societal and cultural changes have transpired in an exponential manner throughout the world. Cultural conflicts and tensions between nations and people seem to be most pronounced where deeply held cultural beliefs and values are in direct conflict with those of an opposing culture.

The cultural conflicts at the macrolevel have their individual or psychological referents in behaviors, customs, and cognition (attitudes, schemas, beliefs, ideas, etc.) of individuals (Berry & Kim, 1988; Cuéllar, Arnold, & González, 1995; Graves, 1967). Changes that transpire in individuals at the microlevel, through some form of continuous contact with others from a different cultural group, are referred to as *psychological acculturation changes*. In geographical zones or meccas where cultures come into continuous contact, acculturation processes and changes are rapid and intense. The frequency and intensity of cultural conflicts at both the micro- and macrolevels in these geographical zones would appear to be proportionate to the extreme differences between cultures, particularly with respect to the system of mores (Stonequist, 1937).

II. CULTURE DEFINED

Culture has been defined in over one hundred ways. The definition used by Anthony Marsella (chapter 1, this volume) is the definition that will be used here as well. It defines culture as shared learned meanings and behaviors that are transmitted from within a social activity context for purposes of promoting individual/societal adjustment, growth, and development. Of much importance in Marsella's definition is the idea that culture is directly related to adjustment, growth, and development.

Cultures can and do vary in terms of several dimensions including, but not limited to, size, power, wealth, worldviews, religious beliefs, traditional views, economic systems, collectivistic versus individualistic cultural identification, among innumerable other ways (Triandis, 1994).

III. ACCULTURATION DEFINED

Acculturation was defined by Redfield, Linton, and Herskovits (1936) as a process represented by all the changes that occur as a result of individuals from two distinct cultures coming into continuous first-hand contact with one another, but particularly those changes that result in changes in the original cultural patterns of either or both groups. If the result of two cultures coming together is that one or both cultures change, then it is said that those changes are the result of acculturation processes. If a culture changes, it has to be that the people of that culture changed in some way as well. This ecological perspective holds that culture is an external variable and an internal variable, with both having influence on behavior. Culture is a multilevel phenomena that operates at various levels simultaneously. Acculturation is an ecological, transactional process that occurs at various levels of human organization and functioning. Acculturation is a stimulus or a causative agent when viewed as a precursor of change at the individual level of functioning. Acculturation is also a process when seen in the context of ongoing learning about our environment. At the macrolevel, acculturation processes, for example, impact language, music, architecture, and values. At the exolevel, acculturation processes influence, for example, institutions and organizations. At the mesolevel it influences, for example, social and group behavior, such as customs, rituals, foods, and folk practices. At the mesolevel it also influences family and social interactions, while the microlevel culture and acculturation processes are believed to influence cognition, emotion, and behavior, as well as perceptions, ideologies, beliefs, values, language use, and other aspects of human behavior and functioning. The degree to which individuals undergoing acculturative processes change their original cultural patterns by means of substitution, addition, integration, syncretism, or whatever other means is the subject of psychological acculturation, a field first developed by anthropologists. (See Marsella, chapter 1, this volume, for an interesting discussion of the historical role given to culture by psychiatry and psychology.)

IV. ACCULTURATION PROCESSES

It is important to have a better understanding of the mental health consequences of acculturation processes. Reaction of some form is not an uncommon response to culture contact. On some extreme positions, people become violent and attempt to extinguish or exterminate others' cultural systems or beliefs, including the people who support those systems. These reactions occur when people are threatened by some cultural feature of others. As the United States becomes increasingly more multicultural or culturally diverse, does this increase risk for psychological conflicts due to acculturation processes and forces?

The United States is a great leader in exportation and dissemination of culture throughout the world. When individuals from one cultural group acquire cultural symbols and features from another culture, this is often referred to as "acculturating" or acquiring cultural elements from the "host" culture. Acculturation is often erroneously viewed as unidimensional, with an imposition of the Immigrant Paradigm of Acculturation. In the Immigrant Paradigm of Acculturation, the adult immigrant acquires characteristics of the host culture in order to adapt, function, and prosper in the new culture. The Immigrant Paradigm of Acculturation applies to immigrants living in the USA. For many second, third- and fourth-generation minority group members, acculturation experiences are bicultural and the Immigrant Paradigm does not apply as well as the Minority Paradigm of Acculturation. In this paradigm, the minority individual is "acculturating" and "enculturating" with regards to at least two cultures. The Minority Paradigm emphasizes biculturalism and bicognitive adaptation. In the Minority Paradigm the subject is required to acculturate simultaneously, but in varying degrees, to their ethnic traditional culture and to mainstream American culture. The Immigrant and the Minority Paradigm apply at distinct developmental stages of the life span. The contextual features of multicultural environments, such as the differences in relative size, power, and other extremes of the two cultures, drive the acculturation engine and determine the speed and qualitative feature of the acculturation experience.

V. CULTURE AND MENTAL HEALTH

The relations of culture and mental health have been of long-standing interest in the fields of psychology, anthropology, sociology, and psychiatry. Culture has been at times given a prominent role in some theories and a minuscule role in others (also see chapters 1 and 2, this volume). Culture has been viewed as having a potential impact on numerous aspects of health, illness, and adaptation. Culture is seen as composing a major component of illness in Kleinman's Illness Model (Kleinman, 1988). In this model, culture is viewed as having a potentiating influence on the definition of illness, the manifestations of illness, the prevalence of illness, and on the treatment of illness, particularly so for the treatment of mental illness. It was the *Diagnostic and Statistical Manual of Mental Disorders* (4th ed.) *(DSM-IV)* that included culture for the first time as an important potentiating variable influencing manifestations, prevalence, and etiological factors in mental disorders.

People and cultures are constantly changing as a result of interactions with others. These changes take place at various ecological levels (Bronfenbrenner, 1989), namely, macrosystem, exosystem, mesosystem, and microsystem. Figure 1 shows a model of the interaction among systems. Many different kinds of changes can transpire as a function of acculturation processes. These changes include changes in multiple systems including social, cultural, architectural, political, economic, and cognitive. Acculturative changes can take place in individuals or can take place at the broader community level (see Figure 1). The point here is that all these changes are termed "acculturative changes." No direction is implied when reference is made to one "acculturating." A majority-group member acculturates to the extent he or she changes as a result of contact with minorities. Minority members in the United States, for example, who are acquiring characteristics of mainstream America are indeed "acculturating," but

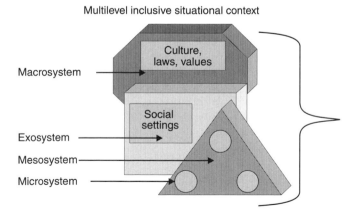

FIGURE 1   Bronfenbrenner's ecological model.

so are majority-group members who change as a result of their contact with the minority group. Although both majority- and minority-group members are acculturating, the rate of acculturation as well as qualitative aspects of the acculturation experience will differ greatly for both groups. In summary, both majority and minority group members are acculturating but in different directions, at different rates, and under very different contextual conditions. Bidirectional changes are sometimes referred to as "transcultural" processes. Most acculturative processes are transcultural to some extent.

VI. MODES OF ACCULTURATION

According to Acculturation Theory (Redfield et al., 1936), people change in at least three basic ways: acceptance, adaptation, and reaction:

1. Acceptance is where the process of acculturation results in the replacement of the older cultural elements with new cultural customs. The end result of Acceptance is not just the assimilation of new behavior patterns but the inner values of the new culture.

2. Adaptation is when both original and foreign traits are combined so as to produce a "harmonious meaningful whole." Adaptation has several variants including blends, or amalgamations, alternating forms, and other means of integrating conflicting cultural elements (Lafromboise, Hardin, Coleman, & Gerton, 1993). Syncretism, a special variant of adaptation, is the reconciliation of two or more cultural systems or elements, with the modification of both (Burger, 1966).

3. Reaction includes all forms of contra-acculturative movements. These include but are not limited to actions to criticize, humiliate, stigmatize, eliminate, and modify contraculture elements.

Some of the terms used by anthropologists sound similar to Piaget's terms of accommodation and assimilation but beware, they are defined very differently by anthropologists. The newer literature on acculturation supports four main modes of acculturation: assimilation, integration, separation, and marginalization (Berry & Kim, 1988).

1. Assimilation is the mode of acculturation that results in the immigrant or minority-group member acquiring the behaviors and values of the host culture and either not acquiring, not relinquishing, not practicing, or not valuing their traditional culture.

2. Integration is a mode of acculturation in which the immigrant or minority member integrates both traditional culture with acquired characteristics of

the host culture. This individual retains traditional culture and integrates it with the host/majority group mainstream culture in such a way that ethnic identity is maintained while endorsing mainstream values as well.

3. Separation is a mode of acculturation in which traditional culture is adhered to and not relinquished, traditional identity is maintained as well, along with a reluctance to accept, change, adapt, or even identify with the host culture in which the individual resides, works, or visits.

4. Marginalization is a mode of acculturation in which the immigrant or minority-group member does not maintain allegiance to traditional beliefs, values, behaviors, and so, while not adopting the values of the host culture. This person is truly marginalized as he or she does not have a good or strong sense of identity with either their traditional culture or with mainstream culture.

These four modes of acculturation are of particular interest to social and behavioral scientists, as each mode has specific mental health implications. There has been a growing interest in the relative health and mental health risks associated with each mode of acculturation. It is known that there are many variants of these cultural adaptations, including phasic, alternating, and syncretic modes of adaptation among others, including the newly identified constructs developed by Buss, Haselton, Shakelford, Bleske, and Wakefield (1998) of "exaptations" and "spandrels." Although used by Buss et al. as inherited characteristics, they have potential heuristic value, minimally, in understanding cultural referents of adaptation as well.

Acculturation changes at the individual level have characteristically included learning new words, idioms, expressions, ideas, customs, values, and behaviors. With the understanding that psychological stressors have individual specific effects, acculturative changes likewise have individual specific effects based on cultural meaning. In some individuals acculturation changes carry an increased risk for mental health-related problems. Stress, for example, is clearly linked as a predisposition for anxiety and depressive forms of illness. One of the most significant psychological studies in the last forty years is the Holmes and Rahe (1967) study showing the stress equivalents of change and assaults on self-integrity. Acculturation processes are replete with changes, and "acculturative stress" increases susceptibility to psychological problems just as does other forms of psychological stress.

Specific behavioral type of acculturative changes, such as eating different foods, learning a new language, enjoying culturally diverse stimuli (e.g., music) are integrated into the self with less psychic effort than participating in a culturally distinct activity or endorsing ideologies with very distinct values from those already held. These changes require greater risk of cognitive dissonance or conflict and are not so easily made.

VII. CULTURE CONFLICT

The notion of conflict is central to survival, adaptation, adjustment, and mental health. The element of conflict is produced within an individual's mind when the acceptance of cultural patterns from another culture are at variance with pre-existing ones. The degree to which this conflict exists represents a stressor to the individual, The successful resolution of this conflict represents a healthy mental adjustment. Cultural conflicts are stress inducing and thus serve as predisposing factors to many forms of psychological and physical illnesses.

It is not easy to change behavior that is firmly adhered to and strengthened gradually over many years of socialization and enculturation. It is perhaps easier to learn something new than to change an entrenched behavior pattern. As previously mentioned, incongruent values cannot be so easily juggled as other cultural elements; neither can commitments to identity, religious ideologies, principles, and worldviews be so easily modified, reinterpreted, or compromised. In some cases, the default may be to lose commitment to both, as hypothesized by Stonequist (1937) in his book, *The Marginal Man*.

A particular mode of acculturation has been theorized as having increased risk for psychic conflict relative to other modes of acculturation. This type or mode occurs in multicultural contexts, where two or more cultures come into continuous interactive contact with one another. This mode of acculturation is referred to as marginalized (Berry & Kim, 1988; Stonequist, 1937). Marginalized individuals do not have a strong affiliation, affirmation, or identification with either of the two main cultures they contact. They are believed to be more susceptible to psychological and adjustment disorders than persons who have adopted traditional, assimilated, integrated, or separation modes of adjustment. The term marginal is applied across a wide range of domains, such as economic status, health status, employment status, social status, and others. Like many biculturals, marginalized individuals live between two cultures; however, in terms of acculturation, marginalized refers specifically to a form of psychological adjustment in which the person does not identify with either culture. High integrated biculturals have a strong sense of identity with both cultures, in contrast to the acculturative marginalized, who don't identify with either.

VIII. ACCULTURATIVE STRESS

Acculturation processes can be challenging or they can be sources of stress and conflict. They can produce eustress or distress to the individual. Cognitive behavior theory has much applicability in understanding psychological acculturation. The same stimulus conditions can have individual meaning, leading to differential reactions and differential mental health consequences.

Acculturative stress, like stress, is defined as either an exogenous factor (stressor) or as an endogenous consequence (e.g., anxiety) of an exogenous process. Acculturative stress is considered to be a significant contributor to risk of illness. In contextual environments in which people live, work, play, and interact socially or digitally with others, there are bound to be acculturative changes at both the societal and the individual level. An important step in understanding acculturative stress was taken by Cervantes, Padilla, and de Snyder (1991) in their development of the Hispanic Stress Inventory. This measure helps partition added stress that comes about by virtue of being Hispanic and living in the United States.

Educational and telecommunication systems are the primary vehicles for acculturation processes. They can also serve as sources of acculturative stress. These stressors include the educational criteria used to successfully compete in elementary grades through high school, vocational school, college, graduate, and professional schools and the like. These hurdles must be overcome in order to fully participate and obtain benefits that accrue with acculturation. The capacity to meet culturally ascribed educational criteria is largely contingent on capacity to acculturate. Achievement of standardized criteria are the foundations for competitive success, higher socioeconomic standard of living, obtaining jobs, positions, or careers that pay better and require less physical strain.

Thus, the economic benefits, which increase capacity to survive, for persons who acculturate are among the major incentives to acculturate, but the criteria required to obtain those benefits are rigorous in the United States. For some, this process can be extremely stressful, whereas for others it is not particularly so. There has to be an incentive for change to occur. The incentives that Western, modern cultures offer to members of minority groups are opportunities to compete for an improved standard of living. This is minimally expressed as an opportunity to acquire goods, services, education, appliances, means of transportation, vehicles, electronic and internet devices, as well as obtain better medical care. Acculturation to U.S. culture is generally viewed as enhancing opportunities for improving quality of life. However, some immigrants and minority members become disillusioned, misguided, become alienated, and feel overwhelmed (Williams & Berry, 1991). This is acculturative stress as well. The list of determinates of acculturation is headed by economic benefits, but can include political dominance, needs for conformity and cogruity, needs to belong, practical advantage, and others.

Although the benefits of acculturation are clearly numerous, there are often hidden costs. An example of how acculturation can increase stress is reported by Ramirez (1987). He found that there were significant differences between traditional Mexicans and acculturated Mexican Americans (second and third generation) with respect to the degree to which parents felt they had control over their children. More acculturated Mexican American parents reported having less control over their children and more problems in wife–husband and parent–child relationships.

There also is individual resistance to acculturate by some minority-group members. Some hold onto traditional cultural beliefs, values, customs, language, behaviors, and so on, while resisting mainstream cultural influences. These are referred to as *separatist,* as there is clear resistance to acculturate. This resistance is confounded, if not caused by, racism, political history, antagonism, and forms of injustice. Another mode of acculturation is to acculturate towards the two cultures simultaneously, as in the case of some second- and third-generation ethnic minorities. This is also true for African Americans who acculturate toward African-American culture and mainstream American culture at the same time. Some individuals relinquish their old beliefs and ideas while replacing them with ideas learned while undergoing acculturative processes. Still other individuals hold on dearly to their traditional culture while trying to integrate the old with the new (integrated biculturals). Although some biculturals are able to integrate elements of both cultures, others are unable to resolve cultural conflicts and have their own individualized reactions. Each of these modes of acculturation represent distinct approaches to conflict resolution and the management of psychological and acculturative stress. Each mode of acculturation with its respective potential for reducing stress have profound implications on the understanding of psychological adjustment.

IX. ACCULTURATION AND PSYCHOLOGICAL ADJUSTMENT

Marsella and Kameoka (1989) describe a model that depicts the relations of culture to pathology. In their interactional model, the environment is divided into physical and cultural components that interact with person variables that are also divided into two components: (a) physiological/genetic component and (b) a sociocultural component (cf. Marsella, chapter 1, this volume). Culture plays a prominent role in this model as it represents both external and internal factors influencing our reactions and behaviors.

Obviously, culture plays a less prominent role for other forms of illness (Marsella & Kameoka, 1989). The base rates for many forms of illness vary by ethnic and cultural groups. There are, for example, higher rates of tuberculosis (TB) in some cultural groups than others. This is true, for example, for Mexican Americans living along the Texas/Mexico border. TB requires both a necessary ingredient (the presence of TB) and a sufficient condition (e.g., unhealthy environment, including unclean or cramped quarters) for it to prosper, and culture plays a role in both the base rate of the necessary condition as well as the base rate of the sufficient condition. Diabetes mellitus, found to have a higher prevalence in some minority groups (e.g., Mexican Americans in South Texas), is another example of how culture plays a role in terms of both the necessary and the sufficient conditions of this illness. Physical illnesses have definite social and psychological impacts on the person afflicted, but also on the person's family, relatives, friends, co-workers, and the like.

The impact of culture and acculturation processes on illness behaviors is commonly seen in the family and social domains of illness as noted in the biopsychosocial model, as well as the more advanced models expounded in chapters 1, 2, and 3 of this volume. As noted elsewhere, however, and particularly by Angel (chapter 2, this volume) the Biopsychosocial Model provides a distal role for culture. As is evident throughout this handbook, culture plays a prominent and central role in how an illness is perceived, how it is accepted, how it is dealt with, what reactions are generated, and what adjustments are made. Issues such as access to health care, compliance with treatment, acceptability and effectiveness of services arise from cultural influences on illness. These are not peripheral, distal, or minor influences. On the contrary, culture is a significant factor with far-reaching influences on illness and health care.

X. ACCULTURATION AND CLINICAL MANIFESTATIONS OF ILLNESS

Depression serves as an excellent example of an illness that is influenced by external factors such as contextual environment, culture, acculturation processes, and social/psychological situations. Depression is also an illness definable by clinical *DSM-IV* criteria. As noted elsewhere in this handbook (see Panigua, chapter 8), culture shapes the manifestations of many illnesses, including those of depressive illness. It also determines the patient's explanatory model of their illness. As Seligman, (1998) points out, some explanatory models of illness have distinct prognostic values. For example, patients who tend to blame others may have a poorer prognosis than those who assume some responsibility for their condition and are willing to invest in their recovery in some meaningful way.

Since culture is tied to many cognitive referents of acculturation, there are multiple entry points for culture to influence illness behaviors. The more common points include perception of illness, manifestations of illness, prevalence rates, susceptibility, acceptance of illness, reactions to illness, adjustment to illness, and its assessment and treatment (Cuéllar & González, 1999).

XI. EMPIRICAL FINDINGS OF
ACCULTURATION AND MENTAL HEALTH

The relations of acculturation and mental health have been studied empirically using reliable and valid indices of acculturation and mental health. These studies have increased in number, complexity, and sophistication as a result of the development of improved acculturation measures (Cuéllar, 1999). Two major reviews of acculturation and mental health are Berry and Kim (1988) and Rogler, Cortes, and Malgady (1991). Both reviews found the relationship between acculturation and mental health to be extremely complex, but with many systematic and important relationships discernible. Rogler et al. (1991) found 30 studies of mental health and acculturation, and the number of studies has grown substantially since then. In addition, Rogler et al. (1991) found acculturation to be significantly related to a number of mental health variables but also found a significant number of studies in which no significant relations were found for acculturation and measures of psychological functioning. Overall, they found the results of empirical studies of acculturation and mental health to be equivocal. Both Rogler et al. (1991) and Cortes (1994) explain that the lack of support for a linear relationship between acculturation and psychological functioning is that the relation is not entirely linear due to forms of adaptation that result in amalgamations or blending of behavior patterns and ideologies.

Among important clinical variables found to be linearly correlated with acculturation or cultural identity are chronicity of illness and prognosis (González & Cuéllar, 1983); alcoholism (Black & Markides, 1993; Caetano, 1987); coping strategies (Montgomery & Orozco, 1985); self-esteem (Salgado de Snyder, 1987); somatization (Escobar, Randolph, & Hill, 1986); alienation (Negy & Woods, 1993); psychopathic deviate, paranoia, psychasthenia, and social introversion on the Minnesota Multiphasic Personality Inventory (2nd Ed.) (MMPI-2) (Lessenger, 1995); perceived stress (Solis, 1991). Ethnic identity, identity achievement, and affirmation and belonging were found to be inversely correlated with linear acculturation (Cuéllar, Roberts, Nyberg, & Maldonado, 1997). Other health risk behaviors found to correlate with acculturation include smoking (Marin, Marin, Otero-Sabogal et al., 1989), Verbal IQ (Garcia-Vazquez, & Ehly, 1994); and age at first sexual intercourse for pregnant teenagers (Reynosa, Felice, & Shragg, 1993). Seat-belt use is another example of a risk factor that is directly related to acculturation, especially along the United States–Mexican border where, among other reasons, traditional individuals tend not to use seat belts, as the use of seat belts is not mandated by law in Mexico.

Significant ethnic group differences in prevalence rates of psychiatric illnesses have been noted that appear to suggest an increased risk for substance abuse and major depressive episodes (Burnam et al., 1987). Despite the many known stressors associated with migration and the lower socioeconomic status of many immigrants, recent studies suggest some immigrants have lower prevalence rates than their native (U.S.-born) ethnic counterparts (Escobar, 1998; Vega, Kolody, Aguilar-Gaxiola, Alderete, Catalano, & Caraveo-Anduaga, 1998). Vega and colleagues compared adjusted lifetime prevalence rates for various mental disorders obtained using the Composite International Diagnostic Inventory (CIDI) from the Mexican American Prevalence and Services Survey (MAPSS), and the National Comorbidity Survey (NCS; Kessler et al., 1994). They compared Mexican immigrants with native-born Mexican Americans and found the native-born lifetime prevalence rate for any disorder (48.1%) was twice that of the immigrants (24.9%). They also found that short-term-stay immigrants (<13 years) had almost half the lifetime prevalence rates for any disorder than long-term immigrants, those having lived in the United States for more than 13 years. In comparing the lifetime prevalence rates for Mexicans in Mexico City with short-term immigrants, long-term immigrants and native-born Mexican origin populations, they found that prevalence rates increased with increased acculturation toward the U.S. culture. They found that those Mexican-origin individuals who were born and raised in the United States, or who had lived the longest in the United States, had higher prevalence rates for depression, affective disorders of any type, and any psychiatric disorder than those who were born in Mexico or had lived the longest in Mexico.

In addition to the evidence of linear relations between acculturation and mental health, noted above, there is a growing body of empirical findings supporting the notion that acculturation, when measured orthogonally, is significantly related to psychological functioning. This is often the case when linear measures show no relationship between acculturation and mental health. The reasons for this apparent paradox can be explained with the same reasoning that applies when a curvilinear correlation is significant when the linear correlation between the two measures is not. The relations of acculturation to other measures are not only linear. The relations of adjustment and acculturation are complex and confounded by many factors, such as (a) the context of acculturation, (b) the determinants of acculturation, (c) the phase of acculturation (Berry & Kim, 1988), and (d) the mode of acculturation. Many of the outcomes of acculturation processes result in traits or states in the form of blends, amalgamates, syncretism, alternating or phasic modes, and other outcomes that are not linearly related to adjustment.

Stonequist (1937) first noted that whereas some immigrants go on to become some of the finest citizens of the United States, others, whom he labeled as "marginal types" have significant acculturation difficulties, Stonequist noted that "marginal types" were at particular risk of experiencing psychological difficulties emanating directly from culture conflicts (Stonequist, 1937). In a comprehensive empirical examinations of Stonequist's hypothesis (Cuéllar, Roberts, Romero, & Leka, 1999), 831 freshmen students, 89% of whom were of Hispanic origin, attending a university in south Texas, were administered a self-report cultural identity survey that included the Acculturation Rating Scale for Mexican Americans—II (ARSMA-II), a linear and orthogonal measure of acculturation, along with four well-established self-report scales of psychological adjustment: (a) The Robert's UCLA Loneliness Scale-8 (RULS-8), (b) the Diagnostic Scale for Depression-26 (DSD-26), (c) the Rosenberg Self-esteem Scale, and (d) an Hispanic Stress Scale. The results showed that orthogonal measures of acculturation are often significantly related to health and adjustment when linear acculturation measures are not. The differences found between the Marginalized group and the High Integrated Bicultural group on all four measures of adjustment were significant. In each case, the High Integrated Bicultural group consistently was found to have the best psychological profile, and the Marginalized group was consistently found to have the worst profile of psychological adjustment. These findings are consistent with the anthropological studies reported by Berry and Kim (1988) in which marginality was found to correlate with stress and with cultural discongruity.

In summary, adjustment to change, adaptation, and resolution of conflict are ongoing processes for all organisms, as Darwin proposed with respect to the struggle for existence, the web of life, and natural selection. Human beings' capacities to build culture and to control the culture of other organisms is central to the struggle for existence. These capacities are, arguably, equally central as well to mankind's position of superiority with respect to other organisms. Every culture developed by humans has some survival value or else its members would not exist to represent that culture. The importance that a specific culture holds for its members cannot be overestimated. It is not uncommon for cultures to come into contact with one another and it is not uncommon for competition, as well as mutual support, along with other possible changes to occur in both cultures and their representatives. Culture conflict, like acculturative stress, has individual, psychological consequences for persons undergoing acculturation. Psychological consequences may entail threats to identity, way of life, values, beliefs, mores, and so on, and they pit the traditional against the modern. Culture conflicts may exacerbate existing symptoms and add to existing stressors and precipitate maladaptive reactions of much mental health significance. Feelings of hostility, racism, loneliness, anxiety, low self-esteem, and depression are but a few of the many symptoms that can be generated from the contingencies of culture conflict.

XII. ECOLOGICAL INTERVENTIONS IN MENTAL HEALTH

The problems frequently associated with minority status and acculturation are numerous. Among some of the characteristics of minorities include, for example, low educational status, high unemployment, high rates of poverty, high risk for some health and mental health problems, high risk for victimization, high rates of incarceration, and high risk for engaging in violence.

Psychology as a profession, according to Shore (1998), is still establishing its identity and more recently has been developing interests and greater involvement in issues of prevention of psychological disorders and the promotion of mental health. These more recent areas of focus of the profession of psychology address such concerns as social issues, ethnic minorities, and ultimately the elaboration of what is needed in a society so that all its members have the opportunity to grow mentally healthy, with appropriate services available if and when problems arise (Shore, 1998). The application of psychological science and methodology to community defines the growing field of Community Psychology. Among the legitimate professional activities of Community Psychology is advocacy, the integration of theory, research, and practice to bring about change to issues of concern for a given community. Theory plays a role in organizing and structuring knowledge. Research plays a role in offering objective data that can clarify and monitor the knowledge from which actions can be taken to ameliorate illness or to promote growth or health. Professional practices in psychology identify issues of concern with respect to access, availability, effectiveness, and acceptability of services and interventions. Practice issues in community psychology are not exclusively directed toward individuals. Community psychology interventions may be broad and may involve development of new programs or modifications to programs, organizations, educational and health systems, litigation and social policy interventions, and the like. An example of how psychological science can be applied to prevention of community-based problems is reported by Caplan, Vinokur, and Price (1997) in their review of the literature. After examining the knowledge that persons experiencing a recent job loss frequently are at greater risk for abuse, depression, alcoholism, poor physical health, violence and mental disruption, resources were directed toward these groups resulting in a clear prevention benefit. Another very direct and concrete example is provided by the advocacy efforts in San Antonio, Texas, leading to changes in local ordinances restricting minors from purchasing spray paint and thus reducing rates of toluene inhalant abuse.

In addition to concern for promotion of health and wellness, an important aspect of community psychology is concerned with directing appropriate resources to prevent or reduce mental health problems. Sue, Funino, Hu, Takeuchi, and Zane (1991), for example, found that ethnic matching of therapist and client led to lower premature termination, greater number of sessions, and better outcomes for African Americans, American Indians, Asian Americans, Mexican Americans, and Whites.

The ecological perspective, an important part of multicultural mental health practice, examines the contexts of both growth and pathology (also see Marsella, chapter 1, this volume). In an ecological perspective, the relations of culture, economic systems, political systems, socialization practices, acculturation stresses, and social problems are related to individual functioning. The macro-level is linked to the individual via such variables as cultural identity, personality, and mental health. Community problems as well as individual mental health problems are intricately intertwined such that in order to effectively prevent or change the individual, the context may require to be changed as well. The prevention and promotion of health activities have particular relevance for children and youth. Whereas it may be too late for some persons, it may not be too late to apply these interventions for young children. Addressing the needs of children is a legitimate advocacy practice in community psychology as are interventions that strengthen the family in society. By incorporating culture and ecological models, the practice of psychology is widened or broadened, and solutions to mental health problems are equally increased in proportion.

REFERENCES

Berry, J., & Kim, U. (1988). Acculturation and mental health. In P. Dasen, J. W. Berry, & Sartorious (Eds.), *Health and cross-cultural psychology: Towards application* (pp. 207–236). London: Sage.

Black, S. A., & Markides, K. S. (1993). Acculturation and alcohol consumption in Puerto Rican, Cuban American, and Mexican American women in the United States. *American Journal of Public Health, 83,*(6), 890–893.

Bronfenbrenner, U. (1989). Ecological systems theory. In R. Vasta (Ed.), *Annals of child development* (Vol. 6, pp. 187–251). Greenwich, CT: JAI Press.

Bronfenbrenner, U. (1997). The ecology of developmental processes. In R. M. Lerner (Ed.), *Handbook of child psychology: Vol. 1, Theoretical models of human development.* New York: Wiley.

Burger, H. G. (1966). Syncretism: An acculturative accelerator. *Human Organization, 25,* 103–115.

Burnam, M. A., Hough, R. L., Escobar, J. I., Karno, M., Timbers, D. M., Telles, C. A., & Locke, B. Z. (1987). Six-month prevalence of specific psychiatric disorders among Mexican Americans and non-Hispanic whites in Los Angeles. *Archives of General Psychiatry, 44,* 687–694.

Buss, D. M., Haselton, M. G., Shakelford, T. K., Bleske, A. L., & Wakefield, J. C. (1998). Adaptations, exaptations, and spandrels. *American Psychologist, 53*(5), 533–548.

Caetano, R. (1987). Acculturation and attitudes toward appropriate drinking among U.S. Hispanics. *Alcohol and Alcoholism, 22*(4), 427–433.

Caplan, R. D., Vinokur, A. D., & Price R. D. (1997). From job loss to reemployment: Field experiments in prevention-focused coping. In G. W. Albee & T. P. Gulotta (Eds.), *Primary prevention works Vol. 6. Issues in children's and families' lives* (pp. 314–380). Thousand Oaks, CA: Sage.

Cervantes, R. C., Padilla, A. M., & de Snyder, N. S. (1991). The Hispanic Stress Inventory: A culturally relevant approach to psychosocial assessment. *A Journal of Consulting and Clinical Psychology, 3,* 438–447.

Cortes, D. E. (1994). Acculturation and its relevance to mental health. In R. G. Malgady & O. Rodriguez (Eds.), *Theoretical and conceptual issues in Hispanic mental health* (pp. 54–68). Malabar, FL: Robert E. Krieger Publishing Co. Inc.

Cuéllar, I., Arnold, B., & Gonzalez, G. (1995). Cognitive referents of acculturation: Assessment of cultural constructs in Mexican Americans. *Journal of Community Psychology, 23,* 339–356.

Cuéllar, I. (1999). Acculturation as a moderator of personality and psychological assessment. In Richard H. Dana (Ed.), *Handbook of cross-cultural/multicultural personality assesssment* (pp. 113–129). Hillsdale, NJ: Lawrence Erlbaum Associates Inc., Publisher.

Cuéllar, I., & González, G. (1999). Cultural identity description and cultural formulation for Hispanics. In Richard H. Dana (Ed.), *Handbook of cross-cultural/multicultural personality assessment* (pp. 605–621). Hillsdale, NJ: Lawrence Erlbaum Associates Inc., Publisher.

Cuéllar, I., Roberts, R. E., Romero, A., & Leka, G. (1999). *Acculturation and marginalization: A test of Stonequist's hypothesis.* Unpublished manuscript.

Cuéllar, I., & Roberts, R. E. (1984). Psychological disorders among Chicanos. In J. L. Martinez & R. H. Mendoza (Eds.), *Chicano psychology,* (2nd ed.). Orlando, FL: Academic Press, Inc.

Cuéllar, I., Roberts, R. E., Nyberg, B., & Maldonado, R. E. (1997). Ethnic identity and acculturation in a young adult Mexican-origin population. *Journal of community Psychology, 25*(6), 535–549.

Darwin, C. (1963). *On the origin of species by means of natural selection.* New York: Heritage Press.

Escobar, J. E., Randolph, E. T., & Hill, M. (1986). Symptoms of schizophrenia in Hispanic and Anglo veterans. *Culture, Medicine and Psychiatry, 10,* 259–276.

Escobar, J. (1998). Immigration and mental health: Why are immigrants better off? *Archives of General Psychiatry, 55,* 781–882.

Garcia-Vazquez, E., & Ehly, S. W. (1994). Acculturation and intelligence: Effects of acculturation on problem-solving. *Perceptual & Motor Skills 78*(2), 501–502.

González, R. & Cuéllar, I. (1983). Readmission and prognosis of Mexican American psychiatric inpatients. *Interamerican Journal of Psychology, 17,* 81–95.

Graves, T. D. (1967). Psychological acculturation in a tri-ethnic community. *Southwestern Journal of Anthropology, 23,* 337–350.

Hawley, A. H. (1950). *Human ecology: A theory of community structure.* New York: The Ronald Press Company.

Holmes, T. H., & Rahe, R. H. (1967). The Social Readjustment Rating Scale. *Journal of Psychosomatic Research, 11,* 213–218.

Kessler, R. C., McGongale, K. A., Zhao, S., Nelson, C. B., Hughes, M., Eshelman, S., Wittchen, H., & Kendler, K. (1994). Lifetime and 12 month prevalence of DSM-III-R psychiatric disorders in the United States: Results of the National Comorbidity Survey. *Archives of General Psychiatry, 51,* 8–19.

Kleinman, A. (1988). *The illness narratives.* New York: Basic Books.

Lafromboise, T., Hardin, L., Coleman, K., & Gerton, J. (1993). Psychological impact of biculturalism: Evidence and theory. *Psychological Bulletin, 114,* 395–412.

Lessenger, L. H. (1995). *The relationship between cultural identity and MMPI-2 scores of Mexican American substance abuse patients.* Unpublished doctoral dissertation, California School of Professional Psychology—Fresno, California.

Marin, G., Marin, B. V., Otero-Sabogal, R., Sabogal, F., et al. (1989). The role of acculturation in the attitudes, norms and expectancies of Hispanic smokers. *Journal of Cross-Cultural Psychology, 20*(4), 399–415.

Marsella, A. J., & Kameoka, V. A. (1989). Ethnocultural issues in the assessment of psychopathology. In Scott Wetzler (Ed.), *Measuring mental illness: Psychometric assessment for clinicians* (pp. 229–256). Washington, DC: American Psychiatric Press.

Montgomery, G. T., & Orozco, S. (1985). Mexican Americans' performance on the MMPI as a function of level of acculturation. *Journal of clinical Psychology, 41*(2), 203–212.

Negy, C., & Woods, D. J. (1993). Mexican- and Anglo-American differences on the Psychological Screening Inventory. *Journal of Personality Assessment, 60*(3), 543–553.

Ramirez, M. (1987). The impact of culture change and economic stressors on physical and mental health of Mexicans and Mexican Americans. In R. Rodriguez & M. Coleman (Eds.), *Mental health issues of the Mexican origin population in Texas: Proceedings of the Fifth Robert L. Sutherland*

Seminar (pp. 181–196). Austin, TX: The Hogg Foundation for Mental Health: The University of Texas at Austin.

Redfield, R., Linton, R., & Herskovits, M. J. (1936). Memorandum for the study of acculturation: Committee Report to the Social Science Research Council. *American Anthropologist, 38*(1), 149–152.

Reynoso, T., Felice, M. E., & Skaggs, G. P. (1993). Does American acculturation affect outcome of Mexican American teenage pregnancy? *Journal of Adolescent Health, 14*(4), 257–261.

Rogler, L. H., Cortes, D. E., Malgady, R. G. (1991). Acculturation and mental health status among Hispanics: Convergence and new directions for research. *American Psychologist, 46*(6), 585–597.

Salgado de Synder, V. N. (1987). Factors associated with acculturation stress and depression symptomatology among married Mexican immigrant women. *Psychology of Women Quarterly, 11,* 477–487.

Seligman, M. (1998). Why therapy works. *American Psychological Association (APA) Monitor,* Oct. pp. 13–14.

Shore, M. F. (1998). Beyond self-interest: Professional Advocacy, and the integration of theory, research and practice. *American Psychologist, 53*(4), 474–479.

Solis, M. L. (1991, November). Parent stress: A cross-cultural comparison between Hispanics and Anglo-Americans. *Dissertation Abstracts International 52/05,* University of Virginia.

Stonequist, E. V. (1937). *The marginal man: A study in personality and culture conflict.* New York: Russell & Russell.

Sue, S., Fujino, D., Hu, L., Takeuchi, D., & Zane, N. (1991). Community mental health services for ethnic minority groups: A test of the cultural irresponsiveness hypothesis. *Journal of Clinical and Consulting Psychology, 59,* 533–540.

Triandis, H. C. (1994). Culture and social behavior. In W. J. Lonner & R. Malpass (Eds.), *Psychology and culture* (pp. 169–173). Boston: Allyn and Bacon.

Vega, W. A., Kolody, B., Aguilar-Gaxiola, S., Alderete, E., Catalano, R., & Caraveo-Anduaga, J. (1998). Lifetime Prevalence of DSD-III-R psychiatric disorders among urban and rural Mexican Americans in California. *Archives of General Psychiatry, 55,* 771–778.

Williams, C. L., & Berry, J. W. (1991). Primary prevention of acculturative stress among refugees. *American Psychologist, 46,* 6, 632–641.

Gender as Subculture: The First Division of Multicultural Diversity

GENEVIEVE CANALES

Department of Hispanic Studies
University of Northern Colorado
Greeley, Colorado

Contrary to the idea that femininity and masculinity are innate, fixed, and universally defined, they are in fact a function of the particular cultural context in which women and men live their daily lives (Wade & Tavris, 1994).

This chapter relates gender and culture in a broad way. The focus is on the four major racial/ethnic minority groups in the United States, namely, African Americans, American Indians, Asian Americans, and Latinas/os. The intent is to show how mental health and adjustment are affected by the gender-role norms of these particular cultures, and further, that different norms are associated with the feminine gender role and the masculine gender role. In some cultures, certain attitudes, behaviors, and characteristics are within the boundaries of the feminine and masculine gender roles; in other cultures, those very same attitudes, behaviors, or characteristics are considered violations of gender-role norms.

Four areas are covered in the present context: (a) key terms and definitions, (b) the relationship between culture and gender-role conflict in the four previously mentioned racial/ethnic minority groups, (c) a discussion on the

Handbook of Multicultural Mental Health: Assessment and Treatment of Diverse Populations

importance of culture as a foundation in the assessment and treatment of mental health and adjustment issues associated with gender-role conflict, and (d) a summary and conclusions.

I. KEY TERMS AND DEFINITIONS

Several important terms to consider in any discussion about culture include gender, sex, femininity/masculinity, and gender role. It is important to point out that one's gender is independent of one's sex. *Gender* refers to characteristics and behaviors considered appropriate for and typical of females and males by a particular culture (Unger, 1979). As such, gender is considered a social construction (Rothenberg, 1998), whereas, *sex* refers to one's status as a female or male, based on anatomical and physiological differences (Baron & Byrne, 1997).

Femininity refers to expressive characteristics and *masculinity* refers to instrumental characteristics (Parsons & Bales, 1955). Both constructs have been operationally defined by Spence, Helmreich, and Stapp (1975) through the Personal Attributes Questionnaire (PAQ). The PAQ is a self-report, paper-and-pencil instrument that measures the degree of an individual's self-ascribed feminine and masculine characteristics. It contains a femininity scale and a masculinity scale. The former includes such characteristics as helpfulness and kindness, whereas, the latter includes such characteristics as independence and competitiveness.

The PAQ, along with the Bem Sex Role Inventory (BSRI, Bem, 1974) are the two most widely used measures of femininity/masculinity. For both the PAQ and the BSRI, a person's femininity score and masculinity scores taken together make it possible to assign the individual to one of four categories: androgynous, feminine, masculine, or undifferentiated. A person with an androgynous classification has a high degree of both feminine as well as masculine characteristics. A person with a feminine classification has a higher degree of feminine than masculine characteristics. A person with a masculine classification has a higher degree of masculine than feminine characteristics. A person with an undifferentiated classification has low degrees of both feminine and masculine characteristics.

Gender role is defined as "behaviors, expectations, and role sets defined by society as masculine or feminine which are embodied in the behavior of the individual man or woman and culturally regarded as appropriate to males or females" (O'Neill, 1990, p. 23). The definition of *gender-role conflict* employed is that of Stillson, O'Neil, and Owen (1991, p. 460): "a set of values, attitudes, or behaviors learned during socialization that causes negative psychological effects on a person or on other people." One of the most widely used measures of gender-role conflict is the Gender-role Conflict Scale (O'Neil, Helms, Gable,

David, & Wrightsman, 1986). It consists of four subscales: (a) Success, Power, and Competition, (b) Restrictive Emotionality, (c) Restrictive Affectionate Behavior between Men, and (d) Conflicts between Work and Family Relations.

The term *majority culture* refers to White, European American individuals and their culture, also known popularly as the dominant culture or as mainstream U.S. culture.

II. TYPES OF GENDER-ROLE CONFLICT AMONG RACIAL AND ETHNIC MINORITY GROUPS

Wade (1996) identified three possible types of gender-role conflict in African-American men. The first type of conflict surrounds attempts to meet the expectations of the majority culture's traditional feminine and masculine gender-role norms. The second type of conflict stems from differences between the majority culture and racial/ethnic minority groups in their conceptions of femininity and masculinity. The third type of conflict arises when the individual's acculturation, ethnic identity, immigrant status, or other similar variables have an impact on the type and degree of gender-role conflict. In addition, a fourth type of gender-role conflict is discussed that has to do with the stress of trying to abide by the gender-role norms of a particular racial/ethnic minority group.

Below is a description and the application of each type of gender-role conflict with examples from African American, American Indian, Asian American, and/or Latino cultures.

A. Gender-Role Conflict Related to Perceived Expectations of the Majority Culture's Gender-Role Norms

Gender-role conflict may occur for racial and ethnic minority groups in trying to live up to the definitions of traditional femininity and masculinity proposed by the majority culture. The word *traditional* is used to differentiate between the former and the more expansive, flexible notions of femininity and masculinity for both women and men since the women's movement of the 1960s and 1970s.

African American men, like their White male counterparts, have valued and tried to meet the requirements of the traditional male role: being a protector, provider, and breadwinner. Racism, however, in every domain of their lives has prevented African Americans from successfully fulfilling their roles as men. In addition, racism, historically and today, has assaulted their very worth as human beings. To cope, Black men have developed a psychological strategy known as "Cool Pose" (Majors & Billson, 1992) which is a facade of postures, gestures, language, and demeanor used to hide their true feelings of fear, hurt, and rage. Cool Pose is the appearance of being emotionless, calm, and detached in the face of pain and atrocities. Cool Pose is beneficial to Black men in that it provides them with dignity, self-worth, and strength. However, it is not without costs. To the extent that Cool Pose becomes deeply internalized, it can be difficult to discard when necessary, for example, in relationships with women. Routinely having to hide their feelings, their needs, and their weaknesses may prevent them from letting down the facade in order to achieve intimacy with women.

Bowman (1992) studied gender-role strain in Black men who were both husbands and fathers. Specifically, Bowman assessed provider role strain, which was operationally defined to include such domains as father-role discouragement, husband-role discouragement, primary provider discouragement, objective employment barriers, and familial subsistence anxiety. The results showed that provider role strain reduced the men's global family satisfaction. Interestingly, two cultural resources were found to mitigate the negative impact of provider role strain, namely, family closeness and religious belief. That is, husband-fathers whose families were very close reported greater global family satisfaction compared to those whose families were less close. Similarly, husband-fathers who were very religious reported greater global family satisfaction than those who were less religious.

B. GENDER-ROLE CONFLICT RELATED TO DIFFERENCES BETWEEN THE MAJORITY CULTURE AND RACIAL AND ETHNIC MINORITIES IN THEIR CONCEPTIONS OF FEMININITY AND MASCULINITY

Although the masculine gender role of African American men includes characteristics found in the masculine gender role of majority culture men, the former also includes characteristics that the majority culture tends to view as more feminine. For example, African American men endorse competition, ambition, and providing for their families; however, they also endorse such characteristics as spirituality, communalism, and emotional sensitivity (Cazenave, 1984; Hunter & Davis, 1992). The differences in the two conceptions of masculinity may create conflict to the extent that Black men may wish to fulfill the masculine gender role as defined by the majority culture, but may also wish to live up to the expectations of the masculine gender role as specified by the African American culture. As Lazur and Majors (1995) point out, all minority men must examine their culture's dictates surrounding masculinity and those of the majority culture in order to arrive at an integrated sense of self that allows them to determine their unique place in society. (In an important chapter on the strains of the masculine gender role for minority men, the authors examine each of the four major racial/ethnic minority groups and its particular gender-role conflict.

LaFromboise, Berman, and Sohi (1994) discuss American Indian sociocultural beliefs and values with respect to a number of areas, including gender roles, family relationships, and developmental stages. They explain American Indians' beliefs concerning wellness and unwellness. Wellness exists when spirit, mind, and body are in balance and harmony. An individual who violates a sacred taboo risks unwellness not only for herself or himself, but for any member of the extended family. One such taboo is for a female to expose her body to others. Thus, a young woman at a non-Indian school who is expected to undress and shower in a locker room as part of the requirements for a physical education class experiences gender-role conflict. She may resolve this conflict by failing the class.

Another source of conflict for the Indian woman may be the opposing demands of school, work, and tribe. Attending to professional or school-related responsibilities may cause her to be absent from important ceremonies. Her absence may have a negative impact on her well-being because participation in sacred tribal rituals is critical in promoting balance and harmony of spirit, mind, and body.

Historically, in their definitions of appropriate gender roles for women, American Indians differed from the majority culture. Interestingly, the majority of Indian women enjoyed far more flexible gender roles and exercised far more power as women, prior to European conquest over indigenous peoples, than did their European female counterparts. There is extensive documentation that, before the conquest, numerous tribes were characterized by a system of egalitarian relations between Indian women and men and power was shared equally (LaFromboise et al., 1994; LaFromboise, Heyle, & Ozer, 1990).

Some tribes gave a great deal of power to women and were matrilineal and matrifocal. Indeed, the institutionalization of alternative roles for women existed among Plains tribes. For example, "manly-hearted women" were independent and aggressive (LaFromboise et al., 1990, p. 458); "crazy women" were sexually adventurous (LaFromboise et al., 1990, p. 458). In many tribes, females could actually assume masculine social and occupational roles. This practice was institutionalized through the "berdache" (LaFromboise et al., 1990, p. 459), which sometimes included marriage to a same-sex partner. In other tribes, there was acceptance of uninhibited sexual expression, and there was social acceptance of nontraditional women and men, lesbian women, and homosexual men.

Gender-role conflict occurred for Indian women from such tribes with flexible gender roles because White European culture was far less tolerant of such flexibility, and many Indian women, accustomed to serving as tribal leaders and participating in tribal councils, lost their right to contribute to the lives of their communities.

American Indian women continue to experience gender-role conflict today. The legacy of European conquest, in some tribes and to varying degree, has been dominance and control over Indian women by Indian men with all the strains that accompany hierarchical relations. In addition, Indian women have had to reassert their rightful place as tribal leaders politically, economically, and socially.

Traditional Latino culture emphasizes expressive (feminine) traits over instrumental (masculine) traits among Latinas, whereas, the majority culture, relatively speaking, is more rewarding of instrumentality in women. Thus, a low degree of instrumentality may place Latinas at greater risk for poor mental health. The results of research on employed Hispanic women provide some support for such a speculation. Using the BSRI (previously described in section I) with a group of professional Hispanic women, Long and Martinez (1994) found a positive correlation between psychological masculinity and both self-esteem and self-acceptance. In other words, the higher the degree of her masculine characteristics, the higher her self-esteem and self-acceptance; conversely, the lower the degree of her masculine characteristics, the lower her self-esteem and self-acceptance. Napholz (1994) reported a negative correlation between depression and both instrumentality and self-esteem among Hispanic working women.

Napholz (1995) also found similar results in a study of midwestern, American Indian working women. Specifically, depression was significantly higher in women with a feminine gender-role orientation than women with an androgynous or a masculine gender-role orientation.

C. GENDER-ROLE CONFLICT RELATED TO INDIVIDUAL DIFFERENCES

The degree of acculturation, racial/ethnic identity, recent immigration, or other conceptually similar factors may affect gender-role conflict for women and men of racial or ethnic minority groups.

The conception of acculturation most relevant to the present discussion is that of Mendoza and Martinez (1981). They define four types of acculturation. Cultural incorporation refers to the process of retaining the original culture while taking on the dominant culture; this definition best describes the experiences of high bicultural individuals who maintain competence in their native culture while simultaneously acquiring competence in the dominant culture. Cultural shift, to which some scholars refer as assimilation, involves the replacement of the culture of origin with the dominant culture. Cultural resistance is the process of actively resisting acculturation, instead embracing the culture of origin. Cultural transmutation occurs when individuals do not identify with either culture; instead, they create a new culture or subculture derived from the combination of the two cultures.

Acculturation and gender-role conflict were studied in a sample of Asian American male college students (Kim, O'Neil, & Owen, 1996). The students included approximately equal numbers of Chinese American, Japanese American, and Korean American men. Gender-role conflict was measured with the Gender-role Conflict Scale (for a description of the scale, see section I). Acculturation was found to correlate significantly with two of the scale's four subscales. Specifically, the more acculturated the Asian American male, the greater his gender-role conflict on the Success, Power, and Competition subscale, but the lower his gender-role conflict on the Restrictive Affectionate Behavior between Men subscale. Thus, the more "traditional" Asian American male is presumably conflicted about pursuing success, power, and competition because traditional Asian culture values cooperation and achievement for the family rather than individual achievement. The more acculturated Asian American male presumably finds it easier to express affection than his less acculturated counterpart. This finding makes sense in light of Chan and Leong's (1994) description of traditional Chinese culture, which places a high value on the suppression of emotion and discourages any public display of affection, even between the sexes, as well as a strong cultural taboo against homosexuality.

Another researcher (Wade, 1996) addressed how racial identity of African American men may be associated with gender-role conflict. He described three possible reference groups for Black men: (a) "Black man's peer group" (p. 19), (b) "the subcultural reference group" (p. 19), and (c) the "societal reference group" (p. 19). The peer group is a response to American racism; it encompasses antifemininity, sexist attitudes, aggressive resolution of conflict, hostility towards other Black males, and an elevation of indicators of material success. African American men of lower socioeconomic status are more likely to identify with this reference group. The subcultural reference group is essentially the Black community, which supports less rigid gender roles for both women and men. The societal reference group refers to the mainstream, dominant society. If the Black man tries to live up to mainstream societal expectations but encounters obstacles in the form of racism and discrimination that prevent him from fulfilling the male provider role, he will experience gender-role strain.

Wade (1996) empirically examined the relationship between gender-role conflict and racial identity in African American men. He measured gender-role conflict with the Gender-role Conflict Scale (described in section I), and assessed racial reference group orientation with the Black Racial Identity Attitudes Scale (RIAS-B, Parham & Helms, 1981).

The RIAS-B is based on the theoretical model that racial identity is a function of various ego statuses associated with different racial identities. For example, in the Preencounter ego status, Blacks are rejected and Whites are elevated as a reference group. The Encounter stage is marked by a preliminary acceptance of

Blacks as a reference group. During Immersion-emersion, Whites are rejected and Blacks are elevated as a reference group. In the fourth stage, Internalization, Blacks are embraced as the principal reference group; this stage is marked by biculturalism. The RIAS-B consists of four subscales. The Preencounter subscale measures the degree to which the individual idealizes White values over Black values and uses Whites as her or his reference group while rejecting Blacks as a reference group. The Encounter subscale measures the degree to which the individual actively subscribes to a Black worldview; the individual experiences elation simultaneously with confusion over racial identity. The Immersion-emersion subscale measures the degree to which the individual has an externally defined Black reference group orientation. The Internalization subscale assesses the degree to which the individual has an internalized Black reference group, but also biculturalism and a transcendent personal identity. It is theorized that in the first three stages, the individual's racial identity is externally defined; whereas, in the fourth stage, racial identity is internally defined.

Wade (1996) obtained the following results. There were significant positive correlations between an Encounter identity and all four gender-role conflict subscales. An Immersion-emersion identity was significantly positively correlated with the Success, Power, and Competition, and the Restrictive Emotionality subscales. A Preencounter racial identity was significantly positively correlated with the Restrictive and the Conflicts between Work and Family Relations subscales. Finally, there was no correlation between an Internalization racial identity and any of the four gender-role conflict subscales. In sum, externally defined racial identity is associated with gender-role conflict because the individual allows her or his own identity to be determined by an outside racial reference group orientation, whereas, an internally defined racial identity is not associated with gender-role conflict. Thus, gender-role conflict is a function of the particular racial identity of the African American individual.

Immigrant status is another variable that may affect gender-role conflict. In a group of immigrant Korean women, depression increased as the women were unable to integrate sucessfully the roles of spouse, mother, and employee (Kim & Rew, 1994).

The interactive impact of gender, culture, acculturation, and immigrant status is especially apparent in interracial and international couples. Kim (1998) presented case studies of marital relationships between Asian women born in Japan, the Philippines, and South Korea and U.S. military men. The couples were in therapy because of major marital distress stemming in large part from cultural/gender-role issues. As Asian-born women, the wives had been socialized according to traditional Asian values. These values are described by Chan and Leong (1994) who provide a comprehensive discussion of the relationship between Asian culture and psychological adjustment among Chinese American immigrant families. They point out that Asian cultures include Chinese, Cambodian, Indian, Japanese, Korean, Pakistani, Filipino, and Vietnamese. It is important to recognize that each Asian cultural group has its unique attitudes, values, and traditions. However, there are sufficient similarities among the various groups that knowledge of Chinese culture may provide some insights into the cultural worldview of the Asian-born wives in therapy with Kim.

In terms of gender roles, religion has a major influence on Asian cultures. Confucianism includes the doctrine of three obediences. Namely, before a woman is married, she must obey her father; once she is married, she must obey her husband; and if she is widowed, she must obey her son. Male dominance is the norm. The husband-father is the disciplinarian and takes care of family business in the world. Sons are valued over daughters and inherit family property. Virginity as well as faithfulness to her husband are strong cultural dictates for the Asian woman.

Because of these Asian cultural values of hierarchical relationships and male dominance, the Asian wife is expected to learn and to adopt her husband's culture. Her husband, given his military background, holds very similar notions of male dominance. The conflicts for the wife are numerous. There is tremendous pressure on her to acculturate. She has lost her support system back home. Her traditional gender-role socialization causes her to be subservient and unassertive. Because she does not know the English language or U.S. culture, she is even more dependent on her American military husband. He may or may not help her in her efforts to learn the culture; having such cultural knowledge is a source of power for him and he may wish to continue to have control over his "exotic Oriental wife" (Kim, 1998, p. 312).

D. GENDER-ROLE CONFLICT RELATED TO GENDER-ROLE NORMS OF A PARTICULAR RACIAL AND ETHNIC MINORITY GROUP

African American, American Indian, Asian American, and Latino cultures have some gender-role expectations that, although found in the majority culture, exert even stronger pressures on its members. All four cultures typically expect females to fulfill a caretaking role, specifically, they are expected to care for younger siblings or the elderly. The stresses associated with being a caretaker are evident in the following examples from African American and Latino cultures.

Watson (1998) describes the caretaking responsibilities of young Black females and the negative impact of such responsibilities on their later relationships with men. Historically, African American women were forced to leave their children in the care of older female children who cared for their younger siblings while their mothers cared for the children of White slaveowners. Over time, such duties were performed for White employers. Because of their responsibilities to younger siblings, Black females were forced to put their own needs aside. Furthermore, greater parental attention was given to the younger children. Consequently, older Black females often failed to receive the love and attention that they, too, needed for proper emotional development. Sadly, these caretakers sometimes came to be perceived as cold and unfeeling. In their later relationships with men, they sometimes had difficulties because they were unable to express their needs or they concentrated excessively on attending to the needs of the male. Intimacy was seriously compromised in these relationships in which reciprocal caring was absent.

Heavy cultural pressures face Latinas too, whether they are Mexican American, Cuban, or Puerto Rican. These pressures can be summed up with one commandment: "Be a good girl!" (Garcia-Preto, 1998). Being a good girl means making motherhood one's major objective in life, protecting one's virginity, living at home with one's parents until marriage or college, acting like a "lady," and caring for children or the elderly. Garcia-Preto provides several case studies based on therapy with clients presenting a variety of gender-role issues. For example, a young Latina wanted to play sports after school. Initially, the parents would not allow the young girl to do so because of their cultural beliefs that girls should sit sedately, be quiet, and not be tomboys. On the other hand, at school the daughter was being encouraged to try out for sports because of her obvious talent and interest. In another study, Claudia, a 24-year-old Cuban, was the youngest daughter living with her parents. Although she wanted to move in with some women friends, she did not want to cause her parents worry. Her initial "solution" was to begin looking for a good man to marry so that she could move away. When she began to experience anxiety attacks, her friend referred her to Garcia-Preto. Still, another study focused on Celia, a 34-year-old "Lati-Negra" from the Dominican Republic. Celia had concerns about being a bad mother because she had to place her 2-year-old son in daycare so that she could go to her job.

Finally, Garcia-Preto discusses the additional burdens of cultural guilt placed on Latina lesbians. "Latina lesbians are perceived not only as rejecting the essence of being female, but as usurping male power; thus, they are a double threat to the culture" (p. 337).

III. IMPLICATIONS OF GENDER-ROLE CONFLICT FOR ASSESSMENT AND TREATMENT OF MENTAL HEALTH AND ADJUSTMENT ISSUES

A. AFRICAN AMERICANS

Because African American culture places considerable emphasis on the caretaking role for its women, therapists should move beyond a Eurocentric model of therapy and consider bringing siblings into the therapy session (Watson, 1998). Siblings who have been caretakers often have more influence on the personality development of younger siblings than parents do. In addition, dynamics of relating to siblings are often carried over into adult relationships. Exploring past sibling relationships could provide valuable insights into current individual as well as relationship issues. One example, particularly relevant, is the situation of the young Black male. The lynching of Black men and other atrocities committed against him are fresh in the psyche of the African American community. Because Black families fear for the very physical survival of their sons, families often overprotect them. Daughters may feel neglected or as if they are held to more rigorous expectations of responsibility and standards of achievement. Exploration of such issues can be extremely beneficial in the therapeutic setting (Watson, 1998).

B. AMERICAN INDIANS

American Indian women are creating ways to address the gender-role conflict resulting, in large part, from the imposition of a restrictive, rigid system of gender relations introduced by the Europeans. One such strategy is "retraditionalization—or the extension of traditional care-taking and cultural transmission roles to include activities vital to the continuity of Indian communities" (LaFromboise et al., 1990, p. 469). Retraditionalization is an effort by Indian women to combine traditional role requirements with contemporary ones in a way that honors past cultural values. Thus, while they pursue professional goals and fill positions of leadership within their tribes, they are also involved in preserving their culture. Ultimately, retraditionalization may promote the kind of egalitarian system of gender roles that Indian peoples had in place before European conquest.

C. ASIAN AMERICANS

Kim (1998), working with interracial, international couples, offers important treatment approaches for use with Asian/Asian American women in powerless (marital) relationships. First, the mental health professional should see the wife first. Doing so communicates to the wife that what she has to say is valued and allows the creation of an alliance between her and the therapist; it also breaks the subordinate–dominant nature of the relationship. Second, the therapist must not use the husband as an intermediary; this will only reinforce for both wife and husband his position of power. Third, the practitioner must be very patient; traditional Asian/Asian American women require a long time to feel comfortable with a therapist and to assert their needs and issues and to self-disclose their pain.

D. LATINAS AND LATINOS

Garcia-Preto (1998) shares her treatment strategies with Latinas. She provides Latinas, who have been socialized to adopt a very traditional gender role, an opportunity to discuss freely the dictates of their culture. For example, when sexuality is an issue, together they examine closely the "virginity myth," that is, the idea that a man will marry and take care of a woman—if she protects her virginity and her reputation until marriage. Further examination of the myth reveals that it is unrealistic to expect a man to take care of her. "Virgins and martyrs go hand in hand in Latino cultures, and their glorification perpetuates male dominance and female oppression" (Garcia-Preto, 1998, p. 335).

When a working Latino expresses conflict over the necessity of leaving her children at daycare or even with family, Garcia-Preto (1998) helps the client reframe the issue by pointing out that going to work to earn money to provide for her children's needs is part of being a good mother. Latinas, whose desire for independence leads them to prioritize searching for a husband, are encouraged by Garcia-Preto to develop their own self-reliance first. In one case, she encouraged a client to take college courses as a way of increasing her self-confidence through the acquisition of marketable skills. In another example, Latino lesbians are reminded that their very marginalization can be a source of tremendous power. Because they are on the periphery of acceptance, they can lead the way as far as critiquing issues important to the Latina community, such as, traditional gender roles, sexuality, and homophobia.

Another issue for Asian American women and Latinas relates to the acceptability of psychological androgyny. African American and American Indian cultures, in general, have promoted masculinity in women. However, Asian/Asian American culture and Latino culture have given more emphasis to femininity in women. Given the negative relationship between masculinity and depression and the positive relationship between masculinity and self-esteem, it would seem wise for therapists working with Asian American women and Latinas to encourage the development of such instrumental characteristics as independence and assertiveness. Besides the aforementioned relationships among instrumentality, depression, and self-esteem, the dominant culture tends to reward masculine characteristics. It is equally important for therapists to point out to clients that femininity need not be replaced by masculinity. Research has shown, generally, that it is not the absence of femininity but the presence of masculinity that contributes to good mental health (Whiteley, 1985).

E. Assessment and Treatment Issues Common to All Racial and Ethnic Minority Groups

When acculturation pressures are part of the problem, the therapist would do well to make the client aware that adjustment to U.S. culture is not a matter of choosing between the culture of origin and the majority culture; the individual can retain the former while mastering the latter. In other words, cultural incorporation is a viable option. Ethnic identity issues can be addressed similarly. In addition, a practitioner can administer acculturation and ethnic identity instruments to the client as part of the initial intake. The resulting information could help the practitioner tailor her or his approach to the client.

Chan and Leong (1994) offer a list of recommendations to treatment approaches with Chinese clients that are generalizable to all racial and ethnic minority groups because of shared cultural values. Their culture-based recommendations include the following: (a) use of a psychosocial rather than a psychological approach, precisely because of cultural issues likely to be present; (b) an autocratic leadership style from the therapist rather than a democratic one; people of racial/ethnic minority groups tend to have respect for teachers or any professionals they perceive as experts; (c) capitalizing on cultural values that will facilitate the therapeutic process; (d) acceptance of modes of treatment that the individual's culture offers, for example, "curanderismo" (folk healing) among Latinas/os; and (e) respect for the client's sometimes dependent demeanor with respect to the therapist: in traditional cultures, respect for authority is an important value.

Finally, all four of the major racial/ethnic minority groups value the extended family; therefore, therapists would do well to make use of group therapy. Having the input and commitment from family members would probably make for better, individual progress in therapy.

IV. SUMMARY AND CONCLUSIONS

Femininity and masculinity are not innate, permanent, or universally defined. The particular cultural context in which racial/ethnic minority groups live their daily lives gives unique meaning to conceptions of femininity and masculinity. Culture and gender work jointly to affect the attitudes, feelings, characteristics, and behaviors experienced by such groups. Knowledge and appreciation of such cultural definitions are as important to effective assessment and treatment of mental health issues with racial/ethnic minority groups as clinical training. African American, American Indian, Asian American, and Latino cultures each have unique perspectives on the meaning of being a woman and being a man. Their perspectives are influenced not only by the worldview of their racial/ethnic minority group but also by the history of their political, economic, and social relationships with the majority culture. For example, although minority men have tried to be effective providers and protectors, they have been severely blocked in their efforts because of racism. In their frustration, they have developed unique survival strategies, for example, Cool Pose in the case of African American men. Modifications, like Cool Pose and others, to majority culture notions of masculinity and femininity, must be taken into consideration by mental health professionals working on gender-role conflicts with women and men who are members of racial/ethnic minority groups.

African Americans, American Indians, Asian Americans, and Latinas/os possess distinctive, rich cultural backgrounds. However, they share many important cultural values that enable them to survive in the racist environments in which they live their everyday lives. The values they have in common include the importance of the extended family, interdependence, cooperation, and spirituality. These are values that every therapist can acknowledge and respect in the therapeutic setting. Doing so can only enhance the interaction between client and therapist as well as promote the goals of assessment and treatment.

ACKNOWLEDGMENTS

I would like to thank Katharine Branham for her extremely valuable help as my research assistant in the preparation of this chapter.

REFERENCES

Baron, R. A., & Byrne, D. (1997). *Social psychology.* Boston: Allyn and Bacon.

Bem, S. (1974). The measurement of psychological androgyny. *Journal of Consulting and Clinical Psychology, 42,* 155–162.

Bowman, P. J. (1992). Coping with provider role strain: Adaptive cultural resources among Black husband-fathers. In A. K. H. Burlew, W. C. Banks, H. P. McAdoo, & D. A. Azibo (Eds.), *African American psychology: Theory, research, and practice* (pp. 135–154). Newbury Park, CA: Sage.

Cazenave, N. A. (1984). Race, socioeconomic status, and age: The social context of American maculinity. *Sex Roles, 11,* 639–656.

Chan, S., & Leong, C. W. (1994). Chinese families in transition: Cultural conflicts and adjustment problems. *Journal of Social Distress and the Homeless, 3* (3), 263–281.

Garcia-Preto, N. (1998). Latinas in the United States: Bridging two worlds. In McGoldrick, M. (Ed.), *Re-visioning family therapy: Race, culture, and gender in clinical practice* (pp. 330–346). New York: The Guilford Press.

Hunter, A. G., & Davis, J. E. (1992). Constructing gender: An exploration of Afro-American men's conceptualization of manhood. *Gender and Society, 6,* 464–479.

Kim, B. C. (1998). Marriages of Asian women and American military men: The impact of gender and culture. In McGoldrick, M. (Ed.), *Re-visioning family therapy: Race, culture, and gender in clinical practice* (pp. 309–319). New York: The Guilford Press.

Kim, E. J., O'Neil, J. M., & Owens, S. V. (1996). Asian-American men's acculturation and gender-role conflict. *Psychological Reports, 79,* 95–104.

Kim, S., & Rew, L. (1994). Ethnic identity, role integration, quality of life, and depression in Korean-American women. *Archives of Psychiatric Nursing, 8* (6), 348–356.

LaFromboise, T. D., Berman, J. S., & Sohi, B. K. (1994). American Indian women. In L. Comas-Diaz & B. Greene (Eds.), *Women of color: Integrating ethnic and gender identities in psychotherapy* (pp. 30–71). New York: The Guilford Press.

LaFromboise, T. D., Heyle, A. M., & Ozer, E. J. (1990). Changing and diverse roles of women in American Indian cultures. *Sex Roles, 22* (7/8), 455–476.

Lazur, R. F., & Majors, R. (1995). Men of color: Ethnocultural variations of male gender role strain. In R. F. Levant & W. S. Pollack (Eds.), *A new psychology of men* (pp. 337–358). New York: BasicBooks.

Long, V. O., & Martinez, E. A. (1994). Masculinity, femininity, and Hispanic professional women's self-esteem and self-acceptance. *Journal of Counseling and Development, 73* (2), 183–186.

Majors, R., & Billson, J. M. (1992). *Cool pose: The dilemmas of Black manhood in America.* New York: Lexington Books.

Mendoza, R. H., & Martinez, J. L. (1981). The measurement of acculturation. In A. Baron (Ed.), *Explorations in Chicano psychology* (pp. 71–82). New York: Praeger.

Napholz, L. (1994). Dysphoria among Hispanic working women: A research note. *Hispanic Journal of Behavioral Sciences, 16* (4), 500–509.

Napholz, L. (1995). Mental health and American Indian women's multiple roles. *American Indian & Alaska Native Mental Health Research, 6* (2), 57–75.

O'Neil, J. M. (1990). Assessing men's gender role conflict. In D. Moore & F. Leafgren (Eds.), *Problem solving strategies and interventions for men in conflict* (pp. 23–38). Alexandria, VA: American Association for Counseling and Development.

O'Neil, J. M., Helms, B., Gable, R., David, L., & Wrightsman, L. (1986). Gender-role conflict scale: College men's fear of femininity. *Sex Roles, 14,* 335–350.

Parham, T. A., & Helms, J. E. (1981). The influence of Black students' racial identity attitudes on preferences for counselor's race. *Journal of Counseling Psychology, 28,* 250–257.

Parsons, T., & Bales, R. F. (1955). *Family socialization and interaction process.* Glencoe: Free Press.

Rothenberg, P. S. (1998). *Race, class, and gender in the United States.* New York: St. Martin's Press.

Spence, J., Helmreich, R., & Stapp, J. (1975). Ratings of self and peers on sex role attributes and their relation to self-esteem and conceptions of masculinity and femininity. *Journal of Personality and Social Psychology, 32,* 29–39.

Stillson, R. W., O'Neil, J. M., & Owen, S. V. (1991). Predictors of adult men's gender-role conflict: Race, class, unemployment, age instrumentality, expressiveness, and personal strain. *Journal of Counseling Psychology 38,* 358–464.

Unger, R. K. (1979). Toward a redefinition of sex and gender. *American Psychologist, 34,* 1085–1094.

Wade, J. C. (1996). African American men's gender role conflict: The significance of racial identity. *Sex Roles, 34* (1/2), 17–33.

Wade, C., & Tavris, C. (1994). The longest war: Gender and culture. In W. J. Lonner & R. Malpass (Eds.), *Psychology and culture* (pp. 121–126). Boston: Allyn and Bacon.

Watson, M. F. (1998). African American sibling relationships. In M. McGoldrick (Ed.), *Re-visioning family therapy: Race, culture, and gender in clinical practice* (pp. 282–294). New York: The Guilford Press.

Whiteley, B. E., Jr. (1985). Sex role orientation and psychological well-being: Two meta-analyses. *Sex Roles, 12,* 207–225.

Multicultural Demographic Developments: Current and Future Trends

Uzzer A. Raajpoot

Department of Sociology
University of Texas—Pan American
Edinburg, Texas

I. INTRODUCTION

An accurate picture of demographics of any society is crucial to assess a variety of health and human needs and planning for the future. Demographic characteristics of a given population, community, or ethnic group provide meaningful indicators of need, risk, and type of service interventions required. For example, if a significant segment of a given population or community is composed of ethnic minorities, and it is known that special needs or risks are associated with that ethnic status, then the service needs for that group can be systematically estimated. Some minority groups are likely to require greater needs for children and youth services simply because minority demographic profiles generally indicate larger families and more children. Likewise, if a given ethnic group has higher rates of poverty, the mental health needs of that community may be greater.

Demographics not only provide indicators of risk and need but also influence the type of services required, such as prevention services, education services, psychosocial interventions, and other delivery components of mental health systems and services. For example, differential rates of infectious disease, drug abuse, gang involvement, school drop-out rates, criminal/illegal behaviors, developmental problems, specific genetic disorders, mental disorders, and the like require differential allocation of resources, interventions, and services. Issues of availability of services, accessibility of services, and acceptability of health and mental health services are all intricately tied to demographic characteristics. Social-demographic characteristics may also dictate the language in which the service should best be delivered. Social-demographic features such as socioeconomic status (SES) have profound influences on all forms of illnesses and social problems.

The changing population structure of American minorities has always been intriguing and dynamic, given the evolving diversity of the U.S. population. The continuous change in the size, composition, and age structure of the U.S. population necessitates the understanding of the dynamic aspects of demographic change. The understanding of the current demographic phenomena of American minorities cannot be completed without comprehending the dynamic interplay of fertility, mortality, and migration, traditionally known as the three factors of population growth. This chapter will examine basic demographic and population growth factors for each of four racial, ethnic minority groups in the United States: African Americans, American Indians, Asian Americans, and Hispanic Americans. Each of these four minority groups is composed of a number of subgroups having a common core of some feature of culture.

Although the focus of this chapter will be on the prior-mentioned minorities, it is important to keep in mind that racial and ethnic boundaries are not fixed. Providers of health and related services to minorities should keep this "fluidity of identity" concept in mind. Most sociologists and demographers agree that ethnic boundaries are fluid in American society. The notion of "ethnic options" implies that many individuals in American society, by virtue of a multiethnic ancestry, can choose among several identities (Waters, 1990). Historically, race has long been considered essentially fixed and immutable. Scholars have generally ignored racial mixing, but more recently racial boundaries are assuming ambiguity and fluidity (Root, 1992; Spickard, 1989). To the degree that racial boundaries are fluid, membership in a particular racial/ethnic category is the outcome of a social process of identification.

Another caveat with respect to demographics of minorities that needs to be kept in mind is the limitations of census data with respect to enumeration methods used by the U.S. Census and their disparate impact on racially and ethnically diverse populations in the United States. In the 1990 Census there was a large undercount of racial and ethnic groups. It is estimated that the census missed 4.4% of African Americans, 5% of Hispanics, 2.3% of Asian and Pacific Islanders, and 12% of American Indians living on reservations (Perine,

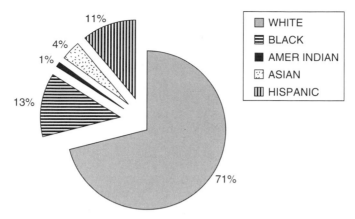

FIGURE 1   Ethnic composition of the U.S. population in the year 2000.

1999). Children under the age of 18 make up 26% of the U.S. population but comprise 52% of the undercount in Census 1990. Because racial and ethnic minorities generally have larger families and more children, they are disparately impacted by undercounting. The undercount in Census 1990 is reported to have been 50% worse than the undercount of Census 1980 (Perine, 1999).

The U.S. population is growing and changing dramatically. Figures 1 and 2 show, respectively, the current and projected racial/ethnic composition of the United States. The Four National Panels on Cultural Competence In Managed Care Mental Health Service, sponsored by the Western Interstate Commission for Higher Education (WICHE, October, 1997), remind us that changes in numbers really represent changes in social structure along with the impact of

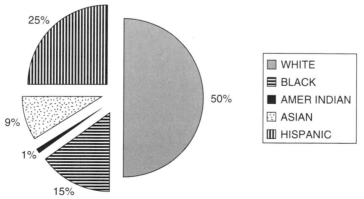

FIGURE 2   Ethnic composition of the U.S. population in the year 2050.

those changes on society and individuals. The four major racial/ethnic groups identified and presented in this chapter (African Americans, Asian/Pacific Islanders, Latino/Hispanic, and American Indian and Alaska Natives) have also been identified as underserved/underrepresented mental health groups (WICHE, 1997).

II. HISPANIC AMERICANS

Hispanic Americans are projected to play an increasing role in American society early on in the 21st century based on demographic growth characteristics. It is widely projected that Hispanic Americans will become the nation's largest minority group by the year 2020 (U.S. Bureau of the Census, 1997), outnumbering the African Americans. The Hispanic population is also projected to form a majority in California's public school enrollment by 2006 (Pinal, 1996). Because of within-group diversity, it is not easy to describe the demographics of Hispanics. As with most ethnic minority labels, there is no single Hispanic population but rather there are, minimally, four distinct subgroups: Mexican Americans, Cuban Americans, Puerto Ricans, and Central/South Americans. These groups are identified through place of birth or country of origin. High migration rates and relatively high birth rates are among some of the variables that separate Hispanics from other minorities. As Romero (chapter 11, this volume) also points out, of the four subgroups of Hispanics, Mexican-Americans make up the largest percentage (63%), followed by Central South Americans (21%), Puerto Ricans (11%), and Cuban Americans 5%. Although these four subgroups of Latinos have many common cultural aspects, they also differ significantly with respect to social, political, economic, and cultural histories and experiences. Their demographic features are not all the same, making for quite a heterogeneous overall picture.

Latino or Hispanic immigration into the United States has been one of the more important streams of immigration of the 20th century. In 1990s, about two-thirds of U.S. Hispanic residents were either immigrants or children of immigrants. Less than one-third were children of U.S.-born parents (Pinal & Singer, 1996). In 1996, a little more than one-third of Hispanics were first-generation Americans (38%), one-third second-generation Americans (30%), and less than one-third were third-generation Americans (32%).

Although international migration is a large contributor to the growth and diversity of the Hispanic population in the U.S., births to Hispanics contributed nearly two-thirds of the increase in the Hispanic population during 1995 (U.S. Bureau of the Census, 1995). Not only does immigration bring in women of reproductive age but foreign-born Hispanic women tend to have substantially higher fertility than U.S.-born Hispanic women. Estimates of Hispanic fertility prior to the mid-1980s were based on scanty data. Systematic collection of Hispanic origin on birth certificates did not begin until 1978, and that data too was available only for few states. By the early 1990s, the size of the Hispanic population was more certain and birth registration by Hispanic origin was much more complete. The recorded dates showed that the fertility of Hispanic women, and of Mexican women in particular, continued to be among the highest of any major racial or ethnic group in the United States. Hispanic fertility is still much higher than that of other racial and ethnic groups. The total fertility rate was three children for Hispanics, in 1995 (NCHS, 1997) and was below 2 for non-Hispanics. Among Hispanics, Mexican Americans had the highest total fertility rate (TFR) (3.3) followed by Puerto Ricans (2.2) and Cubans (1.7) (NCHS, 1997). A TFR is defined as the number of children a woman will have during her reproductive span, given the current birth rates. Cubans were the only major Hispanic group with below replacement level fertility. (A TFR of 2.1 children per woman is required for a generation to replace itself, after allowing for deaths).

Education is a key variable, as it is closely related to fertility through income levels. On average, Hispanics have less education, lower family incomes, and higher poverty rates than non-Hispanics. Among Hispanic women with less than 9 years of education in 1994, the TFR was 4.0 children per woman and 3.8 for 12 years of school (Lee, 1998). Hispanics probably have the lowest rates of high school and college graduation of any major population group. One possible explanation is that Hispanics did not have the same educational opportunities as other groups. Generations of Mexican Americans in the Southwest attended segregated low-quality schools and were not encouraged to excel. Some education specialists see the conflict between Hispanic student's background and the culture promoted in school as the root of Hispanic underachievement. The pressure of assimilation somehow degrades their culture and families that, in turn, give them low-esteem. They are then stereotyped as noncompetitive, lacking "delayed gratification," and family centered rather than individualistic. All these personality characteristics are usually considered hindrances to their academic excellence.

Hispanics are geographically located primarily in the southwestern United States. Hispanic subgroups in the United States are concentrated in different regions, states, and urban areas. For example, Cuban Americans are located primarily in Miami, Mexican Americans are located primarily in the southwest, and the largest mainland population of Puerto Ricans lives in New York. Based on 1995 census projections, 85% of the Hispanic population is concentrated in nine states: California, Texas, New York, Florida, Illinois, New Jersey, Arizona, New Mexico, Colorado. In 1996, one-third of all Hispanics lived in California.

Currently, Hispanics are an overwhelmingly urban population, although the first large stream of migrants came to the United States to work in agriculture in the 1940s (Shafer & Donald, 1981).

Hispanics have a high profile in Los Angeles, San Antonio, and Miami, where Latinos comprise 40% or more of the population. The 1990 census showed Hispanics to be highly concentrated, percentage-wise, around U.S.–Mexico border areas such as Laredo, Texas (85%), Brownsville, Texas (89%), and El Paso, Texas (70%). Also, the McAllen, Brownsville, and Harlingen metropolitan area in south Texas is composed of 87% Hispanic, or Latino, population, with the vast majority being of Mexican origin. The two lower Rio Grande Valley standard metropolitan areas (SMAs), composed of about 90% Hispanics, are ranked the two poorest SMAs in the United States (Neiman, 1999).

Hispanics often share a Spanish-language heritage, a disadvantaged minority status, and a public image as newcomers who are welcomed by some and resented by others. One general conclusion is that Hispanics are not a monolithic group, but rather are a highly diverse and heterogeneous minority group. Based on the U.S. census classification system, Hispanics are not a racial group but are an ethnic group. According to government guidelines, Hispanics prefer to be identified based on their national origin: Mexican, Cuban, Puerto Rican, Salvadoran, or any other term that denotes national origin, place of birth, or community.

Puerto Ricans are U.S. citizens whether they are born on the U.S. mainland or in Puerto Rico. Puerto Ricans may move freely between the mainland and Puerto Rico and are not considered international migrants. Puerto Ricans are not counted as part of the U.S. Hispanic population unless they live in one of the 50 states or the District of Columbia.

The Hispanic population in the United States has steadily increased over the years. Between 1970 and 1980, the Hispanic population in the United States increased by 61%, between 1980 and 1990 there was a 53% increase, and between the intercensal period of 1990 and 1996 by 27%. From 1970–1996, the Puerto Rican proportion of U.S. Hispanics decreased from 16 to 11%. The three major Hispanic subgroups vary in terms of Infant Mortality Rates (IMR) calculated as the number of deaths within the first year of life for every 1000 live births. The Puerto Rican IMR at 78 is the highest among the Cuban, Mexican American, and Puerto Rican subgroups whose rates are, respectively, 51, 59, and 78. A paradoxical finding is that the IMR for Texas border counties (32 in total) is actually lower than the average IMR for the rest of the state of Texas (Texas-Mexico Border Health Coordination Office, 1998). There are other paradoxical health findings, wherein surprisingly lower rates of some diseases and illnesses are found in the Texas-border Mexican American population, such as lower death rates from coronary heart disease, malignant neoplasms, cerebrovascular diseases, and so on (Cuéllar, 1999). Some Mexican immigrant colonies (*colonias*) along the Texas–Mexico border are economically as bad off or worse in some cases than third-world countries (Cuéllar, 1999) and have the highest rates in the state of Texas for numerous infectious diseases such as amebiasis, hepatitis A, shigonelliosis, tuberculosis, chickenpox, and so on (Cuéllar, 1999). There is also an increase in neural tube defects, particularly toward the southernmost tip of Texas along the Rio Grande River (Johnson, 1999).

III. AMERICAN INDIANS

Historically, American Indians tend to fall at the lower end of the socioeconomic spectrum. American Indian reservations have been consistently among the poorest areas in the United States. The standard of living on many reservations, in terms of sanitary conditions, running water, paved roads, and other public facilities is not very different from that in some third-world countries (Ruffing, 1978). Ruffing notes that compared with other minority groups, American Indians, rural or urban, are still among the most poorly housed, poorly nourished, least educated, least healthiest, and most unemployed (See Dillard & Manson, chapter 12, this volume, for additional demographic characteristics of the American Indian and the Alaskan Native population).

The estimates and changes in the American Indian population have been very dramatic from pre-Columbian to modern times. The population of American Indians living above the Rio-Grande river at the time of contact (1492) is estimated to range from a low of 900,000 to a high of 18 million. The Indian population declined sharply from epidemics and warfare after the arrival of Europeans. This decline was precipitous in the early years of European settlement and continued through the late 19th century. Since then, the Indian population has staged a remarkable comeback. As a race, American Indians declined to their smallest number in 1890, at which time their population was about 228,000. From this low point, the population has grown throughout the 20th century (see Table I).

Fear and hostility prevailed in early Euro-American attitudes towards American Indians. Negative statements about Indians as enemies by high-level U.S. military officials served to inflame an existing history of hostile attitudes. In some cases, California tribes were, reportedly, hunted down like animals (Snipp, 1989).

Modern medicine, including vaccines and antibiotics, helped stimulate the expansion of Indian populations, which had been reduced by high incidence of tuberculosis and diabetes (Sorkin, 1971). Sorkin also notes that between 1955 and 1967, IMR among the Indians dropped from 61 per 1000 live birth to 30 per 1000 live births. In 1955, Indian deaths from TB were 41 per 100,000 population, and by 1967 death rates had fallen to 17.

TABLE I   Growth of the American
Indian Population during the 20th
Century[a]

Year	Number (in 100,000s)
1900	237
1910	277
1920	244
1930	343
1940	345
1950	357
1960	524
1970	793
1980	1,367

[a]From Snipp (1989).

Indian life expectancy has also shown a remarkable improvement from 1940–1980. In 1940 the life expectancy was 51.6, in 1950 it was 60, in 1970 it was 65.1, and in 1980 it was up to 71.1 years (U.S. Bureau of the Census, 1985). An American Indian female born after 1980 can reasonably expect to live to the year 2055 based on the current average lifetime of 75 years.

Some other demographic indicators show that the family size of American Indians has reduced over time. There are several demographic indicators available to look at the pace of childbearing in the families. Age-specific fertility and children ever born are two commonly used measures of childbearing behavior (also known as parity), reflecting cumulative, lifetime fertility. This mirrors long-term processes such as changing norms regarding desirable family size and the use of contraceptives.

The age group 20–24 is usually the most fertile age group, and if we look at this group, it seems that their fertility has declined during the recent years. Beginning in 1965, Indian women aged 20–24 gave birth to approximately 2.2 children per woman. Ten years later Indian woman of the same age showed a marked reduction in their fertility by having only 1.6 children per woman (Snipp, 1989). The reduction in American Indian fertility can be seen in terms of overall TFR also. Snipp notes that between 1965 and 1969, their TFR was approximately 3.4 children per woman. Ten years later, it dropped to about 2.4 children per woman, a reduction of 29%.

American Indians, like the other ethnic categories, exemplify the concept of fluidity of ethnic identity (Eschbach, Khalil, & Snipp, 1998), a caveat expressed at the beginning of this chapter. Most American Indians have multiracial identities because of their history of intermarriage among American Indians and members of other racial and ethnic groups (Eschbach, 1995).

Between 1970 and 1990, the American Indian population increased in excess of what might be expected based on fertility, mortality, or immigration factors. The increase noted in the U.S. Census between 1970 and 1990 of American Indians is attributable to changes in ethnic identification, as many multiethnic/ multiracial persons who were reported as members of some other racial/ethnic category in 1970 were identified as American Indians in 1980 and 1990. The American Indian population grew from 827,000 in 1970 to 1.42 million in 1980. More than 62% of the increase in the American Indian population (350,000 persons) is attributable to changes in identification alone (Eschbach et al., 1998). The American Indian and Alaskan Native population in the 1990 census was 1.96 million with about 35% of the increase over the 1980 census figure of 190,000 persons added by identity changes (Passel, 1996).

Demographers distrust the census data because of these changes (Tienda & Jensen, 1988). They note a "dramatic convergence" in the socioeconomic standing of census-enumerated American Indians and Whites in recent decades. They caution against interpreting the change for the American Indian group as representing real improvement in economic status, because of the noncomparability of American Indian population across censuses, especially between 1970 and 1980. Featherman and Hauser (1978) and Hirschman (1983) argue that education is a key indicator of assimilation in American society, and educational gains are a prerequisite for any "real" convergence of health and SES.

It is important to note that the increases noted since 1970 in self-identification of many American Indians may have resulted from attitudinal changes toward American Indians by the U.S. population in general. Beginning in the 1960s, there was a shift from negative to sympathetic and romanticized views of Indians in popular culture. In the 1960s and 1970s, several American Indian organizations and Indian centers sprang up in cities across the country and sought to foster pride in American Indian heritage and identity. Stigma of Indian identity diminished during this period, particularly for fair-skined, urban, and educated metropolitan Indians. As the first inhabitants of the Americas, American Indians and Alaskan Natives deserve to be credited and respected for their heritage, ways of life, worldviews, wisdom, enormous sacrifices, and contributions to America. If the current trends in attitudes toward persons of American Indian heritage continues, further increases in self-identification are likely. This will likewise continue to impact the demographic characteristics of this population.

IV. AFRICAN AMERICANS

African Americans, currently the largest and most visible minority, has a legacy of slavery and legal subjugation. The U.S. Census uses the term *Blacks*. The term "African American" and "Black" will be used interchangeably, in this chapter, depending on the source of data.

Unlike some other immigrants, African Americans were among the earliest settlers of colonial America via slave trade, arriving at Jamestown in 1619, one year before the pilgrims landed at Plymouth Rock (Gill, Glazer, & Thernstrom, 1992). The African American population has grown from an estimated 60 persons in 1630 (Farley, 1970) to a projected number of 35.4 million in the year 2000 (U.S. Bureau of Census, 1997). Forced African migration via slave trade meant the disruption of family, kinship, village, tribal, cultural, and other ties that characterized and made life viable in Africa. The quantity of Africans forced out of Africa via slave trade resulted in a significant change of the demographic makeup of the population in Africa as well as in the United States. In 1700, there were approximately 28,000 Africans and their descendants living in the colonies, nearly 60% in Virginia alone. By the time of the American War of Independence, their numbers had increased greatly. At the time of the first census in 1790, the African population in the United States was estimated at 757,000, of whom 92% were slaves (Gill et al., 1992). In 1990, two centuries later, the estimated African population had risen to over 31 million, which is a very large increase and yet it represents substantial percentage decrease in relation to the U.S. total population. From the first U.S. census until the 1930s, the percentage of Americans who were Africans fell by half. From a height of 19.3% or nearly one-fifth of the U.S. population in 1790, the percentage fell to 9.7% in 1930, or almost exactly half the percentage that it had been 140 years earlier (Gill et al., 1992). Gill also notes that since the 1930s, the percentage has been increasing slowly, rising to an estimated 12.4% in 1990. Middle series Census Bureau Projections (Spencer, 1990) place the percentage at 16.3 in the year 2080. Looking as far ahead as the year 2080, it is probable that the percentage of African Americans will still be below what it was three centuries previously. One of the factors explaining the percentage decline of African Americans is that the slave trade was ended in the early 19th century while the immigrations of other nationalities continued to add to U.S. population growth. The other reason being the high death rate, which limited the rate of natural increase of the African American population along with the unbalanced sex ratio in favor of women.

African Americans have made substantial progress in various spheres of life during the course of their long and difficult history in the United States. Abolition of slavery, passage of civil rights, and three constitutional amendments were crucial steps for the progress of Africans. One of the demographic areas they have made progress in is the increase in longevity. Stunning increases in African American life expectancy have been observed over this century. In 1900, life expectancy at birth was estimated at no more than 33 years. By 1988, it had risen to 69.5 years, or gain of around 111%. In the middle series projection (Spencer, 1990), it is assumed that there is a convergence of African American and white life expectancies at birth at 81.2 years in 2080. It is also assumed that there is a convergence of African American and white fertility rates at 1.8 live births per women in 2080. Life expectancy of African Americans is less than that for all other groups (see Table II).

Although the education, health, living conditions, and incomes have improved since the 1960s, African Americans still rank below whites in many social and economic ways. For example, Black infants are twice as likely to die as White infants (see Table III). Black children are nearly three times more likely to live in a single-parent family than White children. Blacks are half as likely to go to college as Whites. Blacks who migrated to cities in some ways have faced more problems than those who did not. According to Wilson (1987),

TABLE II   Life Expectancy Rates for African Americans
Compared to All Other Races[a]

Year	All other races (years)	Blacks (years)
1970	70.8	64.1
1971	71.1	64.6
1972	71.2	64.7
1973	71.4	65.0
1974	72.0	66.0
1975	72.6	66.8
1976	72.9	67.2
1977	73.3	67.7
1978	73.5	68.1
1979	73.9	68.5
1980	73.7	68.1
1981	74.1	68.9
1982	74.5	69.4
1983	74.6	69.4
1984	74.7	69.5
1985	74.7	69.3
1986	74.7	69.1
1987	74.9	69.1
1988	74.9	68.9
1989	75.1	68.8
1990	75.4	69.1
1991	75.5	69.3
1992	75.8	69.6
1993	75.5	69.2
1994	75.7	69.5
1995	75.8	69.6
1996	76.1	70.2

[a]From NCHS (1998).

TABLE III   Infant Mortality Rates for African
Americans in Comparison to All Other Groups[a]

Year	Non-African Americans	African Americans
1980	12.6	22.2
1981	11.9	20.8
1982	11.5	20.5
1983	11.2	20.0
1984	10.6	19.2
1985	10.6	19.2
1986	10.4	18.9
1987	10.1	18.8
1988	10.0	18.5
1989	9.8	18.6
1990	9.2	18.0
1991	8.9	17.6
1992	8.5	16.8
1993	8.4	16.5
1994	8.0	15.8
1995	7.6	15.1
1996	7.3	14.7

[a]From NCHS (1998).

urban poor became more impoverished and more isolated because of the decline of manufacturing and movement of many blue-collar jobs to suburban
areas. The movement of jobs out of the urban areas eliminated a source of
relatively well-paying, secure jobs for Blacks. Wilson also notes that joblessness
increased among urban Blacks, reducing the pool of marriageable men and
undermining the strength of the family.

Blacks have higher birth rates than whites, but the overall death rate is lower
for Blacks because of a younger age structure, a smaller percentage of Blacks in
the oldest age group most at risk of dying. The median age of Blacks was 27.7
years in 1989, nearly 5 years younger than the median for all Americans
(O'Hare, Pollard, Mann, & Kent, 1991). Birth rates for White and Black men
have declined steadily since 1990. Between 1990 and 1996, the birth rate for
Black men aged 15–54 years dropped 20%.

V. ASIAN AMERICANS

For most non-Asian Americans, "Asian" means Chinese, Japanese, or "Oriental."
This concept of "Asian" accurately reflected the Asian population living in the

United States through 1970, when 96% of Asian Americans were either Japanese, Chinese, or Filipino. As the 21st century approaches, these three groups make up 55% of Asian Americans. Chinese represent the largest Asian subgroup (24%), Filipino is second largest (21%), and Japanese Americans represent 10%. The other 45% of the Asian American population is represented by Asian Indians (13%), Koreans (10%), Vietnamese (11%), Cambodians, Hmong, and Laotian (5%), and other Asian group (6%).

The number of Cambodians, Hmongs, Laotians, and other Asians living in the United States grew rapidly after 1980 because new refugee policies brought a large influx from Southeast Asia. It is also interesting to note that there has been little immigration from Japan in recent decades. Since 1990, the Asian Indians, Koreans, and Vietnamese have all surpassed the number of Japanese Americans.

Although Asian Americans made up less than 4% of the total U.S. population in 1997, this population is growing very rapidly. Asian American numbers nearly doubled between 1980 and 1990 and are likely to double again by the year 2010. Immigration has fueled the dramatic growth of the Asian American population (Barringer, Gardner, & Levin, 1993). Almost 70% of the U.S. Asians counted in the 1990 census were either immigrants who came to the United States after 1970 or the children of these immigrants (Lee, 1998).

Immigration along with fertility and mortality continues to shape the demographic profile and growth rate of Asian American population. Immigration and differences in childbearing patterns have given Asian Americans a young age structure, which is different from other minority groups and from the overall U.S. population. Only about 7% of Asians were aged 65 or older in 1997 compared with 13% of the total U.S. population. U.S.-born Asians also have an extremely young age structure. These young Americans will be forming their own families in the next decade and thus creating the first sizable population of third-generation (grandchildren) Asian Americans.

Aside from immigration, fertility is the major source of growth among the Asian American population. Asian Americans tend to wait longer to have children and eventually have fewer children than other minority groups. Asian mothers are also less likely than other racial and ethnic groups to have a baby out of wedlock. They are more likely to have a high school or college education than mothers in other racial or ethnic groups. These childbearing patterns reflect different age structures, marriage patterns, and cultural influences. The TFR of Asian Americans was 1.9 in 1995, which was lower than the rates of other minority groups. During this period, American Indians, African Americans, and Hispanics had 2.2, 2.5, and 3.0 as their respective TFRs (NCHS, 1997).

Another indicator of population composition is sex ratio (number of males per 100 females), which reflects whether the immigrant flows consisted predominantly of men, women, or families. When the Chinese worked on the railroads during 1850s, there were almost 1400 Chinese men for every 100 Chinese women. The situation has reversed now, as in 1997, the sex-ratio for the Asian American population was 96 to 100 (Lee 1998). Of the various groups of Asian Americans, Asian Indians are an exception whose sex-ratio was 116 to 100 for those who arrived between 1980 and 1990.

Immigration from Asia was transformed after 1965 by two factors: the passage of the Immigration and Nationality Act Amendments of 1965 and the end of the Vietnam War. The Immigration and Nationality Act Amendments (1965) effectively opened the way for new waves of immigrants from China and the Philippines as well as new flows from many other countries, primarily South Korea and India. The post-1965 flow began with highly educated professionals who came to the United States in search of jobs, and it is now dominated by the families of those immigrants. India has been among the leading countries of origin of U.S. immigrants in the 1990s, and the Asian Indian population is now the third largest Asian American ethnic subgroup (Helweg & Helweg, 1990). About 20% of the 1997 population arrived after 1990 (U.S. Bureau of the Census, 1997).

The influence of the Asian American population on U.S. societey is substantial. The Asian American population in general, and some of the Asian American subgroups in particular, has above-average income and educational levels. Both as a group and as individuals they tend to negate the idea that they are a disadvantaged minority. At the same time their diversity in terms of SES contradicts the common stereotype that Asian Americans are a "model minority" (Smith & Edmonston, 1997).

Asian Americans differ from Blacks and Hispanics because a much larger percentage of Asians are in the middle- and upper-income levels. Asian Americans are more likely than Blacks, and as likely as Hispanics, to marry outside their racial and ethnic groups. Some scholars even suggest that Asian's minority status will erode and eventually disappear. By the middle of 21st century, the term "Asian American" may impart no more social distance from the majority population than Italian American or Greek American does today (Lott, 1998).

VI. CONCLUSIONS

Demographic growth characteristics are dynamically interrelated to fertility, mortality, and migration. Each racial and ethnic minority group in the United States has its own history of immigration and specific pattern of growth demonstrated in U.S. census data. There has been an ebb and flow of immigrants into the United States from the four major American minority groups. Each racial and ethnic group is composed of subgroups with each having their own pattern of growth. In general, all four major minority groups are increasing their numbers and percentages in the United States with Latinos and Asians leading growth trends. Increases in assimilation and education are generally accompanied by increases in life expectancy and improved health, concomitant with decreases in fertility and infant mortality. Demographic growth patterns of American minorities indicate that by the middle of the 21st century, the number of all minorities combined (African Americans, Asian Americans, American Indians and Alaskan Natives, and Hispanic Americans) will comprise more than 50% of the total U.S. population. Demographic changes in American minorities are having a profound impact on social structure, health care, educational, legal, and criminal justice systems. A thorough understanding of sociocultural, historical, and demographic characteristics of each racial and ethnic group is essential for understanding the needs of that group. It is also essential in providing effective health and mental health services and for future planning of health-care needs. The United States is rapidly becoming the world's first truly multicultural society. The challenges are great but so are the possibilities. As the United States changes so do its needs, including health and mental health concerns, but changes in demographics also represent opportunities for growth and betterment. When the unique perspectives of diversity, along with the quality and strength that diversity brings with it are factored into the overall picture, optimism prevails. It is important to remember that ethnic minorities bring resiliency, strength of character, a commitment to hard work, and many pluses that add not subtract from America (Suinn, 1999).

REFERENCES

Barringer, R. H., Gardner, R. W., & Levin, M. J. (1993). *Asian and Pacific Islanders in the U.S.* New York: Russell Sage Foundation.

Cuéllar, I. (1999, April). *Border health care overview.* Paper presented as part of the First International Border Health Conference, University of Texas—Pan American, Edinburg, Texas.

Eschbach, K. (1995). The enduring and vanishing American Indian: American Indian population growth and intermarriage in 1990. *Ethnic and Racial Studies, 18,* 89–108.

Eschbach, K., Khalil, S., & Snipp, C. M. (1998). Changes in racial identification and educational attainment of American Indians 1970–1990. *Demography, 35 (1),* 35–43.

Farley, R. (1970). *Growth of the black population.* Chicago, IL: Markham Publishing Company.

Featherman, D., & Hauser, R. (1978). *Opportunity and change.* New York: Academic Press.

Gill, T. R., Glazer, N., & Thernstrom, S. A. (1992). *Our changing population.* Englewood Cliffs, NJ: Prentice Hall.

Helweg, A. A., & Helweg, U. M. (1990). An immigrant success story: *East Indians In America.* Philadelphia, PA: University of Pennsylvania Press.

Hirschman, C. (1983). America's melting pot reconsidered. *Annual Review of Sociology, 9,* 397–423.

Johnson, A. (1999). Birth defect of brain rises again in Cameron County. *The Monitor,* May 4, pg. 1.

Lee, S. (1998). Asian Americans: Diverse and growing. *Population Bulletin, 52*(3).

Lott, J. T. (1998). *Asian Americans: From racial categories to multiple Identities.* Walnut Creek, CA: Alta Mira Press.

National Center for Health Statistics (1997, June). *Monthly vital statistics reports, Vol. 45, Number 11*. Hyattsville, MD: Author.

National Center for Health Statistics (1998, November). *Monthly vital statistics reports, Vol. 47, Number 9*. Hyattsville, MD: Author.

Neiman, P. (1999). Dead last of dead wrong? *The Monitor,* May 7, pg. 1.

O'Hare, W., Pollard, K. M., Mann, T. L., & Kent, M. M. (1991). African Americans in the 1990s. *Population Bulletin, 46*(1).

Passel, J. S. (1996). The growing American Indian population, 1960–1990: Beyond demography (pp. 79–102). In G. Sandefeer, R. Rindfuss, & B. Cohen (Eds.), *Changing numbers, changing needs: American Indians and Public health*. Washington, DC: National Academy Press.

Perine, R. D. (1999). Census 2000: The battle for control of reapportionment continues (pp. 30-36). *COMMUNIQÚE*. Public Interest Directorate, Office of Ethnic Minority Affairs. Washington, DC: American Psychological Association.

Pinal, D. J. (1996, March). *Latinos and California's future: Too few at Schoolhouse Door.* Paper presented at Chicano/Latino policy project and *La Raza Law Journal,* Fifth annual symposium. Berkley, CA.

Pinal, D. J., & Singer, A. (1996). Generations of diversity: Latinos in the United States. *Population Bulletin, 52*(3).

Root, M. (Ed.), (1992). *Racially mixed people in America*. Newbury Park, CA: Sage Publications.

Ruffing, L. T. (1978). Navajo Economic Development: A dual perspective. In S. Stanley (Ed.), *American Indian Economic Development: The Hague Mountain*. New York: Mounton de Gruyter.

Shafer, J. R., & Donald, J. M. (1981). *Neighbors: Mexico and the United States*. Chicago: Nelson Hall.

Smith, P. J., & Edmonston, B. (Eds.). (1997). *The New Americans: Economic, demographic and fiscal effects of immigration*. Washington, DC: National Academy Press.

Snipp, C. M. (1989). *American Indians: The first of this land*. New York: Russell Sage Foundation.

Sorkin, A. (1971). *American Indian and Federal Aid*. Washington, DC: Brookings Institute.

Spencer, G. (1990). Projections of the population of the U.S. by the age, sex, and race: 1988 to 2080; U.S. Bureau of Census, *Current Population Reports,* Series P-25, no. 1018, p. 10.

Spickard, P. (1989). *Mixed blood: Intermarriage and ethnic identity in twentieth century America*. Madison, WI: University of Oklahoma Press.

Suinn, R. M. (1999). The year of our dreams. Commentary (pp. 3–4). *COMMUNIQÚE*. Public Interest Directorate, Office of Ethnic Minority Affairs. Washington, DC: American Psychological Association.

Texas-Mexico Border Health Co-ordination Office. (1998). *Texas-Mexico Border Health Co-ordination Office report*. Edinburg, TX: University of Texas, Pan American.

Tienda, M., & Jensen, L. (1988). Poverty and minorities: A quarter century profile of color and socio-economic disadvantage (pp. 23–61). In G. Sandfeer & M. Tienda (Eds.), *Divided opportunities: Minorities, poverty and social policy*. New York: Plenum Press.

U.S. Bureau of the Census (1985). *Current Population Survey*. Washington, DC: Author.

U.S. Bureau of the Census (1995). *Current Population Reference*. Washington, DC: Author.

U.S. Bureau of the Census (1997). *Current Populations Survey*. Population Reference Bureau. Washington, DC: Author.

Waters, M. (1990). *Ethnic option: Later generation ethnicity in America*. Berkeley, CA: University of California Press.

Western Interstate Commission for Higher Education (WICHE) (1997). *Cultural competence standards in mental health care mental health services for four undeserved/underrepresented racial/ ethnic groups*. Report of the Four National Panels On Cultural Competence In Managed Care Mental Health Service, Boulder, CO, October.

Wilson, J. W. (1987). *The truly disadvantaged: The inner city, the underclass and public policy*. Chicago, IL: The University of Chicago Press.

PART II

Methodology

Culture and Methodology in Personality Assessment

RICHARD H. DANA

Regional Research Institute
Portland State University
Portland, Oregon

Cross-cultural and multicultural psychology both examine group differences, although multicultural psychology refers to domestic or within-country differences rather than between-country differences (Goodstein & Gielen, 1998). Moreover, cross-cultural psychology explicitly seeks general laws of human behavior and is etic or universal in focus on, for example, belief systems and social relationships. Methodology has always been center stage in cross-cultural psychology because scientific purity and its handmaiden objectivity have precluded social priorities and advocacy. Multicultural psychology deals with etics or manifestations of group differences that may be uniquely shaped by a variety of local or national conditions, including identity, oppression, and power. The legacy of human suffering attending these issues and their partisan nature has demanded a wider range of historic and contemporary methodologies, both qualitative and qualitative, with generous infusions from feminist research, anthropology, social psychology, and most recently, cultural psychology.

This chapter begins with an examination of bias in research. Biased methodology has a history in any nation that applies a scientific model developed by the majority culture to all cultural elements within the society. This methodology has been focused on affirming prediction and control elements of a Euro-American worldview. Understanding is also a legitimate scientific objective, but has been relegated to an ancillary position and occurs largely by inference or as a by-product of prediction and control. In a society self-proclaimed as a "melting pot," the scientific establishment has minimized group differences by assuming homogenization to be a fact rather than a fictive outcome of ethnocentrism (Bennett, 1986). As a consequence, bias is omnipresent and has been found in the assumptions made for conventional statistical tests as well as their interpretation, in research designs used for group comparisons and in selection and sampling of research participants (Dana, 1998a, pp. 24–26; Okazaki & Sue, 1995). Bias has also been demonstrated in the instruments used for personality assessment. The Rorschach Comprehensive System (RCS), the Minnesota Multiphasic Personality Inventory (MMPI and MMPI-2), and the Thematic Apperception Test (TAT) will be used to illustrate examples of methodology in test construction, interpretation, and use of normative data that can either exacerbate or reduce bias. Finally, an assessment methodology will be described that supplements test validation per se but can serve to reduce bias in describing or diagnosing persons within a multicultural society.

I. EUROCENTRIC BIAS: REALITY CONSTRUCTION AND A BELIEF SYSTEM UNDERGIRDING RESEARCH

Research bias begins in Eurocentrism, a culture-specific construction of reality that seeks to provide societal cohesion, solidarity, and survival by developing standards for acquisition of knowledge and establishment of universal or etic laws governing human behavior. A Eurocentric reality assumes that human similarities are greater than human differences and invokes prediction and control of nature and human behaviors as primary desiderata for science. This science is motivated by a genuine desire to reduce differences among persons in order to facilitate the development of etic constructs that can be applied worldwide. However, the nature and substance of Eurocentric science also serves national political objectives that are emic or culture-specific in origin. As a consequence, the outcomes of research in the United States on group differences have legitimized invidious comparisons between groups in the name of science and fostered a continuation of stereotypy and discrimination that delays the transition from a mislabeled historic "melting pot" society to a bona fide multicultural society. This dilemma has occurred because the research methodology was, in fact, not etic but a pseudo-etic derivative of a Eurocentric worldview and thus was sensitive to usurpation. Sources of research bias in methodology, test, and interpretation examples will be examined in this section with contiguous suggestions for interim and long-range reduction of bias.

A. SOURCES OF RESEARCH BIAS

1. Selection and Sampling of Research Participants

The selection and sampling of research participants is dependent upon proper definitions that do not degrade samples by overinclusion of nonrepresentative participants and/or underinclusion of representative participants. How the ethnicity of participants is identified is critical and has ordinarily been accomplished by using self-reports or use of surnames without confirmation as well as by inclusion of persons with mixed racial and ethnic identities. Many of the measures used for this purpose have provided data bits too meager to validly reference ethnic origins. This has occurred because it is costly to use more adequately designed instruments or to embed research-based ethnicity content within an interview format. The present status of acculturation research now permits selection of psychometrically acceptable instruments (e.g., Cuéllar, 1999) or derivation of questionnaire contents from item analysis of these instruments for inclusion in interviews (e.g., Zane, 1998).

How the participants are recruited and the settings in which research is conducted provide motivations and incentive for participation in research. College students are typically recruited by forced or voluntary participation and they constitute a captive, nonrepresentative population. The difficulty in recruiting participants of color due to their suspicion and fears of exploitation or negative consequences has led to lumping small "opportunity" samples from different settings using different inducements for participation. Community samples are always preferred to avoid bias from middle-class and socioeconomic status skew. Acquisition of these samples requires understanding of social structures, informed cooperation from within the community, and avoidance of unwitting overrepresentation from subsamples. Finally, the requirement of equal numbers of participants in comparison groups has been frequently flouted by using very small and highly selected samples from cultural and racial groups (Graham, 1992).

2. The Matching of Groups

When groups are matched, conventional wisdom is used to select a small number of variables instead of a representative array of presumably relevant variables.

The identification of these "relevant" variables was decided historically by fiat, and more adequate matching in most studies proved to be neither feasible nor cost-effective. Without adequate matching, comparative group research is unethical by definition because many groups will be misrepresented or pathologized. Azibo (1988) suggested mandatory matching on all relevant variables in concert with use of constructs and measures that have cross-cultural validity. The word "all" is important in this context because psychologists remain unaware of the entire array of these relevant variables until they have been demonstrated by research. For example, "culture" as cultural identification has not been generally included as a relevant variable. General descriptors such as race or ethnicity used for matching purposes omit cultural orientation status or racial identity stage. Because acculturation status and racial identity stages are frequently confounded with psychopathology, participants are at risk whenever these relevant matching variables are omitted in research designs. Moreover, the fact that there are cultural and racial group differences in social class structures as well as in the relative numbers of persons within each class means that social class indices derived from mainstream Anglo-American culture will ordinarily invalidate the matching procedures. I know of no comparative study that has included adequate social class criteria for different cultural and racial groups, or racial identity status for black–white comparisons, or cultural orientation status by generation for Hispanic Americans or Asian Americans. The omission of even these ethically imperative refinements in research design indicates that they have not been considered necessary. Furthermore, as we develop more emic sources of research-based information on cultural and racial groups in the United States, additional variables for matching groups in comparative research will become salient. It is not surprising that critics of the matching process, including, Azibo (1988), call for a burgeoning of emic research instead of continuing comparative research efforts.

3. The Uses of Statistics

Group statistical comparisons are predicated on equal numbers of representative research participants who have been either randomly assigned or matched within a context of control over all relevant variables (Okazaki & Sue, 1995). These necessary conditions are difficult to demonstrate by examination of published research. As a consequence, cultural bias has been appropriately castigated for compromising the assumptions used with conventional statistics, including equal range, variance, and independence of groups (Helms, 1992). Unfortunately, however, there is an overarching problem. Cultural bias occurs in the first place because culture remains a distal variable in most research studies as well as in the biopsychosocial model, for example, rather than the central component. As long as culture remains distal, conventional statistics will fail to detect bias.

Nonetheless, a remedy has been proposed for a ubiquitous source of statistical bias that negatively impacts upon persons of color in the United States (Malgady, 1999; 1996). Social and ethical concerns led Malgady to argue that the directionality of the Null Hypothesis should reflect cultural nonequivalence rather than no cultural difference. The unexamined statistical assumption of minimal group differences is an outcome of focusing on similarities in a general Western research paradigm that has been reinforced by cognitive-behavioral psychology and cross-cultural psychology as the modus operandi in the search for general scientific laws and behavioral universals. Individual difference methodologies represented by qualitative humanistic, existential, anthropological, and recent sociological approaches have been regarded as less scientific in nature and culture-specific in applications. Alternative research paradigms have not been welcomed by the research establishment in the United States (e.g., Hoshmand, 1989).

Almost all of the standard psychological tests developed in the United States are standardized primarily on persons of European cultural backgrounds. Samples from various cultural and racial groups may be included in proportion to their population percentages, but these samples are overinclusive, contain too few persons, and do not control for acculturation status. As a result, these tests are emic psychometric derivatives of a Eurocentric worldview. Nonetheless, these tests are exported worldwide and applied as if they were genuine etics. In fact, however, these standard tests are pseudo-etics disguised as etics and must demonstrate absence of bias or culture-specific validity by "similarity of psychological meaning across cultural groups" (Van de Vijver, 1999, p. 88). Bias is understood by an examination of test scores and their interpretation. Test scores are affected by bias in constructs, items, and methods. To minimize construct bias, all emic parameters required for definition must be specified for each comparison culture prior to any cross-cultural comparisons. The assumption of an underlying universal structure is made in construct validation, and whenever an Anglo-American emic is used as a pseudo-etic, no aspects of the construct definition under consideration can be omitted without excluding culture-specific aspects of psychological functioning in another country. In practice, construct validation has proven immensely difficult to implement even in the United States. As a consequence, exportation of poorly researched and inadequately validated constructs has rendered their cross-cultural validation not only hazardous but infrequently attempted in their new research settings.

This dilemma has restricted the use of some methodologies, such as the multitrait-multimethod matrix to examine convergent-discriminant reliability and validity correlation matrices. Instead, factor analytic methods have been used almost exclusively. Allen and Walsh (1999) have suggested three underutilized statistical procedures as preliminary tools to be used prior to any "significant investment" in cross-cultural construct validation. These tools include confirming factor analysis (i.e., cross-validation of the factor structure across groups), regression analysis to relate test scores to culture-relevant variables and cultural identification measures, and item response theory modeling using a response pattern instead of a linear combination to estimate construct level.

Method bias appears in samples, instruments, and procedures-administrations (Van de Vijver, 1999). As suggested above, genuinely representative samples are infrequently available and difficult to obtain, whereas social class representation may be contradictory or misleading, and language proficiency differences may occur in samples. Instrument bias occurs with differential familiarity of test stimuli across samples. Administration-procedure bias may be due to examiner gender or familiarity of research participants with the examiner and in the form of eisegesis, an intrusion of the examiner's personality into the interpretations of high inference projective tests such as the TAT or the pre-RCS Rorschach.

Metric bias refers to the presence of dissimilar psychometric properties, such as score distributions and ranges of scores in different cultures. Metric bias occurs in the form of item bias or differential item functioning, or the likelihood of unequal item endorsement across groups, has been studied in objective tests and been examined in the Rorschach using the frequencies of scores in different countries. Clear evidence of item bias has been demonstrated for a majority of Rorschach scores and derivative ratios.

Construct-driven approaches are quantitative and ignore methodologies incorporating qualitative approaches. As a consequence, demonstrations of linguistic equivalence are also required. Linguistic bias refers to an absence of linguistic equivalence in translations. Standard assessment instruments should be translated for all persons whose primary language is not English in order to improve construct equivalence or the validity of constructs as rendered by test language, format, and content. There are explicit rules for translations, including simple sentences, repeating nouns rather than pronouns, and avoiding metaphors, colloquialisms, English passive voice, hypothetical phrasings, or subjective moods (e.g., Brislin, 1970). An explicit translation strategy has been recommended for the MMPI/MMPI-2 (Butcher, 1996a).

Translations require a set of explicit, replicable, and consensual procedures to minimize impreciseness or nonequivalency of translated meanings. English is an Indo-European language. Translations to languages very dissimilar from English are much more difficult to accomplish. Target languages from other language families often contain constructs that are attached to subjective emotional states and experiences that stem from patterns of thought and learned verbal or written communication repertoires that have no English equivalents (e.g., English to Hopi). Furthermore, translation difficulties are exacerbated by the intrusion of culture-specific response sets that affect responding to both objective and projective tests. Documentation of intensity, commonality, or range of usage for particular constructs may also be infeasible (Draguns, 1984). To examine the adequacy of translations, Brislin (1970) recommended statistical comparisons of similar responses provided by English and target-language versions to bilinguals with knowledge of either or both versions.

B. INTERPRETATION BIAS

Bias in interpretation occurs in both low-inference and high-inference tests, but in dissimilar ways with different potential remediations. Low-inference tests have formal scoring systems and normative data to use as a frame of reference for interpreting scores and derivative indices. The Rorschach, in RCS format, and the MMPI/MMPI-2 are representative of low-inference tests. High-inference tests include the TAT and the pre-RCS Rorschach. The TAT has been used for many years in the United States without benefit of formal scores (Rossini & Moretti, 1997) in spite of an early history of published formal scoring procedures and normative data that has been resurrected in Spain within a comprehensive scoring system (Avila-Espada, 1999). In Europe there remains controversy concerning the use of the Rorschach, with adherents of high-inference interpretation favoring a psychoanalytic approach, and RCS devotees employing the Rorschach as a low-interpretation test (Andronikof-Sanglade, 1999). High-inference interpretation employs systematic and rigorous hypothesis testing with subsequent organization of hypotheses at descriptive and inferential levels as the basis for personality and diagnostic statements (e.g., Dana, 1982). High-inference interpretation of the Rorschach and TAT relies on guidelines to indicate when formal markers or checkpoints should be inserted into the process of data analysis to increase reliability of interpretations (Dana, 1998b). High-inference procedures are analogous to using cultural formulations to increase the reliability of psychiatric diagnoses (Dana, 1997). The choice of either high- or low-inference interpretation, as Handler suggested (1996), may be based on an assessor's comfort with either or both approaches. This "comfort" is probably related to assessor personality characteristics (see chapter 1, Dana, 1999) that also may result in preferences for prediction-control or understanding as the primary objective of psychological science. Both high- and low-inference interpretation are equally necessary for a science that honors both prediction-control and understanding, and this reconciliation can be achieved within a multi-cultural assessment model (Dana, 1999).

C. REDUCING BIAS IN LOW-INFERENCE INTERPRETATION

Low-inference interpretation relies on norms for the relative meaning of test scores obtained for a particular assessee. Norms provide a rationale for the words and sentences contained either in a personality portrait or in a description of the symptomatology required for a diagnosis of psychopathology. This practice assumes that the norms used for these purposes are representative of the population being assessed and consequently adequate for particular assesses. The history in the United States has been to collect national norms for all kinds of tests and to use these norms as a basis for informed judgments about persons that affect their present lives and future well-being. There has been strong resistance to developing other kinds and sources of normative data, particularly culture-specific norms and local norms. It has been contended that categorizing multiculutral persons by normative data at any point in time is misleading because of extreme within-group heterogeneity and the short life span of such norms due to changes in demographics and societal transformations (Jones & Thorne, 1987). Culture-specific norms effectively mask the inherent range of within-group differences present in any ethnic group in the same manner as so-called representative norms obscure subgroup differences in standard tests. Norms that aggregate Mexican Americans, Puerto Ricans, and Cuban Americans, for example, would be unsatisfactory. As a consequence, separate norms for each country of origin for Hispanics in the United States would be required not merely to represent the heterogeneity of this population, but to provide two sets of normative referents for a particular assessee. In spite of increased assessment fairness, this solution is infeasible at the present time. Nonetheless, sampling deficiencies and omission of critical variables for matching groups in the United States have made the practice of general population norms not only outdated for standard tests but increasingly discriminatory as well. The development of local norms for isolated groups with worldviews that diverge markedly from mainstream North Americans, has both merit and precedent, particularly for some indigenous groups (e.g., Charles, 1988; Le Due, 1982).

However, there is one remedy for the inapplicability of current multicultural population norms. This remedy would be cost-effective, fair, and has a sound basis in empirical research. The development of acculturation status norms rests on the assumption of a linear relationship between an original culture and a host culture. The Acculturation Rating Scale for Mexican Americans (ARSMA), (Cuéllar et al., 1999) the progenitor of many acculturation instruments now used in the United States, was developed as a "correction" for pathologization using the MMPI and other low-inference, norm-referenced standard objective tests (Cuéllar, Harris, & Jasso, 1980). MMPI research with several major cultural and racial groups has documented the confounding of psychopathology with traditional beliefs, values, and behaviors that perdure at least across several generations of family residence in this country. To my knowledge, statistical formulae based on the magnitude of moderator scores have not been applied as formal adjustments for MMPI/MMPI-2 scale elevations. Using moderator scores to provide a statistical correction similar to K was seriously considered at one time and rejected as premature for a specific application (see Hoffmann, Dana, & Bolton, 1985). Test bias can be examined, however, using a statistical analysis methodology. Cuéllar (1999) described slope bias, intercept bias, and an Index for Correction for Culture (ICC). ICC uses acculturation data to estimate how deviant an assessee is from the standardization sample, and several methods for applying the ICC were described. A checklist form of a regression model suggested by Cuéllar includes "Gender+SES (income & education) + group-specific validity coefficient + intercept for a given group + acculturation differences between the subject and the standardized population" (p. 125). Psychologists should be familiar with the rationale, explicit techniques for adjustment, and examples to provide the tools required for implementation of cultural competence in assessment practice and research with multicultural persons. Such techniques not only conform to the scientific mindedness described by Sue (1998) as an essential ingredientof cultural competence, but can become the basis for teaching multicultural assessment using available methodological and statistical skills (López, 1999).

Early MMPI research documented the assertion that as similarity of White and non-White groups increases on a number of matching variables, the frequency of culture-specific item-responding decreases, but never does entirely disappear (Dahlstrom, Lachar, & Dahlstrom, 1986)! This decrease was most evident for research participants of middle-class origins. A more recent comparison of the item responses of the MMPI-2 college sample with the restandardization sample yielded the 29-item MEX scale (Gomez-Maqueo & Reyes-Lagunes, 1994). The MEX scale has a highly patterned relationship to clinical scales and the Harris and Lingoes subscales. These correlates open a narrow cultural window for describing this population.

The argument for development and superimposition of acculturation status norms on all standard objective tests is clearly an interim ethical solution to the problematic use of existing norms. This is particularly relevant because generality across standard tests has been suggested by the successful introduction of acculturation status as a performance correlate on standard neuropsychological tests (Arnold, Montgomery, Castanada, & Longoria, 1994). Nonetheless, there is a hidden caveat to be considered before applying an empirically based and seemingly fair solution to a national assessment establishment *cause célèbre*. I would now contend that piecemeal palliation for standard psychological tests is not necessarily in the best interests of persons of color in the United States. These adjustments, even if ultimately legitimized and adopted by assessors, would preserve the status quo in the assessment of cultural groups in the United States. Standard tests would be retained and culture would remain of peripheral concern in spite of consensus concerning the pervasive discriminatory effects of these tests. However, if adjustments fail to be routinely used (as indeed is my reluctant prediction), their availability remains only a symbolic gesture.

In view of my pessimism, the rationale for adjustments, modifications, and alterations for standard psychological tests to improve the reliability and validity of interpretation requires restatement. This is necessary as a context for the subsequent discussion of bias and bias remediation in specific tests. These recommendations were originally made with particular reference to the MMPI/MMPI-2 (e.g., Dana, 1993, 1995, 1996, 1998d, 1999,a). Included were the use of adjustments for acculturation and acculturation status norms as well as consensual procedures for translations (or test adaptations) and for errors in interpretation resulting from limited sources and availability of cultural knowledge.

Notwithstanding that these suggestions have merit for making the best of a very unfair situation, they were summarily rejected by the MMPI establishment (e.g., Valésquez, Butcher, Garrido, & Cayiba, 1996). I can well understand the cavils of the MMPI establishment in companion chapters from a recent handbook (i.e., Handel & Ben-Porath, 1999; Nichols, Padilla, & Gomez-Macueo, 1999) as noted in the following section on the MMPI. To make matters worse from my perspective, however, to my best knowledge none of these suggestions for improving cross-cultural and multicultural fairness have been acknowledged as acceptable for use in assessment training and practice.

By way of explanation, I would describe an enlarged scenario for the failure of recent multicultural assessment research efforts to penetrate either assessment training or assessment practice. As our society becomes more multicultural, so does the resistance to accommodating these new populations, to sharing the benefits and obligations of a democratic society with persons unable to assimilate or not desiring to assimilate by eschewing their cultural/racial origins. Moreover, a majority of these persons of Latin American, Asian, or African origins are defined as non-White and, therefore, stigmatized by stereotypes and beliefs in their inferiority and potential for disruption of societal stability. The attempt to preserve Euro-American values has been reflected by increased racism and denial that any changes in the status quo are beneficial for the Anglo mainstream population.

The science and profession of psychology shares this general societal reaction to multiculturalism. Hall (1997) has aptly described psychology as culturally incompetent and obsolete for an effective professional role in a multicultural society. The reason for this allegation is that culture remains distal rather than central to psychological training, research, and practice with human beings (Cole, 1996). Malgady's (1996) call for reversal of the Null Hypothesis essentially acknowledged that culture is central to human experience and incorporation of this recognition into the methods of our psychological science has now become mandatory.

D. REDUCING BIAS IN HIGH-INFERENCE INTERPRETATION

High-inference interpretation, often but not exclusively from a psychoanalytic perspective, was practiced prior to the 1974 RCS introduction by John Exner. High-inference interpretation practice was responsible for diminished usage of projective methods. Skepticism increased with regard to the psychometric credibility of these methods as tests were coupled with an increasing preference for objective tests in the United States.

Nonetheless, high-inference interpretation is both theory-driven and rationally sound. This approach to interpretation recognizes the "selectivity of observers and the unsteadiness of facts" (Wyatt, 1967, p. 13). Rychlak (1959) averred that procedural interpretation uses validating evidence that is a coalescence of common sense, intelligibility, and consistency. The intuitive leap from data to inference can be very great and may be accompanied by inadequately defined theoretical concepts. This process thus requires the imposition of a series of checkpoints or steps to increase reliability of interpretation by effectively reducing the opportunities for error. These steps can be introduced in assessment training as well as in assessment practice by use of guidelines.

In assessment training, the use of common data sets enables students to receive multiple sources of feedback on the variety, number, and relevance of concepts contained in their reports from peers, more experienced assessors, and their assesses. This process provides an opportunity to examine personalized contents in their psychological reports of other persons. These ingredients from their own self-contents and personality characteristics appear in the form of eisegesis (Dana, 1966), or personality concepts in their reports that are not shared with other assessors and are also rejected by assessees as relevant to themselves. The research history of this methodology and assessment examples are available in other sources (e.g., Dana, 1982, 1998b, 1999c).

In assessment practice, guidelines are available to invoke caution, reduce stereotypy, and increase assessor confidence that their continued usage of projective methods (e.g., TAT, sentence completions, drawings, etc.) has scientific as well as practical merit and efficacy. Guidelines are available for psychodiagnosis of multicultural persons using cultural formulations (Cuéllar, & Gonzalez, 1999) and for the use of projective methods with Hispanics (Cervantes, & Acosta, 1992; Dana, 1998b).

II. BIAS IN STANDARD PSYCHOLOGICAL TESTS

This section reviews the present status of the MMPI/MMPI-2. RCS, and TAT for cross-cultural and multicultural assessment with particular emphasis on reduction of bias in test construction, more adequate use of available normative data, some mechanics for increasing reliability of interpretations, and current research methodologies applicable to each test. This review separates the interim objective of this chapter—bias reduction—from the long-term issue of whether or not bias reduction per se can serve the best interest of multicultural populations in the United States.

A. MINNESOTA MULTIPHASIC PERSONALITY INVENTORIES

The MMPI was developed to measure psychopathology constructs as defined in the United States using the psychometric technology available during the 1930s (Helmes & Redden, 1993). The nature and specific definitions of these constructs have changed several times over a 60-year period (Castillo, 1996). As a consequence, MMPI interpretation soon relied on established empirical correlates that made the original diagnostic system and Caucasian normative sample "far less relevant to the clinical application of the instrument" (Handel & Ben-Porath, 1999, p. 230). Although the test originated as an Anglo-American emic, the constructs have been accepted as universal dimensions of psychopathology in spite of research-demonstrated cultural differences (e.g., Cheung, Leung, Fan, Song, & Xie, 1996). Worldwide exportation and use in many countries resulted in attention to cross-cultural test validation and the establishment of equivalencies in translations, the meaning of constructs, psychometric properties, and the function of specific behaviors.

Translations, especially of the MMPI-2 sought to retain item meaning and minimize bias by use of a general translation strategy (Butcher, 1996a), although adequate field testing of translations has not occurred (Nichols et al., 1999). Matched cultural groups subsequently were used for comparison of scale scores with tacit acceptance of less than a five-point T-score difference to demonstrate equivalence. However, T-score differences of this magnitude do not necessarily constitute evidence for no differences between groups. In the absence of cross-cultural construct validation, statistical adjustments for culture can provide evidence for the meaning of these T-score differences between groups. Even if means and predictor validities are similar, equivalence of meanings cannot be assumed. As Cuéllar (1999) has emphasized, only by using of statistical adjustments such as the ICC can we obtain more accurate T-scores and T-score differences.

Construct equivalence research has avoided the time-consuming and costly multitrait multimethod approach because neither psychiatric diagnoses nor other psychopathology measures have been validated in this manner in the

United States or in other countries. Nonetheless, avoidance of a methodology that constitutes the "gold standard" for construct validation (Nichols et al., 1999) serves to relegate construct validation to a secondary role. For example, construct validation using a Spanish version of MMPI-2 and the Diagnostic Interview Schedule as the external measure found only moderate hit rates for diagnostic categories (Fantoni-Salvador & Rogers, 1997). Sensitivity and specificity for these categories was variable and moderate at best.

Construct equivalence has been approached using factor similarity indices (e.g., the congruence coefficient), factor score correlations, the comparability coefficient, and confirmatory factor analysis instead (Butcher, 1996b). Serious deficiencies in all of these methods have been acknowledged, and although no one index should be used alone, Butcher reported only two studies with these methods. Statistical equivalency is elusive and even if established "there is no way of knowing whether the items selected are representative of the universe of items within a similar trait in another culture" (Nichols et al., 1999, p. 255). These authors recommend a research focus on group differences in external criteria and how item responses, scale scores, and profile patterns may be affected by such differences. Investigations of possible ethnic differences on supplemental, content, and subscales are also recommended. Finally, the use of K-corrected clinical scales is now controversial, and the applicability of this correction to cultural and racial groups should be examined.

B. RORSCHACH COMPREHENSIVE SYSTEM

Exner (1993) described stages in the Rorschach response process that recognize the origins of perceptual styles and their impact upon the response process. These stages are inextricable from cultural elements in personality. First, the initial visual imput and encoding of the inkblot stimulus is culturally determined. Second, the potential response repertoire always has relevance to daily life within a cultural context. Third, implicit norms and values provide selectivity among possible responses as well as censorship or expression of particular responses. Fourth, the language and learned modes of expression contribute to the manner in which responses are articulated.

Rorschachers generally believe that the ink blot determinants have universal meanings, although only the *Erlebnistypus,* or extraversion–introversion system constructs as defined by movement and color have received validation from a variety of research approaches (see Dana, 1993). Thus, the etic nature of the Rorschach has specific and particularized emic constructions for groups that share a common worldview and cultural values. Rorschach theory has been put to the test of cultural specificity by widespread adoption of the RCS in Latin America and Europe. Researchers in many countries were initially puzzled by the impact of norms developed in the United States upon their normal children and adults. Persons believed to have good psychological adjustment were described by RCS variables as unstable and psychopathological. In the absence of national RCS norms, psychologists in many countries hypothesized explanations that cannot be substantiated without either cross-cultural construct validation studies or the development of national norms for each country. Only Finland (Mattlar & Fried, 1993) and Portugal (Pires, 1999) have developed national norms comparable to U.S. norms. These Finnish norms were originally compared with Klopfer norms, although the significance levels of differences obtained between the two countries were not reported, and RCS rescoring was accomplished at a later date. The Portuguese national norms as well as the diverse samples of Rorschach records collected in many countries were all markedly dissimilar from the Exner norms. These dissimilarities included fewer movement and color responses in contexts of equivalent numbers of total responses, more form responses (and particularly many more poor form responses), and an absence of texture responses. These alterations in RCS responses markedly affected a number of ratios and indices of which they were components. RCS studies from many countries strongly suggested that the use of the RCS with multicultural populations in the United States also may be pathologizing, although this must be documented on the basis of research in this country. Nonetheless, the only description of RCS differences among Hispanic populations in the United States provides information that is remarkably similar to some of the Iberoamerican research conclusions, particularly for use of color (i.e., Costantino, Flanagan, & Malgady, 1995).

The meaning of these substantive differences in Rorschach responding has been accumulating slowly and has been summarized by Andronikof-Sanglade, Ephraim, Pires, and Vinet in chapters 13, 14, 15, and 16, respectively from a recent handbook of cross-cultural and multicultural personality assessment (Dana, 1999,a). The major discrepancies between Exner norms and norms/samples collected throughout Latin America, Portugal and Spain, and Northern Europe will be examined for (a) culture-specific meanings of the test situation and interaction with an examiner, (b) the settings used for RCS administration, and (c) sample differences. The very high-inference statements tendered in this chapter should be viewed in the context of these RCS samples and their earlier culture-specific interpretations.

In the United States, the Rorschach inkblots are relatively well known, particularly among middle-class persons who recognize the implicit social expectations for accommodating their responses to the inkblots. This is also true in Europe, where large populations of middle-class, highly educated, and intellectually sophisticated persons are well informed about the Rorschach as a clinical method. In Latin America, by contrast, the test is more novel, anxiety-producing, and lacking specific rules that could lead to an anticipation of what may constitute acceptable responses. Moreover, Latin Americans live in more authoritarian, nonegalitarian, and frequently inherently unstable societies with much smaller percentages of middle-class and educated persons in the population and infinitely greater differences in income levels. The power differentials between ordinary citizens and authority figures, especially persons representing government in any capacity, are more extreme. The testing situation in these countries is frequently construed as an encounter with authority. This encounter can maximize distrust in a context of cultural values (e.g., respect, obedience, and desire to conform) within a testing process frequently experienced as occurring between an "insider" and an "outsider." In such a setting, it becomes permissible to flout the expectations of outsiders (as long as you do not get caught doing so) when you are an ordinary citizen in a collectivist society. This complex interaction with the examiner damages the cooperative nature of testing by inhibiting responsivity due to defensiveness and reducing affective engagement with the task. Anxiety becomes linked to passivity, and ability to respond is impaired. As a result of these pervasive cultural differences in how the test situation is understood, assessees personalize the inkblots and incorporate them into their inner experiences during the response process.

Many Europeans may also inhibit their responsivity and personalize their RCS responses as a consequence of differing dynamic processes and reasons. These Europeans are more homogeneous in education, income, and middle-class status than samples with other national origins. Many of these persons prize their distinctive national and culturally idiosyncratic differences from one another as exposed by creativity, eccentricity, intellectual sophistication, and a refined and traditional national sense of social etiquette. In Northern Europe, for example, high vista (V) has been interpreted to represent a sophisticated cognitive aspect, whereas use of form (F) responses predominantly may occur as a consequence of preferences for not belaboring the obvious shading and color in the blots among highly educated persons. Similarly, Lambda (L) or a simplification of the world derived from F, has been interpreted to increase with increasing education and intellectual sophistication. An F-dominant approach to the inkblots among Europeans was also recognized by Hermann Rorschach in addition to color and movement approaches.

Exner's (1993) relatively homogeneous and institution-specific normative sample was recruited primarily in workplace settings with encouragement from management or union officials and secondarily through interest organizations and social service agencies. In the United States, more recent unpublished RCS reports on samples collected in the United States have been divergent from Exner's normative data. Pires (1999) recruited Portuguese volunteers from various sites contacted through many local institutions with a range of one to seven subjects per initial contact. Gender, age, geographical area, SES, and education were controlled in both the Exner and Pires sampling strategies.

Studies from other countries used samples of 200–300, usually stratified by SES, included approximately one-half community samples.

Exner's (1993) normative population averaged 13.25 years of education (Range = 8–18 years), with three SES subdivisions for upper (9%), middle (59%), and lower (32%) classes. In Portugal, however, the SES divisions were approximated by levels of formal education that included primary, or zero to seven years (44%), secondary or 7–12 years (36%), and superior or 13+ years (20%). In Portugal, middle-class and upper class status are represented by 20% of this sample as contrasted with 68% of Exner's normative sample from the United States. Educational levels between the United States and Europe are not directly comparable, due to more demanding European educational systems. For example, 12 years of schooling in the United States has been considered to approximate 10 years in Europe. Moreover, there are extreme differences in social class, defined primarily by income levels in the United States and by a more extended range of complex indicators in Portugal, including education. Psychologists who compare normative data cross-nationally should be sensitive to national differences in numbers of social classes, the definitions of each class, and the portion of the population in each class.

As indicated earlier in this section, there is now some consensus concerning interpretation of some cross-cultural RCS scores and ratios. The constructs that these scores and ratios are believed to measure will precede the interpretive conclusions. *Erlebnistypus* (EB) is a complex dimension of human personality that encompasses both M and C. EB evidences the history of internalized personal resources for establishing and maintaining cognitive and affective cohesion as well as the utilization of both cognitive resources and affects for problem solving. This construct has European cultural origins in which there is explicit separation of cognitive and affective portions of personality for acceptable social adaptation. Moreover, Hermann Rorschach recognized three types of sensitivity manifested by a preponderance of movement, color, or form responses. Other cultures may neither recognize a mind–body dichotomy nor localize personality in the head but rather in the heart, or in a fusion of head and heart. These cultural differences speak directly to EB interpretation in non Euro-American cultures. Thus, the etic construct of introversion–extraversion has a variety of emic manifestations in how human personality may be organized and expressed. Exner's (1993) RCS norms categorize EB as extratensive (44%), introversive (36%), and ambient (20%), as contrasted with 22%, 28%, and 50%, respectively, in Portugal (Pires, 1999). Conventional Rorschach interpretation suggests that ambients "are characterized by less consistent, often inefficient problem-solving approaches" (Erdberg, 1996, p. 153). Nonetheless, all samples collected outside of the United States had less M and less C in a context of simplified information processing and more subjective approaches to cognitive mediation. The conclusion that fewer resources are required to cope with the conditions of their lives in collectivist societies requires careful documentation.

Pure F responses make use only of the shape or form of the inkblots, and about 35% F representation is normatively anticipated in the United States. Lambda (L) summarizes F responses relative to all other responses and yields approximately .60 for adults in the United States while Lambda is 1.21 in Portugal. Form quality, as suggested by ordinary (o), unusual (u), and poor quality (-) responses, is scored using X+%, Xu%, and X-%, respectively. In the United States, about 80% of responses in a given record are ordinary form quality, including 30% Popular (P) responses, but 70% ordinary form is suggestive of dysfunction, whereas 60% characterizes inpatient schizophrenics. X+%, Xu%, and X-% are .50, .12, and .37 in Portugal as contrasted with .79, .07, and .14 in the United States, whereas P responses average 2 less in Portugal in records with equivalent numbers of responses. These contrasts are even greater in Latin American countries. Many researchers have concluded from the available data on RCS form that form tables are required for each national population. However, Andronikof-Sanglade (1999) has suggested that F accuracy, the original meaning of the various F responses as accurate assessee recognition of blot shapes, has been altered by Exner to a frequency definition of a specific object, or word, rather than the shape of the blot. Exner's X+% would then measure discrepancy from "average American language use and reference world" (p. 338). This alternative explanation indicates complete disavowal of interpretations involving the conventional meaning of F responses for reality contact and conventionality of thinking processes, including the Schizophrenia Index.

Finally, texture (T) is conventionally interpreted in the United States as signifying need for emotional contact with other persons, and no T suggests absence or scarcity of interpersonal resources in childhood. Sum T in Exner norms is 1.03, whereas in Portugal it is .68, and even closer to zero in Latin America. Southern Europe and Latin America have been described as "contact cultures" in which physical contact and interpersonal warmth and shared feelings are characteristic throughout life. No T in these records would be expected without a major disruption in the person's affectual life and frustration of needs for affection.

RCS research must now focus on the interpretation of the differences noted above that were hypothesized on the basis of this cross-cultural literature. This research would examine the emic manifestations of an RCS etic-emic theoretical model in each country from which norm discrepancies have been reported. Comparison of RCS scores with external correlates or extratest variables should also be accompanied in each country by identification of clusters of scores discriminating normal from clinical groups (Ganellan, 1996).

C. THEMATIC APPERCEPTION TEST

TAT use with multicultural populations in the United States relies on high-inference interpretation in a context of limited training to increase reliability of interpretation or the availability of culture-specific practice guidelines as suggested earlier in this chapter. There is also an ongoing debate concerning the continued utility of the original Murray cards as opposed to the adoption of new culture-specific sets of cards represented by the Tell-Me-A-Story Test for Latino/African American, Asian American, and Anglo-American populations (TEMAS) (Dana, 1999,b). Nonetheless, scoring variables largely developed in the United States in the middle of this century have been coupled with more recent national norms for 12 Murray cards in Spain (Avila-Espada, 1999). The result is a low inference interpretation test that can be imported to the United States initially for research use with Hispanic populations. The scores, ratios, and Spanish norms require similar cross-cultural validation in the United States as the RCS has necessitated in Spain, including translations to Mexican American, Puerto Rican, and Cuban American Spanish, for example.

A second issue, especially germane to the TAT and the RCS, is an etic-emic psychocultural research and practice model described by Ephraim (1999) that can potentially meet many of the requirements for cross-cultural and multicultural assessment. An etic framework with ten basic Murray-derived human needs are represented by instrumental and expressive themes that are reproduced in emic settings. The advantage of etic-emic theoretical models is that they permit a unification of low- and high-inference interpretation to serve scientific objectives of prediction-control and understanding.

III. DISCUSSION

The history of personality assessment methodology can be traced through three ideologies represented by reality orientations of psychologists that dictated preferences for interpretation procedures and objectives of assessment research and practice (see chapter 1, Dana, 1999a). These ideologies were humanistic, normative, and humanistic-normative.

The humanistic ideology began in the 1930s. Projective techniques, including the Rorschach and the TAT, were used by assessment practitioners for an understanding of personality within psychoanalytic or humanistic-existential perspectives. Individual differences were maximized and the assessment process was personal, idiographic, and shared with clients. A credo for practice linked assessor accountability, assessor-assessee phenomenological equality, and the conviction that recipients of assessment findings should learn to use the results of this process for problem solving in their lives (Dana, 1975). This credo was followed by an assessment practice model that included honest feedback of findings (Dana, 1985). These examples of a humanistic ideology were harbingers of a therapeutic assessment model in the 1990s that linked humanistic and normative assessment objectives (Finn & Tonsager, 1992). During this early period, assessees were frequently described within their cultural contexts and the strategy was emic, although group comparisons werre made between culture-specific studies, particularly with the Rorschach (e.g., Abel, 1948). Assessment findings were communicated by means of psychological reports, or personality portraits developed using intuition and high-inference interpretation. In a context of at least four books on how to prepare reports, there were 37 studies on the usefulness and communication adequacy of these reports and 52 studies on virtues and limitations of false feedback and honest feedback to assessees (Dana, 1979, 1980). This was a literature primarily provided by assessment practitioners who understood that validation of a test constituted an interpretation of data, as Cronbach (1971) averred and that the inferences made from test scores were the proper focus of validation research (Wainer & Braum, 1988).

However, this early research history was submerged during the 1970s and early 1980s by a normative ideology when Boulder Model scientist-practitioners began teaching low-inference assessment, first of intelligence tests and then for interpretation of tests of personality and psychopathology, particularly the MMPI and the RCS. The research focus shifted from psychological reports to the validation of tests that produced the inferences subsequently presented in the contents of reports. Scientific objectives of prediction and control eclipsed understanding with acceptance of a normative ideology in professional psychology assessment. This new ideology emphasized objectivity, parsimony, and minimization of differences in a search for general laws to describe human behavior. Because selection of psychology students had also changed from an earlier generation, there were few students and faculty to complain about this ideological transformation (e.g., Lipsey, 1974). This normative ideology excluded culture by an unquestioning acceptance of Eurocentric methodology as universal in applications. Cross-cultural group comparisons were thus legitimized by the false belief that individuals from these groups were highly similar to the normative populations and that the instruments for comparison were indeed etic in application rather than pseudo-etic.

Normative assessment is the currently accepted assessment model, and some limitations of this model are embodied in a quote that suggests what has been lost from the perspective of assessment with multicultural assessees by abandoning the earlier humanistic ideology:

> By methods that objectify, we create method-induced constraints on human data, an artifice of certainty, a derogation of human intent. We learn about others, but we cannot learn how they experience their humanity or how they cope with the ingredients of their living environments. (Dana, 1982, p. 48)

At present in the United States, many psychologists deny that intuition and subjectivity are ingredients necessary for development of a human science. Instead, a pseudo-etic science is favored that finds merit primarily by exercising objectivity in the service of cognitive control over the research enterprise. In light of this ideological transformation, it comes as no surprise that our 1992 code of ethics has been criticized for retreating from a humanitarian stance that recognizes the dignity and worth of all persons (Payton, 1994).

A humanistic-normative assessment model has been proposed to foster a union of low- and high-inference interpretation using norms as well as intuition, with safeguards against eisegesis, to implement an etic-emic perspective.The multicultural U.S. society of the present and immediate future cannot accept an obsolete science of psychology that is oblivious to culture and sanctions "cultural malpractice" in assessment (Hall, 1997). In accord with this new model, Esquivel (1992) has called for a more comprehensive study of the entire psychodiagnostic process moving beyond psychometric validation to incorporate relevant cultural variables during each phase. This suggestion incorporates Malgady's (1996) reversal of the Null Hypothesis to make culture central rather than peripheral in psychological research, and my demonstration of seven critical points during the psychodiagnostic process where relevant questions can lead to infusions of new data and information (Dana, 1997, 1998c, 1999,a, Chap. 1). By the same token, it is feasible to focus once again on the predictive validity of contents in psychological reports (e.g., Dana, Hannifin, Lancaster, Lore, & Nelson, 1963). However, two alterations in current assessment training are necessary. First, multicultural assessment courses will be required to teach students high and low inference interpretation of test data and writing reports on assessees from diverse cultural backgrounds, including Anglo-Americans. Second, a teaching method develops competence by using multiple sources of feedback to students on the concepts contained in their assessment reports using common sets of assessment data (Dana, 1982). Cultural competence is fostered by use of common data sets from multicultural assessees. These feedback sources include assessees, student peers, and more experienced assessors. Accuracy, skill, and eisegesis components are examined by comparisons among student concepts and with concepts contained in criterion reports. Assessee evaluations of the accuracy or inaccuracy of concepts contained in reports on themselves are used in addition.

IV. PERORATION

Bias in assessment methodology has a history of infusing both assessment research and assessment practice with discriminatory effects on multicultural populations in the United States. These sources of bias can be remediated by both interim and long-range considerations of the role of culture in assessment research and practice. On an interim basis, research bias can be remediated by more ethical use of research design and statistical treatments of data as well as by the manner in which standard assessment instruments are used in practice. Both high- and low-inference interpretation procedures can be incorporated into assessment training and practice by means of a humanistic-normative assessment model. This new model incorporates subjectivity and understanding as well as objectivity and prediction-control into a human science that is faithful not only to the history of our discipline but sponsors an etic-emic research paradigm, emphasizing individual and cultural differences as well as general laws.

However, a perspective for the next 50 years requires a transformation in the nature of psychology that places culture at the center of our research and practice attentions. Nothing less can provide relief from the abuses to multicultural populations from bias in the methodology used in assessment research and subsequent assessment practices. Precursors of a paradigm shift have been described in this chapter, and readers are referred to Cole (1996) for a glimpse of this "once and future discipline" of psychology.

REFERENCES

Abel, T. M. (1948). The Rorschach test in the study of culture. *Rorschach Research Exchange,* 12, 79–93.
Allen, J., & Walsh, J. (1999). A construct-based approach to equivalence methodologies for cross-cultural/multicultural personality assessment. In R. H. Dana (Ed.). *Handbook of cross-cultural and multicultural personality assessment* (pp. 63–85). Hillsdale, NJ: Erlbaum.
Andronikof-Sanglade, A. (1999). Use of the Rorschach Comprehensive System in Europe: State of the art. In R. H. Dana (Ed)., *Handbook of cross-cultural and multicultural personality assessment* (pp. 329–344). Hillsdale, NJ: Erlbaum.
Arnold, B. R., Montgomery, G. T., Castanada, I., & Longoria, R. (1994). Acculturation and performance of Hispanics on selected Halstead-Reitan neuropsychological tests. *Assessment, 1,* 239–248.
Avila-Espada, A. (1999). Objective scoring for the TAT. In R. H. Dana (Ed.). *Handbook of cross-cultural and multicultural personality assessment* (pp. 465–480). Hillsdale, NJ: Erlbaum.
Aribo, D. A. Y. (1988). Understanding the proper and improper usage of the comparative research framework. *Journal of Black Psychology,* 15, 81–91.
Bennett, M. J. (1986). Toward ethnorelativism: A development model of intercultural sensitivity. In R. M. Paige (Ed.)., *Cross-cultural orientation: New conceptualizations and applications* (pp. 27–69). Lanham, MD: University Press of America.
Brislin, R. W. (1970) (Ed.). *Translations: Applications and research.* New York: Wiley.
Brislin, R. W. (1970). Back-translation for cross-cultural research. *Journal of Cross-Cultural Psychology,* 1, 185–216.
Butcher, J. N. (1996a). Translation and adaptation of the MMPI-2 for international use. In J. N. Butcher (Ed.). *International adaptations of the MMPI-2* (pp. 26–43). Minneapolis, MN: University of Minnesota Press.

Butcher, J. N. (1996b). Methods of establishing cross-cultural equivalence. In J. N. Butcher (Ed.)., *International adaptations of the MMPI-2* (pp. 44–63). Minneapolis, MN: University of Minnesota Press.

Castillo, R. J. (1996). *Culture and mental illness: A client-centered approach.* Pacific Grove, CA: Brooks/Cole.

Cervantes, R. C., & Acosta, F. X. (1992). Psychological testing for Hispanic Americans. *Journal of Preventive Psychology, 1,* 209–219.

Charles, K. (1988). *Culture-specific MMPI norms for a sample of Northern Ontario Indians.* Unpublished Master's thesis, Lakehead University, Thunder Bay, Ontario, Canada.

Cheung, F. M., Leung, K., Fan, R. M., Song, W. Z., & Xie, D. (1996). Development of the Chinese Personality Inventory. *Journal of Cross-Cultural Psychology, 27,* 181–199.

Cole, M. (1996). *Cultural psychology: A once and future discipline.* Cambridge, MA: Harvard University Press.

Costantino, G., Flanagan, R., & Malgady, R. G. (1995). The history of the Rorschach: Overcoming bias in multicultural projective assessment. *Rorschaciana, 20,* 148–171.

Cronbach, L. J. (1971). Test validation. In R. L. Thorndike (Ed.), *Educational measurement* (2nd ed.). (pp. 443–507). Washington, DC: American Council on Education.

Cuéllar, I. (1999). Acculturation as a moderator of personality and psychological assessment. In R. H. Dana (Ed.), *Handbook of cross-cultural and multicultural personality assessment* (pp. 113–129). Hillsdale, NJ: Erlbaum.

Cuéllar, I., & Gonzales, G. (1999). Cultural identity description and cultural formulations of Hispanics. In R. H. Dana (Ed.)., *Handbook of cross-cultural and multicultural personality assessment* (pp. 605–621). Hillsdale, NJ: Erlbaum.

Cuéllar, I., Harris, I. D., & Jasso, R. (1980). An acculturation scale for Mexican American normal and clinical populations. *Hispanic Journal of Behavioral Sciences, 2,* 199–217.

Dahlstrom, W. G., Lachar, D., & Dahlstrom, L. E. (1986). *MMPI patterns of American minorities.* Minneapolis, MN: University of Minnesota Press.

Dana, R. H. (Ed.) (1999a). *Handbook of cross-cultural and multicultural personality assessment* Hillsdale, NJ: Erlbaum.

Dana, R. H. (1999b). Cross-cultural and multicultural use of the Thematic Apperception Test. In M. L. Geiser & M. Stein (Eds.), *Celebrating the Thematic Apperception Test* (pp. 177–190). Washington, DC: American Psychological Association.

Dana, R. H. (1999c). *Psychological assessment of cultural identity and psychopathology.* Unpublished manuscript.

Dana, R. H. (1998a). *Understanding cultural identity in intervention and assessment.* Thousand Oaks, CA: Sage.

Dana, R. H. (1998b). Projective assessment of Latinos in the United States: Current realities, problems, and prospects. *Cultural Diversity and Mental Health, 4*(3), 165–184.

Dana, R. H. (1998c). Multicultural assessment in the United States: Still art, not yet science, and controversial. *European Journal of Personality Assessment, 14,* 62–70.

Dana, R. H. (1998d). Cultural identity assessment of culturally diverse groups: 1997. *Journal of Personality Assessment, 70,* 1–16.

Dana, R. H. (1997). Multicultural assessment and cultural identity: An assessment-intervention model. *World Psychology, 3* (1–2), 121–142.

Dana, R. H. (1996). *Silk purse or sow's ear: An MMPI commonground.* Unpublished manuscript.

Dana, R. H. (1995). Culturally competence MMPI assessment of Hispanic populations. *Hispanic Journal of Behavioral Sciences, 17,* 305–319.

Dana, R. H. (1993). *Multicultural assessment perspectives for professional psychology.* Boston: Allyn & Bacon.

Dana, R. H. (1985). A service-delivery paradigm for personality assessment *Journal of Personality Assessment, 49,* 598–604.

Dana, R. H. (1982). *A human science model for personality assessment with projective techniques.* Springfield, IL: C. C. Thomas.

Dana, R. H. (1980). Receptivity to clinical interpretation. In R. Woody (Ed.), *Encyclopedia of clinical assessment* (pp. 1042–1049). San Francisco: Jossey-Bass.

Dana, R. H. (1979, March). *The communication of psychologists' assessment interpretations.* Paper presented at the meeting of the Society for Personality Assessment, Scottsdale, AZ.

Dana, R. H. (1975). Ruminations on teaching projective assessment: An ideology, specific usages, teaching practices. *Journal of Personality Assessment, 39,* 563–572.

Dana, R. H. (1966). Eisegesis and assessment. *Journal of Projective Techniques and Personality Assessment, 30,* 215–222.

Dana, R. H., Hannefin, P., Lancaster, C., Lore, W., & Nelson, E. (1963). Psychological reports and juvenile probation counseling. *Journal of Clinical Psychology, 19,* 352–355.

Draguns, J. G. (1984). Assessing mental health and disorders across cultures. In P. Pedersen, N. Sartorius, A. J. Marsella (Eds.), *Mental health services: The cross-cultural context* (pp. 31–57). Beverly Hills, CA: Sage.

Ephraim, D. (1999). A psychocultural approach to TAT scoring and interpretation. In R. H. Dana (Ed.). *Handbook of cross-cultural and multicultural personality assessment.* (pp. 427–445). Hillsdale, NJ: Erlbaum.

Erdberg, P. (1996). The Rorschach. In C. S. Newmark (Ed.), *Major psychological assessment instruments* (2nd ed.) (pp. 148–165). Boston: Allyn & Bacon.

Esquivel, G. (1992). Some needed research on the assessment of Hispanics in clinical settings. In K. F. Geisinger (Ed.), *Psychological testing of Hispanics* (pp. 267–269). Washington, DC: American Psychological Association.

Exner, J. E. Jr. (1993). *The Rorschach: A comprehensive system. Vol. 1: Basic foundations.* (3rd ed.). New York: Wiley.

Fantoni-Salvador, P., & Rogers, R. (1997). Spanish versions of the MMPI-2 and PAI: An investigation of concurrent validity with Hispanic patients. *Assessment, 4,* 29–39.

Finn, S. E., & Tonsager, M. E. (1992). Therapeutic effects of providing MMPI-2 test feedback to college students awaiting therapy. *Psychological Assessment, 4,* 278–287.

Ganellen, R. J. (1996). *Integrating the Rorschach and the MMPI-2 in personality assessment.* Mahwah, NJ: Erlbaum.

Gomez-Maqueo, E. L., & Reyes-Lagunes, L. (1994). New version of the Minnesota Multiphasic Personality inventory MMPI-2 for Mexican college students. *Revista Mexicana de Psicologia, 11,* 45–54.

Goodstein, R., & Gielen, U. P. (1998). Some conceptual similarities and differences between cross-cultural and multicultural psychology. *International Psychologist, 38,* 42–43.

Graham, S. (1992). "Most of the subjects were White and middle-class": Trends in published research on African Americans in selected APA journals, 1970-1989. *American Psychologist, 47,* 629–639.

Hall, C. C. I. (1997). Cultural malpractice: The growing obsolescence of psychology with the changing U.S. population. *American Psychologist, 32,* 642–651.

Handel, R., & Ben-Porath, Y. S. (1999). Multicultural assessment with the MMPI. In R. H. Dana (Ed.)., *Handbook of cross-cultural and multicultural personality assessment* (pp. 229–245). Hillsdale, NJ: Erlbaum.

Handler, L. (1996). The clinical use of drawings: Draw-A-Person, House-Tree-Person, and Kinetic Family Drawings. In C. S. Newmark (Ed.), *Major psychological assessment instruments* (2nd ed.), (pp.206–293). Boston: Allyn & Bacon.

Helmes, E., & Redden, J. R. (1993). A perspective on developments in assessing psychopathology: A critical review of the MMPI and MMPI-2. *Psychological Bulletin, 113,* 453–471.

Helms, J. E. (1992). Why is there no study of cultural equivalence in standard cognitive ability testing? *American Psychologist, 47,* 1083–1101.

Hoffmann, T., Dana, R. H., & Bolton, B. (1985). Measured acculturation and the MMPI-168 performance of Native Americans. *Journal of Cross-Cultural Psychology, 16,* 243–256.

Hoshmand, L. L. S. T. (1989). Alternate research paradigms: A review and teaching proposal. *Counseling Psychologist, 17,* 3–79.

Jones, E. E., & Thorne, A. (1987). Rediscovery of the subject: Intercultural approaches to clinical assessment. *Journal of Consulting and Clinical Psychology, 55,* 488–495.

LaDue, R. A. (1982). *Standardization of the Minnesota Multiphasic Personality Inventory for the Colville Indian reservation.* (Doctoral dissertation, Washington State University, 1982). *Dissertation Abstracts International, 43,* 3033B.

Lipsey, M. W. (1974). Research and relevance: Survey of graduate students and faculty in psychology. *American Psychologist, 29,* 341–353.

Lopez, S. R. (1999). Teaching culturally informed psychological assessment. In R. H. Dana (Ed.), *Handbook of cross-cultural and multicultural personality assessment.* (pp. 669–687). Hillsdale, NJ: Erlbaum.

Malgady, R. G. (1996). The question of cultural bias in assessment and diagnosis of ethnic minority clients: Let's reject the Null Hypothesis. *Professional Psychology: Research and Practice, 27,* 73–77.

Malgady, R. G. (1999). Myths about the Null Hypotehsis and the path to reform. In R. H. Dana (Ed.), *Handbook of cross-cultural and multicultural personality assessment* (pp. 49–62). Hillsdale, NJ: Erlbaum.

Mattlar, C-E, & Fried, R. (1993). The Rorschach in Finland. *Rorschachiana, 18,* 105–125.

Nichols, D. S., Padilla, J., & Gomez-Maqueo, E. L. (1999). Issues in the cross-cultural adaptation and use of the MMPI-2. In R. H. Dana (Ed.), *Handbook of cross-cultural and multicultural personality assessment* (pp. 247–266). Hillsdale, NJ: Erlbaum.

Okazaki, S., & Sue, S. (1995). Methodological issues in assessment research with ethnic minorities. *Psychological Assessment, 7,* 367–375.

Payton, C. (1994). Implications of the 1992 Ethics Code for diverse groups. *Professional Psychology: Research and Practice, 25,* 317–320.

Pires, A. A. (1999). National norms for the Rorschach Comprehensive Test in Portugal. In R. H. Dana (Ed.), *Handbook of cross-cultural and multicultural personality assessment* (pp. 367–392). Hillsdale, NJ: Erlbaum.

Rossini, E. D., & Moretti, R. J. (1997). Thematic Apperception Test (TAT) interpretation: Practice recommendations from a survey of clinical psychology doctoral programs accredited by the American Psychological Association. *Professional Psychology: Research and Practice, 28,* 393–398.

Rychlak, J. F. (1959). Clinical psychology and the nature of evidence. *American Psychologist, 14,* 642–648.

Sue, S. (1998). In search of cultural competence in psychotherapy and counseling. *American Psychologist, 53,* 440–448.

Van de Vijver, F. (1999). The nature of bias. In R. H. Dana (Ed.), *Handbook of cross-cultural and multicultural personality assessment* (pp. 87–106). Hillsdale, NJ: Erlbaum.

Velásquez, R. J., Butcher, J. N., Garrido, M., & Cabiya, J. J. (1996). *Dana's culturally competent MMPI assessment of Hispanics: A case of rounding up the usual suspects.* Unpublished manuscript.

Wainer, H., & Braum, H. I. (1988). *Test validity.* Hillsdale, NJ: Erlbaum.

Wyatt, F. (1967). How objective is objectivity? *Journal of Projective Techniques and Personality Assessment, 31,* 3–19.

Zane, N. (1998, December). *Major approaches to the measurement of acculturation: A content analysis and empirical validation.* Paper presented at the International Conference on Acculturation, San Francisco, CA.

CHAPTER 7

Test Translation and Cultural Equivalence Methodologies for Use with Diverse Populations

BILL R. ARNOLD
YOLANDA E. MATUS
Department of Psychology and Anthropology
The University of Texas—Pan American
Edinburg, Texas

I. INTRODUCTION

Perhaps one of the greatest challenges facing psychology today is addressing the needs of ethnically diverse consumers. Many of the psychological disorders that have been studied widely display a common structure across cultures and language groups (Butcher, Lim, & Nezami, 1998). The *Diagnostic and Statistical Manual of Mental Disorders* (4th ed.; American Psychiatric Association, 1994) now recognizes the importance of integrating the influence of cultural factors into understanding the context of psychopathology and its effective treatment. As well, the American Psychological Association (1991) developed *Guidelines for Providers of Psychological Services to Ethnic, Linguistic, and Culturally Diverse Populations,* to focus awareness on the special vigilance that must be paid in providing services to individuals from different cultures, and individuals different from those on whom assessment instruments were originally developed and normed. In order for psychology to provide effective and useful diagnostic and treatment protocols to the variety of consumers in the population, psychology

Handbook of Multicultural Mental Health: Assessment and Treatment of Diverse Populations

must have more than just an awareness. The decision-making process for collecting information from culturally distinctive groups involves designating the function of the instrument that is being proposed. In other words, how will the information elicited from this instrument be used? Typical functions for these tests involve (a) cross-cultural comparisons of functional abilities; (b) cross-cultural comparisons of personality traits or other characteristics; (c) description of functional abilities within a culture; or (d) description of personality traits or other characteristics within a culture. Methodologies must be utilized that can help provide the necessary data from which psychologists can draw valid conclusions concerning psychological and neuropsychological functioning of culturally diverse consumers. Cultural competence in psychological testing requires first-language assessment of consumers, both to ensure accuracy of data for interpretation and for ethical reasons (Dana, 1993). In addition, mental health professionals in other countries have shown interest in test translations to better serve the needs of their population with valid interpretations of reliable instruments. These professionals are interested in equivalent versions of existing instruments that have been shown to be effective with patients in the United States (Butcher et al., 1998). Logic implies that if an instrument has been shown reliable and valid in one cultural context, it may hold potential for benefiting consumers in other cultures (Van de Vijver & Hambleton, 1996), though the validity cannot be assumed without supportive research. With this in mind, this chapter will focus on a review of test translation and cross-cultural methodologies which will assist researchers and clinicians in choosing how to best address the evaluation needs of ethnically diverse consumers. Along these lines, four domains of guidelines for translating tests from one culture to another will be briefly discussed (International Test Commission, 1993, as reported in Van de Vijver & Hambleton, 1996).

The cultural equivalence of a translated instrument has been generally described as the extent to which a word, concept, scale, or normative structure may be considered relevant and applicable to cultural groups other than the one in which these elements were developed (Marsella & Kameoka, 1989). Helms (1992) additionally describes cultural equivalence as the extent to which constructs hold similar meanings within and across cultural groups. Cross-cultural testing includes the goal of evaluating the commonality, or uniqueness, of a psychological concept, as well as potentially explaining the differences or similarities of functional abilities or personality characteristics from differing cultures (Butcher et al., 1998). Psychometric equivalence is, therefore, the degree to which test instruments measure the same variables at the same level across cultural groups (Helms, 1992). The function that the data will serve will determine the methodology used to develop the instrument utilized. In order to adequately address these objectives, various types of equivalencies need to be considered. These equivalencies include (a) linguistic equivalence; (b) item and scale equivalence; (c) normative equivalence; (d) technical equivalence; and (e) clinical equivalence. Determining the equivalence of a test for use across cultures will lessen the probability for commission of the cultural equivalence fallacy (Helms, 1992).

II. GUIDELINES OF THE INTERNATIONAL TEST COMMISSION

The four domains described by the International Test Commission include (a) Context; (b) Development; (c) Administration; and (d) Documentation/Score Interpretation (International Test Commission, 1993, as reported in Van de Vijver & Hambleton, 1996). Context-domain variables are defined as utilizing test translation methods that minimize or avoid construct bias, method bias, and item bias. Development of a cross-cultural instrument requires an in-depth understanding and knowledge of both the target language and target culture and a translated product that ensures that both are reflected in all aspects of the test. With regard to administration, the item content, stimulus materials, test administration format, and techniques must be familiar to the targeted cultural group. Statistical documentation of the ecological validity of the test is of critical importance in assuring that test results have the potential for accurate score interpretation (Van de Vijver & Hambleton, 1996). Ecological validation involves the ability to observe tested behavior in naturalistic, everyday settings. Sbordone (1996) further defined ecological validity for neuropsychological testing as "the functional and predictive relationship between the patient's performance on a set of neuropsychological tests and the patient's behavior in a variety of real-world settings (e.g., at home, work, school, community)" (p. 16). A measure would demonstrate ecological validity if test results provide correct inferences, or predictions, about an individual's ability to perform a specific task in the home, work, or social settings. Following the guidelines established by this international commission would increase confidence that equivalent and valid test translations have been conducted.

III. LINGUISTIC EQUIVALENCE

In linguistic equivalence, the intent is to ensure that performance requests are identical across cultures, or where regional linguistic variations are observed (Drasgow & Hulin, 1987; Hulin, 1987). Or, as Helms (1992) has suggested, is the language used in test items equalized such that it holds the same meaning in the cultural groups being examined? In terms of methods to increase the likelihood of linguistic equivalence, several have been identified in the literature. Possibilities for test translation include (a) literal translation of the instrument; (b) adaptation of parts of the instrument; and (c) assembling of an entirely new instrument (Van de Vijver & Hambleton, 1996). One method frequently utilized involves translation of the test into the language of the culture, followed by back translation (Brislin, 1970, 1980, 1986; Ellis, 1989). It is of interest, however, that in the field of professional translation, the translation-back translation procedure, unfortunately, is rarely used. Professional translators, typically, first translate, then in teams of competent bilinguals, utilize judgmental methods to assess the accuracy of the new language version (Van de Vijver & Leung, 1997). However, the translation-back translation approach is particularly valuable to researchers and clinicians who do not have proficiency in the translated language, as it can assure some control over the eventual product when the back translation occurs to the source language.

Additionally, in completing a translation, one that is "generic" in nature and broadly reflects the culture of interest would appear most potentially useful (Arnold, Cuéllar, & Guzmán, 1998). Different cultures and subcultures make use of various terms in referring to the same concept. For example, a child may be called 'chilpayate,' 'escuincle,' or 'cabro' in different regions of Mexico, Central, and South America; however, the term 'niño/a' would be a more generic and universally acceptable word choice. This translation approach assumes a rationale that the less complex the verbal performance requests the greater the likelihood it will be meaningful to a larger number of potential patients in the target population. Even so, at times, selection of appropriate words for test items may prove difficult. To illustrate, in some Central and South American countries, corn is referred to as 'choclo,' whereas, in Mexico, 'choclo' is a type of shoe, and the term for corn is either 'elote' or 'maíz.' To complicate test translation issues even further, a simple object such as a pen may have a variety of names, such as, 'pluma,' 'lápiz pasta,' 'lapicero,' or 'bolígrafo.' Following translation, an independent back translation is typically involved. The back translation evaluates translation quality, specifically comparing the original English and the back-translated English (Brislin, 1986; Hulin, Drasgow, & Komocar, 1982; Sinaiko & Brislin, 1973). Subsequent to the back translation of the instrument, review by a panel that adequately reflects the diversity of the targeted population is an important next step. Revisions to the translation are reiterated until reviewers are satisfied that a reliable test has been adapted. When reviewers can agree on adequate similarity of performance requests or statements representing personality traits, field trials with a sample of consumers who represent the population to be tested is conducted.

During these field trials, another method for validation of the translation can be applied that involves establishing functional equivalence by performance testing and knowledge testing (Sinaiko & Brislin, 1973). Functional equivalence refers to dissimilar behavioral competencies that are learned, but aimed at coping with similar problems (Dana, 1993). That is, individuals in dissimilar cultures may develop different coping styles to deal with similar problems. Performance testing includes observing the consumer perform a task using translated instructions, and to the extent that the consumer demonstrates competence in completing the task, the instrument demonstrates equivalency (Sinaiko & Brislin, 1973). The translated test should elicit completely accurate scores in the target culture if the test is sound, and should be independent of individual differences (Sinaiko & Brislin, 1973). Performance testing would appear most appropriate for tests measuring functional abilities that are observable. The second approach to validating translations seems most compatible with tests of functional abilities that are not directly observable, for example, reading comprehension. This approach, labeled "knowledge testing" by Miller and Beebe-Center (1956; Sinaiko & Brislin, 1973), involves targeted consumers reading a translated passage, followed by answering questions concerning the passage. An accurate translation is produced when the target group is able to answer all the questions on the test.

Twelve general guidelines for producing good translations of tests were listed in Brislin, Lonner, and Thorndike (1973), including (a) constructing items using brief, clear and simplified sentences, at times involving elimination of words from the original test to avoid compound thoughts in an item; (b) grammatically phrasing items in the active tense; (c) using nouns in a repetitive manner, if necessary, rather than resorting to pronouns; (d) avoiding the use of metaphors, or regionally specific phrases, idioms, or colloquialisms; (e) not using the subjunctive tense in translated items; (f) using additional phrases to insure comprehension of key meanings in item content; (g) not utilizing items that include adverbs and prepositions; (h) avoiding item content that includes possessive forms of words; (i) being specific and concrete in item content; (j) not using vague descriptors in item content; (k) familiarizing the translator with test item content; and, (l) avoiding inclusion of more than one verb in item content where the two suggest differing actions. Behaviors that have a very low probability of occurring in the target group, or have never been exhibited, should not be included in item content (Hulin, 1987). Translated items that are spelled identically or similarly but have different meanings may cause confusion in careless translators or bilingual test takers and contribute to inequivalencies. By way of illustration, translating 'to assist' from English to Spanish could be easily mistaken for 'asistir,' which means to be present at a function. Similarly, translating "to attend" from English to the Spanish verb 'atender,' meaning to help in a situation, may present problems. Also, poor translations may be due to language that is unique in meaning to a particular culture or region. In the Mexican culture, a "china" is a female of Chinese ethnicity, whereas, in Puerto Rico a "china" is an orange fruit.

Translation of a test from one language to another has the potential for many sources of error, which reduce accuracy and diminish the reliability of the measurement. Potential problem sources include (a) a sound translation can be misinterpreted by an incompetent back translator; (b) a poor translation can be completed with subsequent problems with the back translation. In the latter case, a good translator during the back-translation process may make adjustments to make the back translation more valid, even though the original translation is not a good one (Bontempo, 1993). These potential problems with the translation-back translation procedures require that more measures of equivalence be completed (Sinaiko & Brislin, 1973).

Three important, but rarely utilized designs have been proposed for determining the usefulness of test translations (Hambleton, 1993, 1994; Manuel-Dupont et al., 1992): (a) both target and source versions of the translated test are taken by bilinguals; (b) original and back-translated versions of the test are taken by source language monolinguals; and (c) monolinguals in both target and source language take the test in their respective language. Following implementation of these designs, to determine linguistic equivalence of tests, statistical methods are applied.

IV. ITEM AND SCALE EQUIVALENCE

Items and scales on an instrument must be evaluated to determine measurement equivalency (Drasgow & Hulin, 1987). That is, do the items and scales on the measure represent similar distributions across linguistic and cultural subgroups within the target population? Examining this type of equivalency has sequenced into two stages (Drasgow, 1984; Drasgow & Hulin, 1987). In the first stage, items that display biased properties can be removed because they exhibit different measurement properties from those observed in the original language. Additionally, it is important to determine if individuals from different language groups (original and translated) show significantly similar expected total scores on the target scale.

Statistically, the method of choice for examining measurement and relational equivalencies is based on Item Response Theory, which provides a typically accurate means for detecting item bias, though no means for explaining it (Drasgow & Hulin, 1987). Item Response Theory proposes that there should be a relationship between an individual's response to a particular item on a translated test and the trait measured by the test (Bontempo, 1993; Ellis, 1989). Item bias, or differential item functioning, is said to exist if individuals hold similar scores on the measured construct, but different scores on items contributing to that construct (Hulin et al., 1982). Statistical techniques are employed to remove item bias in translated instruments (Van de Vijver & Hambleton, 1996).

After biased items have been removed during stage one, the second stage focuses on the relationship between performance on the scale and other external variables of importance. Differences between linguistic groups' performances on the translated scale and identical external variables within the different cultures would suggest the scale might be measuring different characteristics across cultures. This culturally based difference implies a relationship between variables within different cultures that the translated instrument cannot adequately represent (Drasgow & Hulin, 1987), even though the translation may be a good one. That is, scale inequivalency would exist due to the lack of familiarity of scale concepts across cultural subgroups. In some cultures, particularly non-Western, there is a lack of familiarity with Western-type interview and survey formats (Marsella & Kameoka, 1989). Test takers from these cultures may not be familiar with Likert-type scales, Thurstone scales, or even true–false scales. An example of this type of bias was provided by Marsella and Kameoka (1989), describing a Filipino male rating his satisfaction with his living conditions using a five-point scale illustrated by a set of stairs, with response options ranging from "very dissatisfied" at the bottom step of the stairs, to "very satisfied" at the top. The illustration continues with the man placing himself on the bottom step. While the examiner interpreted this response as reflecting the man's poor living conditions; when queried for the rationale for his response, the man replied that he did not want to fall down the stairs and get hurt. In order for a test to display scale equivalence across cultures, it must be relevant to both cultures being examined.

V. NORMATIVE EQUIVALENCE

Exploring the normative equivalence of a measure focuses on determining if there is similarity between performance of a norm group on a particular test, and performance of a culturally distinct target group on a translated version of the same test. If the normative distributions of the two culturally different groups are not significantly different, the original norms may prove useful, with caution implied (Cuéllar, 1998). Further, does the translated test discriminate to an acceptable level of confidence between individuals displaying a particular characteristic or functional ability, and those who do not? Statistically, this ability to differentiate is referred to as discriminant validity. However, more importantly, is this ability to statistically discriminate at a level of specificity and sensitivity that is clinically useful? One may find nonsignificant differences between groups regarding normative information, with several possible clinical implications: (a) the original normative data may be used with confidence; (b) the original normative data may be used, but in conjunction with a moderator variable, such as an acculturation measure, which allows development of a formula for adjustment of scores to make them meaningful (Cuéllar, in press). However, in both instances, it is important to determine the sensitivity, specificity, and accuracy of the normative or adjusted normative data used. Adjustment in cutoff scores to maximize correctly classified nonimpaired and impaired participants in the target group will prove essential in making the translated instrument clinically useful in instances where there exist dichotomous clinical categories. Berry (1979, 1980) recommended the use of "ethunits" which would assist adjustment of scores based on dimensions and characteristics that make cultural groups unique. Along these lines, Helms (1992) supported the use of acculturation level as an important variable to include in research on tests of cognitive ability.

If significant differences are discovered between the normative group and the culturally distinct group's performance on the translated test that cannot be useful with adjustments to scores, the original norms may not be appropriate, requiring development of new norms specific to the targeted cultural population and translated instrument. Even so, it will be important to develop cutoff scores that maximize sensitivity and specificity of the translated test to enhance its clinical utility or clinical equivalence.

VI. TECHNICAL EQUIVALENCE

Test-taking behaviors have been hypothesized as culturally learned, providing an inherent disadvantage to those from ethnic backgrounds different from the test source (Geisinger, 1992). Lack of technical equivalence results in method bias. Variations in data collection or test administration procedures can prove to be critical in cross-cultural comparisons of the performance of translated measures. Adapted test administration procedures can produce variability in performance on translated tests that are technical, rather than substantive, but nonetheless, have a significant impact on results of cross-cultural comparisons (Gilmer et al., 1995). If variations in test administration occur on a translated test, these variations typically impact most items on the test, rather than being selective in influence. Discovering method bias can be accomplished by repeated administrations of a translated test. Variations in performance across administrations for individuals who initially hold similar scores can suggest method bias. Additionally, nonstandard administration of a translated test can be deliberately conducted with a variety of instructions, item variations, response alternatives, and prompted motivations to elicit the impact of method bias. Method bias, as well as scale eqivalence, can also be studied utilizing different methods to collect information on the construct of interest, referred to as triangulation. Triangulation is a procedure that emphasizes the use of multiple measures to identify a particular target construct (Van de Vijver & Leung, 1997).

It may also be advantageous to include measures of social desirability to assist evaluation of method bias (Van de Vijver & Hambleton, 1996). It is therefore important that translated versions of tests be administered in the same standardized format, as that described for the original instrument, in order to provide for reliable comparisons across cultures.

At times, the test protocol itself will pose a problem, due to its inherent structure. Aday, Chiu, and Andersen (1980) found that Hispanic respondents were more likely to respond to "yes" answer options than non-Hispanics on a survey. Social desirability has also been shown to affect response patterns of Spanish-speaking consumers (Marin, Gamba, & Marin, 1992). Social desirability test response patterns have been reported for low socioeconomic status, older aged individuals, and individuals of Mexican origin. This response pattern dissipated as acculturation level increased (Guffey, 1997). Additionally, Hui and Triandis (1989) found that Hispanics made more extreme responses than non-Hispanics on a 5-point scale questionnaire, with these differences fading on a 10-point scale questionnaire. Other studies have shown test items with double negatives may prove difficult to translate, or may be confusing (Butcher et al., 1998).

VII. CLINICAL EQUIVALENCE

Clinical equivalence of measures across cultures is an important concept that needs to be more frequently addressed as instruments are developed for use with dichotomous clinical categories. Clinical equivalence is defined as the ability of the translated measure to accurately discriminate impaired and non-impaired individuals in a manner similar to, if not better than, the original instrument. Establishing clinical equivalence involves several data comparisons. First of all, the specificity, sensitivity, and accuracy of the translated instrument is calculated, using available, original, normative information. Acceptable sensitivity and specificity rates are typically viewed at about 85% correct classification. If the translated instrument falls below this level of accuracy, this may be an indication that other linguistically specific norms may be needed. However, data from the original version of the test must also be reviewed for sensitivity and specificity, as the original classification rates may already fall below the 85% range. If these classification rates are provided, comparisons may be conducted fairly easily. If they are not provided, frequency statistics for scores may be provided in original test construction data for impaired and nonimpaired samples. From these frequency statistics, classification rates for available samples may be calculated. Otherwise, if normative equivalence has been shown not to exist, new normative data for nonimpaired individuals will need to be developed, along with the collection of data from clinical samples to establish the specificity, sensitivity, and accuracy of the translated instrument using the linguistically specific, culturally appropriate norms. In some instances, the moderator variable of acculturation may be used to adjust scores to improve classification rates. Acculturation has been described as the extent to which an individual identifies with a culture's customs, social practices, beliefs, and language (Arnold, Montgomery, Castañeda, & Longoria, 1994). Current measures of acculturation recognize the associated multiple dimensions involved, and thus are more sophisticated than earlier linear models of this process (Cuéllar, Arnold, & Maldonado, 1995). Behaviorally anchored factors that may be measured include language use and preference, ethnic identity and classification, cultural heritage and ethnic behaviors, and ethnic interaction. Additionally, modes of the acculturation process may be addressed, as proposed by Berry (1979), including integration, assimilation, separation, and marginalization.

VIII. RELIABILITY AND VALIDITY OF TRANSLATED TESTS

A translated test should always provide information on the reliability and validity of the translation (Geisinger, 1992). Establishing the reliability and the validity of a translated test follows the same statistical format as that provided for any psychological instrument. Reliability statistics aimed at determining the internal consistency of the translated instrument must be included. Internal consistency coefficients should approximate those observed in the test construction of the original measure. Test–retest measures of reliability can be used to determine the stability of the measure over time. Particular interest may be focused, however, on certain types of validation issues. For example, a translated test may be administered to groups with known characteristics in the target population. If the test accurately predicts the known characteristics to a comparable degree as its performance in the normative group, it demonstrates sound criterion validity. In this manner, the translated test is evaluated on its basis to predict behavior in the target population to the same degree as observed in the norm group (Butcher et al., 1998).

Another important validation approach applied to translated tests focuses on determining the factor structure of the translated instrument. In established tests with well-documented factor structures, construct validation of the translated test is possible. In this approach, a factor analysis is first completed with the translated version of the test. A comparison is then made between the resulting factor components derived from the translated test, and those of the original instrument. To the extent the translated test factor structure is similar to that of the original, greater confidence is assured that the translated test and the original test are measuring similar constructs (Dana, 1993). A similar type of factor associated with cultural equivalence is conceptual validity, which is defined as the familiarity of different cultural groups with item content of a test and similar comprehension of their item meanings (Helms, 1992). If dissimilar factor structures are observed, construct bias may be present. Construct bias has been described as being more likely with translations of instruments from a source to a target language or culture, than when an instrument is developed simultaneously for different cultures or languages (Van de Vijver & Hambleton, 1996).

Finally, convergent validity may be used when a test is measuring a trait. A convergent validity approach can be taken where bilingual populations are available. This approach evaluates test scores on the translated and original instruments to determine if they seem to be measuring the same underlying trait, but not in the same manner as does factor analysis with construct validation.

IX. METHODOLOGY ILLUSTRATIONS FOR TRANSLATED TESTS

The Minnesota Multiphasic Personality Inventory—2 (MMPI-2) has 150 translations and is available in 22 of these languages for assessment of psychopathology. Butcher et al. (1998) outlined procedures to attain internal relevance of the MMPI-2 for a culture, as well as cross-cultural equivalence. Translation was conducted in a manner to promote linguistic equivalence using multiple bilingual translators, with a requirement that translators must have lived in a country for 5 years, or demonstrated equivalent experience. Further, at least two translators were involved independently translating from English to the target language, or a committee of professionals independently translated, and then collaborated and discussed items until the best and most socially appropriate of the items were selected for inclusion. Back translation of test items was conducted until all problematic items were satisfactorily translated. Following back translation, the test publisher utilized an independent center to evaluate each translation for accuracy and readability. Bilingual test–retest studies were conducted, similar to those conducted for determining test equivalence of alternative forms of a test or reliability in a test construction design. Statistical analyses were conducted to evaluate for item equivalence, translation equivalence, and measurement equivalence. Factor analysis was conducted for examination of construct validity. Criterion validity of the translated test in the new culture was studied to determine if the test was operating clinically in the target culture in the same manner as in the United States. Normative validity was also assessed to determine if American norms can be used or adapted, or if new norms for the target culture must be developed.

Another scale, the Mattis Dementia Rating Scale, has recently been developed for use with Spanish-speaking elderly (Arnold, Cuéllar, & Guzmán, 1998). This Spanish revision for use across cultures involved adaptation of the test for linguistic equivalence, using several procedures discussed. Linguistic equivalence was established using a translation-back translation procedure. Internal consistency of the adaptation was studied, along with normative equivalence and clinical equivalence of the Spanish version. The concept of clinical equivalence and the utility of the revised instrument in differentiating impaired and nonimpaired individuals was investigated.

In another study, several tests from the Halstead-Reitan neuropsychological test battery were investigated in three linguistically distinct samples: English, bilingual English-Spanish, and Spanish (Arnold et al., 1994). These groups had been composed based on level of Mexican American acculturation to produce culturally distinctive groups. In addition to showing significant group differences based on acculturation level, results suggested that adjustments based on acculturation level could prove clinically useful by improving diagnostic classification and accuracy of information provided by some of the instruments, particularly the Category Test.

A Spanish language version of the Strong Campbell Interest Inventory (SCII-S) was developed using back translation, bilingual field testing, and independent expert opinion to evaluate it. The construct validity of the SCII-S was then explored with both the English and Spanish versions of the Strong Campbell administered to one bilingual group of high school students. A confirmatory factor analysis was then applied to determine if a common factor structure existed for the two versions of the test, with subsequent documentation of both convergent and divergent validity for method and trait factors measured by this test (Fouad, Cudeck, & Hansen, 1984). Development of this patient satisfaction scale began with utilization of the translation-back translation method. Additionally, a decentering technique, with adjustments to either English, or Spanish, or both versions of the scale was completed in order to produce linguistically equivalent versions for cross-cultural use.

Decentering involves enhancement of the readability of both the original and translated instrument by adjusting both as needed (Werner & Campbell, 1970). Reliability and validity coefficients were produced for both English and Spanish versions of the decentered scale. Item and scale score distributions were analyzed using two methods of response dichotomization to compare for differences. Results showed both versions to be reasonably reliable and valid, with the Spanish version less reliable and valid. Problems with the Spanish version of the scale appeared to be associated with response tendencies observed for Spanish-speaking individuals, who tended to respond "good" to items more frequently than their English-speaking counterparts. The important issue of culturally produced response tendencies is referred to in more depth in the prior section focusing on technical equivalence. The MMPI, for example, has been shown to display L-scale elevations that may reflect cultural, rather than clinical test-taking variables (Montgomery & Orozco, 1985). Response format and dichotomization of responses were viewed as important areas to address in developing similar test translations (Hayes & Baker, 1998).

Described as one of the most carefully developed measures of job satisfaction, the Job Description Index scale (Campbell, 1970) began with a target-language translation, followed by back translation to the source language. Measurement equivalence was established with three different groups, item bias analysis completed, and relational equivalence found (Drasgow & Hulin, 1987). Translation effects were observed in comparative analysis. When one culture's population possessed bilingual abilities, translation effects were observed within the culture. Greater differences were found across cultures where test takers spoke the same language (Hulin, 1987).

In a unique study to construct a dementia screening measure for use in two groups with different cultural and linguistic identities, Hall et al. (1993) attempted to develop an instrument independent of culture and language for use with consumers and informants. The approach is described as similar to that used for the neuropsychological battery developed by the World Health Organization (WHO; Maj et al., 1991). This study promoted the use of harmonization (WHO, 1990, as reported in Maj et al., 1991), which indicates that the instrument must be consistent with the cultural, linguistic, and educational norms of the targeted cultural group. Prior to the typical translation-back translation protocol, the study began with identification of cognitive and behavioral dimensions to be measured. The dimensions were selected to be consistent with current diagnostic criteria for dementia. The relevance of each dimension to the target culture was reviewed and discussed by an interdisciplinary, culturally competent team, with draft questions constructed for the target culture. Two independent translators and the interdisciplinary team, who reviewed each item in a manner to promote harmonization, conducted the translation-back translation process. A pretest was conducted in the two culturally distinct groups for acceptability, reliability, and validity. Pretest data were also analyzed both for discriminant function and to determine a cutoff score for dementia. A subsequent community survey and clinical assessments were completed to, again, determine comparability, reliability, and validity, in addition to estimate prevalence rates, sensitivity, and specificity of the new instrument.

X. CONCLUSIONS

Cultural equivalence methodologies are presently developed and available to psychologists interested in providing competent and ethically sound evaluations of individuals from culturally diverse backgrounds. Neglecting the cultural and linguistic dimensions of psychological services can actively harm consumers by providing inaccurate diagnostic information and inappropriate treatments. Assumptions concerning the usefulness of merely translating and using a psychological test should be actively challenged, as this approach is not only potentially dangerous to consumers, but also inconsistent with scientist–practitioner training in professional psychology. Methodologies that promote examination of test construction statistics for the translated instrument are essential, along with specialized methods described in this chapter that examine the influence of linguistic and cultural factors on test performance. Psychologists should become aware of myths associated with cross-cultural testing, and develop competencies that address and correct them (Cuéllar, 1998). Tests provide samples of targeted behavior that are influenced by numerous variables such as language, educational level, cultural affiliation, and socioeconomic status (Ardila, Roselli, & Puente, 1993). Tests are but one source of data that must be added to other routinely collected information, such as developmental history, medical status, and current medications. Culturally competent assessment practices therefore require a thorough exploration of background information about the individual being tested to promote accurate interpretation of test scores (Anastasi, 1988).

REFERENCES

American Psychiatric Association (1994). *Diagnostic and statistical manual of mental disorders* (4th ed.). Washington, DC: Author.
American Psychological Association (1991). *Guidelines for providers of psychological services to ethnic, linguistic, and culturally diverse populations.* Washington, DC: Author.
Aday, L. A., Chiu, G. Y., & Anderson, R. (1980). Methodological issues in health care surveys of the Spanish heritage population. *American Journal of Public Health, 70,* 367.
Anastasi, A. (1988). *Psychological Testing.* New York: Macmillan.
Ardila, A., Roselli, M., & Puente, A. E. (1993). *Neuropsychological evaluation of the Spanish speaker.* New York: Plenum Press.
Arnold, B. R., Cuéllar, I., & Guzmán, N. (1998). Statistical and clinical evaluation of the Mattis Dementia Rating Scale-Spanish Adaptation: An initial investigation. *Journal of Gerontology Psychological Sciences, 53B* (6), 364–369.
Arnold, B. R., Montgomery, G. T., Castañeda, I., & Longoria, R. (1994). Acculturation and performance of Hispanics on selected Halstead-Reitan Neuropsychological Tests. *Assessment, 1* (3), 239–248.
Berry, J. W. (1979). Research in multicultural societies: Implications of cross-cultural methods. *Journal of Cross-Cultural Psychology, 10,* 415–434.
Berry, J. W. (1980). Introduction to methodology. In H. C. Triandis & J. W. Berry (Eds.), *Handbook of cross-cultural psychology* (Vol. 1, pp. 1–28). Boston: Allyn and Bacon.
Bontempo, R. (1993). Translation fidelity of psychological scales: An item response theory analysis of an individualism-collectivism scale. *Journal of Cross-Cultural Psychology, 24* (2), 149–166.

Brislin, R. W. (1970). Back translation for cross-cultural research. *Journal of Cross-Cultural Psychology, 1,* 185–216.

Brislin, R. W. (1980). Translation and content analysis of oral and written material. In H. C. Triandis & J. W. Berry (Eds.), *Handbook of cross-cultural psychology* (Vol. 2, pp. 389–444). Boston: Allyn and Bacon.

Brislin, R. W. (1986). The wording and translation of research instruments. In W. J. Lonner & J. W. Berry (Eds.), *Field methods in cross-cultural research* (pp. 137–164). Newbury Park, CA: Sage.

Brislin, R. W., Lonner, W. J., & Thorndike, R. M. (1973). *Cross-cultural research methods.* New York: John Wiley.

Budgell, G. R., Raju, N. S., & Quartetti, D. A. (1995). Analysis of differential item functioning in translated assessment instruments. *Applied Psychological Measurements, 19* (4), 309–321.

Butcher, J. N., Lim, J., & Nezami, E. (1998). Objective study of abnormal personality in cross-cultural settings. *Journal of Cross-Cultural Psychology, 29* (1), 189–211.

Campbell, J. P. (1970). The way it should be done. *Contemporary Psychology, 15,* 540–542.

Cuéllar, I. (1998). Cross-cultural clinical psychological assessment of Hispanic Americans. *Journal of Psychological Assessment, 70* (1), 71–86.

Cuéllar, I. (in press). Acculturation: A moderator of personality and psychological assessment. In R. H. Dana (Ed.), *Handbook of cross-cultural/multicultural personality assessment.* New Jersey: Lawrence Erlbaum Associates, Inc., Publisher.

Cuéllar, I., Arnold, B. R., & Maldonado, R. (1995). Acculturation rating scale for Mexican Americans-II: A revision of the original ARSMA Scale. *Hispanic Journal of Behavioral Sciences, 17* (3), 275–304.

Dana, R. H. (1993). *Multicultural assessment perspectives for professional psychology.* Boston: Allyn and Bacon.

Drasgow, F. (1984). Scrutinizing psychological tests: Measurement eqivalence and equivalent relations with external variables are the central issues. *Psychological Bulletin, 95,* 134–135.

Drasgow, F., & Hulin, C. L. (1987). Cross-cultural measurement. *Revista Interamericana de Psicología/Interamerican Journal of Psychology, 21* (1), 1–24.

Ellis, B. B. (1989). Differential item functioning: Implications for test translations. *Journal of Applied Psychology, 74* (6), 912–921.

Fouad, N. A., Cudeck, R., & Hansen, J. C. (1984). Convergent validity of the Spanish and English forms of the Strong-Campbell Interest Inventory for Bilingual Hispanic High School Students. *Journal of Counseling Psychology, 31* (7), 339–348.

Geisinger, K. F. (1992). Psychological testing Inventory for Bilingual Hispanic High School Students. *Journal of Counseling Psychology for Hispanics.* Washington, DC: American Psychological Association.

Gilmer, J. S., Tripp-Reimar, T., Buckwalter, K. C., Andrews, P. H., Morris, W. W., Rios, H., Lindenerona, C., & Evers, G. (1995). Technical notes: Translation and validation issues for a multidimensional elderly self-assessment instrument. *Western Journal of Nursing Research, 17* (2), 220–226.

Guffey, A. S. (1997). *Acculturation and response style of Mexican Americans on the Million Index of Personality Styles.* Unpublished master's thesis, University of Texas-Pan American, Edinburg.

Hall, K. S., Hendrie, H. C., Brittain, H. M., Norton, J. A., Rodgers, D. D., & Prince, C. S., et al. (1993). The development of a dementia screening interview in two distinct languages. *International Journal of Methods in Psychiatric Research, 3,* 1–28.

Hambleton, R. K. (1993). Translating achievement tests for use in cross-national studies. *European Journal of Psychological Assessment, 9,* 57–68.

Hambleton, R. K. (1994). Guidelines for adapting educational and psychological tests: A progress report. *European Journal of Psychological Assessment, 10,* 229–244.

Hayes, R. P., & Baker, D. W. (1998). Brief report: Methodological problems in comparing English-speaking and Spanish-speaking patients' satisfaction with interpersonal aspects of care. *Medical Care, 36* (2), 230–236.

Helms, J. E. (1992). Why is there no study in cultural equivalence in standardized cognitive ability testing? *American Psychologist, 47* (9), 1083–1101.

Hui, C. H., & Triandis, H. C. (1989). Effects of culture and response format on extreme response style. *Journal of Cross-Cultural Psychology, 20,* 296–309.

Hulin, C. L. (1987). A psychometric theory of evaluations of items and scale translations: Fidelity across languages. *Journal of Cross-Cultural Psychology, 18* (2), 115–142.

Hulin, C. L., Drasgow, F., & Komocar, J. (1982). Applications of item response theory to analysis of attitude scale translations. *Journal of Applied Psychology, 67* (6), 818–825.

Maj, M., Janssen, R., Satz, P., Zaudig, M., Starace, F., Luabeya, M. K., Ndetei, D., Riedel, R., Shulte, G., & Sartorius, N. (1991). The World Health Organization's cross-cultural study on neuropsychiatric aspects of infection with the Human Immunodeficiency Virus I (HIV-I): Preparation and pilot base. *British Journal of Psychiatry, 159,* 351–356.

Manuel-Dupont, S., Ardila, A., Roselli, M., & Puente, A. E. (1992). Bilingualism. In A. E. Puente & R. J. McCaffrey (Eds.), *Handbook of neuropsychological assessment: A biopsychosocial perspective* pp. 193–210). New York: Plenum Press.

Marin, G., Gamba, R. J., & Marin, B. V. (1992). Extreme response style and acquiescence among Hispanics: The role of acculturation and education. *Journal of Cross-Cultural Psychology, 23* (4), 498–509.

Marsella, A. J., & Kameoka, V. A. (1989). Ethnocultural issues in the assessment of psychopathology. In S. Wetzler (Ed.), *Measuring mental illness: Psychometric assessment for clinicians.* Washington, DC: American Psychiatric Press.

Miller, G. A., & Beebe-Center, J. (1956). Some psychological methods for evaluating the quality of translation. *Mechanical Translation, 3,* 73–80.

Montgomery, G. T., & Orozco, S. (1985). Mexican Americans' performance on the MMPI as a function of level of acculturation. *Journal of Clinical Psychology, 41*(2), 203–212.

Sinaiko, H. W., & Brislin, R. W. (1973). Evaluating language translations: Experiments on three assessment methods. *Journal of Applied Psychology, 57* (3), 328–334.

Sbordone, R. J. (1996). Ecological validity: Some critical issues for the neuropsychologist. In R. J. Sbordone & C. J. Long (Eds.), *Ecological validity of neuropsychological testing,* (pp. 15–41). Delray Beach, FL. St. Lucie Press.

Van de Vijver, F., & Hambleton, R. K. (1996). Translating tests: Some practical guidelines. *European Psychologist, 1* (2), 89–99.

Van de Vijver, F., & Leung, K. (1997). Methods and data analysis of comparative research. In J. W. Berry, Y. H. Poortinga, & J. Pandey (Eds.), *Handbook of cross-cultural psychology: Vol. 1, Theory and method* (2nd ed., pp. 257–300). Boston: Allyn and Bacon.

Werner, O., & Campbell, D. T. (1970). Translating, working through interpreters, and the problem of decentering. In R. Naroll & R. Cohen (Eds.), *A handbook of cultural anthropology* (pp. 398–419). New York: American Museum of Natural History.

PART **III**

Assessment and Treatment

Culture-Bound Syndromes, Cultural Variations, and Psychopathology

FREDDY A. PANIAGUA

Department of Psychiatry and Behavioral Sciences
University of Texas Medical Branch
Galveston, Texas

Inaccuracies in the assessment and diagnosis of psychopathological conditions with culturally diverse groups (i.e., overdiagnosis, underdiagnosis, and misdiagnosis) might result from a lack of understanding of the presence of cultural variants leading to symptoms resembling psychopathology. These variables have generally been described in the case of culture-specific disorders known as "culture-bound syndromes" (Castillo, 1997; Dana, 1993; Dana, 1995; Ivey, Ivey, & Simek-Morgan, 1996; Paniagua, 1998; Pedersen, 1997; Pedersen, Draguns, Lonner, & Timble, 1996; Ponterotto, Casas, Suzuki, & Alexander, 1995; Smart & Smart, 1997). Smart and Smart (1997), for example, pointed out that the glossary (Appendix I) of culture-bound syndromes included in the *Diagnostic and Statistical Manual of Mental Disorders* (*DSM-IV*; American Psychiatric Association, 1994) "are description of 25 forms of aberrant behavior that are referred to as locality-specific troubling experiences that are limited to certain societies or cultural areas" (p. 394). These "locality-specific aberrant experiences," have been given specific names in the cross-cultural literature. Table I shows examples of culture-bound syndromes often-considered specific to a

TABLE I   Summary of Cultural-Bound Syndromes

Name	Group	Description
Ataques de nervios	Hispanics	Out-of-consciousness state resulting from evil spirits. Symptoms include attacks of crying, trembling, uncontrollable shouting, physical or verbal aggression, and intense heat in the chest moving to the head. These *ataques* are often associated with stressful events (e.g., death of a loved one, divorce or separation, or witnessing an accident including a family member).
Amok, Mal de pelea	Malaysia, Laos, Philippines, Polynesia, Papua New Guinea, Puerto Rico	A dissociative disorder involving outburst of violent and aggression or homicidal behavior at people and objects. A minor insult would precipitate this condition. Amnesia, exhaustion, and persecutory ideas are often associated with this syndrome.
Brain fag	African Americans	Problems with concentration and thinking among high school and university students experiencing the challenges of schooling. Symptoms include head and neck pain, blurring of vision, burning, and heat resembling Somatoform, Depressive, and Anxiety Disorders.
Boufée délirante	Haitians	Sudden outburst of aggression, agitation associated with confusion, psychomotor excitement, and symptoms resembling Brief Psychotic Disorder (including visual and auditory hallucinations, paranoid ideation)
Colera	Hispanics	Anger and rage disturbing body balances leading to headache, screaming, stomach pain, loss of consciousness, and fatigue.
Dhat	India, China, Sri Lanka	Extreme anxiety associated with a sense of weakness, exhaustion, and the discharge of semen
Falling-out	African Americans	Seizurelike symptoms resulting from traumatic events such as robberies.
Ghost sickness	American Indians	Weakness, dizziness, fainting, anxiety, hallucinations, confusion, and loss of appetite resulting from the action of witches and evil forces.
Hwa-byung	Asians	Pain in the upper abdomen, fear of death, tiredness resulting from the imbalance between reality and anger

(continues)

TABLE I *(continued)*

Name	Group	Description
Koro	Asians	A man's desire to grasp his penis (in a woman, the vulva and nipples) resulting from the fear that it will retract into his body and cause death.
Latah	Asians	A sudden fright resulting in imitative behaviors that appears beyond control including imitation of movements and speech; the individual often follows commands to do things outside his or her wish (e.g., verbal repetition of obscenities)
Mal de ojo	Hispanics	Medical problems such as vomiting, fever, diarrhea, and mental problems (e.g., anxiety, depression) could result from the *mal de ojo* (evil eye) the individual experienced from another person. This condition is common among infants and children; adults might also experience similar symptoms resulting from this *mal de ojo.*
Ode-ori	Nigeria	Sensations of parasites crawling in the head, feelings of heat in the head, paranoid fears of malevolent attacks by evil spirits.
Pibloktog	Arctic, Subarctic Eskimos	Excitement, coma, and convulsive seizures resembling an abrupt dissociative episode, often associated with amnesia, withdrawal, irritability, and irrational behaviors such as breaking furniture, eating feces, and verbalization of obscenities.
Kyofusho	Asians	Guilt about embarrassing others, timidity resulting from the feeling that the appearance, odor, and facial expressions are offensive to other people.
Mal puesto, hex, root work, voodoo death	African Americans, Hispanics	Unnatural diseases and death resulting from the power of people who use evil spirits
Susto, espanto, miedo, pasmo	Hispanics	Tiredness and weakness resulting from frightening and startling experiences
Wacinko	American Indians	Feelings of anger, withdrawal, mutism, suicide from reaction to disappointment and interpersonal problems
Wind/cold illness	Hispanics, Asians	A fear of the cold and the wind; feeling weakness and susceptibility to illness resulting from the belief that natural and supernatural elements are not balanced

given cultural context or society (Castillo, 1997; Griffith & Baker, 1993; Levine & Gaw, 1995; Price, 1993; Rubel, O'Nell, & Collado-Ardon, 1984; Simons & Hughes, 1993; Westermeyer, 1985).

The same cross-cultural literature, however, suggests that symptoms associated with a given mental disorder may be related to a particular cultural context but the disorder is not considered an example of "culture-bound syndromes" *per se* (e.g., Table I). In this case, clinicians are advised to consider specific cultural variants, which might explain symptoms suggesting the disorder under consideration. Although the *DSM-IV* did not explicitly emphasize this point, a review of the way the *DSM-IV* discusses cultural variants across several disorders suggests a distinction between culture-bound syndromes (e.g., Table I) and the cultural variables contributing to symptoms in a given *DSM-IV* disorder. For example, as noted by Lewis-Fernandez and Kleinman (1995) the Task Force on Culture and *DSM-IV* recommended the inclusion of Dissociative Identity Disorder and Anorexia Nervosa as examples of "culture-bound syndromes" in the Glossary (Appendix I). Apparently, this recommendation was not implemented in the *DSM-IV* because these disorders were not examples of "locality-specific patterns of aberrant behavior and troubling" (*DSM-IV,* 1994, p. 844) resembling culture-bound syndromes included in the Glossary (Appendix I). In the *DSM-IV,* however, cultural variations were considered as potential factors contributing to Dissociative Identity Disorder and Anorexia Nervosa.

Below are examples of disorders (in alphabetical order) which were not specifically included in the *DSM-IV* as examples of "culture-bound syndromes" (Table I), but in which culture-specific contexts were considered to assist clinicians with the application of "*DSM-IV* criteria in a multicultural environment" (*DSM-IV,* 1994, p. 843). It should be noted that in the case of several disorders, the *DSM-IV* suggests that the particular disorder may *resemble* one of the culture-bound syndromes in Appendix I. The term "resemble," however, suggests that in the *DSM-IV* that disorder is not a culture-bound syndrome *per se*. For example, "*boufée délirante*" was included as an example of culture-bound syndromes in Appendix I, and, according to the *DSM-IV,* episodes associated with this culture-bound syndrome "may resemble an episode of Brief Psychotic Disorder" (1994, p. 845). When applicable, this point is also noted in this chapter.

I. ADJUSTMENT DISORDERS

In the case of all subtypes of Adjustment Disorders, the person's cultural setting should be considered to determine whether the individual's response to the stressor is either inappropriate or in excess of what would be expected in his or her culture. Variability exists across cultures with respect to the nature, meaning, and experience of the stressor, and the evaluation of the response to the stressor (*DSM-IV,* 1994, p. 625).

II. ANXIETY DISORDERS

A. PANIC DISORDER

Symptoms resembling panic attacks are common in cultures where members have strong beliefs in witchcraft or evil spirit attacks (Castillo, 1997; Kirmayer, Young, & Hayton, 1995). For example, trembling or shaking, chest pain, fear of dying, palpitations, and other symptoms for Panic Disorder are generally reported by Hispanics with intensive fears of malign magic, malevolent attacks by witchcraft, or evil spirit attacks. These symptoms resemble the culture-bound syndrome named "*ataques de nervios*" among Hispanics (*DSM-IV,* 1994; Kirmayer et al., 1995; see Table I). The *DSM-IV* (1994), however, pointed out that the "association of most ataques with a precipitating event and the frequent absence of the hallmark symptoms of acute fear or apprehensions distinguish [these ataques] from Panic Disorder" (p. 845). Another culture-bound syndrome resembling Panic Disorder is "*Ode-ori*" (Table I), which is often reported among the Nigerian culture and is characterized by sensations of parasites crawling in the head and feelings of heat in the head. Kimayer et al. (1995) recommended that these culture-specific symptoms should not be considered as "indicative of psychopathology" (p. 509). Furthermore, the *DSM-IV* pointed out that the participation of women in public life is sometimes restricted in some ethnic and cultural groups (e.g., Arabic countries), and this situation should be separated from Agoraphobia (*DSM-IV,* 1994, p. 399).

B. SPECIFIC PHOBIA

Although this disorder has been reported across different cultures, the *DSM-IV* (1994) advises clinicians to diagnosis a client with this disorder "only if the fear is excessive in the context of that culture and causes significant impairment or distress" (p. 407). For example, many members of the Hispanic community often share fear of spirits, ghosts, and witches. In this case, if anxiety responses resulting from that fear do not exceed the expected level in that community and the individual is able to control his or her emotions, the diagnosis should not be applied.

C. SOCIAL PHOBIA

In some cultures, social demands may lead to symptoms of Social Phobia. For example, in Japan and Korea an individual may develop persistent and excessive fears of giving offense to others in social situations, instead of being embarrassed (*DSM-IV,* 1994, p. 413). These fears may be expressed in terms of extreme anxiety resulting from the belief that one's body odor, facial expression, or eye contact will be offensive to others. In Table I, these symptoms resemble *taijin kyofusho* (*DSM-IV*, 1994, p. 849).

D. Obsessive-Compulsive Disorder

Behaviors that are culturally prescribed should be differentiated from Obsessive-Compulsive Disorder (OCD), unless these culturally sanctioned behaviors exceed cultural norms, occur at times and places judged inappropriate by other members of the same culture, and interfere with social role functioning (*DSM-IV*, 1994, p. 420). Religious rituals such as repetitive washing, checking and ordering objects, praying, and repetition of words or phrases silently are expected in many cultures (Castillo, 1997; Kirmayer et al., 1995). For example, compulsive praying (e.g., praying five times per day) associated with obsessive rules (e.g., repetition of some words many times during pray) are expected among strict Egyptian Moslems (Bernstein, 1997; Castillo, 1997). These rituals would be considered pathological by clinicians unfamiliar with this culture. Examples of other cultures in which similar OCD behaviors have been observed include Israel, India, Taiwan, and Latin American countries (e.g., Puerto Rico, Dominican Republic, Cuba, Colombia, Venezuela, etc.).

E. Posttraumatic Stress Disorder and Acute Stress Disorder

Immigrants from countries with a high frequency of social unrest, wars, and civil conflicts may show high rates of Posttraumatic Stress Disorder (PTSD) (Boehnlein & Kinzie, 1995). These immigrants may be particularly reluctant to divulge experience of torture and trauma because of their political immigrant status (*DSM-IV*, 1994, p. 426). In the specific case of practitioners providing mental health services to American Indians and Alaska Natives, McNeil, Kee, and Zvolensky (1999) suggested an assessment of historical events leading to cultural abuses and discrimination against these groups (see Paniagua, 1998, pp. 77–81) and how these historical (aversive) events "may lead to intergenerational Posttraumatic Stress Disorder [among members of these groups]" (McNeil et al., 1999, p. 62). In the case of Acute Stress Disorder, the severity of this disorder may be determined by cultural differences in the implications of loss. Coping behaviors may also be culturally determined. For example, many clients from Latin American countries are expected to show symptoms resembling Acute Stress Disorder when they are exposed to stressful events associated with the family (e.g., the death of a close relative, separation and divorce, etc.). Symptoms involving TSD and Acute Stress Disorder may resemble "*ataques de nervios*" and "*susto*" in Table I (Castillo, 1997; *DSM-IV*, 1994, p. 849.

F. GENERALIZED ANXIETY DISORDER

Considerable cultural variations exist in the expression of anxiety. In some cultures, anxiety is expressed predominantly through somatic symptoms, in others through cognitive symptoms. The cultural context should be considered during the evaluation of worries about certain situations as excessive (1994, pp. 433–434). This *DSM-IV* disorder may resemble the culture-bound syndrome termed "*Ode-ori*" (Table I), which has been reported in Nigeria and includes excessive anxiety resulting from the sensation of insects crawling through the body (Castillo, 1997).

III. ATTENTION-DEFICIT AND DISRUPTIVE DISORDERS

A. ATTENTION-DEFICIT–HYPERACTIVITY DISORDER

Although this disorder is known to occur in various cultures (*DSM-IV*, 1994, p. 81), variations in the prevalence of the disorder have been reported. These variations have been explained in terms of two hypotheses (Barkley, 1990). The first hypothesis states that the relatively high rate of Attention-Deficit–Hyperactivity Disorder (ADHD) in developing countries (e.g., the United States) in comparison with underdeveloping countries (e.g., Caribbean, Central American, and South American countries) is a result of increase in the "cultural tempo" in developing countries, which leads to increases in environmental stimulation and significant increases in impulsivity, inattention, and overactivity among individuals exposed to that "cultural tempo." The second hypothesis states that the presence of symptoms suggesting ADHD is a function of consistent versus inconsistent expectations in the "demands made and standards set for child behavior and development" (Barkley, 1990, p. 16). Consistent cultures not only provide clear and consistent expectations and consequences for behaviors that follow expected societal norms, but they also minimize individual differences among children. These two characteristics in consistent cultures are said to result in fewer children with a diagnosis of ADHD. By contrast, inconsistent cultures would result in more children with diagnosis of ADHD because they emphasize individual differences and provide unclear expectations and consequences to children regarding behaviors, which conform to the expected norms.

B. Conduct Disorder

This disorder might be misapplied to individuals residing in settings (e.g., threatening, high-crime, impoverished areas) where undesirable behaviors could be considered as protective. Immigrant youth from countries with a history of aggressive behaviors (necessary for their survival in such countries) resulting from a long history of wars would not warrant the diagnosis of Conduct Disorder. If the behavior were the result of the reaction to the immediate social context, it would not be diagnosed as Conduct Disorder (*DSM-IV*, 1994, p. 88).

IV. DELUSIONAL DISORDERS

The individual's cultural and religious background should be considered in determining the possible presence of Delusional Disorders. The content of delusions varies across cltures (*DSM-IV*, 1994, p. 298). Clinicians should particularly consider the impact of cultural variants in the case of the Jealous Type delusion. For example, a strong belief in the *machismo* cultural variant might suggest this type of delusion in a Hispanic male who feels uneasy with the way his wife begins to show changes in the way she dresses after a number of years residing in the United States. Unfamiliarity with that variant would lead to the conclusion that the case is an example of delusional disorder (Jealous Type), rather than an example of the impact of cultural variables on the case under consideration (e.g., acculturation of the wife to new styles of dressing in this country and the husband's refusal to accept the assimilation of styles by his wife).

V. DISSOCIATIVE DISORDERS

A. Dissociative Identity Disorder

This disorder may be a culture-specific syndrome because it occurs "primarily in persons holding a modern set of cultural schemas" (Castillo, 1997, p. 275). Similarly, the *DSM-IV* (1994) recommended that in the United States this disorder might be an example of culture-specific syndromes because of the "recent relatively high rates of the disorder reported [in this country]" (p. 485).

B. DISSOCIATIVE FUGUE

The sudden and unexpected travel away from home and work and the individual's inability to recall past events associated with this travel is a condition commonly reported among people from the Arctic, Subarctic Skimo, the Miskito Indians of Honduras and Nicaragua, and the Navajo Indians (Castillo, 1997; *DSM-IV,* 1994, p. 842). Some culture-bound syndromes named in Table I may have symptoms resembling this disorder. For example, *pibloktoq* is an episode involving an uncontrollable desire to leave one's home, tear off one's clothes, submit oneself to the Arctic winter, excitement, convulsive seizures, and coma, which is observed primarily in Alaska, the Canadian Arctic, and Greenland (Berry, Poortinga, Segall, & Dasen, 1992; *DSM-IV,* 1994, p. 482).

C. DEPERSONALIZATION DISORDER

In many religions and cultures, induced experiences of depersonalization have been reported. These experiences should not be confused with Depersonalization Disorder (*DSM-IV,* 1994, p. 488).

VI. EATING DISORDERS

Eating disorders are generally more prevalent in industrialized countries, including, for example, the United States, Canada, and Japan. In the case of Anorexia Nervosa, abundance of food and the linkage of attractiveness with being thin may explain high prevalence rates of this disorder in such countries (Castillo, 1997; *DSM-IV,* 1994, pp. 542–543).

VII. MENTAL RETARDATION AND LEARNING DISORDERS

The individual's ethnic or cultural background should be taken into consideration during intellectual testing procedures. Tests in which the person's relevant characteristics are represented in the standardization sample of the test should be considered. Similarly, examiners should be familiar with aspects of the individual ethnic or cultural background (*DSM-IV,* 1994, p. 44). For example, the Wechsler Intelligence Scales are recommended to assess IQ levels and learning problems in children and adults. As noted by Golden (1990), however, these scales are "heavily influenced by cultural and language concepts that reflect the life of the average American, but not that of most [multicultural] groups" (p. 46). This observation is particularly true in the case of the performance of members of these groups on the Information, Comprehension, Vocabulary, Picture Completion, and Picture Arrangement subtests, which are associated with alternate cultural background. For example, a Hispanic client may receive a very low score on the Information subtest (e.g., below 5, where a mean is 10 and the standard deviation is 3) not because the client is not intelligent but because he or she lacks information regarding the total population, height of women, number of senators, and other "general knowledge" expected from the average American in the United States. A similar point could be made in the interpretation of the scores with the Comprehension (the client may not be able to understand basic U.S. customs and situation), Vocabulary (the client cannot define a word using Standard American English), Picture Completion (the client cannot complete the picture because he or she is not familiar with the objects picture in the American culture), and Picture Arrangement subtests (the client cannot arrange the pictures to tell a logical and coherent story, because the social sequence required on the test is not part of the client's cultural background).

VIII. MOOD DISORDERS

A. MAJOR DEPRESSIVE DISORDER

In some cultures, symptoms of depression are not generally recognized as a case for mental disorders. In addition, symptoms of depression might be presented in somatic terms rather than sadness or guilt (Castillo, 1997). For example, among Latin American and Mediterranean cultures depressive experiences might be manifested in terms of complaints of "nerves" and headaches; Asians may show similar experiences in terms of weakness, tiredness, or "imbalance," whereas among people from the Middle East and American Indian tribes these experiences might be shown in terms of difficulties with the "heart" or being "Heartbroken," respectively (see *DSM-IV,* 1994, pp. 324–325). The severity of the depression might also be evaluated differently across cultures (e.g., sadness may lead to less concern than irritability in some cultures). Hallucinations and delusions, which are sometimes part of Major Depressive Disorder, should be differentiated from cultural hallucinations and delusions (e.g., fear of being hexed, feeling of being visited by those who have died). In Table I, the culture-bound syndromes "brain fag" and "*susto*" may resemble symptoms suggesting Major Depressive Disorder (*DSM-IV,* 1994, p. 486, p. 849).

B. Bipolar I and II, Dysthymic, and Cyclothymic Disorders

Differential incidence of Bipolar Disorder I associated with race or ethnicity has not been reported (*DSM-IV,* 1994, p. 352). Some evidence exists suggesting that clinicians may overdiagnose Schizophrenia rather than Bipolar Disorder I in some ethnic groups (*DSM-IV,* 1994, pp. 352–353). The *DSM-IV* (1994) did not provide a description of cultural variants for Bipolar II, Dysthymic, and Cyclothymic Disorders. A major characteristic of Bipolar II and Cyclothymic Disorders is the presence of hypomanic symptoms. As noted by Castillo (1997), these symptoms are culturally accepted in some cultural contexts. For example, members of the Hindu culture generally engaged in "meditative trances to achieve a permanent hypomanic state [during their religious practices]" (Castillo, 1997, p. 219). In the case of Dysthymic Disorder, being depressed most of the time over at least two years could be the result of specific cultural variables such as racial discrimination and severe poverty (Castillo, 1997; Weiss, 1995).

IX. PERSONALITY DISORDERS

A. Paranoid Personality Disorder

Behaviors influenced by sociocultural contexts or specific life circumstances may be erroneously labeled paranoid. For example, immigrants, political and economic refugees, and members of minority groups may show guarded or defensive behaviors because of either unfamiliarity with the language, rules and regulations in the United States, or because of the perceived neglect or indifference of the majority society (*DSM-IV,* 1994, p. 636). Castillo (1997) provided further illustration of this disorder in cultural terms in the case of men in Swat Pukhtun society (tribal people living in the mountains of northern Pakistan). All males in this society own guns and "they trust no one and are constantly vigilant in protecting their honor and their personal interests. Pukhtun men distrust the sexual loyalty of all women to the extent of keeping them confined in their homes" (Castillo, 1997, p. 99). As noted by Castillo (1997), these behavioral patterns among Pukhtun men are examples of normative personality development in this society, and would be considered a maladaptive behavior "not to be constantly on guard and suspicious of everyone [in this society]" (p. 99). For this reason, the diagnosis of Paranoid Personality Disorder is not recommended in the case of the Swat Pukhtun.

B. Schizoid and Schizotypal Personality Disorders

Defensive behaviors, detachment from social activities, and restricted range of emotions displayed by individuals from different cultural backgrounds may be erroneously considered as *schizoid*. For example, individuals who have moved from rural to metropolitan areas may show "emotional freezing" as manifested by solitary activities and constricted affect. Immigrants may also be mistakenly perceived as cold, hostile, and indifferent (*DSM-IV,* 1994, p. 639). In his cross-cultural interpretation of personality disorders in Indians, Castillo (1997) reported that "to be detached and unmoved by good or bad events is considered to be saintly in the Hindu culture... This type of personality development would not be considered pathological in Hindu society. Schizoid personality disorder... would be an inappropriate diagnosis [in this society]" (p. 100). Cognitive and perceptual distortions may be associated with religious beliefs and rituals, which may appear to be *schizotypal* to clinicians uninformed about these cultural variations (*DSM-IV,* p. 643). Examples of these distortions include voodoo ceremonies, speaking in tongues, belief in life beyond death, mind reading, evil eye, and magical beliefs associated with health and illness (Campinha-Bacote, 1992).

C. Antisocial Personality Disorder

Clinicians should consider the social and economic context in which the behaviors occur. Many behaviors associated with this disorder appear to be associated with low socioeconomic status, urban settings, and social contexts in which antisocial behavior functions as a protective survival strategy (*DSM-IV,* 1994, p. 647).

D. Borderline, Histrionic, and Narcissistic Personality Disorders

In the case of Borderline Personality Disorder, the *DSM-IV* suggests that this disorder might not represent a culture-specific disorder because behaviors associated with it have been seen in many cultures around the world (*DSM-IV,* 1994, p. 652). In the case of the second disorder (Histrionic), norms for personal appearance, emotional expressiveness, and interpersonal behavior vary widely across cultures. Symptoms associated with this disorder (e.g., emotionality, seductiveness, impressionability) may be culturally accepted by the community, and it is important to determine whether these symptoms cause clinically significant impairment or distress to the individual in comparison to what is culturally expected. Among Hispanics, this disorder might be confused with the cultural phenomenon of *machismo* in which a Hispanic male would be sexually seductive, feel uncomfortable if he is not the center of attention, and show exaggerated expression of emotions (Castillo, 1997; *DSM-IV*, 1994, p. 656). The *DSM-IV* did not provide descriptions of cultural variables in the case of Narcissistic Personality Disorder. Several symptoms in this disorder, however, might suggest "machismo" in cultures that are hierarchical. For example, symptoms resembling Narcissistic Personality Disorder are common in the Swat Pukhtun culture (Castillo, 1997). These symptoms might also be seen among "macho" Hispanic males, including the need for excessive admiration and the belief that he has unlimited power toward others (particularly females).

E. Avoidant and Dependent Personality Disorders

Variations exist in the degree to which different cultures and ethnic groups regard avoidance as appropriate. Symptoms of this disorder may also result from acculturation problems associated with immigration (*DSM-IV*, 1994, p. 663). The appropriateness of *dependent* behaviors varies across sociocultural groups. Behaviors associated with this disorder (e.g., passivity, difficulty in making everyday decisions) would be considered characteristic of this disorder only when they are clearly in excess of the individual's cultural norms or reflect unrealistic concerns. In addition, some cultures may differentially foster and encourage dependent behaviors in females (Paniagua, 1998). For example, in the Hispanic culture *marianismo* (the opposite of *machismo*) is a cultural value in which women are expected to be submissive, obedient, dependent, timid, docile, and gentle in the presence of Hispanic males, particularly the husband (Paniagua, 1998). A Hispanic female with marianismo characteristics in therapy would most likely display a great deal of "dependent personality" difficulties because she probably would behave in terms of the expected marianismo in the Hispanic community.

F. Obsessive-Compulsive Personality Disorder

Habits, customs, or interpersonal styles culturally sanctioned by the individual's reference groups should not be included when making this diagnosis. The individual may place heavy emphasis on work and productivity because these behaviors are reinforced by the individual's reference group (DSM-IV, 1994, p. 671; Bernstein, 1997).

X. PICA AND SELECTIVE MUTISM

Eating seemingly nonnutritive substances (e.g., paper, dirt, etc.) is considered of value in some cultures (DSM-IV, 1994, p. 95). In the case of selective mutism, immigrant children might refuse to talk to strangers in a new environment because they are unfamiliar or uncomfortable with the new language, the diagnosis of Selective Mutism should not be used (DSM-IV, 1994, p. 114).

XI. SCHIZOPHRENIA AND OTHER PSYCHOTIC DISORDERS

Delusional ideas (e.g., witchcraft) and auditory hallucinations (e.g., seeing the Virgin Mary or hearing God's voice) may be abnormal in one culture and normal in other cultures (Castillo, 1997). For example, in the Nigerian culture, paranoid fears of evil attacks by spirits are part of the local beliefs involving fears of malevolent attacks by evil spirits (Kirmayer et al., 1995). These fears are examples of the culture-bound syndrome named "Ode-ori" in Table I. As noted by Kirmayer et al. (1995), these paranoid fears "might be misdiagnosed as symptoms of psychosis by the uninformed clinician" (p. 509). Variability in language, style of emotional expressions, body language, and eye contact across cultures should be considered when assessing symptoms of Schizophrenia. In the case of Brief Psychotic Disorder, it should be distinguished from culturally sanctioned response patterns. For example, in certain religious ceremonies a person may report hearing voices, which are not considered as abnormal by members of that religion and generally do not persist beyond the termination of such ceremonies (DSM-IV, 1994, p. 303). Temporal visual and auditory hallucinations reported by a client in therapy may also result from the recent death of a loved one. As noted earlier, Brief Psychotic Disorder episodes may resemble the culture-bound syndrome "bouffée délirante" (DSM-IV, 1994, p. 845; see Table I).

XII. SEXUAL DYSFUNCTIONS AND PARAPHILIAS

In the case of Sexual Dysfunctions, the ethnic and religious background of the individual, as well as whether the client's culture emphasizes male dominance and control on female sexuality versus those that reward the opposite view should be considered during the assessment of Sexual Dysfunctions. These cultural variations may affect sexual desire, expectations, and attitudes about performance. In some societies, a female sexual desire is not considered very relevant particularly when fertility is the primary concern (Castillo, 1997; *DSM-IV*, 1994, p. 495). In the case of the paraphilias, the *DSM-IV* (1994, p. 524) only suggests that these disorders might be appropriate in one culture and, at the same time, they may be seen as inappropriate in other cultures; this makes the diagnosis of paraphilias across cultures and religions a complicated task for the clinician.

XIII. SLEEP DISORDERS

A. NIGHTMARES DISORDER

The importance assigned to nightmares may vary with cultural background. In some cultures, nightmares are associated with spiritual or supernatural phenomena; in other cultures, nightmares may be viewed as indicators of mental or physical disturbances (*DSM-IV*, 1994, p. 581).

B. SLEEP TERROR AND SLEEPWALKING DISORDERS

These disorders may differ across cultures; but clear evidence regarding culturally related differences in the presentation of these disorders is lacking (*DSM-IV*, 1994, pp. 584–585 and p. 589).

C. SLEEP DISORDERS RELATED TO ANOTHER MENTAL DISORDER

Sleep complaints may be viewed as less stigmatizing in some cultures than mental disorders. For this reason, individuals from some cultures (e.g., Southeast Asia) may be more likely to show complaints of insomnia or hypersomnia rather than complaints involving symptoms of mental disorders such as depression and anxiety (*DSM-IV*, 1994, p. 594).

XIV. SOMATOFORM DISORDERS

A. SOMATIZATION DISORDER

The frequency and type of somatic symptoms may vary across culture. For example, people from Africa and South Asia tend to show more symptoms of burning hands and feet as well as nondelusional experiences of worms in the head or ants crawling under the skin in comparison to individuals from North America. In cultures in which semen loss is a great concern for their people, symptoms associated with male reproductive function tends to be more prevalent (*DSM-IV,* 1994, p. 447). In India, Sri Lanka, and China, severe anxiety associated with that concern is known as *dhat* (see Table I). Symptoms resembling Somatization Disorder have also been reported in the case of the culture-bound syndromes *Susto* and *Ataques de Nervios* (Table I; *DSM-IV,* 1994, p. 845; Escobar, 1995).

B. CONVERSION DISORDER

Reported to be more common in rural areas and among low-socioeconomic status persons, Conversion Disorder symptoms may reflect local cultural ideas about accepted and credible ways to express distress. Symptoms are common aspects of certain culturally sanctioned religious and healing rituals (*DSM-IV,* 1994, p. 455). Symptoms such as fainting episodes and temporary blindness might resemble the culture-bound syndromes of *ataques de nervios* among Hispanics and "falling-out" among African Americans, respectively (*DSM-IV,* 1994, p. 846; Chaplin, 1997).

C. PAIN DISORDER

Differences across cultural and ethnic groups exist in terms of how these groups react to pain and respond to painful stimuli (Chaplin, 1997; *DSM-IV,* 1994, p. 460). For example, Jewish patients tend to show pain more openly than Asian clients do. The reason for this difference in the expression of pain is that Asians "in general are taught self-restraint and may be more reluctant to express pain" (Castillo, 1997, p. 196). The *DSM-IV* (1994) suggests that cultural variants in the evaluation and treatment of patients with Pain Disorder might be of limited utility because of the great deal of individual differences in the expression of pain across cultures. Another reason for this limitation is that it is extremely difficult to assess the severity of pain with objectivity (Castillo, 1997), which might prevent clinicians from distinguishing pain with sufficient medical justification from pain suggesting either Pain Disorder or culturally related pain in a given culture.

D. HYPOCHONDRIASIS

Continued preoccupation with a given medical problem despite a medical evaluation and reassurance indicating that nothing is wrong should be evaluated relative to the client's cultural background and explanatory models (Chaplin, 1997). For example, traditional healers assisting Hispanics with the management of medical problems might disagree with the medical evaluation and findings provided by a physician. This disagreement could reinforce the client's folk beliefs about disease (DSM-IV, 1994, p. 464). An emphasis on the medical evaluation and the absence of significant findings to confirm the presence of a given disease would probably compete with beliefs among Hispanic clients regarding the role of bad spirits and malevolent witchcraft that could result in medical problems, as well as with the belief regarding the role of healers (curanderos/curanderas) in the solution of medical problems (Paniagua, 1998). As noted by Castillo (1997), clients holding these beliefs would continue looking for the "right" physician if the medical condition is not evaluated and managed with the assistance of healers in a given culture.

E. Body Dysmorphic Disorder

Preoccupation with an *imagined* physical deformity may be determined by cultural concerns about physical appearance and the importance of physical self-presentation (DSM-IV, 1994, p. 467; Castillo, 1997). For example, among some Hispanics "thinner" is associated with being "sick," whereas "hefty" is perceived as "healthy." Among many Anglo-Americans, the opposite is the accepted belief. In this context, a Hispanic client confronting these two conflictive beliefs in the North America culture would be very concerned with a "defect" involving his or her physical appearance in public. This concern, however, might be culturally appropriate in the sense that this client would be responding to racial discrimination and humiliation directed toward an individual's appearance, which differs from those expected in the North American culture.

XV. SUBSTANCE-RELATED DISORDERS

A. Alcohol-Related

Among all substance-related disorders, alcohol-related disorders (e.g., Alcohol Intoxication and Alcohol Withdrawal) have received most attention in the cross-cultural literature (Westermeyer, 1995). Alcohol use patterns could be the result of cultural traditions in which the consumption of alcohol is expected in family, religious, and social settings. For example, many Hispanics consider heavy drinking an acceptable behavior among Hispanic males (Canino, Burnman, & Caetano, 1992). This is particularly true in the case of Hispanics who believe in machismo, which, among other characteristics, refers to Hispanic males' ability to consume an excessive amount of alcohol without getting drunk

(Paniagua, 1998). Castillo (1997) reviewed the literature on this topic and found a similar situation in Ireland, Korea, and Japan and concluded that "in these societies, heavy alcohol use is expected and . . . required by cultural customs for normal social interaction among males" (p. 162). As noted by Castillo (1997), in such societies males who *do not engage in heavy drinking* could be exposed to "negative social and occupational consequences" (p. 162). This observation, of course, is the opposite of what one would expect in the United States, where the negative consequences (both social and occupational) resulting from heavy drinking of alcohol are dramatic (e.g., social rejection, inability to find a job because of a history of alcoholism, etc.).

B. OTHER SUBSTANCES

Other substance-related disorders with brief description of cultural variants in the *DSM-IV* (1994) include Amphetamine-Related Disorders, Cannabis-Related Disorders, Cocaine-Related Disorders, Hallucinogen-Related Disorders, Cocaine-Related Disorders, Inhalant-Related Disorders, Nicotine-Related Disorders, and Opioid-Related Disorders. In general, the *DSM-IV* does not consider these disorders as unique to specific cultures. Cultural acceptability of such disorders, however, might vary across cultures. For example, the hallucinogen peyote is culturally accepted by many American Indians during their religious services, but they rarely abuse this substance; some members in the Southeast Asian community accept opium use, but they do not sanction or promote the use of this substance among members of this community (Westermeyer, 1995).

XVI. DIFFICULTIES IN DISTINGUISHING PSYCHOPATHOLOGY FROM CULTURE-RELATED CONDITIONS

In clinical practice, the distinction between psychopathological conditions and culture-related situations might be difficult to apply for three reasons (Paniagua, 1998). First, managed care companies, Medicaid, and Medicare are demanding a significant reduction in the number of sessions with clients seeking mental health services, and the overall expectancy is that the first session (approximately 45 minutes to one hour) would be devoted to the assessment of the case and diagnosis of symptoms, whereas the majority of sessions (generally six sessions, one hour per session) would be used to treat these symptoms. Under this restriction, clinicians would not have enough time to differentiate psychopathological conditions *unrelated* to a specific cultural context from psychopathology associated with a given cultural context. For example, many Asian clients believe that emotional problems bring shame and guilt to the Asian family, preventing these clients from reporting such problems to others outside the family during the first session (Paniagua, 1998; Sue & Sue, 1990). Under this condition, it would be extremely difficult to conclude that the intense anxiety an Asian client is experiencing during the first session is an example of the culture-bound syndrome "*koro*" (Castillo, 1997; Chowdhury, 1996; see Table I).

Second, assuming that clinicians agree that it is important to consider the impact of cultural variables upon the assessment of multicultural groups, a crucial question would be Why such variables are not currently emphasized by clinicians in their clinical practices? At least two answers may be proposed (Paniagua, 1998). First, current standard clinical ratings such as the Minnesota Multiphasic Personality Inventory, the Child Behavior Checklist, the Zung Depression Scale, and the Schedule of Affective Disorders and Schizophrenia (Rutter, Tuma, & Lann, 1988) and diagnostic instruments such as the *DSM-IV* (1994) *do not require* an assessment of cultural variables that might lead to the identification of culture-bound syndromes (e.g., Table I) or disorders associated with specific cultural contexts (e.g., ADHD, Anorexia Nervosa, etc.). Thus, in clinical practice one would not be concerned with the fact that a given mental health practitioner does not include a screening of cultural variables when making a diagnosis of mental disorders with clients from the multicultural groups generally seen in mental health services (e.g., African American, American Indian, Asian, and Hispanic clients). (As noted above, the *DSM-IV* recommended culture-bound syndromes and specific cultural variants clinicians to be considered in the assessment of psychiatric disorders; practitioners, however, *are not required* to screen these syndromes or cultural variations when making a psychiatric diagnosis using the *DSM-IV*; clinicians are simply *encouraged* to consider that recommendation.)

Third, reimbursement for clinical activities involving the assessment of cultural variables is not a practice among major private insurance, Medicaid, and Medicare. In the case of culture-bound syndromes, for example, a practitioner cannot expect to receive payment for the assessment and treatment of *susto, ghost sickness, mal puesto, koro, ataque de nervios,* and other culture-bound syndromes listed in Table I. For this reason, a clinician in private practice would not be expected to spend time screening such syndromes in those cases when his or her efforts will not lead to reimbursement. (A distinction should be made between considering the assessment of culture-bound syndromes only in those cases when reimbursement for clinical assessment of such syndromes is available and the assessment of these syndromes because it is, indeed, important to assure that a culturally diverse client is experiencing a mental problem and not a given culture-bound syndrome. The first point is a matter of money; the second a matter of ethical standards leading to a recognition of cultural competence in the practice of a clinician involved in the assessment of multicultural groups; American Psychological Association, 1992.)

XVII. GUIDELINES TO DISTINGUISH PSYCHOPATHOLOGY FROM CULTURE-RELATED CONDITIONS

Despite the above difficulties in establishing a distinction between psychopathological conditions unrelated to cultural variants and culturally related disorders, several guidelines exist in the literature to assist practitioners in making that distinction in clinical practice (Castillo, 1997; Paniagua, 1998; Tseng & Streltzer, 1997). Paniagua (1998) suggested four guidelines: (a) consultation with family members, peers, and folk healers within the multicultural group; (b) an examination of practitioner's own biases and prejudice before engaging in the evaluation of clients who do not share the practitioner's race and ethnicity; (c) preventing the use of the term *racism* as an explanation of psychopathological conditions; and (d) clinicians' ability to ask culturally appropriate questions.

In the first guideline, in addition to a familiarity with culture-bound syndromes and cultural variables that may lead to symptoms of mental disorders (as described above) shared by the particular group, consultation with relatives and folk healers (e.g., medicine men and women among American Indians and *curanderos/curanderas* among Hispanics) could assist clinicians in their recognition of symptoms suggesting a culture-bound syndrome in a given client and the identification of the cultural context impacting on the manifestation of *DSM-IV* disorders not included in Appendix I (*DSM-IV*, 1994). For example, if an American Indian client reports that "I believe that my weakness, loss of appetite, fainting are the result of the action of witches and evil supernatural forces" this statement would be an example of schizophrenia in the case of a clinician unfamiliar with the effect of "ghost sickness" among American Indians (see Table I). To determine whether this belief is expected in this specific case, the practitioner is advised to consult with family members, peers, and folk healers in the American Indian community (Simons & Hughes, 1993; Westermeyer, 1993).

In the second guideline, the *Self-Evaluation of Biases and Prejudice Scale* proposed by Paniagua (Paniagua, 1998, pp. 110–111) could assist clinicians with a self-assessment of biases and prejudices when working with culturally diverse clients. For example, in that scale clinicians answering "not at all" to the questions "Are you familiar with the current literature . . . with Hispanics" would suggest unfamiliarity with the impact of cultural variables on the manifestation of mental disorders among Hispanics.

In the third guideline, the fact that culture-bound syndromes have been identified across specific racial groups does not mean that a given member from one of these groups is, indeed, experiencing one of such syndromes during the initial clinical interview. For example, concluding that difficulty in concentrating, remembering, and thinking in an African American student is a case for the culture-bound syndrome known as "brain fag" would be a case of racism. Although it is true that these symptoms are often observed among high school and university African American students (Simons & Hughes, 1993), the generalization of this observation across all African American students receiving mental health services would be a case of racism (i.e., the use of the concept as an explanatory entity).

In the fourth guideline, a culturally appropriate line of questioning should be used to encourage the client and family members to report about culture-related situations they believe could explain the origin of the disorder under consideration. For example, the question "Do you really think a *susto* can explain what is going on with your daughter" would be inappropriate in the case of traditional Hispanic parents who believe that *susto* can, indeed, lead to mental and physical problems among Hispanics.

A major contribution in the *DSM-IV* is the inclusion of four guidelines that clinicians are encouraged to apply when dealing with the screening of cultural variants in the assessment and diagnosis of psychopathological conditions. In the first guideline, practitioners are encouraged to consider culture-bound syndromes (see Table I) to rule out cultural variants impacting the assessment and diagnosis of psychopathological conditions. The second guideline in the *DSM-IV* (1994) is included in a section entitled "Specific Culture, Age, and Gender Features," in which cultural variations are discussed across a small sample of disorders (see Paniagua, 1998, pp. 126–143; Smart & Smart, 1997, p. 75). The third guideline emphasizes culturally sensitive V-Codes. The fourth guideline outlines cultural formulation, which clinicians could use to "supplement the multiaxial diagnostic assessment and to address difficulties that may be encountered in applying *DSM-IV* criteria in a multicultural environment" (*DSM-IV,* 1994, p. 843).

XVIII. *DSM-IV* CULTURAL VARIATIONS AND CULTURALLY SENSITIVE V-CODES

As noted above, cultural variations in the *DSM-IV* were described across a small sample of disorders. In their count of disorders in the *DSM-IV,* Smart and Smart (1997) identified 79 disorders with descriptions of cultural variations among a total of 400 disorders. Paniagua et al. (1996) reviewed the entire *DSM-IV* and found similar results. Table II lists the number of disorders in which *DSM-IV*

TABLE II   Summary of *DSM-IV* Disorders with Description of Cultural Variations

Disorder	Subtype
Adjustment disorders	All subtypes
Alcohol-related disorders	All subtypes
Attention-Deficit and Disruptive Disorders	Conduct Disorder, ADHD
Amnestic disorders	All subtypes

Anxiety disorders	Social Phobia, Posttraumatic Stress Disorder
	Panic Disorder (with or without Agoraphobia),
	    Obsessive-Compulsive Disorder, Acute
	    Stress Disorder
	Generalized Anxiety Disorder

Caffeine-related disorders	All subtypes
Cannabis-related disorders	All subtypes
Cocaine-related disorders	All subtypes
Communication disorders	Expressive Language Disorder Mixed Receptive-Expressive Language Disorder Phonological Disorder
Delirium and dementia	All subtypes
Dissociative disorders	Dissociative Fugue Dissociative Identity Disorder Depersonalization Disorder
Eating disorders	All subtypes
Feeding and eating disorders of infancy or early childhood	Pica
Hallucinogen-related disorders	All subtypes
Inhalant-related disorders	All subtypes
Impulse-control disorders	Intermittent Explosive Disorder Pathological gambling
Impulse-control not elsewhere classified	Trichotillomania
Learning disorders	All subtypes
Mental retardation	All subtypes
Mood disorders	Major Depressive Disorder, Bipolar I Disorder
Nicotine-related disorders	All subtypes
Opioid-related disorders	All subtypes
Other disorders of infancy, childhood, or adolescence	Separation Anxiety Disorder, Selective Mutism
Paraphilias	All subtypes
Parasomnias	Nightmare Disorder, Sleep Terror Disorder, Sleepwalking Disorder

(continues)

TABLE II (continued)

Disorder	Subtype
Personality disorders	All subtypes
Phencyclidine-related disorders	All subtypes
Schizophrenia and other psychotic disorders	All subtypes
Sedative-hypnotic or anxiolytic-related disorders	All subtypes
Sexual dysfunctions	All subtypes
Sleep disorders related to another mental disorder	All subtypes
Somatoform disorders	All subtypes
Tic disorders	Tourette's disorder

provided specific information regarding cultural variations. It should be noted that in the *DSM-IV* (1994) cultural variants were not described across all subtypes of disorders within a set of disorders (Lewis-Fernandez & Kleinman, 1995; Smart & Smart, 1997; Paniagua, 1998, pp. 126–143). For example, in the *DSM-IV* these variants were described in the case of Major Depressive Disorder and Bipolar I Disorder; however, these variants were not described in the case of other subtypes of Mood Disorders (e.g., Dysthymic Disorder). Another example is Attention Deficit and Disruptive Disorders, in which these variations were described in the case of only two subtypes (Conduct Disorder and ADHD); these variations were not mentioned in the case of Oppositional Defiant Disorder. Therefore, in Table II the particular disorder is listed (left-side of table) with a reference to whether these variations are described for only specific subtypes or across all subtypes in the disorder under consideration. Examples of cultural variations across disorders listed in Table II were provided above; a brief summary of these variants across similar disorders can be found in Paniagua (1998, pp. 128–139) and Paniagua et al. (1996).

In the case of culturally sensitive codes in the *DSM-IV,* clinicians are encouraged to use four V-Codes when assessing and treating multicultural groups in mental health services: Partner Relational Problem (V61.1, p. 681), Religious or Spiritual Problem (V62.89, p. 685), Acculturation Problem (V62.4, p. 685), and Parent–Child Relational Problem (V61.20, p. 681).

A. PARTNER RELATIONAL PROBLEM

Cultural variables such as differences in the level of acculturation and the role of machismo and marianismo among Hispanic clients could lead to partner relational problems (Paniagua, 1998). For example, a Hispanic female may experience "negative communication" with her husband regarding their expectations regarding the role the wife should play at home if she does not share the values of machismo and marianismo. Similarly, an acculturated individual (e.g., someone who shares most values, lifestyle situations, and beliefs in the American culture) may experience "marital conflicts" with a less acculturated partner who recently emigrated to the United States from a country with very distinct values, beliefs, and lifestyle situations.

Another example of the application of V-Code 61.1 in a cultural context is the impact of intertribal marriages on the discipline of their children. For example, in the Hopi tribe the wife is primarily responsible for the management of children, whereas in the Cherokee tribe both husband and wife share the discipline of children. Thus, a Cherokee woman who marries a Hopi man would express "marital discord" with her husband if he shows no concerns regarding the discipline of their children (Ho, 1992; Paniagua, 1998).

B. Religious or Spiritual Problems

The *DSM-IV* suggests that a client's religious and spiritual beliefs should be considered in those cases when such beliefs leads to "distressing experiences that involve loss or questioning of faith, problems associated with conversion to a new faith, or questioning of spiritual values" (*DSM-IV,* 1994, p. 685). Religious or spiritual problems may also be the focus of clinical attention in those cases when a clinician believes that such a problem interferes with the overall assessment and treatment of the particular disorder. For example, many Hispanic clients believe that evil spirits cause mental problems and, as a result, the church, not the clinician, has the power to treat these problems (Paniagua, 1998). Hispanics often believe that prayers will cure physical and mental problems, and help from a mental health professional is often sought only when the family has exhausted all religious and folk resources to handle the problem. These religious and spiritual beliefs may directly or indirectly interfere with the assessment and treatment of a client from the Hispanic community.

C. Acculturation Problem

Clinicians should emphasize the process of acculturation as the focus of clinical attention when the problem involves "adjustment to a different culture (e.g., following migration)" (*DSM-IV,* 1994, p. 685). A discrepancy in the level or degree of acculturation among family members may be in itself the focus of clinical attention. This point could be illustrated with the process of dating among Hispanic females (Paniagua, 1996). In this process, a Hispanic female is expected to engage immediate family members in that process (e.g., parents, uncles, brothers, sisters). A highly acculturated Hispanic female residing with less acculturated family members may develop a psychiatric disorder (e.g., depression) because of this discrepancy in acculturation among members. In clinical practice, this discrepancy in acculturation levels should be the focus of clinical attention. Several acculturation scales have been suggested in the literature, which clinicians may use to determine whether or not an acculturation problem should be a focus of clinical attention during the management of a given disorders in Axis I and Axis II in the *DSM-IV* (e.g., Cuellar, Arnold, & Maldonado, 1995; Helms, 1986; Hoffman, Dana, & Bolton, 1985; Norris, Ford, & Bova, 1996; Smither & Rodriguez-Giegling, 1982; Szapocznik, Scopeta, Arnalde, & Kurtines, 1978; Suinn, Rickard-Figeroa, Lew, & Vigil, 1987).

D. PARENT–CHILD RELATIONAL PROBLEM

Parent–child relational problems may include "impaired communication, overprotection, [and] inadequate discipline" (*DSM-IV,* 1994, p. 681). Acculturation problems may lead to parent–child relational problems in the form of impaired communication. For example, later generation Asian and Hispanic adolescents may disagree with their early generation parents in certain issues involving customs and lifestyles (e.g., dressing, dating) because parents are less acculturated than their children into the American society. The phenomenon of *machismo* among Hispanic fathers could lead to the overprotection of their children. Inadequate disciplining of children and adolescents among American Indian parents may be the result of the parents belonging to different tribes. If a practitioner understands that certain cultural variables can easily explain why these parent–child relational problems exist, nothing will be wrong with these examples. In this case, the practitioner should emphasize these variables during the assessment and treatment of the particular family (Paniagua, 1998).

XIX. *DSM-IV* OUTLINE FOR CULTURAL FORMULATION

The Cultural Formation outline is another significant contribution in the *DSM-IV* (1994). Lewis-Fernandez and Kleinman (1995), however, suggested that placing this cultural formulation in Appendix I rather than placing it after the Multiaxial Assessment at the front of the manual would prevent clinicians from seriously considering the relevance of that formulation in their clinical practice.

Despite this critique, the inclusion of an outline for cultural formulation still represents a major step in the historical development of the *DSM* (Smart & Smart, 1997).

In the *DSM-IV*, it is not clear at what stage of the assessment process clinicians should consider cultural variables using five categories of information involving the Cultural Formulation. The *DSM-IV* recommends that "it is important that the clinician take into consideration the individual's ethnic and cultural context in the evaluation of each of the *DSM-IV* axes" (1994, p. 843). This recommendation suggests that clinicians should consider each category in the Cultural Formulation at the moment the particular case is evaluated using *DSM-IV* classification. If true, a clinician using the *DSM-IV* would first make a diagnosis of mental disorder and then would consider each category in that formulation to rule out cultural variables that could explain symptoms suggesting psychopathology. In current clinical practice, however, the overall observation is that most clinicians using *DSM-IV* are not following this recommendation, for two reasons. First, as noted above, busy clinicians would not consider the relevance of that formulation because managed care companies would not cover the time they spend dealing with the cultural assessment of the case. Second, the fact that the Cultural Formulation was included in an appendix (rather than inserted after the Multiaxial Assessment and at the front of the manual) suggests that clinicians are not required to consider cultural variables when making a psychiatric diagnosis using the *DSM-IV*. The outline for Cultural Formulation includes the following five categories (*DSM-IV*, 1994, pp. 843–844; see also Tseng & Streltzer, 1997, pp. 248–251).

A. CULTURAL IDENTITY OF THE INDIVIDUAL

This would include (a) the client's cultural or ethnic preference groups, (b) in the case of immigrants, the degree of involvement with the culture of origin versus the host culture, and (c) language use and preference. For example, a Latino client might prefer the term "Chicano" rather than "Mexican-American" if he or she believes that the first term imply less degrees of acculturation to the Anglo-American Culture. An African American client might report more involvement with the Anglo-American culture and display many behavior patterns (e.g., dress, music) *unrelated* to the African American community (Paniagua, 1998). By contrast, another African American client would not only identify himself or herself with the African American community, but would also prefer to use Black English in communicating symptoms (Paniagua, 1998; Smitherman, 1995).

B. Cultural Explanation of the Individual's Illness

To be included here are (a) idioms of distress used by the individual to communicate symptoms (e.g., "nerves," "spirits"), (b) the meaning of the severity of the symptoms as perceived by the client in relation to the cultural reference groups, (c) the client's perception of the cause of the problem, (d) and names applied to symptoms within the client's culture. For example, a Hispanic client would report that he or she feels "depressed" after being exposed to a *susto* (see Table I). Similarly, among many Hispanics a mental disorder (*enfermedad mental*) is less severe than being insane (*estar loco*). In the first case, the client is suffering from a *crisis nerviosa* or *ataque de nervios* (i.e., a nervous crisis). In the second case, the client shows a complete loss of control or withdrawal or both, requiring hospitalization (Paniagua, 1998).

C. Cultural Factors Related to the Psychosocial Environment and Level of Functioning

Examples include (a) interpretation of social stressors in cultural terms and (b) social supports. For example, the individual's perception of racial discrimination could represent a major stressor leading to symptoms involving depression and anxiety. The extended family is a crucial social support among many clients from culturally diverse groups. For example, among Hispanics the *compadre* (cofather) and *comadre* (comother) are often available to take care of children when their parents are absent; the priest is another important social support in this group. In the case of African Americans, the church is crucial in providing emotional supports. Among American Indians, the medicine man/woman is often consulted when the family is experiencing difficulties; and in the case of Southeast refugees, welfare agencies and community supports are examples of social supports in this group (Gaw, 1993).

D. Cultural Elements of the Relationship between the Individual and the Clinician

Included here are (a) ethnic and racial differences between the client and the clinician, and (b) the negative impact of these differences on the diagnosis and treatment of the client. For example, the fact that the client and the clinician are Hispanics does not necessarily mean that they share the same ethnicity (i.e., values, norms, and lifestyle). In this context, a Hispanic clinician, for example, who does not believe in the cultural values of "machismo" and "marianismo" would diagnosis a Hispanic female with Dependent Personality Disorder when, in fact, this woman is simply behaving according to norms expected in the Hispanic community. In the same case, a treatment plan with emphasis on "social skills training" (teaching a client what to do and say to develop self-assertive behaviors, for example) would be a bad tactic in the treatment of that Hispanic female because the clinician would be recommending an intervention which competes with the value that Hispanic places on *respeto, machismo,* and *marianismo* (Paniagua, 1998).

E. Overall Cultural Assessment for Diagnosis and Care

In this category, clinicians are advised to conclude with a formulation, including a discussion of how cultural variables influence the diagnosis of the case and care. For example, a clinician using this outline for Cultural Formulation would conclude: "Symptoms reported by this client appear to be culture-related. Further assessment is needed with emphasis on acculturation scales recommended with this culturally diverse groups, as well as consultation with members of the social support group identified by the client as part of the extended family. Care of this client should be considered using culturally sensitive treatment modalities."

XX. A FINAL THOUGHT

Despite the importance of considering cultural variables in clinical practices, too much emphasis on these variables may prevent practitioners from considering symptoms as indicative of a severe psychiatric disorders. This emphasis could not only lead to misdiagnosis of real psychiatric disorders but it may also result in turning clients over to folk healers for treatment under the assumption that what the client is experiencing is a set of culturally related symptoms resembling a given *DSM-IV* disorder, which cannot be treated by mental health professionals. As noted by Westermeyer (1993), turning multicultural clients over to folk healers because the presenting symptoms are examples of a culture-related condition may lead to a major error in clinical practices. The assumption here is that, when working with culturally diverse clients in mental health services, overdiagnosis, underdiagnosis, and misdiagnosis of psychopathological conditions could be prevented by emphasizing a combination of cross-cultural assessment strategies (e.g., the *DSM-IV* outline for Cultural Formulation) and traditional psychiatric or psychological evaluations (Castillo, 1997; Lonner, & Ibrahim, 1996; Pope-Davis & Coleman, 1997).

REFERENCES

American Psychiatric Association (1994). *Diagnostic and statistical manual of mental disorders* (4th ed.). Washington, DC: American Psychiatric Association.

American Psychological Association (1992). *Ethical principles of psychologists and code of conduct.* Washington, DC: American Psychological Association.

Barkley, R. A. (1990). *Attention deficit hyperactivity disorder.* New York: Guilford Press.

Bernstein, D. M. (1997). Anxiety disorders. In Wen-Shin Tseng & J. Streltzer (Eds.), *Culture and psychopathology* (pp. 46–66). New York: Brunner/Mazel.

Berry, J. W., Poortinga, Y. H., Segall, M. H., & Darsen, P. R. (1992). *Cross-cultural psychology: Research and applications.* Cambridge, MA: Cambridge University Press.

Boehnlein, J. K., & Kinzie, J. D. (1995). Refugee trauma. *Transcultural psychiatric Research Review, 32,* 223–252.

Campinha-Bacote, J. (1992). Voodoo illness. *Perspectives in Psychiatric Care, 28,* 11–17.

Canino, G., Burnam, A., & Caetano, R. (1992). The prevalence of alcohol abuse/dependence in two Hispanic communities. In J. Helzer & G. Canino (Eds.), *Alcoholism in North America, Europe and Asia* (pp. 131–155). New York: Oxford University Press.

Castillo, R. J. (1997). *Culture and mental illness.* Pacific Grove, CA: Brooks/Cole.

Chaplin, S. L. (1997). Somatization. In Wen-Shin Tseng & J. Streltzer (Eds.), *Culture and psychopathology* (pp. 67–86). New York: Brunner/Mazel.

Chowdhury, A. N. (1996). The definition and classification of Koro. *Culture, Medicine & Psychiatry, 20,* 41–65.

Cuellar, I., Arnold, B., & Maldonado, R. (1995). Acculturation rating scale for Mexicans-II: A revision of the original ARSMA scale. *Hispanic Journal of the Behavioral Sciences, 17,* 275–304.

Dana, R. H. (1993). *Multicultural assessment perspectives for professional psychology.* Boston: Allyn and Bacon.

Dana, R. H. (1995). Culturally competent MMPI assessment of Hispanic populations. *Hispanic Journal of Behavioral Sciences, 17,* 305–319.

Escobar, J. I. (1995). Transcultural aspects of dissociative and somatoform disorders. *The Psychiatric Clinics of North America, 18,* 555–569.

Gaw, A. C. (1993) (ed.). *Culture, ethnicity, and mental illness.* Washington, DC: American Psychiatric Press.

Golden, C. J. (1990). *Clinical interpretation of objective psychological tests,* (2nd ed.). Needham. MA: Allyn and Bacon.

Griffith, E. E. H., & Baker, F. M. (1993). Psychiatric care of African Americans. In A. C. Gaw (Ed.), *Culture, ethnicity, and mental illness* (pp. 147–173). Washington, DC: American Psychiatric Press.

Helms, J. E. (1986). Expanding racial identity theory to cover the counseling process. *Journal of Counseling Psychology, 33,* 62–64.

Ho, M. K. (1992). *Minority children and adolescents in therapy.* Newbury Park, CA: Sage Publications.

Hoffmann, T., Dana, R., & Bolton, B. (1985). Measured acculturation and MMPI-168 performance of Native American adults. *Journal of Cross-Cultural Psychology, 16,* 243–256.

Ivey, A. E., Ivey, M. B., & Simek-Morgan, L. (1996) (Eds.). *Counseling and psychotherapy: A multi-cultural perspective.* Boston: Allyn & Bacon.

Kirmayer, L. J., Young, A., & Hayton, B. C. (1995). The cultural context of anxiety disorders. *The Psychiatric Clinics of North America, 18,* 503–521.

Levine, R., & Gaw, A. C. (1995). Culture-bound syndromes. *The Psychiatric Clinics of North America, 18,* 523–536.

Lewis-Fernandez, R., & Kleinman, A. (1995). Cultural psychiatry: Theoretical, clinical, and research issues. *The Psychiatric Clinics of North America, 18,* 433–448.

Lonner, W. J., & Ibrahim, F. A. (1996). Appraisal and assessment in cross-cultural counseling. In P. B. Pedersen, J. G. Draguns, W. J. Lonner, & J. E. Trimble (Eds.), *Counseling across cultures* (pp. 293–322). Thousand Oaks, CA: Sage.

McNeil, D. W., Kee, M., & Zvolensky, M. J. (1999). Culturally related anxiety and ethnic identity in Navajo college students. *Cultural Diversity and Ethnic Minority Psychology, 5,* 56–64.

Norris, A. E., Ford, K., & Bova, C. A. (1996). Psychometrics of a brief acculturation scale for Hispanics in a probability sample of urban Hispanics adolescents and young adults. *Hispanic Journal of Behavioral Sciences, 18,* 29–38.

Paniagua, F. A. (1998) (2nd edition). *Assessing and treating culturally diverse clients: A practical guide.* Newbury Park, CA: Sage.

Paniagua, F. A. (1996). Cross-cultural guidelines in family therapy practice. *The Family Journal: Counseling and Therapy for Couples and Families, 4,* 127–138.

Paniagua, F. A., Tan, V. T., & Lew, A. S. (1996). A summary of cultural variants in the DSM-IV. *Sociotam: International Journal for the Social Sciences, 6,* 33–57.

Pedersen, P. B. (1997). *Culture-centered counseling interventions: Striving for accuracy.* Newbury Park, CA: Sage.

Pedersen, P. B., Draguns, J. G., Lonner, W. J., & Trimble, J. E. (1996). *Counseling across cultures.* Thousand Oaks, CA: Sage.

Ponterotto, J. G., Casas, J. M., Suzuki, L. A., & Alexander, C. M. (Eds.). (1995). *Handbook of multicultural counseling.* Newbury Park, CA: Sage.

Pope-Davis, D. B., & Coleman, H. L. K. (1997). (Eds.). *Multicultural counseling competencies: Assessment, education and training, and supervision.* Thousand Oaks, CA: Sage.

Price, R. H. (1993). Culture-bound syndromes: The example of social phobias. A. M. Ghadirian & H. E. Lehmann (Eds.), *Environment and psychopathology* (pp. 55–72). New York: Springer Publishing Company.

Rubel, A. J., O'Neill, C. W., & Collado-Ardon, R. (1984). *Susto: A folk illness.* Berkeley: University of California Press.

Rutter, M., Tuma, A. H., & Lann, I. S. (1988). *Assessment and diagnosis in child psychopathology.* New York: The Guilford Press.

Simons, R. C., & Hughes, C. C. (1993). Cultural-bound syndromes. In A. C. Gaw (Ed.), *Culture, ethnicity, and mental illness* (pp. 75–93). Washington, DC: American Psychiatric Press.

Smart, D. W., & Smart, J. F. (1997). DSM-IV and culturally sensitive diagnosis: Some observations for counselors. *Journal of Counseling & Development, 75,* 392–398.

Smither, R., & Rodriguez-Griegling, M. (1982). Personality, demographics, and acculturation of Vietnamese and Nicaraguan refugees to the United States. *International Journal of Psychology, 17,* 19–25.

Smitherman, G. (1995). *Black talk.* Boston: Houghton Mifflin Company.

Sue, D. W., & Sue, D. (1990). *Counseling the culturally different: Theory and practice,* (2nd ed.). New York: John Wiley & Sons.

Suinn, R. M., Rickard-Figueroa, K., Lew, S., & Vigil, S. (1987). The Suinn-Lew Asian Self-Identity Acculturation scale: An initial report. *Education and Psychological Measurement, 47,* 401–407.

Szapocznik, J., Scopetta, M. A., Arnalde, M., & Kurtines, W. (1978). Cuban value structure: Treatment implications. *Journal of Consulting and Clinical Psychology, 46,* 961–970.

Tseng, W. S., & Streltzer, J. (1997). Integration and conclusions. In W. S. Tseng & J. Streltzer (Eds.), *Culture and psychopathology* (pp. 241–252). New York: Brunner/Mazel.

Weiss, M. G. (1995). Eating disorders and disordered eating in different culture. *The Psychiatric Clinics of North America, 18,* 537–553.

Westermeyer, J. (1985). Psychiatric diagnosis across cultural boundaries. *American Journal of Psychiatry, 142,* 798–805.

Westermeyer, J. J. (1993). Cross-cultural psychiatric assessment. In A. C. Gaw (Eds.), *Culture, ethnicity, and mental illness* (pp. 125–144). Washington, DC: American Psychiatric Press.

Westermeyer, J. (1995). Cultural aspects of substance abuse and alcoholism. *The Psychiatric Clinics of North America, 18,* 589–605.

CHAPTER 9

Assessing and Treating Asian Americans: Recent Advances

SUMIE OKAZAKI

Department of Psychology
University of Wisconsin—Madison
Madison, Wisconsin

I. INTRODUCTION

Most book chapters and clinical guidelines for assessing and treating Asian Americans begin with a treatise on the population statistics drawn from the U.S. Census Bureau. Following the descriptions of the number of Asian Americans residing in the United States and their exponential population growth in the past several decades, one typically finds descriptions of Asian cultural characteristics that are relevant to providing culturally competent services to the Asian American population. In writing this chapter, I have chosen not to recapitulate much of the standard discussions of demographic and cultural characteristics of Asian Americans. There are a number of excellent texts that summarize this material (e.g., Dana, 1993, 1998; E. Lee, 1997; D. W. Sue & D. Sue, 1999).

The aim of this chapter is to provide a selective, up-to-date review of relevant resources on Asian American mental health. It is hoped that such a review would assist the clinician in conducting culturally competent assessment and treatment of Asian American clients. The past few years have seen an enormous increase in the availability of texts on multicultural counseling or transcultural treatment (e.g., Dana, 1998; Friedman, 1997; C. C. Lee, 1997; Paniagua, 1994; D. W. Sue & D. Sue, 1999) and assessment (e.g., Butcher, 1996; Dana, 1998; Samuda, 1998; Tseng & Streltzer, 1997). Of particular interest, we have also seen a rise in the publication of texts devoted to psychology of Asian Americans, such as a text on a specific treatment model, *Chinese American Family Therapy* (Jung, 1998), and compendium volumes, *Transference and Empathy in Asian American Psychotherapy* (Chin, Liem, Ham, & Hong, 1993), *Handbook of Asian American Psychology* (edited by L. C. Lee & Zane, 1998), and *Working with Asian Americans* (edited by E. Lee, 1997). There also have been a record number of research and treatment articles in psychology journals and related disciplines concerning Asian Americans. The sheer array of resources can at times be bewildering for a clinician confronted with the task of processing vast amounts of information while facing urgent client needs.

This chapter will first present the salient issues in understanding the phenomenology of distress among Asian Americans, highlighting the latest research findings and pointing to some useful resources. Next, some key concepts that serve as necessary background knowledge will be delineated, followed by guidelines for assessment and treatment. Because of the relative paucity of research on the use of standard tools of personality and cognitive assessment with Asian Americans, the present guidelines will not focus on specific instruments but on strategies for conducting cultural assessment of Asian American clients. Clinicians interested in information regarding the use of standardized measures are referred to other sources (e.g., Okazaki, 1998; Dana, 1993).

Before proceeding, the use of the term *Asian American* deserves brief comments. There exists an enormous diversity within the Asian American population with respect to nationality, language, generational status, income and poverty level, educational and occupational achievement, immigration history, and so on (see Kitano & Daniels, 1995). Accordingly, there is no one clinical approach that works for all, or even most, Asian Americans. In the process of educating oneself regarding the diverse demography (and the psychological correlates associated with demographic characteristics) of Asian Americans, the clinician may begin to wonder if it makes sense to continue discussing Asian Americans as one entity. The answer to this question is a qualified yes. Although one inevitably runs the risk of overgeneralizing and thus stereotyping the clinical picture of Asian Americans by discussing them in a general terms, there are two good reasons for doing so: (a) there are common experiences of being a visible racial minority shared by many Asian Americans, which are potential sources of stress and distress, and (b) there are common cultural characteristics shared by many Asian Americans, which influence the expression of distress and behavior surrounding treatment. These two aspects of the Asian American psychological experience in turn shape the phenomenology of distress. In the next section, I outline how minority status contributes to distress and how cultural forces shape the expression of distress among Asian Americans. In the process, useful resources and clinical implications will be highlighted.

II. PHENOMENOLOGY OF DISTRESS

A. MINORITY AND IMMIGRANT STATUS AS ANTECEDENTS OF DISTRESS

The status of Asian Americans as members of a visible racial minority group in the United States is likely to influence the content of their distress. In an analysis of Asian American–White American differences on various indices of personality patterns (many of which are traits associated with distress), Uba (1994) proposed that the documented ethnic differences can be interpreted on the basis of cultural value differences and the status of Asian Americans as minorities. For example, Uba speculated that the lower levels of assertiveness among Asian Americans compared to non-Asian counterparts may be due to Asian cultural ideals, such as respect for others, modesty, interpersonal harmony, and restraint of hostile and aggressive emotions (cultural basis), but the deferential behavior of Asian Americans may also reflect a strategy for surviving in a racist society or a learned helplessness arising from their experience as minorities.

Although research has been slow to document the relationship between minority status and distress among Asian Americans, the deleterious effects of discrimination, being made to feel different (and deviant, by implication), and the identity conflicts associated with being a minority person in the United States are poignantly documented in many personal narratives and oral histories. Clinicians may wish to sample these writings as one way to appreciate the psychological impact of the minority status on Asian Americans. For example, in a recently published book titled *Leaving Deep Water,* psychotherapist Claire Chow (1998) weaves her own reflections about her life as an Asian American woman with personal narratives of various Asian American women she interviewed. In one chapter entitled "Blending in or standing out: Stories of racism and discrimination," Chow compiles touching examples of Asian American women who remember feeling angry, helpless, powerless, ashamed, and embarrassed in the face of racial slurs or racial harassment. Although the voices featured in this volume represent those of largely middle-class and relatively acculturated Asian American women, the narratives are powerful and poignant illustrations of the lasting impacts of covert or overt experiences of discrimination and racism on Asian Americans. There are many other works that contain personal narratives around the themes of identity and minority status. For example, there is a collection of brief oral histories edited by Joann F. J. Lee (1991) entitled *Asian Americans* that covers the experiences of Asian Americans of various ethnic origins, socioeconomic status, and age. On a more literary side, an anthology edited by Garrett Hongo (1995) entitled *Under Western Eyes* contains a number of eloquent essays by Asian American writers on themes related to stereotyping, ethnic identity, and experiences of marginalization.

Reflections about subtle racism and discrimination are most frequently evident in the personal narratives of younger generations of Asian Americans. However, the difficulty adjusting to an unfamiliar culture and achieving economic success is a source of considerable psychological distress that impacts recent immigrants to the United States, especially older Asian Americans. The personal narratives of Vietnamese American refugees (e.g., Freeman, 1989) and Hmong American refugees (e.g., Chan, 1994) provide insight into the struggles as well as resourcefulness of those Asian Americans who may be most vulnerable to psychological distress due to the multiple traumas they encountered prior to and following their migration.

The preceding recommendation for clinicians who are unfamiliar with Asian American experiences to read personal writings of Asian Americans is issued with a caveat. At the risk of stating the obvious, reading personal accounts or oral histories of Asian Americans cannot substitute for the actual experience of working with Asian American individuals, nor should they be taken as reflecting a typical experience of Asian Americans. However, these first-person narratives may serve as useful qualitative supplements to the standard clinical guideline literature and research reports because they can often convey the subtlety and the complexity of the Asian American psychological experience absent from reports about the general Asian American population.

B. CULTURAL EXPRESSIONS

Asian American mental health research has made strides in dispelling myths that Asian Americans as a population have little or no mental health problems (Uba, 1994). The findings that Asian Americans tend to underutilize outpatient (S. Sue, Fujino, Hu, Takeuchi, & Zane, 1991) and inpatient psychiatric services (Snowden & Cheung, 1990) are no longer interpreted as the Asian Americans' lack of need for such services but as a reflection of various cultural and institutional barriers to Asian Americans' obtaining mental health services. The recent investigations have turned to understanding the phenomenology of distress among Asian Americans. In particular, there have been advances in understanding the cultural idioms of distress surrounding depression.

1. Depression

A number of community studies have documented an elevated level of depressive symptom reports among various segments of the Asian American population using the Center for Epidemiologic Studies—Depression scale (CES-D;

Radloff, 1977). Of note, Korean American community residents have been shown to score particularly highly on the CES-D scale (e.g., Hurh & Kim, 1990; Kuo, 1984; Shin, 1993). These data had been interpreted as reflecting the high level of depression among Asian Americans, particularly those who were recent immigrants and women. However, the analyses of the differential response patterns to the CES-D items between the American sample and the Chinese American residents (Iwamasa, Arean, Miranda, & Muñoz, 1993) or the overseas Japanese adolescents (Iwata, Saito, & Roberts, 1994) suggeests that the higher reports of depressive symptoms among Asian Americans may not be interpreted straightforwardly as indices of higher depression. Researchers from Korea (Cho & Kim, 1998) suggested that while the Korean version of the CES-D appears to be reliable and valid for detecting major depression as defined by the Diagnostic and Statistical Manual of Mental Disorder (3rd ed., rev) (*DSM III-R*) (American Psychiatric Association, 1987) in the Korean population, the cutoff scores are higher than those used in the United States. Cho and Kim argued that the higher cutoff scores in Korea may reflect the Confucian cultural ethics of suppressing positive affect. Along the same line, researchers from Japan found that Japanese responded to positively worded items in a markedly different fashion than the U.S. samples, possibly because the Japanese tended to suppress positive affect (Iwata et al., 1994). In the absence of a more comprehensive assessment of distress, the studies of depressive symptoms in Asian Americans had only provided a tentative picture of the prevalence of distress.

In the last few years, however, extremely valuable data regarding the prevalence rates of the major psychiatric conditions among Asian Americans have begun to emerge. The Chinese American Psychiatric Epidemiological Study (CAPES) is the first large-scale community psychiatric epidemiologic study of an Asian American ethnic group (Takeuchi et al., 1998). The CAPES used a sophisticated multistage probability sampling design and sampled 1,747 Chinese American households in the greater Los Angeles area (at 82% response rate of selected eligible respondents). Using the *DSM III-R* criteria for major depressive episode and dysthymia, the CAPES researchers found that the lifetime prevalence rates of major depressive episode was 6.9%, and the 12-month prevalence rate was 3.4%. The lifetime rate of dysthymia was 5.2%, with the 12-month rate at 0.9% (Takeuchi et al., 1998). These rates of mood disorders among Chinese Americans appear significantly lower than the rates found by the National Comorbidity Study (NCS; Kessler et al., 1994), which also used the same diagnostic instrument with the general U.S. population. The NCS had found the lifetime and 12-month rates of major depression to be 17.1% and 10.3%, respectively, and the lifetime and 12-month rates of dysthymia to be 6.4% and 2.5%, respectively.

A particularly notable finding emerging from the CAPES analyses of mood disorders data was that there were no overall gender differences between Chinese American men and women in the rates of depression or dysthymia (Takeuchi et al., 1998). This lack of overall gender differences stands in stark contrast to most studies in the Western nations, which show that women have much higher rates of depression than men, but is consistent with the lack of gender differences in ethnic minority groups such as African Americans, Southeast Asian refugees, and Korean Americans (see Takeuchi et al., 1998). Interestingly, the CAPES data did show that gender differences emerge with acculturation to the American culture. Among the highly acculturated Chinese American group, women were much more likely to have experienced lifetime dysthymia or depressive episode than men, but no such gender differences were seen among the less acculturated group of Chinese Americans. In sum, the CAPES data suggest that the prevalence of *DSM*-defined mood disorders among Asian Americans may not be as high as previously thought, but that acculturation appears to be a salient factor in the population patterns of rates of depression. The question that arises from such findings is the appropriateness of using the Western-derived diagnostic criteria for assessing distress among Asian Americans, particularly those who are less acculturated to the American culture.

2. Somatic Expressions

Related to the question of the utility of Western psychiatric nosology to individuals from non-Western cultural backgrounds, one of the long-standing debates in the field is whether Asians (and by extension, Asian Americans) tend to somaticize psychological distress (Kleinman, 1982). Clinical anecdotes have long supported the notion that Asian Americans tend to express their psychological distress through somatic symptoms. Such assertions were consistent with many Asian cultures' ideal of not expressing strong emotions that might disrupt interpersonal relationships and roles. One piece of evidence frequently cited for the Asian tendency to somaticize psychological distress was the prevalence of patients in Asian nations diagnosed with neurasthenia, a condition characterized by either fatigue or weakness accompanied by an array of physical and psychological symptoms such as diffuse aches and pains, gastrointestinal problems, sleep problems, irritability, excitability, and so on (Zheng et al., 1997). Kleinman (1982) asserted that most neurasthenia cases in China could be rediagnosed as major depression using the *DSM-III* criteria. Although the popularity of the neurasthenia diagnosis in Asia appears to have waned in the recent decade (S. Lee, 1994), it remains a clinically useful concept among patients and clinicians in Asia. Zheng et al. (1997) examined the prevalence of neurasthenia (as defined by the International Classification of Disease [ICD]-10) in the same sample of Chinese Americans surveyed in the CAPES (Takeuchi et al., 1998) and found that over half of those meeting the diagnostic criteria of neurasthenia did not exhibit any other syndromes associated with current or lifetime *DSM-III-R* diagnoses. Such data suggest that neurasthenia may be clinically distinguishable from *DSM*-defined mood disorders and that neurasthenia may remain a viable way of characterizing the phenomenology of distress among Chinese Americans.

Another idiom of distress that has been examined in the Asian American population is the Korean folk illness label of *hwa-byung*, used by patients suffering from an array of somatic and psychological symptoms including pressing sensations in the chest, palpitations, "heat sensation," flushing, headache, gastrointestinal problems, dysphoria, anxiety, irritability, and difficulty in concentration. In a telephone interview study of 109 Korean American residents in the greater Los Angeles area randomly selected from the Korean language telephone book (Lin et al., 1992), the researchers found that 11.9% of those interviewed regarded themselves as suffering from *hwa-byung*. Moreover, those who labeled themselves as having *hwa-byung* were significantly more likely than other Korean Americans to meet the *DSM* criteria for major depression (Lin et al., 1992). The findings from this study suggest a substantial overlap between the cultural idioms of distress and major depression.

In concluding this section on the phenomenology of distress in Asian Americans, the following two points are underscored: (a) in understanding the Asian American client, it is important to appreciate both the minority status and the cultural bases for distress, and (b) Western psychiatric nosology may not adequately capture the essence of Asian American clients' experience of distress.

III. PREPARATION: A GUIDE TO APPROACHING THE LITERATURE

In describing Asian cultural values and the characteristics of Asian American individuals, clinical literature often errs on the side of overgeneralization. This happens particularly when clinical writers illustrate cultural concepts by emphasizing contrasts between American and Asian cultures (e.g., egalitarian versus hierarchical values, individual versus family, guilt versus shame). A casual perusal of book chapters and clinical articles reveals sentences such as "Chinese find it easy to somatize" or that "An Asian client enters a therapist's office expecting to find an authority who can solve his or her problems." These illustrations can be useful to a clinician who is at the beginning stages of cultural awareness, as many previously unarticulated assumptions about the mainstream American culture are brought to the foreground while being contrasted with various Asian cultural characteristics. However, these characterizations can leave the misimpression that there is such a thing as a monolithic "Asian," "Chinese," or "American" culture. Kwon (1995) pointed out the dangers of such clinical literature in their tendency to overemphasize the between-group differences between Asian Americans and Whites at the cost of minimizing within-group differences among Asian Americans. Kwon further argued that a focus on Asian–White between-group differences may lead the clinician to underestimate the efficacy for Asian American client of general therapeutic techniques used to treat White American clients. Given the potential misuse of clinical guidelines, clinicians are urged to balance broad descriptions at the cultural level with individual accounts. With this caveat, this section describes some key concepts on which culturally competent assessment and treatment with Asian Americans are built; the understanding of the process (credibility) and the acquisition of cultural knowledge.

A. Credibility and the Therapeutic Dyad

In a reformulation of techniques for working with ethnic minority clients, S. Sue and Zane (1987) identified credibility as a process that is central in the beginning stages of treatment for minority clients. In their analysis of credibility, S. Sue and Zane distinguished between credibility that is ascribed and credibility that is achieved. Ascribed credibility derives from the position or role that is assigned by others in society. In Asian cultures, characteristics that often go with higher ascribed status include older age, male sex, and higher expertise or authority (as connoted by titles such as "doctor" and "professor"). Achieved credibility comes from what the clinician actually does to instill faith, trust, confidence, or hope in their clients. S. Sue and Zane further stated that high ascribed credibility may compel the Asian American client to seek mental health services from a particular service provider, but that credibility must also be achieved in early sessions for the client to stay in treatment long enough to gain therapeutic benefits.

These two aspects of credibility are extremely important for Asian American clients, because mental health treatment in general, and Western psychotherapy and psychological assessment (particularly if conducted by non-M.D.s), may be treatment modes that have relatively low ascribed credibility in the minds of many Asian Americans. The clinician must be able to quickly assess to what extent low credibility is an issue for a particular Asian American client, then work to achieve credibility in a culturally appropriate manner in the first session.

What is the role of the clinician's ethnicity in the credibility process? Research with the community mental health services has shown that ethnic and language matching between therapists and clients is associated with the length of treatment for ethnic minority clients but that the relationship between ethnic and language match on treatment outcome is equivocal (S. Sue et al., 1991). Jung (1998) discusses various myths that Asian mental health professionals have toward treatment of Chinese clients, and some of his points are relevant to this discussion of ascribed versus achieved credibility. One such myth is that an Asian American therapist only needs to be bilingual and bicultural to be effective with a particular Asian American client. The consideration of diversity among Asian American clients applies equally to Asian American therapists; thus, an acculturated third-generation Chinese American therapist may not necessarily share the cultural history or value system of a recently immigrated Chinese client from Vietnam. Another myth is that non-Asian therapists cannot be effective in working with traditional Asian clients or families. Jung discusses various techniques he uses in his Chinese American Family Therapy (CAFT) Model to gain the trust of Chinese American clients, many of which can be used by non-Asian clinicians.

On the other hand, it can be argued that the ethnicity of the therapist may play a significant role in the "real" aspects of the therapeutic relationship (i.e., therapeutic alliance) as well as the "projected" aspect of the relationship (i.e., transference relationship). Demographic similarity between clinician and clients increases the likelihood of shared values, beliefs, and experiences (Beutler & Clarkin, 1990), and clinician characteristics such as ethnicity, gender, and age are likely to be used by clients to make rapid appraisals about clinician credibility and empathy. The ability to conduct assessment and treatment in the primary language of the client rather than through translators greatly enhances the therapeutic alliance (Chin, 1993).

On a simple level, Asian American clients' perception of the therapists' capacity to understand the uniqueness of the Asian American psychological experience may facilitate early rapport building. Perceived similarity is also likely to assist in the client's development of trust and rapport, liking for the clinician, openness to being influenced in the treatment context, motivation to commit to working in treatment, and the willingness to make changes that may be initially difficult or painful (Shiang, Kjellander, Huang, & Bogumill, 1998). On a more psychodynamic level, the introduction of race and culture into the therapeutic relationship is likely to invoke a number of transference themes such as self-image, race, social class, identity, and so on. Chin (1993) considers four variations of transference themes concerning Asian American clients:

1. Hierarchical transference (i.e., the therapeutic relationship being colored by Asian emphasis on filial piety and respect for authority)
2. Racial transference (i.e., the therapeutic relationship being affected by power inequalities among the races in the larger American sociocultural context)
3. Self–object transference (i.e., the therapeutic relationship being colored by ethnic self-identification of the client and therapist)
4. Pre-Oedipal transference (i.e., the therapeutic relationship being colored by the dominance of mother–son themes in the Buddhist tradition).

Each of the above-listed transference themes are colored by the individual issues that the client brings to treatment. For example, in a case example of a

24-year-old American-born Chinese woman struggling with issues of autonomy and cultural and personal identity, Yee (1993) discusses both the negative
and positive aspects of racial and ethnic transference. In this case, the fact that
the clinician was also Chinese American contributed to an initial negative
transference, as the client was angry toward her mother and her older sisters
and viewed the clinician as a part of the system that oppressed her. On the other
hand, the fact that the clinician was also Chinese American assisted in the
corrective same-gender relationship that did not involve rejection of the client's
Chinese American heritage. Clinicians working with Asian American clients
should be alert to the possible interaction of cultural factors with transference
and countertransference.

B. CULTURAL KNOWLEDGE

S. Sue and Zane (1987) argued that their recommendation for clinicians to
establish credibility with Asian American client is more proximal to the achievement of the therapeutic goal than the recommendation for clinicians to be
familiar with the client's cultural background. However, a knowledge of cultural
values and behavior are indispensable for conducting cultural assessment and
treatment planning. The essential concepts that would assist in the preparation
of the assessment and treatment of Asian American clients can be broadly divided into three sets: (a) broad cultural concepts about common Asian values,
(b) knowledge of how those broad cultural concepts manifest in Asian American client behavior surrounding mental health treatment, and (c) historical and
demographic information about Asian Americans.

1. Broad Cultural Concepts

The defining psychological characteristics of individuals from non-Western cultures center around the integral relations between the self and others. Cross-
cultural psychology literature provides a theoretical base on which the clinician
can learn to conceptualize Asian American individuals' cognition and behavior
through a cultural lens. There are a number of excellent texts on the central
concepts put forth in cross-cultural psychology to explain broad cross-cultural
differences between the Western industrialized nations (e.g., the United States,
Canada, Western Europe) and non-Western nations (e.g., countries in Asian,
South American, Africa, etc.). Examples of these concepts include individualism versus collectivism (e.g., Triandis, 1995) and independent versus interdependent self-construal (Markus & Kitayama, 1991). Central to these concepts
is the notion that world cultures vary in the extent to which the individual self
and its views, needs, and goals supersede the collective's views, needs, and

goals. For example, the interdependent self-construal, which is thought to characterize the self-concept of individuals from Asian cultures, is fundamentally interrelated with others and cannot be separated from the surrounding social context. The behavior of those with interdependent self is governed by what he or she perceives to be the thoughts, feelings, and actions of others in the relationship, and people with interdependent self-construal derive their self-worth through their abilities to adjust themselves to the social climate, to restrain expressions of their individual wishes or feelings, and to maintain harmony with others. Asian Americans, on average, tend to hold more interdependent self-construal than White Americans (Okazaki, 1997). Other broad cultural concepts that may be useful for understanding the psychology of people from Asian cultures are what Ho (1982) calls "relational" concepts. Ho argues that concepts indigenous to Asian cultures (e.g., filial piety, face, *amae*) all pertain to the relational, reciprocal aspects of social behavior between individuals rather than the traditionally Western focus on individual characteristics (e.g., ego, self-esteem). Many descriptions of Asian psychology in the available clinical literature about Asian Americans make use of these fundamental concepts from the cross-cultural psychology literature; thus, the clinician does well to become familiar with these important works.

2. Behavior Surrounding Treatment

Interdependent self-construal has many behavioral consequences that extend to treatment settings. For example, one of the most cited characteristics of a traditional Asian values is that of modesty and humility in interpersonal contexts in the service of maintaining interpersonal harmony. The culturally normative behavior for many Asian cultures is to downplay one's own accomplishments in group settings, which should not be confused with poor self-esteem (Prathikanti, 1997). The cultural sanction against displaying strong emotions in some interpersonal contexts may manifest as client inexpressivity relative to mainstream American clients. Interdependence, which may be culturally normative for the Asian individual, may be perceived by Western standards as pathological dependency (Kobayashi, 1989).

Clinicians treating Asian American clients must be cognizant of the possible role that stigma plays in the help-seeking and treatment process. For example, an Asian American family may seek treatment in a distant location rather than seek treatment in their own community and risk being seen by someone who may recognize them (which in turn might brand family members as having a mental health problems and thereby lessen the marriageability of family members). Some Asian American parents may not agree to having their child assessed for learning disabilities in schools because they fear that an appointment with a psychologist would imply that the child has mental health problems.

In discussing Indian American families' resistance to seeking mental health treatment, Prathikanti (1997) argues that some Indian families may not wish to undermine the "model minority" myth (which asserts that Asian Americans and Indian Americans have no problems) and may fear that seeking treatment would damage the reputation of the entire ethnic group.

3. Diversity Within

There are many accessible, brief texts that summarize the population characteristics as well as the brief history of the major Asian ethnic groups in the United States (e.g., Cao & Novas, 1996; Kitano & Daniels, 1995). This background knowledge about the demographic characteristics and the history of various Asian ethnic groups serves as a necessary building block for performing culturally competent assessment and treatment. The knowledge of cultural diversity within the Asian American population will make it less likely for the clinician to make broad stereotypical assumptions about their Asian American clients. For example, although many traditional Asian cultures hold Confucian gender roles, the Filipino culture prior to the Spanish domination held much more egalitarian gender roles (Sustento-Seneriches, 1997). By knowing which Asian ethnic groups entered the United States at which points in the history, the clinician is able to narrow the questions needed to assess the particular client's cultural background. For example, a third-generation Japanese American client may be more likely to be English-speaking and have had significant exposure to the various aspects of the American culture, while a first-generation elderly Korean American client may be more likely to be a monolingual Korean-speaker with relatively less exposure to American cultural institutions. A post-1965 Japanese American immigrant may or may not identify with the history of Japanese American internment during the World War II. Knowing the pre- and postmigration history of the various waves of refugees from Southeast Asia will allow the clinician to assess not only the acculturative status of the client but also for possible psychological repercussions of traumatic events following the Vietnam War. Obtaining some basic information about the client (e.g., ethnic origin, generational status) prior to the first session will allow the clinician to review relevant resources about the historical and cultural characteristics of the prospective client.

IV. CULTURAL ASSESSMENT

Given the task of translating general knowledge about Asian cultures and the Asian American population, the clinician must conduct a cultural assessment of each client to determine how applicable the clinical guidelines about traditional Asian Americans (as often characterized in clinical guidelines) are to the particular Asian American client. Although demographic characteristics (such as generational status or length of residence in the United States) can often provide cues as to the prototypical cultural profile and behavioral tendencies of some Asian Americans, it is especially important not to assume cultural-psychological attributes of the Asian American client based on the demographics. For example, the general literature suggests that first-generation immigrant Asian Americans are more likely to adhere to traditional cultural practices, to be reluctant to seek professional mental health services, to terminate treatment prematurely, and to prefer a directive counseling style. However, such general guidelines may not apply well to a first-generation Chinese American immigrant who was born and raised in South America, or to a first-generation Vietnamese American immigrant youth who lives in a largely Hispanic neighborhood and identifies culturally with the Mexican American culture.

It must also be acknowledged that there is an inherent tension in structuring the initial session with an Asian American client. On one hand, a thorough assessment of the client as a "cultural being" is necessary for the clinician to determine how to proceed with further assessment and treatment with this particular client (Dana, 1993). On the other hand, if assessment without any intervention is all that is accomplished in the initial session, the clinician runs a risk of losing the client to premature termination due to lack of achieved credibility (S. Sue & Zane, 1987). In order to balance the need for cultural assessment with the recommendation to achieve credibility, the clinician must become practiced in conducting an expeditious assessment of the client's cultural orientation without resorting to stereotyping. One strategy for conducting an efficient cultural assessment in the initial session is to use a measure of acculturation and ethnic identity.

Why is acculturation such a central variable to assess? Acculturation of the Asian American client, or the extent to which he or she has been exposed to and gained skills for operating within various American cultural contexts, can indicate to the clinician how much cultural modification may be required in order to assess and treat this client. A clinician faced with an Asian American client is typically trained in the Western models of assessment and treatment, hence the clinician is well acculturated to the American and Western culture at least in the mental health system. Western thinking permeates the typical clinician's knowledge of what causes mental health problems and what heals such problems. On the other hand, the Asian American population varies greatly in their level of acculturation to the American culture and to the extent to which they share the Western-trained clinician's conceptualization of what causes mental health problems and what heals such problems. It is generally accepted that the more acculturated an Asian American client is to the American culture, the more appropriate the Western modes of assessment or treatment. For example, the MMPI-2 norms are more likely to be applicable for a fourth-generation Japanese American college graduate than to a recently immigrated Japanese elderly.

Unfortunately, the measurement of acculturation has been extensively contested in the fields of ethnic and cross-cultural psychology, and there is no one standard way to assess acculturation of an Asian American individual. Most researchers agree that acculturation is a multifaceted process that occurs when individuals from two or more cultures have continuous first-hand contact, resulting in changes in the original cultural patterns. However, a number of concerns have been raised regarding the conceptualization and psychometric properties of various written measures to measures this construct among Asian Americans (Nagata, 1994; Ponterotto, Baluch, & Carielli, 1998). For Asian Americans, a myriad of ethnic-specific acculturation and identity measures have been devised for various Asian American ethnic groups (Dana, 1993; Paniagua, 1994), but most such measures have yet to be subjected to wide use or extensive psychometric validation. The most widely accepted scale in Asian American mental health research is the Suinn-Lew Asian Self-Identity and Acculturation Scale (SL-ASIA; Suinn, Rickard-Figueroa, Lew, & Virgil, 1987), a pan-Asian measure of acculturation and identity. In its development, Suinn and his colleagues adopted the format of the original Acculturation Rating Scale for Mexican Americans (ARSMA; Cuéllar, Harris, & Jasso, 1980) and included 21 multiple-choice items covering behavior, language, identity, friendship, generation and geographic history, and attitudes. A total score (the mean of the 21 items) is interpreted to indicate the respondent's level of acculturation, from low acculturation (high Asian identity) to high acculturation (high Western identity or assimilation).

A review of published studies that used SL-ASIA (Ponterotto et al., 1998) highlighted both strengths and shortcomings of this measure as a research instrument. Of note, the lack of conceptual clarity behind SL-ASIA was criticized surrounding the question of whether Asian American acculturation is best conceptualized as a unidimensional or multidimensional construct. The original SL-ASIA classified individuals on a unidimensional index from low to high acculturation, and those individuals scoring in the midrange were labeled as "bicultural." However, it is possible for an individual to identify highly with both the minority and the majority culture (Oetting & Beauvais, 1991). In response to these critiques, Suinn (1998) recently added five additional items to the SL-ASIA to allow for the assessment of acculturation as reflecting Asian and Western values, behavioral competency (i.e., how well one fits in with Asian or Western social contexts), and self-identity as a bicultural person.

Further, despite its limitations as a research tool, potential clinical utility of the SL-ASIA scale has been noted (Dana, 1993; Ponterotto, Baluch, & Carielli, 1998). In particular, Ponterotto and colleagues argued that some of the SL-ASIA items could easily be incorporated into a clinical interview that would assist the clinician in obtaining a quick and general sense of the client's acculturation level. Suinn (1998) himself provided sample scenarios of how the SL-ASIA score may be used in clinical settings to predict outcomes of therapy based on the therapist–client match in cultural orientation. For example, Suinn postulated that an Asian American client with strong Asian values and behavioral competencies in both Asian and Western social contexts may do fine with a non-Asian clinician who encourages self-disclosure, whereas another Asian American client with strong Asian values but behavioral competency only in Asian social contexts may not do as well with a non-Asian clinician who encourages self-disclosure.

In addition to the SL-ASIA, two promising measures of related cultural constructs have been developed recently, which provide additional options for clinicians to assess various aspects of an Asian American client's cultural and ethnic identification. Yamada, Marsella, and Yamada (1998) devised a measure of ethnocultural identity, which the researchers refer to as the behavioral component of ethnic identity (as opposed to the attitudinal and the value components of ethnic identity). The resulting Ethnocultural Identity Behavioral Index (EIBI) is a 19-item self-report measure applicable to any ethnic group. Initial psychometric study with Asian Americans and Pacific Islander Americans in Hawaii suggest that EIBI appears to be a reliable and valid measure for assessing the level of an individual's involvement with an ethnocultural group. In contrast to Yamada et al.'s attempts to develop a behavioral index, Tsai, Ying, and Lee (in press) sought to measure the subjective meanings attached to "being Chinese" and "being American" among a diverse group of Chinese Americans. The researchers developed the Chinese and the American versions of the General Ethnicity Questionnaire (GEQ) to test both the unidimensional and bidimensional models of acculturation. The GEQ samples multiple domains of cultural orientation including language use and proficiency, affiliation with specific ethnic persons (i.e., Chinese or American), participation in ethnic activities, attitudes toward the ethnic group, exposure to specific culture, and preference for ethnic food. The analyses of the responses of Chinese Americans on the GEQ measures found that "being Chinese" and "being American" were unrelated for American-born Chinese Americans but were negatively related for immigrant Chinese. The researchers explained that when immigrants first arrive in the United States, they consider themselves to be "Chinese" and not "American." However, as the immigrants gain more exposure to the American culture, the immigrants may begin to internalize an American identity while "being Chinese" increasingly becomes tied to limited specific contexts in which they have contacts with Chinese people, things, and events. These findings from the Tsai et al. (in press) study underscores the importance of assessing the subjective meanings attached to an individual's cultural identity.

The clinician may wish to administer any of the above-mentioned scales in a written format to the Asian American client prior to the first interview to obtain a rough estimate of the client's acculturation and self-identification, then follow up on some key items regarding cultural orientation and identity in the more thorough cultural assessment during the first session. In particular, the measures that sample multiple domains are particularly useful in identifying the acculturation profiles of the client in different life domains. The clinician should keep in mind that acculturation may not proceed at a uniform rate among the different domains even within an individual, much less among the family members. For example, a South Asian American individual who appears to be highly acculturated with respect to behavior (e.g., adoption of Western dress, manners, English fluency) may still substantially endorse traditional values and behavior within the family system (Prathikanti, 1997).

E. Lee (1982) advocates an approach to the assessment of Asian American families that involves gathering additional information beyond traditional intake data, and many of her suggestions can be also applied to individual cases. Importantly, Lee stresses the importance of gathering information not just about the client system and the family system but also the community system in which the Asian American individual or the family operate, such as formal and informal referral and support network, attitudes toward health and mental illness of community members, impact of immigration and refugee policies, and so on. Similarly, a model of parallel assessment for Asian American children and adolescents has been proposed by Huang (1997), in which the clinician is advised to carry out in parallel the standard assessment and the ethnocultural assessment. The standard assessment consists of evaluating the individual (e.g., appearance, speech, language, affect), family (e.g., composition, subsystems, hierarchy), school (e.g., demographics, philosophy about achievement, cohesiveness), and peers (e.g., nature and degree of involvement, values congruence). The ethnocultural assessment gathers additional information about the individual (e.g., generational status, level of acculturation, ethnicity, and self-concept), family (e.g., migration history, level of acculturation, "generation gaps"), school (e.g., history with cultural differences, ethnic/racial composition), and peers (e.g., ethnicity and race, level of acculturation). Huang provides a detail recommendation for assessing each of these components. Another systematic approach to assessment was suggested by Shiang et al. (1998), who proposed a cultural modification of Beutler and Clarkin's (1990) systematic treatment selection (STS) model of client assessment and treatment planning. Within the STS framework, Shiang et al. suggest a way to make clinical practice decisions that are culturally informed (e.g., what should be the focus of the intervention?) In sum, there are a number of excellent recent innovations in conducting a cultural assessment of Asian American clients and families to assist the clinician in planning a culturally competent intervention.

V. TREATMENT

In this final section, three topics in treating Asian American clients are highlighted: (a) techniques for establishing credibility, (b) importance of maintaining flexibility with respect to the parameters of treatment as well as therapeutic approaches, and (c) availability of case studies that illustrate how to translate broad cultural concepts into cultural formulations of individual cases. These are necessarily broad descriptions that only introduce the reader to potential cultural issues in treatment with Asian Americans. The clinician faced with actual Asian American client cases should consult more specific resources. For example, the volume edited by E. Lee (1997) contains chapters on working with Asian Americans at different stages of the life cycle (children, adolescents, young adults, elderly), with various *DSM-IV* diagnoses (schizophrenia, major depression, posttraumatic stress disorder [PTSD], substance abuse, anxiety disorders), using various treatment approaches (psychoanalytic, group, psychopharmacological, case management, and testing), and other specific topics (gay and lesbian issues, women's issues, intermarriages, domestic violence, spiritual issues, mental health systems, and use of translators). In addition, consultation with cultural informants or professionals with expertise in the specific Asian American group is highly encouraged.

A. ESTABLISHING CREDIBILITY

I have already discussed the supreme importance of establishing and maintaining credibility of mental health treatment with Asian American clients, especially if the clinician determines that the particular client is relatively less acculturated to Western world view. How does a clinician go about establishing credibility? E. Lee (1997) argues that beyond the basics, such as air of confidence, empathic understanding, maturity, and professional mannerisms, there are a number of ways that a clinician can establish credibility and authority with Asian American clients. These recommendations apply especially to those who hold more traditional Asian values concerning the hierarchy of social roles. Lee's list includes using professional titles when making introductions, displaying professional credentials such as diplomas and licenses in the office, obtaining sufficient information about clients and families prior to the initial session, offering some possible explanation for the cause of the problem in the initial session, showing familiarity with the family's cultural background, providing a set of cues for the clients and family to judge the clinician expertise, and providing some immediate solutions to the problems. These recommendations concur with the recommendations for treating Chinese American families given by Jung (1998) and are appropriate for other Asian ethnic clients. Additionally, a strategic disclosure by the clinician of some personal information (e.g., his or her family background, country of origin, academic and professional background) may be helpful in gaining credibility with some Asian American individuals and families (E. Lee, 1997). Jung (1998) gives a number of case examples in the CAFT in which he uses self-disclosure of personal information about his own background at key junctures in the family treatment to establish rapport and to form a cultural alliance with Chinese American clients.

B. MAINTAINING FLEXIBILITY

There is a general agreement that the clinician should maintain flexibility with respect to the traditional "rules" of Western psychotherapy when treating Asian American individuals and families. For instance, not accepting small gifts from clients may be perceived as rude by some Asian Americans. In working with Asian American elderly clients, Kao and Lam (1997) suggest that clinicians practice "mental reservation," which involves deferring the detailed explanation of some Western psychotherapy practices until the client is well engaged in treatment. For example, when an Asian American elderly client initially invites the clinician to lunch, the clinician may respond with a statement such as "I've already eaten" rather than to respond with a detailed explanation of why such actions are inappropriate in psychotherapy. In addition, a clinician working with Asian Americans may need to serve as a cultural broker and provide some concrete assistance (e.g., locating legal aid) or serve functions traditionally not associated with the role of a therapist (e.g., assisting the Cambodian American community in establishing a local Buddhist temple or in initiating a community garden).

There is no one agreed treatment approach or a theoretical orientation that is recommended for treating Asian American clients, just as there is no one treatment approach that is suggested for treating all White clients (Shiang et al., 1998). In treating Asian American clients, the clinician may find it useful to invoke techniques from various schools of psychosocial treatment while still having a coherent framework for understanding the impact of culture and organizing clinical intervention. The treatment recommendations with Asian Americans tend to fall into two categories: (a) an adaptation or a modification of an existing treatment approach, or (b) an integration of various approaches into a new treatment framework. Representative of the former type, a number of clinical writers have described specific modification of theory and techniques of psychoanalytic treatment approach (Bracero, 1994; Wu, 1994; Yi, 1995) or of cognitive-behavioral treatment approach (Chen, 1995) with Asian American clients. For example, Chen (1995) discusses the compatibility of Chinese culture with some aspects of Rational Emotive Therapy (e.g., logical thinking as a principle of life, cognition as the origin of emotion, the counselor as a teacher) while cautioning the clinicians to moderate the Socratic questioning technique for disputing irrational beliefs with Chinese clients. Wu (1994) discusses how her psychoanalytic stance of being a blank slate (i.e., having a "stone face") by not answering a Chinese immigrant client's question about her own background led to a loss of therapeutic rapport and to that client's premature termination.

Taking a more integrative approach, Jung (1998) describes his CAFT model as "an eclectic, multidimensional, comprehensive family therapy model in which family integration theory, general systems theory, and case management act as foundational theories, combined with crisis intervention and social learning theory" (p. 57). Adding to the strategic use of various Western family therapy models and techniques, Jung asserts that "family integration," which is the central goal in the CAFT, is based on the Taoist premise that everything in nature is relative and has an opposite, that life is neither all good nor bad, and that we can all learn from both difficulty and success. The overarching goal for CAFT is for the family members to find peace with each other and with the cultural differences between their country of origin and the country of settlement, and to live harmoniously and ethically with each other. Thus in order to find emotional, psychological, and spiritual harmony within the family, Chinese American families are led to appreciate and accept both the American and Chinese cultural influences on the family.

C. READING CASE STUDIES

Some recent additions to the clinical literature on treating Asian Americans feature more detailed descriptions of the psychotherapy sessions than those that were previously available. These extended case examples provide more holistic pictures of various Asian American client cases in contrast to briefer case examples that can only illustrate a limited number of cultural-clinical phenomenology or cultural intervention. For example, Jung's (1998) text presents case studies of six different Chinese American individuals and families presenting with a variety of problems. The clinician may find particularly useful the extensive, session-by-session description of the Lee family case example. Shiang et al. (1998) also include a clinical case example of an eight-session psychotherapy with a Chinese American woman with somatic complaints. This case lists the relevant concerns for the STS variables for each session alongside the therapist's narrative. Cheung and Lin (1997) present a detailed cultural formulation of a Chinese-Vietnamese woman with multiple somatoform and depressive symptoms. Chin et al.'s (1993) book also contains four case discussions that include not only the client data but mental status evaluation and diagnostic formulation, treatment plan, and summary of sessions for each case.

These case discussions are useful in illustrating the rationale behind major and minor therapeutic decisions and actions (e.g., offering tea and coffee in the initial meeting with a Chinese American family, using or not using the title "doctor" in the initial meeting with an Asian American client, not focusing on immediate expressions of anger in the second session with a sexually assaulted immigrant Chinese woman) in richer cultural contexts of specific individual cases.

VI. CONCLUSION

If the readers can only take home one message from this chapter, I would like to impress upon them the supreme importance of assessing the client's cultural "place" within the context of his or her particular social ecology. That is, clinicians are encouraged to conceptualize each client, as well as themselves, as "cultural beings" (Dana, 1998). The clinician's task of having to translate the literature on the general or modal Asian American characteristics to the individual Asian American client on the basis of an effective cultural assessment presents a formidable challenge. It is hoped that the increased availability of resources for conducting culturally competent assessment and treatment with Asian Americans that have been highlighted in this chapter will facilitate this process.

REFERENCES

American Psychiatric Association (1987). *Diagnostic and statistical manual of mental disorders* (3rd ed., revised). Washington, DC: Author.

Beutler, L. E., & Clarkin, J. F. (1990). *Systematic treatment selection: Toward targeted therapeutic interventions.* New York: Brunner/Mazel.

Bracero, W. (1994). Developing culturally sensitive psychodynamic case formulations: The effects of Asian cultural elements on psychoanalytic control-mastery theory. *Psychotherapy, 31*(3), 525–532.

Butcher, J. N. (Ed.). (1996). *International adaptations of the MMPI-2: Research and clinical applications.* Minneapolis: University of Minnesota Press.

Cao, L., & Novas, H. (1996). *Everything you need to know about Asian American history.* New York: Plume/Penguin.

Chan, S. (Ed.). (1994). *Hmong means free: Life in Laos and America.* Philadelphia: Temple University Press.

Chen, C. P. (1995). Counseling applications of RET in a Chinese cultural context. *Journal of Rational-Emotive and Cognitive Therapy, 13*(2), 117–129.

Cheung, F., & Lin, K. (1997). Neurasthenia, depression, and somatoform disorder in a Chinese-Vietnamese woman migrant. *Culture, Medicine, and Psychiatry, 21,* 247–258.

Chin, J. L. (1993). Transference. In J. L. Chin, J. H. Liem, M. D. Ham, & G. K. Hong (Eds.), *Transference and empathy in Asian American psychotherapy: Cultural values and treatment needs* (pp. 15–33). Westport, CT: Praeger.

Chin, J. L., Liem, J. H., Ham, M. D., & Hong, G. K. (1993). *Transference and Empathy in Asian American Psychotherapy: Cultural values and treatment needs.* Westport, CT: Praeger.

Cho, M., & Kim, K. (1998). Use of the Center for Epidemiologic Studies Depression (CES-D) Scale in Korea. *Journal of Nervous and Mental Disease, 186,* 304–310.

Chow, C. S. (1998). *Leaving deep water: The lives of Asian American women at the crossroads of two cultures.* New York: Dutton.

Cuéllar, I., Harris, L., & Jasso, R. (1980). An acculturation scale for Mexican American normal and clinical populations. *Hispanic Journal of Behavioral Science, 2,* 199–217.

Dana, R. H. (1993). Asian Americans. In *Multicultural assessment perspectives for professional psychology* (pp. 47–64). Boston: Allyn & Bacon.

Dana, R. H. (1998). Asians and Asian Americans. In *Understanding cultural identity in intervention and assessment* (pp. 141–173). Thousand Oaks, CA: Sage.

Freeman, J. M. (1989). *Hearts of sorrow: Vietnamese-American lives.* Stanford, CA: Stanford University Press.

Friedman, S. (Ed.). (1997). *Cultural issues in the treatment of anxiety.* New York: Guilford.

Ho, D. Y. F. (1982). Asian concepts in behavioral science. *Psychologia, 25,* 228–235.

Hongo, G. (Ed.). (1995). *Under Western eyes: Personal essays from Asian America.* New York: Anchor Books.

Huang, L. N. (1997). Asian American adolescents. In E. Lee (Ed.), *Working with Asian Americans: A guide for clinicians* (pp. 175–195). New York: Guilford.

Hurh, W. M., & Kim, K. C. (1990). Correlates of Korean immigrants' mental health. *Journal of Nervous and Mental Disease, 178(11),* 703–711.

Iwamasa, G. Y., Arean, P. A., Miranda, J., & Muñoz, R. (1993, August). *Item bias of the CES-D among African American and Chinese American medical patients.* Paper presented at the annual meeting of the American Psychological Association, Toronto, Canada.

Iwata, N., Saito, K., & Roberts, R. E. (1994). Responses to a self-administered depression scale among younger adolescents in Japan. *Psychiatry Research, 53,* 275–287.

Jung, M. (1998). *Chinese American family therapy: A new model for clinicians.* San Francisco: Jossey-Bass.

Kao, R. S., & Lam, M. L. (1997). Asian American elderly. In E. Lee (Ed.), *Working with Asian Americans: A guide for clinicians* (pp. 208–223). New York: Guilford.

Kessler, R. C., McGonagle, K. A., Zhao, S., Nelson, C. B., Hughes, M., Eshleman, S., Wittchen, H., & Kendler, K. S. (1994). Lifetime and 12-month prevalence of DSM-III-R psychiatric disorders in the United States. *Archives of General Psychiatry, 51,* 8–19.

Kitano, H. H. L., & Daniels, R. (1995). *Asian Americans: Emerging minorities (2nd ed.).* Englewood Cliffs, NJ: Prentice Hall.

Kleinman, A. (1982). Neurasthenia and depression: A study of somatization and culture in China. *Culture, Medicine, and Psychiatry, 6,* 117–190.

Kobayashi, J. S. (1989). Depathologizing dependency: Two perspectives. *Psychiatric Annals, 19(12),* 653–658.

Kuo, W. H. (1984). Prevalence of depression among Asian-Americans. *Journal of Nervous and Mental Disease, 172(8),* 449–457.

Kwon, P. (1995). Application of social cognition principles to treatment recommendations for ethnic minority clients: The case of Asian Americans. *Clinical Psychology Review, 15,* 613–629.

Lee, C. C. (Ed.). (1997). *Multicultural issues in counseling: New approaches to diversity* (2nd ed.). Alexandria, VA: American Counseling Association.

Lee, E. (1982). A social systems approach to assessment and treatment for Chinese American families. In M. McGoldrick, J. K. Pearce, & J. Giordano (Eds.), *Ethnicity and family therapy* (pp. 552–572). New York: Guilford.

Lee, E. (1997). Overview: The assessment and treatment of Asian American families. In E. Lee (Ed.), *Working with Asian Americans: A guide for clinicians* (pp. 3–36). New York: Guilford.

Lee, J. F. J. (1991). *Asian Americans: Oral histories of first to fourth generation Americans from China, the Philippines, Japan, India, the Pacific Islands, Vietnam, and Cambodia.* New York: The New Press.

Lee, L. C., & Zane, N. W. S. (Eds.). (1998). *Handbook of Asian American psychology.* Thousand Oaks, CA: Sage.

Lee, S. (1994). Neurasthenia and Chinese psychiatry in the 1990s. *Journal of Psychosomatic Research, 38,* 487–491.

Lin, K., Lau, J. K. C., Yamamoto, J., Zheng, Y., Kim, H., Cho, K., & Nakasaki, G. (1992). Hwa-Byung: A community study of Korean Americans. *Journal of Nervous and Mental Disease, 180(6),* 386–391.

Markus, H. R., & Kitayama, S. (1991). Culture and the self: Implications for cognition, emotion, and motivation. *Psychological Review, 98,* 224–253.

Nagata, D. K. (1994). Assessing Asian American acculturation and ethnic identity: The need for a multidimensional framework. *Asian American and Pacific Islander Journal of Health, 2(2),* 108–124.

Oetting, E., & Beauvais, F. (1991). Orthogonal cultural identification theory: The cultural identification of minority adolescents. *International Journal of Addictions, 25,* 655–685.

Okazaki, S. (1997). Sources of ethnic differences between Asian American and White American college students on measures of depression and social anxiety. *Journal of Abnormal Psychology, 106,* 52–60.

Okazaki, S. (1998). Psychological assessment of Asian Americans: Research agenda for cultural competency. *Journal of Personality Assessment, 70,* 54–70.

Paniagua, F. A. (1994). *Assessing and treating culturally diverse clients: A practical guide.* Thousand Oaks, CA: Sage.

Ponterotto, J. G., Baluch, S., & Carielli, D. (1998). The Suinn-Lew Asian Self-Identity Acculturation Scale (SL-ASIA): Critique and research recommendations. *Measurement and Evaluation in Counseling and Development, 31,* 109–124.

Prathikanti, S. (1997). East Indian American families. In E. Lee (Ed.), *Working with Asian Americans: A guide for clinicians* (pp. 79–100). New York: Guilford.

Radloff, L. (1977). The CES-D scale: A self-report depression scale for research in the general population. *Applied Psychological Measurement, 1,* 385–401.

Samuda, R. J. (1998). *Psychological testing of American minorities: Issues and consequences (2nd ed.).* Thousand Oaks, CA: Sage.

Shiang, J., Kjellander, C., Huang, K., & Bogumill, S. (1998). Developing cultural competency in clinical practice: Treatment considerations for Chinese cultural groups in the United States. *Clinical Psychology: Science and Practice, 5(2),* 182–210.

Shin, K. R. (1993). Factors predicting depresson among Korean-American women in New York: *International Journal of Nursing Studies, 30,* 415–423.

Snowden, L. R., & Cheung, F. K. (1990). Use of inpatient mental health services by members of ethnic minority groups. *American Psychologist, 45,* 347–355.

Sue, D. W., & Sue, D. (1999). Counseling Asian Americans. In *Counseling the culturally different: Theory and practice (3rd ed.)* (pp. 255–271). New York: Wiley.

Sue, S., Fujino, D. C., Hu, L., Takeuchi, D. T., & Zane, N. W. S. (1991). Community mental health services for ethnic minority groups: A test of the cultural responsiveness hypothesis. *Journal of Consulting and Clinical Psychology, 59,* 533–540.

Sue, S., & Zane, N. (1987). The role of culture and cultural techniques in psychotherapy: A critique and reformulation. *American Psychologist, 42,* 37–45.

Suinn, R. M. (1998). Measurement of acculturation of Asian Americans. *Asian American and Pacific Islander Journal of Health, 6(1),* 7–12.

Suinn, R. M., Rickard-Figueroa, K., Lew, S., & Virgil, P. (1987). The Suinn-Lew Asian self-identity acculturation scale: An initial report. *Educational and Psychological Measurement, 47,* 401–407.

Sustento-Seneriches, J. (1997). Filipino American families. In E. Lee (Ed.), *Working with Asian Americans: A guide for clinicians* (pp. 101–113). New York: Guilford.

Takeuchi, D. T., Chung, R. C., Lin, K., Shen, H., Kurasaki, K., Chun, C., & Sue, S. (1998). Lifetime and twelve-month prevalence rates of major depressive episodes and dysthymia among Chinese Americans in Los Angeles. *American Journal of Psychiatry 155(10),* 1407–1414.

Triandis, H. C. (1995). *Individualism and collectivism: New directions in social psychology.* Boulder, CO: Westview Press.

Tsai, J. L., Ying, Y., & Lee, P. A. (in press). The meaning of "being Chinese" and "being American": Variation among Chinese American young adults. *Journal of Cross-Cultural Psychology.*

Tseng, W., & Streltzer, J. (1997). *Culture and psychopathology: A guide to clinical assessment.* New York: Brunner/Mazel.

Uba, L. (1994). *Asian Americans: Personality patterns, identity, and mental health.* New York: Guilford Press.

Wu, J. (1994). On therapy with Asian patients. *Contemporary Psychoanalysis, 30,* 152–168.

Yamada, A., Marsella, A. J., & Yamada, S. Y. (1998). The development of Ethnocultural Identity Behavioral Index: Psychometric properties and validation with Asian Americans and Pacific Islanders. *Asian American and Pacific Islander Journal of Health, 6(1),* 36–45.

Yee, J. H. Y. (1993). Bridging generations and cultures. In J. L. Chin, J. H. Liem, M. D. Ham, & G. K. Hong (Eds.), *Transference and empathy in Asian American psychotherapy: Cultural values and treatment needs* (pp. 105–117). Westport, CT: Praeger.

Yi, K. (1995). Psychoanalytic psychotherapy with Asian clients: Transference and therapeutic considerations. *Psychotherapy, 32(2),* 308–316.

Zheng, Y., Lin, K., Takeuchi, D. T., Kurasaki, K. S., Wang, Y., & Cheung, F. (1997). An epidemiological study of neurasthenia in Chinese-Americans in Los Angeles. *Comprehensive Psychiatry, 38(5),* 249–259.

CHAPTER 10

Mental Health Assessment and Treatment of African Americans: A Multicultural Perspective

MICHAEL L. LINDSEY

Nestor Consultants, Inc.
Dallas, Texas

ISRAEL CUÉLLAR

Department of Psychology and Anthropology
University of Texas—Pan American
Edinburg, Texas

I. SOCIODEMOGRAPHIC DESCRIPTION

The projected African American population in the year 2000 is 35.4 million, representing 12.9% of the U.S. population (U.S. Bureau of the Census, 1997). African Americans make up the single largest minority group in the United States. African Americans have always been a part of the United States since before the American Revolution. Between 1619 and 1997 the proportion of people of African descent in North America ranged from 5% in 1750 to a high of 19% in 1790. Certain cities or regions of the United States have historically had high proportions of people of African descent; for example, in 1746, New York City's population was one-fifth of African origin, and one-quarter of the population of Newport was of African descent in 1755. In 1790, 35% of the population of the South was of African descent (Farley, 1970).

African-origin slaves were a significant factor in the growth and thriving of the earliest settlements in what is now known as Boston, Newport, New Amsterdam, Philadelphia, and Charleston. These early trading centers depended on manual labor, and African slaves had numerous advantages over indigenous Indians and indentured servants (Farley, 1970). Both the importation of slaves and natural increases are believed to account for the population growth seen between the Revolutionary and the Civil Wars (Farley, 1970).

The African American population in the United States is growing at 1.3%, one of the slowest rates of all populations in the United States. The percentage of African Americans in the United States projected for the year 2020 is 14.0% and for the year 2050 is 15.4%. (U.S. Bureau of the Census, 1997). Immigration of persons of African descent from Egypt, Ethiopia, Ghana, Nigeria, Haiti, Panama, Jamaica, Trinidad, Barbados, and other Caribbean nations has added to the cultural, religious, and language diversity of the African origin people of the United States (U.S. Department of Commerce, 1995).

The average income of African American families in 1995 was $24,698. This was significantly below the national U.S. average of $39,276 and below the European American average of $40,884 (U.S. Bureau of the Census, 1996). Paniagua (1998) notes that 27% of African American families and 30.6% of African American persons fell below the poverty level in comparison to 9.1% of European American families and 11.7% of European American persons.

The average African American living in the U.S. is generally less educated and financially poorer than the average European American. The African American population is generally in poorer physical health (i.e., disproportionate rates of chronic illnesses such as heart and circulatory problems, HIV/AIDS, physical injuries and deaths from violence, than European Americans) (Western Interstate Commission for Higher Education [WICHE], October, 1997). African Americans are at greater risk for substance abuse, one of the most significant health problems in the U.S. according to the Institute for Health Policy (1993).

II. MENTAL HEALTH NEEDS

With respect to mental health, there is a very large and substantial body of research documenting the high rates of utilization of mental health facilities by African Americans, particularly inpatient psychiatric services (Cuéllar, 1977; Manderscheid & Sonnenschein, 1987; Scheffler & Miller, 1989; Snowden & Cheung, 1990; Stolp & Warner, 1987). Admissions to state hospitals, general hospitals with psychiatric units, and community mental health centers by African Americans during the 1970s, 1980s, and early 1990s show consistently higher admission rates for African Americans than European Americans and other racial and ethnic groups. Although the national admission rate to Veterans Administration Hospitals was 70.4 per 100,000, individuals of African descent had a rate of 118.2 per 100,000 (WICHE, 1997). The rate of admission to state psychiatric hospitals for African Americans between the ages of 25–44 was 598 per 100,000, whereas the national rate was 163.6 (Manderscheid & Sonnenschein, 1987). African Americans are also disproportionately misdiagnosed on admission, being diagnosed with more severe mental illnesses than other ethnic or racial populations (Manderscheid & Sonnenschein, 1987).

It is important to note that whereas many community-based epidemiological studies have found both general and specific higher prevalence rates for African Americans across many diagnostic categories, (Holzer, Swanson, & Shea, 1995; Robins, Locke, & Regier, 1991; Warheit, Holzer, & Arey, 1975; Warheit, Holzer, & Schwab, 1973) there are some community-based mental health studies like the National Comorbidity Study (Kessler et al., 1994) and the Washington Needs Assessment Household Survey (WANAHS) that do not report higher prevalence rates for African Americans (also see Holzer & Copeland, chapter 17, this volume, for a discussion of this finding).

The report of the four national panels on cultural competence in managed care mental health services (WICHE, 1997) concludes that African Americans who utilize mental health services tend to drop out of services at significantly higher rates than European American populations. Also in comparison to European Americans, African Americans tend to enter mental health treatment services at a later stage in the course of their illness, are more often misdiagnosed, and are more often diagnosed as having severe mental illness.

Mental health problems and mental illness in any population can be manifested in various ways, including comorbidity with physical illness, substance abuse/dependence, racism, criminal behavior, violence, and through conflicts with institutions, and numerous other means. Mauer (1999) reports that 49% of prison inmates nationally are African American, compared to a 12.9% share in the overall population. This suggests that a large number of black males, in particular, have major problems successfully navigating, using, benefiting, and/ or "buying into" the existing social, educational, legal, financial, health, employment, and other sociocultural systems in the United States.

Like all other communities, the African American community has its own share of problems. Physical illnesses, mental illnesses, drop-out rates, criminal activity, substance abuse and dependence, poverty, and other health and social problems exist in higher proportions than other racial or ethnic groups. What are the causes of these problems and how can mental health systems, health care systems, and providers of mental health care do to improve conditions, prevent problems, rehabilitate or otherwise treat these problems in the African American community? An approach suggested in this chapter and throughout this handbook is multicultural mental health. How can multicultural mental health theory and practies help in the assessment and treatment of African Americans?

III. MULTICULTURAL ASSESSMENT
AND TREATMENT PRACTICES

What does a clinician need to know about the delivery of mental health services to African Americans? What kinds of information and knowledge does the clinician need to know about African Americans, other than general, sociocultural, and demographic patterns obtained from group data? How do general sociocultural and demographic factors relate to the delivery of mental health services for African Americans? Does separating African American patients into ethnic or cultural groups contribute to treating them? These and other questions and concerns will be addressed below specifically for African Americans while at the same time providing guidance in applying multicultural assessment practices with African Americans.

   1. Does multicultural assessment and treatment of mental health problems and disorders in African Americans in any way discredit traditional therapies? The answer is no. Traditional therapies including psychodynamic, behavior therapies, psychotropic therapies, group therapies, insight-oriented, supportive, or behavior-modifying therapies that are used with European American patients also can be used with African Americans. The problem is that traditional approaches sometimes do not seem to work as well for most African Americans as they do for most European Americans. Sometimes traditional approaches have to be modified in some manner or form in order to improve their acceptability and effectiveness. Could it be that systems and therapies are more appropriate in some ways for some consumers than for others? Psychotherapy is not for everybody, it appears to be more effective with more verbal, insightful, and reflective people. Behavior therapies are not for everybody either. Systematic desensitization is appropriate for some problems but not for others. Individuals with different problems respond better to specific therapies. This is nothing new. This is, however, an important clinical skill to learn (i.e., to know what kinds of problems respond best to which therapies). The point here is that African Americans may have very different problems than persons from other groups. Many problems will be in common with all groups, but many problems also are unique onto themselves. It is good for the clinician to have some idea as to the kind of life, psychosocial stressors, problems, burdens, trials, worldviews, and the like that characterize the life of their client.

   At the beginning of the 20th century, it was recognized that psychiatric and psychological care entails communicating with the patient, and the appreciation for the importance of detailed knowledge of the influences the particular culture exerts over the individual. (Also see Marselle, chapter 1, this volume, for a more detailed history of the "struggle" to include the role of culture as a determinant of behavior). Early writers and psychiatrists such as Emil Kraepelin

(1904), Erich Fromm, Wilhelm Reich, Harry Stack Sullivan, and John Dollard (Horney, 1936) recognized the importance of cultural factors as a determining influence in psychological conditions. A physical problem like a broken leg can be treated by anyone trained to treat a broken leg. The racial and ethnic background of the physician or healer doesn't matter, neither does the racial, ethnic, linguistic, or cultural group the patient belongs to for treatment of the patient's broken leg. However, these factors do matter in the provision of mental health care. Assessment of mental status entails sophisticated, structured, nonstructured, standardized, and nonstandardized observations, communication, and testing of the patient in order to assess, among other cognitions and feelings, orientation, reasoning, conceptualization, motivation, thought processes, insight, intelligence, mood, and personality. Often such an assessment has to be conducted within limited time constraints, sometimes limited by reimbursement sources and other times by the setting. An inpatient hospital consultation may need to be accomplished within a 30- or 50-minute period of time. There is a lot to be learned about the patient, and there are many opportunities for miscommunication. Even when the same word is used by two people there can be miscommunication as to meaning.

Miscommunication is exacerbated when expressions of speech, dialects, phrases, metaphors, and the like are used with common meaning between the provider and the consumer of mental health care. The greater the cultural differences existing between the provider and the consumer of mental health care, including socioeconomic, gender, ethnic, language, and worldviews, the greater is the likelihood of misdiagnosis, inappropriate care, or noncompliance with treatment.

The notion that one needs to walk in someone else's shoes to really understand that person has much appeal to many people because it makes intuitive sense. Of course, it is not literally necessary for a professional mental health worker to actually walk in their client's shoes to understand and provide appropriate care and therapy. But if the professional did walk a day, for example, in their patient's shoes, whatever knowledge gained from this act should augment the quality of therapy rendered, and should not in any way discredit the professional's knowledge, skills, and/or training. Communication, empathy, compassion, appreciation, affection, insight, and comprehension increase commensurate with greater knowledge of others.

Traditional therapies have valued directive approaches, individual responsibility, looking inward, self-understanding, personal growth, and improvement in social and occupational functioning, resolution of dependency needs, verbal and emotional expressiveness, and thinking through problems. These same therapies can be used with African Americans; however, some African Americans will respond even more favorably if therapy efforts are directed toward the environment or toward working with the extended family or toward spiritualistic and/or religious interventions, or toward strengthening interdependency, giving direct advice, and to special symbolic approaches.

Cognitive therapy for depression can be used as an example. The basic principles of cognitive therapy are the same for individuals suffering from depression regardless of their racial and ethnic background. It is a traditional form of psychological therapy appropriate for African Americans as it is for Hispanics, Asian Americans, American Indians, Native Americans, and European Americans. An example of the way in which cognitive therapy could be applied across diverse populations from a multicultural perspective is that individual explanatory models are linked to the cultural background of the person. For example, in culture "A," needs for achievement, individual responsibility, and guilt may be intricately tied to a patient's explanatory model, whereas in culture "B," needs for acceptance, interdependence, and fatalistic beliefs may be linked to their explanatory model. An individual clinical assessment in the development of a cognitive therapy plan that does not identify such cultural differences between a patient for culture "A" and "B" would most likely not lead to effectual treatment.

2. Does multicultural assessment and treatment of mental health problems and disorders in African Americans presume that most practitioners are racist? The answer is no. Multicultural Therapy understands the reality that people with racist attitudes exist in the real world. It also recognizes that people have biases and that people harbor negative stereotypes. What Multicultural Therapy stresses is that whenever working cross-culturally with individuals from racial/ethnic/cultural groups different from oneself, it is essential to routinely ask oneself, "Do I have any conflicting values with this consumer?" Some people who have racist attitudes are not consciously aware of their racism while others are. Some people who are not racist, nonetheless, have strong conflicting values with their consumers. There is no presumption of racism in multicultural therapies and interventions. For the therapist to ask himself or herself if they hold any racist, discriminating, or prejudicial attitudes toward members of their client's ethnic and racial group is not to presume racism. It is a healthy question for all therapists to ask of themselves. Questions such as, "Would I view this client differently if they were from my own ethnic group?" These questions do not presume that the therapist is racist. What they do presume is that everybody is human and we all hold biases from time to time. Furthermore, it is important for therapists to be in touch with their own feelings, attitudes, and values held with respect to their own culture and other ethnic group(s). Most therapists are not racist, as racism strives to oppress people, whereas mental health strives to empower people, the same goal of psychotherapy. Oppression and empowerment are incompatible goals. However, trainees are people and like many people may come into their training programs with prejudicial and racist attitudes

toward other groups. It is not a minor point that multicultural sensitivity training is promoted by the American Psychological Association, the American Psychiatric Association, and other mental health professional organizations and associations. It is not because of a presumption of racism but a presumption of need for some kinds of cultural training when assessing and treating people from different ethnocultural groups. It cannot even be presumed that because a trainee is from a given racial or ethnic cultural group that they do not require knowledge or training with that group.

A multicultural therapist, like a good psychotherapist requires knowledge of self in order to provide appropriate help for others. Multicultural therapy practices emphasize the importance of learning about self and others. Like other good scientific practices, it requires objectivity, stepping back, reflecting, relating, and integrating formal practice knowledge with applied experiential knowledge.

3. Does multicultural assessment and treatment of mental health problems and disorders in African Americans require the acceptance of stereotypes as the basis of therapy? The answer is no. A frequently heard criticism of multicultural psychotherapy and related professional practices is that it requires the acceptance of blatant ethnic stereotypes as the basis for psychological treatment. Paniagua (1998) in his book on *Assessing and Treating Culturally Diverse Clients* is careful to warn the reader in the Preface that descriptions of cultural variables reflect generalizations. They don't apply to everyone who is a member of that group, and they represent heterogeneous constructs that vary both within and across groups. Paniagua indicates that for any group there are cultural commonalities with other cultural groups as well as cultural differences reflected in diversity. These generalizations about a group are not stereotypes. Stereotypes are "something conforming to a fixed or general pattern" according to *Webster's Ninth New Collegiate Dictionary* (Webster, 1991). These general descriptions, like the ones provided at the beginning of this chapter, about African Americans are acknowledged to be nonfixed descriptions and clearly do not characterize all members of that group. Cultural descriptions obtained from multicultural approaches do not impose a one-size-fits-all cultural diagnosis to be used with all persons from that group. Neither do they establish rigid rules of treatment based on groupthink.

Group-based generalizations represent knoweldge used as cultural variables to better understand members of that group. Group-based generalizations when obtained using sound scientific methods should represent relative truths. Knowing, for example, that historical hostility is a pattern of responses (rage, violence, crime, and substance abuse) found in many African Americans (Vontress & Epp, 1997) is important clinical information to know. If this information were used as a stereotype, the clinician would think and behave according to that stereotype, and would treat each African American client as though he or she automatically had "historical hostility." The way that information about "historical hostility" can be used constructively is to prepare therapeutic techniques or strategies that break through this defense, or stance, if historical hostility is or becomes a therapeutic barrier during assessment and treatment. From a preventive perspective, historical hostility could be studied. It would be of interest to research its etiology and development in African Americans: who has it worse, how it is learned or taught, and how is it dysfunction, and how can it be channeled into positive, proactive growth and development?

4. Does multicultural assessment and treatment of mental health problems and disorders in African Americans excuse dysfunctional behavior as misunderstood cultural behavior? The answer is no. A frequently used example of multiculturalism excusing dysfunctional behavior is the concept of "healthy paranoia." An African American client having paranoid ideation (feelings and thoughts that others are conspiring to do one harm) is seen as expressing defensive behavior in response to discrimination or racism. By relabeling paranoia as defensive behavior, this excuses important symptoms of mental disorder. Another manner in which multicultural approaches are supposed to excuse dysfunctional behavior is to label it as "cultural" and thus acceptable. For example, because it is normal in some neighborhoods for juveniles to steal does not mean that stealing is acceptable. These are examples of how multicultural perspectives change the meaning or relative importance of cultural elements and the role they exert on behavior. This is not meant to minimize the clinical importance of certain behaviors, but rather to arrive at a more comprehensive, and perhaps more balanced perspective on matters. There are, however, also many examples of multicultural practices identifying unhealthy patterns, attitudes, cultural practices, morals, and beliefs that have adverse consequences or are maladaptive for a specific group. The identification of high rates of substance abuse/dependence, poverty, mental illness, criminal behavior, violence, and other unhealthy and maladaptive behaviors patterns in African Americans does not excuse these patterns. On the contrary, their identification helps to target resources, advocacy efforts, policies, programs, services, and interventions aimed at their reduction, correction or modification, and elimination where possible.

Multicultural mental health helps to develop a body of knowledge about diverse populations and to use that body of knowledge in constructive ways to improve psychological, social, and occupational functioning. Multiculturalism does not excuse dysfunctional behavior. On the contrary, multicultural theory and practices are concerned with the identification of factors related to high levels of personal, social, and occupational functioning within and across contexts. Multiculturalism actually expands the role of mental health systems to include many forms of dysfunctional and maladaptive behavior.

Mental health, like physical health, is not defined simply by the absence of symptoms. Mental health requires the presence of a healthy environment that promotes health and well-being. Mental health and multiculturalism, like science, aim to control, maximally, features of the physical or cultural environment that have adverse impacts on growth and development. Thus, behaviors such as (a) dropping out of school before completion, (b) refusing to work for a living, (c) violence to self or others, (d) criminal behavior, (e) substance abuse and dependence, and other behaviors including (f) inability to financially support self or to take responsibility for self are examples of behaviors that indicate there is a dysfunction, a failure to adapt to either the environment, the culture, or its institutions, specifically those designed to promote growth and well-being. Spiritual development and moral development are also included when mental health is defined broadly.

Broadly defined, mental health includes such behaviors as violence, criminal behavior, substance abuse, and irresponsibility. These behaviors when found to exist in relative high rates in any group become indicators of mental health needs. Behaviors such as violence and criminal behavior result from interactional conflicts between the self and the environment. In interactional problems, sometimes the individual is to blame (i.e., the responsibility lies with the self), whereas at other times it is not the individual's fault at all (i.e., fault lies with the environment, physical and/or cultural, and at other times, neither the individual nor the environment can be singularly blamed (i.e., responsibility lies with both to some varying degree, as neither people nor their cultures are perfect). Interactional behaviors, by their very nature, involve to some extent dynamism. For some reason, the concept of shared responsibility is very threatening to those persons who adhere to the belief that the individual is solely responsible for his or her behavior. The few exceptions to individual responsibility generally allowed for in U.S. culture are (a) insanity or mental illness, (b) extreme youth, and (c) physical disease or other organic illness.

An important feature of multicultural approaches is that culture and person–environment interactions are taken into consideration in explaining behavior. Regression analyses conducted in the social sciences are frequently used to empirically demonstrate the relative contribution of various factors, variables, or predictors on some criterion variable(s). Cultural variables such as acculturation and ethnic identity have been empirically demonstrated in numerous studies to make significant contributions and influences on a variety of behaviors (Dana, 1993, 1998; Paniagua, 1998). Although this is far from saying that cultural variables cause behavior, the evidence shows there are strong empirically demonstrated relations among cultural variables and many behaviors. Because multiculturalism at times finds fault with both the environment and the individual, this does not mean it excuses or diminishes personal or individual responsibility. Criminal behavior, for example, may result from both individual or psychological dysfunction and sociocultural dysfunction. Macro- and meso-level system failures can generate individual dysfunctional behavior, as when a family system fails to instill moral behavior. The problem is that some systems work well for most individuals but do not work well for all individuals. Not all systems function perfectly for all. It appears that most systems (educational, health, criminal justice, economic, etc.) work best for defined cultural groups, and even so not for all from any given cultural group. When a system that works well for most persons from a specific cultural group doesn't work well for a specific individual, is it always the fault of the individual? Because individual differences are, generally, normally distributed in any given population, there will always be some persons who don't seem to fit into any given system. Take the educational system, for example, early on at the turn of the century, around 1905, Alfred Binet and others saw the need to identify persons with special needs (mental deficiency) in order to devise special educational systems for them. This concept of identifying subgroups with special needs has now been expanded for other special education populations, and lately is being used to assign special educational settings for those who exhibit behavioral problems in school (e.g., Alternative Behavior Schools/programs). In the Criminal Justice System there are continuums of security facilities with restrictions of individual liberties, depending on the nature and severity of the crime. Not everyone is treated the same. Economic systems do not market the same product to every-body. Stores provide a variety of prices, goods, and services. The food and entertainment industry likewise tailor their products to special groups because they know that not everybody has the same likes and needs. If a widget doesn't sell it is not always the consumer who is to blame. Likewise, mental health system interventions and therapies need to be tailored to the diverse needs and problems of that population. Does the automobile blame the consumer when a particular vehicle doesn't do well in the marketplace? Why should the mental health field assume that all its traditional therapies should work equally well for all consumers of mental health care regardless of the consumer's cultural background? The truth is that some traditional therapies (i.e., psychoanalysis, Adlerian, analytical, person-centered, rational-emotive, behavioral, etc.) work well for all persons, others not so well for some, and not at all for others. It is part of a good clinician's repertoire of skills to know what works best for what kinds of problems across what kinds of settings and populations. The general tendency initially is to blame the individual or victim for failures to comply, engage, and benefit from system interventions. Mental health is a system intervention as well as an individual intervention. Objective functional analyses of the mental health, social, and other problems of African Americans clearly reveal system as well as individual failings in most cases of noncompliance and mismatching of needs.

5. Does multicultural assessment and treatment of mental health problems and disorders in African Americans undermine serious discussion? The answer again is no. The shortcomings of the established mental health service delivery systems, training programs, and models are at times highlighted in discussions of treatment of African Americans and other racial or ethnic minorities. For example, there are some professionals with strong opinions that certain racial and ethnically diverse groups in the United States are not being served adequately (i.e., are underserved or inappropriately served). There is also evidence as noted in the introduction of this chapter that African Americans are being disproportionately misdiagnosed. Some professionals would like to revamp many service and training programs to include specialist training in multiculturalism.

When opposing views are expressed, multicultural practitioners examine the scientific evidence in support of the differing views. Practitioners certainly do not automatically reject traditional scientific practices. Debate over the issue of the role of culture gets at the very heart of multicultural practices. To what extent does the environment and our culture influence who we are, what we believe in, and what we do? This is an ongoing discussion in the fields of psychology, sociology, psychiatry, and other behavioral sciences. There are those that believe that we are human beings not "cultural puppets," and that we are responsible for our own actions not the environment or our culture. Efforts that blame the environment lessen or overlook responsibility that rightfully belongs with the individual. Furthermore, they warn that disavowing individual responsibility is a dangerous and disastrous road to take. Multiculturalism does not run from this debate and in no way supports the lessening of individual responsibility. It promotes the application of scientific practices and analysis as the basis for determining the most appropriate, efficient, and effective ways to treat mental illness in any given population. It promotes the use of scientific methods to arrive at the truth of these and other matters.

In the early 1970s it was not unusual for a supervisor to instruct their trainee to delete the label Black as a description of the patient from the psychological report. This rationale often had to do with labeling. By labeling the client as Black you could be found guilty, or accused, of discriminating against him or her. You could also be accused of placing an unacceptable label on the client, the very person to whom services and help are being directed. To some extent this is still true today. How to label people from different racial and ethnic groups has always been problematic, and there seldom is any clear consensus. There are risks involved in labeling, particularly mislabeling people.

Dr. Richard H. Dana's book, *Understanding Cultural Identity in Intervention and Assessment* (1998) makes a strong case for assessing ethnic identity, cultural identity, and other cultural variables in professional practices. His point is that the failure to assess ethnic identity and cultural identity in our patients is to leave out much about who our patients are as human beings. Dana and others believe that one's sense of self is formulated from our experiences, our cultural upbringing, membership in racial and ethnic groups, as well as other commitments and ideologies. Ethnic identity is more salient for some people than others. It is particularly salient for some racial/ethnic groups (Phinney & Alipuria, 1990), and is an important part of the psychological makeup of all human beings.

IV. CONCLUSIONS ABOUT MULTICULTURAL ASSESSMENT AND TREATMENT PRACTICES FOR AFRICAN AMERICANS

It appears that multicultural professional practices in the mental health field have significant implications for African American consumers of mental health care as well as the providers of mental health care. Multicultural practices for African Americans advocate for the following:

1. More studies on African Americans so as to better understand their history, and to add to the growing body of knowledge on African Americans and their families, children, dialects, ideas, customs, practices, beliefs, worldviews, problems of living, health and mental health risks, as well as their strengths and potentialities.

2. Better understanding of the role of culture on both wellness and illness.

3. An understanding of factors that contribute to dysfunction and maladjustment in African Americans.

4. An understanding of positive factors that lead to competency, self-reliance, responsibility, healthy growth and development, and the pursuit of happiness in African Americans.

5. The development of models, measures, practices, and clinical techniques appropriate and acceptable for African Americans in addition to the use of traditional therapies.

6. Preventive strategies to reduce high rates of pathology, maladjustment, discontent, and dysfunction where they are found.

7. The identification of negative risk factors associated with criminal behavior, substance abuse and dependence, violence, and the like.

8. Research to help identify factors related to racism, oppression, and marginalization.

9. The understanding of bicultural and biracial development, as well as racial identity development in various contexts throughout the life span.

10. The advancement of scientifically derived knowledge that empowers African Americans with self-efficacy to live better lives, particularly those who suffer from poor mental health, from poverty, from depression, from apathy, hopelessness, helplessness, high crime rates, violence, poor schools and the like.

11. The strengthening of existing mental health systems while researching and developing new systems of delivery that include the prevention of social problems related to mental health, as well as interventions that ameliorate and rehabilitate those afflicted with mental and emotional problems and disorders.

These goals necessitate (a) comprehensive understanding of the psychological life of African Americans, including all factors related to risk and maladjustment, be they cultural or not, (b) and all factors related to positive outcomes, growth and development, and (c) objective understanding of what therapies work best for whom, under what conditions, and across what specific settings.

REFERENCES

Cuéllar, I. (1977). The utilization of mental health facilities by Mexican Americans: A test of the underutilization hypothesis (Doctoral Dissertation, University of Texas at Austin, 1977). *Dissertations Abstracts International, 38,* 3364–3365B.

Dana, R. H. (1993). *Multicultural assessment practices for professional psychology.* Boston: Allyn and Bacon.

Dana, R. H. (1998). *Understanding cultural identity in intervention and assessment.* Thousand Oaks, CA: SAGE Publications.

Farley, R. (1970). *Growth of the Black population: A study of demographic trends.* Chicago, IL: Markham Publishing Company.

Holzer, C. E., III., Swanson, J. W., & Shea, B. M. (1975). Ethnicity, social status, and psychiatric disorder in the epidemiologic catchment area survey. In R. K. Price, B. M. Shea, & H. N. Mookherjee (Eds.), *Social psychiatry across cultures: Studies from North America, Asia, Europe, and Africa.* Plenum Press, New York.

Horney, K. (1936). Cultural and psychological implications of neuroses. In K. Horney (Ed.), *The neurotic personality of our time,* (pp. 13–29). New York: W. W. Norton & Co., Inc.

Institute for Health Policy, Brandeis University (1993). *Substance abuse: The nation's number one health problem: Key indicators for policy.* Princeton, NJ: The Robert Wood Johnson Foundation.

Kessler, R. C., McGonagle, K. A., Zhao, S., Nelson, C. B., Hughes, M., Eshleman, S., Wittchen, H. U., & Kendler, K. S. (1994). Lifetime and 12-month prevalence of DSM-III-R psychiatric disorders in the United States. *Archives of General Psychiatry, 51,* 8–19.

Kraepelin, E. (1904). *Vergleichende psychaitrie. Zentralblatt fur Nervenherlkande und Psychiatrie, 15,* 433–37.

Manderscheid, R. W., & Sonnenschein, M. A. (1985). *Mental health, United States, 1985.* Rockville, MD: National Institute of Mental Health.

Mauer, M. (1999). *The crisis of the young African male and the Criminal Justice System.* U. S. Commission on Civil Rights Conference, Washington, DC.

Paniagua, F. A. (1998). *Assessing and treating culturally diverse clients* (2nd ed.). Thousand Oaks, CA: SAGE Publications.

Phinney, J. S., & Alipuria, L. L. (1990). Ethnic identity in college students from four ethnic groups. *Journal of Adolescence, 13,* 171–183.

Robins, L. N., Regier, D. A., & Freedman, D. K. (Eds.). (1991). *Psychiatric disorders in America.* New York: Free Press.

Scheffler, R. M., & Miller, A. B. (1989). Demand analysis of service use among ethnic subpopulations. *Inquiry, 26,* 202–215.

Snowden, L. R., & Cheung, F. K. (1990). Use of inpatient health services by members of ethnic minority groups. *American Psychologist, 45,* 347–355.

Stolp, C., & Warner, D. (1987). Mental health service utilization of California hospitals by age, ethnicity, and sex in 1983. In R. Rodriguez and M. T. Coleman (Eds.), *Mental health issues of the Mexican American origin population in Texas* (pgs. 116–134). Austin, TX: Hogg Foundation for Mental Health, the University of Texas at Austin.

U.S. Bureau of the Census (1996). *Statistical abstract of the United States.* Washington, DC: Government Printing Office.

U.S. Bureau of the Census (1997). *Statistical abstract of the United States.* Middle series projections. Washington, DC: Government Printing Office.

U.S. Department of Commerce (1995). *Statistical abstract of the United States.* Washington, DC: U.S. Department of Commerce.

Vernon, S. W., & Roberts, R. E. (1982). Prevalence of treated and untreated psychiatric disorders in three ethnic groups. *Social Science Medicine, 116,* 1575–1582.

Vontress, C., & Epp, L. R. (1997). Historical hostility in the African American client: Implications for counseling. *Journal of Multicultural Counseling and Development, 25,* 170–184.

Warheit, G. J., Holzer, C. E., III, & Arey, S. A. (1975). Race and mental illness: An epidemiologic update. *Journal of Health & Social Behavior, 16.* 243–256.

Warheit, G. J., Holzer, C. E., & Schwab, J. J. (1973). An analysis of social class & racial differences in depressive symptomatology: A community study: *Journal of Health & Social Behavior, 14.*

Webster's Ninth New Collegiate Dictionary 1991). Springfield, MA: Merriam-Webster Inc.

Western Interstate Commission for Higher Education (WICHE, October 1997). *Cultural competence standards in mental health care; mental health services for four underserved/underrepresented racial/ethnic groups.* Report of the Four National Panels On Cultural Competence In Managed Care Mental Health Service, Boulder, CO.

CHAPTER 11

Assessing and Treating Latinos: Overview of Research

ANDREA J. ROMERO

Stanford Center for Research
in Disease Prevention
Stanford University School of Medicine
Palo Alto, California

The United States population is becoming increasingly diverse; as of 1990 there were 30 million Blacks, 22 million Hispanics, 7 million Asians, and 2 million Native Americans living in the United States (U.S. Bureau of the Census, 1990). Additionally, based on current fertility and immigration rates, it is projected that Latinos will become the largest non-European American ethnic group in the United States by the year 2020 (Davis, Haub, & Willette, 1988). Also, this burgeoning population is relatively young; in 1993 the median age for Latinos was 27 years old. It is projected that by the year 2010 Latinos will account for 42% of the country's new population growth (U.S. Bureau of the Census, 1990).

Given these population trends, issues of cultural appropriateness appear to be very timely. It has been argued that culture has an impact on numerous aspects of mental illness (American Psychiatric Association, 1994) and its treatment (Angel & Thoits, 1987; Cuéllar, 1982; Draguns, 1984; Lopez, 1989; Marsella, 1987; Marsella & Kameoka, 1989). In this chapter I will present an overview of research on cultural theories and mental health in the Latino community. I will argue that current conceptualizations of cultural models may help the mental health services communities move beyond stereotypes and oversimplifications of the Latino culture. The measurement of cultural constructs will be briefly discussed in order to understand how to assess individuals as cultural beings. Finally, recommendations for when and how to tailor diagnosis and treatment to be culturally appropriate will be provided. It will be argued in this chapter that a multicultural approach will bring more clarity to our research and more effective treatment of mental health problems within the Latino community.

I. LEARNING FROM THE PAST

There is much to be learned from the evolution of the history of mental health research on Latinos and the emergence of more comprehensive models of culture. Originally, culture was a topic of consideration only for immigrants and was discussed in terms of their assimilation to the new society. Early psychological approaches to culture were based on the dominant majority model, which reflected the assumption of the U.S. American "melting pot." In the sense that individuals were expected to sufficiently "melt" into one homogeneous society, the dominant majority model assumed that individuals were expected to assimilate into the dominant culture (Born, 1970). The very nature of acculturation was conceptualized as stressful, such as reflected in constructs as culture stress, culture shock, culture fatigue, role shock, and language shock (see Smart & Smart, 1995, for a review). Therefore, it was assumed that all immigrants underwent some form of psychological distress due to the stressful nature of acculturation.

Several studies supported the hypothesis that Latinos who were less acculturated experienced more psychological distress (Burnam, Hough, Karno, Escobar, & Telles, 1987; Cuéllar, Roberts, Nyberg, & Maldonado, 1997; Cuéllar & Roberts, 1999; Kaplan & Marks, 1990; Roberts & Chen, 1995; Roberts, Roberts, & Chen, 1997; Rogler, Cortes, & Malgady, 1991). Largely because of the interpretations of these findings, it was argued that the treatment for these types of mental problems was complete assimilation into the U.S. culture.

In the early 1980s the unidimensional bipolar framework was introduced, and culture was represented by a continuum with the new culture on one end and the culture of origin on the other end (Keefe & Padilla, 1987). This model still implicitly suggested that as Latinos became more acculturated they would necessarily have to lose their ties to their culture of origin. The unidimensional model defined culture as primarily based on English language use and generation level (Marin, 1992; Negy & Woods, 1992; Padilla, Alvarez, & Lindholm, 1986).

However, as this new model was introduced, the findings on the association between acculturation and mental well-being of Latinos became less obvious. For example, there were many studies supporting the hypothesis that higher acculturation is associated with increased stress, which is contradictory to the original hypothesis that less acculturated individuals will have more psychological distress (Kaplan & Marks, 1990; for a review, see Rogler et al., 1991; Vega et al., 1998). Subsequently, several meta-analyses and review articles have summarized the findings between acculturation and mental well-being in Latinos, and reported that findings were equivocal (Cervantes & Castro, 1985; Kaplan & Marks, 1990; Molina & Aguirre-Molina, 1994; Negy & Woods, 1992; Rogler et al., 1991). Researchers postulated that the reliance on the measurement of English language use and generation level had too much noise to accurately reflect the complexities of the migration experience or the cultural experience (Rogler, Cortes, & Malgady, 1994; Stiffman & Davis, 1990). Trimble (1990–91) and Phinney (1996) both argued that the measurement and conceptualization of ethnicity needs to encompass the distinct lifeways and thoughtways that reflect the complexity of culture, as represented by cultural norms, values, ethnic identity, and minority status.

II. CURRENT MODELS

Given the new articulations on the complexity of culture, researchers began to search for more valid representations of culture within the United States that more accurately reflected the multidimensionality of the immigration and culture change process. Keefe and Padilla (1987) introduced the idea of multiple dimensions in their conceptualization of the measurement of Chicano culture. They argued that knowledge of the Mexican culture, following traditions, socializing with individuals of the same ethnic background, and ethnic pride were key elements of culture to consider in psychological models. The multidimensional model was an important breakthrough in the conceptualization of culture; it shifted the focus of cultural theories and measurement beyond language.

Further, in recent advancements of cultural conceptualizations, Oetting and Beauvais (1990–91) introduced the orthogonal model of cultural orientation based on their work with Native American adolescents. Their model consisted of one axis reflecting adherence to the culture of origin and another perpendicular axis reflecting adherence to the new culture. This conceptualization has extended models of culture a step beyond that of Keefe and Padilla (1987), by no longer being predicated on a bipolar continuum of cultural change. Rather, Oetting and Beauvais (1990–91) argue that maintenance or acceptance of different cultures may occur completely separate from each other. In other words, these two potentially orthogonal change processes make it possible to assess bicultural individuals or conversely individuals marginalized from both cultures.

The multidimensional and orthogonal conceptualization appears to provide a representation of culture that may be more consistent with the experiences of Latino youth today, who are exposed to multiple cultures and who are expected to navigate cultural borders and live competently in multiple cultural worlds (Delgado-Gaitan, 1994). Supporting this model, Keefe and Padilla (1987) presented evidence that later generations often maintained their ethnic social orientation and their ethnic pride, despite their change in language preference and their lack of knowledge of cultural history. Stated differently, individuals could be bicultural, such that they adopt behaviors of the new culture while maintaining behaviors of the culture of origin. In relation to mental health, it has been reported that the healthiest outcome was for bicultural individuals; on the other hand, the least healthy outcomes seem to be associated with marginalization (Buriel, 1984; Cuéllar, Roberts, Romero, & Leka, 1999; Negy & Woods, 1992; Richman, Gaviria, Flaherty, Birz, & Wintrob, 1987). Marginalization is when individuals do not identify with either culture (Cuéllar et al., 1999).

The recent evidence suggests that being bicultural is the optimum mental health outcome possible, whereas marginalization may be the outcome that puts individuals most at-risk for deleterious mental health. In reviewing the extant literature on Latinos and mental health, it is recommended that culture be conceptualized as a multidimensional framework that be measured orthogonally on multiple dimensions. Additionally, it is important to remember that culture is complex and that other associated variables, such as socioeconomic status, may account for influences on mental health (Rogler et al., 1994). In summary, when assessing and treating the Latino community, researchers and clinicians would be wise to address culture and migration as complex processes, to take social context of socioeconomic status into consideration, and to use reliable multidimensional orthogonal measures of culture.

III. MOVING BEYOND STEREOTYPES

Clearly, there is still a lot to learn about the implications of culture on mental health within the Latino population. There are many lessons to learn from the changes in models of culture and findings of mental health research. These lessons can inform our future research and our assessment and treatment of Latinos. The first step is to begin to understand Latinos as a cultural group and individuals as cultural beings. One such issue is concerned with how to utilize these concepts in a more applied setting. We need to first move beyond stereotypes or oversimplified descriptions of the Latino culture, so that researchers and clinicians begin to understand and assess individuals as cultural beings (Dana, 1998).

To begin with there has been much discussion concerning the limited utility of ethnic labels as descriptors of culture. Cultural psychology argues that ethnicity is complex and involves the lifeways and thoughtways of individuals that reach far beyond ethnic labels (Phinney, 1996 Shweder, 1993; Trimble, 1990–91). Moreover, there are a variety of measurement issues surrounding ethnic labels, such as misclassification or inaccurate labels. For example, racial and ethnic groups are generally listed together, as such Latinos often are categorized within racial groups (e.g., Black or Caucasian), instead of their ethnic group. Additionally, diverse ethnic subgroups are often clumped together under one pan-ethnic label, such as the labels "Latino" or "Hispanic." When in fact, the U.S. Latino population is very heterogeneous; as of 1991 the Latino population was composed of the following subgroups: 63% Mexican, 11% Puerto Rican, 5% Cuban, and 21% other Latino (Central/South American). Therefore, it is clear that if ethnic labels are used they need to include specific ethnic groups distinct from racial groups; members of an ethnic group are defined by common exposure to *cultural elements*, whereas racial groups are biologically based (Atkinson, Morten, & Sue, 1983). However, it is important to remember that despite improved measurement, ethnic labels still do not accurately represent cultural differences, and should not be used alone for the assessment of culture.

Although the pan-ethnic term "Latino" is used throughout this chapter, it is important to acknowledge that there is great variation within the Latino population. Of course there are certain commonalities, such as the majority of Latino ethnic groups come from Spanish-speaking countries and as many as 90% of Latinos continue to speak Spanish (Dana, 1993). Although many aspects of Latino culture are common, there are also significant differences between ethnic groups due to socioeconomic, sociocultural, and historical influences.

Specifically, many Mexican Americans have migrated to the United States for economic reasons and many have served as a source of labor in farming communities or as factory workers, though there is still great variation in the cultural experiences of Mexican Americans. For example, there are many individuals of Mexican descent who were originally living in the southwest when the land was still Mexico. These individuals, Tejanos and Hispanos, retained their culture and their language, although they officially became U.S. citizens. Mexican culture is a mixture of Spanish and many indigenous Indian cultures. In terms of location, Mexican Americans generally have stayed closer to the U.S./Mexican border areas, in the states of California, Arizona, New Mexico, and Texas.

Whereas Puerto Ricans, although they have continued to maintain commonwealth status with the United States rather than statehood, have often migrated to the eastern states of New York, New Jersey, and Florida. Puerto Rico is a mixture of European, African, Taino Indian, and American cultures (Dana,

1993). Both Puerto Ricans and Mexicans continue to have high rates of poverty and have relatively low education/occupation status despite easy access to the United States and many generations of U.S. American-born children.

The Cuban migration to the United States was primarily a result of the Castro revolution in 1959, and many were treated as political refugees (Dana, 1993). This generation of Cubans was older, well educated, and affluent; they created ethnic enclaves and have created and sustained a strong economy for themselves. However, there was another large migration in the early 1980s of individuals from Cuba who were working class or socially disadvantaged individuals (prison inmates and mental patients) (Dana, 1993). Consequently, Cubans are a very diverse ethnic group within the United States; overall they are less likely to be living in poverty and more likely to be educated. Other Latino groups are still migrating to the United States; in fact there is a growing population of Central Americans in many major cities (Leslie, 1992). However, there is much less known about Central Americans in the United States and their social contexts.

The specific nature of Latino culture is defined by specific ethnic groups, who have created their own beliefs, norms, shared symbols, physical objects, and a shared set of learning experiences (Foster & Martinez, 1995; Triandis, 1980). Culture is created by ethnic groups and is taught from generation to generation; thus, culture is a learned construct. Culture has been conceptualized as a complex, dynamic, multidimensional, and multidirectional process with a variety of psychological outcomes. If culture is conceptualized as more than language, there are important implications for mental health research and treatment, such as the understanding of the self, demonstration of illness, and methods of treatment.

IV. LATINO CULTURAL SELF-CONSTRUAL

In order to understand the complexities of the Latino cultural experience, we need to begin to conceptualize the deeper structure of the culture. The concept of cultural self-construal has important relevance for understanding and measuring cultural aspects of the Latino community. The conceptualization of a cultural self and cultural values tapes into key psychological components of culture that have been theorized to impact cognitions, emotions, behaviors, and motivations (Markus & Kityama, 1991; Triandis, 1996). Clearly, if culture influences the individual at the basic level of self-construal it will have important implications for mental illness. Subsequently, cultural values can inform us concerning the application to the understanding of Latino mental health service utilization, manifestation of illness, and treatment.

There are two basic construals of the self that have been linked to the study of most all cultures: individualistic or independent versus collectivistic or interdependent (Markus & Kityama, 1991; Triandis, 1996). The independent self tends to construe the self as separate from all others within the social realm, and prefers to view behaviors and emotions as consistent across all situations and with all individuals. The individualist will focus more on the importance of the individual and becoming autonomous and independent as part of the development process. The independent perspective has been described as representative of the U.S. American value system and self-construal (Markus & Kityama, 1991). Therefore, it is anticipated that as Latinos become more acculturated they are more likely to demonstrate and adhere to more of these individualistic values.

Alternately, the collectivistic culture is more representative of Latino culture, and construes the self as more interdependent with other important people within one's social realm. Social roles are highly important and are central identities of the self. Typically, the Latino culture has been described as being defined by traditional gender roles for men and women, and a high regard for parental roles, which is consistent with the collectivistic nature (Delgado-Gaitan, 1994). Other traditional Latino values of *respeto* (respect) and *dignidad* (dignity) are complementary to the use of social roles, because they help establish the role boundaries and allow individuals to maintain their roles through respect and consideration of dignity (Molina & Aguirre-Molina, 1994). Also, collectivist individuals will be more likely to focus on the importance of relationships and connectedness between individuals. For example, Latino social interactions are guided by *personalismo* or the establishment of trust and rapport through developing warm friendly relationships (Cuéllar et al., 1995). It is important to remember these types of social expectations will influence how patients will expect to be dealt with on the basic level of social interaction.

Another demonstration of the collectivistic nature of the Latino culture is in the understanding and value in the family. Research has demonstrated that the cultural value of *la familia* (the family) is pervasive in most Latino cultures and influences child psychopathology and help seeking (Abad, 1987; Badillo-Ghali, 1977; Canino & Canino, 1980; Comas-Diaz, 1988; Cuéllar & Glazer, 1995). Additionally, the family is an important context for the Latino culture, the family is perceived as highly interdependent and the members are highly valued, and often an extended family is set up through the roles of *padrinos* (godparents) and grandparents (Sabogal, Marin, Otero-Sabogal, Marin, & Perez-Stable, 1987). Generally, family members live close by and have a sense of obligation towards each other (Molina & Aguirre-Molina, 1994); thus reflecting the interdependent nature of the Latino culture. Family is such a ubiquitous context in Latino culture that health and sickness both become family affairs. Generally the family is looked to first in terms of help seeking, which will influence mental health service utilization. It is recommended that families be included and welcomed into the treatment process if possible, as a show of respect towards their interdependent functioning.

Additionally, there are other collectivistic cultural attributes that will influence service utilization. For example, the development goals of collectivistic individuals tend to be voluntary control of inner attributes. In Latino culture a strong individual is defined as being able to control oneself (*controlarse*), which includes *aguantarse* or being able to withstand stress during bad times (Dana, 1993). These factors in particular will have direct relevance for service utilization. For example, if individuals perceive that they are weak because they cannot control their emotions they may be less likely to pursue help. This recognition of the global representation of culture shows promise for future research and practice, and it provides a framework for understanding the deeper structure of the Latino culture and the individual as a cultural being.

V. ASSESSING THE CULTURAL BEING

Because people within any culture are likely to vary substantially, it is critical to assess the individual as a cultural being before diagnosis and treatment (Dana, 1998). Not all Latinos are the same or adhere to the culture of their ethnic subgroup to the same extent. Therefore, it is necessary to understand to what extent culture of origin plays a role in self-identity, behaviors, and values. These factors will influence how illness is manifested and what the most appropriate method of treatment will be. Ethnic identity, cultural values, and acculturation are constructs that can be used to assess the degree to which an individual integrates their cultural background into their self-identity and behaviors. These are important tools for understanding the individual as a cultural being and acknowledging individual differences in identification with culture. Additionally there is empirical evidence that positive ethnic identity and biculturalism are related to higher self-esteem, less depression, better mental well-being, and less drug use (Felix-Ortíz, Newcomb, & Myers, 1994; Phinney, 1991; Roberts, Phinney, Romero, & Chen, 1999).

A. CULTURAL VALUES AND CULTURAL SELF

As discussed earlier, cultural values and cultural selves describe the individual in an orthogonal manner with the two axes being collectivistic and individualistic. Triandis and colleagues (1995) have multiple methods that can be utilized for this purpose. Additionally, there are several more culture-specific measures of cultural values, or cultural schemas, such as *familism, machismo,* or *personalismo* (see Cuéllar, Arnold, & González, 1995).

B. ETHNIC IDENTITY

Ethnic identity will impact an individual's social construction *of their world and their degree of identification with their culture of origin.* Ethnic identity is the self-concept that is derived from the membership in one's ethnic group and the emotional value of belonging to this group (Phinney, 1991). There are several measures of ethnic identity available, such as the Bernal, Knight, Ocampo, Garza, and Cota (1993) measures of ethnic identity in Chicano children, Phinney's (1991) universal Multigroup Ethnic Identity Measure, or components of other acculturation measures, such as the Acculturation Rating Scale for Mexican Americans (ARSMA-II) (Cuéllar, Arnold, & Maldonado, 1995) or Keefe and Padilla's (1987) Chicano cultural orientation measure.

C. ACCULTURATION

Another measure of within-group variation is that of acculturation. Acculturation can provide information about the extent to which individuals engage in behaviors of their culture of origin or U.S. culture. Acculturation is the process of culture change. Several current measures reflect the most recent conceptualization of culture as orthogonal and multidimensional, such as the ARSMA-II (Cuéllar, Arnold, & Maldonado, 1995), Marin's (1966) bidimensional scale, or Felix-Ortíz, Newcomb, and Myers (1994) adolescent cultural identification scale.

D. SOCIAL CONTEXT

Minority status and socioeconomic realities of the Latino community within the United States are important to understand in relation to culture. In the United States, a significant percentage of Mexicans and Puerto Ricans are likely to be living in poverty. As of the 1992 Census, 40% of Latino children live in poverty. Therefore, it is likely that Latino youth are at increased risk for mental health problems due to their combination of low socioeconomic status, less access to human services, and often violence-ridden environments (Castañeda, 1994; Roberts, Treviño, & Holzer, 1990). The social context of culture in the U.S. is critical to the understanding of culture and mental health for the Latino population. Socioeconomic status is strongly correlated with certain Latino ethnic groups in the United States; thus, it is necessary to acknowledge that poverty, rather than culture, may be impacting outcomes.

VI. CULTURALLY APPROVED ILLNESS MANIFESTATION

Once we know to what extent individuals adhere to the Latino culture or the U.S. culture, it is important to understand how to culturally tailor further diagnosis and treatment. It would be inappropriate to use Latino culture-specific methods of diagnosis or treatment if the individual is highly assimilated, just as it would be inappropriate to ignore culture-specific methods if the individual is less acculutrated. Culture has been purported to have influences on the perception and definition of mental illness (Kleinman & Good, 1985) and the manifestation and expression of the symptoms (Draguns, 1973; Kleinman, 1988). Some researchers have identified culture-specific disorders in Latino cultures, and have demonstrated the inseparable connection between the mental and physical well-being in the Latino culture (see Molina & Aguirre-Molina, 1994). Some Latinos practice folk medicine and self-medicate through herbs and home remedies. Some examples of folk illness are *mal de ojo* (evil eye), *empacho, el calor, ataque de nervios, susto, caida de mollera* (Molina & Aguirre-Molina, 1994). In general, *ataque de nervios* is a culturally appropriate demonstration of strong emotions due to stressful life events; it is an outlet for anger, grief, and family disruptions. This is often characterized by shouting, swearing, and striking out at others and falling to the ground. Often *ataque de nervios* proceeds to a worsened condition of *susto,* which is a more prolonged and chronic condition, which might be considered similar to depression. *Susto* is described as having lost one's soul due to a traumatic life event. It is clear that these symptoms could be understood in different forms in different cultures.

VII. SERVICE UTILIZATION

As a result of such culture-specific representations of illness, service utilization may be impacted by how Latinos understand and attribute causes to mental illness. General lay theories of causation are guided by the holistic view of illness and are often attributed to supernatural causes, environmental causes (bad air), or strong emotions (embarrassment, envy, and others) (Molina & Aguirre-Molina, 1994). Because it is more socially appropriate for women or children to manifest illness (they are perceived as weaker), it is consistent that studies have found that more often Latina women report higher rates of depression than men do. Additionally, there are very low service utilization rates for Latino men, which is consistent with cultural norms that men are expected to be strong and able to control their inner feelings. Consequently, it may be important not only to educate the community about causes of mental illness symptoms, but also to use methods of out-reach that allow individuals to retain their *dignidad* and cultural norms.

Clearly, cultural values also will play a role in how individuals perceive treatment and finding treatments and interventions that work best. It will be important to culturally tailor treatments and interventions that are responsive to the types of cultural experiences that are relevant for the target audience. Of course, at a basic level it is crucial to use the correct language in order to begin to address relevant cultural issues. To date, relatively few culture-specific treatments have been empirically tested. One example is Constantino and colleagues (1994) who used storytelling as a form of treatment in Latino youth with success. Other individuals have suggested utilizing the natural family support system for improving mental health or at least including family members in therapy sessions (Molina & Aguirre-Molina, 1994). Additionally, Dana (1993) discusses folk healers or spiritual healing, such as *curanderismo* and *espiritismo,* as a culture-specific form of treatment that may legitimately help improve mental status of individuals who have strong beliefs that are consistent with these types of treatments.

VIII. WHERE DO WE GO FROM HERE?

Basic recommendations for future assessment and treatment of Latinos include the following five aspects: (a) being informed by previous literature and cultural models, (b) acknowledging diversity within ethnic groups, (c) assessing the cultural being, (d) awareness of cultural values and culture-specific illness manifestation, (e) culturally tailored treatment as appropriate. In order for mental health service providers to become culturally aware it is important to understand the complex nature of culture, so that the target audience not be viewed in a stereotypical manner. Individuals should be assessed to find out to what degree different cultures need to be taken into account in their treatment, through measurement of cultural values, ethnic identity, and acculturation. Based on the information of the individual as a cultural being, it is important to then proceed with not only the appropriate language, but also the appropriate assessments of mental illness, considering culture-specific forms of distress when appropriate. Finally, it is critical to be willing to explore culture-specific means of treatment as may be appropriate for certain individuals. As mentioned previously, socioeconomic status often plays a strong role in health outcomes, primarily in that individuals may not have access to health care or may not be aware of the resources available to them.

IX. CONCLUSION

I have argued in this chapter that culture is a social element that permeates every aspect of an individual, similar to the water that a fish swims through; as such, it is crucial to understand culture and its influences. Moreover, if we are to be guided by a truly comprehensive biopsychosocial model of health research, we need to begin to take into account not only the patient, but also their social context, such as socioeconomic and sociocultural stressors. Individual, group, and cultural differences should be an essential and systematic aspect of applying principles of human behavior to promote wellness.

REFERENCES

Abad, V. (1987). Mental health delivery systems for Hispanics in the U.S.: Issues and dilemmas. In M. Gavira & J. Arana (Eds.), *Simon Bolivar Research Institute monograph: Hispanic American psychiatric research program* (Serial no. 1, pp. 278–293). Chicago: University of Illinois.

American Psychiatric Association (1994). *Diagnostic and statistical manual of mental disorders—4th ed.* Washington, DC: Author.

Angel, R., & Thoits, P. (1987). The impact of culture on the cognitive structure of illness. *Culture, Medicine and Psychiatry, 11,* 465–494.

Atkinson, D., Morten, G., & Sue, D. W. (1983). *Counseling American minorities.* Madison, WI: Brown and Benchmark.

Badillo-Ghali, S. (1977). Culture sensitivity and the Puerto Rican client. *Social Casework, 58(8),* 459–468.

Bernal, M. E., Knight, G. P., Ocampo, K. A., Garza, C. A., & Cota, M. K. (1993). *Ethnic Identity: Development of Mexican American Identity.* Albany: SUNY Press.

Born, D. O. (1970). Psychological adaptation and development under acculturative stress: Toward a general model. *Social Science & Medicine, 3,* 529–547.

Buriel, R. (1984). Integration with traditional Mexican culture and sociocultural adjustment. In J. E. Martinez (Ed.), *Chicano Psychology (2nd Ed.)* (pp. 95–129). Academic Press.

Burnam, M. A., Hough, R. L., Karno, M., Escobar, J. I., & Telles, C. A. (1987). Acculturation and lifetime prevalence of psychiatric disorders among Mexican Americans in Los Angeles. *Journal of Health and Social Behavior, 28(3),* 89–102.

Canino, I. A., & Canino, G. (1980). Impact of stress on the Puerto Rican family: Treatment considerations. *American Journal of Orthopsychiatry, 50(3),* 535–541.

Castañeda, D. M. (1994). A research agenda for Mexican-American adolescent mental health. *Adolescence, 29(113),* 225–239.

Cervantes, R. C., & Castro, F. G. (1985). Stress, coping, and Mexican American mental health: A systematic review. *Hispanic Journal of Behavioral Sciences, 7,* 1–73.

Comas-Diaz, L. (1988). Hispanics. In L. Comas-Diaz & E. E. Griffith (Eds.), *Clinical guidelines in cross-cultural mental health* (pp. 183–268). New York: John Wiley.

Costantino, G., Malgady, R. G., & Rogler, L. H. (1994). Storytelling through pictures: Culturally sensitive psychotherapy for Hispanic children and adolescents. *Journal of Clinical Child Psychology, 23*(1), 13–20.

Cuéllar, I. (1982). The diagnosis and evaluation of schizophrenic disorders among Mexican Americans. In R. Becerra, M. Karno, & L. Escobar (Eds.), *Mental health and Hispanic Americans: Clinical perspectives* (pp. 61–81). New York: Grune & Stratton.

Cuéllar, I., & Glazer, M. (1995). The impact of culture on the family. In M. Harway (Ed.), *Treating the changing family* (pp. 17–36). New York: Wiley and Sons.

Cuéllar, I., Arnold, B., & González, G. (1995). Cognitive referents and acculturation: Assessment of cultural constructs in Mexican Americans. *Journal of Community Psychology, 23*(4), 339–356.

Cuéllar, I., Arnold, B., & Maldonado, G. (1995). Acculturation rating scale for Mexican Americans–II: A revision of the original ARSMA scale. *Hispanic Journal of Behavioral Sciences, 17*(3), 275–304.

Cuéllar, I., Roberts, R., Nyberg, B., and Maldonado, R. E. (1997). Ethnic identity and acculturation in a young adult Mexican origin population. *Journal of Community Psychology, 25,* 535–549.

Cuéllar, I., & Roberts, R. E. (1999). *Relations of depression, acculturation and SES in a Latino sample.* Unpublished manuscript.

Cuéllar, I., Roberts, R. E., Romero, A., & Leka, G. (1999). Acculturation and mental health: A test of Stonequist's hypothesis. *Journal of Cross-Cultural Psychology.*

Dana, R. H. (1993). *Multicultural assessment perspectives for professional psychology.* Boston: Allyn and Bacon.

Dana, R. H. (1998). *Understanding cultural identity in intervention and assessment.* Thousand Oaks, CA: SAGE Publications.

Davis, C., Haub, C., & Wilette, J. L. (1988). U.S. Hispanics: Changing the face of America. In E. Acosta-Belén & B. R. Sjostrom (Eds.), *The Hispanic experience in the United States: Contemporary issues and perspectives* (pp. 3–55). New York: Praeger.

Delgado-Gaitan, C. (1994). Socializing young children in Mexican American families: An intergenerational perspective. In P. M. Greenfield & R. R. Cocking (Eds.), *Cross-cultural roots of minority child development* (pp. 55–86). Hillsdale, NJ: Lawrence Erlbaum.

Draguns, J. G. (1973). Comparisons of psychopathology across cultures. *Journals of Cross-cultural Psychology, March,* 10–47.

Draguns, J. G. (1984). Assessing mental health and disorder across cultures (pp. 31–58). In P. B. Peterson, N. Sartorius, & A. J. Marsella (Eds.), *Mental health services: The cross-cultural context.* Beverly Hills, CA: Sage.

Felix-Ortíz, M., Newcomb, M. D., & Myers, H. (1994). A multidimensional measure of cultural identity for Latino and Latina adolescents. *Hispanic Journal of Behavioral Sciences, 16*(2), 99–115.

Foster, S. L., & Martinez, C. R., Jr. (1995). Ethnicity: Conceptual and methodological issues in child clinical research. *Journal of Clinical and Child Psychology, 24*(2), 214–226.

Kaplan, M. S., & Marks, G. (1990). Adverse effects of acculturation psychological distress among Mexican American young adults. *Social Science Medicine, 31*(12), 1313–1319.

Keefe, S., & Padilla, A. (1987). *Chicano ethnicity.* Albuquerque: University of New Mexico Press.

Kleinman, A. (1988). *Rethinking psychiatry.* New York: Free Press.

Kleinman, A. M., & Good, B. (1985). *Culture and depression.* Berkeley, CA: University of California Press.

Leslie, L. A. (1992). The role of informal support networks in the adjustment of Central American families. *Journal of Community Psychology, 20*(3), 243–256.

Lopez, S. R. (1989). Patient variable biases in clinical judgement: Conceptual overview and methodological considerations. *Psychological Bulletin, 106*(2), 184–203.

Marin, G. (1992). Issues in the measurement of acculturation among Hispanics. In K. F. Geisinger (Ed.), *Psychological testing of Hispanics* (pp. 235–251). Washington, DC: American Psychological Association.

Marin, G., & Gamba, R. J. (1996). A new measurement of acculturation for Hispanics: The bidimensional acculturation scale for Hispanics (BAS). *Hispanic Journal of Behavioral Sciences,(18*(3), 297–316.

Markus, H. R., & Kityama, S. (1991). Culture and the self: Implications for cognition, emotion, and motivation. *Psychological Review, 98,* 224–253.

Marsella, A. (1987). The measurement of depressive experience and disorder across cultures. In A. J. Marsella, R. M. A. Hirschfeld, & M. M. Katz (Eds.), *The measurement of depression* (pp. 376–397). New York: The Guilford Press.

Marsella, A. J., & Kameoka, V. A. (1989). Ethnocultural issues in the assessment of psychopathology. In S. Wetzler (Ed.), *Measuring mental illness: Psychometric assessment for clinicians* (pp. 231–256). Washington, DC: American Psychiatric Press, Inc.

Molina, C. W., & Aguirre-Molina, M. (1994). *Latino Health in the U.S.: A growing challenge.* Washington, DC: American Public Health Association.

Negy, C., & Woods, D. J. (1992). The importance of acculturation in understanding research with Hispanic Americans. *Hispanic Journal of Behavioral Sciences, 14,* 224–247.

Niemann, Y. F., Romero, A. J., Arredondo, J., & Rodriguez, V. (1999). What does it mean to be "Mexican" or "Mexican American": Lay person's construction of their ethnic identity. *Hispanic Journal of Behavioral Sciences, 21*(1), 47–60.

Oetting, E. R., & Beauvais, F. (1990–91). Orthogonal Cultural Identification Theory: The cultural identification of minority adolescents. *The International Journal of Addictions, 25*(5a & 6a), 655–685.

Padilla, A. M., Alvarez, M., & Lindholm, K. J. (1986). Generational status and personality factors as predictors of stress in students. *Hispanic Journal of Behavioral Sciences, 8,* 275–288.

Phinney, J. S. (1991). Ethnic identity and self esteem: A review and integration. *Hispanic Journal of Behavioral Sciences, 13*(2), 193–208.

Phinney, J. S. (1996). When we talk about American ethnic groups, what do we mean? *American Psychologist, 51,* 1–10.

Richman, J. A., Gaviria, M., Flaherty, J. A., Birz, S., & Wintrob, R. M. (1987). The process of acculturation: Theoretical perspectives and an empirical investigation in Peru. *Social Science Medicine, 25,* 839–847.

Roberts, R. E., & Chen, Y-W. (1995). Depressive symptoms and suicidal ideation among Mexican origin and Anglo adolescents. *Journal of American Academy of Child and Adolescent Psychiatry, 34*(1), 81–90.

Roberts, R. E., Roberts, C. R., & Chen, Y-W. (1997). Ethnocultural differences in prevalence of adolescent depression. *American Journal of Community Psychology, 25*(1), 95–110.

Roberts, R. E., Treviño, F. M., and Holzer, C. III (1990). Research on the mental health of minorities in Texas: Past, present, and future. In C. M. Bonjean & D. J. Foss (Eds.), *Mental health research in Texas: Retrospect and prospect* (pp. 270–285). Austin, TX: Hogg Foundation for Mental Health.

Roberts, R. E., Phinney, J. S., Masse, L. C., Chen, Y. R., Roberts, C. R., & Romero, A. (1999). The structure of ethnic identity of young adolescents from diverse ethnocultural groups. *Journal of Early Adolescence, 19*(3), 301–322.

Rogler, L. H., Cortes, D. E., & Malgady, R. G. (1991). Acculturation and mental health status among Hispanics: Convergence and new directions for research. *American Psychologist, 46,* 585–597.

Rogler, L. H., Cortes, D. E., Malgady, R. G. (1994). The mental health relevance of idioms of distress. *Journal of Nervous and Mental Disease, 182*(6), 327–330.

Sabogal, F., Marin, G., Otero-Sabogal, R., Marin, B., & Perez-Stable, E. (1987). Hispanic *familism* and acculturation: What changes and what doesn't? *Hispanic Journal of Behavioral Sciences, 9(4),* 397–412.

Shweder, R. A. (1993). The cultural psychology of the emotions. In M. Lewis & J. M. Haviland (Eds.), *Handbook of emotions* (pp. 417–431). New York: The Guilford Press.

Smart, J. F., & Smart, D. W. (1995). Acculturative stress among Hispanics: Loss and challenge. *Journal of Counseling and Development, 73,* 390–396.

Stiffman, A. R., & Davis, L. E. (Eds.). (1990). *Ethnic issues in adolescent mental health.* Newbury Park, CA: Sage Publications.

Triandis, H. C. (1980). Reflections on trends in cross-cultural research. *Journal of Cross-Cultural Psychology, 11(1),* 35–58.

Triandis, H. C. (1996). The psychological measurement of cultural syndromes. *American Psychologist, 51(4),* 407–415.

Triandis, H. C., Chan, D. K. S., Bhawuk, D. P. S., Iwao, S., & Sinha, J. B. P. (1995). Multimethod probes of allocentrism and idiocentrism. *International Journal of Psychology, 30,* 461–480.

Trimble, J. E. (1990–91). Ethnic specification, validation prospects, and the future of drug use research. *International Journal of the Addictions, 25,* 149–170.

U.S. Bureau of the Census (1990). *Census data for United States.* Washington, DC: Government Printing Office.

Vega, W. A., Kolody, B., Aguilar-Gaxiola, S., Alderete, E., Catalano, R., & Caraneo-Anduaga, J. (1998). Lifetime prevalence of *DSM-III-R* Psychiatric disorders among urban and rural Mexican Americans in California. *Archives of General Psychiatry, 55,* 771–778.

CHAPTER 12

Assessing and Treating American Indians and Alaska Natives

DENISE ANNE DILLARD
Apache Behavioral Health Services
Whiteriver, Arizona

SPERO M. MANSON
National Center for American Indian
and Alaska Native Mental Health Research
Department of Psychiatry
University of Colorado Health Sciences Center
Denver, Colorado

This chapter begins with a discussion of general factors that might impact the assessment and treatment of American Indians and Alaska Natives.[1] The history of American Indians and Alaska Natives is briefly summarized and followed by a description of the unique demographic, socioeconomic, and health characteristics of the population. Some common cultural values among American Indians and Alaska Natives are then outlined. The chapter concludes with a shift to specific recommendations and guidelines to aid clinicians in accurately assessing and successfully treating their Indian and Native clientele.

[1]For the sake of brevity, the terms *Indian* and *Native* will periodically be used.

Handbook of Multicultural Mental Health: Assessment and Treatment of Diverse Populations
Copyright © 2000 by Academic Press. All rights of reproduction in any form reserved.

I. GENERAL FACTORS THAT MIGHT IMPACT ASSESSMENT AND TREATMENT

A. HISTORY

Although American Indians of the lower 48 United States and Alaska Natives are separated by at least a thousand miles, these groups share a set of common historical experiences. Both have suffered decimation of their people, loss of ancestral lands, and destruction of language, culture, and religion at the hands of U.S. citizens or others visiting or settling their land (Norton & Manson, 1996).

It is estimated the American Indian population before European contact numbered approximately 9 million. In 1900, approximately 400 years after contact, 240,000 Indians remained. This loss of over 95% of the population is attributed to wars, genocide, and diseases such as smallpox and influenza (Nies, 1996; Trimble, Fleming, Beauvais, & Jumper-Thurman, 1996). In Alaska, the statistics are similar. For example, in the first 50 years after contact with Russian explorers, the Aleut population (one of the Alaska Native groups) experienced a 90% reduction from 16,000 to 1,600 individuals (Krauss, 1980). By 1900, American Indians also lost over 95% of the land holdings they held in 1800 (Nies, 1996).

These losses of life and land both contributed to the destruction of traditional ways of obtaining food, governance, and practicing religion. For example, the Sioux, traditionally nomadic hunter–gatherers, were relocated onto reservations in the late 1800s and forced to rely on commodity foods distributed by government Indian agents. In addition to replacing tribal leaders as the source of authority, Indian agents often banned traditional religious ceremonies such as the Sundance. The aftereffects of European diseases also have been linked to conversion to Christianity (e.g., Paniagua, 1994). Besides killing leaders and elders who practiced traditional religions, the "failure" of the "old" ways to stop the epidemics might have increased openness to other faiths. Religious conversion, however, was not all voluntary. Also in the 1800s, boarding schools were created as part of a federal policy of Assimilation and Civilization. Indian children were subsequently forced to attend these schools and required to speak English, follow Christian teachings, cut their hair, and wear "citizen" clothing (Nies, 1996).

Although reservations were not created in Alaska, Alaska Natives experienced similar losses of land to settlers (e.g., Russians) as well as comparable losses of culture. Missionaries, for instance, arrived in Alaskan lands in the late 1700s (Nies, 1996) and created English-only boarding schools that persisted in suppressing Native languages until the 1960s (Krauss, 1980).

More recent history depicts continued attempts at assimilation by the U.S. government. In the 1950s, the Bureau of Indian Affairs (BIA) relocated more than 35,000 American Indians from reservations to urban areas. The aim of this urban relocation movement was the integration of American Indians into the larger capitalistic society through vocational training and assistance (Olson & Wilson, 1984). For some, the Alaska Native Claims Settlement Act of 1971 (ANCSA) provides another example. Although ANCSA compensated Alaska Natives monetarily for lands that were lost and set aside some subsistence land, this compensation was given to corporations that were required to develop a business. Beyond forcing adherence to capitalism, the traditional lifestyle organized around hunting and fishing was further jeopardized as ANCSA failed to provide fish or wildlife rights (Berger, 1985; Nies, 1996).

B. Impact of Historical Factors

Given this distant as well as recent history, it is not surprising many American Indians and Alaska Natives are distrustful of others. History has taught Indians and Natives that others may act in ways that threaten their physical safety or the survival of their culture. The impact of this historical backdrop on therapy is aptly described by Lockhart (1981):

> For an Indian person to entrust himself to an Anglo counselor, or to someone . . . representative of the dominant society, may be extremely difficult given the results of past trust relationships. . . . No longer is the issue of trust necessarily based in the present; it takes on a historical perspective that is even harder to deal with. It is essential that the conscientious counselor be aware of the existence of this distrust and its basis, and try to understand its magnitude in order that the counseling relationship be effective. (pp. 31–32)

In other words, some level of mistrust is normative and perhaps adaptive for the Indian or Native client beginning psychological treatment, especially when a clinician is White. Even an Indian or Native clinician, however, will likely experience distrust, probably being seen as having given up traditional ways or otherwise becoming part of the White establishment given his or her level of education. A clinician who minimizes, denies, or pathologizes this historical mistrust will likely weaken or perhaps preclude the establishment of a productive therapeutic alliance. For example, some clinicians might attempt to assuage the suspicion of their American Indian client by stating their intentions are to help Indians to improve their lives. To the client, these efforts might sound eerily familiar to words spoken by missionaries, politicians, and others expressing a desire to help while acting in destructive ways. These words might also sound like those of White liberals who can exhibit patronizing beliefs about "poor" Indians or Natives needing considerable help from more capable Whites to "improve their situation."

The therapist who attributes mistrust to a personality flaw within the Indian or Native client is similarly counterproductive by ignoring the context that contributes to this mistrust. Instead, the clinician should aspire to gain an empathic understanding and acceptance of the distrust. This respectful and nonjudgmental approach will likely serve as an important building block in the foundation of trust necessary to other therapeutic work.

In a related point, clinicians should always be cognizant of the potential damage they can cause because of the inherent power differential between therapist and client. A clinician can dramatically effect how a client thinks, feels, and acts with respect to themselves, significant others, and their environment through various means (e.g., suggesting changes, confronting certain thoughts). For the Indian or Native client, the power differential takes on an added historical dimension. American Indians and Alaska Natives long have suffered at the hands of powerful others and been told that, as an individual and group, they are somehow "less-than." The clinician can unwittingly become another oppressor, an additional source of discrimination or devaluation. Devaluation can happen when a clinician applies Western ideas about proper behaviors, thoughts, and emotions unthinkingly to an Indian or Native client or views his or her client as powerless to help themselves or their people. Once again, Indians and Natives have been viewed historically as needing to adopt White ways, which were somehow better, and as needing a lot of help from more knowledgeable others in this effort to "improve their lot" and become "civilized."

An additional way that history can impact the assessment and treatment process relates to internalized racism or conflicts about ethnic identity. An Indian or Native client might (independent of the clinician) devalue themselves and their culture and/or be confused about their ethnicity. Three to four generations of Indians and Natives have existed in an environment that has necessitated difficult "choices" in a variety of contexts. One "choice" has involved adopting Western ways and/or "passing" as White with the benefits of survival and perhaps acceptance by those with more power. Some Indians and Natives have internalized the belief that the Western way is somehow superior after being bombarded with messages from source after source. Another "choice," maintaining "traditional" ways, has evoked sanctions ranging from social marginalization to death. Understandably, the former has been the "choice" of some Indians and Natives in various contexts (e.g., the workplace, in school). Note that the word "choice" is enclosed in quotes, however, because racism and discrimination are barriers preventing Indian and Native success in the Western world regardless of desire.

To complicate matters, there has always been some level of rejection within Indians and Natives of members who have attempted to "assimilate," and, more recently, there has been a movement encouraging American Indians and Alaska Natives to be proud of their roots and traditions (Trimble & LaFromboise, 1985). For the 60% of Indians and Natives who are of mixed heritage (e.g., Alaska Native/Mexican), rejection by "full-bloods" or those with higher Indian blood quantum also occurs (Trimble, Fleming, Beauvais, & Jumper-Thurman, 1996). It is thus not surprising many Indians and Natives today struggle, whether attempting to negotiate two cultures, to accept the sanctions in choosing to live according to the ways of one, or not feeling a sense of true belonging in any social or cultural sphere. Addressing internalized racism and conflicts about cultural identity are important themes for clinicians to address in treatment with most Indian or Native individuals.

C. DEMOGRAPHIC, SOCIOECONOMIC, AND HEALTH CHARACTERISTICS

According to the 1990 Census, the number of American Indians and Alaska Natives living in the United States is just under 2 million. Based on the total United States population, Indians and Natives thus comprise slightly less than 1% of the American population (U.S. Bureau of the Census, 1995a). The American Indian and Alaska Native population is projected to reach 4.3 million by 2050 (Paisano, 1997).

Despite these small numbers, there are more than 250 federally recognized American Indian tribes and 225 Alaska Native villages (Bureau of Indian Affairs [BIA], 1998). There are also 65 tribes recognized at the state level and dozens of other communities not recognized by any form of government (Norton & Manson, 1996). About one-quarter (21%) of Indians and Natives speak one of 135 American Indian languages or 20 Alaska Native languages at some level of fluency. Fluency levels vary greatly, with 85% of Navajos reporting the traditional language was being spoken in their homes in 1990, whereas only 2 Alaska Native languages are being transmitted to the next generation in a similar capacity (Crawford, 1994).

Geographically, half the Indian and Native population lives in the Western United States, with highest concentrations in Oklahoma, California, Arizona, and New Mexico. Twenty-two percent of American Indians and Alaska Natives live on one of 314 reservations or trust lands with only the Navajo Reservation supporting more than 100,000 residents (Norton & Manson, 1996; Paisano, 1997). Statistics further indicate >60% of the total Indian population is non-rural (BIA, 1998; Manson, Bechtold, Novins, & Beals, 1997), although a more recent study suggests higher concentrations in and around reservations than previously thought (Beals, Keane, & Manson, in press). With respect to Alaska

Natives, approximately 17% live in Anchorage, the only locale within the state considered an urban setting (U.S. Bureau of the Census, 1995c, 1995d).

In terms of other demographics, the Indian and Native population is young, with a median age of 26 years compared to the U.S. median age of 33. More than a quarter (28%) of the Indian and Native population are children and adolescents, with only 6% aged 65 years or older. In contrast, the 1990 general population was evenly distributed with 13% under 18 and 13% 65 or greater (U.S. Bureau of the Census, 1995a). These statistics reflect a fertility rate at least twice the general U.S. population as well as significantly higher death rates among certain Indian and Native age groups (Manson et al., 1997). For example, the Indian/Native birth rate between 1991 and 1993 was 67% higher than the U.S. all-races rate. About half (45%) of Indian mothers are under 20 when they have their first child compared to about one-fifth (21%) in the U.S. White-only population (Indian Health Service [IHS], 1997).

In terms of mortality, Indians and Natives under 54 have a death rate 1.4 to 1.8 times higher than the overall U.S. rate. Although the leading causes of death for the population as a whole are heart disease and cancer, young Indians and Natives are significantly more likely than their U.S. counterparts to die from nondisease-related conditions (e.g., homicide, cirrhosis). (See Table I for a list-

TABLE I   Leading Causes of Death[a]

Group	Two leading causes of death in U.S. all races population	Two leading causes of death in American Indian and Alaska Native population	Ratio American Indian and Alaska Native to U.S. all races[a]
Ages 1 to 4	1. Accidents	1. Accidents	2.3
	2. Congenital anomalies	2. Homicides	2.2
Ages 5 to 14	1. Accidents	1. Accidents	1.8
	2. Malignant neoplasms	2. Homicides	1.4
Ages 15 to 24	1. Accidents	1. Accidents	2.4
	2. Homicides	2. Suicides	2.4
Ages 25 to 44	1. Accidents	1. Accidents	3.4
	2. Human immunodeficiency virus (HIV)	2. Chronic liver disease and cirrhosis	5.5

Source: Indian Health Services, 1997.

[a] Ratio for two leading causes of American Indian and Alaska Native deaths.

ing of the two leading causes of Indian and Native deaths compared to the top causes within the U.S. all-Races population). Thus, accidents and homicides are the leading causes of death for Indian and Native youth ages 1 to 14. An Indian or Native child between 1 and 4 is 2.3 times more likely to die in an accident than his or her general U.S. counterpart and 2.2 times more likely to be murdered. Statistics also indicate elevated rates of death due to tuberculosis (5.3 times higher than the general population), diabetes (2.7 times higher), and pneumonia and influenza (1.5 times higher) (IHS, 1997).

Socioeconomically, Indians and Natives are twice as likely to live in poverty than their general counterparts. This economic gap increases when only female-headed households are considered. Not only are Indian and Native families more likely to have no husband present as compared to the general American population (26% and 16%, respectively) (U.S. Bureau of the Census, 1995a), half of these Indian and Native families are poor compared to a 31% rate for female-headed households nationwide (Paisano, 1997). The average unemployment rates for reservation Indians ranges from 15% to 40%, whereas, the urban Indian unemployment rate is double that of all other races (BIA, 1998; IHS, 1997).

Educationally, two-thirds of the 1990 Indian population over 25 have completed high school and approximately 9% completed at least a bachelor's degree (Paisano, 1997). These rates are significantly lower than the nationwide averages of 75% and 20%. Statistics specific to the urban Indian population paint an even more dismal picture, suggesting a 75% high school drop-out rate (BIA, 1998).

In terms of housing data, one in five American Indian households surveyed in the 1990 Census did not have complete plumbing (e.g., a flush toilet), 18% of those on reservations did not have complete kitchens (e.g., a refrigerator), and 53% did not have phones. Nationally, one percent of households lacked complete plumbing or complete kitchens, and 5% lacked telephones. Twenty-two percent of American Indians on reservations also did not own a car in 1990 (U.S. Bureau of the Census, 1995b).

D. Impact of Demographic, Socioeconomic, and Health Characteristics

Of the demographic factors discussed, perhaps the one with the greatest influence on assessment and treatment is the tremendous diversity in tribal or group affiliation. As so eloquently said by Mary Ann Broken Nose (1992):

> In truth, the Indian nations of North America are as different from one another as are the countries of Europe. . . . Barring the intervening influence of the dominant Anglo-American culture, a Seminole has as much in common with a Sioux as does a Sicilian with a Swede. Each tribe has its own language, religious beliefs, traditions, and way of life (p. 380)

Thus, it is very difficult to make generalizations about Indians or Alaska Natives for clinicians to use in the assessment and treatment process. It is essential clinicians take the initiative to learn about the unique aspects of their client's tribe or Native group for several reasons. First, this information can assist in more accurately assessing the presence or absence of pathology. Cultural information offers the clinician a normative context in which to evaluate the client and determine if the client is thinking, acting, or feeling in an expected fashion. Second, this knowledge can prevent the clinician from offending the client and unnecessarily jeopardizing rapport as well as helping the clinician choose a culturally compatible therapeutic approach.

As an example of how clients with different tribal or group affiliations can vary, several American Indian tribes, including the Navajo, have strong taboos against speaking of individuals who are dead or the manner in which death occurred. In contrast, the Oglala Sioux, although reticent to talk about death, do not have the same strong prohibitions. A clinician working with an Oglala Sioux tribal member whose relative has been murdered might be able to do in-depth grief work of a cathartic manner once sufficient trust has developed. However, a clinician working with a Navajo tribal member who has suffered loss would be wise to refrain from talking about the specifics of the murder regardless of the level of trust.

To offer a brief (but important) caveat, despite the utility of learning about a client's culture, clincians must always remember that groups and tribes vary tremendously according to factors such as degree of identification with Western ways, education, and even personality. As with any client, an Indian or Native needs to be seen and understood as unique.

Secondary to tribal or group affiliation, assessment and treatment can be significantly affected by language. Language barriers can impede the process whether the client is monolingual (necessitating the use of a translator) or mostly bilingual. Bilingual clinicians or professional translators are rarely available, and family, friends, or community members frequently are the only option. Significant others as translators can increase the client's comfort in discussing distressing topics. The former may also offer clinicians useful information about the client but there are potential downfalls. Besides the obvious limits to confidentiality, family or friends can minimize or exaggerate client's symptoms or avoid uncomfortable topics such as suicidality (Westermeyer, 1987). In addition, certain emotional states are very difficult or even impossible to translate. For example, words for "depressed" and "anxious" are absent from certain Indian and Native groups (Manson, Shore, & Bloom, 1985). In sum, translators may not be able to accurately solicit or convey information (e.g., the presence of depressed affect) or can present the client in distorted manner.

Even for the bilingual client, communication problems may continue to be present. For example, McNabb (1990) documented difficulties in achieving semantic equivalence for common self-report terms such as "somewhat satisfied" across four Alaska Native groups. When "somewhat satisfied" was translated into Central Yup'ik, the resulting phrase meant "approve of it partly" while translated into Siberian Yup'ik it meant "insufficiently satisfied." Thus, a bilingual Yup'ik male who endorses he is "somewhat satisfied" with his marriage on a questionnaire might not need to discuss his relationship. But it is equally possible he is rather unhappy with his marriage and that relationship issues should be a predominant treatment theme.

It is further important to remember emotional states such as anxiety and thought problems will affect a client's communication in a second language more dramatically than the first, as facility with a second language is more tenuous. A Sioux male who learned English second might look highly disturbed and in need of hospitalization to an English-speaking clinician. If this same client were able to speak with a clinician familiar with his first language, however, it might become evident the client is highly stressed but not in need of emergent intervention. Suzuki and Kugler (1995) also warn that the dysfluencies common when acquiring a new language can look like symptoms of a language disorder such as dyslexia.

In addition to considering group differences and the effect of language, the clinician should use demographic and socioeconomic factors as additional pieces of data when assessing for health and pathology. For example, it is common for Indian or Native females to have children at a young age and, within some tribes and groups, this behavior is encouraged. A seventeen-year-old Indian female with two children has not necessarily experienced family or peer disapproval, stress related to dropping out of high school, or be considered irresponsible. In a similar vein, because of higher unemployment rates, a jobless Inupiaq male should not automatically be considered as meeting the Antisocial Personality Disorder criterion C(1) ("inability to sustain consistent work behavior"). The availability of jobs in his village and the norms in his community regarding employment should be explored first. Subsistence remains the primary way many Inupiaq Eskimos provide for themselves with seasonal employment undertaken only to obtain enough money to maintain equipment.

On a more practical level, demographic and socioeconomic factors can create logistical barriers to treatment, especially when implemented in the traditional manner with the client attending a session at the clinician's office. First, the considerable distances that frequently exist between clients' homes and clinics make access to treatment difficult, as many reservation Indians do not own cars. In Alaska, many Natives live in villages accessible only via airplane. Even contacting a client to set up appointments can be challenging given the lack of telephones. If treatment is available on reservations or in villages, many Indians and Natives then worry about confidentiality and the stigma that can occur in seeking out mental health treatment. The size of most communities makes clinicians very visible and their clientele perhaps even more visible. For rural Native Americans who live far from IHS facilities or who choose to seek treatment elsewhere, the standard fees of private clinicians may simply be impossible given limited financial resources.

For the urban Indian or Native, many of the barriers present for their rural counterparts also exist (e.g., lack of transportation, inadequate finances). Urban Indians and Natives also may have difficulty in developing a sense of community, which might serve to protect them against developing psychological or physical problems.

E. CULTURAL VALUES

As mentioned previously, it is difficult to generalize about American Indians and Alaska Natives given the significant between-group as well as within-group differences. Yet, many clinicians are unfamiliar with the Indian and Native population and how their cultural values might differ from other groups. Some possible cultural differences for clinicians to consider are thus presented, but should not be taken as true about all Indians or Natives.

Generally speaking, Indian and Native cultures are "sociocentric" rather than "egocentric." In "egocentric" cultures such as many Western, industrialized nations (including the U.S.), individuals are viewed as autonomous from other individuals. In contrast, "sociocentric" cultures view individuals as part of an interdependent collective (Manson, 1995). For many Indians and Natives, identity and definitions of self are closely tied to one's family, tribe, or group (Blanchard, 1983). Decisions are strongly influenced by others (Horejsi & Pablo, 1993), and cooperation and humility are often more valued than competition or individual success (Richardson, 1981). As harmony with others is central, mores against interfering with others, disagreement, or otherwise creating conflict might exist (Sue & Sue, 1990).

Indians and Natives also tend to have a more holistic and fatalistic view of the world. Thus, the physical, mental, emotional, spiritual, or social aspects of self are not seen as distinct (Richardson, 1981). Humans, other creatures, spirits, and nature are seen as highly interwoven (Locke, 1992). Indians and Natives are more likely, for instance, to emphasize harmony with nature and respecting the land rather than controlling nature or using its resources (Horejsi & Pablo, 1993; Sue & Sue, 1990). Time was traditionally demarcated according to natural phenomenon such as seasons (Richardson, 1981) and, along with a belief that one had little control over what was meant to happen, events were thought to happen according to a natural schedule (Horejsi & Pablo, 1993). Within Indian and Native culture, mores often emphasize living patiently in the here-and-now versus continual concern with planning for the future or with "wasting" time (Richardson, 1981).

Along these same lines, learning is often seen as a process that will happen without interference as an individual experiences the natural consequences of their decisions and behavior. Learning is not necessarily viewed in a Western way, as needing to be highly "active" where consequences or limits are imposed on children by others such as parents. Observational learning is an important mode in addition to learning from the wisdom of others through listening, not only those physically present but one's ancestors via oral myths and legends (Horejsi & Pablo, 1993; Locke, 1992; Paniagua, 1994).

F. IMPACT OF CULTURAL VALUES

Cultural values effect the assessment and treatment process in terms of clinical judgments about normalcy. Erroneous judgments can lead to misunderstanding, overpathologization, or implementation of a treatment plan that is not culturally consistent. In addition, clinicians who lack understanding of these differences might unknowingly act in a manner that jeopardizes rapport and trust.

Misunderstandings within the therapeutic relationship not only occur because of the language-related issues covered earlier, but result as well from differences in the experience and expression of affect. As indicated, Indians and Natives are less likely to separate aspects of themselves such as their physical, mental, and social selves (Richardson, 1981). Typically, affect is more contextual and related to interpersonal difficulties rather than the "ego-oriented, context-less self-statements of dysphoria (e.g., I feel blue) or worry (e.g., I fear things)" (p. 490) present in more egocentric cultures (Manson, 1995). Discussing difficulties in determining the presence of depressed affect among American Indian Vietnam Veterans, Norton (1997) wrote, "It is as if the interviewer and veteran are having two separate conversations, the interviewer is asking about an interior life of emotions, and the veteran is telling her about an outer life of social relationships" (p. 26). Thus, if a clinician asks an Indian or Native client to identify and label his or her feelings, this probing might produce confusion or a paucity of information. It might be more helpful for the clinician to first inquire how things have been socially for the client and then ask how any difficulties noted have affected him or her in a feeling or emotional way. Indian or Native clients are also more likely to express affective concerns in somatic terms given the lack of differentiation between somatic and other aspects of one's being (Manson, 1995). Clinicians might gain insight into the emotional states of Indian or Native clientele, therefore, by attending to changes in physical well-being.

Moving to typical situations open to overpathologization, numerous authors warn against labeling commonly occurring hallucinations or delusions as signs of schizophrenia or other serious psychopathology (Manson et al., 1985; O'Nell, 1989; Pollack & Shore, 1980). It might not be at all unusual for Indians or Natives to "see" or "hear" a recently deceased person or, in some tribes, to believe one has been inhabited or cursed by a witch. Manson et al. (1985), for example, found 20% of a group of clinically depressed Hopi individuals experienced these types of hallucinations without significant social or cognitive impairment.

Indians and Natives can also present with a subdued manner and lack of eye contact that seems "withdrawn," "passive," or indicative of "flat affect" to the inexperienced clinician. Downcast eyes and a composed demeanor are cultural expressions of interpersonal respect within many tribes and groups. O'Nell (1989), in fact, postulates in her review of the literature the "flat affect" displayed by many Indians and Natives is often mislabeled as a symptom of schizophrenia rather than a cultural difference in the display of emotion. She warns of the dangers inherent in committing "category fallacy" or the application of Western categories of illness to a non-Western culture. She writes clinicians cannot validly "rule out the possibility that the converse of these manifestations, i.e. 'emotional lability,' 'inability to contact the spirit world,' . . . indicate a great degree of pathology . . . than the original 'signs'" (p. 78) of flat affect or delusions.

The application of Western ideas about separation-individuation, child rearing, achievement, and problem solving can also be problematic as depicted in the following scenarios. First, Indians or Natives often live with their nuclear or extended family throughout most of their lives (Staples & Mirande, 1980). A 35-year-old Ute male who lives with his family in his parents' home is thus not necessarily "dependent," "insufficiently individuated," or otherwise pathological. He is also not "passive" or "too focused on what others think" if he makes decisions based on the preferences of his wife and grandparents or "conflict-avoidant" if unwilling to share angry feelings with his family. Labeling him as "codependent" and encouraging him to "set boundaries" with his family might cause considerable psychological distress as well as rejection from members of his culture. Given more fatalistic beliefs, it is not uncommon for Indians, especially more traditional ones, to cope with stress such as anger towards family by waiting for a solution to appear (Trimble et al., 1996) rather than being "proactive" and planning how to cope differently in the future. Clinically, Indian or Native clients might be prone to missing appointments, especially if their presenting concerns have improved. This is not sufficient evidence to deem the client irresponsible or "crisis-oriented," a term with highly negative connotations among treatment providers. The here-and-now emphasis of the culture as well as the multitude of stressors present in many Indian and Native lives might lead the client to quite reasonably decide something else is more of a priority than an appointment.

Second, given the different philosophies about learning, a Native husband and wife should not be automatically considered "permissive" parents in need of a strict behavioral plan if they rarely discipline their children. Culturally, this couple is also not considered neglectful if the children's grandparents take as much responsibility in child rearing. Lastly, a 10-year-old Ojibwe boy who is reluctant to participate in competitive activities at school isn't necessarily unable to complete the task or suffering from low self-esteem. In his family and tribal life, it might be highly offensive to try to look better than others.

On the clinician's part, interrupting a client who digresses from something seemingly more important could be highly offensive as could actively confronting the client. A clinician who spends considerable time talking about their credentials or their thoughts or beliefs might also be seen as a "know-it-all" or rude because of lack of humility.

The previous paragraph concludes the discussion of more contextual and global factors related to therapeutic work with American Indians and Alaska Natives. These factors were presented to facilitate the development of empathy, respect, and understanding on the part of clinicians, especially those unfamiliar with the Indian or Native population. Without these qualities, a strong therapeutic alliance is unlikely to ensue between the Indian/Native client and clinician, and even the best assessment and treatment approaches will likely fail. With this backdrop in place, the chapter now shifts to specific assessment and treatment suggestions to help clinicians more successfully enact their role as diagnosticians and treatment providers.

II. SPECIFIC ASSESSMENT AND TREATMENT SUGGESTIONS

Included in this discussion are common disorders to anticipate, guidelines regarding the use of standardized measures, and the benefits of alternative sources of information. Once again, these suggestions are meant to supplement the contextual information presented in the first half of this chapter rather than stand on their own.

A. COMMONLY OCCURRING DISORDERS

Prior to considering the prevalence of mental disorders among Indians and Natives, it is important to note that few epidemiological studies have been completed with this population. Moreover, those available to use frequently suffer from methodological problems such as flawed sampling methods, outdated samples, and limited cultural sensitivity (Manson et al., 1997). However, in the interest of clues regarding which psychological problems might be common and deserving of attention in the assessment/diagnostic phase, the current state of knowledge will be presented.

Indian and Native youth and adults are at high risk for or have a high prevalence of the following: mental retardation, speech impediments, learning disabilities, developmental disabilities, Attention Deficit Hyperactivity Disorder, Conduct Disorder, psychoactive substance abuse and dependence, depression, simple phobias, social phobias, separation anxiety, overanxious disorder, obsessive-compulsive disorder, and posttraumatic stress disorder (Manson et al., 1997; Manson & Brenneman, 1995; Manson, Walker, & Kivlahan, 1987). In addition, American Indian and Alaska Native youth experience high rates of Fetal Alcohol Effects or Fetal Alcohol Syndrome, otitis media, which can contribute to language and speech delays (McShane, 1982), suicide (Blum, Harmon, Harris, Bergeisen, & Resnick, 1992), and child abuse and neglect (Manson et al., 1997).

It is important to mention the high rates of traumatic stress experienced by Indian/Natives as abuse victims and witnesses of the abuse of others, for they are related to the development of psychiatric symptomatology. As an example, Piasecki et al. (1989) found significantly higher rates of development disorders, conduct disorders, drug use disorders, depressive disorders, and anxiety disorders in abused Indian and Native youth than those without similar histories.

B. Use of Standardized Methods

For many clinicians (especially psychologists), self-report instruments (e.g., the Minnesota Multiphasic Personality Inventory [MMPI]) and clinician-administered psychological tests (e.g., the Wechsler intelligence scales, the Rorschach) are invaluable sources of information in the assessment phase. The majority of standardized measures have not been normed on American Indian or Alaska Native populations, however. Lacking such norms, it is difficult to judge whether elevated symptomatology indicate psychopathology or nonpathological cultural variation. For example, Pollack and Shore (1980) reported consistent elevations in the F, Pd, and Sc scales of the MMPI within urban Indian psychiatric patients regardless of gender, age, tribal affiliation, or diagnosis (including schizophrenia and depression). They concluded, "It appears that cultural influence overrides individual pathology and personality differences in influencing the pattern of the MMPI" (p. 948). In a similar vein, the commonly observed discrepancies between the Verbal and Performance Intelligence Quotients of the Wechsler scales might be an expression of a learning disability but could also indicate cultural differences in learning, environment, or language barriers (Manson et al., 1997).

Other doubts have been expressed about the cross-cultural validity of various personality and intellectual tests beyond lack of norms. As summarized by Suzuki and Kugler (1995), the following are the common concerns: (a) the content of items as well as constructs measured reflect White middle-class values; (b) minorities might not be as accustomed to test-taking, and issues of test-practice and motivation may influence test results (c) clinicians unfamiliar with the culture of the client may inadvertently stereotype the client and bias the results; and (d) oppression and discrimination may contribute to the elevation or depression of various scores rather than an individual deficit. Ideally, as proposed by Pollack and Shore (1980), "It is not only cultural norms for standard tests that need development but cultural research that identifies culturally appropriate instruments from the outset" (p. 949).

Given that norms are typically nonexistent and that such culturally appropriate instruments are also lacking, clinicians using standardized measures should approach results with caution. As a general rule, clinicians should interpret and report data consistent across measures in an assessment battery. For example, it is probably reasonable to conclude an American Indian male is depressed if he indicates depressed affect and other depressive symptoms such as insomnia during a clinical interview and testing further reveals an elevated D scale on the MMPI, a positive Depression Index on the Rorschach, and a very slow processing speed within the Performance subtests of the Weschler Adult Intelligence Scale (WAIS). As described below, however, clinicians should routinely utilize other sources of information beyond standardized measures and incorporate this data into any diagnostic formulation.

C. Use of Alternative Sources of Information

Family members (including extended family) and community members such as medicine men can be invaluable sources to consult (with a client's consent). As part of the culture and the client's daily life, these individuals possess a rich understanding of the client's social, emotional, physical, and spiritual functioning, both currently and across time. In addition, these individuals are perhaps most able to render culturally sensitive and accurate judgments as to the existence of pathology. For example, it can be quite difficult for Anglo clinicians to decipher whether an Indian male's high level of mistrust stems from a realistic need to protect oneself from the dangers and injury associated with discrimination or if he is paranoid in a delusional sense. Family and community members might rather effortlessly be able to tell the clinician whether the man's level of mistrust is normal or pathological.

To give another example, O'Nell and Mitchell (1996) ethnographically investigated teen drinking in a North Plains community through in-depth interviews with teens as well as other community members. They found that the definition of pathological drinking in this community was not related to frequency of use or quantity of alcohol consumed. Instead, local norms define an adolescent as having a drinking problem when drinking interferes with the adolescent's acquisition of cultural values such as courage, modesty, humor, generosity, and family honor. Thus, in assessing a potential alcohol problem, asking a Northern Plains adolescent if she or he felt these values were effected by alcohol use might prove more fruitful than asking how often or how much the youth drinks.

Other sources to consider consulting include clinicians with Indian and Native experience, anthropologists who have researched the particular tribe or group of the client, and the academic literature (ethnographies, histories, and the literature of the culture) (Westermeyer, 1987). Home or school observations might also help capture for the clinician the "flavor" of a client's life beyond the capabilities of any test. Observing an Indian or Native client engaging in hobbies can help provide a balanced view of the client as possessing strengths in addition to weaknesses. For example, an American Indian child might be performing well below average in academics and seem to be severely delayed according to intellectual testing and teacher observations. However, during a home visit, a clinician might observe the child has a strong facility in beadwork, making highly complex patterns. The "delay" thus might not be as severe as thought and more related to cultural issues such as activity preferences and language rather than innate ability.

On a final note, assessing the client's level of acculturation to Western ways and ethnic identity should be a focus with most every American Indian and Alaska Native client. As mentioned by Trimble et al. (1996), "For some individuals who are otherwise fairly healthy, the conflicts surrounding movement between cultures may be what brings them into counseling. . . . These issues become more salient for Indian people who are living in an urban or other nonreservation environment (p. 204)." Some of these conflicts were described earlier in this chapter. In addition, scholars (Grieger & Ponterotto, 1995; Trimble et al., 1996) argue understanding the client's ethnic identity and level of acculturation can increase the effectiveness of treatment. A client who is fairly acculturated, for example, may have previous counseling experience and be quite comfortable with the process and roles of the therapist and client. In contrast, a very traditional Indian male will likely have not been in counseling before and may be highly uncomfortable with some aspects of his role as a client (e.g., self-disclosure) as well as some of the behaviors of the therapist (e.g., direct questioning). The content and structure of therapy with this client thus might be very different and involve rather informal meetings at the client's home with limited self-disclosure over a substantial amount of time.

There are several models of how to assess level of acculturation. Trimble et al. (1996) recommend clinicians develop a line of open-ended questions to obtain information about education, employment, religion, language, political participation, urbanization, media influence, social relations, daily life, and past significant events and their causes. Grieger and Ponterotto (1995) suggest approaching the entire family and asking about (a) the client's level of Western psychological mindedness (e.g., awareness of Western view and experience of depression); (b) the family's level of psychological mindedness; (c) the client and family's attitude towards counseling; (d) the client's level of acculturation; (e) the family's level of acculturation; and (f) the family's attitude towards acculturation.

Another useful framework is presented in the *DSM-IV* Outline for Cultural Formulation, a tool for clinicians to systematically evaluate the impact of culture on diagnosis and treatment. This outline (in *DSM-IV,* Appendix I) addresses the cultural identity of the individual, cultural explanations of the individual's illness, cultural factors related to the psychosocial environment and levels of functioning, and cultural elements of the relationship between the individual and clinician (American Psychiatric Association, 1994). Although the Outline has limitations and weaknesses (Novins et al., 1997), the reader is encouraged to consult Fleming (1996), Manson (1996), and O'Nell (1998) as useful applications to the American Indian population. One could also see Choney, Berryhill-Paapke, and Robbins (1995) for a more in-depth presentation and discussion of acculturation frameworks.

D. SPECIFIC TREATMENT SUGGESTIONS

1. Modality

Given the aforementioned lack of transportation as well as the distances between clinics and clients' homes, the first step in treatment with American Indians and Alaska Natives should be to identify where intervention should occur. In some instances, sessions will not occur or will occur inconsistently unless the clinician is willing and able to visit the client's home (Willis, Dobrec, & Bigfoot Sipes, 1992). In addition to transportation concerns, some individuals and families may be very uncomfortable visiting a clinic. For some, the bureaucracy embodied in clinics can symbolize historical and current attempts of forced assimilation. For others, concerns about confidentiality predominate.

In addition, because of the cultural emphasis on others, family or group therapy might fit better with an Indian or Native client's background and expectations than individual treatment (Sue & Sue, 1990; Trimble et al., 1996). In fact, many Indian and Native cultures have a long tradition of employing groups for social and religious activities, which have strong similarities to the techniques used in group therapy. For instance, it is rather easy to identify the parallels between "talking circles" and group therapies (Neligh, 1990). Clients might bring others with them to treatment spontaneously and the composition of who attends sessions might be fluid across treatment. Other clients, however, might feel uncomfortable discussing concerns in a group setting or request individual treatment to discuss anger or other uncomfortable affect related to disrupted interpersonal relationships. The preferences of the client should be ascertained and accommodated to the best of the therapist's ability.

Clinicians should also consider that weekly sessions lasting for 1 hour might not be an effective option for many American Indians and Alaska Natives. Given the cultural emphasis on living in the here-and-now, Indian and Native individuals and families often present with significant distress and a highly pressing issue to discuss. Not attending to these "crisis" situations at the time or soon after for lack of time or other duties (e.g., paperwork, administrative meetings) will likely seem uncaring and offensive. As further cited in Trimble et al. (1996), American Indians are more likely than other ethnic groups to underuse mental health services and/or drop out of treatment. Allowing for more lengthy sessions on an as-needed basis may be one way clinicians can make mental health services more appealing in addition to preventing premature termination. For example, if a family presents because of a recent suicide of a family member, an immediate session of several hours could be undertaken followed by a contact every day for the first week. The clinician might continue seeing all of the family or certain members on a long-term basis. Others might have gained the assistance they needed to never return to treatment.

As a final note, it is highly recommended that clinicians inform American Indians and Alaska Natives of other resources available in their communities and encourage clients to utilize these other services. Trimble and LaFromboise (1985) suggest that one reason American Indians and Alaska Natives underuse services is simply they do not know what is available. They further suggest that family and other community members can offer valuable mental health-related assistance in addition to organizations such as B.I.A. and I.H.S. Others (e.g., Manson et al., 1997; Solomon, 1992; Trimble et al., 1996) are strong proponents for using traditional methods of healing such as ceremonies, talking circles, and sweat lodges in conjunction with Western psychological treatment.

2. Content

Numerous suggestions have already been outlined with regard to session content. For example, the benefits of discussing historical mistrust, cultural identity, and internalized racism have been considered to some detail. The relative predominance of affect and emotions in therapeutic sessions has also been discussed as needing to vary according to tribal or group membership. Sue and Sue (1990) also propose that describing the typical course of therapy as well as the role of the clinician and client at the beginning of treatment might prevent premature termination and increase treatment effectiveness.

Another suggestion is that clinicians working with American Indians and Alaska Natives spend as much time discussing areas of strength as areas of pathology. Clinicians are often struck with the resilience of most American Indian and Alaska Native clients in the face of tremendous hardship. Identifying such strengths is usually an easy task to achieve with this prompting. Focusing on positive experiences or capacities engenders trust in the therapeutic relationship and also facilitates the client's ability to use adaptive coping mechanisms in other problem areas. This respectful belief in and focus on the client's inherent capacity as part of the healing process is especially important given Indian's and Native's history of devaluation and discrimination.

3. Treatment Method

The literature offers contradictory evidence about effective methods or approaches to counseling with American Indians and Alaska Natives. For example, Trimble and LaFromboise (1985) argue that a directive approach is the most useful stance to adopt with an Indian or Native client, whereas others argue a nondirective approach is more effective (e.g., Tanaka-Matsumi & Higginbotham, 1996; Wise & Miller, 1983). Some clinicians state that psychodynamically oriented therapy is less useful than behavioral approaches as it (dynamic therapy) emphasizes internal conflicts rather than how environmental events impact behavior (e.g., Paniagua, 1994; Tanaka-Matsumi & Higginbotham, 1996). However, interpersonal therapy, rooted in psychodynamic theory, has been seen as a promising treatment approach with American Indians (Neligh, 1990).

Given the lack of outcome studies with this population as well as the considerable diversity between and within tribes and groups, it is not surprising definitive guidance is lacking in regard to effectiveness of one treatment approach over another. Despite these controversies, however, a review of the literature supports the following propositions about therapy with Indians and Natives: (a) therapist warmth, genuineness, respect, and empathy are significantly related to successful therapeutic outcomes, and (b) therapists will need to be adaptive and flexible rather than unthinking in their application of convention counseling techniques (e.g., Neligh, 1990; Trimble et al., 1996; Trimble & LaFromboise, 1985).

The first point is generally true in treatment with all clients (Trimble et al., 1996), but considerable effort has been spent in this chapter to facilitate an empathic understanding specific to American Indians and Alaska Natives. The dangers in relying uncritically upon Western ideas about mental health and pathology also have been considered in detail. The remainder of the chapter will provide more discussion of how to adapt conventional treatment models.

From the general cross-cultural literature, Tanaka-Matsumi and Higgin-botham (1996) argue that an effective cross-cultural intervention should incorporate culture-specific definitions of deviancy, accepted norms of role behavior, and approved behavior change agents. Thus, a 16-year-old American Indian male who is brought to treatment by his parents for rebellious behavior may require treatment different from a 16-year-old White male with the same presenting issue. Unlike the White male, separation-individuation is a less important developmental task for Indians and it is socially taboo to not listen or be disrespectful of those more elderly regardless of developmental age. One's first inclination might be to teach the parents how to apply consequences when the adolescent misbehaves or to normalize the adolescent's behavior as "just part of being a teenager." It would make more sense culturally, however, to explore aspects of identity formation. If the youth identifies more strongly with and aspires the values of American Indian culture, discussing and predicting the social rejection which will inevitably result from his rebellious behavior might facilitate change. Linking this adolescent with an influential male family member, a more traditional community member, or a traditional healer might also prove effective in addition to encouraging attendance at traditional events like sweats and pow-wows.

From the American Indian literature more specifically, both Trimble (1992) and Manson and Brenneman (1995) present descriptions of how conventional cognitive-behavioral treatment programs were adapted for use with American Indian youth and elders. Manson and Brenneman (1995), for instance, adapted the Coping with Depression course created by Lewinsohn, Munoz, Youngren, and Zeiss (1986) with the aim of preventing the psychological sequelae associated with chronic disease in American Indian elders. Culturally salient examples of symptom expression and mood descriptors were incorporated into each component, and the program was expanded from 12 to 16 sessions to compensate for language and cultural barriers. The utility of this treatment and its adaptations were evident in the diminishment of depressive symptoms between pre- and posttest for those elders participating in this project. Trimble (1992) likewise modified a cognitive-behavioral skills enhancement program to prevent drug use among Indian adolescents via consultation with an Indian advisory committee, the incorporation of local Indian values, customs, and lifestyles into the intervention, and training Indian community residents in implementation of the curriculum.

III. CONCLUSION

This chapter has presented a mixture of general knowledge about the American Indian and Alaska Native population, weaving in specific suggestions more pointedly related to psychological assessment and treatment. As stated, possessing an understanding of the context in which Indians and Natives live will be invaluable in enabling clinicians to provide the empathy and respect essential for an Indian/Native client to trust and remain in treatment. The relative emphasis on more general factors also reflects the authors' belief that critical thinking and analysis are among the most useful tools for clinicians working with American Indian and Alaska Native clients to possess. The current state of knowledge as well as the diversity among Indians and Natives currently preclude a "standard" approach to assessment or treatment. Having read this chapter, hopefully clinicians will better appreciate that it can be challenging to work effectively and sensitively with Indians or Natives, but that such challenges offer exciting and potentially rewarding opportunities to enhance one's skills as a care provider.

REFERENCES

American Psychiatric Association. (1994). *Diagnostic and Statistical Manual of Mental Disorders (4th ed.)*. Washington, DC: American Psychiatric Association.

Beals, J. B., Keane, E. M., & Manson, S. M. (in press). Population studies of older American Indians and Alaska Natives: Challenges for survey sampling. *The Gerontologist.*

Berger, T. R. (1985). *Village journey: The report of the Alaska Native Review Commission.* New York: Hill and Wang.

Blanchard, E. L. (1983). The growth and development of American Indian and Alaska Native children. In G. J. Powell, J. Yamamoto, A. Romero, & A. Morales, (Eds.), *The psychosocial development of minority group children* (pp. 115–130). New York: Brunner/Mazel.

Blum, R. W., Harmon, B., Harris, L., Bergeisen, L., & Resnick, M.D. (1992). American Indian-Alaska Native youth health. *Journal of the American Medical Association, 267*(12), 1637–1644.

Broken Nose, M. A. (1992). Working with the Oglala Lakota: An outsider's perspective. *Families in Society: The Journal, 73,* 380–383.

Bureau of Indian Affairs. (1998). *Answers to frequently asked questions.* (On-line). Available Internet: http://www.doi.gov/bia/aitoday/q_and_a.html.

Choney, S. K. Berryhill-Paapke, E., & Robbins, R. R. (1995). The acculturation of American Indians: Developing frameworks for research and practice. In J. G. Ponterotto, J. M. Casas, L. A. Suzuki, & C. M. Alexander (Eds.), *Handbook of multicultural counseling* (pp. 73–92). Thousand Oaks, CA: Sage Publications, Inc.

Crawford, J. (1994). *Endangered Native American languages: What is to be done, and why?* (On-line). Available Internet: http://www.ncbe.gwu.edu/miscpubs/crawford.

Fleming, C. M. (1996). Cultural formulation of psychiatric diagnosis: Case No. O1. An American Indian woman suffering from depression, alcoholism, and childhood trauma. *Culture, Medicine, & Psychiatry, 20*(2), 145–154.

Grieger, I., & Ponterotto, J. (1995). A framework for assessment in multicultural counseling. In J. G. Ponterotto, J. M. Casas, L. A. Suzuki, & C. M. Alexander (Eds.), *Handbook of multicultural counseling* (pp. 357–374). Thousand Oaks, CA: Sage Publications, Inc.

Horejsi, C., & Pablo, J. (1993). Traditional Native American cultures and contemporary U.S. society: A comparison. *Human Services in the Rural Environment, 16*(3), 24–27.

Indian Health Service. (1997). *Trends in Indian Health—1996.* (On-line). Available Internet: http://www.tucson.ihs.gov/PublicInfo/publications/trends96.asp.

Krauss, M. E. (1980). *Alaska Native languages: Past, present, and future.* (Alaska Native Language Center Research Papers No. 4). Fairbanks, AK: Alaska Native Language Center.

Lewinsohn, P. M., Munoz, R. F., Youngren, M. A., & Zeiss, A. M. (1986). *Control your depression* (2nd ed.). Englewood Cliffs, NJ: Prentice-Hall.

Locke, D. L. (1992). Native Americans. In D. C. Locke (Ed.), *Increasing multicultural understanding* (pp. 46–61). Newburg Park, CA: Sage Publications, Inc.

Lockhart, B. (1981). Historic distrust and the counseling of American Indians and Alaska Natives. *White Cloud Journal, 2*(3), 31–34.

Manson, S. M. (1995). Culture and major depression: Current challenges in the diagnosis of mood disorders. *The Psychiatric Clinics of North America, 18*(8), 487–503.

Manson, S. M. (1996). The wounded spirit: A cultural formulation of post-traumatic stress disorder. *Culture, Medicine, and Psychiatry, 20,* 489–498.

Manson, S. M., Bechtold, D. W., Novins, D. K., & Beals, J. (1997). Assessing psychopathology in American Indian and Alaska Native children and adolescents. *Applied Developmental Science, 1*(3), 135–144.

Manson, S. M., & Brenneman, D. L. (1995). Chronic disease among older American Indians: Preventing depressive symptoms and related problems of coping. In D. K. Padgett (Ed.), *Handbook on ethnicity, aging, and mental health* (pp. 284–303). Westport, CT: Greenwood Press.

Manson, S. M., Shore, J. H., & Bloom, J. D. (1985). The depressive experience in American Indian communities: A challenge for psychiatric theory and diagnosis. In A. Kleinman & B. Good (Eds.), *Culture and depression: Studies in the anthropology and cross-cultural psychiatry of affect and disorder* (pp. 331–368). Berkeley, CA: University of California Press.

Manson, S. M., Walker, R. D., & Kivlahan, D. R. (1987). Psychiatric assessment and treatment of American Indians and Alaska Natives. *Hospital and Community Psychiatry, 38*(2), 165–173.

McNabb, S. L. (1990). Self-reports in cross-cultural contexts. *Human Organization, 49*(4), 291–299.

McShane, D. (1982). Otitis media and American Indians: Prevalence, etiology, psychoeducational consequences, prevention, and intervention. In S. M. Manson (Ed.), *New directions in prevention among American Indian and Alaska Native communities* (pp. 265–297). Portland, OR: Oregon Health Sciences University.

Neligh, G. (1990). Mental health programs for American Indians: Their logic, structure, and function. *The Journal of the National Center Monograph Series, 3*(3).

Nies, J. (1996). *Native American history: A chronology of a culture's vast achievements and their links to world events.* New York: Ballantine Books.

Norton, I. M. (1997). *The validity of DSM-III-R major depression among American Indians.* Unpublished manuscript.

Norton, I. M., & Manson, S. M. (1996). Research in American Indian and Alaska Native communities: Navigating the cultural universe of values and process. *Journal of Consulting and Clinical Psychology, 64*(5), 856–860.

Novins, D. K., Bechtold, D. W., Sack, W. H., Thompson, J., Carter, D. R., & Manson, S. M. (1997). The DSM-IV® Outline for Cultural Formulation: A critical demonstration with American Indian children. *Journal of the American Academy of Child and Adolescent Psychiatry, 36*(9), 1244–1251.

Olson, J. S., & Wilson, R. (1984). *Native Americans in the twentieth century.* Urbana, IL: University of Illinois Press.

O'Nell, T. D. (1989). Psychiatric investigations among American Indians and Alaska Natives: A critical review. *Culture, Medicine, and Psychiatry, 13,* 51–87.

O'Nell, T. D. (1998). Cultural formulation of psychiatric diagnosis: Psychotic depression and alcoholism in an American Indian male. *Culture, Medicine, and Psychiatry, 22,* 123–136.

O'Nell, T. D., & Mitchell, C. M. (1996). Alcohol use among American Indian adolescents: The role of culture in pathological drinking. *Social Science and Medicine, 42*(4), 565–578.

Paisano, E. L. (1997). *The American Indian, Eskimo, and Aleut population.* [On-line]. Available http://www.census.gov/population/www/pop-profile/amerind.html

Paniagua, F. A. (1994). *Assessing and treating culturally diverse clients: A practical guide.* Thousand Oaks, CA: Sage Publications, Inc.

Piasecki, J. M., Manson, S. M., Biernoff, M. P., Hiat, A. B., Taylor, S. S., & Bechtold, D. W. (1989). Abuse and neglect of American Indian children: Findings from a survey of federal providers. *American Indian and Alaska Native Mental Health Research, 3*(2), 43–62.

Pollack, D., & Shore, J. H. (1980). Validity of the MMPI with Native Americans. *American Journal of Psychiatry, 137*(8), 646–650.

Richardson, E. H. (1981). Cultural and historical perspectives in counseling American Indians. In D. W. Sue (Ed.), *Counseling the culturally different: Theory and practice* (pp. 216–255). New York: John Wiley & Sons.

Solomon, A. (1992). Clinical diagnosis among diverse populations: A multicultural perspective. *Families in Society: The Journal of Contemporary Human Services, 73,* 371–377.

Staples, R., & Mirande, A. (1980). Racial and cultural variations among American families: A decennial review of the literature on minority families. *Journal of Marriage and the Family, 6,* 887–900.

Sue, D. W., & Sue, D. (1990). Counseling American Indians, In D. W. Sue, & D. Sue (Eds.), *Counseling the culturally different: Theory and practice* (pp. 175–188). New York: John Wiley & Sons.

Suzuki, L. A., & Kugler, J. F. (1995). Intelligence and personality assessment: Multicultural perspectives. In J. G. Ponterotto, J. M. Casas, L. A. Suzuki, & C. M. Alexander (Eds.), *Handbook of multicultural counseling* (pp. 493–515). Thousand Oaks, CA: Sage Publications, Inc.

Tanaka-Matsumi, J., & Higginbotham, H. N. (1996). Behavioral approaches to counseling across cultures. In P. B. Pedersen, J. G. Draguns, W. J. Lonner, & J. E. Trimble (Eds.), *Counseling across cultures* (4th ed.) (pp. 265–292). Thousand Oaks, CA: Sage Publications, Inc.

Trimble, J. E. (1992). A cognitive-behavioral approach to drug abuse prevention and intervention with American Indian youth. In L. A. Vargas & J. D. Koss-Chioino (Eds.), *Working with culture: Psychotherapeutic interventions with ethnic minority children and adolescents* (pp. 246–275). San Francisco, CA: Jossey-Bass Publishers.

Trimble, J. E., Fleming, C. M., Beauvais, F., & Jumper-Thurman, P. (1996). Essential cultural and social strategies for counseling Native American Indians. In P. B. Pedersen, J. G. Draguns, W. J. Lonner, & J. E. Trimble (Eds.), *Counseling across cultures* (4th Ed.) (pp. 177–209). Thousand Oaks, CA: Sage Publications, Inc.

Trimble, J. E., & LaFromboise, T. (1985). American Indians and the counseling process: Culture, adaptation, and style. In P. Pedersen (Ed.), *Handbook of cross-cultural counseling and therapy* (pp. 127–133). Westport, CT: Greenwood Press.

U.S. Bureau of the Census. (1995a). *Selected social and economic characteristics for the 25 largest American Indian tribes.* (On-line). Available Internet: http://www.census.gov/population/socdemo/indian/ailang2.txt.

U.S. Bureau of the Census. (1995b). *Census Bureau reports on status of American Indians' housing on reservations.* (On-line). Available Internet: http://www.census.gov/Press-Release/Cb95-74.txt.

U.S. Bureau of the Census. (1995c). State—Urbanized Area, Anchorage, AK. (On-line). Available Internet: http://venus.census.gov/cdrom/lookup.

U.S. Bureau of the Census. (1995d). State—Alaska. (On-line). Available Internet: http://venus.census.gov/cdrom/lookup.

Westermeyer, J. (1987). Clinical considerations in cross-cultural diagnosis. *Hospital and Community Psychiatry, 38*(2), 160–165.

Willis, D. J., Dobrec, A., & Bigfoot Sipes, D. S. (1992). Treating American Indian victims of abuse and neglect. In L. A. Vargas & J. D. Koss-Chioino (Eds.), *Working with culture: Psychotherapeutic interventions with ethnic minority children and adolescents* (pp. 276–299). San Francisco, CA: Jossey-Bass Publishers.

Wise, F., & Miller, N. B. (1983). The mental health of the American Indian child. In G. J. Powell, J. Yamamoto, A. Romero, & A. Morales (Eds.), *The psychosocial development of minority group children* (pp. 344–361). New York: Bruner/Mazel.

CHAPTER 13

Multicultural Issues in Treating Clients with HIV/AIDS from the African American, American Indian, Asian, and Hispanic Populations

Freddy A. Paniagua

Department of Psychiatry and Behavioral Sciences
University of Texas Medical Branch
Galveston, Texas

In the United States, the first description of cases resembling symptoms for the acquired immunodeficiency syndrome (AIDS) was reported in 1981 in a group of homosexual men residing in Los Angeles (California) and New York City (Centers for Disease Control [CDC], 1981a, 1981b). The virus that causes AIDS was first identified in 1983–1984 (Gallo & Montagnier, 1988). This virus has received several names (see McCombie, 1990, p. 12), but the name commonly used in biomedical and social research is "human immunodeficiency virus" or HIV (Flaskerud & Ungvarski, 1999).

In the last 10 years, the biomedical and psychosocial literature on HIV/AIDS indicate three general findings. First, the metaphors "Gay-Related Immune Deficiency" and "Gay Plague" used during the earlier days of the epidemic facilitated the spread of HIV disease because the health-care system in this country failed to identify other risks for HIV disease (in addition to sexual behavior among homosexuals). For example, as noted by Landau-Stanton and Clements (1993) "American researchers initially missed the signs of the disease in intravenous drug users, in recipients of [blood] transfusions, in hemophiliacs, in babies and children, and in women" (p. 5). The current finding is that HIV disease does not discriminate against race, sex, age, or geographical locations around the world (Shannon, Pyle, & Bashur, 1991). Second, in comparison to Anglo-Americans with HIV/AIDS, in this country "HIV/AIDS is a major public problem for racial and ethnic minorities" (Ward & Duchin, 1998). Third, a crucial aspect of HIV/AIDS ignored during the earlier signs of this disease was the psychosocial and social impact of the disease on individuals affected by HIV/AIDS as well as on the family and community structures of such individuals (Hoffman, 1996). Today, the current thought is that HIV is not only a physical entity but also a major psychosocial problem in society. This point led to the development of a biopsychosocial approach specific to the assessment and treatment of persons with HIV/AIDS (Flaskerud & Miller, 1999).

In the biopsychosocial approach toward HIV/AIDS, a crucial factor is the inclusion of cultural similarities and variations across racial groups. These cultural similarities and variations are illustrated in this chapter, with emphasis on four culturally diverse groups in the United States: African American, American Indian, Asian, and Hispanic communities (National Commission on AIDS, 1992; Medrano & Klopner, 1992). The need to emphasize these racial groups was assessed in a study including 2,121 mental health professionals, who were surveyed regarding their opinion about the inclusion of HIV/AIDS topics they would recommend in educational programs targeting this professional group (Paniagua et al., 1998). The inclusion of these four racial groups was among the highest endorsed topic in the "strongly recommended" scale: African American (56.1%), American Indian (44.8%), Asian (43.2%), and Hispanic (54.7%) communities.

I. THE EPIDEMIOLOGY OF HIV/AIDS

A. AGE, SEX, AND EXPOSURE CATEGORY IN THE GENERAL POPULATION

As of June 1997 report of AIDS cases in the United States totaled 612,078 (CDC, 1997), including 604,176 adults/adolescents (511,934 males and 92,242 females) and 7,902 children (<13 years old). From 1981 through 1997, approximately 374,656 and 4,602 adults/adolescents and children (<13 years old) have died because of AIDS, respectively (CDC, 1997). Table I (CDC, 1997) shows a summary of exposure category in adults/adolescents and children in the general U.S. population. In Table I (see also Tables II–IV), other exposures include HIV-infected blood, body fluids, or concentrated virus in health care,

TABLE I.   AIDS Cases by Exposure Category in Adults/Adolescents
and Children in the U.S. Population through June 1997[a]

Exposure category	Total	%
Adults/Adolescents		
Men who have sex with men	298,699	49
Injecting drug use	154,664	26
Heterosexual contacts	54,571	9
Men who have sex with men and injecting drug use	38,923	6
Hemophilia/coagulation disorder	4,567	1
Receipt of blood transfusions, blood components, or tissue	8,075	1
Other risks	44,677	7
Adult/adolescent subtotal 604,176		
Children (< 13 years old)		
Mother with/at risk for HIV infection	7,157	91
Receipt of blood transfusions, blood components, or tissue	375	5
Hemophilia/coagulation disorder	232	2
Other risks	138	2
Children subtotal 7,902		
Total 612,078		

[a] CDC: HIV Surveillance Report (1997, Vol. 9, No. 1).

laboratory, or household settings as supported by seroconversion, epidemiologic, and/or laboratory evidence (CDC, 1997).

Although the percentage of AIDS cases (Table I) resulting from heterosexual contacts among adults and adolescents is still low (95%), relative to other major risk factors, the number of AIDS cases in this subgroup is increasing rapidly (Ward & Duchin, 1998). For example, from 1990 through 1995, the incidence of AIDS (i.e., new cases within a given period) increased 189% for individuals infected with HIV because of heterosexual contacts with persons infected with this virus or at risk for HIV, in comparison with 12% for bisexual and homosexual men (Ward & Duchin, 1998). In these findings, adults/adolescent women are being significantly affected, compared to the rate of HIV infection among men. For example, from 1990 through 1995 the rate of AIDS resulting from heterosexual contacts among men in the general population increased by 27%, whereas the rate for women was 103% (Ward & Duchin, 1998).

Similarly, from 1995 through 1997, a total of 6,606 new cases of AIDS among adults/adolescent men were reported to the CDC (1997), compared to 11,399 of cases among adults/adolescent women. These findings probably explain the fact that the main risk factor for HIV infection among children has involved mothers with HIV or at risk for HIV infection (i.e., 91% in Table I). These findings suggest the need for the development of mental health services tailored to persons with HIV/AIDS from the subgroup of heterosexuals, with particular emphasis on heterosexual women who appeared to be at a higher risk for HIV infection, relative to the rate of this disease among men.

It should be noted that among adults/adolescent AIDS cases reported to the CDC through 1997, only 5% represent persons 13–25 years of age. Persons within this age range, however, are at highest risk for HIV infection (Paniagua, O'Boyle, & Wagner, 1997; Ward & Duchin, 1998). Because symptoms suggesting AIDS are generally developed 10 to 15 years after the acquisition of the virus, most clients with AIDS cases seen by mental health professionals were probably infected with the HIV virus during their adolescence or young adult stage (i.e., 13–25 years).

B. RACIAL GROUPS AND HIV/AIDS

Epidemiological findings show that HIV/AIDS is a major health problem among all racial groups in the United States. The magnitude of this problem, however, has a profoundly disporportionate impact on African Americans and Hispanics (Brown & Sankar, 1998; Flaskerud, 1999; Flaskerud & Ungvarski, 1999; Ory & Mack, 1998; Ward & Duchin, 1998). For example, 69,151 adults/adolescents AIDS cases were reported in 1996, in which 38% were whites (approximately 75% of the U.S. population), 41% African Americans (13% of the U.S. population), and 19% Hispanics (10% of the U.S. population) (Ward & Duchin, 1998). In addition, whereas the proportion of newly reported AIDS cases among whites decreased from 60% in 1985 to 40% in 1995, the proportion of newly reported cases among African Americans and Hispanics within the same period increased from 25% to 40% and 15% to 19%, respectively (Flaskerud & Ungvarski, 1999).

In general, American Indians and Asian Americans are yet underrepresented among HIV/AIDS cases in proportion to their number in the total population in the United States. For example, although African Americans and Hispanics constitute approximately 22% of the U.S. population in 1992 (National Commission on AIDS, 1992), these racial groups represented nearly 47% of AIDS cases reported in 1992. By contrast, in the same year American Indians and Asian Americans made up 3% of the total population in the U.S., but accounted for only 0.6% of the AIDS cases. Similar results were reported by the CDC (1998) and Sy, Chng, Choi, and Wong (1997).

In the specific case of women, approximately 77% of AIDS cases reported in this gender group has been African Americans or Hispanic (Ward & Duchin, 1998). These findings suggest those mental health professionals interested in serving persons with HIV/AIDS in the United States should expect a significant number of African Americans and Hispanics in their clinical practice.

Table II shows a summary of exposure category in male adults/adolescents across racial groups. In general, a greater number of African American and Hispanic males have been reported with AIDS through 1997, compared with Asian and American Indian males. In the case of "men who have sex with men" as a risk factor for HIV infection, whites have taken the lead since 1981 (first year when AIDS symptoms were reported to the CDC). It should be noted, however, that African Americans and Hispanics have historically constituted a small number in the United States compared to whites. Therefore, 32% and 44% of AIDS cases among African Americans and Hispanics, respectively (Table II), reported through 1997 is in disproportion to the number of persons from these two racial groups in the U.S. population (Ward & Duchin, 1998). Another significant finding is that the number of AIDS cases resulting from heterosexual contacts (Table II) have been higher among African American and Hispanic males relative to whites, Asians, and American Indians.

Table III shows a summary of exposure category in female adults/adolescents across racial groups. In general, in comparison with white females, African American and Hispanic women have been dramatically affected by the HIV/AIDS epidemic. For example, in a total of 92,424 AIDS cases reported to the CDC (1997), African American and Hispanic women represented 51,410 and 18,663 cases, respectively. These figures together represent 76% of AIDS cases reported to the CDC as of June 1997 (CDC, 1997).

Table IV shows a summary of exposure category in children (<13 years old) across racial groups. In general, a greater number of African American children have been diagnosed with AIDS relative to other racial groups in Table IV. In addition, in the case of the "mother with/at risk for HIV infection" category (Table IV) the percentage of AIDS among African American and Hispanic children is disproportionally higher for these groups, relative to white, Asian, and American Indian children. Because injecting drug use and heterosexual contacts have been the major risk factors for HIV infection among African American and Hispanic women (see Table III), it is not surprised to find out (Table IV) that most AIDS cases among children in these two racial groups have been associated with vertical transmission (i.e., transmission of HIV from mother to infant; Ward & Duchin, 1998).

In terms of results in Tables II–IV, mental health professionals interested in providing services to racial minority groups would probably have the largest number of HIV/AIDS cases from the African American and Hispanic communities, relative to the Asian and American Indian groups. In addition, in the process of individual, family, and group therapy, injecting drug use and heterosexual contacts would constitute two critical variables to consider during the management of emotional or psychological problems resulting from knowing about the HIV or AIDS status among members from such groups.

TABLE II.   AIDS Cases by Exposure Category in Male Adults and Adolescents across Racial Groups through June 1997[a]

Category	White N(%)	African American N(%)	Hispanic N(%)	Asian N(%)	American Indian N(%)	Total N(%)
Men who have sex with men	194,042(76)	61,251(32)	38,765(44)	2,884(75)	822(59)	298,699(58)
Injecting drug use	22,962(9)	57,409(36)	32,724(37)	203(5)	210(15)	113,635(22)
Men who have sex with men and injecting drug use	20,385(8)	12,246(8)	5,915(7)	128(3)	231(17)	38,923(8)
Heterosexual contacts	3,881(2)	10,511(7)	4,263(5)	111(3)	28(2)	18,811(4)
Hemophilia/coagulation disorder	3,442(1)	466(0)	376(0)	61(2)	231(17)	4,378(1)
Receipt of blood transfusions, blood components or tissue	3,043(1)	960(1)	516(1)	98(3)	7(1)	4,634(1)
Other risks	8,598(3)	17,498(11)	6,197(7)	365(9)	65(5)	32,854(6)
Total	256,353(100)	160,984(100)	88,766(100)	3,850(100)	1,390(100)	511,934(100)

[a] CDC: HIV Surveillance Report (1997, Vol. 9, No. 1).

TABLE III.   AIDS Cases by Exposure Category in Female Adults and Adolescents across Racial Groups through June 1997[a]

Category	White N(%)	African American N(%)	Hispanic N(%)	Asian N(%)	American Indian N(%)	Total N(%)
Injecting drug use	9,156(43)	23,646(46)	7,984(43)	80(17)	124(48)	41,029(44)
Heterosexual contacts	8,338(39)	18,482(36)	8,595(46)	219(46)	95(36)	35,760(39)
Hemophilia/coagulation disorder	89(0)	8(0)	32(0)	4(1)	15(0)	189(0)
Receipt of blood transfusion, blood components, or tissue	1,733(8)	1,098(2)	508(3)	87(18)	12(5)	3,441(4)
Other risks	2,003(9)	8,121(16)	1,543(8)	89(19)	29(11)	11,823(13)
Total	21,319(100)	51,410(100)	18,663(100)	479(100)	261(100)	92,242(100)

[a] CDC: HIV Surveillance Report (1997, Vol. 9, No. 1).

TABLE IV. AIDS Cases by Exposure Category in Children (<13 years old) across Racial Groups through June 1997[a]

Category	White N(%)	African American N(%)	Hispanic N(%)	Asian N(%)	American Indian N(%)	Total N(%)
Mother with/at risk for HIV infection	1,037(11)	4,374(95)	1,679(93)	27(66)	25(96)	7,157(91)
Hemophilia/coagulation disorder	157(11)	34(1)	37(2)	3(7)	1(4)	232(3)
Receipt of blood transfusions, blood components/tissue	183(13)	90(2)	92(5)	10(24)	—	375(5)
Other risks	23(2)	88(2)	25(1)	1(2)	—	138(2)
Total	1,400(100)	4,586(100)	1,833(100)	41(100)	26(100)	7,902(100)

[a]CDC: HIV Surveillance Report (1997, Vol. 9, No. 1).

II. MULTICULTURAL ISSUES ACROSS CULTURALLY DIVERSE CLIENTS WITH HIV/AIDS

In the present context, multicultural issues are often classified into two areas: (a) general issues shared by all racial minority clients with HIV/AIDS (Boyd-Franklin, Aleman, Jean-Gilles, & Lewis, 1995; Hoffman, 1996; Jue & Kain, 1989) and (b) issues specific to the particular racial group (Medrano & Klopner, 1992).

A. GENERAL MULTICULTURAL ISSUES

1. Development of a Therapeutic Relationship

As noted by Hoffman (1996), persons with HIV/AIDS from the four culturally diverse groups discussed in this chapter often believe that they are oppressed, stigmatized, or discriminated because of their HIV/AIDS status. Because of this general belief, clients from these groups seeking mental health services to deal with the spectrum of medical and psychological difficulties resulting from HIV/AIDS might be reluctant to discuss sensitive issues during therapy (e.g., how specifically the client believes he or she got the HIV virus; whether or not the client is engaged in preventive strategies to avoid infecting other members in his or her community). Thus, the development and maintenance (throughout the entire process of therapy) of a trusting client–therapist relationship is a critical issue to consider when assessing and treating clients with HIV/AIDS from the African American, American Indian, Asian, and Hispanic communities.

Paniagua (1998) proposed three levels (i.e., conceptual, behavioral, and cultural) to develop this therapeutic relationship with clients from such communities. The conceptual level includes, for example, the client's perception that the mental health professional is effective and trustworthy and the client's recognition that the therapist has provided something of value in the client–therapeutic relationship. These two elements of the conceptual level are known as *credibility* and *giving* (Sue & Sue, 1990). The *behavioral* level includes the client's perception of a mental health professional as competent in terms of his or her training in providing mental health services to persons with HIV/AIDS from culturally diverse groups.

The *cultural* level generally includes two approaches (Lonner & Ibrahim, 1996; Paniagua, 1996; Tharp, 1991). In the *cultural compatibility* approach, a client–clinician therapeutic relationship would be enhanced if racial differences between the client and the clinician were minimized. Thus, as these differences approach zero, the provision of both cultural and sensitive interventions are enhanced with a given racial group (Lopez, Lopez, & Fong, 1991). For example, this approach suggests that the assessment and treatment of Hispanic clients with HIV/AIDS would be enhanced if the therapist is also a member of the Hispanic community. Despite the apparent utility of this approach in the present context, clinicians are advised to use this approach with caution.

Among other problems with the compatibility approach (see Paniagua, 1998, pp. 6–7), the compatibility approach fails to distinguish between race and ethnicity concepts (Paniagua, 1998; Waytt, 1991; Wilkinson, 1993). In general, *race* "is a category of persons who are related by a common heredity or ancestry and who are perceived and responded to in terms of external features or traits" (Wilkinson, 1993, p. 19). Ethnicity, *however,* often refers to "a shared culture and lifestyles" (Wilkinson, 1993, p. 19). In terms of this distinction, the client and the therapist may share the same racial group (e.g., both Hispanics), but they may not share the same ethnicity (e.g., they have different values and lifestyles). Failure to appreciate this distinction when providing mental health services to culturally diverse groups may have a profound negative impact in such services. For example, highly acculturated Hispanic clinicians working with less acculturated Hispanic clients with HIV/AIDS may not agree with the cultural values of *machismo* (e.g., a sense of masculinity, respect from others, submission by others among Hispanic men) and *marianismo* (e.g., a sense of submission, obedience, dependence among Hispanic women) regardless of the fact that both therapists and client share the same racial group. This disagreement may lead to culturally inappropriate interventions with these clients. For example, a sense of marianismo in a Hispanic woman would prevent her from asking her Hispanic sexual partner to use a condom during sexual intercourse (Boyd-Franklin et al., 1995).

In the *universalistic* approach (Lonner & Ibrahim, 1996; Paniagua, 1998; Tharp, 1991) what appears relevant in the development of a trusting client–clinician therapeutic relationship is evidence that the clinician can display both *cultural sensitivity* (i.e., awareness of cultural variables that may affect assessment and treatment) and *cultural competence* (i.e., translation of this awareness into behaviors leading to effective assessment and treatment of the particular racial minority group). Thus, according to this approach a clinician's ability to provide mental health services to culturally diverse clients with HIV/AIDS in a culturally sensitive manner and to exhibit cultural competency during the assessment and treatment of these clients is more important than the similarity in the clinician's and client's racial membership (Tharp, 1991).

2. The Extended Family

Among culturally diverse clients described in this chapter, the extended family is a critical component of their community (Paniagua, 1998; Sue & Sue, 1990).

In this context, the extended family includes both biological (e.g., parents, uncles, aunts, sisters, brothers) *and* nonbiological (e.g., friends, the minister) individuals who could provide instrumental supports (e.g., money, clothing, housing) and emotional supports (e.g., counseling and advice). In the case of Hispanic clients, these nonbiological members often include the *compadre* (cofather) and the *comadre* (comother). Among the American Indian clients, the elders in the tribe (particularly the head of the tribe) and traditional medicine men and women have a special place in the family, and they are also seen as integral part of the extended family. In the case of African-Americans, church membership is an essential element in the family, and it is expected that church members (particularly the minister) would be involved in the solution of family issues. In this group, grandparents, sisters, and brothers often play a major role in the extended family (Boyd-Franklin, 1989). Among Asian American clients, the extended family does not generally include individuals (e.g., friends, minister, etc.) outside the core family structure (i.e., parents, children, grandparents, and relatives). This is because public admission of problems (including mental health problems) is generally not allowed in these groups (Sue & Sue, 1990). Finally, many Southeast Asian refugee clients (Vietnamese, Cambodians, and Laotians) may place more emphasis upon the availability of nonbiological persons (e.g., friends) or social agencies (e.g., welfare agencies, community supports) in their definition of the extended family, in comparison with an emphasis upon the nuclear family (e.g., parents). The reason for this is that many refugees either left their family behind in their country of origin when entering the United States or their family members were killed during war (Mollica & Lavelle, 1988).

Because of the historical and significant role the extended family had played among culturally diverse groups discussed in this chapter, the overall assumption is that the extended family should also be emphasized when working with HIV/AIDS infected clients from these groups (Boyd-Franklin et al., 1995). Clinicians, however, are advised to consider two points before deciding to include members of the extended family in the assessment and treatment of these clients. First, because of the stigma of HIV/AIDS and misconceptions regarding the transmission of HIV (Paniagua et al., 1997), some members of the client's extended family may not cooperate with the assessment and treatment of the case. For example, among many Hispanics, homosexuality is viewed as a sin against God (Jue & Kain, 1989). When this belief is combined with the misconception that the main risk for the transmission of HIV is homosexual relationships (Paniagua et al., 1997), a clinician working with a Hispanic client with HIV/AIDS should not be surprised to find out that this client is rejected by many members of the extended family. Similarly, among many Asians homosexuality is an unacceptable behavior. Therefore, Asian men engaged in homosexual relationships would maintain these relations secretly (Medrano & Klopner,

1992), which could prevent clinicians from including members of the extended family in the assessment and treatment of Asian clients with HIV/AIDS.

The second point to consider prior to a decision to include the extended family in the present context is *not to assume* that the client and the therapist share the same definition of an extended family. For example, it may be a mistake to assume that an aunt is viewed by an African American client as a member of the extended family (in the client's mind) simply because she is biologically related with the client. A guideline to understand the client's definition of "extension" in the interpretation of the client's extended family is to listen to the client's description of instrumental and emotional supports provided by any member of the community. Persons mentioned by the client with a fundamental role in the provision of such assistance should be considered in the client's extended family. These persons may include a brother (but not a sister), the priest (but not the grandfather), a friend (but not an uncle), the case manager assigned to the case by welfare agencies (but not the director of these agencies).

3. Acculturation

Acculturation is another crucial cultural variant in the assessment and treatment of culturally diverse clients with HIV/AIDS (Marin, 1991). In general, acculturation may be defined in terms of the degree of integration of new cultural patterns into the original cultural patterns. Paniagua (1998) proposed two processes of acculturation. In the *internal* process of acculturation, changes in cultural patterns may occur when an individual moves from a U.S. region to another region in the United States (e.g., from a city to another within the same state or across states). For example, when American Indians living in Arizona, New Mexico, or other states with a large number of reservations move from their reservations to cities, they experience the impact of a societal lifestyle quite different from their societal lifestyle they experienced in the reservations. For example, competition and individualism are two values with little relevance among American Indians who reside on reservations. These values, however, are extremely important for anyone who resides outside a reservation. In this example, the group simply moves from one area to another within the United States, and the assimilation of new values and lifestyles in the new area is a function of the process of internal acculturation.

The impact of the internal process of acculturation, however, would be minimal if an American Indian were to move from one reservation to another reservation in the United States. The internal process of acculturation is further illustrated by Hispanics residing in certain areas of New York City who move to certain areas in Florida (e.g., Miami). The impact of acculturation as an internal process would be minimal in comparison with a move from New York City to another city, such as Lawrence, Kansas, with few shared cultural patterns between the Hispanics and local residents. Another example is Mexican-Americans who reside on the U.S.–Mexican border (particularly in the lower Rio Grande Valley of Texas, including Edinburg, Brownsville, McAllen, and Harlingen). Mexican-Americans who move from this region of the United States to another region resembling little of Mexican-American cultural patterns (e.g., Washington, DC) would experience a difficult internal acculturation process. Mexican Americans who move from the U.S.–Mexican border into San Antonio, Texas, though, would not experience that internal process of acculturation (or its impact would be minimal) because many Mexican Americans residing in the U.S.–Mexican border and Mexicans Americans residing in San Antonio share similar cultural patterns.

In the *external process* of acculturation, a person moves from his or her country of origin into another country. This is the process generally used in the acculturation literature (Dana, 1993) in the case of immigrants who move from their country of origin to the United States (e.g., Hispanics and Asians). The effects of the external acculturation process are less dramatic when immigrants move into the United States and reside in cities that resemble norms, cultural patterns, and values of their country of origin. This is the case of most Hispanics from Cuba, Dominican Republic, and Puerto Rico residing in New York City and Miami, as well as Mexicans who move to the U.S. cities located in the U.S.–Mexican Border. Hispanics residing in such U.S. cities not only encounter people who can understand their language, but also find people from their countries of origin who share many of their cultural values (e.g., folk beliefs, customs, music, etc.). The effect of the external acculturation process is more dramatic in those cases when a person moves into the United States and resides in a city with little similarity to that person's original cultural patterns.

It is also important to determine the potential impact of different levels of acculturation upon the assessment and treatment of a client. These levels can be defined in terms of number of years in the internal or the external acculturation process, age at which the client enters such process, and country of origin. The general assumption is that younger clients are more easily acculturated than older clients, and that as the number of years in those process increases the level of acculturation also increases. In terms of the country of origin, the main assumption is that a racial group tends to show a higher level of acculturation depending on their country of origin. For example, a client from the Dominican Republic residing in New York City is more easily acculturated than a client from Vietnam residing in the same city because the Dominican client has already experienced (in his or her country of origin) a great deal of U.S. cultural values prior to entering the United States, including dressing style, music, language (many of them speak English prior to entering the United States), and a competitive approach.

As noted above, the assessment of acculturation could be a significant variable in the clinician's decision to implement a given treatment modality with culturally diverse clients with HIV/AIDS. For example, Marin and Marin (1990) found that less acculturated Hispanics tended to have less correct knowledge about HIV transmission than highly acculturated Hispanics. In the case of American Indians, Schinke (1996) suggested that the high prevalence of alcohol abuse among members of this racial group could be explained in terms of the effect of acculturation. (It should be noted that alcohol abuse is considered a risk factor for the transmission of HIV disease because alcohol is often associated with unprotected sexual activities, which is another risk for HIV transmission; Hoffman, 1996.) Schinke pointed out that many American Indians living in cities outside their reservations "may feel multiple pressures related to conflicts between their own culture and the dominant society. Such pressures demand a coping response ... [and American Indians may] adopt ... alcohol use as a coping mechanism against acculturation stress" (p. 371). This is another example of the negative effect of the internal process of acculturation (i.e., American Indians moving from their reservations into U.S. cities representing the dominant culture).

Examples of acculturation scales recommended in the present context can be found in Paniagua (1998, see Table 8.1, p. 102). The *Brief Acculturation Scale* shown in Table V could assist busy clinicians to conduct a preliminary assessment of the level of acculturation clients with HIV/AIDS from the above culturally diverse groups, before using more extensive scales (e.g., Cuéllar, Arnold, & Maldonado, 1995). In Table V, three variables are emphasized: generation, language preferred, and social activity. For example, family members in the fifth generation are considered highly acculturated, in comparison with members in the first generation. In terms of language preferred, the client should be asked a general question covering most situations in which a certain language is preferred (e.g., with children, with parents, with co-workers, etc.). In the case of social activity, a similar approach is recommended. For example, a Mexican American client may be asked, "When you listen to music and go to a restaurant to eat, would you do these things with Mexican Americans only, mostly with Mexican Americans, with Mexican Americans and other racial groups mostly (e.g., African Americans, whites, Asians, American Indians), with a different racial group of your own (e.g., whites), or only with a different racial group?"

The following acculturation scores are recommended in the Brief Acculturation Scale: 1 to 1.75 = low acculturation; 1.76 to 3.25 = medium acculturation; 3.26 to 5 = high acculturation. To obtain these scores, add all values checked across variables and divide them by the total number of items checked. For example, if the client checked 1 for the first item across each variable, the total score would be 1 (or 3/3 = 1, or low acculturation score). If the client checked 2, 2, and 3 for the generational, language, and social activity variables, the overall acculturation score would be 2.3 (medium acculturation score).

Results with this scale could assist clinicians in making culturally sensitive decisions. For example, Hispanic clients who scoring 1.0 in Table V would tend

TABLE V.   Brief Acculturation Scale[a]

Instruction: Please check only one item from the group of Generation items, Language Preferred items, and Social Activity items.[b]

My generation is

First	Second	Third	Fourth	Fifth
(1)	(2)	(3)	(4)	(5)

The language I prefer to use is:

Mine	Mostly	Both mine and	Mostly	Only
only	mine	English	English	English
(1)	(2)	(3)	(4)	(5)

I prefer to engage in social activity with:

Only	Mostly	Within/	Mostly with	Only with
within	within	between	a different	a different
racial	racial	racial	racial	racial
group	group	groups	group	group
(1)	(2)	(3)	(4)	(5)

[a] Reprinted with permission from: Paniagua, F. A. (1998). *Assessing and Treating culturally diverse clients: A practical guide.* Thousand Oaks, CA: Sage Publications (Fig. 2.1).

[b] To obtain the overall score, add all values checked across variables and divide them by the total number of items checked (e.g., checking No. 1 for the first item across each variable will result in a score = 1, or 3/3 = 1).

to speak Spanish and emphasize traditional cultural values in comparison to those Hispanics who are more acculturated (e.g., a score = 3.0, in Table V). In this example, an assessment of HIV/AIDS knowledge in Spanish would be culturally sensitive because language could be a barrier in the assessment of this knowledge among Hispanics (Marin & Marin, 1990). Similarly, lower scores on the Brief Acculturation Scale may also suggest strong belief in the cultural values of *machismo* and *marianismo* and, as noted above, these values could have a significant impact on the assessment and treatment of Hispanic clients with HIV/AIDS (Boyd-Franklin et al., 1995).

4. Religious Beliefs

In the study by Paniagua et al. (1998), 55.1% of participants agreed that a discussion regarding the role of the church should be a "recommended" topic in HIV/AIDS educational programs; but only 34.2% of respondents endorsed this topic in the "strongly recommended" scale. (The top four selected topics, i.e., 84% and above, included psychosocial issues = 84.1%; grief, loss, and death = 84.2%; ethical issues = 82.6%; and psychosocial crisis associated with learning that one is HIV-positive = 92.8%.) The results in the Paniagua et al.

(1998) study suggest that although mental health professionals interested in learning about strategies to deal with clients with HIV/AIDS might not perceive the role of the church as critical as other issues (e.g., learning how to counsel clients who just learned about their HIV positive status), the role of the church should not be minimized in the present context. Regardless of racial and/or ethnic membership, all major religious denominations in the United States have taken a leading role in helping their members to deal with emotional difficulties resulting from life-threatening diseases, including HIV disease (Landau-Stanton, Clements, Tartaglia, Nudd, & Spaillat-Pina, 1993). In the case of culturally diverse groups discussed in this chapter, the role of the church is considered the most important social support among many individuals with HIV infection. This is particularly true with African American and Hispanic clients with HIV/AIDS (Boyd-Franklin et al., 1995).

Regardless of the client's race and/or ethnic status, mental health professionals are advised to explore three key areas before deciding to include the church in the assessment and treatment of clients with HIV/AIDS (Landau-Stanton et al., 1993). First, an extensive religious history with each client and his or her family should be conducted, with emphasis on how this history reveals the role of religion in facilitating healing (e.g., the role of the church in helping the family deal with other life-threatening disease or severe emotional difficulties such as a divorce or sudden death of a loved one). Second, an understanding of the importance of the blending of culture and religion from the client's and family's perspective would tell clinicians whether or not to emphasize the inclusion of the church in the assessment and treatment plan. For example, although for many African American families the church is a central aspect in their culture (Paniagua, 1998), this observation should not be generalized across all African Americans with HIV/AIDS seen in mental health services. Third, clinicians should conduct an evaluation of the client's and family's perception of emotional, physical, and social needs provided by the church in the past (i.e., it is crucial to determine that the client and the family perceive the church as part of the extended family).

5. Spiritual Issues

Regardless of racial and/or ethnic membership, the distinction between "spiritual" and the "religious" is a crucial point in the assessment and treatment of individuals with HIV/AIDS (Flaskerud & Miller, 1999). A universal agreement, however, is lacking regarding the parameters used to make that distinction. For example, Landau-Stanton et al. (1993) pointed out that the "spiritual" is a case for "finding meaning of existence" (p. 269) whereas the "religious" emphasizes "communal creeds and practice" (p. 269). A more detailed application of this distinction can be found in Hoffman (1996): "Spirituality [deals with] a basic value around which one's life is focused" (p. 123) including "being concerned with issues of meaning, hope, self-identity, self-worth, one's image of God, forgiveness, and reconciliation" (p. 123). The "religious" includes "a more formal framework for an institutionalized system of beliefs, values, and code of conduct" (Hoffman, 1996, p. 123). The applicability of this distinction in the present context can be appreciated in the following case vignette reported by Landau-Stanton et al. (1993). The case involved a homosexual diagnosed with AIDS who said to the chaplain (third author, in Landau-Stanton et al., 1993), "I have become spiritual, not in the traditional religious sense, but in a very personal way . . . the church [was, after all, one of the institutions that] condemned me and my (gay) lifestyle" (p. 268).

The difference between the "spiritual" and the "religious" is particularly significant in the case of culturally diverse clients with HIV/AIDS. For example, as noted in Table II, homosexual relationships (men who have sex with men) are a major the risk for the transmission of HIV infection among African American and Hispanic communities. Despite the fact that the church is a crucial social support among these communities, it is important to remember that an emphasis on the family and procreation among church denominations in such communities makes homosexual relationships unacceptable (Medrano & Klopner, 1992). Therefore, African American and Hispanic clients with knowledge of the acquisition of the AIDS virus (HIV) through homosexual contacts would not seek help from their church and, instead, would emphasize the "spiritual" in terms described above. Under this circumstance, mental health professionals working with HIV-infected individuals from these groups would not bring the church into the assessment and treatment of the case, but would rather emphasize the "existential questions" the client brings to the therapist (e.g., "Am I Safe?" "Am I Worthy?" "Am I valued?" "Am I Safe?"; see Landau-Stanton et al., 1993, pp. 269–270).

6. Modality of Therapy

In general, African Americans, American Indians, Hispanics, and Asians prefer a therapy process that encompasses an approach that is *directive* (i.e., what is the problem the therapist wants to solve), *active* (i.e., what role would the client play in solving that problem), and *structured* (i.e., what exactly is the therapist recommending to solve that problem; see Paniagua, 1998, pp. 17–18). This approach has been strongly recommended in the assessment and treatment of culturally diverse clients with HIV/AIDS (Jue & Kain, 1989). For example, the main problem might not be to help the HIV-infected client to deal with the anxiety resulting from knowing about his or her HIV status but fear that the client's revelation of this disease would lead to rejection from the extended family (including the church). In the absence of symptoms suggesting AIDS, however, the client might not agree to report that he or she has the AIDS virus (HIV) to anyone, minimizing the active role the client should play in making that report. Knowing that the client is heavily involved in church activities and that the client has already revealed to the therapist that he is homosexual, the practitioner might suggest that the client's perception of rejection could be "real" in the case of the church (for reasons explained above) but "imaginary" in the case of other members of the extended family and encouraged the client to play an active role in making that report at least in the case of family members he "trusts." In this case, the therapist would recommend a "reunion" (i.e., family therapy) including those individuals the client identified as examples of extended family members who have provided instrumental and emotional supports to the client in the past.

7. Language

A client's difficulty in expressing his or her feelings about HIV/AIDS using his or her primary language can be a critical barrier to assessment and treatment of the case. This is particularly true in the case of Asian American, Southeast Asian refugees, and Hispanic clients (Boyd-Franklin et al., 1995; Musser-Granski & Carrillo, 1997). Two significant findings resulting from a client's inability to speak and understand English include increased drop-out rates from therapy and noncompliance behavior with the treatment plan (see Paniagua, 1998, p. 12). In the specific case of clients with HIV/AIDS, these are two critical findings to consider in the effort to prevent the spread of HIV among clients unable to use their primary language in mental health services. For example, a fundamental difference between HIV disease and other life-threatening conditions (e.g., cancer) is that individuals with HIV can transmit this disease by engaging in specific behaviors (e.g., sexual contacts without the use of condoms). When a client with HIV infection drops out from therapy or does not follow the treatment plan because of limited English proficiency, HIV-prevention strategies would not be implemented with this client. The resulting negative outcome of this failure to implement such strategies would be an increase in the probability that this client might continue to engage in risky behaviors leading to the spread of the virus among healthy individuals in his or her community. The use of mental health professionals who speak the language of such clients is, of course, the best alternative to the problem of language barrier in this context. This alternative, however, is not cost-effective in many instances (e.g., not enough Hispanic clinicians to handle the number of Hispanic clients in a given mental health service for people with HIV/AIDS).

The use of translators is another alternative, but it may lead to three errors: omissions, additions, and substitutions during the process of translation from the primary language into English (Musser-Granski & Carrillo, 1997). Despite these errors, the use of translators may be unavoidable in clinical practices. For this reason, several guidelines have been proposed to minimize the effect of such errors and prevent clients from dropping out from therapy or refusing to follow the treatment plan (see Paniagua, 1998, pp. 12–13), including the use of translators who share the client's racial and ethnic background (e.g., Mexican-American clients-Mexican American translators) and assessment of the level of acculturation of the translator in relation to the client's level of acculturation. In general, bilingual children should also be avoided in the process of translation because children's bilingualism could reverse the hierarchical role of parents who are monolingual or who have a limited domain of English. In the context of HIV/AIDS, however, Boyd-Franklin et al. (1995) proposed another reason why children should not be used as translators: "One can only begin to imagine the burden and stress placed . . . on a young boy who has to translate for his mother that his newborn baby sister is HIV-infected" (p. 61).

B. Specific Multicultural Issues

In addition to general multicultural issues shared by many individuals identified as members of the four culturally diverse groups discussed in this chapter, cultural variables specific to each group have also been described in the literature (e.g., Paniagua, 1998) and suggested in the assessment and treatment of clients with HIV/AIDS from the above groups (e.g., Boyd-Franklin et al., 1995; Medrano & Klopner, 1992; Worth, 1990). Examples of such variables are provided across groups.

1. African American Community

Among the cultural variables to consider with African American individuals with HIV/AIDS, five appeared to be critical: (a) racial labels, (b) folk beliefs, (c) healthy paranoia, (d) discussion of racial differences, and (e) family secrets.

a. Racial Labels

Racial labels have been a concern to African Americans for many years (Smith, 1992). Terms which emphasize skin color should be avoided (e.g., colored, black) when assessing and treating clients from this community infected (e.g., the client per se) and affected (e.g., family members) with the HIV/AIDS. The term *African American* is gaining acceptability in this community because it is less stigmatizing, does not emphasize skin color, and formalizes the African connection with emphasis on cultural heritage (see Paniagua, 1998, p. 21).

b. Folk Beliefs

Folk beliefs are part of the belief system of many African Americans, and clinicians should be prepared to include this system in the overall assessment and treatment of the case. Problems experienced by many members of this community might be perceived not only as resulting from physical (e.g., HIV) and environmental causes (poverty, racism) but also from occult or spiritual factors (e.g., evil spirits, supernatural forces, violation of sacred beliefs, or sin). In the second case, folk healers might be consulted for treatment.

c. Healthy Paranoia

The healthy paranoia phenomenon is the result of a history of slavery and racism experienced by the African American community (Gregory, 1996). African American clients with HIV/AIDS might present themselves as highly suspicious of others with different color and values, and this could interfere with the client–therapist relationship during the assessment and treatment of such clients (Boyd-Franklin et al., 1995).

d. Discussion of Racial Differences

The effect of the healthy paranoia phenomenon in therapy could be minimized with a discussion of racial differences between the therapist and the client. In those cases when the clinician is Anglo-American, Boyd-Franklin (1989) recommends an open-ended question in the form, "How do you feel about working with a white therapist" (p. 102). This question might not only reduce racial tension between the client and the clinician but also may help the therapist to appear less anxious, more comfortable, and sensitive to the client's expectations and beliefs (Paniagua, 1998). Under certain circumstances, a discussion of racial differences is also suggested in those cases when both the therapist and the client are African Americans. For example, Boyd-Franklin (1989) pointed out that many African Americans often find it difficult to discuss personal matters (e.g., homosexual activities, drug use) in front of an African American therapist. Thus, it is important for African American clinicians to understand that racial similarity *would not necessarily* lead to lesser perception of the healthy paranoia phenomenon in the mind of an African American.

e. Family Secrets

The ability to handle *family secrets* among African Americans is a critical issue under any context involving individuals from this community (Paniagua,

1998). This issue is even more critical in mental health services involving African American clients with HIV/AIDS. Boyd-Franklin et al. (1995) noted that among many African Americans "the cause of death of a family member who has died of AIDS is treated as a toxic family secret" (p. 57). Family secrets involving homosexuality and drug abuse (two leading risks for HIV infection) might have to be revealed to family members when a diagnosis of HIV or AIDS is made. The family of an individual with HIV/AIDS might not reveal these secrets to their church (e.g., the minister) because of the shame and stigma associated with this disease. In the case of the therapist, these secrets are not expected to be revealed during the first encounter with the client who is seeking help to deal with symptoms of depression after knowing that he or she has HIV infection.

As noted by Paniagua (1998), the revelation of family secrets among African American clients in mental health services is a matter of *timing* (i.e., do not pressure these clients to discuss their secrets; rather, wait until the client is ready to reveal that secret). An overall approach to handle family secrets among African American families in the present context, including three elements (Paniagua, 1998, p. 31): (a) listen carefully to what the client and/or the family is saying (e.g., are they interested in talking about the etiology of the disease or about ways to help the client to deal with a current episode of depression after knowing about the HIV status); (b) attend to the amount of silence when the client is questioned about an issue that appears to be sensitive (e.g., questions regarding sexual activities, substance use), and (c) do not ask questions leading to the revelation of family secrets. For example, the question "Do you know that HIV can be transmitted through sexual relationships between two men?" is very inappropriate because it might imply an invitation to talk about the client's personal sexual experience in this context.

2. Hispanic Community

Four critical cultural variables to consider with Hispanics seeking mental health services to deal with HIV/AIDS issues are (a) folk beliefs and *fatalismo*, (b) *machismo* and *marianismo*, and (c) *personalismo* (Paniagua, 1998).

a. Folk Beliefs and Fatalismo

Many Hispanics with HIV/AIDS may believe that this disease is the result of certain forms of behavior such as *envidia* (envy), *mal puesto* (hex), *mal de ojo* (evil eye), and sins against a divine providence (e.g., God). Among traditional (less acculturated) Hispanic families, professional help to deal with physical and mental problems are not generally considered until all religious (e.g., prayers) and folk belief resources have been exhausted. Examples of folk belief resources include *el curandero* (for men) or *la curandera* (for women) and *el brujo* or *la bruja* (witch doctor). For example, these folk healers may recommend that Hispanics with HIV/AIDS wear "statues of saints or beads around the necks or wrists . . . to protect the individuals from supernatural causes of illness" (Boyd-Franklin et al., 1995, p. 66).

Knowledge of these folk beliefs among Hispanics may help clinicians to understand the impact of these beliefs on the client's sense of *fatalismo* (fatalism) and how this cultural variable may negatively impact on the assessment and treatment of Hispanics with HIV/AIDS.

In general, among many Hispanics, spirits, a divine providence, or supernatural events govern the world and the individual cannot control or prevent adversity resulting from these events. This belief may result in a sense of vulnerability and lack of control in the presence of adverse events, which may compete with the goals of therapy. For example, if a Hispanic with HIV (not AIDS) believes that no protections exist against problems with a root in *fatalismo,* a treatment plan with the goal to create a sense of hope by emphasizing positive events in the future would fail. In many instances, AIDS is developed 10 to 15 years after the individual has been infected with HIV and a significant percentage of persons with HIV have died because of other problems including drug abuse, injuries, suicide, homicide, and lung cancer (see Hoffman, 1996, p. 19). A sense of *fatalismo* would prevent Hispanic clients with HIV infection to see that despite the progressive course, absence of curative treatment, and poor prognosis of HIV infection, the virus might still have a long way to go before leading to AIDS.

b. Machismo and Marianismo

These cultural variables should carefully be assessed prior to the design of a treatment plan to assist Hispanic clients with HIV/AIDS and their families. As noted by Medrano and Klopner (1992) a sense of masculinity, respect (*respeto*) from others, and submission by others (i.e., a sense of machismo among many Hispanic men) may contribute to the presence of risks for HIV infection. For example, three risks for HIV disease are extramarital relationships with multiple partners among heterosexual men, sexual relationships with prostitutes (who are already engaged in multiple sexual relationships without knowledge of the HIV status of sexual partners), and refusal to use condoms during sexual intercourse (Paniagua et al., 1994; Paniagua et al., 1997). Medrano and Klopner (1992) suggested that the "oversexed-male myth" (p. 120) among Hispanics who perceive themselves as "*machistas*" may facilitate the presence of these risks for HIV disease in a given context. In the case of many Hispanic women, the acceptance of the *machismo* is expressed in their sense of submission, obedience, dependence (i.e., a sense of *marianismo*) toward Hispanic men. This sense of *marianismo* could also lead to significant risks for HIV disease (Medrano & Klopner, 1992; Boyd-Franklin et al., 1995). For example, Hispanic women who believe in the machismo–marianismo demarcation would not negotiate safe-sex practices with their husband or boyfriends because of a fear of rejection. An attempt to engage in such negotiations might also lead to physical abuse and verbal abuse (Medrano & Klopner, 1992).

As noted above, clinicians with lack of understanding of the significance of machismo and marianismo in the Hispanic culture might just be on the wrong track when suggesting therapeutic interventions from standard textbooks. For example, the general goal of social skill training interventions (e.g., Lang & Jakubowski, 1976) is to teach the client to be assertive in his or her expression of feelings, emotions, and behaviors. Hispanic women who believe in *marianismo* and *machismo* as culturally appropriate values in her community would probably drop out from therapy in those cases when they are told that they will be trained to be "self-assertive" and to "negotiate" safe-sex practices with the assistance of these interventions (Paniagua, 1998).

It should be noted that Hispanics' belief in the cultural value of machismo could have a positive side: it might encourage Hispanics to engage in safe-sex practices. To appreciate this point, it is important to understand that *machismo* also implies a sense of "protection" of a Hispanic man's family. Therefore, a Hispanic man who believes in the machismo–marianismo demarcation may agree to use condoms with his wife "as a way to reduce the threat of HIV to his family, thus insuring its survival" (Medrano & Klopner, 1992, p. 120).

c. Personalismo

In general, Hispanics are more oriented toward people than impersonal relationships. This phenomenon is known as *personalismo* (Paniagua, 1998). This cultural variable might also have a positive impact on the assessment and treatment of Hispanics with HIV/AIDS (Medrano & Klopner, 1992). Examples of a lack of *personalismo* (as it is perceived by a Hispanic client) include a feeling that he or she is being treated as a "thing" or "abstraction," lack of "warmth" because the client is not hugged when shaking hands with the therapist, and the therapist's refusal to self-disclose personal information (excluding intimate aspects of the therapist's life), such as food preferences, music, hobbies (Paniagua, 1998).

3. Asian and American Indian Communities

As noted earlier, Asian Americans and American Indians are two racial groups underrepresented among HIV/AIDS cases in proportion to their number in the total population in the United States. For this reason, very little information is available regarding the provision of mental health services to individuals with

HIV/AIDS from these groups. A substantial amount of information, however, is available in terms of cultural variables specific to these groups, which could be integrated in the assessment and treatment of such individuals (e.g., Gaw, 1993, pp. 245–430; Paniagua, 1998, pp. 57–90). Clinicians are encouraged to include these variables when assessing and treating clients with HIV/AIDS from these groups.

a. Asian Americans: Shame and Guilt

For example, among many Asians, *shame* and *guilt* are mechanisms used to enforce norms in the family (Dana, 1993). These mechanisms prevent many Asian families from reporting or admitting their problems in public. Because of this norm, Asian families often refuse to seek professional mental health and tend to wait for many years before seeking such help (Fujii, Fukushima, & Yamamoto, 1993). Thus, when an Asian client with HIV/AIDS is brought to the attention of the clinician, family members are probably in a state of crisis because of their inability to handle a case that has developed into a chronic and severe condition over time (i.e., a chronic symptomatic HIV disease suggesting a progression into AIDS). In addition, this sense of shame and guilt may cause some Asians with HIV/AIDS to "choose between dying in isolation or suffering the rejection of family and community" (Medrano & Klopner, 1992, p. 135). This situation could minimize the role of the family and other social supports a clinician would consider in the treatment plan of an Asian client with HIV/AIDS.

b. Asian Americans: Family Secrets

Similar to African American families, the importance of *family secrets* among many Asian families is another variable to consider in the assessment and treatment of Asians with HIV/AIDS. In the present context, homosexual relationships are the key family secret a therapist should approach carefully when working with Asians with HIV/AIDS. As noted earlier, homosexuality is an unacceptable behavior among many Asian families. In addition, many Asian families still believe that HIV/AIDS disease is transmitted primarily through homosexual contacts (Medrano & Klopner, 1992). Thus, for these families the individual with HIV/AIDS not only brings shame and guilt to the family by reporting to people outside the family his or her HIV/AIDS status, but this report would also be a disgrace to the family because it implies the individual's engagement in homosexual relationships.

c. Asian Americans: Somatic Terms for Psychological Problems

Another significant finding among many Asians is that their efforts to prevent bringing shame and guilt to the family often leads to the *expression of psychological problems in somatic terms* (Chun, Enomoto, & Sue, 1996; Sue & Sue, 1990). The reason for this is that reports about physical conditions (e.g., chest pain, headaches, fatigue) are often more acceptable (i.e., result in less shame and guilt) than reports about psychiatric disorders. This situation may be problematic in those cases when a clinician suspects that an Asian client is experiencing a severe depression (including suicidal ideation and/or attempts) because of his or her knowledge of having HIV (not AIDS), but the client elects to talk about physical conditions (unrelated to this disease) rather than the depression resulting from having that knowledge.

Specific clinical guidelines to handle the above situations are lacking in the cross-cultural literature involving HIV disease. In general, however, two approaches have been recommended to handle the expression of mental disorders in somatic terms among many Asians (see Paniagua, 1998, pp. 62–63). First, the clinician should acknowledge these somatic complaints and inform the client that medical consultations will be arranged to assess physical disorders reported by the client. This suggestion would be particularly appropriate in those cases when the client's reports do not include a clear picture of symptoms suggesting AIDS. Second, the clinician should gradually introduce statements that allow the client to move from verbalizations of somatic complaints to verbalizations involving mental problems. In the case of clients with HIV (but not AIDS), this second recommendation could be enhanced with a brief summary of symptoms suggesting AIDS (e.g., Kaposi's sarcoma, pneumocystis pneumonia, AIDS wasting syndrome; see Kotler & Grunfeld, 1996, and Hoffman, 1996, pp. 10–15) versus symptoms commonly reported in the general population not infected with HIV (e.g., fever, fatigue, loss of appetite).

a. American Indians: Negative Historical Events

In the case of American Indian clients seeking mental health services to deal with HIV/AIDS issues, four specific cultural variables should be emphasized. First, clinicians are encouraged to have a clear understanding of the impact of *negative historical events* on this community and how these events had shaped American Indians' conflictive relationships with members of the dominant society. For example, in 1492–1890, American Indians passed through a period historically known as the "Manifest Destiny Period" (see Paniagua, 1998, pp. 78–79). During this period, European diseases (e.g., smallpox, malaria, pneumonia, syphilis) were introduced by earlier explorers into the life of American Indians leading to a massive number of deaths among Indians. This period also led to racism and discrimination, with the creation of the reservations and the boarding schools. American Indians were promised vast amounts of land and protection from the influence of whites by agreeing to relocate their tribes to reservations in areas remote from white settlements. These promises, however, were broken many times, including the reduction in lands, elimination of existing reservations, introduction of legislation making the language, religion, and customs of Indians illegal, and the exiling of tribal leaders (Walker & LaDue, 1986). The main goal of the boarding schools created by the government and non-Indian religious groups was to replace the practice of Indian language, dress, beliefs, religion, and custom with the practice of the white civilization. In these schools, children were physically punished for speaking their own language and the overall message was that "to be Indian was to be bad" (Walker & LaDue, 1986, p. 157). This period was followed by the "Assimilation Period" (1890–1970), which served to reinforce the development of racism and discrimination to the extreme. Indians had two choices: death or the assimilation of the white culture. Thus, many Indians moved away from their old traditions not only to avoid death but also as a result of the deaths of the Great Chiefs, who were instrumental in the transmission of such traditions to their people (Walker & LaDue, 1986). A familiarity with these events could help practitioners to understand why many American Indian clients are still very suspicious of white people and tend to mistrust anyone outside their society (particularly whites) who make promises to them concerning socioeconomic, political, and cultural opportunities outside their own lands.

b. American Indians: Perception of Secrets

Because of the negative impact of such historical events, a second cultural variable to consider is American Indians' *perception of secrets* in the client–therapist relationship. Because of the stigma of HIV/AIDS in the general population, this variable is particularly critical to remember when serving clients with HIV/AIDS from this community. Thus, the therapist should avoid "pseudo-secrecy statements" such as "Feel free to tell me . . ." or "You can rest assured I will not discuss your problems with . . ." (Paniagua, 1998, p. 84). As noted by Walker and LaDue, 1986), American Indians have heard these statements many times from the Great White Father and the federal bureaucrats, and each time they have been deceived.

c. American Indians: Confidentiality

The third variable involves American Indian's *understanding of confidentiality statements*. These statements are generally used by clinicians (e.g., "I want to inform you that in this clinic clients' reports about their emotional difficulties are strictly confidential") because of ethical and/or licensing boards' guidelines. As noted by Thompson, Walker, and Silk-Walker (1993), an American Indian client would not answer questions dealing with his or her priviate life if he or she knows that relatives and friends are working in the clinic or hospital (e.g., the medical record room). Under this specific case, the client would not consider his or her reports as "confidential." Again, because of the great stigma attached to HIV/AIDS by the public, an understanding of the way an American Indian client with this disease understands what is "strictly confidential" should be carefully assessed prior to reaching the conclusion that this client's refusal to reveal confidential information (e.g., engagement in homosexual relationships, multiple heterosexual contacts, or injection of drugs) is an indication of "resistance" from the client or "mistrust" toward the therapist (Paniagua, 1998).

d. American Indians: Role of Healers and Tribal Leaders

The fourth variable involves the *role of healers and tribal leaders* in the life of many American Indians. American Indians seeking professional assistance to deal with their physical and emotional problems will expect the professionals to be familiar with and ready to integrate traditional healing practices with Western healing practices. The overall finding is that health promotion and the management of physical and emotional difficulties among American Indians are less likely to succeed in the absence of a collaborative effort involving traditional healers (e.g., the medicine man/woman) and tribal leaders in a given reservation (Schinke, 1996). Therefore, when providing mental health services to American Indian clients with HIV/AIDS, that level of collaboration is strongly recommended in the assessment and treatment of such clients (Barney, 1996; Duran & Barney, 1996; Lidot, 1996).

III. SUMMARY AND ADDITIONAL THOUGHTS

Regardless of a client's racial and/or ethnic status, a biopsychosocial approach is the recommended strategy in the assessment and treatment of persons with HIV/AIDS. This chapter summarized examples of epidemiological and multicultural issues to consider when using this approach with clients from the African American, American Indian, Asian, and Hispanic communities. For example, the recognition that HIV/AIDS is a critical health problem in these communities suggests the need to assure the availability of culturally competent clinicians during the programming and implementation of biopsychosocial programs with clients with HIV/AIDS from these communities. This need is even more crucial in the case of African Americans and Hispanics, who continue to represent a disproportionate number of HIV/AIDS cases in epidemiological research relative to other culturally diverse groups discussed above.

The following two examples show the interrelationship between multicultural issues and the goals of the biopsychosocial approach in the present context. Participation in HIV antibody testing is a major goal in this approach not only to assure that symptoms presented by the client are actually indicative of AIDS but also to minimize and/or prevent emotional difficulties resulting from the fear of having HIV/AIDS. Many clients from the above culturally diverse groups, however, do not take that test because they are generally skeptical "about medical researcher and medical professionals" (Flaskerud, 1999, p. 345). This is particularly true in the case of an African American client who believes in the "healthy paranoia" phenomenon described above. Furthermore, Medrano and Klopner (1992) reported that "many Asians and Pacific Islanders still believe that HIV/AIDS is a white, gay men's disease" (p. 134) and, as noted above, homosexuality is an unacceptable behavior among many Asian families. Under this condition, an Asian male might not agree to take that test because of fear that his homosexual status could be revealed to the public, particularly his family. The same conclusion would apply to Hispanics who might not take that test to avoid being rejected by family members who believe that homosexuality is a "sin" against God.

Another example is the role of *fatalismo* in the HIV disease progression toward AIDS among Hispanics. Biopsychosocial researchers know that HIV and AIDS are not the same thing, that at least 5% of persons diagnosed with HIV have not progressed toward AIDS, that the interval between HIV and the developing of AIDS symptoms could be 10 or more years, and that in between this period the HIV-infected individual could die because of reasons other than AIDS (Hoffman, 1996; Kalichman, 1995). Many Hispanic clients who believe in *fatalismo* (as defined above) would show a sense of vulnerability and lack of control with the notification that he or she is HIV positive. Therefore, medical and psychosocial interventions to assist this client to cope with this disease would probably fail because of that sense of *fatalismo*.

Finally, regardless of the client's race and/or ethnicity status, the clinical management of clients with HIV/AIDS in mental health services require not only a clear understanding of medical, psychosocial, and multicultural variables, but it is also important to assess and treat the most significant emotional or psychological problems resulting from (a) thinking that one is HIV positive (or that one has AIDS) because of engagement in behaviors considered at risk for HIV infection (e.g., multiple sexual partners, sex without using condoms, anal intercourse, injecting drug use, etc.); (b) being told that one is HIV positive; (c) experiencing symptoms suggesting progression toward AIDS, and (d) a recognition that one is about to die because of AIDS (Flaskerud & Miller, 1999; Kalichman, 1995). For example, in the first case Anxiety and Panic Disorders would be expected in many clients seeking mental health services because they "think" that they has been infected with the virus. In the second and third cases, the client would show most symptoms for Major Depression, particularly suicidal ideation and/or attempts. In the last case, psychosis and neuropsychiatric complications would be expected in the final state of the illness. In the assessment and management of these psychological difficulties, the contribution of cultural variables should also be considered (Gaw, 1993; Paniagua, 1998).

REFERENCES

Barney, D. D. (1996). Effective case management for HIV-infected American Indians and Native Hawaiians. *International Conference on AIDS, 11,* 208 (abstract No. 1918).

Boyd-Franklin, N. (1989). *Black families therapy: A multisystem approach.* New York: Guilford.

Boyd-Franklin, N., Aleman, J., Jean-Gilles, M. M., & Lewis, S. Y. (1995). Cultural sensitivity and Competence. In N. Boyd-Franklin, G. L. Steiner, & M. G. Boland (Eds.), *Children, families, and HIV/AIDS* (pp. 53–77). New York: The Guilford Press.

Brown, D. R., & Sankar, A. (1998). HIV/AIDS and aging minority populations. *Research on Aging, 20,* 865–884.

Centers for Disease Control (1981a). Pneumocystis pneumonia—Los Angeles. *MMRW, 30,* 250–252.

Centers for Disease Control (1981b). Karposi's sarcoma and pneumocystis pneumonia. Among homosexual men—New York City and California. *MMWR, 30,* 305–308.

Centers for Disease Control (1997). *HIV/AIDS surveillance report* (Midyear edition). Atlanta, GA: CDC Division of HIV/AIDS-Surveillance and Epidemiology.

Centers for Disease Control (1998). HIV/AIDS among American Indians and Alaskan Natives-United States, 1981–1997. *MMWR, 47,* 154–160.

Chun, C., Enomoto, K., & Sue, S. (1996). Health care issues among Asian Americans: Implications of somatization. In P. M. Kato & T. Mann (Eds.), *Handbook of diversity issues in health psychology* (pp. 347–365). New York: Plenum Press.

Cuéllar, I., Arnold, B., & Maldonado, R. (1995). Acculturation rating scale for Mexicans-II: A revision of the original ARSMA scale. *Hispanic Journal of Behavioral Sciences, 2,* 199–217.

Dana, R. H. (1993). *Multicultural assessment perspectives for professional psychology.* Boston: Allyn and Bacon.

Duran, B. E., & Barney, D. D. (1996). Traditional healing and spirituality in HIV-care services for American Indians, Alaska Natives, and Native Hawaiians. *International Conference on AIDS, 11,* 425 (abstract No. 5128).

Flaskerud, J. H. (1999). Culture and ethnicity. In P. J. Ungvarski & J. H. Flaskerud (Eds.), *HIV/AIDS: A guide to primary care management* (pp. 328–360). Philadelphia: W. B. Saunders.

Flaskerud, J. H., & Miller, E. N. (1999). Psychosocial and neuropsychiatric dysfunction. In P. J. Ungvarski & J. H. Flaskerud (Eds.), *HIV/AIDS: A guide to primary care management* (pp. 255–291). Philadelphia: W. B. Saunders.

Flaskerud, J. H., & Ungvarski, P. J. (1999). Overview and update of HIV disease. In P. J. Ungvarski & J. H. Flaskerud (Eds.), *HIV/AIDS: A guide to primary care management* (pp. 1–25). Philadelphia: W. B. Saunders.

Gallo, R. C., & Montagnier, L. (1988). AIDS in 1988. *Scientific America, 259,* 40–51.

Gaw, A. C. (1993). *Culture, ethnicity, and mental illness.* Washington, DC: American Psychiatric Press.

Gregory, S. (1996). "We've been down this road already." In S. Gregory & R. Sanjek (Eds.), *Race* (pp. 18–38). New Brunswick, NJ: Rutgers University Press.

Hoffman, M. A. (1996). *Counseling clients with HIV disease: Assessment, intervention, and Prevention.* New York: The Guilford Press.

Jue, S., & Kain, C. D. (1989). Culturally sensitive AIDS counseling. In C. Kain et al. (Eds.), *No longer immune: A counselor's guide to AIDS* (pp. 131–148). Alexandria, VA: American Association for Counseling and Development.

Kalichman, S. C. (1995). *Understanding AIDS: A guide for mental health professionals.* Washington, DC: American Psychological Association.

Kotler, D. P., & Grunfeld, C. (1996). Pathophysiology and treatment of the AIDS wasting syndrome. In P. Voldberding & M. A. Jacobson (Eds.), *AIDS clinical review: 1995/1996* (pp. 229–275). New York: Marcel Dekker, Inc.

Landau-Stanton, J., & Clements, C. D. (1993). *AIDS Health and mental health: A primary sourcebook.* New York: Brunner/Mazel.

Landau-Stanton, J., Clements, C. D. Tartaglia, A. F., Nudd, J., & Spaillat-Pina, E. (1993). Spiritual, cultural, and community system. In J. Landau-Stanton & C. D. Clements (Eds.), *AIDS health and mental health: A primary sourcebook* (pp. 267–299). New York: Brunner/Mazel.

Lang, A. J., & Jakubowski, P. (1976). *Responsible assertive behavior.* Champaign, IL: Research Press.

Lidot, T. (1996). HIV/AIDS services integrated with native traditional medicine for urban vs. reservation Native populations: What's the difference? *International Conference on AIDS, 11,* 425 (abstract No. 5127).

Lonner, W. J., & Ibrahim, F. A. (1996). Appraisal and assessment in cross-cultural counseling. In P. B. Pedersen, J. G. Draguns, W. J. Lonner, & J. E. Trimble (Eds.), *Counseling across cultures* (pp. 293–322). Thousand Oaks, CA: Sage Publications.

Lopez, S. R., Lopez, A. A., & Fong, K. T. (1991). Mexican Americans' initial preferences for counselors: The role of ethnic factors. *Journal of Counseling Psychology, 38,* 487–496.

Marin, B. V. (1991). Hispanic culture: Effects on prevention and care. *Focus: A guide to AIDS research and counseling, 6,* 2–3.

Marin, B., & Marin, G. (1990). Effects of acculturation on knowledge of AIDS and HIV among Hispanics. *Hispanic Journal of Behavioral Sciences, 12,* 110–112.

McCombie, S. C. (1990). AIDS in cultural, historical, and epidemiological context. In D. A. Feldman (Ed.), *Culture and AIDS* (pp. 9–27). New York: Prager.

Medrano, L., & Klopner, M. C. (1992). AIDS and people of color. In H. Land (Ed.), *A complete guide to psychosocial intervention* (pp. 117–139). Milwaukee, WI: Family Service of American, Inc.

Mollica, R. F., & Lavelle, J. (1988). Southeast Asian refugees. In L. Comas-Diaz & E. E. H. Griffith (Eds.), *Clinical guidelines in cross-cultural mental health* (pp. 262–293). New York: John Wiley.

Musser-Granski, J., & Carrillo, D. F. (1997). The use of bilingual, bicultural professionals in mental health services: Issues for hiring, training, and supervision. *Community Mental Health Journal, 33,* 51–60.

National Commission on AIDS (1992). *The challenge of HIV/AIDS in communities of color.* Washington, DC: National AIDS Clearinghouse.

Ory, M. G., & Mack, K. A. (1998). Middle-aged and older people with AIDS. *Research on Aging, 20,* 653–664.

Paniagua, F. A. (1996). Cross-cultural guidelines in family therapy practice. *Family Journal: Counseling and Therapy for Couples and Families, 4,* 127–138.

Paniagua, F. A. (1998). *Assessing and treating culturally diverse clients: A practical guide* (2nd ed.). Thousand Oaks, CA: Sage Publications.

Paniagua, F. A., Grimes, R. M., O'Boyle, M., Wagner, K. D., Tan, V. L., & Lew, A. S. (1998). HIV/AIDS education survey for mental health professionals. *Psychological Reports, 82,* 887–897.

Paniagua, F. A., O'Boyle, M., & Wagner, K. D. (1997). The assessment of HIV/AIDS knowledge, attitudes, self-efficacy, and susceptibility among psychiatrically hospitalized adolescents. *Journal of HIV/AIDS Prevention and Education for Adolescents and Children, 1,* 65–104.

Paniagua, F. A., O'Boyle, M., Wagner, K. D., Ramirez, S. Z., Holmes, W. D., Nieto, J. F., & Smith, E. M. (1994). AIDS-related items for developing and AIDS questionnaire for children and adolescents. *Journal of Adolescent Research, 9,* 311–399.

Schinke, S. (1996). Behavioral approaches to illness prevention for Native Americans. In P. M. Kato & T. Mann (eds.), *Handbook of diversity issues in health psychology* (pp. 367–387). New York: Plenum Press.

Shannon, G., Pyle, G. F., & Bashshur, R. L. (1991). *The geographic of AIDS*. New York: The Guilford Press.

Sue, D. W., & Sue, D. (1990). *Counseling the culturally different: Theory and practice* (2nd ed.). New York: John Wiley.

Sy, F. S., Chng, C. L., Choi, S. T., & Wong, F. Y. (1998). Epidemiology of HIV and AIDS among Asian and Pacific Islander Americans. *AIDS Education & Prevention, 10*, 4–18.

Tharp, R. G. (1991). Cultural diversity and treatment of children. *Journal of Consulting and Clinical Psychology, 59*, 799–812.

Thompson, J., Walker, R. D., & Silk-Walker, P. (1993). Psychiatric care of American Indians and Alaska Natives. In A. C. Gaw (Ed.), *Culture, ethnicity, and mental illness* (pp. 189–243). Washington, DC: American Psychiatric Press.

Walker, R. D., & LaDue, R. (1986). An integrative approach to American Indian mental health. In C. B. Wilkinson (Ed.), *Ethnic psychiatry* (pp. 143–199). New York: Plenum.

Ward, J. W., & Duchin, J. S. (1998). The epidemiology of HIV and AIDS in the United States. In P. A. Volberding & M. A. Jacobson (Eds.), *AIDS clinical review* (pp. 3–45). New York: Marcel Dekker.

Waytt, G. E. (1991). Examining ethnicity versus race in AIDS related sex research. *Social Science and Medicine, 33*, pp. 37–45.

Wilkinson, D. (1993). Family ethnicity in America. In H. P. McAdoo (Ed.), *Family ethnicity: Strength in diversity* (pp. 15–59). Newbury Park, CA: Sage Publications.

Worth, D. (1990). Minority women and AIDS: Culture, race, and gender. In D. A. Feldman (ed.), *Culture and AIDS* (pp. 111–135). New York: Prager.

CHAPTER 14

The History, Current Status, and Future of Multicultural Psychotherapy

RICHARD M. LEE
Department of Educational Psychology
University of Texas at Austin
Austin, Texas

MANUEL RAMIREZ III
Department of Psychology
University of Texas at Austin
Austin, Texas

At the start of the 1990s, Pedersen (1991) asserted multiculturalism as the fourth force in psychology. This bold statement positioned multiculturalism for the first time beside the traditional schools of psychoanalysis, behaviorism, and person-centered humanism in the field of counseling and psychotherapy. It also served to legitimize a movement that began in the 1960s and early 1970s when psychologists started to examine the role of culture in the therapy hour (Jackson, 1995). The development and refinement of multicultural psychotherapy has evolved since from the recognition to serve culturally different populations to specific counseling models for these populations. Multicultural psychotherapy is now applicable to all groups of people because individual and cultural differences are integrated into the basic therapeutic philosophy and approach. The purpose of this chapter is to address these theoretical and professional developments in the field of multicultural psychotherapy.

I. CULTURAL CONSIDERATIONS
IN TRADITIONAL THEORIES

Traditional theories of psychotherapy (e.g., psychoanalysis, cognitive-behaviorism, humanistic-existentialism) historically have received criticism for their lack of sensitivity to cultural diversity. The criticism has centered justifiably on the fact that these theories were developed according to Euro-American and middle- and upper-class assumptions of human behavior and well-being (D. Sue & Sue, 1999). The very notion of a talking cure for psychological problems is an excellent example of a Eurocentric value. Other culture-bound behaviors and values that pervade traditional theories of psychotherapy include the intrapsychic etiology for psychological problems, sharing intimate feelings and thoughts with a nonfamily member (e.g., therapist), and separation and autonomy from the family. These assumptions mistakenly have been thought to apply to all groups of people, regardless of gender, race, sexual orientation, religion, and physical abilities (Atkinson, Morten, & Sue, 1998). Cultural deviations from these norms of behavior and well-being consequently have been viewed as abnormal or pathological (Szasz, 1970) and not simply a reflection of cultural differences or variations (D. Sue & Sue, 1999). Likewise, clients who have not responded to Western-based interventions oftentimes have been viewed as resistant or not amendable to treatment (Draguns, 1989). The theories and models of traditional psychotherapy, however, rarely have been viewed as Eurocentric or insufficient for use across cultural groups (Jackson, 1995).

As the multicultural movement in the field of psychology gained momentum in the United States of America of the 1960s and 1970s, considerations of cultural differences were developed ironically in the context of these existing theories of psychotherapy. Culture for the most part was viewed as a nuisance variable or ancillary to the basic psychotherapy process. Culturally different clients were seen as lacking the appropriate education and cultural sophistication to benefit from psychotherapy. This mistakenly led some therapists who worked with culturally diverse populations to assume a benevolent role as if they were helping the less fortunate. Other therapists recognized the salience of culture in the psychotherapy process, but refused to abandon the traditional psychotherapy paradigm. The responsibility remained with the culturally different clients to adjust to the psychotherapy process, rather than therapists adjusting the models to the needs of the clients.

Riessman (1962), for example, had described people of color as "culturally deprived" and lacking the resources to manage life challenges effectively. This attitude, according to W. Ryan (1971), was based on a "blaming the victim" orientation that was common among the traditional psychotherapy theories. Helms (1990) similarly described this early attempt to address multiculturalism in psychotherapy as locating psychological problems within the client. The effects of racial oppression and discrimination were acknowledged as psychologically meaningful experiences, but these experiences were assumed to reside solely within the person. The person was subsequently viewed inaccurately as "culturally scarred" and "culturally paranoid" (Helms, 1990). A similar argument continues to be made about non-English-speaking immigrants to this country. Their struggles with culture shock and the acquisition of a second culture sometimes have been turned against them as a sign of their inability to adapt to mainstream society (LaFromboise, Coleman, & Gerton, 1993). From this perspective, culturally different people were and continue to be viewed as inferior with few personal strengths and social resources to handle the racism and discrimination in society. These supposed deficiencies within people were expected to conflict with the psychotherapy process. Traditional models of psychotherapy consequently were not likely to be effective with culturally different people, yet few alternative models were suggested.

As the multicultural movement continued to develop and mature in psychology, there was a shift from the client-as-problem to the therapist-as-problem (Helms, 1990). This perspective recognized that another reason for the lack of success in treating culturally different people was the therapist's own cultural insensitivity and possible racial biases and prejudices. The therapist as a perceived barrier to working with culturally diverse clients remains a salient issue today. D. W. Sue and Sue (1999) state that therapists trained in traditional or mainstream Euro-American models of psychotherapy often hold certain values and assumptions that are distinct from those held by culturally different people. Some therapists may be aware of their own biases and prejudices, but they use this awareness to excuse their inability to work effectively with culturally different clients. Other therapists may recognize cultural differences with clients, but they nonetheless insist that clients maintain a certain degree of psychological mindedness, which is itself a culture-bound characteristic. If clients did not adequately understand the meaning and process of psychotherapy, therapists might educate them about traditional Western-based psychotherapy goals, strategies, and techniques. This education about psychotherapy was and remains a common approach to working with culturally different clients. Yet similar to blaming the victim, it shifts the responsibility from the therapists to the clients. It forces clients to conform to the worldviews of the therapists. As Sue and Sue (1999) noted, this pressure for clients to conform to the standards and expectations of therapists is exemplified best in therapist preferences for YAVIS clients (young, attractive, verbal, intelligent, and successful) (YAVIS acronym coined by Schofield, 1964). But YAVIS clients represent a narrow band of the population that traditionally has consisted of the White Euro-American college-educated middle class. Few therapists, D. W. Sue and Sue contend (1999), have a

preference for QUOID clients (quiet, ugly, old, indigent, and dissimilar culturally) even though this latter population likely represents the majority of people
in the world (QUOID acronym coined by Sundberg, 1981).

Fortunately, cultural considerations in traditional theories of psychotherapy
are increasing without necessarily viewing the client-as-problem or therapist-as-
problem. Renfrey (1992), for example, described the use of cognitive-behavior
therapy with Native American clients. Antokoletz (1993) proposed a psychoanalytic framework to understand the immigration experience. Ibrahim (1984)
described an existential psychotherapy model that highlights the role of culture
in the change process. Ivey, Ivey, and Simek-Morgan (1997) also have written a
textbook that incorporates cultural diversity into the psychodynamic, cognitive-behavioral, and existential-humanistic psychotherapies. These new considerations are now trying to adjust the dominant paradigms or models of
psychotherapy to the cultural expectations and needs of the client. This transition to more culturally responsive forms of traditional psychotherapies remains
a work in progress.

A serious consequence of the persistent lack of appropriate cultural considerations in traditional psychotherapy, however, has been the underutilization
of mental health services by ethnic/racial minority populations (Cheung &
Snowden, 1990; Sue, Fujino, Hu, Takeuchi, & Zane, 1991). Numerous studies
have reported a consistent pattern of low service use for African Americans,
Asian Americans, and Hispanics despite the fact that these groups report similar
and sometimes more symptoms of distress (Hu, Snowden, Jerrell, & Nguyen,
1991; Hough et al., 1987; Snowden & Cheung, 1990). Sue et al. (1991) have
suggested that a major reason for the underutilization of mental health services
is the limited availability of culturally competent psychotherapists and culturally responsive services. Akutsu, Snowden, and Organista (1996), for example,
found higher referral and usage rates by ethnic minorities at agencies that were
more culturally responsive. This need to better serve culturally different populations has slowly been addressed by scholars, practitioners, and professional
governing bodies (e.g., American Psychological Association [APA], 1993).

II. MULTICULTURAL COUNSELING
AND SUPERVISION COMPETENCIES

The lack of cultural considerations in traditional psychotherapy and the rising
need for culturally responsive services for all people led to a call to the psychological profession in 1982 by D. W. Sue et al. (1982). They argued for a more
comprehensive effort to incorporate cultural differences into the field of counseling and psychotherapy. They particularly advocated for the development of

multicultural counseling competencies for psychotherapists, since the responsibility to best serve culturally diverse clients rests with the therapist and not the client. Similarly, Cross, Bazron, Dennis, and Issac (1989) advocated that all human service providers need to be culturally competent and, more specifically, share the positive value of cultural diversity, be responsive to the cultural needs of clients, and deliver services in a way that empowers the client.

The multiculturally competent therapist and mental health service provider is characterized by (a) an awareness of one's own assumptions, values, and biases and how they might impact work with culturally different clients, (b) an understanding and respect of the worldviews of clients, and (c) the development of culturally appropriate interventions, strategies, and techniques (D. W. Sue et al., 1982). These characteristics additionally are manifested across the domains of knowledge, beliefs and attitudes, and skills to create nine areas of cultural competency (3 characteristics × 3 domains). Sodowsky, Taffe, Gutkin, and Wise (1994) have suggested that in addition to knowledge, beliefs and attitudes, and skills, the culturally-competent therapist and provider is able to establish a multicultural counseling relationship with consideration of past inequalities and the ability to provide credibility and empowerment. This additional domain creates twelve areas of cultural competency (3 characteristics × 4 domains). These cultural-competency standards now serve as the benchmark for ensuing appropriate and adequate multicultural psychotherapy and human services (APA, 1993; D. Sue, Arredondo, & McDavis, 1992).

Another critical but often overlooked multicultural-counseling competency component is supervision (Leong & Wagner, 1994; Martinez & Holloway, 1997). Leong and Wagner (1994) made an important distinction between cross-cultural supervision and multicultural supervision. *Cross-cultural supervision* refers to the relationship between a supervisor and the supervisee who are from different cultural groups. This type of supervisory relationship primarily focuses on the dynamics within the supervisory relationship itself. *Multicultural supervision,* on the other hand, refers to supervisory situations that are affected by multiple cultural factors, including cross-cultural supervision dyads. In multicultural supervision, one might see an African American trainee assigned to an Asian American client, seeking advice from another therapist with more experience working with Asian American populations. It might also include a Latino supervisor–supervisee dyad addressing countertransference toward a White client who made a racist comment in the therapy hour. In these relationships, there are multiple layers of culture that need to be discussed between the supervisor and supervisee for the benefit of the client.

Multicultural supervision represents a hands-on opportunity for therapists and trainees to gain more cultural knowledge, explore their own attitudes and beliefs about multicultural issues, and acquire more culturally responsive skills and interventions. Ryan and Hendricks (1989) suggested that multicultural supervision requires (a) awareness of differences in cognition, motivation, and communication, (b) open discussion of racial content and experiences in counseling, (c) setting mutually agreed upon expectations for supervision, and (d) recognition of differences as a learning and growth experience. Multicultural supervision also directs attention to ways in which ethnic and racial identity development impacts both the counseling and supervision process (D'Andrea & Daniels, 1997). For example, an Asian American supervisee who does not perceive race as a salient issue in his own life may be challenged by his supervisor to explore this identity issue in the context of professional development. At the same time, Martinez and Holloway (1997) recognized the important role of power in multicultural supervision. It is important for the supervisee to feel empowered enough to likewise empower the culturally different client. The multiculturally competent supervisor therefore must be aware of the parallel process that is occurring in the supervision hour and the therapy hour.

Although multicultural counseling competency has been proposed and adopted by many professional organizations as a professional aspiration, they have not yet been adopted as ethical standards for treatment. As such, supervision serves as the true gatekeeper into the profession and, as such, is an important place to demonstrate multicultural counseling competency and ensure culturally responsive services. Unfortunately, there has been little research on multicultural supervision (Leong & Wagner, 1994). Lee et al. (1999), for instance, noted in a recent survey of predoctoral internship training programs that the majority of programs relied upon supervisors to evaluate multicultural counseling competencies. They cautioned, however, that it remains unknown whether or not the supervisors themselves are culturally competent service providers.

III. UNIVERSAL VERSUS CULTURE-SPECIFIC DEBATE

Although some scholars and practitioners have sought to accommodate culture within traditional theories of psychotherapy and others have established external criteria to ensure cultural fairness in psychotherapy, many have developed culturally sensitive theories that either complement or supplant traditional theories. The revision of traditional models and the development of new multicultural models of psychotherapy have been influenced by an ongoing debate between two approaches to understanding culture. The study of culture in psychology has been approached from both a universal and culture-specific orientation. This distinction between a universal and culture-specific orientation also is known as the "etic–emic" dichotomy. These terms originate from the study of structural linguistics (Pike, 1967). *Etic* is derived from the term *phonetic,* which refers to sounds assumed to be universal across all languages. *Emic* is derived from the term *phonemic,* which refers to particular sounds within one language. In cross-cultural psychology, etic and emic refer to universal versus culture-specific behaviors. Likewise in psychotherapy, etic and emic have become synonymous with universal and culture-specific approaches to multicultural psychotherapy, respectively.

Fukuyama (1990) and others (e.g., Fischer, Jome, & Atkinson, 1998; McFadden, 1999; Patterson, 1996) posit a universal or etic approach to multicultural psychotherapy. She argues that this approach "recognizes universal processes that transcend cultural variations" and also "provides a broad and inclusive perspective for understanding the influences of culture in counseling" (p. 7). It is important to note that Fukuyama is not endorsing the simple use of traditional, Western-based models of counseling and psychotherapy for work with culturally different clients. In fact, she notes the cultural bias of Western-style counseling. Fukuyama instead emphasizes the inherent role of culture in all theories of psychotherapy. She, along with McFadden, Patterson, and Fischer et al., articulate a transcultural approach that acknowledges common experiences among these different populations (e.g., discrimination and oppression, matching worldviews, different forms of communication, need for identity, and value of validation and empowerment) and integrates this knowledge into existing theories and processes of psychotherapy.

Locke (1990), in a counterpoint article to Fukuyama's, challenges the universal approach to counseling and psychotherapy. He, along with others (e.g., Baruth & Manning, 1999), argues that a universal understanding of cultural issues is insufficient without expertise knowledge in specific cultural groups. Locke articulates a culture-specific or emic approach to multicultural psychotherapy. Accordingly, it is important to understand clients at both the individual level and as members of culturally different groups. This "focused approach" requires therapists to possess self-awareness, an understanding of global influences, the role of the dominant culture, and cultural differences between racial groups (Locke, 1992). This approach to psychotherapy has led to revisions in traditional models, as well as to the development of indigenous or culture-specific psychotherapy models.

Despite the ongoing debate between these two camps, many scholars and practitioners, such as Koss-Chioino and Vargas (1992) and Dana (1993), feel that the dichotomous paradigm of universal versus culture-specific is insufficient altogether for understanding multicultural psychotherapy. First, the universal or etic concept is itself culturally embedded and thus not truly universal or culture-free. According to Berry (1989), this type of universal approach is often an "imposed etic," that is, a Western emic assumed to be universal. Second, universal or culture-specific approaches can be used to polarize scholars and practitioners who in defense of their positions may overlook the true needs of clients. For example, advocates for women, gays, and people with disabilities complain that universalist and culture-specific proponents often fail to consider the salience of gender, sexual orientation, and disability in culture (Atkinson & Hackett, 1997; Fassinger & Richie, 1997). Third, multicultural psychotherapy is simply a more complex process than a simple understanding of universal and culture-specific features. There is a need for models of psychotherapy that balance the benefits of both universal and culture-specific approaches.

A multidimensional approach serves as a more appropriate basic building block in the development of multicultural psychotherapy models. This perspective requires therapists to acknowledge culture as a critically important variable that must be incorporated thoroughly into the psychotherapy process. Cultural difference should not be viewed as a nuisance variable. Koss-Chioino and Vargas (1992) argue that a multidimensional perspective allows multicultural psychotherapy models to develop without the previous constraints of either traditional theories or false etic–emic dichotomies. They suggest that the content of approaches (i.e., universal or culture-specific) and the process and form of counseling are equally salient factors for effective work with the culturally different. S. Sue and Zane (1987) also have stated the need to move beyond the issue of universal or culture-specific approaches to multicultural psychotherapy. According to them, these approaches are too distant from the actual counseling and psychotherapy experience. There is a greater need to focus on the proximal processes of psychotherapy. For example, they state the importance of establishing therapist credibility and having clients feel the direct benefit of counseling as more proximal techniques. Similarly, dynamic assessment procedures that encourage a joint/collaborative inquiry with clients is another example of proximal techniques that have a more direct benefit to clients (Dana, 1993; Jones & Thorne, 1987). This multidimensional approach to multicultural psychotherapy has led to the development of more comprehensive multicultural psychotherapy models.

IV. A MULTICULTURAL METATHEORY

Multicultural psychotherapy models now include modifications of traditional theories, universal or culture-specific approaches, and multidimensional forms of psychotherapy. D. W. Sue, Ivey, and Pedersen (1996) have articulated the need for a metatheory or theory of theories to provide an organizational framework to study the salience or relevance of each multicultural psychotherapy model. A metatheory offsets the potential for a "crisis of relativism" (Cooper & Lewis as cited by Fukuyama, 1990) when too many theories are available to therapists and the salience of multiculturalism becomes trivialized. A multicultural metatheory seeks to unify disparate approaches to multicultural psychotherapy by highlighting the common features of each model or approach. Relatedly, the metatheory is culture-centered and multidimensional but not exclusively culture-specific nor universal. It therefore accommodates the variety of worldviews that serve as the foundation for each theory.

The metatheory complements the past call to the profession for multicultural counseling competencies by providing a "buyer's guide" for therapists who are becoming culturally competent and consequently seeking to employ culturally sensitive models of psychotherapy. It serves as another benchmark to examine the comprehensiveness of existing models of multicultural psychotherapy and the development of new models. In brief, the six multicultural counseling and psychotherapy (MCT) propositions are (a) "MCT is a metatheory of counseling and psychotherapy"; (b) "Both therapist and client identities are formed and embedded in multiple levels of experiences and contexts"; (c) "Development of cultural identity is a major determinant of therapist and client attitudes toward the self, others of the same group, others of a different group, and the dominant culture"; (d) "The effectiveness of MCT theory is most likely enhanced when the therapist uses modalities and defines goals consistent with the life experiences/cultural values of the client"; (e) "MCT theory stresses the importance of multiple helping roles developed by many culturally different groups and societies"; and (f) "The liberation of consciousness is a basic goal of MCT theory" (Sue et al., 1996, pp. 23–29).

V. FOUR MULTICULTURAL APPROACHES

The majority of contemporary multicultural models (see Table I) can be categorized into one of four approaches—*culture-matching, acculturation/adaptation, racial identity,* and *person–environment*—that are consistent with the six propositions and respective corollaries of MCT metatheory. The four approaches, however, are not mutually exclusive of each other. They instead emphasize different aspects of multicultural psychotherapy. In this regard, they carefully balance the universal and culture-specific qualities of psychotherapy. They recognize the uniqueness or emic nature of each culture, but they acknowledge some universal or etic characteristics of the psychotherapy process. To reach their goals and objectives, they borrow generously from many theoretical traditions and consequently tend to be multidimensional and eclectic in their employment of roles, strategies, and interventions. For instance, Atkinson, Thompson, and Grant's (1993) three-dimensional model of counseling recommends that psychologists understand the client's level of acculturation, goals of helping, and locus of problem etiology in order to work effectively with culturally different clients. Using this framework, multicultural therapists can assume

TABLE I Selection of Multicultural Psychotherapy Models

Model	General multicultural approach	Reference	Primary goals and strategies
Multicultural or mestizo psychotherapy	Person–environment	Ramirez (1999)	Assess client and therapist on values and cognitive styles; develop cultural and cognitive flexibility; empower client to be an agent of social change.
Counseling culturally different	Culture match	D. W. Sue & Sue (1999)	Identify cultural barriers to therapy, therapeutic relationship factors, cultural identity, and conditions for culturally skilled therapist.
Using race and culture in counseling	Racial identity	Helms & Cook (1999)	Assess racial identity of therapist and client; identify racial and cultural themes in therapy and in client's life.
Liberation psychotherapy	Person–environment	Ivey (1994, 1995); Ivey, Ivey, & Simek-Morgan (1997)	Educate and empower client to recognize and overcome oppression in personal life and in society; adapt different intentional communication styles to match client.
Culture-centered counseling interventions	Culture match	Pedersen (1997)	Understand client in cultural context; emphasis is on process and relationship rather than solution to problem.
Worldview	Culture match	Ibrahim (1985); Treviño (1996)	Identify shared and unique worldviews; change occurs by establishing congruence at general worldview level and discrepancy at specific worldview level.
Transcultural counseling	Acculturation and adaptation	McFadden (1999)	Transcend cultural differences while acknowledging cultural identity and context; help client to live and survive satisfactorily in multicultural world.
Synergetic counseling	Culture match	Axelson (1999); Herring (1996)	Mutual process of working toward goals that are applicable to client in cultural context
Network and link therapy	Acculturation and adaptation	Attneave (1969); Landau (1982)	Empower clients by accessing immediate and extended families to help cope with life crisis.
Optimal theory and Belief systems analysis	Person–environment	Speight, Myers, Cox, & Highlen (1991)	Holistic view of client that emphasizes self-knowledge and acceptance of others.
Minority identity development model	Racial identity	Atkinson, Morton, & Sue (1998)	Identify role of oppression in identity development, recognize within-group variability, and potential each client has for change in identity.
Bicultural effectiveness training and counseling	Acculturation and adaptation	Coleman (1995); LaFromboise, Coleman, & Gerton (1993); Szapocznik & Kurtines (1993)	Assist client to cope with cultural diversity via bicultural orientation.

different roles depending on the client's position along the three dimensions (e.g., therapist, counselor, consultant, advisor, advocate). These roles may be culture-specific (facilitator of indigenous healing) or more traditional (e.g., psychotherapist, counselor). Similarly, multicultural therapists may modify traditional psychotherapy interventions, adapt indigenous healing methods, and utilize alternative sources of help to meet the needs of the clients (Ivey, Ivey, & Simek-Morgan, 1997; LaFromboise, Trimble, & Mohatt, 1990).

A. CULTURE MATCHING

Culture-matching psychotherapy models remove the pressure on clients to fit into dominant psychotherapy paradigms and worldviews. The culture-matching model of psychotherapy represents the broadest multicultural framework in that it is easily adaptable to traditional theories. It holds the basic assumption that effective psychotherapy requires therapists to be sensitive to the client's cultural worldview and experiences (Ibrahim, 1985). D. W. Sue and Sue (1999) describe two independent psychological orientations—locus of control and locus of responsibility—that create four possible worldviews or orientations to life. Although most traditional psychotherapy models subscribe to an internal locus of control and internal locus of responsibility orientation, they argue that culturally different clients may possess other worldviews (e.g., external locus of control and external locus of responsibility). Therapists must use this cultural awareness and sensitivity to match their worldviews with the clients in order for change to occur in psychotherapy. The client should not be forced to match the therapists' worldview, although it is acknowledged that a mutual shift in worldviews will occur.

Treviño (1996) emphasizes the need for therapists to match clients in their general and specific worldviews. According to her, psychological problems often reside in the specific worldviews of clients. As such, therapists must work toward resolving the cognitive dissonance at this level and assisting clients to move toward more congruent worldviews. Toward this end, culture matching subsumes both etic and emic approaches to psychotherapy and acknowledges the value of culture-specific knowledge and universal healing processes (Ibrahim, 1984). Once therapists and clients are able to match worldviews and overcome cultural barriers, then they are able to work collaboratively toward the resolution of common life problems (e.g., career choice, depression, anxiety, marital conflicts).

B. ACCULTURATION AND ADAPTATION

Culturally different people experience various challenges to living as a minority in a diverse society (Berry & Sam, 1997; Coleman, 1995). Some of these challenges can be chronic environmental stressors, such as poverty or discrimination, whereas other stressors can be more acute and circumscribed, such as a new job or migration to a new country. Anderson (1991) notes that perhaps the most powerful yet overlooked stressors are day-to-day hassles of being a minority that often are "accepted as a price of being human" (p. 692). All these life challenges can be construed as forms of acculturative stress for the culturally different. People manage acculturative stress in their daily lives by employing specific cultural coping strategies to negotiate living in two or more cultures (Berry & Sam, 1997; LaFromboise, Coleman, & Gerton, 1993). Berry and Sam (1997), for instance, described four acculturation strategies for maintaining one's traditional culture and participating in the dominant culture: integration, assimilation, separation, and marginalization. When these strategies are no longer effective for individuals, they are no longer able to balance the demands of two cultures that are competing with each other for priority in life. This acculturative stress is a serious health concern that unfortunately often is ignored and accepted as a part of immigrant life.

The primary focus of the acculturation and adaptation approach to multicultural psychotherapy therefore is helping people overcome their acculturative stresses and better adjust and adapt to their environments. At the same time, the acculturation and adaptation approach recognizes the importance of respecting clients' worldviews and addressing other psychological needs. Coleman (1995), for example, proposed that therapists must work toward helping people deal more effectively with these strains of cultural diversity. He suggests that after identifying people's dominant acculturation strategy, therapists must help clients develop better coping strategies to succeed in their given environments. In some instances, this may require emic interventions such as the mobilization of indigenous resources (Atteneave, 1969; Landau; 1982). It also requires etic techniques such as validating the acculturative struggles and stress that clients experience. In the end, the acculturation and adaptation models of multicultural psychotherapy work toward the alleviation of acculturative stress via more successful coping strategies.

C. Ethnic and Racial Identity

For culturally different people who are ethnic and racial minorities in this country, the experience of racism and discrimination has a powerful impact on identity development. These experiences remind people of color that many individuals and institutions in society view them as perpetually different and oftentimes inferior. Over time, the experiences become incorporated into one's perceptions about oneself in the form of ethnic and racial identities. Ethnic and racial identities specifically refer to social identities based on experiences as a member of an ethnic or racial group (Atkinson et al., 1998; Cross, 1978; Helms, 1990). An important feature of ethnic or racial identification relevant to psychotherapy is the stage-like process that people invariably move through depending on their life circumstances. Helms (1990), for example, posits that racial minorities move through at least five stages of racial identification: pre-encounter, encounter, immersion/emersion, internalization, and internalization/commitment. Similarly, Euro-Americans also move through various stages of racial identification: contact, disintegration, reintegration, pseudo-independence, and autonomy (Helms, 1990). For all groups of people, these stages differentially affect people's attitudes and beliefs about themselves as ethnic/racial minorities, other people of the same ethnic/racial heritage, and people of the dominant ethnic/racial group vacillate over time (Atkinson, Poston, Furlong, & Mercado, 1989). It is usually an ethnic or racial incident directed toward the individual or instigated by the individual that moves a person to another ethnic/racial identity stage. Sometimes these experiences can produce a significant amount of psychological and interpersonal distress that can impair one's ability to lead a productive life.

The focus of ethnic and racial identity models of psychotherapy, therefore, is helping people become conscious of their ethnic/racial identity and understand its origin, development, and impact on their lives. In this regard, it is a specialized version of culture matching and acculturation and adaptation models of multicultural psychotherapy. One important feature is the emphasis on the identity status of both the client and the therapist (Helms, 1984; Sabnani, Ponterotto, & Borodovsky, 1991). Both Comas-Diaz and Jacobsen (1991) and Yi (1995), for example, describe cases in which cultural transference and countertransference developed because of the interaction of client and therapist racial identities. The interpersonal dynamics of the client–therapist racial relationship consequently can be used as a therapeutic intervention. For this reason, Helms and Cook (1999) strongly recommend that therapists carefully examine their own racial and cultural assumptions and biases. They further recommend that therapists directly address the sociopolitical and personal meaning of race and culture with clients. This open and honest discussion can ameliorate cultural mistrust of psychotherapy and establish therapist credibility.

D. PERSON–ENVIRONMENT

The culture-matching, acculturation and adaptation, and racial identity approaches to multicultural psychotherapy remind us that people live in the context of culture. These approaches consequently focus on specific cultural experiences, including validating different worldviews, assisting in cultural transitions, and facilitating racial identity development. The person–environment approach goes a step further by acknowledging that people live in a cultural context and, more importantly, by placing this reality at the center of psychotherapy (Fanon, 1963; Friere, 1972; Ramirez, 1999; D. Sue et al., 1996). The basic goal of person–environment psychotherapy therfore is the liberation of consciousness or "learning to see onself and others in relation to cultural context" (Ivey, 1995, p. 56). It moves beyond assisting clients in their adjustment and adaptation to life as a culturally different minority in an Euro-American dominant society and toward creating empowered individuals who are capable of transforming society into a more pluralistic society.

The person–environment approach to multicultural psychotherapy emphasizes the inherent resilience in people. This resilience is embedded within the interdependence among people, including collective wisdom, shared resources, and commitment to community. People are encouraged to embrace the cultural differences in others' lives and to work cooperatively with each other. Similarly, therapists work with clients in a mutually collaborative manner to discover additional strengths and assets (Ivey, 1995). The balance of multiple roles and identities in people's lives, for example, is identified and reinforced as a positive individual and collective characteristic (LaFromboise et al., 1993). The person–environment approach also encourages the development of an internalized and committed racial identity that empowers clients with an understanding of themselves as relational agents of change. Fanon (1963) and Friere (1972), for instance, were early proponents of empowering culturally different people living in an oppressive society. They emphasized the importance of finding one's own voice and language to describe personal experiences and life conditions. The power of language allows clients to recognize the unfair conditions and contradictions in life and moves them toward greater racial consciousness. Clients are encouraged to understand the self-in-relation concept and personally examine their own cultural strengths and assets. Cuento therapy, for example, is a form of storytelling that helps Puerto Rican children understand their lives in the context of their cultural heritage (Constantino, Malgady, & Rogler, 1986). At the same time, it is important for therapists to help clients see life from multiple perspectives and in the context of others. Clients are encouraged to understand life beyond their own inidividual needs and eventually work toward the societal good.

VI. THE MULTICULTURAL WORLDVIEW: THE FUTURE OF MULTICULTURAL PSYCHOTHERAPY

We believe that the person–environment approach to multicultural psychotherapy marks a turning point in the evolution of multicultural psychotherapy models. It represents the emergence of a comprehensive, culture-centered world-view that is the future of multicultural psychotherapy. This worldview acknowledges the central role of culture in individuals and communities, but is not limited by culture-specific or universal frames of reference. As Pedersen and Ivey (1993) comment,

> Culture is within the person, develops as a result of accumulated learning from a complexity of sources, depends on interaction with others to define itself, changes to accommodate the experiences in a changing world, provides a basis for predicting future behavior of self and others, and becomes the central control point for any and all decisions. (p. 2)

Ramirez (1998, 1999) similarly posits that culture in this sense refers to the inclusion and synthesis of diverse perspectives, values, and lifestyles. He further suggests that the new worldview is a blending of different cultures and philosophies that are based on the social, political, and historical forces that have helped shape the Americas.

According to Ramirez (1998, 1999), two important historical forces have contributed to the development of this new worldview—Jose Vasconcellos's (1925, 1927) *la raza cosmica* (the cosmic race) and Crevecoeur's (1904) inclusive melting pot concept of the Americas. Ivey (1995) also has emphasized the important contributions of two modern oppositionists to colonial oppression—Paolo Friere (1972), a Brazilian educator, and Franz Fanon (1963), an African Martinequian psychiatrist—in the shaping of this new multicultural worldview.

The concept of *la raza cosmica* is the belief that the utmost development of humanity could be achieved only through the amalgamation of different races and cultural perspectives (Vasconcellos, 1925, 1927). Vasconcellos extolled the advantages of diversity reflected in the development of the mestizo race (i.e., the intermarriage of Europeans and native American Indians) and observed that in the mestizo race lies the greatest hope for the future of the Americas and the world. The development of the cosmic race, of which the mestizo race was the first developmental stage, would emerge to fulfill what he referred to as the divine mission of the American continent. This cosmic race would represent the product of the synthesis of, "the black, the brown, the yellow, and the white" (1925, pp. 52–53). Vasconcellos predicted that each member of the new race would be a "whole human."

The French writer Crevecoeur (1904) posited the early Americas' social philosophy to be the inclusive melting pot. Crevecoeur conceived of the evolving United States society not as a slightly modified Europe, but as a totally new cultural and biological blend that rejected the class-bound and colonialist institutions brought by the British colonists. In this new world, the genetic strains and folkways of Europe mixed indiscriminately in the political pot of the emerging nation and were fused by the fires of American influence and interaction into a distinctly new American personality. For example, the early European settlers were influenced by the democratic practices they observed in the Native Indian peoples they encountered on the East Coast. They also were influenced by the need to cooperate and negotiate with the indigenous peoples. From these experiences, institutions were developed that were uniquely American and represented more acceptance of cultural and individual differences than the European institutions. It is unfortunate, however, that over time this originally culturally inclusive concept became synonymous with the assimilation, exclusion, and oppression of indigenous and later immigrant peoples (Ramirez, 1998).

Among modern-day oppositionists to colonial oppression, Paolo Friere (1972) stands out for his work with the poor and uneducated peoples of Brazil. Friere's lifelong commitment to education as a means to transform society was a step toward restoring the humanitarian balance that was lost when the Americas became exclusionary and oppressive toward the indigenous people. Friere specifically advocated for the development of *conscientizacáo,* or critical consciousness, as the starting point for liberating people from the oppression of their environments. *Conscientizacáo* refers to "learning to perceive social, political, and economic contradictions, and to take action against the oppressive elements of reality" (p. 19). Toward this end, he emphasized the need for people to become educated and thereby more aware of themselves in their social contexts. Education, according to Friere, was a co-intentional process in which two or more people work together in an egalitarian fashion toward finding new meaning and new ways of being (Ivey, 1995). By achieving *conscientizacáo,* people become empowered and learn to co-construct a new reality that is free of the bonds of oppression.

Franz Fanon (1963, 1967), similar to Friere, emphasized the importance of sociocultural realities and the influence of racism and oppression in the personality development of colonized people. He saw racism as a form of patriarchal domination "in which oppressors actually inscribe a mentality of subordination in the oppressed" (Ivey, 1995). Fanon therefore emphasized the need for people to fight oppression by finding meaning in their experiences as racial minorities. He specifically encouraged people to name and describe their conditions as a means to liberate themselves from the mentality of the oppressed. Fanon furthermore sought to explain all personality dynamics in terms of sociohistorical and cultural realities. For example, he saw neurosis as the expression of a given culture: "Even neurosis, every abnormal manifestation . . . is the product of the cultural situation" (Fanon, 1967, p. 152).

Critical contributions to the multicultural worldview also came from the pioneers in the fields of community psychology (e.g., Rappaport, 1977), ethnopsychology (e.g., Sanchez, 1932), and feminist psychology (e.g., Horney, 1937). These psychologists disclaimed the emphasis on universals in psychology, instead looking to the importance both of sociocultural environments and the effects of minority status and oppression on personality development and functioning. Rappaport, for example, emphasized respect for human diversity and the right to be different, and the belief that human problems are those of person–environment fit rather than of incompetent, inferior people or psychological and cultural environments. Sanchez was the first psychologist to question the use of intelligence tests to assert racial superiority of White children over Mexican and African American children. He showed that environmental and linguistic factors were related significantly to performance on intelligence tests. Horney similarly challenged the sexist bias in society and in psychology and pointed out that Freud's theory ignored important cultural realities: the powerless position of most women in society and the central role of culture in personality dynamics.

Taken altogether, the above influences helped shape a new multicultural worldview that is based on the respect for cultural and individual differences and the inclusion and synthesis of all cultures. The multicultural worldview also emphasizes personal empowerment and the development of institutions in society that are free of inequality and oppression. The following principles or tenets outline the multicultural worldview (Ramirez, 1998) and are consistent with the metatheoretical propositions for multicultural counseling theories set forth by Sue et al. (1996):

- There are no inferior peoples, cultures, or groups in terms of gender, ethnicity, race, economics, religion, disabilities, region, sexual orientation, or language.
- Problems of adjustment are not the result of inferior peoples or groups, but rather of a mismatch between people, or between people and their environment.
- Every individual, group, or culture has positive contributions to make to personality development and to a healthy adjustment to life.
- People who are willing to learn from others and from groups and cultures different from their own acquire multicultural coping techniques, philosophies, and perspectives that are the basis of multicultural personality development and multicultural/multiracial identity.
- The synthesis and amalgamation of personality assets acquired from different peoples, groups, and cultures occur when people with multicultural potential work towards the goals of understanding and cooperation in the context of a pluralistic society.
- Synthesis and amalgamation from diverse origins contribute to the development of a multicultural/multiracial personality functioning, and to the ultimate in psychological adjustment in a pluralistic society.

The multicultural worldview, as defined above, can serve as the foundation to enhance the quality of life for culturally different people. At the psychotherapeutic level, the multicultural worldview moves beyond the traditional goal of helping people as individuals toward helping people become more active citizens and leaders in a pluralistic society. To achieve this goal, it acknowledges culture-specific and universal aspects of counseling and development and incorporates the key elements of the four approaches to multicultural psychotherapy. Perhaps most importantly, multicultural therapists also are challenged to define themselves beyond their traditional roles as psychotherapist and counselor (Atkinson et al., 1993) and to see themselves as social engineers in an increasingly multicultural society (Ramirez, 1999).

VII. THE MULTICULTURAL PSYCHOTHERAPIST AS SOCIAL ENGINEER

The multicultural psychotherapist should aspire to be a social engineer or community leader in the movement toward an inclusive, culture-centered pluralistic society. But this view, according to Draguns (1989), is a delicate charge for the contemporary multicultural psychotherapist. As psychotherapists, "our knowledge . . . is far greater about changing people than changing societies" (p. 15). We therefore must realistically and sensitively balance our responsibilities to help culturally different clients learn to adapt and cope with their lives in a majority culture and to serve as social agents of change to improve the overall quality of life for all peoples.

To achieve this delicate balance in roles and responsibilities, therapists must encourage in their own lives and the lives of their clients the development of multicultural identities and lifestyles that reflect a transcendent perspective on life. Peter Adler (1974) defined a transcendent orientation as the ability to be a part of and apart from the cultures and groups a multicultural person is identified with. The transcendent person is capable of appreciating the cultures and groups she or he belongs to, and at the same time can stand at a distance to objectively determine what is negative about these groups. For example, a multicultural person could be very closely identified with a sociocultural group, but also realize that the group may be sexist or perhaps prejudiced against certain sexual orientations or disabilities. The transcendent person encourages individuals, groups/and or cultures to break from the bonds of racism, sexism, and prejudice in general and to move toward greater openness, inclusiveness, and acceptance of diversity. In this sense, the multicultural, transcendent person is a citizen of the world. He or she is a person who is capable of identifying weaknesses in societies and then has the motivation and ability to promote societal changes.

It is of foremost importance that psychotherapists have the necessary multicultural skills to insure cooperation, harmony, and effective group functioning in a pluralistic society even under conditions of disagreement and conflict. Likewise, clients who participate in multicultural psychotherapy are encouraged to develop these same skills for satisfying and effective living in a pluralistic society. Ramirez, Cox, and Castaneda (1977) and Garza, Romero, Cox, and Ramirez (1982) identified these multicultural skills in their leadership studies on ethnically mixed groups. They found that multicultural leaders, as compared to monocultural leaders, were more effective in increasing effectiveness of communication between mixed-ethnic group members, in making efforts to reduce interpersonal conflict, in flexibility of use of leadership behaviors, and in being more democratic in their orientation to leadership. High multicultural leaders were active and assertive, but they combined these behaviors with tactfulness and personableness. Low multicultural leaders, on the other hand, tended either to behave in an authoritarian fashion, rudely interrupting the members of their groups by shouting them down, or to adopt a very passive and laissez-faire management style, allowing time to be wasted in unproductive arguments among group members. Postgroup interviews conducted with the leaders showed that high multicultural leaders were more accurate in reporting what actually transpired in their groups. When asked to speculate as to why their groups had failed to achieve consensus in the allotted time, the high multicultural participants expressed more optimism for success if they were given a second chance. In general, high multicultural leaders appeared to have more behavioral and perspective repertoires or resources available to them. They also made sure that all members in their groups expressed their opinions and that they all understood each others points of view.

Ramirez (1999) has observed other personality characteristics in clients who have participated in multicultural psychotherapy. For example, as clients develop a cultural awareness of themselves and others, they tend to adopt the role of *multicultural educator.* That is, they introduce others to the groups and cultures that they are familiar with. They also create other educational opportunities for people to develop effective communication strategies and exchange sociocultural knowledge. Another important set of behaviors observed in clients who have participated in multicultural therapy is the ability and desire to function as *multicultural peer counselors* for friends and acquaintances who are experiencing psychological adjustment problems related to living, working, and relating in pluralistic environments. The problems may range from problems of identity to interpersonal conflicts due to misunderstandings in a variety of settings. In these roles, the multicultural person draws on coping techniques and perspectives that they have developed in their own working through of cultural problems in multicultural psychotherapy. The highest level of functioning in multicultural psychotherapy is the transformation of clients into multicultural ambassadors. *Multicultural ambassadors* serve as social catalysts who establish environments that encourage understanding and cooperation among different peoples and groups. Multicultural ambassadors specifically create environments in which the synthesis and amalgamation of cultures and the subsequent synergy that is produced by the melding of cultures help forge pluralistic identities and lifestyles. The ambassadors serve as facilitators for the forging of new ways of viewing the world, solving problems, and developing pluralistic life philosophies. Like the multicultural therapist, they, in turn, will be the social engineers of the future.

VIII. RESEARCH CONSIDERATIONS IN THE ADVANCEMENT OF MULTICULTURAL PSYCHOTHERAPY

If the new multicultural worldview and approach to psychotherapy is to establish itself as the dominant paradigm for the new century, empirical research will be needed to validate the applicability and limitations of traditional and multicultural approaches to psychotherapy with culturally different peoples (Casas, 1995). Unfortunately, the current status of this research suggests that there is still much work to be done in evaluating the different therapy approaches (Atkinson & Lowe, 1995; Helms & Cook, 1999). To date, multicultural psychotherapy research has focused primarily on client preferences for and perceived credibility of ethnically or racially similar or dissimilar therapists. Research attention also has focused on the development and refinement of multicultural assessment instruments and procedures and, to a more limited extent, the utilization of specific multicultural techniques or interventions. There have not been, however, systematic studies that have examined the overall effectiveness and efficacy of multicultural psychotherapy models as compared with conventional, Western psychotherapies.

A. CLIENT–THERAPIST PREFERENCES

Harrison (1975) was among the first to review client–therapist preferences when he found that Black clients generally preferred Black therapists. Although subsequent reviews have supported Harrison's findings for other ethnic and racial groups (e.g., Atkinson, 1983, 1985; Coleman, Wampold, & Casali, 1995), it is important to note that personal characteristics of therapists have been found to be even more important to therapist preference than ethnic and racial factors (e.g., similar attitudes and values, personality, education, age; Atkinson et al., 1989). Researchers also have identified racial identity status and acculturation as critical variables in influencing therapist preference (Helms & Carter,

1990; Morten & Atkinson, 1983). Among African Americans, for instance, it appears that clients with an Immersion/Emersion racial identity, compared to clients with a more Internalized racial identity, prefer racially similar African American counselors. Research with Hispanic and Asian Americans, on the other hand, have more mixed results when examining the role of acculturation in therapist preferences (Atkinson & Lowe, 1995). But using a more sophisticated statistical procedure for paired comparisons, Atkinson, Wampold, Lowe, Mathews, and Ahn (1998) recently found that Asian Americans' counselor preferences varied by problem type, acculturation, and sex of clients. In brief, the research on client–therapist preferences affirms the view that multicultural therapists do not necessarily have to be the same race or ethnicity to validate the life experiences of and provide therapeutic healing for culturally different clients.

B. Perceived Therapist Credibility

As research questions and methodologies have become more sophisticated, researchers have shifted their attentions from client preference for ethnically and racially similar therapists to perceived therapist credibility (S. Sue, 1988). Atkinson and Lowe's (1995) review of the role of ethnicity in counseling, for example, found credibility in some instances to be more salient than ethnic or racial match. Recent research on perceived therapist credibility have confirmed its salience in the psychotherapy process and also have focused on within-group variability in perceptions of therapist credibility (e.g., client's language usage and cultural orientation) (Ramos-Sánchez, Atkinson, & Fraga, 1999; Ruelas, Atkinson, & Ramos-Sánchez, 1998). In brief, this research highlights the importance of moving beyond the static constructs of race and ethnicity in psychotherapy and toward understanding the general cultural process of psychotherapy—that is, recognizing individual difference within cultural groups, matching cultural worldviews, and impressing upon clients that psychotherapy will be beneficial to them (S. Sue & Zane, 1987). Once multicultural therapists demonstrate and establish their credibility with culturally different clients, they will be better able to help clients achieve a more optimal personality by creating a more congruent person–environment fit.

C. Assessment Instruments

The assessment of within-group variability in client–therapist preferences and perceived therapist credibillity has burgeoned in the past decades as a result of the development and refinement of specific multicultural assessment instruments

(Dana, 1993; Okazaki, 1998). These instruments include, but are not restricted to, the measurement of acculturation status, racial and ethnic identity status, and acculturative stress. The assessment of these within-group variables allows multicultural therapists to have a more complete understanding of the uniqueness of each individual's multicultural worldview. More specifically, it allows multicultural therapists to understand how people perceive and define themselves and their relationships in the social, cultural, and political contexts of their daily living. This information then can be used to develop a more congruent person–environment fit that will contribute to positive mental health and adjustment.

Acculturation status, for example, is no longer construed as a unidimensional or static construct in which people replace their traditional cultural values, attitudes, and lifestyles with the majority culture's. Scholars now emphasize the potential bicultural experiences of immigrants who are able to maintain in varying degrees contact with the traditional and majority cultures over the course of their lives (LaFromboise et al., 1993). Cuellar, Arnold, and Maldonado (1995), for instance, have developed a measure of acculturation—Acculturation Rating Scale for Mexican Americans-II (ARSMA-II)—that is based on orthogonal dimensions of Mexican and Anglo cultural orientation. Interestingly, when Ruelas et al. (1998) used the ARSMA-II in their study of counselor helping models and perceived counselor credibility, they found that loss of Mexican culture, but not acquisition of Anglo culture, was related to less positive perceptions of counselor credibility. Using a semistructured life history procedure, Ramirez (1983, 1998) have identified different developmental pathways to stages of acculturation that they have referred to as Historical Development Patterns. These stages are based on time and degree of exposure to two cultures (e.g., early Latino/gradual mainstream, early Latino/abrupt mainstream, early mainstream/gradual Latino, and early mainstream/abrupt Latino). Drawing upon case studies, they have found that these historical developmental patterns are related to degree of commitment to take certain diversity challenges in the course of multicultural psychotherapy. Taken together, multicultural psychotherapists can use both acculturation frameworks—multidimensional and developmental—to help clients achieve a greater cultural flexibility in their everyday lives.

Ethnic and racial identity are aspects of the self that are greatly influenced by the process of acculturation. People's own identification with their cultural reference groups has a powerful impact on mental health and ability to function effectively in a multicultural environment. Numerous models and self-report instruments have been developed to better assess these particular worldviews of clients. Although early racial identity models focused exclusively on African Americans (Cross, 1971), more recent models have been developed to measure Asian American, Hispanic, and White or European American racial identification

(Atkinson, Morten, & Sue, 1998; Helms & Parham, 1996). Similarly, Phinney (1992) developed the Multicultural Ethnic Identity Measure to assess orientation toward one's ethnic cultural group, as well as one's orientation to the dominant cultural group. Although the convergent and discriminant validity of some of these scales have been questioned (e.g., Fischer, Tokar, & Serna, 1998; Pope-Davis, Vandiver, & Stone, 1999), the inclusion of ethnic and racial identity measures into the assessment of multicultural psychotherapy remains critical (Helms, 1995, Helms & Carter, 1990). Richardson and Helms (1994), for example, found racial identity plays a role in emotional reactions, but not cognitive reactions, to counselors. In particular, if a long-term goal of multicultural psychotherapy is to empower culturally different clients and to create a new pluralistic society, it is critical that therapists encourage the facilitation of a more secure, internalized, or synthesized racial identity status. As Ramirez (1998) describes,

> Persons identified as synthesized biculturals/multiculturals exhibited similar personality characteristics, including positive attitudes toward Latino and other minority cultures and mainstream cultures; competent functioning in both Latino, mainstream, and other cultures with an ability to 'shuttle' between the cultures; evidence of close interpersonal relationships with members of different age, sex, and socioeconomic groups from different cultures; behaviors demonstrating a commitment to assisting in the continued development of the cultures they participate in; and a trascendent philosophy of life. (pp. 150–151).

In addition to the assessment of acculturation and racial identity status, it is important for therapists to assess the acculturative stress that culturally different clients may experience when the person–environment fit is poor. Two reliable and validated measures of acculturative stress are the Social, Attitudinal, Familial, and Environmental Acculturation Stress Scale (SAFE) by Mena, Padilla, and Maldonado (1987) and Padilla, Wagatsuma, and Lindholm (1985) and the Hispanic Stress Inventory by Cervantes, Padilla, and Salgado de Snyder (1990, 1991). These measures examine the amount of distress experienced when cultural conflicts occur within and outside the family. The development of these acculturative stress measures hopefully will encourage multicultural psychotherapy researchers to look at the effectiveness of their culturally sensitive interventions in improving the person–environment fit vis-à-vis acculturative stress.

D. MULTICULTURAL TECHNIQUES
AND INTERVENTIONS

As this review of multicultural psychotherapy has shown, most approaches rely upon an assortment of techniques and interventions drawn from different theoretical orientations when working with culturally different clients. This eclectic practice has made it more difficult to validate empirically any given multicultural psychotherapy model. Furthermore, research on the value and effectiveness of universal and culture-specific therapeutic strategies is limited and mixed at best. Atkinson and Lowe's (1995) review of multicultural therapy, for example, found moderate support for the use of a directive style of counseling when working with Hispanic/Latino and Asian American populations. They did not find compelling evidence, however, for the use of therapist self-disclosure with culturally diverse populations. Among American Indians, LaFromboise (1992) found moderate support for the use of self-disclosure and clarification techniques, but found negative reactions to therapist guidance and advice giving. Perhaps most exciting is the potential for incorporating culture-specific healing models into multicultural psychotherapy. Constantino et al.'s (1986) study using Cuento therapy, for example, suggests that use of Puerto Rican folktales can reduce anxiety, decrease aggression, and increase reading comprehension compared to traditional therapy and no therapy.

E. FUTURE RESEARCH DIRECTIONS

If multicultural psychotherapy is to be the fourth force in psychology, clearly more empirical research on process and outcome will need to be standardized and repeatedly replicated. Multicultural psychotherapy research must follow the benchmark that was set forth over 30 years ago when Paul (1967) and Kiesler (1966) both articulated the need to study the effectiveness of psychotherapy in terms of what types of treatments work best for particular types of clients across different settings. It also will be important to look at controlled comparisons of multicultural with conventional models, as well as culture-specific models with culture-universal models (Constantino et al., 1986).

We also need to look beyond logical positivistic models of empirical research and incorporate alternate research methodologies that better assess the contextual nature or person–environment fit of psychological adjustment and mental health. Ethnography, life history, and other narrative forms are qualitative approaches that can enrich our understanding of the synthesis and amalgamation of different cultures. Ramirez (1998), for instance, has over the years developed a life history interview format that incorporates autobiography, family history, self-report attitudes, and the social-historical-political context of individual lives. Ainslie's (1995) ethnographic study of a small Texas community also exemplifies the value to look beyond race in isolation and to understand individuals of different racial backgrounds in the context of their unique and shared communities.

In addition, Betancourt and Lopez (1993) have recommended two research approaches—bottom-up and top-down—to account for specific aspects of culture that are thought to influence behavior. The "bottom-up" approach requires the investigator to begin with a phenomenon observed in the study of a culture and then apply it cross-culturally to test theories of human behavior. By contrast, the "top-down" requires the investigator to begin with a theory that traditionally has ignored culture and incorporate cultural elements to broaden the theoretical domains. Speight and Vera (1997), for example, have proposed the use of attraction and repulsion theory to explain the role of ethnic similarity and difference in client–therapist preferences. Vega (1992) also has suggested evaluating the cultural appropriateness of theoretical premises and hypotheses, field testing instruments to be used, and, most importantly, sharing research findings with members of communities in which the data were collected. This last recomendation exemplifies the multicultural worldview on individual and societal empowerment and change.

IX. CONCLUSION

In the introductory section of this chapter we agreed with Pedersen's observation that multiculturalism is the fourth force in psychology. Throughout the chapter, we have attempted to show the positive contributions of multiculturalism in psychotherapy. We began with a review of early considerations of cultural differences in traditional or mainstream psychotherapy. We also highlighted the importance of multicultural counseling and supervision competencies, as well as a metatheoretical framework, to guide the development and ensure the success of multiculturalism in psychotherapy. In our review of multicultural psychotherapy models, we classified most into one of four major approaches—culture matching, acculturation and adaptation, ethnic and racial identity, and person–environment—and detailed the significance of each approach. Perhaps most striking, we have tried to show that multicultural psychology is a revolutionary force that has the potential to create broad changes in the social sciences and mental health because of its emphases on inclusion, synthesis, and synergy. The future of multicultural psychotherapy, in our view, rests upon the success of the multicultural therapist and client to be co-intentional social engineers of the future, to be active participants in the lives of culturally different people who are striving to live effectively and efficiently in a pluralistic society. To achieve this goal, we conclude with the need for scholars and practitioners to actively engage in research that will validate this multicultural way of life.

REFERENCES

Adler, P. S. (1974). Beyond cultural identity: Reflections on cultural and multicultural man. In R. Brislin (Ed.), *Topics in cultural learning: Vol. 2.* Honolulu, HI: University of Hawaii, East-West Cultural Learning Institute.

Ainslie, R. C. (1995). *No dancin' in Anson: An American story of race and social change.* Northvale, NJ: Jason Aronson, Inc.

Akutsu, P. D., Snowden, L. R., & Organista, K. C. (1996). Referral patterns in ethnic-specific and mainstream programs for ethnic minorities and Whites. *Journal of Counseling Psychology, 43,* 56–64.

American Psychological Association (1993). Guidelines for providers of psychological services to ethnic, linguistic, and culturally diverse populations. *American Psychologist, 48,* 45–48.

Anderson, L. P. (1991). Acculturative stress: A theory of relevance to Black Americans. *Clinical Psychology Review, 11,* 685–702.

Antokoletz, J. C. (1993). A psychoanalytic view of cross-cultural passage. *The American Journal of Psychoanalysis, 53,* 35–54.

Atkinson, D. R. (1983). Ethnic similarity in counseling psychology: A review of research. *The Counseling Psychologist, 11,* 79–92.

Atkinson, D. R. (1985). A meta-review of research on cross-cultural counseling and psychotherapy. *Journal of Multicultural Counseling and Development, 13,* 138–153.

Atkinson, D. R., & Hackett, G. (1997). *Counseling diverse populations.* Boston: McGraw Hill.

Atkinson, D. R., & Lowe, S. M. (1995). The role of ethnicity, cultural knowledge, and conventional techniques in counseling and psychotherapy. In J. G. Ponterotto, J. Manual Casas, L. A. Suzuki, & C. M. Alexander (Eds.), *Handbook of multicultural counseling* (pp. 387–414). Thousand Oaks, CA: Sage.

Atkinson, D. R., Morten, G., & Sue, D. W. (Eds.) (1998). *Counseling American minorities* (5th ed.). Boston: McGraw Hill.

Atkinson, D. R., Poston, W. C., Furlong, M. J., & Mercado, P. (1989). Ethnic group preferences for counselor characteristics. *Journal of Counseling Psychology, 36,* 68–72.

Atkinson, D. R., Thompson, C. E., & Grant, S. K. (1993). A three-dimensional model for counseling racial/ethnic minorities. *The Counseling Psychologist, 21,* 257–277.

Atkinson, D. R., Wampold, B. E., Lowe, S. M., Matthews, L., & Aha, H. (1998). Asian American preferences for counselor characteristics: Application of Bradley-Luce model to paired comparison data. *Journal of Counseling Psychology, 26,* 101–123.

Atteneave, C. L. (1969). Therapy in tribal settings and urban network intervention. *Family Process, 8,* 192–210.

Axelson, J. A. (1999). *Counseling and development in a multicultural society* (3rd ed.). Pacific Grove, CA: Brooks Cole.

Baruth, L. G., & Manning, M. L. (1999). *Multicultural counseling and psychotherapy: A lifespan perspective* (2nd ed.). Upper Saddle River, NJ: Merrill/Prentice Hall.

Berry, J. W. (1989). Imposed etics-emics-derived etics: The operationalization of a compelling idea. *International Journal of Psychology, 24,* 721–734.

Berry, J. W., & Sam, D. (1997). Acculturation and adaptation. In J. W. Berry, M. H. Segall, & C. Kagitcibasi (Eds.), *Handbook of cross-cultural psychology (vol. 3): Social behavior and applications* (pp. 291–326). Boston: Allyn and Bacon.

Betancourt, H., & Lopez, S. R. (1993). The study of culture, ethnicity, and race in American psychology. *American Psychologist, 28,* 629–637.

Casas, J. M. (1995). Counseling and psychotherapy with racial/ethnic minority groups in theory and practice. In B. M. Bongar & L. E. Beutler, (Eds.), *Comprehensive textbook of psychotherapy: Theory and practice* (pp. 311–335). New York: Oxford University Press.

Cervantes, R. C., Padilla, A. M., & Salgado de Snyder, N. (1991). The Hispanic Stress Inventory: A culturally relevant approach to psychosocial assessment. *Psychological Assessment: A Journal of Consulting and Clinical Psychology, 3,* 438–447.

Cervantes, R. C., Padilla, A. M., & Salgado de Synder, N. (1990). Reliability and validity of the Hispanic Stress Inventory. *Hispanic Journal of the Behavioral Sciences, 12,* 76–82.

Cheung, F., & Snowden, L. R. (1990). Community mental health and ethnic minority populations. *Community Mental Health Journal, 26,* 277–291.

Coleman, H. L. K. (1995). Strategies for coping with cultural diversity. *The Counseling Psychologist, 23,* 722–740.

Coleman, H. L. K., Wampold, B. E., & Casali, S. L. (1995). Ethnic minorities' ratings of ethnically similar and European American counselors: A meta-analysis. *Journal of Counseling Psychology, 42,* 55–64.

Comas-Diaz, L., & Jacobsen, F. M. (1991). Ethnocultural transference and countertransference in the therapeutic dyad. *American Journal of Orthopsychiatry, 61,* 392–402.

Constantino, G., Malgady, R. G., & Rogler, L. H. (1986). Cuento therapy: A culturally sensitive modality for Puerto Rican children. *Journal of Consulting & Clinical Psychology, 54,* 639–645.

Cooper, T. D., & Lewis, J. A. (1983). The crisis of relativism: Helping counselors cope with diversity. *Counselor Education and Supervision, 22,* 290–295.

Crevecoeur, J. H. St. J. (1904). *Letters from an American farmer.* New York: Fox Duffield.

Cross, W. E. (1971). The Negro to Black conversion experience: Towards a psychology of Black liberation. *Black World, 20,* 13–27.

Cross, W. E. (1978). The Cross and Thomas models of psychological nigrescence. *Journal of Black Psychology, 5,* 13–19.

Cross, T. L., Bazron, B. J., Dennis, K. W., & Isaac, M. R. (1989). *Towards a culturally competent system of care.* Washington, DC: Child and Adolescent Service System Program Technical Assistance Center.

Cuellar, I. B., Arnold, B., & Maldonado, R. (1995). Acculturation rating scale for Mexican-Americans-II. A revision of the original ARSMA scale. *Hispanic Journal of the Behavioral Sciences, 17,* 275–304.

D'Andrea, M., & Daniels, J. (1997). Multicultural counseling supervision: Central issues, theoretical considerations, and practical strategies. In D. B. Pope-Davis & H. L. K. Coleman (Eds.), *Multicultural counseling competencies: Assessment, education, training, and supervision* (pp. 290–309). Thousand Oaks, CA: Sage.

Dana, R. H. (1993). *Multicultural assessment perspectives for professional psychology.* Needham Heights, MA: Allyn & Bacon.

Draguns, J. G. (1989). Dilemmas and choices in cross-cultural counseling: the universal versus the culturally distinctive. In P. B. Pedersen, J. G. Draguns, W. J. Lonner, & J. E. Trimble (Eds.), *Counseling across cultures* (pp. 3–21). Honolulu, HI: University of Hawaii Press.

Fanon, F. (1963). *The wretched of the earth.* New York: Grove Wheatland.

Fanon, F. (1967). *Black skin, White masks.* New York: Grove.

Fassinger, R. E., & Richie, B. S. (1997). Sex matters: Gender and sexual orientation in training for multicultural counseling competency. In D. B. Pope-Davis & H. L. K. Coleman (Eds.), *Multicultural counseling competencies: Assessment, education, training, and supervision* (pp. 83–110). Thousand Oaks, CA: Sage.

Fischer, A. R., Jome, L. M., & Atkinson, D. R. (1998). Reconceptualizing multicultural counseling: Universal healing conditions in a culturally specific context. *The Counseling Psychologist, 26,* 525–588.

Fischer, A. R., Tokar, D. M., & Serna, G. S. (1998). Validity and construct contamination of the Racial Identity Attitude Scale-Long Form. *Journal of Counseling Psychology, 45,* 212–224.

Friere, P. (1972). *Pedagogy of the oppressed.* New York: Herder & Herder.

Fukuyama, M. A. (1990). Taking a universal approach to multicultural counseling. *Counselor Education and Supervision, 30,* 6–17.

Garza, R. T., Romero, G. J., Cox, B. G., & Ramirez, M. (1982). Biculturalism, locus of control, and leader behavior in ethnically mixed small groups. *Journal of Applied Social Psychology, 12,* 227–253.

Harrison, D. K. (1975). Race as a counselor-client variable in counseling and psychotherapy: A review of the research. *The Counseling Psychologist, 5,* 124–133.

Helms, J. E. (1984). Toward a theoretical explanation of the effects of race on counseling: A Black and White model. *The Counseling Psychologist, 12,* 153–165.

Helms, J. E. (1990). Three perspectives on counseling and psychotherapy with visible racial/ethnic group clients. In F. Serafica et al. (Eds.), *Mental health of ethnic minorities.* New York: Praeger.

Helms, J. E. (1995). Update of Helms' racial identity models. In J. G. Ponterotto, J. Manuel Casas, L. A. Suzuki, & C. M. Alexander (Eds.), *Handbook of multicultural counseling* (pp. 181–198). Thousand Oaks, CA: Sage.

Helms, J. E., & Carter, R. T. (1990). Development of the White racial identity attitude inventory. In J. E. Helms (Ed.), *Black and White racial identity: Theory, research, and practice* (pp. 67–80). Westport, CT: Greenwood.

Helms, J. E., & Cook, D. A. (1999). *Using race and culture in counseling and psychotherapy: Theory and process.* Boston: Allyn & Bacon.

Helms, J. E., & Parham, T. A. (1996). The Racial Identity Attitude Scale. In R. L. Jones (Ed.), *Handbook of tests and measurements for Black populations* (Vol. 2, pp. 167–174). Hampton, VA: Cobb & Henry Publishers.

Herring, R. D. (1996). Synergetic counseling and Native American Indian students. *Journal of Counseling and Development, 74,* 542–547.

Horney, K. (1937). *The neurotic personality of our time.* New York: W. W. Norton.

Hough, R. L., Landsverk, J. A., Karno, M., Burnam, M. A., Timbers, D. M., Escobar, J. I., & Regier, D. A. (1987). Utilization of health and mental health services by Los Angeles Mexican Americans and non-Hispanic Whites. *Archives of General Psychiatry, 44,* 702–709.

Hu, T., Snowden, L. R., Jerrell, J. M., & Nguyen, T. D. (1991). Ethnic populations in public mental health: Services choice and level of use. *American Journal of Public Health, 81,* 1429–1434.

Ibrahim, F. A. (1984). Cross-cultural counseling and psychotherapy: An existential-psychological approach. *International Journal for the Advancement of Counselling, 7,* 159–169.

Ibrahim, F. A. (1985). Effective cross-cultural counseling and psychotherapy: A framework. *The Counseling Psychologist, 13,* 625–638.

Ivey, A. E. (1994). *Intentional interviewing and counseling: Facilitating client development in a multicultural society.* Pacific Grove, CA: Brooks Cole.

Ivey, A. E. (1995). Psychotherapy as liberation: Toward specific skills and strategies in multicultural counseling and therapy. In J. G. Ponterotto, J. Manuel Casas, L. A. Suzuki, C. M. Alexander (Eds.), *Handbook of multicultural counseling* (pp. 181–198). Thousand Oaks, CA: Sage.

Ivey, A. E., Ivey, M. B., & Simek-Morgan, L. (1997). *Counseling and psychotherapy: A multicultural perspective* (4th ed.). Boston: Allyn & Bacon.

Jackson, M. L. (1995). Multicultural counseling: Historical perspectives. In J. G. Ponterotto, J. Manuel Casas, L. A. Suzuki, & C. M. Alexander (Eds.), *Handbook of multicultural counseling* (pp. 181–198). Thousand Oaks, CA: Sage.

Jones, E. E., & Thorne, A. (1987). Rediscovery of the subject: Intercultural approaches to clinical assessment. *Journal of Consulting and Clinical Psychology, 55,* 488–495.

Kiesler, D. J. (1966). Some myths of psychotherapy research and the search for a paradigm. *Psychological Bulletin, 65,* 110–136.

Koss-Chioino, J. D., & Vargas, L. A. (1992). Through the cultural looking glass: A model for understanding culturally responsive psychotherapies. In J. D. Koss-Chioino & L. A. Vargas (Eds.), *Working with culture: Psychotherapeutic interventions with ethnic minority children and adolescents.* San Francisco: Jossey-Bass.

LaFromboise, T. D. (1992). An interpersonal analysis of affinity, clarification, and helpful responses with American Indians. *Professional Psychology: Research and Practice, 23,* 281–286.

LaFromboise, T., Coleman, H. L. K., & Gerton, J. (1993). Psychological impact of biculturalism: Evidence and theory. *Psychological Bulletin, 114,* 395–412.

LaFromboise, T. D., Trimble, J. E., & Mohatt, G. V. (1990). Counseling intervention and American Indian tradition: An integrative approach. *The Counseling Psychologist, 18,* 628–654.

Landau, J. (1982). Therapy with families in cultural transition. In M. McGoldrick, J. K. Pearce, & J. Giordano (Eds.), *Ethnicity and family therapy* (pp. 552–572). New York: Guilford.

Lee, R. M., Chalk, L., Conner, S. Kawasaki, N., Jannetti, A., LaRue, T., & Rodolfa, E. (1999). The status of multicultural counseling training at counseling center internship sites. *Journal of Multicultural Counseling and Development, 27,* 58–74.

Leong, F. T. L., & Wagner, N. M. (1994). Cross-cultural counseling supervision: What do we know? What do we need to know? *Counseling Education and Supervision, 34,* 117–131.

Locke, D. (1990). A not so provincial view of multicultural counseling. *Counselor Education and Supervision, 30,* 18–25.

Locke, D. C. (1992). The Locke paradigm of cross cultural counseling. *International Journal for the Advancement of Counselling, 14,* 15–25.

Martinez, R. P., & Holloway, E. L. (1997). The supervision relationship in multicultural training. In D. B. Pope-Davis & H. L. K. Coleman (Eds.), *Multicultural counseling competencies: Assessment, education, training, and supervision* (pp. 325–349). Thousand Oaks, CA: Sage.

McFadden, J. (1999). Historical approaches to transcultural counseling. In J. McFadden (Ed.), *Transcultural counseling* (2nd ed.). Alexandria, VA: American Counseling Association.

Mena, F. J., Padilla, A. M., & Maldonado, M. (1987). Acculturative stress and specific coping strategies among immigrant and later generation college students. *Hispanic Journal of the Behavioral Sciences, 9,* 207–225.

Morten, G., & Atkinson, D. R. (1983). Minority identity development and preference for counselor race. *Journal of Negro Education, 52,* 156–161.

Okazaki, S. (1998). Psychological assessment of Asian Americans: Research agenda for cultural competency. *Journal of Personality Assessment, 70,* 54–70.

Padilla, A., Wagatsuma, Y., & Lindholm, K. (1985). Acculturation and personality as predictors of stress in Japanese and Japanese Americans. *Journal of Social Psychology, 125,* 295–305.

Patterson, C. H. (1996). Multicultural counseling: From diversity to universality. *Journal of Counseling and Development, 74,* 227–231.

Paul, G. L. (1967). Strategy of outcome research in psychotherapy. *Journal of Consulting Psychology, 31,* 109–118.

Pedersen, P. B. (1991). Multiculturalism as a fourth force in counseling [Special issue]. *Journal of Counseling and Development, 70.*

Pedersen, P. B. (1997). *Culture-centered counseling interventions: Striving for accuracy.* Thousand Oaks, CA: Sage.

Pedersen, P. B., & Ivey, A. E. (1993). *Culture-centered counseling and interviewing skills: A practical guide.* Westport, CT: Praeger.

Phinney, J. S. (1992). The Multigroup Ethnic Identity Measure: A new scale for use with diverse groups. *Journal of Adolescent Research, 7,* 156–176.

Pike, K. L. (1967). *Language in relation to a unified theory of the structures of human behavior* (2nd ed.). The Hague: Mouton.

Pope-David, D. B., Vandiver, B. J., & Stone G. L. (1999). White racial identity attitude development: A psychometric examination of two instruments. *Journal of Counseling Psychology, 46,* 70–79.

Ramirez, M. (1983). *Psychology of the Americas: Mestizo perspectives in personality and mental health.* New York: Pergamon.

Ramirez, M. (1998). *Multicultural/multiracial psychology: Mestizo perspectives in personality and mental health.* Northvale, NJ: Aronson.

Ramirez, M. (1999). *Multicultural psychotherapy: An approach to individual and cultural differences* (2nd Ed.). Boston: Allyn & Bacon.

Ramirez, M., Cox, B. G., & Castaneda, A. (1977). *The psychodynamics of biculturalism.* Unpublished technical report to Office of Naval Research, Arlington, VA.

Ramos-Sánchez, L., Atkinson, D. R., & Fraga, E. D. (1999). Mexican Americans' bilingual ability, counselor bilingualism cues, counselor ethnicity, and perceived counselor credibility. *Journal of Counseling Psychology, 46,* 125–131.

Rappaport, J. (1977). *Community psychology: Values, research, and action.* New York: Holt, Rinehart, & Winston.

Renfrey, G. S. (1992). Cognitive-behavior therapy and the Native American client. *Behavior Therapy, 23,* 321–340.

Richardson, T. Q., & Helms, J. E. (1994). The relationship of the racial identity attitudes of Black men to perceptions of "parallel" counseling dyads. *Journal of Counseling and Development, 73,* 172–177.

Riessman, F. (1962). *The culturally deprived child.* New York: Harper & Row.

Ruelas, S. R., Atkinson, D. R., & Ramos-Sánchez, L. (1998). Counselor helping model, participant ethnicity, and acculturation level, and perceived counselor credibility. *Journal of Counseling Psychology,* 98–103.

Ryan, A. S., & Hendricks, C. O. (1989). Culture and communication: Supervising the Asian and Hispanic social workers. *The Clinical Supervisor, 7,* 27–40.

Ryan, W. (1971). *Blaming the victim.* New York: Random House.

Sabnani, H. B., Ponterotto, J. G., & Borodovsky, L. G. (1991). White racial identity development and cross-cultural counselor training: A stage model. *The Counseling Psychologist, 19,* 76–101.

Sanchez, G. I. (1932). Group differences and Spanish-speaking children—a critical review. *Journal of Applied Psychology, 18,* 756–772.

Schofield, W. (1964). *Psychotherapy: The purchase of friendship.* Englewood Cliffs, NJ: Prentice-Hall.

Snowden, L. R., & Cheung, F. (1990). Use of inpatient mental health services by members of ethnic minority groups. *American Psychologist, 45,* 347–355.

Sodowsky, G. R., Taffe, R. C., Gutkin, T. B., & Wise, S. L. (1994). Development of the Multicultural Counseling Inventory: A self-report measure of multicultural competencies. *Journal of Counseling Psychology, 41,* 137–148.

Speight, S. L., & Vera, E. M. (1997). Similarity and difference in multicultural counseling: Considering the attraction and repulsion hypotheses. *The Counseling Psychologist, 25,* 280–298.

Speight, S. L., Myers, L. J., Cox, C. I., & Highlen, P. S. (1991). A redefinition of multicultural counseling. *Journal of Counseling and Development, 70,* 29–36.

Sue, D. W., Arrendondo, P., & McDavis, R. J. (1992). Multicultural competencies/standards: A call to the profession. *Journal of Counseling and Development, 70,* 477–486.

Sue, D. W., Bernier, J. B., Durran, M., Feinberg, L., Pedersen, P., Smith, E., Vasquez-Nuttal, E. (1982). Position paper: Cross-cultural counseling competencies. *The Counseling Psychologist, 10,* 45–52.

Sue, D. W., Ivey, A. E., Pedersen, P. B. (1996). *A theory of multicultural counseling and therapy.* Pacific Grove, CA: Brooks Cole.

Sue, D. W., & Sue, D. (1999). *Counseling the culturally different: Theory and practice* (3rd ed.). New York: John Wiley & Sons.

Sue, S. (1988). Psychotherapeutic services for ethnic minorities: Two decades of research findings. *American Psychologist, 43,* 301–308.

Sue, S., Fujino, D. C., Hu, L., Takeuchi, D. T., & Zane, N. W. S. (1991). Community mental health services for ethnic minority groups: A test of the cultural responsiveness hypothesis. *Journal of Consulting and Clinical Psychology, 59,* 533–540.

Sue, S., & Zane, N. (1987). The role of culture and cultural techniques in psychotherapy: A critique and reformulation. *The American Psychologist, 42,* 37–45.

Sundberg, N. D. (1981). Cross-cultural counseling and psychotherapy: A research overview. In A. J. Marsella & P. B. Pedersen (Eds.), *Cross-cultural counseling and psychotherapy* (pp. 29–38). New York: Pergamon.

Szapocznik, J., & Kurtines, W. M. (1993). Family psychology and cultural diversity: Opportunities for theory, research, and application. *American Psychologist, 48,* 400–407.

Szasz, T. S. (1970) The crime of commitment. In *Readings in Clinical Psychology Today* (pp. 167–169). Del Mar, CA: CRM Books.

Treviño, K. G. (1996). Worldview and change in cross-cultural counseling. *The Counseling Psychologist, 24,* 198–215.

Vasconcellos, J. (1925). La raza cosmica: Mision de la raza iberoamericana (The cosmic race: Mission of the Iberoamerican race). Mexico: D. F. Espasa-Calpe Mexicana S. A.

Vasconcellos, J. (1927). *Indologia: Una interpretaction de la cultura iberoamericana* [The study of Indian cultures: An interpretation of Iberoamerican culture]. Barcelona, Spain: Agencia Mundial de Liberia.

Vega, W. A. (1992). Theoretical and pragmatic implications of cultural diversity for community research. *American Journal of Community Psychology, 20,* 375–391.

Yi, K. (1995). Psychoanalytic psychotherapy with Asian clients: Transference and therapeutic considerations. *Psychotherapy, 32,* 308–316.

.

CHAPTER 15

Conducting the Cross-Cultural Clinical Interview

Cervando Martinez

Department of Psychiatry
University of Texas Health Science Center
San Antonio, Texas

I. INTRODUCTION AND GENERAL CONSIDERATIONS

Writing and, in turn, reading a chapter such as this is fraught with difficulties. It is difficult to write about cross-cultural issues, in this case the clinical interview, from a general point of view that is relevant to most, if not all, cultural groups encountered clinically. Even if one is limited to the cultural groups that are most common in the United States (African Americans, Hispanics, Asian Americans, Native Americans), there are serious questions about whether one can (or should) generalize across groups or across social classes. Recognizing these difficulties one can still attempt to discuss general problems, issues, and approaches. Furthermore, as I will do in this chapter, one can single out a cultural group, in this case Mexican Americans, and use it as an example.

Also, I have always found learning about interviewing from a book to be difficult. Probably the best way to learn how to be a good interviewer is to watch good interviewers (and bad ones, too). Observing different styles and techniques can then be gradually blended into one's own style. As described later, the three most basic elements in becoming a good interviewer are (a) attaining a constant attitude of care, (b) having empathy, and (c) having compassion for those to whom we provide mental health care. This is not to say that techniques and reading are unimportant, but these should build upon the above stated three basic underlying ideal attributes of a good health care professional.

Thus my focus in this chapter will be on the general and of necessity is derived from my own training, experiences, and present clinical work. I am a physician and psychiatrist. My psychiatric training was at an institution with a pervasive classic psychoanalytic orientation, although I am not a psychoanalyst. Almost all of my clinical work has been in psychiatric outpatient clinics of a county hospital system for the medically indigent in a city (San Antonio, Texas) where over 60% of the population is of Mexican origin (Mexican Americans or Chicanos). For these reasons the individuals that I see are usually moderately to severely ill, often have comorbid medical conditions, may be taking medications, and are called patients not clients. About a third speak predominantly Spanish; somewhat less than this were born in Mexico. Thus, I see recent immigrants from Mexico as well as multigeneration Texans of Mexican descent. Of interest is that many of the latter still speak Spanish a great deal—sometimes exclusively—although not necessarily "Mexican" in customs.

Finally, I elected not to make this a reference rich-work. I have done this elsewhere (Martinez 1982, 1993, 1994). Instead I chose to make this an experience-based chapter in the hope that this would be equally, if not more, meaningful. The most common clinical interview that I conduct is not entirely structured nor is it nonstructured, but rather a combination of some structured components designed to gather specific information, such as the presenting problem, symptom presentation, history, insight, cognitive functioning, and the like. The nonstructured part is where I ask questions in order to pursue a particular matter or direction during the interview based on previously elicited or observed behavior. In this respect, the clinical interview is a dynamic process, individually tailored to each patient. This is not too much unlike the process of obtaining psychological and psychiatric information when conducting a structured clinical interview with a defined probe module, as in the case of the Composite International Diagnostic Inventory (CIDI) wherein, depending on whether a question is answered affirmatively or negatively, the interviewer follows up with a different defined set of questions.

The need to be evaluating information while conducting the interview is an important part of the clinical interview. I have labeled this the "stepping-back" process, and by necessity it is a reoccurring process throughout the clinical interview. It is precisely this stepping-back process that makes the cross-cultural clinical interview particularly interesting and challenging for the clinician.

Othmer and Othmer (1994) identify five phases of the Clinical Interview:

1. Warm-up and screening
2. Follow-up on preliminary impressions
3. Psychiatric history and database
4. Diagnosis and feedback
5. Prognosis and treatment

I will utilize these five phases of the Clinical Interview to present some of my observations and experiences with respect to conducting culturally competent cross-cultural clinical interviews. It is my understanding that cultural competence in conducting a clinical interview, or in any other aspect of the delivery of mental health services, is not a place but a developmental process. It is also my understanding that the fundamental basis of developing this competency lies in respect for others, their ways of life, their religious practices, their worldviews, and their individual autonomy.

II. WARM-UP AND SCREENING

A. LANGUAGE OF INTERVIEW

There are several things to keep in mind when initiating a cross-cultural clinical interview. These are the same irrespective of whether the interview is for diagnostic, assessment, psychotherapy, pharmacological management, or any other purpose.

The first is for the clinician to determine in which language to conduct the interview, assuming that the clinician knows more than one language. When either the clinician or the patient speak more than one language, a language has to be decided upon to start with. This may simply be a matter of selecting the language that the patient speaks best, or feels most comfortable with, and that can also be understood and spoken by the clinician. This selection sometimes occurs spontaneously or intuitively at the time the two individuals meet or initiate contact. The selection may be determined for good then without any future deviations. However, in a significant number of cases there needs to be somewhat more attention paid to this issue initially and in a few cases it (the language of the interview) persists as a recurring and, sometimes nettlesome, problem.

If the patient and clinician have more than one language in common, then they have to settle on one language for most if not all of the interview. Usually this determination can be made simply by asking the patient which language is preferred or is most comfortable. It is also acceptable for the therapist to guess which language might be the patient's choice and proceed to use it but remain alert to discomfort or awkwardness in the patient if the guess is wrong. With individuals who are recent immigrants or with many elderly minority patients, it may be safe to initiate conversations in what is considered the native language for that group on the assumption that English is not their primary language.

In my experience I have not sensed that a "wrong" guess on this matter of choice of initial language has adversely affected the remainder of the interview. My tendency is always to err on the side of using Spanish initially with patients who either look Hispanic or have Spanish last names, Exceptions are younger patients, especially adolescents, and patients that I know for certain do not speak Spanish well or at all. Also, I always ask the patient which language he or she prefers because many Hispanics are equally fluent in both languages but usually have a preference. I do not usually impose the use of one language or the other, and I have encountered patients who are clearly more dominant in Spanish (they still speak English with an accent) yet they insist on speaking English. I will accede to their wish at least initially as I assess the possible underlying motivation for this behavior. In most of these cases I determine that this insistence on using the less than best language is part of an overall attempt at denial or avoidance of painful experiences or emotions or an effort to control the interview and guide the interviewer away from certain areas. Sensitive insistence that the more appropriate, although direct and powerful, language be used may suffice to overcome this resistance.

B. CLINICAL VIGNETTE

A 62-year-old married woman who was born in Mexico as on previous occasions became tearful as she described a recent interaction with a married daughter who was going through a divorce. She spoke in English, although it is clearly not her best language, as she described a series of interactions where she invariably ended up being hurt or rejected, made to feel unloved, adding to her chronic sadness, bitterness, and unforgiving nature. I had heard her speak this way before many times, and perhaps with some exasperation, proceeded to make my intervention in a switch to Spanish as I encouraged her to try to be more understanding of her daughter's plight and not accumulate yet one more grudge. I did this because I sensed that by continuing our conversation in English I would not be able to reach her core self as well as in Spanish, which in this case felt to me like the more honest and mature voice (language).

A more difficult situation is when the clinician does not speak (or poorly speaks and understands) the patient's primary and best language. I will not discuss here the indications and specific techniques of the use of interpretors in health and mental health settings, but rather comment on the situation when there is an imperfect yet useful common language. Most commonly this will involve a clinician who has a moderately good ability to communicate in the patient's language of choice and decides not to use an interpreter. This situation is a challenging yet potentially rewarding one both in terms of therapeutic efficacy and personal fulfillment. Even though two people may be "understanding" one another less than optimally, if there is a joint sense of common mission (to obtain help for a troubling problem) it is surprising how often effective communication can take place. The intense effort of attempts to understand one another's communication can result in an important sense of closeness and empathic contact. Repetition and clarification, effective techniques in traditional psychotherapy, are usually necessary when trying to communicate with less than optimal common language facility.

C. Presenting Problem

Language issues aside there are other basic steps that are important in initiating all clinical interviews but are of greater importance in the early cross-cultural interview. One of these is deterimining "why is the patient here?" There are usually several components to this question with all patients: What is the reason this person gives for seeking help now, and more importantly, what is the real reason help is being sought? As reasonably good clinicians we know that there are often unspoken or unconscious reasons why persons seek help and that we should be alert for these. In the cross-cultural clinical setting this also occurs, but the fact that the patient is from a different cultural group may add other layers of complexity to the question. Depending on the type of clinical setting, patients may present their problems in different terms. For example, in a medical/psychiatric clinic type of setting the patient may describe the presenting problem in terms of physical symptoms or psychological complaints (i.e., insomnia, anxiety, etc.), or more general yet related terms (i.e., nervousness, stress). In a family social service environment the patient (or client in this case) may start with an emphasis on family, economic or other social problems. A patient may come for help with distressing symptoms which at first are attributed to one underlying process (medical illness, family problem), but which are really the result of another process (spousal abuse, serious depression).

D. Symptom Presentation

Misidentification of causal sources may be more common in cross-cultural settings because of the recognized tendency among some groups to somatize their distress. This can be treacherous ground even for the medically trained clinician. Assuming that a somatic symptom is due to somatization of distress may be just as erroneous as the opposite focusing on a somatic symptom as though

it had no emotional component and perhaps needlessly pursuing it diagnosti-
cally. I recently saw a Mexican American man with what to me were bizarre
somatic abdominal complaints that did not conform to any recognized medical
condition, who had undergone an exploratory laparotomy in a fruitless search
for organic pathology. None was found.

E. Vague, General Complaints

More important than determining the underlying, perhaps unconscious, reasons for seeking help, is the immediate task of discerning what is distressing
the patient and converting that expression in the patient's own words, language,
and concepts to the clinician's terminology and frame of reference. Many individuals from ethnic minority groups will express their distress in nonspecific
terms: "I feel bad," "I feel upset," "I am nervous" (*nervios*), and so on. It is thus
important to attempt to have the patient elaborate on what they are experiencing, by asking them to say more about their distress without suggesting any
specific symptom. This requires patience because among some cultural groups
emotional distress is often described in terms of physical symptoms or by referring to a specific disturbed organ or body part. Even with careful attempts to
elicit greater subjective elaboration, an individual may not provide the necessary information for the clinician to conclude that a particular affect is being
described (i.e., depression). Collateral observation may be needed (e.g. insomnia, lack of interest), as reported by patient or family member.

III. FOLLOW-UP ON PRELIMINARY
IMPRESSIONS

As in all clinical interviews, perhaps more in cross-cultural settings, we should
attend to our own inner mental state as we enter the interview process. By this
I mean that clinicians should first examine themselves for tensions, biases,
preoccupations, and worries that distract and affect our perceptions and responses to the person we are trying to help. These distractions come in many
forms: some fully conscious and modifiable, others not so evident, hopefully
accessible and unfortunately having the potential to interfere with clear clinicial
thinking. They occur during our interactions with all patients but should be
more carefully searched for when working with patients from certain groups
(e.g., minority groups, the elderly, individuals with personality disorders, and
others). Persons from these broad groups (and from others depending on our
experience) tend to stimulate these distracting biases and reactions. They re-

mind us of something or we stereotype them: "All old people are demented." "The poor are all suffering and unhappy." "She is a borderline."

Another good practice in interviewing any patient but particularly patients from socioeconomic classes or ethnic groups other than one's own is what can best be called "stepping back" or being in the moment. Often as clinicians we tend to lose our concentration, the intense focus on the patient's subjective experience, that allows us to make full use of the power of the clinical interpersonal interaction, even if the interview is a brief one. The human tendency is to rush along (even if unhurried), listen less closely and intently, allow our empathic powers to wane, and miss opportunities for discernment of important nuances in the interview and only slightly hidden signals from our patients. These missed empathic opportunities and lost signals obviously make the encounter less helpful and meaningful for both clinician and patient. Lapses cannot be completely avoided. We all do this. However, it may be that in the cross-cultural setting this heightened focus needs to be more consciously called forward. In many sensitive clinicians the heightened attention may occur as a result of the perceived challenge of the cross-cultural interview. On the other hand, it is also easy in a cross-cultural setting to fall into a less attentive mode because of frustration and difficulty encountered in such a setting. My call is for clinicians to strive to achieve this attitude at all times.

A. Psychiatric History and Database

During the greater part of the clinical interview one has to move back and forth between approaches allowing the patient to speak his or her mind and letting the interview go wherever it may or exerting more direction to elicit specific details, symptoms, and issues, and guiding the interview into other areas. The degree and type of directiveness is determined by the purpose of the interview and other factors. In this section I will focus on three areas of culturally influenced patient–clinician interaction: traditional versus nontraditional values, autonomy issues, and the manifestation of religious belief in the interview.

B. Social Class Factors Impinging the Interview

Most of the techniques recommended for conducting a sound general clinical interview (empathic listening, a nonjudgmental attitude, sensitive interventions, nondirectiveness versus judicious directiveness) are equally applicable to a cross-cultural setting. However, as was pointed out earlier, there are issues of attitude set and language that are encountered in a cross-cultural (including "cross socioeconomic class") interview that must be navigated as well. During the main body of the interview other types of issues arise. These issues generally have to do with determining whether an observation should be considered pathological or whether it is culturally determined. This chapter assumes that there exist social class and cultural differences between clinician and patient. A word of explanation is needed. It is assumed that in most countries of the world, certainly in the United States, there exist different social and economic classes in the population and that clinicians because of their usually greater education, the socialization that accompanies it, and perhaps their own class origins may find themselves interacting with patients from a distinct social class. (It also occurs that some clinicians find themselves working with patients from a higher social class, but in this discussion the emphasis is on working with lower socioeconomic status persons.) Furthermore, many countries, even fairly homogenous ones, have groups of individuals of distinct ethnic/national origin. Certainly this is the case in the United States. Similarly, the clinician may be a member of this group but because of acculturation may now have moved apart from involvement (and understanding) of the group's customs, beliefs, and so on. This dissonance arising from class or cultural differences between clinicians and because of their presumably somewhat greater education and the socialization that accompanied it and perhaps class origins may find themselves interacting with patients from a distinct social class. Awareness of the degree of this sociocultural distance is important and may only be determined as the interview progresses. For example, the cultural distance between an American clinician and a foreign-born patient may be somewhat neutralized if they are from similar social classes (i.e., health professionals).

C. Value Differences Impinging the Interview

At least in the United States, most immigrant groups come from less developed countries or rural/small town communities where, what are called "traditional" values still have strong influence. These values are described as consisting of greater emphasis on family ties (as well as subservience of the individual to the will or benefit of the family or community), more strictly defined gender roles and beliefs in folk explanations for natural phenomena. (This is not an exhaustive list of the characteristics of traditional societies.) Not all minority/ethnic group members will subscribe to these values to the same degree; in fact, some may be in frank rebellion against these, may seem not to subscribe to them at all, or may appear completely acculturated to the 20th-century North American style (if such a thing can be characterized). The point is that, regardless of the apparent degree of acculturation, these values and their emotional and behavioral manifestation continue to effect many individuals at some level. The clinician should be aware of these traditional values (they tend to be similar around the world), particularly how they affect family relationships. For example, the notion of respect for elders and the sharp divisions between what men and women do are very noticeable, at least in the cultural group that I work with. For example, there may seem to be excessive concern about caring for a sick family member at home or keeping an elderly parent at home rather than in a nursing home. Or within the nuclear family, the husband may appear to rule, the wife seem subservient, and the children supposed to be very respectful of, or even dominated by, both. The clinician should not only be mindful and respectful of these attitudes but should exercise caution in interpreting them as problematic, although they can certainly be that. Interventions to attempt to change tradition-based values should also be considered with care.

Related to this area of traditional values is the important principle of autonomy of the individual in society and in health care. This principle is one of the basic principles underlying decision making in medical ethics. It has, however, been criticized as being in conflict with traditional values of decision making as guided equally if not more by family needs, wishes, and expectations. In the mental health arena we see this issue arising in terms of apparent excessive dependence on family. It is important that the clinician not be too quick to consider dependency as pathologic, although it can certainly be so. Too great an emphasis on pushing the patient to decide a personal issue on their own, to fulfill their own needs by declaring their freedom from a seemingly oppressive relationship, or to unburden themselves of a tiring obligation may push the person into more acute and perhaps unresolvable conflict, or worse still may not be a solution at all. One must be careful not to impose one's culturally determined notions about self-autonomy upon others. On a more practical level, this issue plays out in determining whether to speak to family and, whether to be directive with the patient about adherence to or need for therapy, and around the question of advice giving in psychotherapy.

IV. DIAGNOSIS AND FEEDBACK

During the course of the clinical interview the clinician strives to elicit, observe, and note the patient's psychopathology and personal customs while simultaneously placing these in a social and cultural context determined by the person's background and development. The elaboration of psychopathology is affected by social and cultural factors, as is the expression of personal concerns. Individual defenses and personality development of course also intervene.

Thus, one is commonly left attempting to determine whether a particular observed behavior should be considered predominantly pathological or cultural. Religious beliefs and behavior sometimes raise this issue, as do unique (folk) ways of describing causation of mental disorders.

This process of evaluating previously obtained information from the patient is done in large part when one "steps back" and objectifies the situation, context, and information that was just obtained. As mentioned previously, it is an ongoing process throughout the interview. The process of evaluating whether or not something is cultural versus pathological is done during this stepping-back process as well and is part of conducting a cultural formulation. A cultural formulation is the clinician's account of the individual's cultural and social reference group and ways in which the cultural context is relevant to clinical care. The essentials of the cultural formulation require the interviewer to be aware of the cultural identity of the individual, any cultural explanations the individual may have of their illness, cultural factors related to psychosocial functioning, the differences between the clinician and the individual with respect to social class and culture, and possible confounds in assessment and treatment stemming from the individual's cultural background (American Psychiatric Association, 1994).

A. How to Handle Religious Concerns

Many patient's religious beliefs and behavior may seem extreme or pathologic to the clinician. There was a time when modern psychologic thought considered almost all forms of religious expression a form of neurosis. Thankfully this time is past. However, now during a time of heightened spiritual yearning the issue assumes great relevance. Among some minority patients, rigidly held religious views are common and are not in and of themselves pathologic, although some fundamentalist Christian subgroups do have an antimedical, antipsychological bent. The leaders of some of these congregations may openly encourage troubled or mentally ill church members not only to seek cure in prayer but also to abandon all other nonprayer treatment. It is helpful to inquire of the patient whether these type of views are expressed by their church.

Some patients may have had personal religious experiences, especially contact with a divine presence that may markedly affect them and that seems puzzling to a clinician especially a skeptical clinician.

B. Case Vignette

Carlos is a 35-year-old Mexican American gay man with AIDS whose relationships to his parents were ambivalent and problematic and who, starting in adolescence, led a life of substance abuse, street existence, abusive/dependent relationships where he was "the wife", and menial if any employment. As his disease became unmistakably manifest, he sank into a profound, hopeless depression. While in this state and perhaps affected by the concomitant use of prescribed opioids he had a life-transforming religious experience. He saw, communicated with, and was comforted by the Holy Family. There followed a brief period of excitement, fervor, and agitation that was considered by some clinicians a psychotic state. Antipsychotic medication was given and his agitation subsided. His excitement and awe about the experience continued, and when I examined him what was most notable were his unrealistic judgment about his day-to-day existence and his intensely ambivalent feelings toward his mother, mostly rejecting and hostile. Several months passed and he continued to be deeply affected by his contact with the divine, becoming intensely prayerful and reflective. Equally striking was that he began to handle his relationships in a surprisingly mature and balanced way very unlike before.

This vignette illustrates not only the apparent psyche-transforming effect of an intense religious event, but also how a religious preoccupation can fluctuate, becoming pathologic in its all-absorbing effect at one moment and then settling into a more "normal," in fact, enhancing, tendency.

V. PROGNOSIS AND TREATMENT

A. Closing the Interview

During the course of the interview as the clinician has tried to discern what ails the patient, what life concerns are most preoccupying, and what diagnoses best fit, he or she is also trying to get an idea of how the patient puts together the various elements of the history to explain what is being felt and experienced. This latter process has been called determining the patient's explanatory model of illness. It is important not only for the clinician to make this determination in his or her own mind but also for this process to involve the patient so that a shared concept can occur. This can be done fairly directly by inquiring about what the patient believes is the matter or how the patient explains what is happening. Once an explanation has been elicited, it is also important to ask what the patient thinks will make it worse or better and what type of treatment is felt to be needed. In many cases the explanation offered and shared is fairly similar to that used by clinicians. In my experience, many of my patients' "explanatory models" are similar to what clinicians might call the stress-and-coping paradigm. Having this shared explanation makes the treatment easier to plan and carry out.

Difficulties with treatment compliance may be reduced, the explanation may be shared with the family if indicated, and, importantly, the patient may benefit psychologically knowing that there is a logic or reasonableness to the distressing and confusing feelings and perceptions that have been occurring and that this explanation is being shared with a helpful professional and a way out is possible. The shared model may still accommodate idiosyncratic elements or culturally determined aspects. For example, among the Mexican American patients that I see, some still adhere to folk notions and practices. Some of these are used at times as part of the explanation for their problems. A common such notion is that of the *mal puesto* or hex. The belief is that another person, usually because of jealousy, has placed a hex on the patient. The patient and/or family, if they believe in hexes, may believe that a hex was involved in the production of their illness while simultaneously attributing causality to psychologic factors and readily accepting a talking and/or medication treatment. There will of course be many patients who have limited insight about the underlying reasons for their distress, but I have found the stress/coping approach very useful with most patients. It is useful because it avoids the "chemical imbalance" explanation at one extreme as well as the sometimes threatening development/psychodynamic explanation at the other extreme. I often end an interview by trying to briefly describe to the patient how I understand the problem and a recommended treatment. Whenever possible I use the patient's own concepts or words as I give this feedback and I often describe treatment simply in terms of two parts: talk and/or medications. Most patients intuitively understand that talking helps, and in the setting where I work they are not surprised to be offered medication as well.

Finally, I usually err on the side of formality rather than informality in addressing my patients by referring to them as Mister, Miss, or Mrs. and using their last name. This practice is related to my sense that individuals from other cultural groups who are not very acculturated are often more traditional in their interpersonal relations.

VI. CONCLUSION

In closing I want to remind the reader of my caveat at the beginning of this chapter: that it is difficult, if not impossible, to learn sound clinical interviewing from a book.

My own most valuable learning about interviewing occurred by observing seasoned clinicians conduct an interview and then discuss why they did what they did. I have tried to present a few basic principles that may be helpful in all cross-cultural settings, but there are many more valuable principles and techniques. In addition, family interviewing and teaching of interviewing were not covered. I have also tried to describe an inner attitude that clinicians should strive to attain: one of self-awareness and examination, caring attention, and honest communication. The final arbiter of our skills, the patient, is always the first to sense our attitudes. This is why it is important to attend carefully to your inner state. I hope the lessons in this chapter will help some of us to be judged less harshly by our patients.

REFERENCES

American Psychiatric Association *Diagnostic and Statistical Manual of Mental Disorders,* 4th ed. Washington, DC: Author.

Martinez, C. (1982). Interviewing across cultural and language differences. In R. L. Leon (Ed.), *Psychiatric interviewing: A primer* (pp 66–73). New York: Elsevier North Holland, Inc.

Martinez, C. (1993). Psychiatric care of Mexican Americans. In A. C. Gaw (Ed.), *Culture, ethnicity, and mental illness* (pp 431–466), Washington, DC: American Psychiatric Press, Inc.

Martinez, C. (1994). Psychiatric treatment of Mexican Americans: A review. In C. Telles & M. Karno (Eds.), *Latino mental health: Current research and policy perspectives* (pp. 227–239). Los Angeles: Neuropsychiatric Institute, University of California.

Othmer, E., & Othmer, S. C. (1994). *The clinical interview using DSM-IV: Vol. 1. Fundamentals.* Washington, DC: American Psychiatric Press, Inc.

CHAPTER 16

The Mental Health of Culturally Diverse Elderly: Research and Clinical Issues

SANDRA A. BLACK

Center on Aging and Department of Internal Medicine
University of Texas Medical Branch
Galveston, Texas

One of the greatest challenges facing mental health care is the need for competent assessment and treatment of the growing numbers of older adults, particularly minority elders. The aging of the population and the increasing diversity of the elderly, coupled with increasingly limited health care resources, has resulted in the need for appropriate research as well as effective mental health services. This chapter provides an overview of mental disorders in minority elderly, as well as issues relevant to research and clinical issues. As in any population, it is important to remember that there is often as much diversity within groups as between groups, whether on the grounds of age, gender, social class, or culture. Effective treatment must address not only mental disorders, but also the factors influencing differences across ethnically and culturally diverse groups of older adults.

I. WHO ARE THE MINORITY ELDERLY?

Older adults constitute the fastest growing portion of the population, as well as the most heterogeneous. By 2000, over 35 million Americans will be aged 65 or older, comprising 13% of the total U.S. population. The numbers of older adults are projected to exceed 53 million by the year 2020 and over 80 million by the year 2050, constituting over 20% of the entire population (U.S. Bureau of the Census, 1997).

The largest contributing factors to the increasing numbers and diversity of older adults are race, ethnicity, and minority status. Over the next few decades African Americans, Hispanic Americans, Asian Americans, and Native Americans will comprise increasingly substantial proportions of the aging population (U.S. Bureau of the Census, 1997). In 2000, 16% of all older Americans, or an estimated 5.5 million individuals will be minority elderly. By 2025, the proportion of minority elderly is estimated to have increased to over 24% (14.6 million), and by 2050 over 33% (26.4 million) older adults will be from culturally diverse groups. African American elders are currently the largest group of minority elderly in the United States, numbering 2.6 million. This population is expected to double over the next few decades, with a projected number of 5.6 million by 2025. Hispanic Americans, currently the second largest group of minority elderly, will experience an even greater growth rate, from 1.9 million in 2000 to over 6.1 million by 2025. The older Asian American/Pacific Islander population is projected to increase from 780,000 to over 2.6 million, and the numbers of Native Americans, Eskimos, and Aleuts are expected to increase from 149,000 to over 320,000 during the same time period. As these populations grow, so will their mental health care needs.

II. FACTORS INFLUENCING THE MENTAL HEALTH OF ALL OLDER ADULTS

Mental disorders fall into two broad categories: primary mental disorders and disorders that result from physical illness, disability, loss, and other stresses (American Psychiatric Association, 1994). Older adults in general, and older minorities, in particular, are at elevated risk for secondary mental disorders, especially those resulting from physical illness and disability. In addition, many risk factors for mental disorders occur more frequently among older adults (Markides, 1986).

Advances in biopsychosocial research have identified a number of factors that influence the mental health of older adults in general (Engel, 1997). Social factors (such as gender, socioeconomic status, marital status, and social support), psychological factors (such as stress and bereavement), and biological factors (such as physical illness and disability) have been found associated with mental illness and disorders among older adults of all ethnocultural groups. Few of these factors are unique to the elderly; rather, the majority of these factors are the same as those that influence the mental health of younger adults. What differs is the distribution of risk factors among the elderly: older adults are more likely to be female, less educated, impoverished, widowed, and live in social isolation (Blazer, Burchett, Service, & George, 1991).

Older adults are also much more likely to suffer from physical illness and disability than younger adults. Over 75% of older adults have at least one chronic health condition, and 50% have multiple conditions (Fried & Wallace, 1992). Disability also increases with age: the rates of disability in everyday functioning range from 10% of adults aged 65–74 to over 50% of those aged 85 and older (Hobbs & Damon, 1996). Hearing and visual impairment are particularly common among older adults and are strongly associated with mental disorders.

It is imperative that any examination of the mental health of older adults include assessment of medical conditions, particularly chronic health conditions, and functional status. It has been well established that diseases such as cancer, heart disease, stroke, arthritis, diabetes, and kidney disease, conditions that become increasingly prevalent with age, have strong influence on the mental well-being of older adults (Black, Goodwin, & Markides, 1998; Finch, Ramsay, & Katona, 1992). For example, poor physical health has been found to be one of the strongest predictors of depression in the elderly, with the rates two to three times higher among physically ill elders than among healthy elders (Black, Markides, & Miller, 1998; Finch et al., 1992). Further evidence has demonstrated that the risk of depression is greater among older individuals with functional disability than among the healthier aged (Black, Markides, & Miller, 1998; Pennix et al., 1996).

III. FACTORS UNIQUE TO OLDER MINORITIES

Much of the variation in rates of mental disorders among minority elderly groups can also be attributed to the differential distribution of standard risk factors across ethnic groups: older minorities are more likely to be less educated, impoverished, living alone with fewer social contacts, and to be physically ill and disabled than mainstream elderly (Blazer, Burchett, et al., 1991). This can be misleading, however, in that variations across ethnic groups can be considerable. Hispanics, for example, are more likely to have greater social support available, and Asian Americans are less likely to be of low socioeconomic status (Paniagua, 1998).

More importantly, the profiles of disease and disability vary substantially across ethnic and cultural groups. Whereas the most prevalent chronic conditions among older non-Hispanic whites are cardiovascular disease, stroke, and cancer, African American elderly evidence elevated rates of hypertension and renal disease, and Hispanic elderly evidence increased rates of diabetes, cirrhosis, and gallbladder disease (Fried & Wallce, 1992; Markides, Rudkin, Angel, & Espino, 1997). Differences in disability rates are also apparent. In comparison to older non-Hispanic whites, for example, older African Americans and Hispanics appear to experience greater rates of disability, whereas the rates among older Asian Americans appear to be lower (Guralnik & Simonsick, 1993). Differences in other factors such as health behaviors associated with mental disorders are also evident. Older African American males, for example, have higher rates of smoking, and older Hispanics have elevated rates of obesity, behaviors that have both been linked to elevated rates of mental disorders (Berkman & Mullen, 1997).

Research has also identified certain factors unique to older minorities that influence the development of mental disorders among the elderly. Many groups of minority elderly are largely composed of immigrants: almost 50% of older Hispanic Americans and 66% of older Asian Americans, for example, are immigrants (Hobbs & Damon, 1996). Studies on immigration have demonstrated both positive and negative effects regarding health and mental health. Overall, immigrants tend to be healthier than nonimmigrants, referred to as the healthy immigrant effect or migration selection (Moscicki, Locke, Rae, & Boyd, 1989). Immigration is also, however, a stressful event with lasting consequences such as reduced resources and social support. A recent study of older Mexican Americans (Black, Markides, & Miller, 1998) demonstrated that older male immigrants reflect the healthy immigrant effect in that they experience lower rates of depressive symptoms than males born in the United States. Among older females, however, immigrants experienced considerably higher rates of depressive symptoms than the U.S. born. Furthermore, both males and females who were recent immigrants (previous 5 years) evidenced the highest rates of depressive symptoms. It has been postulated that females and recent immigrants do not reflect the healthy immigrant effect, because they came to the United States at later ages and for different reasons than male immigrants, whereas the majority of older males migrated to the United States in childhood or early adulthood, the majority of females migrated in later life to be with spouses or adult children (Black, Markides, & Miller, 1998).

Acculturation, the process of adaptation and adjustment to the dominant society, as well as linguistic and cultural barriers, have also been found to play substantial roles in the mental health of older minorities. Low acculturation has been found to be associated with increased rates of cognitive impairment, depression, and anxiety (Griffin, 1983; Henderson, 1996; Masten, Penland, & Nayani, 1994). The process of acculturation is recognized as stressful, a primary factor in the adjustment of immigrants to their new society (Moyerman & Forman, 1992). Furthermore, the acculturating individual can become caught between the two cultures, attempting to maintain the behaviors of the traditional culture while adapting to the new culture (Paniagua, 1998).

Other cultural factors such as social support and family structure, religion, integration of belief systems, cultural norms, and the expression of distress have been recognized as having dramatic influence on the mental well-being of older adults. The level of adaptation or ease of functioning in the dominant society has been found to influence the mental health of predominantly nonimmigrant minorities such as African Americans and Native Americans, as well as Hispanic Americans and Asian Americans (Gutman, 1992). Beliefs systems also influence the mental health, as well as the assessment, of older minorities. Among the Chinese, for example, cognitive impairment and dementia are much less likely to be viewed as illness than as a normal part of aging (Elliott, DiMinno, Lam, & Tu, 1996), whereas the Japanese are more likely to view such a condition as a stigma (Tempo & Saito, 1996). In either case, older individuals, as well as their families, are less likely to seek assessment or treatment.

IV. SPECIAL PROBLEMS FOR RESEARCH AND CLINICAL CARE

A. WITHIN-GROUP VARIATION

Differences in both the standard and cultural factors result in considerable variation in the rates and manifestation of mental disorders across ethnocultural groups, and can present special problems both for research and clinical care. Foremost among these issues is the problem of collapsing different groups into one ethnic category. Puerto Ricans, Cuban Americans, Mexican Americans, and other groups with roots in Latin America are all classified as Hispanic Americans. Although they share a common language, they vary greatly in terms of history, culture, and immigration experience, which is reflected in physical and mental health status. Asian Americans and Pacific Islanders comprise an even more varied category, with even greater variation in terms of language, history, and health status. Native Americans, Eskimos, and Aleut include over 500 federally recognized nations and tribes from very different geographic regions (Kramer, 1996). Even those living in the same region of the United States are widely different in terms of language, belief systems, and health status (e.g., the Navajo, Hopi, and Puma Indians of the Southwest). African Americans are also not a homogeneous group, with distinct variations evident between Jamaicans, Haitians, recent African immigrants, and the majority of African Americans who are descendants of slaves (Paniagua, 1998).

B. BETWEEN-GROUP VARIATION

These within-group differences can present problems in sampling minority elderly for research. Research into the mental health and mental health needs of diverse elders is a relatively new phenomena: African Americans began being systematically studied in the 1950s, Hispanic Americans in the 1970s and 1980s, Asian Americans and Native American studies began even more recently (Markides, 1986). Furthermore, large-scale studies that have included minority elderly, such as the Duke and Hispanic Established Populations for the Epidemiologic Study of the Elderly surveys, have as yet only been conducted among African American and Hispanic American elders (Cornoni-Huntley et al., 1992; Markides et al., 1997).

C. EQUIVALENCE ISSUES

More critical issues include achieving equivalence in measurement across groups and the development of standard assessment instruments that are not biased when applied to older minorities. Equivalence in measurement can be assessed in a number of ways (Paniagua, 1998), including content equivalence (are items or criteria equally relevant across cultures); semantic equivalence (is the meaning of items the same across translations); technical equivalence (is the method of assessment comparable across cultural groups); criterion equivalence (would the interpretation of measures remain the same when compared to the norm for each culture); and conceptual equivalence (are the same theoretical constructs being measured across cultures). In reality, no culture-free measurements or instruments exist (Paniagua, 1998). The use of standard instruments is important, however, because they provide a common language for both assessment and treatment, enabling comparisons to be made (see Arnold & Matus, chapter 7, this volume). Table I provides a listing of standardized assessment instruments for cognitive status, depression, and anxiety, that are commonly employed in both research and clinical settings.

Assessment of cognitive status and dementia provides the clearest example of the need for equivalence and the potential problems that can occur when attention is not paid to noncognitive factors. The standardized assessment of

TABLE I   Selected Standardized Screening and Assessment Instruments Used with Older Adults

Disorder assessed	Instrument	Source
Cognitive status/ dementia	Mini-Mental State Examination (MMSE)	Folstein, Folstein, & McHugh, 1975
	Blessed Information-Concentration-Attention Test	Blessed, Tomlinson & Roth, 1968
	Wechsler Adult Intelligence Scale-II (WAIS-III)	Wechsler, 1981
	Wechsler Memory Scale-III (WMS-III)	Wechsler, 1987
	Short Portable Mental Status Questionnaire (SPMSQ)	Pfeiffer, 1975
	Washington University Battery	Storandt et al., 1984
	Dementia Rating Scale	Mattis, 1989
Delirium	Delirium Symptom Interview	Levkoff, 1991
	Delirium Rating Scale	Rockwood, Goodman, Flynn, & Stolee, 1996
Depression/ other mood disorders	Center for Epidemiologic Study of Depression (CES-D)	Radloff, 1977
	Hamilton Depression Rating Scale	Hamilton, 1969
	Geriatric Depression Scale (GDS)	Yesavage, Brink, Rose, & Lum, 1983
	Beck Depression Scale	Beck, Ward, Medelson, Mock, & Erbaugh, 1961
	Diagnostic Interview Schedule (DIS)	Robins, Helzer, Croughan, & Ratcliff, 1981
	Composite International Diagnostic Instrument (CIDI)	Robins et al., 1988
Anxiety	Zung Self-Administered Anxiety Scale	Zung, 1971
	Hamilton Anxiety Rating Scale	Hamilton, 1959
	Beck Anxiety Rating Scale	Beck, Epstein, Brown, & Steer, 1988
	Hopkins Symptoms Checklist	Derogatis, 1975
	Diagnostic Interview Schedule (DIS)	Robins, Helzer, Croughan, & Ratcliff, 1981
	Composite International Diagnostic Instrument (CIDI)	Robins et al., 1988

cognitive status includes not only level of consciousness and focal cognitive functions, but thought processes, memory, language facility, attention, judgement, and abstraction, as well. These factors are all strongly associated with language, education, and level of acculturation, characteristics that vary widely across ethnic groups, particularly minorities. If variation in these noncognitive variables are not taken into account, minority elders generally perform more poorly than mainstream elderly. An example can be found in data from a tri-ethnic study of 600 adults aged 75 and older living in Galveston County, Texas (Goodwin, Jakobi, Black, & DiNuzzo, 1998). Using the Pfieffer Rating Scale, the rates of cognitive impairment (when not controlling for noncognitive factors) were over 20% among older African Americans and Hispanic Americans, in comparison to 5% of older non-Hispanic whites. When adjustment was made for the level of education, however, the rates are much more comparable: among individuals with less than 8 years of education, rates of impairment ranged from 18% among non-Hispanic whites to 23% of Hispanics and 26% of African Americans, whereas among those with 12 or more years of education, rates ranged from 2% to 6%.

D. STANDARDIZING DISABILITY DEFINITIONS ACROSS DIFFERENT CULTURAL GROUPS

Another critical issue is the absence of a uniform definition of disability among older adults, which also impacts elderly adults from diverse cultural groups. The standard assessment of disability generally includes identification of the impaired ability to perform daily tasks, such as those measured by Activities of Daily Living (AOLs) (self-care skills including walking, bathing, eating, grooming, dressing, transferring from bed to chair, and toileting) and Instrumental Activities of Daily Living (IADLs) (skills necessary for independent living including using a telephone, managing money, taking medications, doing heavy and light houework, driving a car, shopping, preparing meals, and walking some distance), as well as sensory impairments (such as hearing and vision loss), social dysfunction, and cognitive impairment (Guralnik & Simonsick, 1993). One problem that is often encountered with this approach is that some of these tasks may not be relevant for many older minorities. Older women, for example, are often less likely to drive a car or manage finances, and older men often have never had to shop for food or prepare meals for themselves. Indeed, in many cultures, many of these tasks are more closely bound to gender roles than is typical in mainstream America. Furthermore, older minorities often receive assistance from spouses and other family members (e.g., with meal preparation, driving, and housework) that is considered a normal part of family life and not perceived as an impairment in ability on the part of the older individual. In assessing mental illness in older adults, these issues can cloud the assessment of true and meaningful disability versus cultural norms for behavior.

V. CRITICAL MENTAL DISORDERS AMONG OLDER ADULTS

A. DEMENTIA, DELIRIUM, AND COGNITIVE STATUS

Overall, reported rates for dementia among older adults have ranged from 4% to 7% (Pfeffer, Afifi, & Chance, 1987), although more recent studies have estimated rates as high as 10% (Evans et al., 1989). The rates increase with age, with estimates of 3–5% among adults aged 65 to 74, 18–20% of those aged 75–84, and as many as 50% of those aged 85 and older. It has been estimated that as much as 90% of dementia is of the Alzheimer's type, with another 10% accounted for by vascular dementia (Evans et al., 1989; Tatemichi, Sacktor, & Mayeau, 1994). In comparison to non-Hispanic whites, however, the rates of vascular dementia among African Americans, Chinese Americans, and Japanese Americans, appear to be 2–4 times higher, as a result of higher rates of conditions such as hypertension, whereas the rates among Hispanics are lower, a result of lower rates of cardiovascular disease (Hasegawa, Homma, & Imai, 1985).

Based on the results of screening instruments such as the Mini-Mental State Examination (MMSE; Folstein, Folstein, & McHugh, 1975), the rates of cognitive impairment have been reported to be twice as high among African Americans and Hispanic Americans as among non-Hispanic whites (Black et al., 1999; Escobar et al., 1986). The rates among Native Americans may be considerably lower, although data are available from only a very limited number of studies (Hendrie et al., 1993). Using data from the five Epidemiologic Catchment Area (ECA) study sites, for example, George, Landerman, Blazer, and Anthony (1991) reported unadjusted rates of cognitive impairment to be 42% for African Americans and 29% of Hispanic Americans, in comparison to 12% for non-Hispanic whites. The rate differences found in the ECA data were much less dramatic for severe impairment (8% for African Americans and 3% for Hispanics, compared to 2% for non-Hispanic whites), than the rate differences for mild impairment (33% for African Americans, 26% for Hispanics, and 10% for non-Hispanic whites).

The issue then arises as to whether these are true differences, or inaccurate reflections of impairment resulting from sociodemographic and cultural bias, particularly confounded by level of education and adaptation into the mainstream society. On the basis of education alone, the validity of assessments among older minorities becomes questionable. A substantial amount of convincing research has demonstrated that older individuals who are poorly educated or illiterate perform poorly on screening instruments such as the MMSE

(Taussig, Henderson, & Mack, 1996), and will score like brain-damaged individuals on neuropsychological tests (Ardila, Roselli, & Puente, 1994).

B. MOOD DISORDERS

Estimates of the rates of depression and other mood disorders among older adults vary substantially, primarily as a result of different assessment methods. The two foremost methods of assessment are the use of (a) diagnostic interview schedules, such as the Diagnostic Interview Schedule (DIS; Robins, Helzer, Croughan, & Ratcliff, 1981), and the Composite International Diagnostic Interview (CIDI; Robins, et al., 1988), and (b) symptom rating scales, such as the Center for Epidemiologic Studies of Depression (CES-D; Radloff, 1977) and the Geriatric Depression Scale (GDS; Yesavage, Brink, Rose, & Lum, 1983). Comparing the results of the two methods reveals paradoxical differences: The rates of diagnosed disorders appear to decline with age after age 60, whereas the rates of depressive symptoms appear to increase (Newman, 1989).

In studies employing diagnostic interview schedules, older African Americans, Hispanic Americans, and Native Americans appear to experience higher rates of depression than older non-Hispanic whites, whereas the rates of older Asian Americans are more comparable. The ECA data indicate that the lifetime rates of any affective disorder of 1.9% for older African Americans and 4.3% for older Hispanic Americans, in comparison to 1.5% for older non-Hispanic whites (Weissman, Bruce, Leaf, Florio, & Holzer, 1991). Within-group variation can be substantial, however: data from the Hispanic Health and Nutrition Examination Survey indicates lifetime rates of major depressive epidose of 3.9% among older Cuban Americans and 4.2% among older Mexican Americans, whereas the rate among older Puerto Ricans was 8.9% (Moscicki, Rae, Regier, & Locke, 1987).

Studies employing symptom checklists have also found much more elevated rates among older minorities. The rates of high levels of depressive symptoms measured with the CES-D, for example, have been reported to be as high as 22% older African Americans (Jones-Webb & Snowden, 1993), and 26% among older Mexican Americans (Black, Markides, & Miller, 1998), in contrast to rates ranging from 9% to 16% among older non-Hispanic whites (Berkman et al., 1986; Blazer, Burchett, et al., 1991). Ethnic group variation is also evident, with rates ranging from 11% among older Cuban Americans to 28% among older Puerto Ricans (Black, Markides, & Miller, 1998; Moscicki et al., 1987). Among the less studied minorities, an estimated rate of 19% has been reported for older Asians and Pacific Islanders; however, intergroup variation was substantial, with rates highest among older Koreans, followed by Filipinos, Japanese, and

Chinese (Kuo, 1984), also a more recent study reported a rate of 24% for older Chinese (Ying, 1988). A rate of 32% has been reported for older Native Americans (Manson, 1995).

C. ANXIETY DISORDERS AND OTHER MENTAL DISORDERS

Available data on the rates of anxiety, substance abuse, schizophrenia, and other mental disorders among minority elders is more limited. Using data from the ECA, Eaton, Dryman, and Weissman (1991) report lifetime rates of panic disorder of less than 1% among older African Americans and between 1% and 3% among older Hispanics, rates that are not substantially different from those found among older non-Hispanic whites. The lifetime rates of phobic disorder, however, were found to be considerably higher among older African Americans (15% to 24%) than among older Hispanics (5% to 10%) or non-Hispanic whites (7% to 13%). Blazer, Hughes, George, Swartz, and Boyer (1991) reported that the rates of generalized anxiety disorder were 1% to 3% among older African Americans, and less than 1% among older Hispanics, rates comparable to those reported for older non-Hispanic whites. In a recent study of older Asian Americans, Harada and Kim (1995) reported rates of anxiety disorders ranging from 5% among the Japanese elderly to 13% among older Vietnamese, rates of psychotic disorders ranging from 13% among older Vietnamese to 29% of older, Japanese, and rates of adjustment disorders ranging from 15% among older Filipinos to 20% among older Chinese.

The rates of alcohol abuse and dependency are reportedly higher in older minorities than non-Hispanic whites, particularly among older males. Data from the ECA (Helzer, Burnam, & McEvay, 1991), for example, indicate lifetime rates of 17.8% among older African American males, in comparison to 10.8% among older Hispanics and 10.4% among non-Hispanic whites. Both older African American and Hispanic males, however, are reported to have higher current rates of alcoholism (2.9% and 6.6%, respectively) than non-Hispanic white males (2.8%). The rates are highest, however, among older Native Americans, particularly older males. The rates of alcohol abuse and dependency, as well as alcoholism are generally much lower in all groups of older females. The rates of drug abuse and dependency are very low among virtually all older adults, although they constitute a serious problem (Gaw, 1993). Both alcohol and drug abuse, however, may be underecognized in older adults, due to symptoms that may be attributed to medical conditions or to the reluctance of clinicians to identify such problems in older adults (Zarit & Zarit, 1998).

VI. SUMMARY

Culture and ethnicity are powerful forces in our society, influencing the lives and the health of all individuals, including older adults. While it is clear that ethnicity, culture, and minority status are associated with very real differences in the rates of mental disorders among the elderly, it is also clear that these variations are the result of differences in socioeconomic status, gender, age, and social class, coupled with cultural differences. These factors can compound diagnostic formulation and complicate the delivery of mental health services to older minorities. Many mental disorders that occur among the elderly can be effectively treated, however, and even in the case of disorders such as dementia, for which treatment is lacking, understanding and culturally appropriate intervention can improve the functioning of older adults and their families.

REFERENCES

American Psychiatric Association. (1994). *Diagnostic and statistical manual of mental disorders (4th ed. Revised) (DSM-IV).* Washington, DC: American Psychiatric Association.

Ardila, A., Rosselli, M., & Puente, A. E. (1994). *Neuropsychological evaluation of the Spanish speaker.* Plenum Press: New York.

Beck, A. T., Epstein, N., Brown, G., & Steer, R. (1988). An inventory for measuring clinical anxiety: Psychometric properties. *Journal of Consulting and Clinical Psychology, 56,* 893–897.

Beck, A. T., Ward, C. H., Mendelson, M., Mock, J., & Erbaugh, J. (1961). An inventory measuring depression. *Archives of General Psychiatry, 4,* 561–571.

Berkman, L. F., Berkman, C. S., Kasl, S., Freeman, D. H., Leo, L., Ostfeld, A. M., Cornoni-Huntley, J., & Brody, J. (1986). Depressive symptoms in relation to physical health and functioning in the elderly. *American Journal of Epidemiology, 124,* 372–388.

Berkman, L. F., & Mullen, J. M. (1997). How health behaviors and the social environment contribute to health differences between black and white older Americans. In L. Martin & B. Soldo (Eds.), *Racial and ethnic differences in the health of older Americans* (pp. 163–182). Washington, National Academy Press.

Black, S. A., Espino, D. V., Mahurin, R., Lichtenstein, M., Hazuda, H., Fabrizio, D., Ray, L. A., & Markides, K. S. (1999). The influence of non-cognitive factors on the Mini-Mental State Exam in older Mexican Americans: Findings from the Hispanic EPESE. *Journal of Clinical Epidemiology, 52,* 1095–1102.

Black, S. A., Goodwin, J. S., & Markides, K. S. (1998). The association between chronic diseases and depressive symptomatology in older Mexican Americans. *Journals of Gerontology: Medical Science, 53A,* M188–M194.

Black, S. A., Markides, K. S., & Miller, T. Q. (1998). Correlates of depressive symptomatology among older community-dwelling Mexican Americans: The Hispanic EPESE. *Journals of Gerontology: Social Science, 53B,* S198–S208.

Blazer, D., Burchett, B., Service, C., & George, L. K. (1991). The association of age and depression among the elderly: An epidemiologic exploration. *Journals of Gerontology, 46,* M210–M215.

Blazer, D., Hughes, D., George, L. K., Swartz, M., & Boyer, R. (1991). Generalized anxiety disorder. In L. N. Robins & D. A. Regier (Eds.), *Psychiatric disorders in America: The Epidemiologic Catchment Area Study* (pp. 180–203). New York: Free Press.

Blessed, G., Tomlinson, B. E., & Roth, M. (1968). The association between quantitative measures of dementia and of senile change in the cerebral grey matter of elderly subjects. *British Journal of Psychiatry, 114*, 797–811.

Cornoni-Huntley, J., Blazer, D. G., Lafferty, M. E., Everett, D. F., Brock, D. B., Farmer, M. E. (Eds.), (1990). *Established populations for epidemiologic studies of the elderly, Volume II.* USDHHS: National Institute on Aging.

Derogatis, L. R. (1975). *The SCL-90-R.* Baltimore: Clinical Psychometric Research.

Eaton, W. W., Dryman, A., & Wiessman, M. M. (1991). Panic and phobia. In L. N. Robins & D. A. Regier (Eds.), *Psychiatric disorders in America: The Epidemiologic Catchment Area Study.* New York: Free Press.

Elliott, K. S., DiMinno, M., Lam, D., & Tu, A. M. (1996). Working with Chinese families in the context of dementia. In G. Yeo & D. Gallagher-Thompson D. (Eds.), *Ethnicity and the Dementias.* Washington, DC: Taylor & Francis.

Engel, G. L. (1997). From biomedical to biopsychosocial: Being specific in the human domain. *Psychosomatics, 38*, 521–528.

Escobar, J., Burnam, A., Karno, M., Forsythe, A., Landsverk, J., & Golding, J. M. (1986). Use of the Mini-Mental Status Examination (MMSE) in a community population of mixed ethnicity: Cultural and linguistic artifacts. *Journal of Nervous and Mental Disease, 174*, 607–614.

Evans, D. A., Funkenstein, H. H., Albert, M. S., Scherr, P. A., Cook, N. R., Chown, M. J., Hebert, L. E., Hennekens, C. H., & Taylor, J. O. (1989). Prevalence of Alzheimer's disease in a community population of older persons: Higher than previously reported. *JAMA, 262*, 2551–2556.

Finch, E., Ramsay, R., & Katona, C. (1992). Depression and physical illness in the elderly. *Clinics in Geriatric Medicine, 8*, 275–287.

Fried, L. P., & Wallace, R. B. (1992). The complexity of chronic illness in the elderly: From clinic to community. In R. B. Wallace & R. F. Woolson (Eds.), *The epidemiologic study of the elderly* (pp. 10–19). New York: Oxford Press.

Folstein, M. F., Folstein, S. E., & McHugh, P. R. (1975). "Mini-Mental State." A practical method for grading the cognitive state of patient for the clinician. *Journal of Psychiatric Research, 12*, 189–98.

Gaw, A. C. (1993). *Culture, ethnicity, and mental illness.* American Psychiatric Press: Washington, DC.

George, L. K., Landerman, R., Blazer, D. G., & Anthony, J. C. (1991). Cognitive Impairment. In L. N. Robins & D. A. Regier (Eds.), *Psychiatric disorders in America: The Epidemiologic Catchment Area Study.* New York: Free Press.

Goodwin, J. S., Jakobi, P. L., Black, S. A., & DiNuzzo, A. R. (1998). *A Health and Social Services needs assessment of community-dwelling Galveston County residents aged 75 and over.* Galveston, Texas: UTMB Center on Aging.

Griffin, J. (1983). Relationship between acculturation and psychologic impairment in adult Mexican Americans. *Hispanic Journal of Behavioral Sciences, 5*, 431–459.

Guralnik, J. M., & Simonsick, E. M. (1993). Physical disability in older Americans. *Journals of Gerontology, 48 (Special Issue)*, 3–10.

Gutman, D. (1992). Culture and mental health in later life revisited. In J. E. Birren, R. B. Sloane, & G. D. Cohen (Eds.), *Handbook of mental health and aging.* San Diego: Academic Press. pp. 75–97.

Hamilton, M. (1959). The assessment of anxiety states by rating. *British Journal of Psychiatry, 32*, 50–55.

Hamilton, M. (1969). Standardized assessment and recording of depressive symptoms. *Psychiatria, Neurologia, Neurochirurgia, 72*, 201–205.

Harada, N. D., & Kim, L. S. (1995). Use of mental health services by older Asian and Pacific Islander Americans. In D. K. Padgett (Ed.), *Handbook on ethnicity, aging, and mental health* (pp. 185–202). Westport: Greenwood Press.

Hasagawa, K., Homma, A., & Imai, Y. (1985). An epidemiologic study of age-related dementia in the community. *International Journal of Geriatric Psychiatry, 1,* 45–55.

Helzer, J. E., Burnam, A., & McEvay, L. T. (1991). Alcohol abuse and dependence. In L. N. Robins & D. A. Regier (Eds.), *Psychiatric disorders in America: The Epidemiologic Catchment Area Study.* New York: Free Press.

Henderson, J. N. (1996). Cultural dynamics of dementia in a Cuban and Puerto Rican population in the United States. In G. Yeo & D. Gallagher-Thompson D. (Eds), *Ethnicity and the dementias* (pp. 153–166). Washington DC: Taylor & Francis.

Hendrie, H. C., Hall, K. S., Pillay, N., Rodgers, D., Prince, C., Norton, J., Brittain, H. M., Nath, A., Blue, A., Kaufert, J., Shelton, P., Postl, B., & Osuntokun, B. O. (1993). Alzheimer's disease is rare in Cree. *International Psychogeriatrics, 5,* 5–14.

Hobbs, F. B., & Damon, B. L. (1996). *65+ in the United States. Current Population Report P23-190.* Washington, DC: U.S. Government Printing Office.

Jones-Webb, R. J., & Snowden, L. R. (1993). Symptoms of depression among Blacks and Whites. *American Journal of Public Health, 83,* 240–244.

Kramer, B. J. (1996). Dementia and American Indian Populations. In G. Yeo & D. Gallagher-Thompson (Eds), *Ethnicity and the dementias* (pp. 175–181). Washington DC: Taylor & Francis.

Kuo, W. H. (1984). Prevalence of depression among Asian Americans. *Journal of Nervous and Mental Disease, 172,* 449–457.

Levkoff, S., Liptzin, B., Cleary, P., Reilly, C. H., & Evans, D. (1991). Review of research instruments and techniques used to detect delirium. *International Psychogeriatrics, 3,* 253–271.

Manson, S. M. (1995). Mental health status and needs of the American Indian and Alaskan native elderly. In D. K. Padgett (Ed.), *Handbook of ethnicity, aging, and mental health* (pp. 132–141). Westport: Greenwood Press.

Markides, K. S. (1986). Minority status, aging, and mental health. *International Journal of Aging and Human Development, 23,* 285–300.

Markides, K. S., Rudkin, L., Angel, R. J., & Espino, D. V. (1997). Health status of Hispanic elderly in the United States. In L. Martin & B. Soldo (Eds.), *Racial and ethnic differences in the health of older Americans* (pp. 285–300). Washington, DC: National Academy Press.

Masten, W. G., Penland, E. A., & Nayani, E. J. (1994). Depression and acculturation in Mexican American women. *Psychological Reports, 75,* 1499–1503.

Mattis, S. (1989). *Dementia Rating Scale.* Odessa, Florida: Psychological Assessment Resources.

Moscicki, E. K., Locke, B. Z., Rae, D. S., & Boyd, J. H. (1989). Depressive symptoms among Mexican Americans: The Hispanic Health & Nutrition Examination Survey. *American Journal of Epidemiology, 130,* 348–360.

Moscicki, E. K., Rae, D. S., Regier, D. A., & Locke, B. Z. (1987). The Hispanic Health and Nutrition Examination Survey: Depression among Mexican Americans, Cuban Americans, and Puerto Ricans. In M. Gaviria M & J. D. Arana (Eds.), *Health and behavior: Research agenda for Hispanics* (pp. 145–159). Chicago: University of Illinois.

Moyerman, D. R., & Forman, B. (1992). Acculturation and adjustment: A meta-analytic study. *Hispanic Journal of Behavioral Sciences, 14,* 63–200.

Newman, J. P. (1989). Aging and depression. *Psychology and Aging, 4,* 150–165.

Paniagua, F. A. (1998). *Assessing and treating culturally diverse clients: A practical guide (2nd ed.).* Sage: Thousand Oaks.

Pennix, B. W. J. H., Beekman, A. T. F., Ormel, J., Kriegsman, D. M. W., Boeke, A. J. P., van Eijk, J.Th.M., & Deeg, D. J. H. (1996). Psychological status among elderly people with chronic diseases: Does type of disease play a part? *Journal of Psychosomatic Research, 40,* 521–534.

Pfeffer, R. I., Afifi, A. A., & Chance, J. M. (1987). Prevalence of Alzheimer's disease in a retirement community. *American Journal of Epidemiology, 125,* 420–436.

Pfeiffer, E. (1975). A short portable mental status questionnaire for the assessment of organic brain deficit in elderly patients. *Journal of the American Geriatrics Society, 23,* 433–439.

Radloff, L. S. (1977). The CES-D Scale: A self-report depression scale for research in the general population. *Journal of Applied Psychology and Measurement, 1,* 385–401.

Robins, L. N., Helzer, J. E., Croughan, J., & Ratcliff, K. (1981). National Institute of Mental Health Diagnostic Interview Schedule. *Archives of General Psychiatry, 38,* 381–389.

Robins, L. N., Wing, J., Wittchen, H. U., Helzer, J. E., Babor, T. F., Burke, J., Farmer, A., Jablenski, A., Pickens, R., Rieger, D. A., Satorius, N., & Towle, L. H. (1988). The Composite International Diagnostic Interview: An epidemiologic instrument suitable for use in conjunction with different diagnostic systems and in different cultures. *Archives of General Psychiatry, 45,* 1069–1077.

Rockwood, K., Goodman, J., Flynn, M., & Stolee, P. (1996). Cross-validation of the delirium rating scale in older patients. *Journal of the American Geriatrics Society, 44,* 839–842.

Storandt, M., Botwinick, J., Danziger, W. L., Berg, L., & Hughes, C. P. (1984). Psychometric differentiation of mild senile dementia of the Alzheimer's type. *Archives of Neurology, 41,* 497–499.

Tatemichi, T. K., Sacktor, N., & Mayeau, R. (1994). Dementia associated with cerebrovascular disease, other degenerative disease, and metabolic disorders. In R. D. Terry, R. Katzman, & K. L. Bicks (Eds.), *Alzheimer's disease* (pp. 123–166). New York: Raven Press.

Taussig, I. M., Henderson, V. W., & Mack, W. (1996). Concurrent validity of Spanish-language versions of the Mini-Mental State Examination, Mental Status Questionnaire, Information-Memory-Concentration Test, and Orientation-Memory-Concentration Test: Alzheimer's disease patients and non-demented elderly subjects. *Journal of International Neuropsychological Society, 2,* 286–298.

Tempo, P. M., & Saito, A. (1996). Techniques of working with Japanese American families. In G. Yeo & D. Gallagher-Thompson (Eds), *Ethnicity and the dementias.* Washington, DC: Taylor & Francis.

U.S. Bureau of the Census. *Statistical Abstract of the United States, 1997.* Washington, DC: U.S. Government Printing Office.

Weissman, M. M., Bruce, M. L., Leaf, P. J., Florio, L. P., & Holzer, C. (1991). Affective disorders. In L. N. Robins & D. A. Regier (Eds.), *Psychiatric disorders in America: The Epidemiologic Catchment Area Study.* New York: Free Press.

Wechsler, D. (1981). *Wechsler Adult Intelligence Scale—Revised.* New York: The Psychological Corporation.

Wechsler, D. (1987). *Wechsler Memory Scale—Revised.* San Antonio: The Psychological Corporation.

Yesavage, J. A., Brink, T., Rose, T. L., & Lum, O. (1983). Development and validation of the Geriatric Depression Scale: A preliminary report. *Journal of Psychiatric Research, 17,* 37–49.

Ying, Y. W. (1988). Depressive symptomatology among Chinese-Americans as measured by the CES-D. *Journal of Clinical Psychology, 44,* 739–746.

Zarit, S. H., & Zarit, J. M. (1998). *Mental disorders in older adults.* New York: Guilford Press.

Zung, W. W. K. (1971). A rating instrument for anxiety disorders. *Psychosomatics, 12,* 371–379.

CHAPTER 17

Race, Ethnicity, and the Epidemiology of Mental Disorders in Adults

CHARLES E. HOLZER III

Department of Psychiatry and Behavioral Sciences
University of Texas Medical Branch
Galveston, Texas

SAM COPELAND

School of Social Work
Stephen F. Austin State University
Nacogdoches, Texas

I. INTRODUCTION

The relationship of race and ethnicity to the etiology and prevalence of mental disorders has been of great interest historically and in the present. From the late 1800s through the middle of the 20th century, both race and ethnicity, usually identified by national origin, were largely seen as constitutional influences on mental health. As we come forward to the present, studies of race and ethnicity have become increasingly linked to the study of ethnic minorities, and particularly those designated as underserved by the mental health services system. In examining race and ethnicity, we will attempt to examine some of the earlier ideas that link national origins and particularly immigration experience to the processes that operate within American society. It is clear that neither race nor ethnicity operate solely or even substantially as constitutional factors in the formation of mental disorders.

Thus any discussion of race or ethnicity with regard to most mental disorders in the United States should include a discussion of culture and the historical

Handbook of Multicultural Mental Health: Assessment and Treatment of Diverse Populations
Copyright © 2000 by Academic Press. All rights of reproduction in any form reserved.

experiences of peoples who have come freely or have been brought to this country. Such a discussion should also take into account the range of current experiences, such as acculturation, socioeconomic status, poverty, discrimination, and minority status as well as many individual experiences that may or may not be influenced by group membership. Among these is the availability of treatment for those becoming ill. Thus the prevalence of disorder in a group is a result of many different influences that can only partially be attributed to the group identity. This ambiguity has resulted in many conflicting results and the need for a great deal of caution in interpreting any proffered finding of ethnic or racial differences. We will also see that the results of ethnic comparisons are strongly influenced by research methodologies that have variously relied on treatment records or direct assessments in communities, on sampling methods that compare groups of similar or vastly differing social and economic backgrounds, and on assessment methodologies that may or may not take into account the culture and beliefs about mental health of those being surveyed.

In this chapter we will generally conform to a convention that substitutes current usage for designation of ethnic or racial groups. Thus we will generally refer to persons of African descent as African American or black, although historically studies have used different conventions. The term Hispanic will encompass multiple Spanish-speaking groups, sometimes called Chicano or La Raza, unless the particular studies designate persons of Mexican, Puerto Rican, or Cuban heritage, usually with "-American" appended to differentiate residents of the United States from nationals of the various countries of origin. Asian American will be used as the generic term to refer to persons with cultural origins in Asia, although the vast differences among countries in culture and national origin must be recognized. Native American will be used to include the many tribes of American Indians as well as Aleut, Inuit, and Eskimo peoples. The largest group of persons in the United States, those generally of Caucasian race and European origin will be designated as White or Anglo because European American is too cumbersome and fails to convey a sense of the degree to which the "melting pot" versus "salad bowl" views of these groups apply. Apologies are made in advance to all those who would not choose to be categorized in such a limited scheme, which divides humanity excessively while not capturing the richness of diversity.

A. IMMIGRATION

One of the recurrent themes in the examination of ethnic groups is that of immigration. The most visible ethnic group is frequently the last to arrive. In his seminal volume, *Emigration and Insanity,* Ödegaard (1932) describes the history of concerns with regard to mental health and immigration. From the earliest days of the American colonies, concern was expressed to keep out persons who were infirm and thus could become a public burden. In the late 1800s it was documented that along with criminals and paupers, the insane were being sent from various European and non-European countries. In 1882, the first federal immigration act banned entry to lunatics and idiots, with extensions in 1907 and 1917 adding more disorders and requiring an examination determining the mental condition of all arriving immigrants. Yet it was concluded that the screening was not particularly effective based on the small numbers excluded and that indeed there were persons with mental disorder arriving in the United States with disorders or acquiring disorders over their subsequent lifetimes.

Concerns about immigrant mental health were reflected in state hospital statistics of the time, which showed higher proportions of immigrants in hospitals than were represented in the population. Some of this effect was explained as a result of statistics that did not adjust for the younger age of the immigrant population, their concentration in the northeastern United States, where more hospital beds were available, nor their poverty, which led to public and state hospitals rather than private ones. Nonetheless, the statistics of the time raised concern, which fed and was reinforced by the then thriving eugenics movement.

Interestingly, Ödegaard's primary concern was about the mental health of Norwegians and particularly the deleterious effects on them of emigration from Norway to the United States. His careful analysis of rates of disorder among those emigrating to the United States and even some returning home led him to conclude that rates of mental disorder were higher for Norwegians moving to the United States than for either those staying in Norway or those born in the United States. Furthermore, for Norwegians and many of the groups reviewed, the highest rates of disorder were for those present in the United States for a number of years and not those newly arrived. Thus elements in the experiences of immigrants to the United States seemed to tend more to disorder than the experiences of those born here, even those of immigrant parentage. It was observed that often the persons having disorder had been in the United States for 5 or more years before onset of disorder, and in many cases the higher rates of disorder showed up in the elderly.

Ödegaard's focus was on Norwegians, and the literature reviewed focused mostly on Europeans. It is ironic that most of the groups of concern then are now routinely lumped into a general classification of "white," "white-non-Hispanic," and sometimes "Anglo." This discussion leads to two principles that should always be taken into account, but often are not. The first is that one cannot assume homogeneity for a racial or ethnic group just because it has a label. The usual categories such as African American, Asian American, Native American, and Hispanic are exceedingly broad even if they are used in official designations. We cannot assume a common history or common culture or even a common genetic heritage. Yet most studies are forced to deal with the broad designations because of limitations of sample size and the unavailability of adequate background information for those being studied.

II. STUDIES PRIOR TO THE EPIDEMIOLOGIC CATCHMENT AREA STUDY

A. AFRICAN AMERICANS

African Americans have largely been identified as the descendants of slaves brought to the Americas during the centuries prior to the Civil War, with their ultimate emancipation, but ongoing degrees of discrimination through the present era. Other groups with origins in Black Africa have continued to arrive, but in smaller numbers and with frequent identification by nation of origin to identify their differing histories and economic circumstances. Most studies in the United States have focused on the former group and few studies, if any, have attempted to differentiate the experience of the more recent immigrants.

The prevalence of mental disorder among African Americans has been a source of ongoing controversy for over a century. Prior to emancipation, treatment for mental disorders was largely not available for slaves and so rates of treated disorder were not representative of true prevalence. Dain (1964) notes that the U.S. Census of 1840 reported a higher frequency of insanity for free northern Blacks (along with the Irish) than for the entire white population, but substantially lower rates for Black slaves of the South. He further discusses the politically motivated arguments of the time that the care provided by slave owners and a simple agrarian life without responsibility would bring low rates. Such arguments ignored the harsh treatment and demeaning elements of slavery.

The realities regarding mental health services appeared in Samuel Gridley Howe's (1863) *American Freedmen's Inquiry Commission,* which inquired of asylum (Dain, 1964) superintendents in the North about the number of insane Blacks, only to find that most asylums even in the North did not admit Blacks and that insane Blacks were more likely to be found in almshouses (Dain, 1964). Malzberg (1944) points out that after 1910 census data on the insane came primarily from institutions, and that in the South the availability of beds in asylums was considerably less than in the North, and many beds were White only. It was not until 1930 that the census reported rates from state hospitals, and those rates were higher for Blacks than for Whites (Warheit, Holzer, & Arey, 1975). This history of the relationship between service availability and reported prevalence rates continues to be an issue, although prisons have substituted for almshouses as a place to put the mentally ill. Either way, examination of rates of treated disorder usually provide biased estimates of true prevalence.

Faris and Dunham (1939) examined first admission rates for schizophrenia in Chicago and found higher rates (per 100,000) for Blacks (41.4) as compared to native-born Whites (28.0), and foreign-born Whites (38.1). Malzberg (1944, 1959) examined hospitalization rates for New York State, where there was no official segregation or discrimination and found higher rates for Blacks than others even controlling for age. Between 1940 and 1950, Malzberg (1959) reported a decrease in rates of first admissions for Blacks for all illnesses except involutional psychoses and schizophrenia, which he attributed to improved living conditions for Blacks.

Dohrenwend and Dohrenwend (1969) reviewed eight studies with race comparisons and found that four of them reported higher rates for Whites (Lemkau, Tietze, & Cooper, 1942; Roth & Luton, 1943; and Pasamanick et al., 1959) and four with higher rates for Blacks (Cohen, Fairbank, & Greene, 1939; Hyde & Chisholm, 1944; Leighton, Harding, Macklin, Macmillan, & Leighton, 1963; and Rosanoff, 1917). Dohrenwend's review marks a transition from treatment-based statistics to those based on community surveys.

Warheit, Holzer, and Schwab (1973) and Warheit et al. (1975) conducted analyses of symptomatology in a southern community, and found higher mean depressive symptom scores for Blacks than Whites on several symptom measures including depression, anxiety, phobias, and general psychopathology. In regression models that controlled for age, sex, and socioeconomic status, however, the race effect became nonsignificant for all but the phobia scale. Thus, both age and socioeconomic status should be considered in making ethnic comparisons. Similar findings of higher symptom scores for Blacks than Whites but decreased or even reversed comparisons when controls for age and/or socioeconomic status were added (Comstock & Helsing, 1976; Husaini, 1983; Roberts, 1980, 1981; Weissman & Myers, 1978). Vernon and Roberts (1982) showed higher depressive symptoms and diagnosed major depression (SADS-RDC) among Blacks and Mexican Americans than Whites in Alameda, California. Overall rates of mental illness, however, were lower in Blacks than Whites or Mexican Americans because of other diagnoses.

B. HISPANICS

There are several large groups of Hispanics in the United States, including those with different historical experiences regarding immigration. Historically, Hispanics and particularly Mexican Americans have been underrepresented in inpatient and outpatient populations (Roberts, 1981), a trend that has persisted through the last decade (Swanson, Holzer, & Ganju, 1993). Population-based studies of psychological symptoms have provided a mixed picture. Quesada, Spears, and Ramos (1978) showed lower Zung depression scores for Mexican Americans (mean = 37.8) than Blacks (mean = 41.4) in the Southwest. Antunes and colleagues (1974) as well as Gaitz and Scott (1974) reported lower scores on the Langner symptom scale for Mexican Americans than for Anglos and the lowest scores for Blacks. Roberts (1980) reported lower rates of emotional or mental illness for Mexican Americans than either Anglos or Blacks. In a second study, Roberts (1980) reported that unadjusted rates were higher for Mexican Americans but lower once adjusted for age, sex, education, family income, marital status, and physical health. Vernon and Roberts (1982) reported higher rates of depression for Mexican Americans (28.9%) on the Center for Epidemiologic Studies—Depression (CES-D) scale than for Blacks (18.1%) or Anglos (14.6%). On the SADS-RDC diagnostic interview, Mexican American (9.8%) rates were higher than for Blacks (7.5%) and Anglos (5.5%). For total disorder, however, Mexican Americans (22.1%) were nearly the same as Anglos (21.0%), and Blacks (17.6%) had lower rates.

III. DIAGNOSTIC COMMUNITY SURVEYS

A. THE EPIDEMIOLOGIC CATCHMENT AREA STUDY

In order to obtain diagnostic assessments of specific disorders without treatment selection bias, one needs to conduct a community survey using some form of diagnostic assessment. The National Institute of Mental Health (NIMH)-funded ECA was the first large-scale study to do that, and used a lay-administered diagnostic instrument based on Diagnostic and Statistical Manual of Mental Disorders (3rd ed.) (DSM-III) (American Psychiatric Association, 1980) called the Diagnostic Interview Schedule (DIS). It included five sites, including New Haven, Baltimore, St. Louis, North Carolina, and Los Angeles. Approximately 4,697 African Americans were included in the ECA samples, or about 10.5% (after weighting) of the nearly 20,862 respondents, including an oversample of Blacks in the St. Louis sample. The ECA also included approximately 1428 Hispanics, mostly Mexican Americans, who were oversampled at the Los Angeles site. Relatively small numbers of Asians (about 239) and Native Americans (about 148) were included in the ECA samples, and are considered too small for presentation in most ECA analyses. The details of the ECA methodology are reported in Eaton and Kessler (1985), and the main results are found in Robins and Regier (1991).

In the ECA study, Robins, Locke, and Regier (1991) report lifetime prevalence rates for any disorder of 32% for Whites, 38% for Blacks, and 33% for

TABLE I   Weighted 6-Month Rates per 100 of Psychiatric Disorder by Ethnicity[a]

Psychiatric disorder	White N = 11,900	Black N = 4,190	Hispanic N = 1,428
Any disorder	10.4	11.9	11.7
Alcohol abuse or dependence	4.5	4.8	6.2
Major depressive episode	2.8	2.9	3.1
Schizophrenia or schizophreniform	0.9	1.5	0.4
Phobias	7.9	13.7	7.7
Cognitive impairment	0.9	3.2	1.4

[a] Adapted from Holzer, Swanson, and Shea (1995).

Hispanics. The corresponding rates for a 1-year prevalence period were 19%, 26%, and 20%, respectively. In both instances the rates are significantly higher for Black than for White respondents. More detailed analyses of lifetime and 6-month prevalence for Mexican Americans have been presented by the Los Angeles ECA group (Burnam et al., 1987; Karno et al., 1987).

In subsequent ECA analyses, Holzer, Swanson, and Shea (1995) presented ethnic comparisons for a 6-month prevalence period, as shown in Table I. These crude rates, weighted to population composition, are higher for Blacks than Whites in every group and higher than Hispanics in all but alcohol abuse or dependence and major depressive episode.

In order to test the ethnic differences, Holzer et al. (1995) created logistic regression models for any disorder that included age, sex, race, and socioeconomic status, as well as their two-way interactions. In the first model using socioeconomic status as a categorical variable, the main effect for race was not significant, although there were significant age-by-race and race-by-socioeconomic status interactions. In a second model, which used socioeconomic status as a linear variable, race and the interactions remained significant, indicating that the ethnic differences are not cancelled by simple demographic controls.

B. THE NATIONAL COMORBIDITY STUDY

The National Comorbidity Study (NCS, Kessler et al., 1994) was the first to use a psychiatric diagnostic instrument on a U.S. national sample. The instrument used was the Composite International Diagnostic Instrument (CIDI), which is closely related to the DIS, although it adds diagnostic criteria from the International Classification of Diseases. The NCS sample included persons ages 15 to 55. The survey resulted in 8098 interviews, of which the respondents were about 75% White, 12.5% Black, 9.1% Hispanic, and 3.3% other. Separate results

TABLE II   Ethnic Comparison Odds Ratios by Lifetime Disorder
in the National Comorbidity Study[a]

Disorder	White	Black	Hispanic
Any affective disorder	1.00	0.63*	0.96
Any anxiety disorder	1.00	0.77	0.90
Any substance disorder	1.00	0.35*	0.80
Antisocial personality	1.00	0.89	1.43
Any disorder	1.00	0.50*	0.86
Three or more disorders	1.00	0.67*	0.99

[a] Adapted from Kessler et al. (1994, p. 15).

are not usually presented for Asians or Native Americans because of their small numbers.

Overall, the NCS reports higher rates of any disorder than the ECA in all groups and substantially higher rates for certain disorders, such as major depression. Rather than presenting specific rates of lifetime disorder for ethnic comparisons, rates are compared as odds ratios with Whites as the reference group. These are summarized in Table II. For each of the categories of disorder, Blacks have lower rates than Whites, with the differences being significant for any affective disorder, any substance disorder, any disorder reported, and having three or more disorders. Similarly, the reported rates are nonsignificantly lower for Hispanics for all disorders except antisocial disorder, which was nonsignificantly higher. These comparisons appear quite contradictory to those of the ECA, although some of the differences may be due to the different age range and the inclusion of the whole country and not just the five ECA sites.

C. THE WASHINGTON NEEDS ASSESSMENT HOUSEHOLD SURVEY

The Washington Needs Assessment Household Survey (WANAHS) was conducted in the State of Washington by Washington State University for The Washington State Department of Social and Health Services. Although primarily a substance abuse survey, it included assessments for major depression, mania, anxiety, panic attacks, and psychosis using a CIDI-based screener developed by Kessler from the NCS. The WANAHS differs from the ECA and NCS in several significant ways: first, it was a telephone survey; second, it covered only one state; and third, it provided significant oversamples of five major ethnic groups, including White, Black, Asian, Native, and Hispanic.

TABLE III   Weighted Annual Prevalence for a Summary Variable and Depression by Ethnicity[a,b]

	White	Black	Asian	Native	Hispanic
Summary rate					
ECA	14.3	19.6	9.5	18.5	14.1
NCS	23.3	19.7	19.1	22.4	26.3
WANAHS	12.1	9.6	5.6	18.5	9.0
Depression					
ECA	3.6	3.2	2.5	1.9	4.0
NCS	10.2	8.4	6.3	8.5	14.1
WANAHS	7.9	6.7	4.1	11.7	6.6
Sample size					
ECA	12424	4268	239	148	1433
NCS	6079	1009	141	98	756
WANAHS	1655	1173	1341	1174	1658

[a] From Holzer et al. (1998).

[b] ECA, Epidemiology Catchment Area; NCS, National Comorbidity Study; WANAHS, Washington Needs Assessment Household Survey.

Table III presents a comparison of 1-year prevalence rates of disorder between the ECA, NCS, and WANAHS surveys for each of five ethnic classifications. The table is adapted from a presentation by Holzer, Kabel, Nguyen, and Nordlund (1998). The datasets for the ECA and NCS are available publicly and have been incorporated into the following analyses. The summary variable includes all the disorders assessed in WANAHS and disorders selected from the ECA and NCS to approximate that summary. The variable for depression is *DSM-III* or *DSM-III-R* major depressive episode from each survey. For WANAHS, the scoring omits one low prevalence symptom. Further, one must be cautioned that the denominators for Asian and Native American are small in the ECA and NCS, but are presented for the purpose of comparison.

Examination of Table III reveals many inconsistencies among the surveys, both for the larger ethnic groups and the smaller ones. For the summary variable and for depression, the NCS usually has the highest rates. WANAHS generally has intermediate rates, and the ECA has the lowest rates. In the ethnic comparisons for the summary of disorder, the ECA shows higher rates for Black than White respondents, whereas both the NCS and WANAHS show the reverse. For Hispanic respondents, rates in WANAHS are lower than for Whites, as is seen in the ECA, but are substantially higher in the NCS. Interestingly, the Hispanics in the ECA and WANAHS are mostly Mexican American, whereas the NCS also includes other Hispanic groups. The summary rates of disorder are lower for Asians in all three studies than for other groups. This is expected from the literature. It should be noted that through the use of telephone methods that permitted callbacks in a variety of Asian languages, the WANAHS was able to interview large numbers of Asians who did not speak English and thus would have been excluded from other studies. The summary rates of any disorder for Native Americans are also interesting because they are substantially higher than for Whites, Asians, and Hispanics in the ECA, and are higher than any other group in the WANAHS, but were substantially lower than Hispanics and slightly lower than Whites in the NCS survey.

The prevalence rates for depression are more consistent than those for any disorder. In all three surveys, lower prevalence of depression was found for Blacks than Whites, and Asians were even lower than Blacks. Rates for Hispanics were higher than for Whites in the ECA and NCS, but about the same as for Blacks in the WANAHS. Native Americans had low rates of depression in the ECA, were about the same as Blacks in the NCS, and had the highest rates in the WANAHS. The high rate of depression for Native Americans in the WANAHS is of concern because it is based on a large sample size and is in a state where there has been ongoing tension around issues such as fishing rights for Native Americans.

D. MEXICAN AMERICANS AND IMMIGRATION

It is useful at this point to turn to a study by Vega et al. (1998), which addresses the prevalence of disorder in a Mexican American sample and relates that prevalence to immigration. This study used methods based on the CIDI, with a Spanish-language translation, to conduct a survey of Mexican Americans in Fresno County, California. They focused primarily on issues of migration, with the overall finding that rates of disorder were higher among the U.S.-born Mexican Americans than among those who had immigrated, and that rates of disorder generally were higher for immigrants who had spent more time in the United States. They generally found that the lowest rates of most disorders were for those born in Mexico who had come to the United States within 13 years of the interviews, with somewhat higher rates for those immigrants who had been in the United States for 13 years or more, and the highest rates were for Mexican Americans born in the United States. For reference, these rates are compared to a survey done in Mexico by Medina-Mora, Conver, Sepulveda, and Otero (1989) and to the NCS. The Mexican rates were most comparable to the low rates for recent immigrants, as would be expected if there were not strong selection effects for immigration or trauma associated with it. The high lifetime rates for Mexican Americans born in the United States were most comparable to the NCS sample as a whole and to the Hispanics in the NCS. It would be useful to see similar comparisons for current instead of lifetime disorder.

These findings bring us back to consideration of Ödegaard, who looked at emigration from Norway. Clearly the process of immigration can have elements of selection and elements of stress, as can experiences once one is resident in the United States. In California, the reason for immigration may be largely economic, with the poor of Mexico coming to work for a better wage, only to find that their new home brings its own problems, including hard physical labor, prejudice, substance abuse, and other urban stressors. That theme would be familiar to Ödegaard's Norwegians, although the circumstances are not the same.

E. ASIAN AMERICANS

Asian Americans have been called the "model minority" because overall they have done well economically and have relatively low levels of social pathology. With regard to mental health, they show low overall rates of service utilization, leading to the speculation that they have lower rates of psychopathology. Sue, Sue, Sue, and Takeuchi (1995) have challenged this assumption, saying that from the information available at the time it was not possible to make accurate comparisons. Aside from the inclusion of small numbers Asian Americans in the ECA and NCS, and the larger sample in WANAHS, we have been able to locate only one large diagnostic community survey of Asian Americans. That is the Chinese American Psychiatric Epidemiological Study (Takeuchi et al., 1998). Most other studies are smaller, focus on specific Asian groups, and use symptom scales rather than diagnostic assessments. There are several possible reasons for the small number of diagnostic surveys in the U.S. Asian community. The first of these is the degree of cultural and linguistic difference among Asian cultures and the differences between them and the U.S. mainstream. This necessitates not only translation of instruments, but also some degree of adjustment to differing conceptions of mental disorder.

There are approximately twenty distinct groups designated as Asian. Another is the difficulty in developing sampling frames to identify persons distributed sparsely across larger communities. Thus, there is a tendency to focus on communities with larger Asian populations. Another reason is that a large proportion of Asians are recent immigrants from areas with differing recent histories. Many persons have come from Southeast Asia as refugees from Vietnam, Cambodia, and Laos, but each of these has a somewhat different experience and period of arrival. Within those coming from Vietnam are minority groups such as Hmong who have differing language, culture, and problems from the majority Vietnamese. All this has led studies to focus on particular groups that have been highly visible as refugees. Less visible have been the Chinese Americans, some of whom who have been in the United States for a century, whereas others are new waves of immigration from Hong Kong, Taiwan, and the Chinese mainland. A final factor making it difficult to do large Asian studies has been the reluctance of some Asian groups to permit intrusive questioning about mental illness, which is typically highly stigmatized. As a consequence of these reasons, there appear to be more attempts to conduct studies of Asians in Asia than in the United States. Examples are the study of Compton and colleagues (1991), which compared results from a survey in Taiwan to the ECA and found much lower rates for most disorders.

There are a number of studies that document symptoms among refugees and immigrants from southeast Asia. These have included the work by a number of investigators, including Kinzie, Westermeyer, and Beiser. Many studies have been conducted in conjunction with refugee-oriented treatment programs rather than being representative community samples. Many studies have used adaptations of standard symptom scales such as the SCL-90, the CES-D, and the Hopkins Symptom Checklist. In our own work with refugees, we have used a translation of the DIS with Vietnamese, although with a small sample (Holzer et al., 1988). Typically, the studies of refugee samples are able to document substantial trauma in the countries of origin. There is frequently additional trauma while a displaced person is in refugee camps. Adaptation to life in the United States is frequently an additional burden, with loss of status and economic means at the same time that one needs to adapt to a new culture. Thus, although rates of service utilization have been relatively low, higher symptom levels are often found than in other Asian groups or the U.S. population at large. Yet this is variable depending on the circumstances of becoming a refugee.

In marked contrast to most of the refugee studies is the Chinese American Psychiatric Epidemiological Study (CAPES, Takeuchi et al., 1998), a large survey of Chinese Americans in Los Angeles. Based on a community probability sample of 1747 Chinese Americans ages 18 to 65, CAPES interviewers were fluent in English and either Mandarin or Cantonese and administered translated versions of the CIDI. Results were weighted for the sampling probabilities.

The prevalence rates for major depression was 6.9% for lifetime and 3.4% for the past year (Takeuchi et al., 1998). The lifetime rates for dysthymia was 5.2%, whereas the 1-year prevalence was only 0.9%. These rates are much lower than found in either the NCS or the WANAHS, which used comparable instrumentation and slightly higher than the rates found in the ECA (see Table III).

Most other studies of Asians groups, such as the Chinese, Japanese, or Koreans, especially studies of those who have been in the United States for a longer time or have come as immigrants rather than refugees, report lower symptom levels than the rates for refugees or other U.S. groups. These findings fit into a more generalized understanding of Asian culture in which mental disorder is severely stigmatized. Deviations in psychological symptoms or functioning are often hidden or else seen in a more holistic view of health than the Western focus on psychological processes. Such views have been shown to influence patterns of help seeking and generally result in lower levels of utilization of Western-style mental health services.

F. NATIVE AMERICANS

Community data on the mental health of Native Americans is sparse, but several types of statistics provide some cause for concern. High rates of suicide have been reported for Native Americans, particularly those who live on reservations. Manson, Beals, Disk, and Duclos (1989) reported that 23% of students in an Indian boarding school had attempted suicide and that 33% reported suicidal ideation in the past month. Similarly, high rates of alcoholism are reported in national arrest statistics for public intoxication and driving under the influence of alcohol. Beals et al. (1997) report high rates of disorder in a sample of 251 American Indian adolescents who were interviewed with the DIS for Children. They also found behavioral and substance use disorders.

With this background, it is not surprising that high rates of depression and overall disorder are found in the WANAHS survey, but that rates from the ECA and NCS, which had much smaller sample sizes for this group, were highly inconsistent. Thus much more epidemiologic work needs to be done with this population.

IV. ISSUES LIKELY TO INFLUENCE RATES USED IN ETHNIC COMPARISONS

In closing this chapter it is useful to review some of the issues that make comparisons among ethnic groups difficult at best and otherwise quite misleading. The first of these is the specification of the ethnic group or population being studied. For the most part "ethnic" groups are inadequately identified by broad categories. Subgroups within broad categories are likely to differ in cultural as well as social and economic circumstances. One of these elements is their historical experience with mental health services, which may serve to offer definitions and models for understanding psychological processes.

There are numerous sampling issues. The greatest of these is whether the locations of samples from the different groups are comparable. A national sample may include Blacks from the rural south and northern cities, Mexican Americans from the Southwest, and Asians from the far West. One must ask whether these populations are from comparable circumstances. Do they have comparable demographics such as age, sex, and socioeconomic status? Are there local neighborhood stress or contagion effects? One would expect different results for Native Americans living on reservations from those who have moved to the cities. Ultimately, sampling deals with the generalizability of results.

Interview methods are also likely to make a difference in observed rates of disorder, and may effect ethnic differentials because the methods may be experienced differentially by the groups being compared. Major choices are between face-to-face and telephone interview methods. Face-to-face interviews are preferred because they provide more direct interaction with respondents, visual observation of responses, and direct observation social contexts. Telephone interviews usually cost less and may facilitate the use of native language interviewers, but telephones introduce issues of who can be reached by telephone, and who is willing to disclose personal information through that mode of communication.

Telephone interviews hide many characteristics of the interviewer and may introduce a sense of social distance or cultural neutrality that may help or hurt disclosure. Any perceived risk of loss of confidentiality is important. Complicated sentences and lists are difficult to communicate over the telephone thus changing some of the modes of interaction. The biggest ongoing controversy over telephone interviewing is who can be reached by telephone and whether sampling methods such as random digit dialing can find a representative population sample. Often the poorest minorities lack residential telephones, and the most mobile may have pager and/or cell phones instead. One should note, however, that telephone usage is not limited by language spoken, so telephone access to immigrant groups may actually be easier than access through a more intrusive and potentially threatening attempt to contact in person.

The content of a mental health interview is also likely to influence results. Familiarity with current mental health concepts and linguistic identifiers varies among ethnic groups and by cohort within those groups. The recall and communication of mental health symptoms is strongly influenced by prior familiarity with the language and concepts of mental health, so that just as there is a generational effect in symptom reporting in the mainstream, it is likely that the reporting of symptoms and diagnostic criteria may be less developed in new immigrants from regions with less psychologically oriented discourse. These cultural norms may also make some concepts more stigmatizing and less socially acceptable to report. The availability of mental health concepts to individuals and groups is influenced by the availability and utilization of mental health services in the past, so that groups with historically high mental health service availability are also more likely to report certain kinds of symptoms.

Finally, we return to the issue of nature versus nurture and ultimately whether any of the ethnic differences reported in mental health surveys reflect constitutional or other intrinsic factors of ethnic group membership versus being direct consequences of the experiences of a group and its membership. Although there are some well-documented genetic influences on mental illness, their relationship to group ethnicity is largely unknown. From an epidemiologic perspective, one would want to know whether or not ethnicity is an independent risk factor. More likely, it is a surrogate for historical and recent experience of many other risk factors that change the true prevalence of disorders in a population. That is the reason that analyses of ethnic differences usually attempt to discover whether statistical controls for risk factors such as age, sex, socioeconomic status, trauma, recent life events, immigration and acculturation reduce or modify the differences among groups. Finding reduced differences removes the stigma of mental illness from a particular ethnic group and redirects the concern toward inequities in our nation and the world. From a services perspective, however, the observation of ethnic differences should lead the mental health services system to direct resources to where the need is greatest.

REFERENCES

American Psychiatric Association. (1982). Diagnostic and statistical manual of mental disorders (3rd ed.). Washington, DC: Author.

Beals, J., Piasecki, J., Nelson, S., Jones, M., Keane, E., Dauphinais, P., Shirt, R. R., Sack, W. H., & Manson, S. M. (1997). Psychiatric disorder among American Indian adolescents: Prevalence in northern plains youth. *Journal of the American Academy of Child and Adolescent Psychiatry, 36*(9), 1252–1259.

Burnam, M. A., Timbers, D. M., & Hough, R. L. (1984). Two measures of Antunes psychological distress among Mexican Americans, Mexicans and Anglos. *Journal of Health and Social Behaviors, 125,* 24–33.

Burnam, M. A., Hough, R. L., Escobar, J. I., Karno, M., Timbers, D. M., Telles, C. A., & Locke, B. Z. (1987). Six-month prevalence of specific psychiatric disorders among Mexican Americans and non-Hispanic whites in Los Angeles. *Archives of General Psychiatry, 44,* 687–694.

Cohen, B. M., Fairbank, R., & Greene, E. (1939). Statistical contributions from the mental hygiene study of the Eastern Health District of Baltimore: III. Personality disorder in the Eastern Health District in 1933. *Human Biology, 11,* 112–129.

Compton, W. M., Helzer, J. E., Hwu, H. G., Yeh, E. K., McEvoy, L., Tipp, J. E., & Spitznagel, E. L. (1991). New methods in cross-cultural psychiatry: Psychiatric Illness in Taiwan and the United States. *American Journal of Psychiatry, 148,* 12, December 1991.

Comstock, G. W., & Helsing, K. J. (1976). Symptoms of depression in two communities. *Psychological Medicine, 6,* 551–563.

Dain, N. (1964). *Concepts of Insanity in the United States 1789–1865.* New Brunswick, NJ: Rutgers University Press.

Dohrenwend, B. P., & Dohrenwend, B. S. (1969). *Social status and psychological disorder: A causal inquiry.* New York: John Wiley and Sons, Inc.

Dohrenwend, B. P. (1975). Sociocultural and social-psychological factors in the genesis of mental disorders. *Journal of Health & Social Behavior, 6,* 4.

Eaton, W. W., & Kessler, L. G. (Ed.). (1985). *Epidemiologic field methods in psychiatry: The NIMH Epidemiologic Catchment Area Program.* Orlando, FL: Academic Press Inc.

Faris, R., & Dunham, H. W. (1939). *Mental disorders in urban areas. Chicago.* (pp. 55). The University of Chicago Press.

Gaitz, C. M., & Scott, J. (1974). Mental health of Mexican-Americans: Do ethnic factors make a difference? *Geriatrics, 29,* 103–10.

Gordon, C. M., Gaitz, C., & Scott, J. (1974). Ethnicity, socioeconomic status and the etiology of psychological distress. *Sociology & Social Research, 58,* 361–368.

Gould, S. J. (1981). *The mismeasure of man.* New York: Norton.

Holzer, C. E., Kabel, J. R., Nguyen, H. T., & Nordlund, D. (1998, July). *Comparisons of mental illness in Washington State.* Presented at the International Sociological Association, XIV World Congress of Sociology, Montreal, Canada.

Holzer, C. E., Swanson, J. W., HuynHa, M. Q., Ganju, V. K., Jono, R. T., & Le, C. K. (1988). *Psychiatric disorder among the Vietnamese-origin population in Texas: A diagnostic survey of 100 households in Harris and Galveston Counties.* Final report to the Texas Department of Mental Health and Mental Retardation, September 12, Austin, TX: Texas State University.

Holzer, C. E., III, Swanson, J. W., & Shea, B. M. (1995). Ethnicity, social status, and psychiatric disorder in the Epidemiologic Catchment Area survey. In *Social psychiatry across cultures: Studies from North American, Asia, Europe, and Africa.* R. K. Price, B. M. Shea, & H. N. Mookherjee, (Eds.), New York: Plenum Press.

Husaini, B. A. (1983). *A study of health needs of rural blacks in Tennessee. Mental Health of Rural Blacks.* Cooperative Agricultural Research Program, Tennessee State University, Nashville.

Hyde, R. W., & Chisholm, R. M. (1944). The relation of mental disorders to race and nationality. *New England Journal of Medicine, 231,* 612–618.

Karno, M., Hough, R. L., Burnam, M., Escobar, J. I., Timbers, D. M., Santana, F., & Boyd, J. H. (1987). Lifetime prevalence of specific psychiatric disorders among Mexican Americans & non-Hispanic Whites in Los Angeles. *Archives of General Psychiatry, 44,* pp. 687–694.

Kessler, R. C., McGonagle, K. A., Zhao, S., Nelson, C. B., Hughes, M., Eshleman, S., Wittchen, H. U., & Kendler, K. S. (1994). Lifetime and 12-month prevalence of *DSM-III-R* psychiatric disorders in the United States. *Archives of General Psychiatry, 51,* 8–19.

Leighton, D., Harding, J., Macklin, D., MacMillan, & Leighton, A. (1963). *The character of danger.* New York: Basic Books.

Lemkau, P., Tietze, C., & Cooper, M. (1942). Mental hygiene problems in an urban district. *Mental Hygiene, 26,* 100–119.

Malzberg, B. (Ed.) (1944). Mental disease among American Negroes a statistical analysis. In O. Klineberg (Ed.), Characteristics of the American Negro (pp. 373–402). New York: Harper.

Malzberg, B. (Ed.) (1959). Important statistical data about mental illness. In S. Arieti (Ed.), *American handbook of Psychiatry* (pp. 161–174). New York: Basic Books.

Malzberg, B. (1965). Marital status and mental disease among Negroes in New York State. *Journal of Nervous Mental Disorders, 123,* 457–465.

Manson, S. M., Beals, J., Disk, R. W., & Duclos, C. (1989). Risk factors for suicide among Indian adolescents as to boarding school. *Public Health Reports, 104,* (6), 609–14.

Medina Mora, M. E., Conver, R. T., Sepulveda, J., & Otero, M. R. (1989). Extension del consumo de drogas en Mexico encuesta Nacional de Adicciones resultados nacionales *Salud Mental, 12,* 7–12.

Ödegaard, O., (1932). *Emigration and insanity: A study of mental disease among the Norwegianborn population of Minnesota.* Copenhagen: Levin & Munksgaards Publishers.

Pasamanick, B. (1959). *Epidemiology of mental disorder.* Washington, DC: American Association for the Advancement of Science.

Quesada, M., Spears, W., & Ramos, P. (1978). Interracial depressive epidemiology in the Southwest. *Journal of Health & Social Behavior, 19,* 77–85.

Roberts, R. E. (1980). Prevalence of psychological distress among Mexican Americans. *Journal of Health and Social Behavior, 21,* 134–145.

Roberts, R. E. (1981). Prevalence of depressive symptoms among Mexican Americans. *Journal of Nervous Mental Disorders, 169,* 213–219.

Robins, L. N., & Regiere, D. A. (1991). *Psychiatric disorders in America: The epidemiologic catchment area study.* New York: Free Press.

Robins, L. N., Locke, B. Z., & Regier, D. A. (1991). *An overview of psychiatric disorders in America. Psychiatric disorders in America:* The Epidemiologic Catchment Area Study (pp. 333).

Rosanoff, A. (1917). Survey of mental disorders in Nassau County, New York. *Psychiatric Bulletin,* Vol. 2 (109–231.

Roth, W. F., & Luton, F. B. (1943). The mental hygiene program in Tennessee. *American Journal of Psychiatry, 99,* 662–675.

Sue, S., Sue, D. W., Sue, L., & Takeuchi, D. T. (1995). Psychopathology among Asian Americans: A model minority? *Cultural Diversity & Mental Health, 1,* (1), 39–51.

Swanson, J. W., Holzer, C. E., & Ganju, V. K. (1993). Hispanic Americans and the state mental hospitals in Texas: Ethnic parity as a latent function of a fiscal incentive policy. *Social Science and Medicine, 37,* (7), 917–926.

Swanson, J. W., Linskey, A. O., Quintero-Salinas, R., Psych, M., Pumariega, A. J., & Holzer, C. E. (1992). A binational school survey of depressive symptoms, drug use, and suicidal ideation. *Journal of the Academy of Child Adolescent Psychiatry, 31,* (4).

Takeuchi, D. T., Chung, R. C., Lin, K. M., Shen, H., Kurasaki, K., Chung, C. A., & Sue, S. (1998). Lifetime and twelve-month prevalence rates of major depressive episodes and dysthymia among Chinese Americans in Los Angeles. *American Journal of Psychiatry, 155,* 10.

Telles, C., & Karno, M. (1994). Latino mental health: Current research and policy perspectives. Neuropsychiatric Institute, University of California, Los Angeles.

Vega, W., & Warheit, G., & Auth, J., & Meinhardt, K. (1984). The prevalence of depressive symptoms among Mexican Americans and Anglos. *American Journal of Epidemiology, 120,* 592–607.

Vernon, S. W., & Roberts, R. E. (1982). Prevalence of treated and untreated psychiatric disorders in three ethnic groups. *Social Science Medicine, 116,* 1575–1582.

Warheit, G. J., Holzer III, C. E., & Arey, S. A. (1975). Race and mental illness: An epidemiologic update. *Journal of Health Social Behavior, 16,* 243–256.

Warheit, G. J., Holzer, C. E., & Schwab, J. J. (1973). An analysis of social class & racial differences in depressive symptomatology: A community study: *Journal of Health & Social Behavior, 14,* 291–299.

Weissman, M. M., & Myers, J. K. (1978). Affective disorders in a United States urban community: The use of research diagnostic criteria in an epidemiological survey. *Archives of General Psychiatry, 35,* 1304–1311.

Westermeyer, J., Williams, C. L., & Nguyen, A. N. (1991). *Mental health services for refugees* (DHHS Publication No. [ADM] 91-1824). Washington, DC: U.S. Government Printing Office.

CHAPTER 18

Depression and Suicidal Behaviors among Adolescents: The Role of Ethnicity

ROBERT E. ROBERTS

Departments of Behavioral Sciences and International and Family Health
School of Public Health
The University of Texas, Houston
Houston, Texas

For some years now I have carried out a program of research directed at under-standing the role of ethnic culture in the epidemiology of psychopathology, in particular depression and suicidal behaviors. The question is whether and how ethnic culture operates to increase or reduce the risk for depression and suicide. More recently, the focus has been on adolescents.

From several perspectives, the concept of ethnicity would appear to facilitate research on the epidemiology of psychological and behavioral disorders (in this case, depression and suicidal behaviors) occurring in adolescence. First, as I noted some years ago (Roberts, 1988), "ethnicity" is a multifactorial construct, encompassing several cultural aspects defined by psychological, sociological, historical, geographical, and biological dimensions. Second, there seems little doubt, given our current state of knowledge, that psychological and behavioral disorders are the result of lifelong interactions among psychological, sociological, and biological factors (Cooper & Morgan, 1973; Regier & Allen, 1981). Third, psychological disorders, particularly functional disorders, primarily involve disturbances of mood, cognition, and behavior; and culture has been found

Handbook of Multicultural Mental Health: Assessment and Treatment of Diverse Populations
Copyright © 2000 by Academic Press. All rights of reproduction in any form reserved.

to directly influence emotion, behavior, and cognitive expectations (Campos, Mumme, Kermoian, & Campos, 1994). Given these three basic premises, it should follow that ethnicity constitutes a preeminent construct for organizing research on the causes and consequences of psychological dysfunction, in this case, depression and suicide. Ethnicity would appear to be particularly salient in the development and successful adaptation of adolescents in a culturally diverse society (Aries & Moorehead, 1989; Bernal, Knight, Ocampo, Garza, & Cota, 1993; Helms, 1985; Phinney & Alipuria, 1990).

The possible effects of ethnicity on mental health are that mental health may differ across ethnocultural groups due to (a) different risk factors operating in the groups; (b) the same generic factors that operate differentially across groups; (c) the effects of both unique factors and common factors; or (d) mental health may not differ across groups.

What is the evidence concerning ethnocultural differences in adolescent depression and suicidal behaviors? Unfortunately, the evidence we have does not even allow us to say with any degree of confidence whether some ethnic groups are at greater risk of depression or suicidal behaviors and others are at lesser risk. For most ethnic groups in the United States, we do not know either the prevalence or incidence of affective disorders in general or specific affective disorders such as major depression or of suicidal behaviors, be they ideation, plans, attempts, or completed suicide. Since we do not have good data on incidence or prevalence, it follows that we do not understand the etiology or consequences of depression and suicidal behaviors in the many ethnocultural groups that make up American society.

Ethnicity is a central theme of the American experience. And, it may be, as Alba (1990) has argued, that ethnic differences form a possibly permanent substructure, if not the ultimate bedrock of American society. However, in spite of the acknowledged role of race and ethnicity in the United States, and the increasing diversity of our population, there have been remarkably few epidemiological studies of adolescent mental health in diverse ethnic groups.

The question remains as to whether ethnic culture affects the risk for depression and suicidal behavior among adolescents and, if so, how? What is the evidence in this regard?

I. ETHNICITY AND ADOLESCENT DEPRESSION

A. PREVALENCE

There are few data on depression among minority children and adolescents in the United States. The dearth of data on minority adolescents is not surprising, given the lack of data on adolescent depression in general. For example, there have been few community-based epidemiologic studies of adolescent depression. Perusing the studies that have been done, it is difficult to identify a coherent empirical pattern due to the great diversity in research designs, study populations, and methods of case ascertainment.

For example, Fleming and Offord (1990) identified nine epidemiologic studies of clinical depression and report that prevalence of current depression ranged from 0.4–5.7% in the five studies reporting such data. The mean prevalence of current major depression was 3.6%. Subsequent to that review, several other articles have appeared. Lewinsohn, Hops, Roberts, Seeley, and Andrews (1993) reported data from a large sample of high school students indicating a point prevalence for *Diagnostic and Statistical Manual of Mental Disorders* (3rd. rev. ed.) (DSM-III-R) (American Psychiatric Association, 1987) major depression of 2.6%. Garrison et al. (1992) reported 1 year prevalence rates of about 9% for *DSM-III* major depressive disorder in a large sample of middle-school students. Based on an epidemiologic survey of youths 6–17 years of age, Jensen et al. (1995) estimated prevalence of depression (Major Depressive Episode/Dysthymia) to be 1.9% based on parent report and 2.8% based on child report. Adjusting for impairment, prevalences were 1.9% for both parent and child reports of depression. The Methods for the Epidemiology of Child and Adolescent Mental Disorders (MECA) study (Shaffer et al., 1996) combined data from four sites for subjects 9–17 years of age and reported that the prevalence of major depression was 3.1% based on parent report and 4.8% based on youth report. Using their recommended impairment criteria, prevalence of major depression reported by the parent was 2.4% and by the youth was 2.6%.

What about studies that focus on depressive symptoms? School-based studies using the Beck Depression Inventory (BDI) have reported mean scores ranging from 6.0 to 103; the average was 8.6 across five studies (Baron & Parron, 1986; Doerfler, Felner, Rowlison, Raley, & Evans, 1988; Gibbs, 1985; Kaplan, Hong, & Weinhold, 1984; Teri, 1982). At least eight studies, all school-based, have used the Center for Epidemiologic Studies Depression Scale (CES-D; Doerfler et al., 1988; Garrison, Jackson, Marsteller, McKeown, & Addy, 1990; Manson, Ackerman, Dick, Baron, & Fleming, 1990; Roberts, Andrews, Lewinsohn, & Hops, 1990; Roberts & Chen, 1995; Schoenbach, Kaplan, Grimson, & Wagner, 1982; Swanson, Linskey, Quintero-Salina, Pumanega, & Holzer, 1992; Tolor & Murphy, 1985). These studies have reported mean scores for the CES-D in the range of 16–20, with an overall mean of about 17. Prevalence of depressive symptoms using a CES-D caseness criterion of 16 or greater is in the range of 45–55%.

Given the limited number of epidemiologic studies of adolescent depression in general, it is not surprising that there have been few studies published focusing on race or ethnic status. Again, even among this small subset of studies the findings are not cohesive. Although some studies find no evidence of ethnic differences in adolescent depression (Garrison et al., 1990; Kandel & Davies, 1982; Manson et al., 1990), others report that minority adolescents report greater levels of depressive symptoms (Emslie, Weinberg, Rush, Adams, & Rintelman, 1990; Schoenbach et al., 1982), and still others that minority youth have lower levels of depression (Doerfler et al., 1988). But again, it is difficult to draw any firm conclusions concerning ethnic status and risk of depression from these studies, because they employ different measures of depression, and they also focus on different ethnic minority adolescents (African American, Hispanic American, Native American, etc.).

A number of studies have included Mexican-origin adolescents. For example, Weinberg and Emslie (1987) reported that in their sample of high school students, Anglos had the lowest rates of depression on both the BDI and the Weinberg Screening Affective Scale (WSAS), African Americans were intermediate, and Mexican Americans had the highest rates. Swanson et al. (1992) conducted a school-based survey in three cities in Texas and three in Mexico along the U.S.–Mexico border. The U.S. sample, comprising over 95% Mexican-origin adolescents, had a prevalence of 48% using the score of 16 or more on the CES-D.

Roberts and Sobhan (1992) analyzed data from a national survey of persons 12–17 years of age, comparing symptom levels of Anglo, African, Mexican-origin, and other Hispanic Americans using a 12-item version of the CES-D. Mexican-origin males reported more depressive symptoms than other males and the same was true for Mexican-origin females, although to a lesser extent. Roberts (1994) examined depression rates among Mexican-origin and Anglo adolescents sampled from middle schools in Las Cruces, New Mexico. The minority youth had significantly higher rates of depressive symptoms on both the 20-item CES-D and the WSAS. In a second analyses of these data, Roberts and Chen (1995) examined depressive symptoms among Anglo and Mexican-origin adolescents. The minority adolescents reported significantly more symptoms of depression than their Anglo counterparts. Prevalences were highest for Mexican-origin females.

Hovey and King (1996) report that 22.9% of a small sample ($N = 70$) of first- and second-generation Latino American adolescents reported critical levels of depressive symptoms using the Reynolds Adolescent Depression Scale (RADS; Reynolds, 1986). As a comparison, 12% of the standardization sample of RADS (Reynolds, 1988) reported a critical level of depression. Those adolescents experiencing a high level of acculturative stress were more likely to be depressed. Similar results were found in another study by Hovey (1998), which focused on Mexican American adolescents.

Roberts, Roberts, and Chen (1997) used data from an ethnically diverse sample of middle school students ($N = 5,423$) to examine ethnic differences in major depression. The point prevalence of *DSM-IV* major depression was 8.4%

without and 4.3% with impairment. Data were sufficient to calculate prevalences for nine ethnic groups. Prevalences adjusted for impairment ranged from 1.9% for youths of Chinese descent to 6.6% for those of Mexican decent. African and Mexican American youths had significantly higher crude rates of depression without impairment, but only the latter had significantly higher rates of depression with impairment. Multivariate (logistic regression) analyses, adjusting for the effects of age, gender, and socioeconomic status (SES), yielded significant odds ratios (OR) for only one group. Mexican American youths were at elevated risk for both depression without (OR = 1. 74, $p < .05$) and depression with impairment (OR = 1.71, $p < .05$). There was no significant interaction of ethnicity and SES in relation to depression.

In a recent study, Siegel, Aneshensle, Taub, Cantwell, and Driscoll (1998) examined whether there was an impact of race ethnicity on depressed mood among adolescents, independent of SES. A three-stage, area probability sampling frame was utilized to select 877 adolescents, ages 12–17 years, for an in-person interview. Compared with European, African, or Asian Americans, Latinos reported more symptoms of depressed mood, a finding that was independent of SES.

Katragadda and Tidwell (1998) studied 240 Hispanic high school students in rural California using the CES-D to assess depressive symptoms. Using the standard score of 16 or more, 50.8% met the criteria for depression. Defining scores of 21–30 as "moderate depression," the prevalence was 17.5% and for "severe depression," (scores of 31 and above), prevalence was 15.8%. These rates are higher than most other studies have found.

A recent review by Cole, Martin, Peeke, Henderson, and Harwell (1998) identified eight studies comparing African and European American youths on measures of depression. The studies all included or were entirely adolescent populations. The results were quite disparate. Two studies reported that African American youths scored higher on depression measures than did European American youths (Garrison et al., 1990; McDonald & Gynther, 1963). Five studies found no significant differences between African American and European American youth on measures of depression (Helsel & Matson, 1984; Lubin & McCollum, 1994; Reynolds & Graves, 1989; Treadwell, Flannery-Schroeder, & Kendall, 1995; Wrobel & Lachar, 1995). One study (Doerfler et al., 1988) revealed that Europeans scored higher than African American youths.

Cole and his colleagues (1998) obtained yearly self-report, peer nomination, and teacher-rating assessments of depression symptoms, anxiety symptoms, and social acceptance on two cohorts of African American (N = 139 and 184, respectively) and European American school children (N = 328 and 339, respectively), yielding a total of six waves of data between 3rd and 8th grade. Analyses demonstrated that the measures were equally valid across ethnic groups. Peer-nomination measures of depression and anxiety symptoms appeared to be biased, however, leading to the underestimation of psychopathology in African American children. Adjusting for this, African American youths evinced more signs of depression and anxiety in grades three, four, and five than did European American children. Such differences were not significant in grades six, seven, and eight.

Other ethnic groups have been studied much less. For example, Prescott et al. (1998), based on a two-stage epidemiologic survey of high school students in Hawaii, found no differences between Hawaiian and non-Hawaiian youths in terms of the prevalence of *DSMR-III-R* major depressive disorder and dysthymic disorder. For example, the prevalence of MDD (6 months) was 8.4 for Hawaiians and 8.5 for non-Hawaiians. Greenberger and Chen (1996) examined perceived parent–adolescent relationships and depressed mood among 173 early adolescents and 297 college students, all of European or Asian American background. Ethnic differences in depressed mood, not evident in the early adolescent sample, emerged in the college sample, with Asian Americans reporting more symptoms. Ethnic differences in depressed mood were reduced to nonsignificance when quality of parent–adolescent relationships was statistically controlled. The magnitude of associations between measures of parent–adolescent relationships and depressed mood was similar for European and Asian Americans at the same phase of adolescence.

B. DISCUSSION

The only consistent finding thus far is that Mexican American youth appear to be at greater risk for depression. Why might Mexican American youths have elevated risks for depression? One possible explanation relates to the possible role of Mexican culture in the epidemiology of depression. For example, Ross, Mirowsky, and Cockerham (1983) reported that persons of Mexican origin are more fatalistic, and that fatalism, in turn, increases psychological distress. In a second paper, Mirowsky and Ross (1984) reported that Mexican culture has contradictory effects on mental health, increasing symptoms of depression and decreasing symptoms of anxiety. Increased risk for depression is attributable to a higher prevalence of belief in external control among persons of Mexican heritage. A more recent paper by Neff and Hoppe (1993) suggests that ethnic differences in depression are the result of the complex interaction of acculturation, fatalism, and religiosity. Fatalism, or feelings of a lack of control, may lead to impaired coping effort, which in turn leads to psychological distress because fatalistic beliefs destroy both the will and the ability to cope with life's problems (Kohn, 1972; Pearlin & Schooler, 1978; Wheaton, 1980). Although fatalism appears to be one possible explanation for the higher prevalence of depression observed for Mexican American youths, no studies have yet examined this issue in adolescent samples.

There are other possibilities, of course. One possible explanation appeals to the response-style theory of depression formulated by Nolen-Hoeksema (1991). She argued that ruminative response styles are more deleterious to the course and severity of depression than are distractive responses. Because prevalence rates are a function of incidence plus duration, any process that prolongs depression would increase prevalence, all other things equal. Since Mexican American youths report higher prevalence of depression, particularly Mexican American girls, and women are more likely to use ruminative coping (see Nolen-Hoeksema & Girgis, 1994; Schwartz & Koenig, 1996), such coping styles may be operant. Again, however, no studies of minority adolescents have addressed this question.

Essentially all studies of ethnic status and psychological disorder among adolescents have relied on nonclinical or nondiagnostic measures of dysfunction, to the exclusion of clinical disorder (for an exception, see Bird et al., 1988). Symptoms of depression are highly prevalent among adolescents in general, and they are the source of considerable suffering. A better understanding of their etiology and consequences is needed. However, absence of a measure of clinical depression omits the more serious forms of depressive illness. From an epidemiological perspective, the differences in prevalences are substantial. For example, studies indicate the prevalence of clinical depression among adolescents is perhaps 3–4% (Fleming & Offord, 1990; Roberts, Lewinsohn, & Seeley, 1991). In the only study of clinical depression among Hispanic youth, Bird et al. (1988) reported the 6-month prevalence of depression/dysthymia in Puerto Rico was 2.8%. By contrast, prevalence rates based on data from depression scales are 4–10 times greater than those derived from clinical interviews. My own results, which are generally consistent with other findings, are limited in some respects because of the nature of the measures of psychopathology used. In our study of multiple ethnic groups (Roberts, Roberts, & Chen, 1997), the measure of depression operationalizes *DSM* criteria and is derived from a structured psychiatric interview, but it still is a self-report instrument. The resulting prevalence rates are not derived from clinical psychiatric assessments, employing the full range of *DSM* criteria.

C. RISK FACTORS   General

There is an extensive and growing body of literature on risk and protective factors in depression. Presentation of the details of this literature is beyond the scope of this review. Interested readers are referred to a number of reviews that are available (see for example, Birmaher et al., 1996; Fleming & Offord, 1990; Gotlib & Hammen, 1992; Harrington, 1993; Kashani & McNaul, 1997;

Lewinsohn, Rhode, & Seeley, 1996). Rather, I would like to note several themes that have emerged from this body of research.

First, there appears to be a strong genetic and family aggregation component to depression, particularly early-onset depression. For example, twin and adoption studies have provided evidence that genetic factors account for up to 50% of the variance in transmission of mood disorders. Children of depressed parents are about three times more likely to have a lifetime episode of major depression. Finally, lifetime prevalence of depression in first-degree relatives of depressed children and adolescents are estimated to be 20–46% (for a review, see Birmaher et al., 1996).

Second, psychosocial factors also clearly play a role. Depressed adolescents, drawn from community and clinical samples, have lower self-esteem, higher self-criticism, increased cognitive dysfunction, negative attributions, hopelessness, a tendency to attribute outcomes to external causes, and social skills deficits compared with nonaffective psychiatric and normal controls (see, for example, Birmaher et al., 1996; Lewinsohn et al., 1996).

Research also has demonstrated that depression is a recurrent condition, with almost three-fourths of adolescents having a recurrence within 5 years of the initial episode, and with almost an equal probability of the risk of depression episodes persisting into adulthood (Birmaher et al., 1996).

Comorbidity of other psychiatric disorders is one of the hallmarks of depression, including depression in adolescence. Half or more of depressed youths have comorbid psychiatric disorders, and 20% to 50% have two or more comorbid disorders. The most frequent comorbid diagnoses are dysthymia, anxiety disorders, disruptive disorders, and substance abuse. Except for substance abuse, major depression is more likely to occur after the onset of other psychiatric disorders (see Birmaher et al., 1996; Lewinsohn et al., 1996).

A number of studies have documented a range of psychosocial deficits among formerly depressed adolescents, which no doubt account in large part for future vulnerability for episodes of depression. One of the critical sequelae of depressive episodes among adolescents is the increased risk of suicidal behaviors (see Birmaher et al., 1996; Kashani & McNaul, 1997; Lewinsohn et al., 1996). I revisit this point in more depth below in my discussion of suicidal behaviors.

II. ETHNICITY AND ADOLESCENT SUICIDE BEHAVIORS

A. PREVALENCE

In spite of the acknowledged role of race and ethnicity in the United States, and the increasing diversity of our population, there have been remarkably few epidemiological studies of adolescent suicidal behaviors in the diverse groups that make up American society.

Suicide is a major public health problem in the United States. For example, suicide is the third leading cause of death for persons 15–24 years old (the rate was 13.1 per 100,000 in 1991; National Center for Health Statistics, 1994; Moscicki, 1997). Suicidal behavior has been reported as a leading cause of psychiatric emergencies among children and adolescents (Robinson, 1986) and one of the strongest predictors of psychiatric hospital admissions for adolescents (Hillard, Slomowitz, & Deddens, 1988).

In the United States, as well as worldwide, suicide rates differ by age, gender, race or ethnicity, marital status, and SES (Moscicki, 1995). Most of these studies have had adults as their focus. For example, mortality statistics in the United States indicate that American Indians and Alaska Natives have the highest suicide rates of any ethnic group, about 50% higher than the overall rates (Moscicki, 1997). Although there have been studies of suicidal behaviors of adolescents (see reviews by Reynolds & Mazza, 1994; Shaffer & Hicks, 1994), there are virtually no data on suicidal behaviors among minority adolescents. This is surprising, since epidemiological studies suggest such behaviors are not uncommon.

Concerning suicide mortality, Smith, Mercy, and Warren (1985) compared suicide rates among Anglos and Latinos (of which 86% were Mexican American) in five southwestern states and found that, for all ages, the suicide rate for Latinos (9.0) in the areas was less than that for Anglos (19.2). This discrepancy between groups, however, was less for adolescents ages 15–19, as the suicide rate for Latino adolescents was 9.0 compared to 11.9 for Anglo adolescents. Suicides, moreover, occurred at a younger age for Latinos (32.9% under age 25) than for Anglos (17.3% under age 25). A recent report examined the epidemiology of trauma deaths in Los Angeles County (Demetriades et al., 1998). Excluding poisonings (17.7% of all trauma deaths) and drownings, the suicide rates for those under 15 years of age were 5.2 and 5.3 per 100,000 for African American males and females, 4.6 and 4.1 for Hispanic males and females, and 2.9 and 1.9 for European American males and females, compared with 3.8 and 3.9 for all males and females under 15. Overall, for all ages, there were no differences across the three largest ethnic groups for either males or females.

Recent community-based, epidemiological studies report prevalence of suicidal ideation for adolescents ranging from about 2% to as high as 60% (Garrison, Addy, Jackson, McKeown, & Waller, 1991b). The prevalence of suicide attempts tends to be much lower, with lifetime prevalence for adolescents ranging from 3.5% to 11% (Andrews & Lewinsohn, 1992). Results from the few studies that have examined ethnic differences have been equivocal, with several studies reporting no difference between European and African American adolescent suicidal behaviors (Dubow, Kaush, Blum, Reed, & Bush, 1989; Garrison et al., 1991b) and several reporting higher suicidal behavior among African American adolescents (Garrison et al., 1991a; Harkavy, Friedman, Asnis, Boeck,

& DiFore, 1987). Garrison, McKeown, et al. (1993), reporting data from a statewide survey in South Carolina, found that although suicide attempts were higher for Europeans than for African Americans, African American females reported the highest frequency of attempts requiring medical treatment. African Americans were less likely to report plans, but significant ethnic differences were not found for suicidal thoughts.

Lester and Anderson (1992), using data from a very small school-based sample in New Jersey, report that Hispanic students had higher scores on both depression and suicidal ideation than did African American students. Most of the Hispanic students were of Puerto Rican origin. Vega, Gil, Zimmerman, and Warheit (1993), using data from a large school-based survey of Cuban, Nicara-guan, other Hispanic, African American, and Anglo American males in grades six and seven, report that African Americans had the highest prevalence of suicidal ideation in the previous 6 months. Nicaraguans and other Hispanics had the highest levels of lifetime suicide attempts.

Roberts and Chen (1995) examined suicidal ideation in a large sample of European and Mexican American middle school students. Mexican Americans had rates of ideation almost twice as high as those of their Anglo counterparts. Adjusting for the effects of covariates such as age, gender, language use, and household structure, Mexican American adolescents still had 1.7 times the risk of suicidal ideation. The percentage of Mexican American youths reporting they had thought about killing themselves on one or more days during the past week was 25.2%. This is similar to a rate of 23.4% reported by Swanson et al. (1992) for Mexican American students.

Reynolds and Mazza (1992) assessed suicidal behaviors in a sample of junior and senior high schools in eight states. The highest rate of a history of suicide attempts was found for Native American adolescents (25.5%) and the lowest rate was among African American youths. Hispanic youths also reported a high rate (16.3%) of lifetime suicide attempts. Walter et al. (1995) report that 14% of Hispanics reported suicidal behaviors compared to 12.8% of African Ameri-cans and 12.0% for "Other" ethnicities in a survey ($N = 3,738$) of four middle schools in New York City. The primary risk factor for suicidal behaviors was depression. The Hispanic students were largely Dominicans (they were 73.7% of the overall sample). Suicidal behavior was defined as intent to commit sui-cide or having attempted suicide ever in their lifetime.

Hovey and King (1996) report that 24.3% of a small sample ($N = 70$) of first- and second-generation Latino American adolescents reported critical lev-els of suicidal ideation on the Suicidal Ideation Questionnaire-Junior (SIQ-JR). As a comparison, 11% of the standardization sample exceeded a score of 31 (Reynolds, 1988). Hovey and King (1996) then explored the relationship be-tween acculturative stress, depressive symptoms, and suicidal ideation. They found that perceived family dysfunction and nonpositive expectations for the future were significant predictors of acculturative stress; and that acculturative stress, perceived family dysfunction, and nonpositive "expectations for the future" were significant predictors of depression and suicidal ideation. Their overall results suggest that some acculturating Latino adolescents experience high levels of acculturative stress, and that these adolescents are also "at risk" for experiencing critical levels of depression and suicidal ideation.

Warheit et al. (1996) report no association between ethnicity (White non-Hispanic, Hispanic, African American) and suicidal ideation in South Florida. The study examined the relations between disaster-related stresses, depression scores, and suicidal ideation among adolescents ($N = 4,978$) all of whom have been exposed to Hurricane Andrew. Regression analysis showed that being female, hurricane-generated stresses, low levels of family support, pre-hurricane suicidal ideation, and post-hurricane depression scores were significant predictors of post-hurricane suicidal ideation. Ethnic status was not a significant predictor of suicidal ideation.

Howard-Pitney, LaFromboise, Basil, September, and Johnson (1992) studied Zuni adolescents and found significant correlations between a measure of suicide ideation and past suicide attempt behavior, drug use, depression, hopelessness, stress, psychological symptomatology, social support, liking for school, and interpersonal communication. Significant differences between the 30% of the students who reported having previously attempted suicide and the non-attempters were also found on these measures. The rate of suicide attempt (30%) was much higher than the 4–13% attempt rate found in general population youth studies but consistent with American Indian/Alaska Native boarding school population studies (Dinges & Duong-Tran, 1990; Manson, Beals, Dick, & Duclos, 1989). A striking gender difference pattern in suicide attempts was found at the Zuni pueblo that mirrored findings from the U.S. youth population (Kinkel, Bailey, & Josef, 1989), indicating that girls attempt suicide two to three times more than boys. Other research on Indian populations, such as Pueblo Indians (Biernoff, 1970) and the more recent boarding school studies, have suggested that gender differences in attempt rates are not as large.

Novins, Beals, Roberts, and Manson (1999) analyzed data from self-report surveys of 1,353 high school students representing three culturally distinct American Indian tribes for tribal differences in factors associated with suicidal ideation. Overall, 3.5% screened positive for suicidal ideation, but differences between groups were not statistically significant. Prevalences were 2.3% for Southwest, 5.0% for Northern Plains, and 3.8% for Pueblo youths. No single correlate of suicidal ideation was common to all three tribes. The correlates of suicidal ideation were consistent with each tribes' social structure, conceptualization of individual and gender roles, support systems, and conceptualizations of death. These results underscore the heterogeneity of suicidal ideation across three distinct American Indian tribes consistent with their cultural heterogeneity.

In one of the few studies of Asian-Pacific Islander adolescents in the United States, Yuen et al. (1996) found a 6-month prevalence of suicide attempts of 4.3% among Native Hawaiian high school students ($N = 1,779$). There were no significant differences between boys and girls, similar to some reports on Native American youths (Manson et al., 1989).

Roberts, Chen, and Roberts (1997) used data from an ethnically diverse sample of middle school students ($N = 5,423$) to examine differences in suicidal ideation, thoughts about suicide in the past 2 weeks, suicide plans, and suicide attempts. Ideation was examined using a four-item scale and a single item on suicidal thoughts. Ideation was higher among females, older youths, and lower status youths. The same general pattern held for recent suicidal plans and attempts, with the exception of gender, where the trend was for males to report more attempts. Lifetime plans and attempts were higher for females, older youths, and lower status youths. Data were sufficient to compare nine ethnic groups. Multivariate logistic regression analyses, adjusting for the effects of age, gender, and SES, yielded significant odds ratios using the Anglo group as the reference for suicidal ideation for the Mexican (OR = 1.76, $p < 0.01$), Pakistani (OR = 2.0, $p < .01$), and Vietnamese (OR = 1.48, $p < .05$) American groups. For thoughts about suicide in the past 2 weeks, only Pakistani and Mixed Ancestry youths had elevated risk. For suicidal plans in the past 2 weeks, Mixed Ancestry youths (OR = 2.02, $p < .05$) and Pakistani youths (OR = 3.20, $p < .01$) had elevated risk. For recent attempts, only the Pakistani American youths had elevated risk (OR = 3.19, $p < .01$).

Grunbaum, Basen-Enquist, and Pandey (1998), using data from 1,786 high school students (6.5% were Mexican American), report no significant differences between European and Mexican Americans in terms of suicide plans and suicide attempts in the past year. For males, the rates of attempted suicide were 6.3% for European and 6.9% for Mexican Americans; for females the rates were 11.2% for European and 14.9% for Mexican Americans. Substance use increased risk of suicidal behaviors, but not consistently across groups. Depression, a known significant risk factor for suicidal behaviors, was not examined.

Kann et al. (1998), using data from the Youth Risk Behavior Surveillance System of the Centers for Disease Control, report that 2.5% of students had seriously considered attempting suicide during the 12 months preceding the survey. Overall, Hispanic students (23.1%) were significantly more likely than African American students (16.4%) to have considered attempting suicide. More serious suicidal ideation was observed among the 15.7% of students nationwide who, during the 12 months preceding the survey, had made a specific plan to attempt suicide. Overall, Hispanic students (19.6%) were significantly more likely than European and African American students (14.3% and 12.5%, respectively) to have made a suicide plan. Hispanic female students (23.9%) were significantly more likely than African Female female students (16.0%) to have made a suicide plan. Hispanic male students (16.0%) were significantly more likely than European and African American male students (11.0% and 8.8%, respectively) to report this behavior. Nationwide, 7.7% of students had attempted suicide one or more times during the 12 months preceding the survey. Overall, Hispanic students (10.7%) were significantly more likely than white students (6.3%) to have attempted suicide. Hispanic male students (7.2%) were significantly more likely than European male students (3.2%) to report this behavior. Nationwide, 2.6% of students reported having made a suicide attempt during the 12 months preceding the survey that resulted in an injury, poisoning, or overdose that had been treated by a doctor or nurse. No ethnic differences were reported for such serious attempts.

B. DISCUSSION

As this review of studies shows, there are still relatively few data on prevalence of suicidal ideation, plans, or attempts in specific ethnocultural groups. Available results suggest minority status may increase the risk of suicidal behaviors, but also that the effects vary depending on the outcome examined (ideation vs. attempts vs. plans) and the group studied. For example, in one of our studies (Roberts, Chen, & Roberts, 1997), Mexican American, Pakistani American, Vietnamese American, and Mixed Ancestry youths all had elevated prevalences on one or more indicators of suicidal behavior. Adjusting for the effects of age, gender, and SES, Pakistani American students reported higher prevalences of recent ideation, plans, and attempts. An intriguing finding was that youth of Mixed Ancestry appear to be at elevated risk of several suicidal indicators. To our knowledge, this is the first report of such an effect.

We are unaware of any published research that has reported risk of suicidal behaviors among Pakistani American adolescents. At this point, it is not clear why this is so. Likewise, the Chinese youths appear to be at lower risk of all three forms of suicidal behaviors. Why this is so is not apparent, although some studies have reported lower risk of depression for Chinese as well (Chang, Morrissey, & Koplewicz, 1995; Klienman, 1982; Kuo, 1984; Leung, Chan, & Cheng, 1992; Lin, 1953; Shen, 1981; Xia & Zhang, 1984). Mexican American adolescents had higher rates of suicidal behaviors, whereas those of Central American origin did not. What accounts for this differential risk also needs clarification.

Results suggest that risks of suicidal behaviors vary somewhat, depending on the ethnic group and the indicator of suicidal behaviors. That is, there were differential effects across groups observed for suicidal ideation, plans, and attempts. Data support the contention by some that suicidal behaviors are complex, ranging from ideation to attempts to completed suicide (see Reynolds &

Mazza, 1994), with presumed severity in terms of risk of death in that order. For example, prevalence rates in our 1997 study reflect that. Prevalence in the past 2 weeks was 16.7% for ideation, 5.7% for plans, and 3.6% for attempts (Roberts, Chen, & Roberts, 1997).

Findings are limited in some respects by the measures of suicidal behaviors. Although studies often include a range of suicidal behaviors, measures are imprecise. This is particularly problematic in the case of reported suicide attempts. As Reynolds and Mazza (1994) point out, suicide attempters represent a heterogeneous population that includes youths who have made serious and life-threatening attempts as well as youngsters whose attempts are very mild or of limited lethality potential. These two extremes probably represent very different risk groups for completed suicide. For example, Meehan et al. (1992) report that of those young adults who reported ever attempting suicide, 44% actually suffered injury, 25% sought medical care, and 10% were admitted to the hospital. Garrison et al. (1991b) report 5.9% of high school students reported a suicide attempt in the past year not requiring medical care in the past year, and 1.6% reported attempters requiring medical treatment.

The study of nonfatal suicidal behavior has been impeded by the lack of standard nomenclature (Garrison, 1989; Moscicki, 1997; O'Carroll et al., 1996) and by the lack of clear operational definitions when collecting epidemiologic data (Garrison, Lewinsohn, et al., 1991; Moscicki, 1989, 1997). Two critical elements in the study of nonfatal suicidal behaviors are suicidal intent and lethality of the method used (Beautrais et al., 1996; Brent, 1987; Lewinsohn et al., 1996; Moscicki, 1997; Roberts, Chen, & Roberts, 1997). Very few epidemiologic studies of adolescent suicidal behaviors have done so (for exceptions, see Garrison et al., 1991a; Lewinsohn et al., 1996). Recent U.S. studies that have incorporated lethality as of the measure of attempts among adolescents report estimates ranging from 1.6 to 2.6 per 100 (Andrews & Lewinsohn, 1992; Garrison et al., 1993; Meehan, Saltzman, & Sattin, 1991). None of these studies focused on ethnic differences.

Many surveys have been school-based; however, in most school-based surveys it is not possible to assess methods used to attempt suicide or to judge severity of the attempts. Thus, in the case of the many observed ethnic differences in reported suicide attempts, it is not possible to determine whether the increased risk observed for some groups, for example, would remain if method and severity were controlled.

C. NATURAL HISTORY OF SUICIDAL BEHAVIORS

Epidemiological research on adolescent suicide historically has focused on etiology. That is, the research questions driving the inquiry concern identifying which factors under what circumstances increase the likelihood that youths will kill themselves. However, epidemiology is not just the study of the distribution and the causes of diseases. Epidemiology also focuses on the natural history of disease, including its consequences (Friis & Sellers, 1996; Sackett, Haynes, Guyatt, & Tugwell, 1991). So it is with adolescent suicide. Suicidal behaviors represent a continuum, ranging from thoughts to plans to attempts to completions (Kosky, Sillburn, & Zubrick, 1990; Lewinsohn et al., 1996; Pfeffer, 1986, 1997; Reynolds & Mazza, 1994). Although data are scarce, available evidence suggests that the ratio of attempts to completions is high. That is, relatively few suicide attempts among adolescents are successful. For example, studies have found lifetime prevalence rates of suicide attempts reported by adolescents ranging from 3.5% to 11% (Andrews & Lewinsohn, 1992; Dubow et al., 1989; Velez & Cohen, 1988). The 1-year prevalence of serious suicide attempts, of course, is lower, being 1% to 3% in one community study (Garrison et al., 1993). The rate of completed suicides is magnitudes lower, typically in the range of 12 to 15 per 100,000 (see Kachur, 1995; Pfeffer, 1997; Shaffer et al., 1996).

If one assumes a 1-year prevalence of 3% for attempts and a 1-year suicide rate of 12 per 100,000, the prevalence ratio of attempts to completions is approximately 300 to 1. The overwhelming proportion of youths who attempt suicide do not die from their attempts. Thus, there is a relatively large population of adolescents at any given time who have a history of one or more suicide attempts. What are the epidemiological consequences? Are attempters different from nonattempters in terms of their subsequent life course?

Although epidemiological data relevant to this question also are scarce (Shaffer & Hicks, 1994), the evidence available suggests that a history of suicide attempts substantially increases the risk of psychopathology and psychosocial dysfunction among adolescents (see Brent et al., 1993; Garrison et al., 1991a; Lewinsohn et al., 1993; Pfeffer, 1997; Roberts et al., 1998). In perhaps the most systematic epidemiological study of the consequences of unsuccessful suicide attempts, Lewinsohn et al. (1993) found that youths with a history of attempts subsequently are more likely to be depressed and to be experiencing significant psychosocial deficits, particularly in the cognitive and interpersonal spheres. There was a near dose–response effect, with the probability of past suicide attempt increasing substantially as a function of the number of current risk factors.

A small but growing body of epidemiological literature on the subsequent life experience of adolescents who make nonfatal suicide attempts indicate that such youths are at very high risk of continued suicidal behaviors, including ideation and plans for committing suicide. As noted above, youths with a history of attempts also evidence an array of psychosocial deficits, in particular depression. Substantial evidence exists for the role of depression in suicidal behaviors (see Lewinsohn et al., 1996; Pfeffer, 1997; Roberts & Chen, 1995;

Shaffer & Hicks, 1994). Lewinsohn et al. (1993) as well as Roberts, Roberts, & Chen (1998) report that current depression was significantly associated with a history of suicide attempters among adolescents.

The strong association between a history of suicide attempts, current ideation, and current depression suggests that a past suidice attempt in adolescents occurs in the context of other signs of psychopathology (see Birmaher et al., 1996; Lewinsohn et al., 1993; Roberts, Roberts, & Chen, 1998; Shaffer et al., 1996). Indeed, the role of depression is so pervasive that Lewinsohn and his colleagues argue that suicide behavior should be considered an expression of severe depression. Evidence for this hypothesis is of two types. On the one hand, there is the association between the two phenomena. On the other, there are data reported by Lewinsohn et al. (1993) as well as my colleagues and I (Roberts et al., 1998), that the psychosocial characteristics associated with a past attempt are essentially the same as risk factors associated with adult and adolescent depression (e.g., Barnett and Gotlib, 1988; Birmaher et al., 1996; Gotlib & Hammen, 1992; Harrington, 1993; Lewinsohn et al., 1994; Roberts, 1987). To date, there have been no community-based, prospective studies with long-term follow-up of the subsequent functioning of adolescent suicide attempters. Albeit the low base rate of suicide attempts and the fact that the period of risk is not finite make epidemiological follow-up studies difficult, such studies are needed (Shaffer & Hicks, 1994). Although retrospective or prevalence studies provide evidence for covariation of suicide attempts and poor functioning, they do not permit us to address the question of the true temporal relationship of attempts and functioning. To answer that question, we need prospective studies that examine indicators of poor functioning and suicidal behaviors at baseline and then examine the occurrence of future functioning in those with and without attempts, with and without poor functioning at baseline. This is critical, since it is generally assumed that the causal structure producing morbidity is different before and after suicide attempts have occurred. In other words, factors that cause the problem may be different from those that sustain or prolong it (Eaton, 1995; Roberts, 1990). Fortunately, we do have some data, albeit not a lot, from longitudinal or prospective clinical studies. These studies clearly indicate that suicide attempters are at greatly increased risk of poor subsequent psychosocial functioning, including future suicide attempts (Shaffer & Hicks, 1994). In one study, 70% of attempters ultimately committed suicide (Otto, 1972).

Given the paucity of epidemiological data on the natural history of suicidal behaviors among youths (see Lewinsohn et al., 1996; Shaffer & Hicks, 1994), more epidemiological studies of the antecedents and consequences of the range of suicidal behaviors among children and adolescents are needed. Given the very high risk of subsequent suicidal behaviors by youths who have attempted but not completed suicide, this constitutes a high-risk population on which future research should focus.

But, once again, data on adolescents from differing ethnocultural groups are conspicuous by their absence. And again, the question is what is the role of ethnic culture in the natural history of adolescent suicide?

D. Risk Factors

Myriad articles and books have been published on factors that are known or believed to increase the risk of suicidal behaviors. Limitations of space precludes discussion of this body of literature here. The interested reader is referred to recent reviews of this literature (see for example Bell & Clark, 1998; Birmaher et al., 1996; King, 1998; Lewinsohn et al., 1996; Moscicki, 1997; Pfeffer, 1997; Reynolds & Mazza, 1994; Shaffer & Hicks, 1994).

Rather, I would like to reiterate a key point that has emerged from this body of research, and then place ethnic culture in the context of risk and protective factors for suicidal behaviors among adolescents.

The association between psychiatric disorders and suicidal behaviors is so pronounced that Moscicki (1997) asserts that psychiatric dysfunction is a necessary condition for suicide to occur. Moscicki (1997) has succinctly summarized this literature.

> Findings from psychological autopsy studies from the United States and Europe consistently indicate that more than 90% of completed suicides in all age groups are associated with mental or addictive disorders. . . . These disorders are also the strongest observed risk factors for attempted suicide in all age groups. . . . Mood disorders, frequently comorbid with other psychiatric and medical diagnoses, are the most commonly found diagnoses in psychological autopsy studies of completed suicides for both men and women, across all age groups. . . . Substance abuse and behavioral disorders, such as antisocial personality and conduct disorder, are found in much larger proportions in adolescent suicides than in older suicides, which are dominated by depressive disorders. . . . The same psychiatric diagnoses, depression, substance abuse, and aggressive behavior disorders, also have been found to distinguish suicide attempters from nonattempters in carefully controlled studies of both community and clinical populations of adolescents and adults . . . Comorbidity of mental, addictive, and physical disorders has been found in approximately 70% to 80% of completed suicides. . . . Comorbid diagnoses, of mood and substance abuse disorders in particular, also greatly increase the likelihood of attempted suicide. . . . Persons with more than one psychiatric diagnosis are at greatly increased risk for attempted suicide. . . . Prior suicide attempts are among the strongest risk factors for completed suicide and, in retrospective studies, may be the best single predictor of completed suicide. (pp. 506–508)

The implications for research on suicidal behaviors among adolescents is clear. Any study attempting to estimate risk for adolescent suicide must include measures of psychiatric dysfunction, in particular internalizing disorders, such as depression, and externalizing disorders, such as conduct and substance abuse disorders. Failure to do so omits major explanatory variables, as well as potential targets for intervention.

III. ETHNICITY AS AN ETIOLOGIC AGENT

From an epidemiologic perspective, depression and suicidal behaviors can be viewed as the product of the same general factors believed to be involved in the etiology of both psychiatric and somatic disorders (see Cohen, Kessler, & Gordon, 1995; Dohrenwend, 1998). In general, disease outcomes are believed to result from the interaction over time of three etiologic forces: biological, psychological, and social-environmental. Employing this framework, both depression and suicidal behaviors can be hypothesized to most likely occur in populations where (a) there is a family history of such disorders; (b) risk further depends upon social placement factors such as age, gender, and ethnic status; (c) lifetime and current stressors (see Turner, Wheaton, & Lloyd, 1995), such as somatic and comorbid psychiatric disorders in the child or current somatic, psychiatric disorders in the parent; and (d) upon personal and social resources available such as high self-esteem, social support from family and friends, coping style, a sense of control over external events (i.e., mastery), and socioeconomic resources.

What is the role of ethnicity in this conceptual framework? By extension, given a particular family history constellation, and given a particular combination of placement factors such as age, gender, and ethnic status, to the extent ethnic experience reduces stressors and enhances resources, its impact on health should be positive. To the extent ethnicity increases stressors and decreases resources, its impact on health should be negative.

At a basic level, ethnicity can be subdivided into three components: natal, behavioral, and subjective (Trimble, 1995). Typically, in past research, the natal component has been the primary measure of ethnicity or ethnic identity, based on self-identification of ethnicity, birthplace, and generational level (Garcia, 1981; Kitano, 1976). Although these measurements are reliable, the assessment remains at a superficial level of the cultural experience, because social and psychological factors are not taken into account. Therefore, research has moved toward assessing behavioral components with acculturation models, which measure the degree to which changes in cultural patterns occur when two distinct cultures interact (Berry, Trimble, & Olmedo, 1986). The fundamental acculturative behaviors measured are language usage, ethnic affiliation, and knowledge of country of origin (Cuéllar, Harris, & Jasso, 1980; Keefe & Padilla, 1987; Marin et al., 1987). However, acculturation scales have been unable to account for cultural change with simultaneous retention and maintenance of ethnic identification (Glazer & Moynihan, 1970). Acculturation assesses the relationship between an individual's group and another group, whereas ethnic identity assesses the relationship between an individual and their own group. Ethnic identity has been conceptualized as ethnic pride affiliation, belonging, way of life, and loyalty to culture (Alba, 1990; Felix-Ortiz, Newcomb, & Myers, 1994; Mendoza, 1989; Oetting & Beauvais, 1990–91; Phinney & Rotheram, 1987).

In addition to these three basic categories (natal, behavioral, subjective), additional factors have emerged, particularly in relation to health. In regard to acculturation, the concept of acculturative stress has been proposed as more clearly distinguishing specific acculturative stressors (Cervantes, Padilla, & Salgado de Snyder, 1991; Vega et al., 1993). There are additional subjective components of ethnicity which may be influential, such as personal importance of ethnicity, perceived power status of group, perceived discrimination, and ethnic esteem. Salience of ethnicity may be a potential mediator in utilizing ethnicity as a predictor. In other words, the perceived meaningfulness and intensity of ethnic identity may indicate the centrality of ethnicity within the adolescent's identity (Alba, 1990; Bernal, Saenz, & Knight, 1991; Stryker, 1987). Perception of prejudice and discrimination has been identified as another potential aspect of ethnic identity, and in particular may influence psychological stress (Aries & Moorehead, 1989; Keefe & Padilla, 1987; Roberts, Roberts, & Chen, 1995a, 1995b; Semons, 1991). Previous measures of ethnic identity assume that high ethnic identity equates with a positive image of the ethnic group and positive identification; however, it may be possible for individuals to identify with their ethnic group and maintain negative stereotypes and negative images of the group.

Studies of the relation between ethnicity and psychological distress or psychiatric disorder implicitly examine two competing hypotheses, one of which argues that observed ethnic differences are due primarily to social class effects and the other that there are ethnic effects (both positive and negative) on mental health over and above social class effects. Mirowsky and Ross (1980) have labeled these two arguments, respectively, the minority status perspective and the ethnic culture perspective. The former argument asserts that to the extent an ethnic group is both a minority group and disadvantaged, there are chronic social stressors associated with disadvantaged position that produce greater distress. The latter argument, the ethnic culture perspective, assumes that psychological well-being varies with different cultural patterns in terms of beliefs, values, and lifestyles. Thus, disadvantaged social class does not necessarily place members of an ethnic collectivity at greater risk for psychological disorder. Essentially these two arguments turn on a single question of fact: Are the rates of psychological disorder in ethnic minority populations different than the rates in the dominant ethnic population, when social class is controlled? If so, then the ethnic culture hypothesis is supported; if not, the minority status hypothesis is sustained (Roberts & Vernon, 1984).

More recently, attempts to examine this question have extended the analytic strategy to examine both main and interactive effects of ethnic status and SES. For example, Kessler and Neighbors (1986) and Ulbrich, Warheit, and Zimmerman (1989) reported that the effects of social class and the effect of minority status on distress is more pronounced at lower income levels than at higher income levels. The explanations for this relation is that lower status minorities are exposed to more environmental stressors than others and/or they are more emotionally responsive to such stressors, hence higher prevalence of psychological dysfunction (see Kessler, 1979; Ulbrich et al., 1989). However, Somervell, Leaf, Weissman, Blazer, and Bruce (1989) found no evidence of significant or consistent interaction of race (White/Black) with household income or age for depression using data on adults from the five-site ECA study. My own research on adolescents (Roberts & Sobhan, 1992; Roberts, Roberts, & Chen, 1997) also has failed to find interaction effects in samples of European, African, and Mexican American as well as other adolescent groups. Given that the evidence on interaction effects from studies of adults is mixed, and my own studies of adolescents that examine this question have found no evidence for such an effect, additional inquiry clearly is needed. Is this effect a general effect, or conditioned by place, population, or procedures?

There are significant differences in SES among different ethnic groups, which may imply that findings related to "ethnicity" may be essentially due to SES differentials. Therefore, it is important to separate effects of "ethnicity" from effects of SES or at a minimum control for SES when using ethnocultural variables. More specifically, SES appears to be highly correlated with acculturation level and generational level, where less acculturated individuals tend to be of earlier generational levels and lower SES (Cuéllar, 1995; Keefe & Padilla, 1987). Furthermore, there is no literature detailing the relation between SES and subjective ethnocultural variables such as ethnic identity, salience, or perceived discrimination, although there are some indications that ethnic affiliation, pride, and perceived discrimination may be relatively stable across SES and generation levels (Keffe & Padilla, 1987; Phinney, 1990).

There is a particular set of constructs that may increase vulnerability for disordered behavior, including depression and suicidal behaviors. These constructs are fatalism and coping style. Fatalism is the belief that external forces control one's life, which results in a lack of confidence in ability to exert personal control over events and situations (Wheaton, 1982). This belief in external control increases risk of emotional and behavioral problems because it reduces both the will and the ability to cope (Pearlin, Lieberman, Menaghan, & Mullen, 1981; Wheaton, 1980). A fatalistic worldview and passive coping have been found to be more prevalent in lower status groups and in some minority groups (Farris & Glenn, 1976; Kohn, 1974; Lewis, 1961; Wheaton, 1980). In particular, persons of Mexican origin in the United States have been found to have a greater tendency toward fatalism and passive coping, which is related in turn to more depression (Mirowsky & Ross, 1984; Neff & Hoppe, 1993). In fact, Mirowsky and Ross (1984) present data showing that fatalism among Mexican Americans increases risk for depression but reduces risk for anxiety.

IV. CONCLUSIONS

Perusing the literature reviewed in this chapter, it is clear that there are a number of fundamental epidemiologic questions for which as yet we have no empirical answers. The basic questions focus on issues of incidence, prevalence, natural history, and etiologic factors in regard to depression and suicidal behaviors and how ethnicity plays out in this regard.

1. The available data on prevalence are quite limited. For example, there are almost no data on the prevalence of clinical depression among diverse ethnic minorities, different socioeconomic strata, and rural compared with urban populations. The same is true for the spectrum of suicidal behaviors.

2. From the perspective of prevention and treatment as well as epidemiology, understanding the natural history of child and adolescent disorders is critical, yet there are essentially no data on incidence, duration, and recurrence of clinical depression and suicidal behaviors in minority populations.

3. Comorbidity is increasingly recognized as a key phenomenological feature of psychiatric disorders among children and adults (Bird, Gould, & Staghessa, 1993; Brady & Kendall, 1992), yet there are basically no community-based epidemiologic data on the prevalence, incidence, and natural history of comorbid disorders with depression and suicidal behaviors in minority adolescents.

4. A key to understanding disorders is understanding the role of developmental factors (Costello & Angold, 1993), but at present there are few data on the role of development in the manifestation of psychiatric problems, because there are few data from epidemiologic studies examining the relation between developmental milestones of stages and psychiatric syndromes such as depression and suicide.

5. Ultimately, the goal of psychiatric epidemiology is to explain the etiology of mental disorders. A necessary requisite is data from prospective, longitudinal studies assessing the roles of multiple risk factors drawn from both psychosocial and biological domains in specific disorders and the specificity of effects of these factors. Few such data are available on depression or suicidal behaviors among minority youths.

6. In addition to examination of the role of risk factors in etiology, there also is a need for community-based epidemiologic studies aimed at understanding the factors affecting duration and recurrence of child disorders, in particular, depression and suicidal behaviors.

7. To date, the role of biological factors has been little studied and is poorly understood vis-à-vis child and adolescent disorders. Fuller knowledge of the etiology of such disorders will require inclusion of biological and genetic variables in our conceptual models (Cohen et al., 1995; Roger, 1995; Uchino, Cacioppo, & Kiecolt-Glaser, 1996).

8. We need more research on the role of ethnicity in depression and suicidal behaviors, but future research should focus on an expanded conceptualization of the ethnic experience. Reliance on ethnic status as the sole measure of the ethnic experience has yielded limited explanatory power (see Trimble, 1990–91; Roberts & Chen, 1995). Ethnicity is a complex biopsychosocial construct that is only partially operationalized by demographic categories of race or ethnic status. Trimble (1990–91) has argued that ethnicity can (should) be examined using measures that assess three domains: natal, behavioral, and subjective. There have been few epidemiological studies that have incorporated such a strategy, examining the question of what is is about ethnicity that increases or decreases risk for psychiatric disorder.

I submit that these research issues constitute central research challenges that need to be met successfully if we are to better understand depression and suicidal behaviors among adolescents. By this, I mean *all* adolescents, including those from the diverse cultural streams that constitute American society.

REFERENCES

Alba, R. D. (1990). *Ethnic identity: The transformation of White America*. New Haven, CT: Yale University Press.

American Psychiatric Association. (1987). *Diagnostic and statistical manual of mental disorders* (3rd ed. rev.), Washington, DC: Author.

Andrews, J. A., & Lewinsohn, P. M. (1992). Suicidal attempts among older adolescents: Prevalence and co-occurrence with psychiatric disorders. *Journal of the American Academy of Child and Adolescent Psychiatry, 31,* 655–662.

Aries, E., & Moorehead, K. (1989). The importance of ethnicity in the development of identity in Black adolescents. *Psychological Reports, 65,* 75–82.

Barnett, P. A., & Gotlib, I. H. (1988). Psychosocial functioning among older adolescents: Prevalence and co-occurrence with psychiatric disorders. *Psychological Bulletin, 14,* 97–126.

Barron, P., & Parron, L. M. (1986). Sex difference in the Beck Depression Inventory scores of adolescents. *Journal of Youth and Adolescents, 15,* 165–171.

Beautrais, A. L., Joyce, P. R., Mulder, R. T., Fergusson, D. M., Deavoll, B. J., & Nightingale, S. K. (1996). Prevalence and comorbidity of mental disorders in persons making serious suicide attempts: A case-control study. *American Journal of Psychiatry, 153*(8), 1009–1014.

Bell, C. C., & Clark, D. C. (1998). Adolescent suicide. *Pediatric Clinics of North American, 45*(2), 365–380.

Bernal, M. E., Knight, G. P., Ocampo, K. A., Garza, C. A., & Cota, M. K. (1993). Development of Mexican American identity. In M. E. Bernal & G. P. Knight (Eds.), *Ethnic identity* (pp. 31–46). Albany: SUNY Press.

Bernal, M. E., Saenz, D. S.., & Knight, G. P. (1991). Ethnic identity and adaptation of Mexican-American youths in school settings. *Hispanic Journal of Behavioral Sciences, 13*(2), 135–154.

Berry, J., Trimble, J., & Olmedo, E. (1986). Assessment of acculturation. In W. Lonner & J. Berry (Eds.), *Field methods in cross-cultural research* (pp. 291–324). Newbury Park, CA: Sage.

Biernoff, M. A. (1970). *A survey of Pueblo Indian suicide.* Unpublished manuscript. Indian Health Service Alcohol Program, Albuquerque, NM.

Bird, H. R., Canino, G., Rubio-Stipec, M., et al. (1988). Estimates of the prevalence of childhood maladjustment in a community survey in Puerto Rico. The use of combined measures. *Archives of General Psychiatry, 45,* 1120–1126.

Bird, H. R., Gould, M. S., & Staghessa, B. M. (1993). Patterns of diagnostic comorbidity in a community sample of children aged 9 through 16 years. *Journal of the American Academy of Child and Adolescent Psychiatry, 32,* 361–368.

Birmaher, B., Ryan, N. D., Williamson, D. E., Brent, D. A., Kaufman, J., Dahl, R. E., Perel, J., & Nelson, B. (1996). Childhood adolescent depression: A review of the past 10 years. Part I. *Journal of the American Academy of Child and Adolescent Psychiatry, 35*(11), 1427–1439.

Brady, E. U., & Kendall, P. C. (1992). Comorbidity of anxiety and depression in children and adolescents. *Psychological Bulletin, 111,* 244–255.

Brent, D. A. (1987). Correlates of medical lethality of suicide attempts in children and adolescents. *Journal of the American Academy of Child and Adolescent Psychiatry, 26,* 87–89.

Brent, D. A., Johnson, B., Bartle, S., et al. (1993). Personality disorder, tendency to impulsive violence, and suicidal behavior in adolescents. *Journal of the American Academy of Child and Adolescent Psychiatry, 32,* 69–75.

Campos, J. J., Mumme, D. L., Kermoian, R., & Campos, R. G. (1994). A functionalist perspective on the nature of emotion. In N. A. Fox (Ed.), *Monographs of the Society for Research in Child Development, 59* (2-3, Serial No. 240, pp. 284–303). Berkeley, CA: Institute of Human Development.

Cervantes, R. C., Padilla, A. M., & Salgado de Snyder, N. (1991). The Hispanic Stress Inventory: A culturally relevant approach to psychosocial assessment. *Journal of Consulting and Clinical Psychology, 3,* 438–447.

Chang, L., Morrissey, R. F., & Koplewicz, H. S. (1995). Prevalence of psychiatric symptoms and their relation to adjustment among Chinese-American youth. *Journal of the American Academy of Child and Adolescent Psychiatry, 34*(1), 91–99.

Cohen, S., Kessler, R. C., & Gordon, L. U. (1995). Strategies for measuring stress in studies of psychiatric and physical disorders. In S. Cohen, R. C. Kessler, & L. U. Gordon (Eds.), *Measuring stress: A guide for health and social scientists* (pp. 3–28). New York: Oxford Press.

Cole, D. A., Martin, J. M., Peeke, L., Henderson, A., & Harwell, J. (1998). Validation of depression and anxiety measures in White and Black youths: Multitrait-multimethod analyses. *Psychological Assessment, 10*(3), 261–276.

Cooper, B., & Morgan, H. G. (1973). *Epidemiologic psychiatry.* Springfield, IL: Charles C. Thomas.

Costello, E. J., & Angold, A. (1993). Toward a developmental epidemiology of the disruptive behavior disorders. *Developmental Psychopathology, 5,* 91–101.

Cuéllar, I. (1995). Acculturation rating scale for Mexican-Americans II: A revision of the original ARSMA scale. *Hispanic Journal of Behavioral Sciences, 17*(3), 275–304.

Cuéllar, I., Harris, L. C., & Jasso, R. (1980). An acculturation scale for Mexican American normal and clinical populations. *Hispanic Journal of Behavioral Sciences, 2,* 199–217.

Demetriades, D., Murray, J., Sinz, B., Myles, D., Chand, L., Sathyaragiswaran, L., Noguchi, T., Bongard, F. S., Vryer, G. H., 7 Gaspard, D. J. (1998). Epidemiology of major trauma and trauma deaths in Los Angeles County. *Journal of the American College of Surgery, 187*(4), 373–383.

Dinges, G., & Duong-Tran, Q. (1990, October). *Suicide ideation and suicide attempt among American Indian and Alaska Native boarding school adolescents.* Paper presented at the American Indian/Alaska Native Adolescent Suicide Research Conference, Estes Park, CO.

Doerfler, L. A., Felner, R. A., Rowlison, R. T., Raley, P. A., & Evans, E. (1988). Depression in children and adolescents: A comparative analysis of the utility and construct validity of two assessment measures. *Journal of Consulting and Clinical Psychology, 56,* 769–772.

Dohrenwend, B. P. (Ed.). (1998). *Adversity, stress, and psychopathology.* New York: Oxford University Press.

Dubow, E. F., Kaush, D. F., Blum, M. C., Reed, J., & Bush, E. (1989). Correlates of suicidal ideation and attempts among older adolescents: Prevalence and co-occurrence with psychiatric disorders, *Journal of the American Academy of Child and Adolescent Psychiatry, 32,* 655–622.

Eaton, W. W. (1995). Studying the natural history of psychopathology. In M. T. Tsuang, M. Tohen, & G. E. P. Zahner (Eds.), *Textbook of psychiatric epidemiology* (pp. 157–177). New York: Wiley-Liss.

Emslie, G. J., Weinberg, W. A., Rush, A. J., Adams, R. M., 7 Rintelmann, J. W. (1990). Depressive symptoms by self-report in adolescence: Phase I of the development of a questionnaire for depression by self-report. *Journal of Child Neurology, 5,* 114–121.

Farris, B. E., & Glenn, N. D. (1976). Fatalism and familism among Anglos and Mexican-Americans in San Antonio. *Sociology and Social Research, 60,* 393–402.

Felix-Ortiz, M., Newcomb, M. D., & Myers, H. (1994). A multi-dimensional measure of cultural identity for Latino and Latina adolescents. *Hispanic Journal of Behavioral Sciences, 16*(2), 99–115.

Fleming, J. E., & Offord, D. R. (1990). Epidemiology of childhood depressive disorders: A critical review. *Journal of the American Academy of Child and Adolescent Psychiatry, 29*(4), 571–580.

Friis, R. H., & Sellers, T. A. (1996). *Epidemiology for public health practice.* Gaithersburg, MD: Aspen.

Garcia, J. A. (1981). Self-identity among Mexican origin populations. *Social Science Quarterly, 62,* 88–98.

Garrison, C. Z. (1989). The study of suicidal behavior in the schools. *Suicide and Life-Threatening Behavior, 19,* 120–130.

Garrison, C. Z., Addy, C. L., Jackson, K. L., McKeown, R. E., & Waller, J. L. (1991a). A longitudinal study of suicidal ideation in young adolescents. *Journal of the American Academy of Child and Adolescent Psychiatry, 30*(4), 597–603.

Garrison, C. Z., Addy, C. L., Jackson, K. L., McKeown, R. E., & Waller, J. L. (1991b). Suicidal behaviors in young adolescents. *American Journal of Epidemiology, 133*(10), 1005–1014.

Garrison, C. Z., Addy, C. L., Jackson, K. L., McKeown, R. E., & Waller, J. L. (1992). Major depressive disorder and dysthymia in young adolescents. *American Journal of Epidemiology, 135,* 792–802.

Garrison, C. Z., Jackson, K. L., Marsteller, F., McKeown, R. E., & Addy, C. L. (1990). A longitudinal study of depressive symptomology in young adolescents. *Journal of the American Academy of Child and Adolescent Psychiatry, 29,* 581–585.

Garrison, C. Z., Lewinsohn, C. Z., Lewinsohn, P. M., Marsteller, F., et al. (1991). The assessment of suicidal behavior in adolescents. *Suicide and Life-Threatening Behavior, 21,* 217–230.

Garrison, C. Z., McKeown, R. E., Valois, R. F., et al. (1993). Aggression, substance use, and suicidal behaviors in high school students. *American Journal of Public Health, 83,* 179–184.

Gibbs, J. T. (1985). Psychological factors associated with depression in urban adolescents females: Implications for assessment. *Journal of Youth and Adolescence, 14,* 47–60.

Glazer, N., & Moynihan, D. (1970). *Beyond the melting pot.* Cambridge, MA: Harvard University Press.

Gotlib, I., & Hammen, C. (1992). *Psychological aspects of depression: Toward a cognitive-interpersonal integration.* Chichester, U.K.: John Wiley & Sons.

Greenberger, E., & Chen, C. (1996). Perceived family relationships and depressed mood in early and late adolescence: A comparison of European and Asian Americans. *Developmental Psychology, 32*(4), 707–716.

Grunbaum, J. A., Basen-Engquist, K., & Pandey, D. (1998). Association between violent behaviors and substance use among Mexican-American and non-Hispanic White high school students. *Journal of Adolescent Health, 23,* 153–159.

Harkavy, J., Friedman, M. N., Asnis, G. M., Boeck, M., & DiFore, J. (1987). Prevalence of specific suicidal behaviors in a high school sample. *American Journal of Psychiatry, 144,* 1203–1206.

Harrington, R. C. (1993). *Depressive disorders in childhood and adolescence.* New York: John Wiley.

Helms, J. (1985). Toward a theoretical explanation of the effects of race on counseling: A Black and White model. *The Counseling Psychologist, 12,* 153–165.

Helsel, W., & Matson, J. (1984). The assessment of depression in children: The internal structure of the child depression inventory (CDI). *Behavioral Research and Therapy, 22,* 289–298.

Hillard, J. R., Slomowitz, M., & Deddens, J. (1988). Determinants of emergency psychiatric admission for adolescents and adults. *American Journal of Psychiatry, 145,* 1416–1419.

Hovey, J. D. (1998). Acculturative stress, depression, and suicidal ideation among Mexican American adolescents: Implications for the development of suicide prevention programs in schools. *Psychological Reports, 8,* 249–250.

Hovey, J. D., & King, C. A. (1996). Acculturative stress, depression, and suicidal ideation among immigrant and second-generation Latino adolescents. *Journal of the American Academy of Child and Adolescent Psychiatry, 35*(9), 1183–1192.

Howard-Pitney, B., LaFromboise, T. D., Basil, M., September, B., & Johnson, M. (1992). Psychological and social indicators of suicide ideation and suicide attempts in Zuni adolescents. *Journal of Consulting and Clinical Psychology, 60*(3), 473–476.

Jensen, P. S., Wantanabe, H. K., Richters, J. E., Cortes, R., Roper, M., & Liu, S. (1995). Prevalence of mental disorder in military children and adolescents: Findings from a two-stage community survey. *Journal of the American Academy of Child and Adolescent Psychiatry, 34,* 1514–1524.

Kachur, S. P. (1995). *Suicide in the United States, 1980–1992.* Atlanta: National Center for Injury Prevention and Control.

Kandel, D. B., & Davies, M. (1982). Epidemiology of depressive mood in adolescents. *Archives of General Psychiatry, 39,* 1205–1212.

Kann, L., Kinchen, S. A., Williams, B. I., Ross, J. G., Lowry, R., Hill, C. V., Grunbaum, J. A., Blumson, P. S., Collins, J. L., & Kolbe, L. J. (1998). Youth risk behavior surveillance—United States, 1997. *Journal of School Health, 68*(9), 355–369.

Kaplan, G. A., Hong, G. K., & Weinhold, C. (1984). Epidemiology of depressive symptomology in adolescence. *Journal of the American Academy of Child Psychiatry, 23,* 91–98.

Kashani, J. H., & McNaul, J. P. (1997). Mood disorders in adolescence. In J. M. Wiener (Ed.), *Textbook of child and adolescent psychiatry* (pp. 343–384). New York: John Wiley & Sons.

Katragadda, C. P., & Tidwell, R. (1998). Rural Hispanic adolescents at risk for depressive symptoms. *Journal of Applied Social Psychology, 28*(20), 1916–1930.

Keefe, S., & Padilla, A. (1987). *Chicano ethnicity.* Albuquerque: University of New Mexico Press.

Kessler, R. C. (1979). Stress, social status, and psychological distress. *Journal of Health and Social Behavior, 20,* 259–273.

Kessler, R. C., & Neighbors, H. W. (1986). A new perspective on the relationship among race, social class, and psychological distress. *Journal of Health and Social Behavior, 27,* 107–115.

King, C. (1998). Suicidal behavior in adolescence. In R. W. Maris, M. M. Silverman, et al. (Eds.), *Review of Suicidality, 1997* (pp. 61–95). New York: Guilford.

Kinkel, R. J., Bailey, C. W., & Josef, N. C. (1989). Correlates of adolescent suicide attempts: Alienation, drugs, and social background. *Journal of Alcohol and Drug Education, 34,* 85–96.

Kitano, H. (1976). *Japanese Americans: The evolution of a subculture.* Englewood Cliffs, NJ: Prentice Hall.

Klineman, A. (1982). Neurasthenia and depression: A study of somatization and culture in China. *Culture, Medicine, and Psychiatry, 6,* 117–190.

Kohn, M. (1972). Class, family, and schizophrenia. *Social Forces, 50,* 295–304.

Kohn, M. (1974). Social class and schizophrenia: A critical review and reformulation. In P. Roman & H. Trice (Eds.), *Explanations in psychiatric sociology* (pp. 113–137). Philadelphia: F. A. Davis.

Kosky, R., Silburn, S., & Zubrick, S. R. (1990). Are children and adolescents who have suicidal thoughts different from those that attempt suicide? *Journal of Nervous and Mental Disorders, 178,* 38–43.

Kuo, W. H. (1984). Prevalence of depression among Asian-Americans. *Journal of Nervous and Mental Disease, 172,* 449–457.

Lester, D., & Anderson, D. (1992). Depression and suicidal ideation in African American and Hispanic American high school students. *Psychological Reports, 71,* 618.

Leung, C. M., Chan, K. K., & Cheng, K. K. (1992). Psychiatric morbidity in a general medical ward: Hong Kong's experience. *General Hospital Psychiatry, 14,* 196–200.

Lewinsohn, P. M., Hops, H., Roberts, R. E., Seeley, J. R., & Andrews, J. A. (1993). Adolescent psychopathology I: Prevalence and incidence of depression and other DSM-III-R disorders in high school students. *Journal of Abnormal Psychology, 102,* 133–144.

Lewinsohn, P. M., Rhode, P., & Seeley, S. R. (1996). Adolescent suicidal ideation and attempts: Prevalence, risk factors, and clinical implications. *Clinical Psychology: Science and Practice, 3,* 25–46.

Lewinsohn, P. M., Roberts, R. E., Seeley, J. R., Rhode, P., Gotlib, I. H., & Hops, H. (1994). Adolescent depression II: Psychosocial risk factors. *Journal of Abnormal Psychology, 103,* 302–315.

Lewis, O. (1961). *The children of Sanchez: Autobiography of a Mexican family.* New York: Random House.

Lin, T. (1953). A study of the incidence of mental disorders in Chinese and other cultures. *Psychiatry, 16,* 313–336.

Lubin, B., & McCollum, K. (1994). Depressive mood in Black and White female adolescents. *Adolescence, 29,* 241–245.

Manson, S. M., Ackerman, L. M., Dick, R. W., Baron, A. E., & Fleming, C. M. (1990). Depressive symptoms among American Indian adolescents: Psychometric characteristics of the CES-D psychological assessment. *Journal of Consulting and Clinical Psychology, 2,* 231–237.

Manson, S. M., Beals, J., Dick, R., & Duclos, C. (1989). Risk factors for suicide among Indian adolescents at a boarding school. *Public Health Reports, 104,* 609–614.

Marin, G., Sabogal, F., Van-Oss-Marin, B., Otero-Sabogal, R., & Perez-Stable, E. J. (1987). Development of a short acculturation scale for Hispanics. *Hispanic Journal of Behavioral Sciences, 9,* 183–205.

McDonald, R., & Gynther, M. (1963). MMPI differences associated with sex, race, and class in two adolescent samples, *Journal of Consulting Psychology, 27,* 112–116.

Meehan, P. J., Saltzman, L. E., & Sattin, R. W. (1991). Suicides among older United States residents: Epidemiologic characteristics and trends. *American Journal of Public Health, 81,* 1198–1200.

Meehan, P. J., Lamb, J. A., Saltzman, L. E., et al. (1992). Attempted suicide among young adults: Progress toward a meaningful estimate of prevalence. *American Journal of Psychiatry, 149,* 44–41.

Mendoza, R. H. (1989). An empirical scale to measure type and degree of acculturation in Mexican-American adolescents and adults. *Journal of Cross-Cultural Psychology, 20*(4), 372–385.

Mirowsky, J., & Ross, C. E. (1980). Minority status, ethnic culture, and distress: A comparison of Blacks, Whites, Mexicans, and Mexican Americans. *American Journal of Sociology, 86,* 479–495.

Mirowsky, J., & Ross, C. E. (1984). Mexican culture and its emotional contradictions. *Journal of Health and Social Behavior, 25,* 2–13.

Moscicki, E. K. (1989). Epidemiologic surveys as tools for studying suicidal behavior: A review. *Suicide and Life-Threatening Behavior, 19,* 131–146.

Moscicki, E. K. (1995). Epidemiology of suicidal behavior. *Suicide and Life-Threatening Behavior, 25,* 22–35.

Moscicki, E. K. (1997). Identification of suicide risk factors using epidemiologic studies. *Psychiatric Clinics of North America, 20*(3), 499–517.

National Center for Health Statistics. (1994). Advance report of final mortality statistics, 1991. *Monthly Vital Statistics Report, 42*(2, Suppl.). Hyattsville, MD: U.S. Public Health Service.

Neff, J. A., & Hoppe, S. K. (1993). Race/ethnicity, acculturation, and psychological distress: Fatalism and religiosity as cultural resources. *Journal of Community Psychology, 21*, 3–20.

Nolen-Hoeksema, S. (1991). Responses to depression and their effects on the duration of depressive episodes. *Journal of Abnormal Psychology, 100*, 569–582.

Nolen-Hoeksema, S., & Girgis, J. S. (1994). The emergence of gender differences in depression during adolescence. *Psychological Bulletin, 115*, 424–443.

Novins, D. K., Beals, J., Roberts, R. E., & manson, S. M. (1999). Factors associated with suicidal ideation among American Indian adolescents: Does culture matter? *Suicide and Life-Threatening Behavior.* (in press).

O'Carroll, P. W., Berman, A. L., Maris, R. W., et al. (1996). Beyond the Tower of Babel: A nomenclature for suicidology. *Suicide and Life-Threatening Behavior, 26*, 237–252.

Oetting, E. R., & Beauvais, F. (1990–91). Orthogonal cultural identification theory: The cultural identification of minority adolescents. *The International Journal of the Addictions*, 655–685.

Otto, U. (1972). Suicidal acts by children and adolescents: A follow-up study. *Acta Psychiatrica Scandinavica, 233*, 7–123.

Pearlin, L. E., Lieberman, M. A., Menaghan, E. G., & Mullan, J. T. (1981). The stress process. *Journal of Health and Social Behavior, 22*, 337–356.

Pearlin, L. E., & Schooler, C. (1978). The structure of coping. *Journal of Health and Social Behavior, 19*, 2–21.

Pfeffer, C. R. (1986). *The suicidal child.* New York: Guilford.

Pfeffer, C. R. (1997). Suicide and suicidality. In J. M. Weiner (Ed.), *Textbook of child and adolescent psychiatry* (pp. 727–738). Washington, DC: American Psychiatric Press.

Phinney, J. S., & Alipuria, L. L. (1990). Ethnic identity in college students from four ethnic groups. *Journal of Adolescence, 13*, 171–183.

Phinney, J. S. (1990). Ethnic identity in adolescents and adults: Review of research. *Psychological Bulletin, 108*, 499–514.

Phinney, J. S., & Rotheram, M. J. (Eds.). (1987). *Children's ethnic socialization: Pluralism and development.* Newbury Park, CA: Sage.

Prescott, C. A., McArdle, J. J., Hishinuma, E. S., Johnson, R. C., Miyamoto, R. H., Andrade, N. N., Edman, J. L., Makini, G. K., Nahulu, L. B., Yuen, N. Y. C., & Carlton, B. S. (1998). Prediction of major depression and dysthymia from CES-D scores among ethnic minority adolescents. *Journal of the American Academy of Child and Adolescent Psychiatry, 37*(5), 495–503.

Regier, D., & Allen, G. (1981). *Risk factor research in the major mental disorders* (DHHS Publication No. ADM 81-1068). Washington, DC: U.S. Government Printing Office.

Reynolds, W. M. (1986). *Reynolds Adolescent Depression Scale.* Odessa, FL: Psychological Assessment Resources.

Reynolds, W. M. (1988). *Suicidal Ideation Questionnaire (SIQ): Professional manual.* Odessa, FL: Psychological Assessment Resources.

Reynolds, W., & Graves, A. (1989). Reliability of children's reports of depressive symptomology. *Journal of Abnormal Child Psychology, 17*, 647–655.

Reynolds, W. M., & Mazza, J. J. (1992, July). *Suicidal behavior in non-referred adolescents.* Paper presented at the International Conference for Suicidal Behavior, Western Psychiatric Clinic, Pittsburgh, PA.

Reynolds, W. M., & Mazza, J. J. (1994). Suicide and suicidal behaviors in children and adolescents. In W. M. Reynolds & H. J. Johnson (Eds.), *Handbook of depression in children and adolescents* (pp. 525–580). New York: Plenum.

Roberts, R. E. (1987). Epidemiological issues in measuring preventive effects. In R. F. Munoz (Ed.), *Depression prevention: Research directions* (pp. 45–78). Washington, DC: Hemisphere.

Roberts, R. E. (1988). The epidemiology of depression in minorities. In P. Muehrer (Ed.), *Research perspectives on depression and suicide in minorities* (pp. 1–20). Washington, DC: National Institute of Mental Health.

Roberts, R. E. (1990). Special population issues in screening for depression. In C. C. Attkisson & J. M. Zich (Eds.), *Depression in primary care: Screening and detection* (pp. 183–216). New York: Routledge.

Roberts, R. E. (1994). Research on the mental health of Mexican origin children and adolescents. In C. Telles & M. Karno (Eds.), *Latino mental health: Current research and policy perspectives* (pp. 17–39). Los Angeles: University of California.

Roberts, R. E., Andrews, J. A., Lewinsohn, P. M., & Hops, H. (1990). Assessment of depression in adolescents using the Center for Epidemiologic Studies Depression Scale. *Psychological Assessment: A Journal of Consulting and Clinical Psychology, 2,* 122–128.

Roberts, R. E., & Chen, Y.-W. (1995). Depressive symptoms and suicidal ideation among Mexican-origin and Anglo adolescents. *Journal of the American Academy of Child and Adolescent Psychiatry, 34,* 81–90.

Roberts, R. E., Chen, Y. R., & Roberts, C. R. (1997). Ethnocultural differences in prevalence of adolescent suicidal behaviors. *Suicide and Life-Threatening Behavior, 27*(2), 208–217.

Roberts, R. E., Lewinsohn, P. M., & Seeley, J. R. (1991). Screening for adolescent depression: A comparison of depression scales. *Journal of American Academy Child and Adolescent Psychiatry, 30,* 58–66.

Roberts, R. E., Roberts, C. R., & Chen, Y-W. (1995a, October, November). *Ethnocultural differences in adolescent depression and suicidal behaviors.* Paper presented at American Public Health Association Meeting, San Diego, CA.

Roberts, R. E., Roberts, C. R., & Chen, Y-W. (1995b, May). *Ethnicity as a risk factor for adolescent depression.* Paper presented at the World Psychiatric Association Meeting, New York, N.Y.

Roberts, R. E., Roberts, C. R., & Chen, Y. R. (1997). Ethnocultural differences in the prevalence of adolescent depression. *American Journal of Community Psychology, 25,* 95–110.

Roberts, R. E., Roberts, C. R., & Chen, Y. R. (1998). Suicidal thinking among adolescents with a history of attempted suicide. *Journal of the American Academy of Child and Adolescent Psychiatry, 37*(12), 1294–1300.

Roberts, R. E., & Sobhan, M. (1992). Symptoms of depression in adolescence: A comparison of Anglo, African, and Hispanic Americans. *Journal of Youth and Adolescence, 21*:639–651.

Roberts, R. E., & Vernon, S. W. (1984). Minority status and psychological stress re-examined: The case of Mexican Americans. *Research in Community Mental Health, 4,* 131–164.

Robinson, J. (1986). Emergencies I. In K. S. Robson (Ed.), *Manual of clinical child psychiatry* (pp. 185–211). New York: Oxford University Press.

Roger, D. (1995). Emotion control, coping strategies, and adaptive behavior. In C. D. Spielberger, I. G., Sarason, Brebner, J. M. T., Greenglass, E., Laungani, P., & O'Roark, A. M. (Eds.), *Stress and emotion: Anxiety, anger, and curiosity* Vol. 15 (pp. 255–264). Washington, DC: Taylor & Francis.

Ross, C. E., Mirowsky, J., & Cockerham, W. C. (1983). Social class, Mexican culture, and fatalism: Their effects on psychological distress. *American Journal of Community Psychology, 11,* 383–399.

Sackett, D. L., Haynes, R. B., Guyatt, G. H., & Tugwell, P. (1991). *Clinical epidemiology.* Boston: Little, Brown.

Schoenbach, V. J., Kaplan, B. H., Grimson, R. C., & Wagner, E. H. (1982). Use of a symptom scale to study the prevalence of a depressive syndrome in adolescence. *American Journal of Epidemiology, 116,* 791–800.

Schwartz, J. A. J., & Koenig, L. J. (1996). Response styles and negative affect among adolescents. *Cognitive Therapy and Research, 20*(1), 13–36.

Semons, M. (1991). Ethnicity in the urban high school: A naturalistic study of student experiences. *The Urban Review, 23,* 137–157.

Shaffer, D., & Hicks, R. (1994). *Suicide.* In I. B. Pless (Ed.), *Epidemiology of childhood disorders* (pp. 339–365). New York: Oxford University Press.

Shaffer, D., Gould, M. S., Fisher, P., et al. (1996). Psychiatric diagnosis in child and adolescent suicide. *Archives of General Psychiatry, 53,* 339–348.

Shen, Y. (1981). The psychiatric services in the urban and rural areas of the People's Republic of China. *Bulletin of the Neuroinformation Laboratory of Nagasaki University, 8,* 131–137.

Siegal, J. M., Aneshensle, C. S., Taub, B., Cantwell, D. P., & Driscoll, A. K. (1998). Adolescent depressed mood in a multiethnic sample. *Journal of Youth and Adolescence, 27*(4), 413–427.

Smith, J. C., Mercy, J. A., & Warren, C. W. (1985). Comparison of suicides among Anglos and Hispanics in five Southwestern states. *Suicide and Life-Threatening Behavior, 15*(1), 14–26.

Somerville, P. D., Leaf, P. J., Weissman, M. M., Blazer, D. G., & Bruce, M. L. (1989). The prevalence of major depression in Black and White adults in five United States communities. *American Journal of Epidemiology, 130,* 725–735.

Stryker, S. (1987). Identity theory: Developments and extension. In K. Yarkley & T. Honess (Eds.), *Self and identity: Psychosocial perspectives* (pp. 83–108). New York: Wiley.

Swanson, J. W., Linskey, A. O., Quintero-Salinas, R., Pumariega, A. J., & Holzer, C. E. (1992). A binational school survey of depressive symptoms, drug use, and suicidal ideation. *Journal of the American Academy of Child and Adolescent Psychiatry, 31,* 669–678.

Teri, L. (1982). The use of the Beck Depression Inventory with adolescents. *Journal of Abnormal Child Psychology, 10,* 277–284.

Tolor, A., & Murphy, V. V. (1985). Stress and depression in high school students. *Psychological Reports, 57,* 535–541.

Treadwell, K., Flannery-Schroeder, E., & Kendall, P. (1995). Ethnicity and gender in relation to adaptive functioning, diagnostic status, and treatment outcome in children from an anxiety clinic. *Journal of Anxiety Disorders, 9,* 373–384.

Trimble, J. E. (1990–91). Ethnic specification, validation prospects, and the future of drug use research. *International Journal of the Addictions, 25,* 149–170.

Trimble, J. E. (1995). Toward an understanding of ethnicity and ethnic identity and their relationship with drug use research. In G. J. Botvin, S. Schinke, & M. Orlandi (Eds.), *Drug abuse prevention with multi-ethnic youth* (pp. 176–202). Thousand Oaks, CA: Sage.

Turner, R. J., Wheaton, B., & Lloyd, D. A. (1995). The epidemiology of social stress. *American Sociological Review, 60,* 104–125.

Uchino, B. N., Cacioppo, J. T., & Kiecolt-Glaser, J. K. (1996). The relationship between social support and physiological processes: A review with emphasis on underlying mechanisms and implications for health. *Psychological Bulletin, 119*(3), 488–531.

Ulbrich, P. A., Warheit, G. J., & Zimmerman, R. S. (1989). Race, socioeconomic status, and psychological distress: An examination of differential vulnerability. *Journal of Health and Social Behavior, 30,* 131–146.

Vega, W. A., Gil, A., Zimmerman, R. S., & Warheit, W. J. (1993). Risk factors for suicidal behavior among Hispanic, African American, and non-Hispanic White boys in early adolescence. *Ethnicity and Disease, 3,* 229–241.

Velez, C. N., & Cohen, P. (1988). Suicidal behavior and ideation in a community sample of children: Maternal and youth reports. *Journal of the American Academy of Child and Adolescent Psychiatry, 27,* 349–356.

Walter, H. J., Vaughan, R. D., Armstrong, B., Krakoff, R. Y., Maldonado, L. M., Tiezzi, L., & McCarthy, J. F. (1995). Sexual, assaultive, and suicidal behaviors among urban minority junior high school students. *Journal of the American Academy of Child and Adolescent Psychiatry, 34*(1), 73–80.

Warheit, G. J., Zimmerman, R. S., Khoury, E. L., Vega, W. A., & Gil, A. G. (1996). Disaster related stress, depressive signs and symptoms, and suicidal ideation among a multi-racial/ethnic sample of adolescents: A longitudinal analysis. *Journal of Child Psychology and Psychiatry, 37*(4), 435–444.

Weinberg, W. A., & Emslie, G. J. (1987). Depression and suicide in adolescents. *International Pediatrics, 2,* 154–159.

Wheaton, B. (1980). The sociogenesis of psychological disorder: An attributional theory. *Journal of Health and Social Behavior, 21,* 100–124.

Wheaton, B. (1982). Uses and abuses of the Langner Index: A reexamination of findings on psychological and psychophysiological distress. In D. Mechanic (Ed.), *Psychosocial epidemiology: Symptoms, illness behavior, and help-seeking* (pp. 25–53). New York: Neale Watson.

Wrobel, N., & Lachar, D. (1995). Racial differences in adolescent self-report: A comparative validity study using homogeneous MMPI content measures. *Psychological Assessment, 7,* 140–147.

Xia, Z. Y., & Zhang, M. (1984). Affective psychoses. In Z. Y. Xia et al. (Eds.), *Clinical Psychiatry,* Volume 2 (in Chinese: pp.) Shanghai: Jingshenyixuecongshu.

Yuen, N., Andrade, N., Nahulu, L., Makini, G., McDermott, J. F., Danko, G., Johnson, R., & Waldron, J. W. (1996). The rate and characteristics of suicide attempters in the Native Hawaiian adolescent population. *Suicide and Life-Threatening Behavior, 26*(1), 27–36.

CHAPTER 19

Culturally Competent Use of the Minnesota Multiphasic Personality Inventory-2

ROBERT J. VELÁSQUEZ
GUADALUPE X. AYALA
Joint Doctoral Program in Clinical Psychology
San Diego State University-University of California, San Diego
San Diego, California

SONIA MENDOZA
California School of Professional Psychology
San Diego, California

ELAHE NEZAMI
Institute for Health Promotion and Disease Prevention Research
University of Southern California
Los Angeles, California

IDALIA CASTILLO-CANEZ
Joint Doctoral Program in Clinical Psychology
San Diego State University-University of California, San Diego
San Diego, California

TERRY PACE
Counseling Psychology Program
University of Oklahoma
Norman, Oklahoma

SANDRA K. CHONEY
Behavioral Health Services
Muscogee (Creek) Nation
Okmulgee, Oklahoma

FRANCISCO C. GOMEZ, JR.
San Diego, California

LAURALYN E. MILES
Joint Doctoral Program in Clinical
Psychology
San Diego State University-
University of California, San Diego
San Diego, California

In this chapter, we examine the use of the Minnesota Multiphasic Personality Inventory-2 (MMPI-2) with ethnically diverse minorities in the United States including Puerto Rico. We have intentionally designed our chapter to answer a series of questions regarding the MMPI-2 and its application to minority populations. These questions are frequently posed by both researchers and clinicians who consider using this instrument in the evaluation of minority group members. These questions are also frequently asked by graduate students who are enrolled in psychological assessment courses and by colleagues who attend MMPI-2 training workshops. For example, in the first section of this chapter, we attempt to answer the following question: To what extent has the MMPI-2 been applied to ethnic minorities? We continue by addressing these additional questions in successive order: What are the trends or patterns of MMPI-2 research with minorities? What types of research still need to be conducted with the MMPI-2? What constitutes a culturally competent approach to the use of the MMPI-2 with minorities? In addition, we discuss six case studies that illustrate culturally competent approaches to MMPI-2 use and interpretation.

Handbook of Multicultural Mental Health: Assessment and Treatment of Diverse Populations

It is important to note that in this chapter we only focus on the MMPI-2, thus, only adult populations. The MMPI-A, for adolescents, was published in 1992 (see Butcher, Williams, et al., 1992). Research with ethnic minority adolescents has begun to emerge (Butcher, Cabiya, et al., 1998; Gumbiner, 1998; Negy, Leal-Puente, Trainor, & Carlson, 1997; Pena, 1996; Tyson, 1997).

I. TO WHAT EXTENT IS THE MMPI-2 USED WITH AMERICAN ETHNIC MINORITIES?

Since 1989, when the MMPI-2 was published as the revision of the original MMPI (see Butcher, Dahlstrom, Graham, Tellegen, & Kaemmer, 1989), 58 studies have been conducted with ethnic minority groups in the United States (including Puerto Rico). Table I presents studies on ethnic/racial groups using the MMPI-2. The subgroup entitled "multiple groups" indicates that the studies included more than one ethnic group. Unlike research with the MMPI, which primarily focused on African Americans (see Dahlstrom, Lachar, & Dahlstrom, 1986; Greene, 1987), it appears that the current focus of research for the MMPI-2 is on Latinos, with Mexican-Americans or Chicanos being the most studied subgroup. African-Americans rank second, with Asians, American Indians, and Iranian Americans receiving minimal attention (see Table I).

Unlike the Rorschach, Personality Assessment Inventory (PAI), or Millon Clinical Multiaxial Inventory (MCMI), the MMPI-2 is frequently employed by

TABLE I   MMPI-2 Research with American Minorities:
Studies by Ethnicity/Race (1989–1998)[a]

Ethnic/racial group	Number of studies
Latinos	24
Mexican Americans/Chicanos	19
Puerto Ricans	2
Other Latinos	3
African Americans	17
American Indians/Native Americans	1
Asian Americans	2
Iranian Americans	1
Multiple Ethnic/Racial Groups	12
Total	57

[a] This includes published and unpublished studies, master's theses, dissertations, and conference papers. The MMPI-2 was published in 1989.

psychologists to assess culturally and linguistically diverse clients (Velásquez et al., 1998). Most recently, it has been increasingly used with "new" minorities like Iranian Americans (Butcher, Lim, & Nezami, 1998; Nezami, Bernous, Ghassemi, & Nezami, 1998). The MMPI-2 is used to assess these clients in community mental health centers, forensic settings, substance abuse treatment programs, and inpatient psychiatric facilities. It is also frequently used to assess minorities involved in child custody disputes, disability or worker's compensation claims, or the job application process (i.e., fitness for employment).

Other reasons why the MMPI-2 is widely applied to culturally diverse groups in this country include (a) a tradition of research on minority groups, especially African Americans and Latinos, with the original MMPI; (b) ethnic minorities were included in the development of the norms for the MMPI-2; (c) special efforts have been made to develop translations (e.g., Spanish, Hmong, Farsi, Vietnamese, Chinese, etc.) that cannot only be applied abroad, but also in the United States; and (d) innovations such as the development of norms on the Spanish adaptation of the MMPI-A for Latino adolescents living in the United States and Puerto Rico. Also, there is a growing interface or linkage between MMPI-2 research conducted in the United States and in other parts of the world. This is especially relevant to the assessment of immigrants who come from countries where the MMPI-2 is used in both research and practice (e.g., Mexico, Israel, and China). At the same time, it is important to acknowledge that controversy still continues regarding the potential for bias of the MMPI-2 as it relates to ethnic minorities (see Butcher, Graham, & Ben-Porath, 1995; Dana, 1995; Grillo, 1994; Okazaki, 1995; Sturmer & Gerstein, 1997). Yet, the controversy does not appear to be as heated as it once was with the MMPI because cross-cultural differences have been lessened on the MMPI-2 (Gynther, 1972; Gynther & Green, 1980; Pritchard & Rosenblatt, 1980).

II. WHAT ARE THE TRENDS OF MMPI-2 RESEARCH WITH MINORITIES?

In our systematic review of the literature, we found the following five trends in the literature on minority groups. It is important to note that these trends are largely based on research with Latinos and African Americans, since studies on other ethnic groups are extremely limited.

A. TREND #1

Researchers continue to compare ethnic minority groups to majority or White counterparts on the MMPI-2 (see Table I). This trend has carried over from research with the original MMPI. The primary aim of these types of studies is to answer the following questions: Are there differences between an ethnic group, such as American Indians, and Whites on the MMPI-2 scales? Or, does culture somehow differentially impact the performance of minorities and Whites on the MMPI-2?

The prototypic study involves comparing one or more ethnic minority groups to a White group on the validity and clinical scales of the MMPI-2. Rarely do researchers consider additional scales such as the Content or Supplementary scales, which we have found very useful with culturally diverse persons. To date, the majority of the studies have been conducted on college populations, which are samples of convenience, and which have limited generalizability when extended to the clinical domain. There remains a major absence of research with clinical or psychiatric populations. In particular, there is a need to determine whether minorities with different psychiatric diagnoses perform differently on the MMPI-2 scales, and/or whether they obtain different scale configurations including codetypes. Outside indicators can help to examine the validity of codetypes.

Table II presents a summary of the findings on cross-cultural MMPI-2 comparisons. It is important to note that studies, which have controlled for such variables as culture or race, socioeconomic status, and education, do suggest minimal overall differences. In our analysis there emerged only one salient finding across ethnic groups. It appears that minorities, and in particular Latinos, consistently score higher than White counterparts on the L (Lie) scale (see Callahan, 1997; Garrido, Velásquez, Parsons, Reimann, & Salazar, 1997; Haskell, 1996; Hernandez, 1994; Whitworth & McBlaine, 1993; Whitworth & Unterbrink, 1994). This pattern was also present in research with the original MMPI (see Velásquez, 1984; Velásquez, Ayala, & Mendoza, 1998). This leads us to believe that Latinos may respond differentially on the L scale, which may suggest a tendency toward "cultural defensiveness," an approach toward presenting oneself in the best light to strangers, including the evaluator, and a culturally based attitude of "not airing one's laundry in public." Hence, psychologists should not reach conclusions that deal with intent to lie or deceive without first considering potential culturally related approaches illustrated in the MMPI-2 profile (see Table II).

B. TREND #2

Unlike research with the MMPI, there appears to be a stronger emphasis on intracultural variation with the MMPI-2. That is, there is now a growing interest in the diversity that exists within ethnic and racial groups on such variables as gender, geographic location, and cultural subgroups (e.g., tribes). For example,

TABLE II Cross-Cultural Comparisons on the MMPI-2

Author(s)	Participants[a]	Key findings[b]
Latinos		
Callahan (1997)	88 L 62 W	Mexican Americans obtained higher scores on the L and Pa scales, whereas Whites obtained higher scores on the Pt, Sc, and Si scales. It is important to note that this study included three types of samples: psychiatric patients, college students, and community subjects. This study also considered acculturation using the ARSMA.
Callahan et al. (1995)	20 L 20 W	No differences were found between Mexican American and White college students.
Cook (1996)	90 L 90 W	Compared Latino and White mental health outpatients on item-response rates. Similar biased items were found for both ethnic groups, which were minimal. This is the first study to examine item-endorsement rates for Latinos.
Garrido et al. (1997)	22 L 53 W	Latino child abusers obtained higher scores on the L, Hs, D, Sc, and Si scales in comparison to White counterparts. The majority of the Latino sample was Puerto Rican and Central American.
Haskell (1996)	57 L 57 W	Mexican Americans obtained higher scores on the L, D, and Pt scales.
Hernandez (1994)	58 L 124 W	Compared Mexican American and White college students, Mexican American males obtained higher scores on the L scale, and White males had higher scores on the Mf, Pt, and Si scales.
Whitworth & McBlaine (1993)	173 L 110 W	Mexican Americans obtained higher scores on L scale, whereas Whites obtained higher scores on the K, Hy, Pd, and Mf scales.
Whitworth & Unterbrink (1994)	200 L 200 W	Mexican Americans obtained higher scores on the L, F, D, Pd, Sc, and Ma scales, whereas Whites obtained a high score on K.
African Americans		
Ben-Porath et al. (1996)	121 AA 551 W	African American males obtained higher scores on the L scale, females on the Pt, and all on the Ma scale compared to Whites.
Ben-Porath et al. (1995)	47 AA 137 W	No differences were found between Whites and African Americans.
Frueh et al. (1996)	88 AA 118 W	African Americans obtained higher scores on the Pa and Sc scales.
Grillo (1992)	173 AA 247 W	African Americans obtained higher scores on L, F, K, Pa, Pt, and Si scales, whereas Whites obtained a higher score on the Mf scale.

(continues)

TABLE II (*continued*)

Author(s)	Participants[a]	Key findings[b]
African Americans (continued)		
Lopez (1997)	58 AA 91 W	African Americans obtained higher Pa scale scores than Whites. The most frequently occurring code-type for homeless African Americans was "6-8/8-6" (17%).
McClinton et al. (1995)	60 AA 60 W	No differences were found between African Americans and Whites.
McNulty et al. (1997)	123 AA 561 W	African American males obtained higher scores on the L scale and females on the Ma scale.
Timbrook & Graham (1994)	140 AA 1468 W	African American females obtained higher scores on the Pd, Mf, and Ma scales, whereas males obtained a higher score on the Sc scale.
Multiple group comparisons		
Frank et al. (1997)	101 L 27 AA 89 W	Mexican American sex offenders obtained higher scores than Whites on the L, D, and Si scales, and African Americans obtained higher scores than Whites on the Pt and Sc scales.
Garrido et al. (1998)	29 L 41 AA 97 W	Latinos were found to obtain higher scores on the FRS scale. African Americans obtained higher scores on the CYN and ASP scales, and Whites obtained higher scores on the Pd scale.
Ladd (1994, 1996)	21 L 48 W 69 AA	No differences were found between the three groups on the MMPI-2.
Lapham et al. (1995)	1066 L 996 W 225 NA	No differences were found between the three ethnic groups. All had drug or alcohol problems.
Lapham et al. (1997)	620 L 619 W 113 NA	Elevations on the MAC-R alcohol scale differentiated DWI offenders at risk for recidivism across all three ethnic groups.
Maiocco (1996)	42 L 32 W 34 AA	Latinos obtained higher scores on the L scale than Whites or African Americans. Latinos and African Americans obtained higher scores than Whites on the Sc scale.
Robers (1992)	98 AA 1115 W 157 A 50 NA	Asians obtained higher scores on the F, Hs, D, Pa, Pt, Sc, Ma, and Si compared to Whites and African Americans.
Rowell (1992)	102 L 98 AA 96 W	No differences were found between the three groups on the MAC-R scale.

(*continues*)

TABLE II *(continued)*

Author(s)	Participants[a]	Key findings[b]
Multiple group comparisons (continued)		
Schinka et al. (1998)	153 Non-W 347 W	Examined the effects of demographic variables, including ethnicity and presence of mental illness on the variance of MMPI-2 scale scores. The demographic variables contribute little incremental variance for the validity and clinical scales. No comparisons were made by ethnicity and race, and no exact numbers are given by ethnicity.
Steinman (1993)	7 L 16 AA 66 W	No differences were found between the three groups. Please note the small sample size of Latinos.
Wexler (1996)	43 L 43 AA 48 W	African Americans were elevated on the Pd and Ma scales when compared to Whites and Latinos. African Americans were twice as likely to be disqualified for hire.

[a] L, Latino; W, White; AA, African American; NA, Native American; Non-W, non-White.

[b] L, Lie; Pa, Paranoia; Pt, Psyasthenia; Si, Social Introversion; ARSMA, Acculturation Rating Scale for Mexican Americans; Hs, Hypochondriasis; D, Depression; Sc, Schizophrenia; Mf, Masculinity-femininity; K, Defensiveness; Hy, Hypochondriasis; Pd, Psychopathic Deviate; MA, mania; F, Infrequency; CYN, Cynician; FRS, fears; ASP, Antisocial Practices.

Fantoni-Salvador and Rogers (1997) found that Puerto Rican psychiatric patients obtained higher scores on the psychotic- and anxiety-related scales when compared to Mexican American counterparts (as well as other Latino subgroups). Pace, Choney, Blair, Hill, and Lacey compared two different groups of American Indian tribes from Oklahoma, the Plains and Eastern Woodlands Indians, and found that these two groups differed on scales L and Infrequency (F), with the Plains obtaining higher scores. The Plains were also found to have higher scores on the F, Hypochondriasis (Hy), Paranoia (Pa), Schizophrenia (Sc), and Mania (Ma) scales when contrasted to the small American Indian sample from the MMPI-2 norms. Incidentally, this norm sample was primarily from a tribe in the state of Washington. In both of these studies, the respective authors concluded that variations in subculture, attitudes, and lifestyle most likely accounted for these differences.

These findings, while clearly limited, indicate that psychologists must always be sensitive to variations that may be present within particular ethnic groups. For example, the concepts of ethnic identity or acculturation may vary tremendously with respect to Puerto Ricans who reside in the United States versus those who reside in Puerto Rico. Puerto Ricans who live in this country may be more apt to feel like a "minority" than those who live on the island. Thus, those who reside on the mainland may be more sensitive to issues of discrimination, prejudice, or racism than those who live in Puerto Rico (see Table III).

C. TREND #3

Researchers have examined the role of acculturation on the MMPI-2 performance of ethnic minority groups, with an emphasis on non-Puerto Rican or non-Cuban Latinos. Although findings on the effects of acculturation remain equivocal, it does appear that acculturation can impact MMPI-2 performance. Canul (1993), for example, found that Mexican Americans who were pro-White and anti-Mexican in their orientations tended to score higher on the L scale, whereas those with a positive view toward their own group and a negative view toward the White majority were more likely to obtain lower K (defensiveness) or defensiveness scores. Quintana (1997) and Lessenger (1997), using the Acculturation Rating Scale for Mexican Americans-II (ARSMA-II; Cuéllar, Arnold, & Maldonado, 1994) found no relationship between acculturation and the MMPI-2 scales. Pace et al. (1997) found that Americans Indians who were more traditional were more likely to score higher on the F and Sc scales, whereas those who were less traditional were more likely to score higher on the K scale. Our research and clinical experiences have led us to consider a new scale, the Acculturative Stress Index (ASI), which is derived from the MMPI-2 item pool, and which may help clarify the role of acculturation through the lenses of stress and coping. For these reasons, researchers are employing measures like the Hispanic Stress Inventory (HSI) developed by Cervantes and colleagues (Cervantes, Padilla, & Salgado de Snyder, 1991), to better understand the impact of stress during the acculturation process.

D. TREND #4

Research has examined the equivalence of linguistic translations to the English version of the MMPI-2. Again, the majority of research has focused on Latinos, with one investigation of Iranian Americans. The results of these investigations suggest high linguistic equivalence of the Spanish and Farsi translations to the English-language MMPI-2, and the potential for use with monolingual and bilingual Latinos and Iranians in the United States. Cabiya (1994), in his study, reported on the adaptation of the Chilean version for use in Puerto Rico. Although 22 items had to be modified for the new adaptation, the overall results indicated strong equivalence. Karle (1994) and Velásquez, Chavira, Karle, Callahan, and

TABLE III Intracultural Comparisons on the MMPI-2: Key Findings

Author(s)	Participants	Key findings[a]
Latinos		
Alamo et al. (1995)	107	Victims of assault scored higher than nonvictims on all scales except for MF. Major elevations (>75T) were found on F, Hs, D, Pa, Pt, Sc, PK, PS, FRS, and BIZ. Examined Puerto Ricans in Puerto Rico.
Anderson et al. (1993)	15	Veterans with PTSD were given the MMPI-2. The mean high point pair was SC-Pt and modal pair was Sc-Pa.
Cabiya (1994)	271	Adapted the Chilean MMPI-2 for use in Puerto Rico. Twenty-two items had to be modified for the new adaptation.
Canul (1993), Canul & Cross (1994)	48	Less acculturated who were pro-White and anti-Mexican scored higher on L. A low K was linked to positive view toward own group and negative view toward Whites.
Chavira, Montemayor, et al. (1995)	34	Applied two Spanish translations, U.S. and Mexican versions. Differences were found for the U.S. version with participants obtaining higher scores on F and Sc, and a higher score on Mexican translation's PS scale.
Chavira et al. (1996)	31	On U.S. Spanish version, low acculturated participants scored higher on Mf than high acculturated.
Colon (1993)	125	Compared psychiatric patients to students on the Content scales. Psychiatric males obtained higher scores on all scales except ANG. Psychiatric females scored higher on all scales except DEP and SOD. Study conducted in Puerto Rico.
Fantoni-Salvador & Rogers (1997)	105	MMPI-2, PAI, and DIS were administered to all psychiatric patients in Spanish. MMPI-2 yielded greater specificity but lower sensitivity than PAI scales on two of four diagnostic categories, major depression and schizophrenia. Participants were also compared by ethnic subgroup. Puerto Ricans obtained higher scores than Mexican Americans on psychotic- and anxiety-related scales.
Flores et al. (1996)	82	Substance abusers obtained two-point codes that included Sc most frequently. Age of onset of substance abuse was negatively correlated with OBS, PK, Sc, PS, Pt, ANG, CYN, and Hs,
Greenwood et al. (1998)	14	MMPI-2 was administered to seven mothers and MMPI-A to their respective daughters. The daughters were clients with severe problems. They

(continues)

TABLE III (continued)

Author(s)	Participants	Key findings[a]
Latinos (continued)		
Greenwood et al. (1998)	14	obtained only one elevation on the MMPI-A, scale L. The mothers obtained elevations over 65T on scales HS, Hy, and Sc.
Karle (1994)	57	Administered the MMPI-2 in English and Spanish to bilingual subjects to determine equivalency. No differences were found between language versions except on MF scale, with higher score on Spanish translation.
Lessenger (1997)	100	No relationship was found between MMPI-2 performance and acculturation. Elevated scores (>65T) were found on F and Sc only.
Mason (1997)	200	Veterans with PTSD with higher levels of distress displaced higher elevations on F, A, and R. Substance abuse, as noted by the AAS, was found to be highly correlated to greater assimilation.
Netto et al. (1998)	60	Compared participants with traumatic brain injury to those with no injury on MMPI-2. Those with injury had higher elevations on all validity and clinical scales except K, Mf, Ma, and Si. Age, education, SES, language, and acculturation were not related to MMPI-2 scores for the injury sample.
Pena et al. (1995)	117	Prison inmates were administered the MMPI-2 twice, before and after therapy. Scores decreased significantly on the F and D scales, and all of the Content scales except for FRS, HEA, ANG, SOD, and FAM. An expected increase was noted on K. Study was conducted in Puerto Rico.
Pena et al. (1996)	339	Applied MMPI-2 to male and female prison inmates in Puerto Rico. Found the Megargee classification system not useful in discriminating between different profiles.
Quintana (1997)	135	The relationship between acculturation and MMPI-2 performance was examined for college students. No relationship was found between the ARSMA and MMPI-2.
Velásquez et al. (1998)	27	A bilingual MMPI-2, consisting of both English- and Spanish-language items was administered to bilingual participants. Results indicated that the two linguistic versions are comparable.

(continues)

TABLE III (*continued*)

Author(s)	Participants	Key findings[a]
Latinos (*continued*)		
Velásquez et al. (in review)	96	The results of two studies are presented. The first study examined bilinguals' performance on the English and Spanish MMPI-2, whereas the second study considered Spanish speakers performance on two Spanish versions, the U.S. and Mexican.
African Americans		
Bellamy (1994)	Unk	Compared a noncriminal to a criminal sample on the Pd scale. Results indicated that the scale demonstrated good predictive validity.
Bowler et al. (1996)	310	Used 60 items from the MMPI-2 to create two scales, for anxiety and PTSD, to assess participants.
Holland (1993)	88	Investigated MMPI-2 differences by gender for adult children of alcoholics
Reed et al. (1996a, 1996b)	78	Used the MMPI-2 to determine if MMPI-2 pathologized college women. Results indicated that 76% had elevations on at least one scale, and 40% had two point codetypes (>65 T).
Speca (1994)	153	Confirmatory factor analysis was conducted for groups of men and women on the MMPI-2. These factors were compared to those from the MMPI-2 norms. Results indicated a lack of identical factor structures.
Native Americans		
Pace et al. (1997)	87 Plains 84 Woodlands	Compared both tribes to MMPI-2 norms. Plains were higher than norms on L, F, Hs, Pd, Pa, Sc, and Ma. Eastern Woodlands were higher than norms on the F, Hs, Pa, Sc, and Ma. Plains were higher on L and F than Woodlands. Also, traditionally acculturated scored higher on the F and Sc, and high acculturated on K.
Iranian Americans		
Nezami et al. (1998)	50 Iranian	Iranian Americans were given the MMPI-2 in English and Farsi within one week. No differences were found between both versions, suggesting equivalence.

[a] Mf, Masculinity-Femininity; F, Infrequency; H, Hypochondriasis; D, Depression; Pa, Paranoia; Pt, Psychasthenia; Sc, Schizophrenia; Pk, Posttraumatic Stress; PS, Posttraumatic Scale; FRS, Fears; Biz, Bizarre Mentation; PTSD, Posttraumatic Stress Disorder; L, Lie; K, Defensiveness; ANG, Anger; DEP, Depression; SOD, Social Discomfort; PAI, Personality Assessment Inventory; DIS, Diagnostic Interview Schedule; OBS, Obsessiveness; CYN, cynicism; Hy, Hypochondriasis; A, Anxiety; R, Repression; AAS, Addiction Admission Scale; MA, Mania; Si, Social Introversion; D, Depression; HEA, Health Beliefs; FAM, Family Problems; Pd, Psychopathic Deviate.

Garcia (in press) found good comparability between the U.S. Hispanic Spanish adaptation and the English version. They also found high comparability, as defined by the lack of scale differences, between two Spanish-language adaptations, the U.S. Hispanic and "official" Mexican adaptation. Nezami et al. (1998) obtained similar findings when they administered the Persian or Farsi adaptation and the English version to bilingual Iranian Americans. Clearly there remains a need for more investigations that take into consideration item endorsement rates.

E. TREND #5

Although most studies continue to focus on the validity and clinical scales, a few investigations have considered additional subscales or indices. Colon (1993), in a dissertation conducted in Puerto Rico, found that male psychiatric patients obtained higher scores than male college students on all Content scales except the Anger (ANG) scale. A similar finding was obtained with female patients obtaining higher scores on all scales except Depression (DEP) and Social Discomfort (SOD). Flores, Chavira, Perez, Engel, and Velásquez (1996) found that age of onset of alcohol use was negatively correlated with the Obsessiveness (OBS), Posttraumatic Stress Disorder (PK), ANG, and (CYN) scales for Mexican immigrants. Hernandez (1994) found that more traditional Mexican American males obtained higher scores than those assimilated to Anglo values on the Fears (FRS) subscale. Mason (1997) found a strong positive relationship between the Addiction Admission Scale (AAS) and greater acculturation toward mainstream values in a group of Latino veterans with Posttraumatic Stress Disorder (PTSD). In our clinical experience, we have found that the additional MMPI-2 scales often yield greater information or clinical hypotheses than the validity or clinical scales alone when assessing ethnic minority clients.

III. WHAT TYPES OF RESEARCH STILL NEED TO BE CONSIDERED WITH THE MMPI-2?

Our impressions of the literature, which spans the last 10 years, leads us to the following seven recommendations for future research:

1. There is a need for studies that examine nonclinical community samples in order to strengthen or supplement the current MMPI-2 norms. For example, Latinos and Asians are currently underrepresented; only 73 Latinos and 19 Asians were included in the norms.

2. There is a need for investigations that not only consider the distribution of code types for minorities, but the meaning of these codetypes through empirical clinical correlates.

3. There is a need for studies that reflect methodological sophistication and which take into consideration the role of socioeconomic status, education, ethnic subgroup, and marginalization in ethnic minorities. The role of acculturative stress should also be examined on the MMPI-2 performance of immigrants.

4. There is a need for investigations in traditional clinical settings, such as community mental health centers where minorities are widely served. These studies should also consider how quality of life relates to MMPI-2 performance.

5. There remains a strong need for validation-type studies. A major problem with many studies conducted with minorities is that the MMPI-2 is the only psychodiagnostic measure used. There is a need for investigations that utilize multiple measures.

6. There is a need for further studies on the role of language on MMPI-2 performance. Although a few studies indicate "comparability," it is not clear to what extent translations are equivalent.

7. There is a need to study culture-bound syndromes like "*nervios*" with the MMPI-2.

IV. WHAT DEFINES A CULTURALLY COMPETENT APPROACH WITH THE MMPI-2?

In recent years, psychologists like Dana (1995) have strongly advocated for the culturally competent use of the MMPI-2 with ethnic minority individuals. Dana has argued that the MMPI-2 is so widely used by psychologists to assess individuals from different cultural and linguistic backgrounds that some standards, guidelines, or recommendations are needed in order to ensure that the MMPI-2 is not misapplied to these groups. Although we agree with Dana in principle, we disagree with his approach, which advocates that special corrections be applied when interpreting an ethnic minority's MMPI-2. The corrections focus on taking into account the potential effects of acculturation on MMPI-2 scale scores, without providing a clear discussion of how one should go about making such corrections. The other approach advocated by Dana is to develop new "emic-based" tests like "a reconstructed and restandardized MMPI for Hispanics" (p. 314). Following this logic, a reconstructed MMPI-2 would be required for all other ethnic minority groups. Unfortunately, this may not be tenable at this time. *but fair !!*

Our definition of the culturally competent use of the MMPI-2 is more thorough and comprehensive, and reflects the realities of clinical practice (see Velásquez et al., 1997). If one is to follow Dana's suggestions, then one would be remiss in not dealing with other issues that are just as important, such as the culturally incompetent or inappropriate practice of using translators, using personal and unvalidated translations, extracting and administering only certain scales, having the client take the MMPI-2 at home, and giving instructions that create a socially desirable or defensive response style.

The following eight points are provided to guide the psychologist in the administration and interpretation of the MMPI-2 across cultures:

1. Prior to using the MMPI-2 with culturally and linguistically diverse individuals, psychologists are encouraged to reflect upon the following set of questions:

   a. Is the MMPI-2 the most appropriate measure for my client?
   b. Are there any potential barriers to obtaining a valid MMPI-2 measure?
   c. At what point in treatment should I use the MMPI-2 with my client?
   d. Should "trust" be established prior to administering the MMPI-2?
   e. Is my client currently experiencing significant acculturative stress?
   f. Is my client accustomed to responding to questions about his or her mental health status via a structured questionnaire requiring a True-False response?
   g. Has my client been previously evaluated with the MMPI or MMPI-2, and was this a positive or negative experience?
   h. Should I administer the MMPI-2 in English or another language?
   i. In what language is the client most likely to report emotionally laden issues?
   j. How should I structure the feedback session in order to establish "cultural collaboration" between the client and myself?
   k. To what extent should I consider making the feedback a psychoeducational experience for the client?
   l. What types of mental disorders or syndromes are most common in the client's cultural group and how can I use this information in formulating diagnostic and treatment impressions?
   m. Is there any prevalence data on this client's ethnic or racial group?
   n. Are there culturally based syndromes that I must be aware of and which may impact my interpretation of the MMPI-2?

2. Psychologists should always administer the MMPI-2 to culturally diverse clients following standardized procedures. In our collective experience, we have observed that many of the problems that frequently occur in the interpretation of the MMPI-2 are related to how the MMPI-2 was administered to an ethnic minority client. For example, we have witnessed situations in which psychologists have used translations of the original MMPI. Research on many of these translations suggests that these adaptations were more likely to overpathologize minorities than the original English version (see Velásquez, Ayala, & Mendoza, 1998).

3. Psychologists are cautioned against *depending* on computerized or "canned" interpretive reports when evaluating ethnic minorities. It is very tempting for both research and clinical psychologists to depend on the comments generated by such software programs. We have observed on many occasions that psychologists simply "lift" sections from these reports without questioning if culture does, or does not, play an important role. Without examining the validity of such interpretive comments, the psychologist may make inaccurate diagnoses. To our knowledge, there exist no interpretive reports that have integrated correlates associated with culturally diverse populations.

4. Psychologists are advised to use more than just the traditional validity and clinical scales of the MMPI-2 when assessing culturally diverse individuals. We have observed many situations in which psychologists simply depend on the validity and clinical scales in the interpretation process. In our collective experience, we have found that oftentimes additional indices such as the Content and Supplementary scales, or the Harris-Lingoes subscales, are the most useful in understanding the performance of ethnic minorities. At the end of this chapter, we present the case of Michael whose performance on the validity and clinical scales only made sense when some of the Supplementary scales were considered. Some of the scales that can be affected by a person's culture include the L, F, K, Hs, Psychopathic Deviate (Pd), Masculinity-Feminity (Mf), PA, Sc, Ma, Social Introversion (Si), Bizarre Mentation (BIZ), CYN, Low Self-Esteem (LSE), SOD, and Family Problems (FAM). For example, the PD scale is often elevated for African Americans. Does this mean that this group is more likely to report symptoms that are related to criminality, and thus be antisocial? No, a culturally competent psychologist would examine the Harris-Lingoes Pd subscales to determine if this scale is artificially elevated by the Familial Discord (Pd1), Authority Problems (Pd2), or Social Alienation (Pd4) subscales. In our research and clinical work, we have observed that ethnic minority clients who are more psychologically connected to their traditional culture, both male and female, are more likely to obtain very low Mf scores. They are also more likely to feel culturally defensive, less likely to initially self-disclose, or more likely to feel pressure to to present themselves as emotionally healthy or free of pathology as indicated on both the L and K scales. In nonclinical settings, it is not uncommon for African Americans or American Indians to obtain elevations on the Pa, CYN, and SOD scales, given potential histories of feeling oppressed or misunderstood. Should this be considered surprising and interpreted as abnormal?

5. Psychologists are advised to always consider the potential for a language factor in the MMPI-2 assessment of culturally diverse persons. This is especially important when evaluating immigrants. For monolingual persons who cannot function in English, we strongly recommend that the psychologist administer a linguistic adaptation of the MMPI-2 that has undergone a back-translation (Butcher, 1996). Butcher (1996) documents the numerous translation projects

from around the world that also have relevance for use in the United States. The psychologist should always avoid situations in which an interpreter or translator is employed. We have witnessed countless mishaps in which psychologists, with good intentions, misapplied the MMPI or MMPI-2 only to be embarrassed in such arenas as court. There now exist numerous translations that can be employed with clients in this country. For example, there exist many adaptations of the Spanish-language MMPI-2, including "Mexican" and "Puerto Rican" versions, which can be used with immigrants who come from these respective countries.

For bilingual persons, there exist even greater options. The person can be administered either the English version or an adaptation suited to his or her native language (e.g., a Puerto Rican client administered a Puerto Rican adaptation). Yet, the psychologist needs to determine the language in which the client is most likely to feel psychologically and culturally comfortable. We have observed many immigrants preferring to initially take the MMPI-2 in English because of a desire to appear socially competent. Yet, high elevations on scales such as F and F-back (Fb) may suggest invalidity, exaggeration, or malingering, when in reality the person experienced difficulty in comprehending or reading the items. Thus, we recommend that psychologists consider administering both linguistic versions in order to make such a determination, which ultimately has an impact on diagnosis and treatment planning. The cases of Sandra and Maria presented later in this chapter, serve to illustrate the challenges that can be encountered when evaluating a bilingual person with the MMPI-2.

6. Psychologists should always consider the impact of acculturation, or better yet acculturative stress, on the mental status of the client they are evaluating. Although we consider acculturation to be a very important issue, as evidenced by the amount of research on this concept (see Choney, Berryhill-Paapke, & Robbins, 1995; Cuéllar et al., 1995; Ghaffarian, 1987; Landrine & Klonoff, 1995; Suinn, Knoo, & Ahuna, 1995), the reality is that the results of investigations that have considered the role of acculturation on MMPI-2 performance remain equivocal. Some studies indicate an effect, whereas others do not. It is our opinion, based on both research and clinical practice, that the psychologist who evaluates culturally diverse clients is more likely to benefit from knowing the extent to which the client is experiencing acculturative stress than simply knowing the stage or level of acculturation. The recent work of Cervantes and colleagues (Cervantes, Padilla, & Salgado de Snyder, 1991) indicates that acculturative stress indices can be developed and applied in a clinical context. Although the concept of acculturation can be useful in understanding variation within specific ethnic or racial groups, current measures of acculturation do not offer practical clinical applications.

7. Psychologists are advised to always consider the prospect of giving MMPI-2 feedback to culturally diverse individuals. It is easy for the psycholo-

gist to apply the language that is unique to psychological assessment (e.g., codetypes, Variable Response Inconsistency Scale [VRIN], True Response Inconsistency Scale [TRIN], etc.) without considering that an evaluation must always yield useful information for the client. More importantly, this information should have some real-life practicality in light of the fact that psychologists are now more likely to both assess and treat their clients because of the constraints placed by managed care. The ethnic minority client, like all clients, has expectations that the results of an evaluation are likely to yield valuable information. At the same time, ethnic minority clients often expect that the MMPI-2 results will assist them in understanding their problems or issues through their cultural lenses. Collectively, we believe that maintaining this stance or attitude keeps us on our cultural toes at all times.

8. Finally, psychologists are encouraged to seek out consultation from those who possess expertise in the assessment of culturally diverse persons. We have observed, firsthand, the benefits of consulting with each other when confronted with the prospect of evaluating a client whose cultural background is different (or even similar) from our individual backgrounds. Typically, we use a consultation model that includes a two-step process, with consultation prior to and after the evaluation. In the initial consultation, an environment is created in which the examiner is invited to discuss potential psychometric and clinical barriers. Postconsultation, the examiner is encouraged to consider both mainstream and culturally based options in the interpretation of the client's MMPI-2 performance. Questions related to whether certain scale elevations are expected or not, due to acculturative stress for example, are discussed within the context of the target culture.

V. CASE STUDIES WITH THE MMPI-2

The following are six case studies illustrating some of the potential problems of not considering culture and ethnicity in the use and interpretation of the MMPI-2, as well as solutions to these problems.

A. CASE #1: SANDRA

Sandra is a 24-year-old female college student who was born and raised in Mexico until the age of 13, when her family moved to the United States. Sandra entered therapy in English, but quickly switched to Spanish because she felt more comfortable self-disclosing in her native language. Her therapist identified herself as Mexican American and Spanish-speaking. In total, she was administered the MMPI-2 three times. At intake she was administered the MMPI-2 in

English. She obtained a valid profile suggesting severe psychopathology and perhaps a psychotic disorder. This was evidenced in her profile configuration, which included elevations on the Sc, Psychasthenia (Pt), and Pa scales, an "8-7-6" codetype. An additional elevation on the Si scale also suggested the potential for severe withdrawal and isolation. If these results were allowed to stand alone, the likely diagnosis would have suggested the possibility of hospitalization and the use of psychotropic medications. However, this was unlikely based on the clinical impressions of the therapist. Given the fact that she had "language-switched" after the third session, the decision was made to readminister the MMPI-2 in Spanish. This time she obtained a profile more suggestive of interpersonal problems and not psychosis. She obtained a codetype with elevations on Pt, Sc, and Psychopathic Deviate (Pd) scales, an "7-8-4" codetype. Her Si scale was significantly lower and not suggestive of isolation but of social involvement. Many of the Content scale scores dropped by at least 10 T-score points including BIZ, Antisocial Practices (ASP), and SOD scales, also affecting the diagnostic impression.

She was readministered the MMPI-2 in Spanish about 8 months later as part of treatment. Although there was a drop in some scores, like the Pt scale, her codetype remained essentially the same, supporting the hypothesis that Sandra's problems were more long-standing and interpersonally related. Clearly, she did not appear to be in need of hospitalization or medication, but instead required long-term psychotherapy (see Figure 1).

B. CASE #2: *MARIA*

Maria was a 39-year-old Mexican American woman who was referred for individual counseling by her couple's therapist. Maria was born and raised in Mexico, until the age of 16, when she and her family moved to the United States. Maria's primary complaint was her inability to understand herself and her husband of 12 years. She described feelings of depression, anxiety, hopelessness, and frustration. Maria endured emotional and physical abuse by her husband for many years, but continued to feel an obligation to stay with him, and care for him and their children.

At intake, Maria was administered the MMPI-2 in English because she presented using the English language. Her profile appeared to be valid, and suggested that Maria likely had a serious thought disorder with paranoid features, possibly Paranoid Schizophrenia. After several therapy sessions, the therapist's clinical impressions did not substantiate the client's profile and the MMPI-2 was readministered in Spanish. In both the Spanish and English versions, Maria reported a significant amount of distress, yet it appeared that she expressed her concerns more openly in Spanish, due to a lower K scale on the Spanish version.

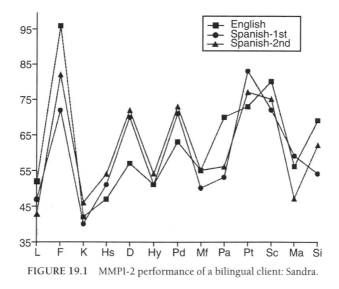

FIGURE 19.1   MMPI-2 performance of a bilingual client: Sandra.

The Spanish version also yielded decreased scores on eight clinical scales. Between the two versions, four of the scale scores differed by at least one standard deviation. The greatest difference was evident in the Pa scale, on which there was a decrease of two standard deviations. In addition, the Depression (D) and Pd scales decreased by approximately 15 and 13 points, respectively, in the Spanish version. Despite such drastic decreases in several of the clinical scales, Maria's profile remained elevated on six clinical scales.

In addition to decreases on clinical scales, four Content scales dropped to the subclinical level in the Spanish version. These differences were evidenced on the LSE, Work Interference (WRK), FAM, and Negative Treatment Indicators (TRT) scales. This suggests that Maria's MMPI-2 performance in English reflected greater problems. This provides further evidence for identifying the client's "comfort zone" with respect to language for self-disclosure.

C. CASE #3: *PARVIN*

Parvin is a 35-year-old Iranian woman who was referred for a psychological evaluation. She was born in Iran and immigrated to the United States in 1979, after the fall of the Shah. Her chief complaints included sadness, anguish, and feeling alienated from family members. She was married for only one year, and divorced because her husband wanted her to "be a more traditional Iranian wife, who would stay at home and care for his children from a previous marriage."

Instead, she rebelled by not being subservient to him. He forced her to obtain a divorce. Her history also included a brutal rape by a neighbor when she was age 17. She subsequently continued a relationship with this neighbor for about two years. She noted that in her culture it is not acceptable to be a divorcée or a victim of rape. She was administered the Farsi (Persian) translation of the MMPI-2 as part of her evaluation for treatment planning. While her F scale score was elevated at 79T, her profile was considered valid. Eight of the 10 clinical scales were significantly elevated over 65T, with the Mf scale being very low. This number of elevations made it very difficult to discern a codetype. Instead, one can see both the neurotic and psychotic triads elevated, as well as the Pd and Si scales (see Figure 2).

Although the psychologist who evaluated Parvin was sensitive enough to use the correct linguistic version of the MMPI-2, his conclusions that "this person must be either psychotic or malingering" were incorrect. An Iranian-American psychologist asked to consult on this case came up with an alternative interpretation, which began with her consideration of the low Mf scale. The psychologist indicated that the low Mf scale,

> probably suggested a significant struggle with her sex role in and out of her Iranian culture. The profile also reflected tremendous feelings of being alone (Si), active chaos and inefficiency in her lifestyle, and significant feelings of guilt possibly related to her religious beliefs. The combination of elevations on the Marital Distress Scale (MDS) and Posttraumatic Scale (PS) possibly indicated significant confusion related

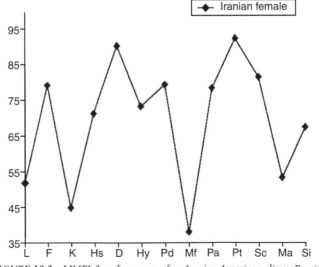

FIGURE 19.2   MMPI-2 performance of an Iranian American client: Parvin.

to her relationship within her culture, which were probably affected by her trauma related to rape.

D. Case #4: Mr. and Mrs. Gonzalez

Mr. and Mrs. Gonzalez were evaluated for couple's therapy. The couple had been married for one year. She was born in the United States and he was born in Mexico. She had a college degree in business, while he had a high school education from Mexico. The primary concern voiced by Mrs. Gonzalez was that "since being married, we have discovered that we are very different, because of our culture and where we were born." She stated that "it is like being married to someone from another race. We always seem to argue about our values, including my goal to achieve a career. He would prefer to have me stay at home."

As part of the evaluation, both were administered the MMPI-2, Mr. Gonzalez in Spanish and Mrs. Gonzalez in English. Their MMPI-2 performance reflected both similarities and differences (see Figure 3). For example, both had highly elevated L scales, suggestive of a need to appear socially competent and free of major problems. This is consistent with research findings and clinical data, which suggest that it is not unusual for Latinos to obtain high elevations on the L scale. On the other hand, there were major differences on the Mf scale, which appeared to reflect differences in values, sex role ideologies, and perhaps more

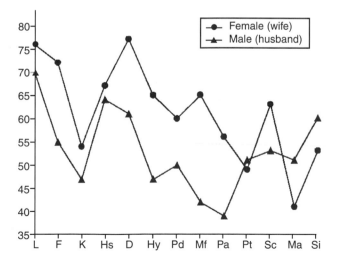

FIGURE 19.3   MMPI-2 performance of a Latino couple: Mr. and Mrs. Gonzalez.

importantly, acculturation. Mr. Gonzalez appeared to possess a more traditional masculine worldview, whereas she appeared to possess a more nontraditional feminine perspective. In addition, it appeared that Mrs. Gonzalez's issues included a mood component, while Mr. Gonzalez appeared to minimize any problems. In this case, it was very important to work with the couple around issues of communication, sex role expectations, and long-term family goals.

E. CASE #5: *MICHAEL*

Michael is a 21-year-old African American male who was initially evaluated by a clinical psychologist upon request of his attorney. His attorney wanted to determine if there were any problems related to substance abuse and aggression as he was charged with domestic violence. The clinical psychologist decided to administer only the first 370 items of the MMPI-2 "because the shortened version is just as good with ethnic minorities as the full version." Michael's profile appeared to be valid with only one elevation, on the Ma scale (70T). Michael had denied any use of substances or aggressive behavior to the psychologist in a clinical interview. Based on this data, and his MMPI-2 profile, he concluded that Michael was only "immature and irresponsible, with a tendency to act out from time to time, but not prone to violence or outbursts of anger."

The psychologist did not bother to consider any additional MMPI-2 data, including the Content or Supplementary scales. The attorney was not satisfied with this psychologist's conclusion, and requested a second opinion. The second time, Michael was administered the complete MMPI-2 (i.e., 567 items). His scores on the validity and clinical scales were identical to his prior performance. Unlike the first psychologist, the examiner evaluated additional scores "because additional scales can enhance an MMPI-2 profile interpretation for African-Americans." In addition to a spiked elevation on the Ma scale, two scores were highly elevated on the supplementary scales, the MacAndrew Alcoholism Scale-Revised (MAC-R) at 80T and Overcontrolled-Hostility (O-H) at 70T. Unlike the first psychologist, the latter examiner concluded that "Michael may be prone to minimizing his use of substances, and may become aggressive and abusive towards family members under these circumstances." Ultimately, these latter findings had a significant impact on Michael's legal defense.

F. CASE #6: *BRENDA*

Brenda is a 54-year-old American Indian female member of an Eastern Woodland tribe. She was referred to a psychologist for evaluation by her family physician. The physician was requesting confirmation of her diagnosis of severe depression and support for the administration of antidepressant medication. The psychologist administered the MMPI-2 and conducted an in-depth clinical interview.

A standard interpretation of the MMPI-2 scores obtained for Brenda questioned the validity of the test due to her F score, and further suggested that if the results were valid, there was an increasing probability of serious psychological and emotional problems. A "best fit" codetype of 1-3/3-1 indicated that Brenda most likely engaged in somatization, was manipulative, expressed her anger in passive and indirect ways, and lacked genuine interest in others. Her prognosis was noted to be poor due to lack of insight, a tendency to resist psychological interpretation, and a tendency to abuse prescribed medication.

Interview data revealed Brenda to be a person who heavily identified herself as an "Indian" person because of her upbringing in a rural, predominantly Indian setting. Yet she had moved away from her Native community as a young woman and had not participated in cultural activities since that time. In spite of her dropping out of high school in her junior year and experiencing two failed marriages, she reported earning a college degree in marketing. She had recently been caring for her 32-year-old son who had suffered a paralyzing injury in a car accident the previous year. One month before, Brenda was involved in a failing business venture and was contributing to the financial support of her 38-year-old daughter. Brenda expressed worry about her son's care and about her ability to continue to help her daughter in light of the inevitable closing of her business. Of equal concern was her ability to meet her own basic needs of food, clothing, and shelter. During the interview, she failed to express any physical complaints, revealed only a cautious willingness to accept prescribed psychotropic medications from her physician, and requested additional appointments with the psychologist to work through her current problems.

Had the psychologist relied on the standard interpretation of the MMPI-2, this client would probably have received a diagnosis included in the Somatoform or Anxiety disorders. Compulsive and Passive-Aggressive Personality Disorders would also have been considered. Importantly, these diagnostic possibilities seemed a poor fit with information generated in the clinical interview. Recent research evaluating the MMPI-2 American Indian norms, however, offers data that could have added clarity to this otherwise puzzling clinical situation. This research suggests that the client's scores may best be interpreted when compared to average scores and standard deviations obtained from an Eastern Woodland sample. Thus, Brenda's F score of 75T would have fallen well within "normal" bounds, removing the questions of profile validity and negating the suggestion of serious psychological problems. Further, the HS score was below 69T, D below 66T, and Pt below 68T, suggesting normative functioning. That is, the elevations were not as extreme as standard interpretation procedures might indicate. Similar to the F score, Brenda's Pa score of 67 would have been considered to be within the normal range for American Indians.

Consistent with Brenda's culturally modified MMPI-2 interpretation, the psychologist treated her for simple mild-moderate reactive depression. Brenda declined to continue on antidepressant medication and actively participated in 12 sessions of individual psychotherapy over a 6-month period. At the end of treatment, her depression had remitted, she had resolved her family and business conflicts, and had obtained a new job.

VI. CONCLUDING REMARKS

This review of the use of the MMPI-2 with ethnic minorities, as well as presentation of the case studies, illustrates that progress is being made toward culturally competent assessment of ethnic minorities. In order to continue such progress, researchers and clinicians alike are encouraged to reexamine their standards of practice when using and interpreting standardized measures with ethnic minorities. An understanding of within- and between-group differences is necessary to provide a frame of reference for culturally competent interpretation of MMPI-2 profiles with ethnic minorities. Likewise, sociocultural and environmental factors should always be considered before psychopathology is attributed to a client on the basis of an elevated MMPI-2 scale. It is hoped that this chapter helps to expand our horizons and improve our practices with ethnic minority clients.

REFERENCES

Alamo, R. R., Cabiya, J. J., & Pedrosa, O. (1995, March). *Utility of the MMPI-2 in the identification of emotional indicators in a sample of Puerto Ricans who experienced armed assault.* Paper presented at the Annual Symposium on Recent Developments in the Use of the MMPI-2, St. Petersburg, FL.

Anderson, T. R., Thompson, J. P., & Boeringa, J. A. (1993, August). *MMPI-2 and Mississippi scale profiles of Hispanic veterans with post-traumatic stress disorder.* Paper presented at the 101st Annual Meeting of the American Psychological Association, New Orleans, LA.

Bellamy, F. (1994). An investigation of the Minnesota Multiphasic Personality Inventory-2 Pd and Pd subscales in African American males. *Dissertation Abstracts International, 55,* 1660B.

Ben-Porath, Y. S., Graham, J. R., McNulty, J. L., & Stein, L. A. R. (1996, June). *A comparative study of the validity of the MMPI-2 scores of African-American and Caucasian outpatients.* Paper presented at the Annual Symposium on Recent Developments in the Use of the MMPI-2, Minneapolis, MN.

Ben-Porath, Y. S., Shondrick, D. D., & Stafford, K. P. (1995). MMPI-2 and race in a forensic diagnostic sample. *Criminal Justice and Behavior, 22,* 19–32.

Bowler, R. M., Mergler, D., Huel, G., & Cone, J. E. (1996). Adverse health effects in African American residents living adjacent to chemical industries. *Journal of Black Psychology, 22,* 470–497.

Butcher, J. N. (1996). *International adaptations of the MMPI-2.* Minneapolis: University of Minnesota Press.

Butcher, J. N., Cabiya, J., Lucio, G. M., E., Pena, L., Reuben, D. L., & Scott, R. (1998). *MMPI-A: Inventario Multifasico de la Personalidad- para Minnesota, Adolescentes.* Minneapolis, MN: University of Minnesota Press.

Butcher, J. N., Dahlstrom, W. G., Graham, J. R., Tellegen, A., & Kaemmer, B. (1989). *Manual for the restandardized Minnesota Multiphasic Personality Inventory: MMPI-2, an administrative and interpretive guide.* Minneapolis, MN: University of Minnesota Press.

Butcher, J. N., Graham, J. R., & Ben-Porath, Y. S. (1995). Methodological problems and issues in MMPI, MMPI-2, and MMPI-A research. *Psychological Assessment, 7,* 320–329.

Butcher, J. N., Lim, J., & Nezami, E. (1998). Objective study of abnormal personality in cross-cultural settings. The Minnesota Multiphasic Personality Inventory (MMPI-2). *Journal of Cross-Cultural Psychology, 29,* 189–211.

Butcher, J. N., Williams, C. L., Graham, J. R., Archer, R. P., Tellegen, A., Ben-Porath, Y. S., & Kaemmer, B. (1992). *Minnesota Multiphasic Personality Inventory-Adolescent: Manual for administration, scoring, and interpretation.* Minneapolis, MN: University of Minnesota Press.

Cabiya, J. J. (1994, May). *Application of the Hispanic MMPI-2 in Puerto Rico.* Paper presented at the Annual Symposium on Recent Developments in the Use of the MMPI-2, Minneapolis, MN.

Callahan, W. J. (1997). Symptom reports and acculturation of White and Mexican-Americans in psychiatric, college, and community settings. *Dissertation Abstracts International, 58(8-B),* 4439.

Callahan, W. J., Velásquez, R. J., & Saccuzzo, D. P. (1995, August). *MMPI-2 performance of university students by ethnicity and gender.* Paper presented at the 103rd Annual Meeting of the American Psychological Association, New York, NY.

Canul, G. D. (1993). The influence of acculturation and racial identity attitudes on Mexican Americans' MMPI-2 performance. *Dissertation Abstracts International, 54,* 6442B.

Canul, G. D., & Cross, H. J. (1994). The influence of acculturation and racial identity attitudes on Mexican Americans' MMPI-2 performance. *Journal of Clinical Psychology, 50,* 736–745.

Cervantes, R. C., Padilla, A. M., & Salgado de Snyder, N. (1991). The Hispanic Stress Inventory: A culturally relevant approach to psychosocial assessment. *Psychological Assessment, 3,* 438–447.

Chavira, D. A., Montemayor, V., Velásquez, R. J., & Villarino, J. (1995, August). *Comparison of two Spanish translations of the MMPI-2 with Mexican Americans.* Paper presented at the 103rd Annual Meeting of the American Psychological Association, New York, NY.

Chavira, D. A., Velásquez, R. J., Montemayor, V., & Villarino, J. (1995, August). *U.S. Latinos' performance on the Spanish language MMPI-2 and acculturation.* Paper presented at the Annual Symposium on Recent Developments in the Use of the MMPI-2, St. Petersburg, FL.

Chavira, D. A., Malcarne, V., Velásquez, R. J., Liu, P. J., & Fabian, G. (1996, August). *Influence of ethnic experience on Spanish MMPI-2 performance.* Paper presented at the 103rd Annual Meeting of the American Psychological Association, Toronto, Canada.

Choney, S. K., Berryhill-Paapke, E., & Robbins, R. R. (1995). The acculturation of American Indians: Developing frameworks for research and practice. In J. G. Ponterotto, J. M. Casas, C. Alexander, & L. Suzuki (Eds.), *Handbook of multicultural counseling* (pp. 73–92). New York: Sage.

Colon, C. C. (1993). *Relationship between the MMPI-2 content scales and psychiatric symptoms with Puerto Rican college students and psychiatric patients.* Unpublished doctoral dissertations, Caribbean Center for Advanced Studies, San Juan, Puerto Rico.

Cook, W. A. (1996). Item validity of the MMPI-2 for a Hispanic and White clinical sample. (Doctoral dissertation, Texas A&M University). *Dissertation Abstracts International, 56B,* 5761.

Cuéllar, I., Arnold, B., & Maldonado, R. (1995). Acculturation Rating Scale for Mexican Americans-II: A revision of the original ARSMA scale. *Hispanic Journal of Behavioral Sciences, 17,* 275–304.

Dahlstrom, W. G., Lachar, D., & Dahlstrom, L. E. (1986). *MMPI patterns of American minorities.* Minneapolis, MN: University of Minnesota Press.

Dana, R. H. (1995). Culturally competent MMPI assessment of Hispanic populations. *Hispanic Journal of Behavioral Sciences, 17,* 305–319.

Fantoni-Salvador, P., & Rogers, R. (1997). Spanish versions of the MMPI-2 and PAI: An investigation of concurrent validity with Hispanic patients. *Assessment, 4,* 29–39.

Flores, L., Chavira, D. A., Perez, J., Engel, B., & Velásquez, R. J. (1996, June). *MMPI-2 codetypes of Spanish-speaking Hispanic DUI offenders: Preliminary findings.* Paper presented at the Annual Symposium on Recent Developments in the Use of the MMPI-2, Minneapolis, MN.

Frank, J. G., Velásquez, R. J., Reimann, J., & Salazar, J. (1997, June). *MMPI-2 profiles of Latino, Black, and White rapists and child molesters on parole.* Paper presented at the Annual Symposium on Recent Developments in the Use of the MMPI-2, Minneapolis, MN.

Frueh, B. C., Smith, D. W., & Libet, J. M. (1996). Racial differences on psychological measures in combat veterans seeking treatment for PTSD. *Journal of Personality Assessment, 66,* 41–53.

Garrido, M., Gionta, D., Diehl, S., & Boscia, M. (1998, March). *The Megargee MMPI-2 system of inmate classification: A study of its applicability with ethnically diverse prison inmates.* Paper presented at the Annual Symposium on Recent Developments in the Use of the MMPI-2, Clearwater, FL.

Garrido, M., Velásquez, R. J., Parsons, J. P., Reimann, J., & Salazar, J. (1997, June). *MMPI-2 performance of Hispanic and White abusive and neglectful parents.* Paper presented at the Annual Symposium on Recent Developments in the Use of the MMPI-2, Minneapolis, MN.

Ghaffarian, S. (1987). The acculturation of Iranians in the United States. *Journal of Social Psychology, 127,* 565–571.

Greene, R. L.. (1987). Ethnicity and MMPI performance: A review. *Journal of Consulting and Clinical Psychology, 55,* 497–512.

Greenwood, K., Velásquez, R. J., Suarez, R., Rodriguez-Reimann, D., Johnson, A., Flores-Gonzalez, R., & Ledeboer, M. E. (1998, March). *MMPI-2/MMPI-A profiles of Latino mother and daughter dyads in an outpatient community mental health center.* Paper presented at the Annual Symposium on Recent Developments in the Use of the MMPI-2, Clearwater, FL.

Grillo, J. (1992). The influence of ethnicity on the validity and clinical scales of the Minnesota Multiphasic Personality Inventory-2. *Dissertation Abstracts International, 52,* 3905B.

Grillo, J. (1994, August). *Underrepresentation of Hispanic Americans in the MMPI-2 normative group.* Paper presented at the 102nd Annual Meeting of the American Psychological Association, Los Angeles, CA.

Gumbiner, J. (1998). MMPI-A profiles of Hispanic adolescents. *Psychological Reports, 82,* 659–672.

Gynther, M. D. (1972). White norms and Black MMPIs: A prescription for discrimination? *Psychological Bulletin, 78,* 386–402.

Gynther, M. D., & Green, S. B. (1980). Accuracy may make a difference, but does a difference make for accuracy?: A response to Pritchard and Rosenblatt. *Journal of Consulting and Clinical Psychology, 48,* 268–272.

Haskell, A. (1996). Mexican American and Anglo American endorsement of items on the MMPI-2 Scale 2, the Center for Epidemiological Studies Depression Scale, and the Cohen-Hoberman Inventory for Physical Symptoms. *Dissertation Abstract International, 57,* 4708B.

Hernandez, J. (1994). *The MMPI-2 performance as a function of acculturation.* Unpublished master's thesis, Houston State University, Huntsville, TX.

Holland, J. A. (1993). MMPI-2 profile differences in Black male and female children of alcoholics. *Dissertation Abstracts International, 53,* 2248A.

Karle, H. R. (1994). *Comparability of the English and Spanish versions of the MMPI-2: A study of Latino bilingual-bicultural students.* Unpublished master's thesis, San Diego State University, San Diego, California.

Ladd, J. S. (1994). Codetype agreement between MMPI-2 and estimated MMPI profiles in chemically dependent inpatients. *Psychological Reports, 75,* 367–370.

Ladd, J. S. (1996). MMPI-2 critical items norms in chemically dependent inpatients. *Journal of Clinical Psychology, 52,* 367–372.

Landrine, H., & Klonoff, E. A. (1995). The African American Acculturation Scale II: Cross-validation and short form. *Journal of Black Psychology, 21,* 124–152.

Lapham, S. C., Skipper, B. J., Owen, J. P., Kleyboecker, K., Teaf, D., Thompson, B., & Simpson, G. (1995). Alcohol abuse screening instruments: Normative test data collected for a first DUI offender screening program. *Journal of Studies on Alcohol, 56,* 51–59.

Lapham, S. C., Skipper, B. J., & Simpson, G. L. (1997). A prospective study of the utility of standardized instruments in predicting recidivism among first DWI offenders. *Journal of Studies on Alcohol, 58,* 524–530.

Lessenger, L. H. (1997). Acculturation and MMPI-2 scale scores of Mexican-American substance abuse patients. *Psychological Reports, 80,* 1181–1182.

Lopez, C. M. (1997). Psychological adjustment of Black and White homeless veterans and nonveterans on the MMPI-2. *Dissertation Abstracts International, 58(3-B),* 1538.

Maiocco, M. (1996). The relationship between ethnicity and somatization in workers' compensation claimants (African-American, Hispanic). *Dissertation Abstracts International, 57,* 2199B.

Mason, K. (1997). Ethnic identity and the MMPI-2 profiles of Hispanic male veterans diagnosed with PTSD. *Dissertation Abstracts International, 58(4-B),* 2129.

McClinton, B. K., Graham, J. R., & Ben-Porath, Y. S. (1995, March). *Ethnicity and MMPI-2 substance abuse scales.* Paper presented at the Annual Symposium on Recent Developments in the Use of the MMPI-2, St. Petersburg, FL.

McNulty, J., Graham, J. R., Ben-Porath, Y. S., & Stein, L. A. R. (1997). Comparative validity of MMPI-2 scores of African American and Caucasian mental health center clients. *Psychological Assessment, 9,* 464–470.

Negy, C., Leal-Puente, L., Trainor, D. J., & Carlson, R. (1997). Mexican American adolescents' performance on the MMPI-A. *Journal of Personality Assessment, 69,* 205–214.

Netto, D. S., Aguila-Puentes, G., Burns, W. J., Sellars, A. H., & Garcia, B. (1998, August). *Brain injury and the MMPI-2: Neurocorrection for Hispanics.* Paper presented at the 106th Annual Meeting of the American Psychological Association, San Francisco, CA.

Nezami, E., Bernous, B., Ghassemi, A., & Nezami, M. A. (1998). *A bilingual study of the Farsi translation of the MMPI-2.* Paper presented at the International Association of Applied Psychology, San Francisco, CA.

Okazaki, S. (1995, August). *Cultural differences underlying Asian-White differences on the MMPI-2.* Paper presented at the 103rd Annual Meeting of the American Psychological Association, New York, NY.

Pace, T. M., Choney, S. K., Blair, G. M., Hill, J. S. H., & Lacey, K. (1997, August). *Evaluating the MMPI-2 American Indian norms.* Paper presented at the 105th Annual Meeting of the American Psychological Association, Chicago, IL.

Pena, L. (1996, June). *Spanish MMPI-A and Cuban Americans: Profiles of adolescents using the Spanish version of the MMPI-A.* Paper presented at the Annual Symposium on Recent Developments in the Use of the MMPI-2, Minneapolis, MN.

Pena, C., Cabiya, J. J., & Echevarria, N. (1995, March). *Changes in mean MMPI-2 T scores of violent offenders in a social learning treatment program.* Paper presented at the Annual Symposium on Recent Developments in the Use of the MMPI-2, St. Petersburg, FL.

Pena, C., Cabiya, J. J., & Echevarria, N. (1996, November). *MMPI-2 scores of a representative sample of statement inmates in Puerto Rico.* Paper presented at the 43rd Convention of the Puerto Rican Psychological Association, Mayaguez, P.R.

Pritchard, D. A., & Rosenblatt, A. (1980). Racial bias in the MMPI: A methodological review. *Journal of Consulting and Clinical Psychology, 48,* 263–267.

Quintana, J. P. (1997). Acculturation of Hispanic-American college students and its relationship to MMPI-2 scores. *Dissertation Abstracts International: 57(11-B),* 7265.

Reed, M. K., McLeod, S., Randall, Y., & Walker, B. (1996a). Depressive symptoms in African-American women. *Journal of Multicultural Counseling and Development, 24,* 6–14.

Reed, M. K., Walker, B., Williams, G., McLeod, S., & Jones, S. (1996b). MMPI-2 patterns in African-American females. *Journal of Clinical Psychology, 52,* 437–441.

Robers, H. R. H. (1922). Ethnicity and the MMPI-2: Cultural implications and limitations for Chinese Americans. *Dissertation Abstracts International, 53,* 2095B.

Rowell, R. K. (1992). Differences between black, Mexican American, and White probationers on the revised MacAndrew Alcoholism Scale of the MMPI-2. *Dissertation Abstracts International, 54,* 821A.

Schinka, J. A., LaLone, L., & Greene, R. L. (1998). Effects of psychopathology and demographic characteristics on MMPI-2 scale scores. *Journal of Personality Assessment, 70,* 197–211.

Speca, M. (1994). A factor analytic test of racial bias in the Minnesota Multiphasic Personality Inventory-2. *Dissertation Abstracts International, 55,* 2412B.

Steinman, D. (1993). MMPI-2 profiles of inpatient polysubstance abusers. *Dissertation Abstracts International, 54,* 3354B.

Sturmer, P. J., & Gerstein, L. H. (1997). MMPI profiles of Black Americans: Is there a bias? *Journal of Mental Health Counseling, 19,* 114–129.

Suinn, R. M., Knoo, G., & Ahuna, C. (1995). The Suinn-Lew Asian Self-Identity Acculturation Scale: Cross-cultural information. *Journal of Multicultural Counseling and Development, 23,* 139–148.

Timbrook, R. E., & Graham, J. R. (1994). Ethnic differences on the MMPI-2? *Psychological Assessment, 6,* 212–217.

Tyson, B. B. (1997). MMPI-A differences between African American and Caucasian adolescents in a shelter or detention center. *Dissertation Abstracts International, 57,* 4767B.

Velásquez, R. J. (1984). *An atlas of MMPI group profiles in Mexican Americans.* (Occasional Paper No. 19). Los Angeles: Spanish Speaking Mental Health Research Center, University of California, Los Angeles.

Velásquez, R. J., Ayala, G. X., & Mendoza, S. A. (1998). *Psychodiagnostic assessment of U.S. Latinos with the MMPI, MMPI-2, and MMPI-A: A comprehensive resource manual.* East Lansing, MI: Julian Samora Research Institute, Michigan State University.

Velásquez, R. J., Callahan, W. J., Reimann, J., & Carbonell, S. (1998, August). *Performance of bilingual Latinos on an English-Spanish MMPI-2.* Paper presented at the 106th Annual Meeting of the American Psychological Association, San Francisco, CA.

Velásquez, R. J., Chavira, D. A., Karle, H., Callahan, W. J., & Garcia, J. A. (in press). Assessing Spanish-speaking Latinos with translations of the MMPI-2: Initial data. *Cultural Diversity and Ethnic Minority Psychology.*

Velásquez, R. J., Gonzales, M., Butcher, J. N., Castillo-Cañez, I., Apodaca, J. X., & Chavira, D. (1997). Use of the MMPI-2 with Chicanos: Strategies for counselors. *Journal of Multicultural Counseling and Development, 25,* 107–120.

Wexler, A. K. (1996). Gender and ethnicity as predictors of psychological qualifications for police officer candidates. *Dissertation Abstracts International, 57,* 2924B.

Whitworth, R. H., & McBlaine, D. D. (1993). Comparison of the MMPI and MMPI-2 administered to Anglo- and Hispanic-American university students. *Journal of Personality Assessment, 61,* 19–27.

Whitworth, R. H., & Unterbrink, C. (1994). Comparison of MMPI-2 clinical and content scales administered to Hispanic- and Anglo-Americans. *Hispanic Journal of Behavioral Sciences, 16,* 255–264.

CHAPTER 20

Neuropsychological Assessment of Ethnic Minorities: Clinical Issues

ANTONIO E. PUENTE
Department of Psychology
University of North Carolina at Wilmington
Wilmington, North Carolina

MIGUEL PEREZ-GARCIA
Department of Psychology
Universidad de Granada
Granada, Spain

The psychology of individual differences underscores the importance of understanding the unique qualities of the person. Of particular importance is the issue of understanding the role of culture in the assessment of psychological abilities and disabilities. Indeed, the third article ever published in English on psychological assessment (Willey & Herskovits, 1927) was entitled "Psychology and Culture." In that article the influence of culture on human behavior as measured by psychological testing is debated. Over the last quarter of a century, it has become widespread knowledge that ethnic minorities represent a unique challenge to psychological assessment. Whether the issue is that of bias (e.g., Jensen, 1980) or cultural equivalence (e.g., Helms, 1992), most scientists and professionals have come to understand the unique challenges that must be faced to develop a comprehensive understanding of all individuals. Indeed, that is the purpose of this volume.

Although the preceding argument has become commonplace, its application to all areas of psychological assessment has not been realized (Betancourt & Lopez, 1993). This is clearly the case in one of the fastest and most important

Handbook of Multicultural Mental Health: Assessment and Treatment of Diverse Populations
419

areas of psychological assessment, the evaluation of the behavioral, cognitive, and emotional sequalae of injury to the brain. Over the last 20 years, clinical neuropsychology has grown to become an important area of professional psychology (Puente, 1992; Puente & Marcotte, in press). Despite its unprecedented growth and impact, both in psychology and in medicine (most notably in neurology), the field has not considered the important variable of culture in its unique approach to the measurement of humans. Whether this ignorance is due to a willful disregard of ethnic minorities and cultural variables or simply historical inertia is rarely speculated (Puente & Perez-Garcia, in press) and not the topic of this chapter.

The purpose of this chapter is to attempt to alleviate this gross misunderstanding. Initially, we will outline the objectives and development of what is now being called cross-cultural neuropsychology. Traditionally, cross-cultural psychology has dealt with the comparisons of persons across distinct cultures (e.g., North Americans Europeans). In this case, we will expand the approach to subsume the contrast and comparisons of individuals from a majority group to those of a minority group. In fact, we define ethnicity much in the same way one would define culture. After outlining the objectives and development of the discipline, we will turn our attention to the application of these principles to neuropsychological evaluation. Issues such as illiteracy and adaptation will be considered. In addition, specific strategies for interviewing, testing, and interpreting results will be presented. Finally, suggestions for future training and research in the area will be considered.

It is important to note that although we look forward to presenting a new model as a solution to a long-standing problem in neuropsychology and the understanding of ethnic minorities, we realize the unique nature of our assumptions, model, and implications. To that end, we trust that the reader will consider this chapter as an introduction to a complex issue in neuropsychology and the psychological assessment of nonmajority group members. Further, we invite the reader to critique, revise, and expand this important and new area in neuropsychology and the assessment of the ethnic minority.

I. OBJECTIVES AND DEVELOPMENT OF A CULTURALLY SENSITIVE CLINICAL NEUROPSYCHOLOGY

The application of clinical neuropsychology to people of diverse cultural heritage is a relatively newfound scientific and professional enterprise. This development was due, among other factors, to both the growth of professional neuropsychology along with increasing societal concerns, both here and abroad, of the importance of understanding individuals in a broader cultural context (Puente & McCaffrey, 1992). The application of psychometric instruments standardized on White individuals from the majority culture resulted in larger than expected false-positives both in terms of psychopathological and neuropsychological variables. As a consequence, the lack of the universality of the instrument prevented not only the use of those instruments with individuals of varied cultural backgrounds but the limitations of theories of human function, especially brain, that were similarly universal in nature (Ardila, 1995; Greenfield, 1997).

The development of culturally sensitive clinical neuropsychology was a direct function of increasing interests in cultural concerns in the assessment and treatment of psychological problems (Brislin, 1980; Phinney, 1996). Indeed, over the last 10 years an ever increasing concern for these issues has been noted in the general psychological literature as well as within the American Psychological Association (APA) (Fowers & Richardson, 1996; Hall, 1997). From these concerns, cross-cultural psychology has begun to describe the differences in performances and treatment of individuals from different cultures. The rationale for this has been that differences from the majority culture have been compared to a constant—the majority culture—as if other forms of behaving were of interest, at best, or pathological, at worst. Greenfield, among others, have suggested that appropriate comparison, therefore, can only be realized if both cultures are at least generally understood before any form of comparison can be made.

Assessment of diverse groups within clinical neuropsychology will be, as suggested earlier, defined as cross-cultural neuropsychology. In other words, we are expanding the traditional concepts of cross-cultural psychology to address the issues of how one group, a minority group, compares and contrasts to that of a larger group. The rationale for this expanded concept is that we believe that understanding ethnic minorities in the United States should subscribe to the same principles as understanding a minority group in any other national or international setting. For example, the basic principles of neuropsychological comparisons between White, European-Americans to Hispanics in the United States should reflect similar approaches when Portuguese-speaking, city-dwelling Brazilians are compared to indigenous people living in the Amazon.

By expanding the scope accordingly, our comprehension of brain–behavior relationships will be similarly expanded. We are, after all, in search of a "neuropsychological g," much like Cattell was envisioning for a general intelligence. Thus, we should be able to factor the role of culture and minority status in understanding brain function. We do not want to confound adaptation with brain dysfunction as the two are, at least theoretically, different. Of course, the argument could be proposed that, after all, the reason for a difference is academic and that brain dysfunction and adaptation are different words for the same thing—an inability to process information in a goal-directed fashion.

If this approach is considered, then a literature clearly has been developing over the last 5 or so years. Examples include Ardila (1993a, 1993b) and Pontius (1993), an excellent example of this work. Pontius (1993) attempted to compare a variety of neuropsychological tests with indigenous people of New Guinea. In this study, he compared indigenous individuals living in traditional rural settings with those living in less traditional (i.e., Western) urban settings. In this and related studies, the conclusions are that the environment played a crucial role at least in visual processing.

An interesting and potentially useful source of comparisons can be found in recent work with AIDS patients across different cultures. This work, completed under the auspices of the World Health Organization, has been realized in five different countries located in Europe, North America, South America, Asia, and Africa (Maj, 1993; Maj et al., 1991, 1993). One of the findings is that the original versions of some of these tests, such as the Rey Auditory Verbal Learning Test, are affected significantly. For example, the standard deviation of across-national differences sometimes masked the differences noted between AIDS and non-AIDS patients (Maj et al., 1993, 1994a, 1994b).

A. CULTURAL ADAPTATION AND EDUCATIONAL ATTAINMENT

Without doubt, one of the most salient lines of research has been the exploration of the role of cultural adaptation and educational attainment on neuropsychological functioning. The changing demographics of American society alone beg the importance of attending to the role of adaptation alone. However, review of the demographics show an interesting pattern. Whereas during the early 20th century immigrants emigrated primarily from Europe, during the later part of this century, immigrants come from either Asia or the Americas. There is evidence to suggest that sometime during the next century, ethnic minorities will actually become the majority in the United States (Hall, 1997). Hence, understanding the minority group culture in light of changing demographics is clearly becoming more evident. There is ample evidence, however, that at present ethnic minorities do more poorly on most neuropsychological tests. Although most of this evidence appears anecdotal and clinical in nature, there is a growing body of data on intelligence (Helms, 1992; Greenfield, 1997; Puente & Perez-Garcia, in press; Puente & Salazar, 1998). More careful analysis of these findings indicate that cultural adaptation might be the salient variable that explains group differences (Berry, 1990; Magana et al., 1996).

In addition to cultural adaptation, there is growing evidence that educational attainment may help in explaining a significant aspect of cultural differences. Examples of this line of research include Roselli (1993), Roselli and Ardila (1991,

1993), Roselli, Ardila, and Rosas (1990), Ardila, Roselli, and Puente (1994) and Ostrovski-Solis, Ardila, Rosselli, Lopez-Arango, and Uriel-Mendoza (1998). In general, these studies suggest that low educational attainment produces low performance on neuropsychological tests. In the Ardila et al.'s (1994) book, norms are published for a variety of tests using both age, education, and status of brain function (i.e., brain-damaged vs. non-brain-damaged). As with many other types of psychological test results across a sample, a bell curve emerges. However, the results are particularly important when brain-damaged versus non-brain-damaged patients are compared. What is particularly unusual is that non-brain-damaged illiterates appear highly similar to brain-damaged but literate patients. That is, education, either directly or otherwise, appears to be a prophylactic for brain injury. Conversely, illiteracy appears much like brain damage.

B. Ecological Validity

Besides cultural adaptation and educational attainment, another important issue is that of biopsychosocial context—now referred to as ecological validity. The question of validity moves us away from what variables affect brain function to how they affect brain dysfunction. In other words, we now begin to focus not on questions as to whether ethnic minorities are slower on neuropsychological tests nor if education mediates brain function. Ardila (1995) has stated that "cultures dictate what is and what is not situationally relevant. What is relevant and worth learning for an Eskimo does not necessarily coincide with what is relevant and worth learning for an inhabitant of New York, Mogadishu, Manus, or Bogota" (p. 144). Hence, the mechanism is to potentiate the development of whatever cognitive and related abilities are necessary to be successful within a given culture. Ardila (1995) believes that there are common or universal abilities and that these abilities are molded by the specific cultural context around the person. This point is elaborated upon towards the end of this chapter.

As a consequence, it is the purpose of this chapter to address more specifically cultural issues in clinical neuropsychology. We will address later how these factors play a role in the expression of neuropsychological pathology in disorders such as AIDS and Alzheimer's dementia. In addition, specific and pragmatic considerations for the evaluation of the culturally dissimilar will be considered.

II. NEUROPSYCHOLOGICAL EVALUATION OF THE CULTURALLY DISSIMILAR PERSON

Because the theoretical aspects of several studies on cultural issues were briefly reviewed in the preceding section, we now turn to the more pragmatic aspects of the evaluation itself. Specifically, what are the variables that affect correct assessment of the culturally dissimilar person and how can they be understood and controlled.

A. ROLE OF CULTURAL ADAPTATION AND EDUCATIONAL ATTAINMENT

The role of acculturation in neuropsychological functioning has been realized with a variety of diverse populations, including individuals with schizophrenia (Chen, Lam, Chen, & Nguyen, 1996; Karno & Jenkins, 1993), AIDS patients (Maj et al., 1993, 1994a, 1994b), and dementia (Jacobs et al., 1997; Loewenstein, Rubert, Arguelles, & Duara, 1995; Mahurin, Espino, & Hollifield, 1992). Of these, dementias have probably received the most attention and, thus, might reveal the most critical aspects of culture and educational attainment in individuals of a minority status.

The effects of culture on neuropsychological function has basically focused on Hispanics. This ethnic group is expected to reflect anywhere between 33 and 38% of the population of the United States growth projected to occur between 1990 and the year 2020 (Campbell, 1994). In fact, between 1979 and 1980, Hispanics over the age of 65 grew by over 75% (Cuellar, 1990). Initial studies tended to focus on the use of screening measures for this population (Glosser et al., 1993; Loewenstein, Arguelles, Barker, & Duara, 1993; Mahurin et al., 1992; Taussig, Henderson, & Mack, 1992). A common finding across studies is that Hispanic elderly perform at a lower level on most screening measures. Further, this effect is more pronounced when the individual is either nonacculturated or of low educational attainment. Further, these authors suggest that possibly the use of nonverbal tests might be of greater value, and they intuitively have less cultural weight attached to them. In addition, others have recommended that analysis of neuropsychological dysfunction be based on more functional tests, such as observation of actual behavior in a home setting (Loewenstein, Ardila, Roselli, Hayden & Eisdorfer, 1992; Loewenstein et al., 1995).

In some studies, acculturation has been controlled statistically. However, other problems arise. For example, sample selections have not allowed for adequate generalization. One illustration of this is the use of Hispanics as a unified or cohesive ethnic group when Hispanics reflect a heterogeneous population. Indeed in attempting to establish proverbs for a Spanish translation of the WISC, a panel of experts from different countries of Latin America, consensus could not be reached over a proverb that was universal to all different Hispanic groups. To compensate for these problems, Jacobs et al. (1997) designed a study that controlled most of these confounds. Of the 14 measures used, Hispanic elderly scored poorer on 5 of the 14 measures. Surprisingly, most of these measures were nonverbal (i.e., Identities and Oddities, Benton Visual Retention Test matching (BVRT), and recognition. After obtaining these findings, the authors then grouped individuals according to three different acculturation groups. Acculturation was measured according to ease or fluidity of the English language. The three groups include adapted Hispanics (those that spoke good or very good English), a second group that was not acculturated (spoke little or no English), and a group that were native English speakers. The three groups were equal in terms of age and educational attainment. The results indicated that no differences were found between either the acculturated Hispanics or the English speakers. However, differences were noted between the non-acculturated Hispanics and the English speakers. Based on these findings, Jacobs's team is now exploring whether elderly Hispanics have different processing capabilities on geometric figures since that is the foundation of the BVRT.

Ostrovski-Solis et al. (1998) have chosen not to control but to manipulate educational attainment in neuropsychological test situations. She and her colleagues have found that educational level and acculturation has a negatively accelerated curve that eventually stabilizes or plateaus. Some neuropsychological tests, such as comprehension of language or verbal fluidity, are affected by as little as one to 2 years of formal education. Various hypotheses have been proposed by Ostrovski-Solis and colleagues, including the limited number of occasions that illiterate individuals come in contact with tests, the lack of familiarity with test protocol and performance (e.g., time), and, most likely, that education affects cerebral organization.

An excellent example of this type of study is found with the previously described WHO studies on AIDS patients (Maj et al., 1993, 1994a, 1994b). One of the more interesting results is found when comparing asymptotic HIV-1 zeropositive and HIV-1-zero-negative controls in Kinshaha and Sao Paolo. These two groups, as compared to the other locations, perform worse, regardless of HIV status of their counterparts. In another instance, Maj et al. (1994b) reported that in Kinshasa and Nairobi, decreased functioning on neuropsychological tests was only evident in individuals with a very limited (versus high levels) of education. Maj et al. (1994b) have hypothesized that high levels of education augment a "cerebral reserve" potentiating cerebral circuits and synaptic connections. In addition, low educational attainment appears highly correlated with the prevalence of other medical problems including, but not limited to, infectious diseases and malnutrition as well as with morbidity. In other words, illiteracy, again, appears to equate, in one fashion or another, with brain dysfunction.

B. CONTROLLING CULTURAL AND EDUCATIONAL VARIABLES IN NEUROPSYCHOLOGICAL EVALUATIONS

According to Ardila (1995) and Greenfield (1997), tests are not cultural or educationally isolated. Some tests, more than others, have attempted to be less affected by education and culture (Jensen, 1980; Greenfield, 1997). However, it must be understood that even before the actual testing, these variables begin to affect our understanding of the patient. As a consequence we begin by addressing the review of records, then the interview, and finally the actual testing.

1. Records

Every neuropsychological evaluation begins with a review of existing records. These records might include school, prison, service, and vocational ones. By design, individuals with limited educational background and different cultural heritage pose significant difficulties for a number of reasons, including existence of such records, obtaining them, appreciating the American equivalence, and so on. For example, recently the senior author was asked to complete an evaluation of an Arabic woman. Because premorbid intelligence is an important factor to be addressed and because educational attainment is often considered a good measure of premorbid intelligence, review of school records is a must. However, in some Arabic cultures, especially the more traditional ones, formal education for women is not considered appropriate for middle and upper classes. However, it is important to note that formal education in some Arabic countries does not equate with intellectual abilities. In fact, in some cases, education is considered for those not intelligent enough to be able to marry early and adequately.

When records are available, it is important to realize that things are not equivalent simply because face validity appears evident. For example, a college education in non-North American countries usually equals to a Master's degree in the United States. Hence, some understanding of the culture of origin and the educational system is in order. Otherwise, mistakes will be made in estimating premorbid functioning.

2. Interview

For starters, let us begin by addressing the issue of interpreters. In order of preference, we propose, that all things being equal (and they are not often the case), that the evaluation be done by a culturally similar individual (Spanish patient and Spanish evaluator) in the native tongue of the patient. Next best would be a translator. However, unusual care must be taken in that two common errors are often made. One is that the translator, though qualified, could be literal and miss the cognitive equivalence of the intended question. A second issue is that it is often easier to use available family members. Such individuals are apt to provide their own interpretation as they are not entirely objective. Finally, one could conceivably argue that it would be better to attempt a neuropsychological evaluation without any understanding of the culture or language of the person rather than not do an evaluation at all. In this case, extreme caution should be taken and any final report should address explicitly these concerns. What it comes down to is the clinician weighing Type 1 versus Type II errors. Is it better to have some flawed data than none?

As Velasquez et al. (1997) have suggested, however, a lack of understanding of language and culture will invariably produce errors in the interview process. These errors could include specific terms or concepts, cognitive equivalence issues, and subtle meanings only deciphered with a fluid understanding of the language and culture. If at all possible, the major cultural issue should be understood. Among other variables, Greenfield (1997) has suggested that the following variables should be considered in an interview.

1. *The value and significance of specific cultural concepts.* For example, educational systems in Spanish cultures may reflect more social ability than formal education.

2. *Modes of knowledge.* Mode of knowledge is the collective form of knowing. It is common for a head of a family to speak on behalf of the rest of the family. Hence, better information might be ascertained not from the patient but from the head of the family.

3. *Modes of communication.* It is important to note the role and strategies of communicating. Sometimes apparently important and straightforward questions can be construed as an invasion of privacy, eventually affecting the success of the later testing.

In addition to these considerations, the following information should be obtained, as it may help in appreciating the role of acculturation and education in neuropsychological functioning.

1. *Prior testing history.* Considering that individuals with either cultural or educational differences are often not exposed to standardized testing, it would be valuable to determine prior knowledge with these modes of understanding.

2. *Level of education.* Clearly, educational attainment affects neuropsychological functioning. It is imperative that the level and type of education be obtained and understood. However, as Loewenstein, Arguelles, Arguelles, & Linn-Fuentes (1994) have argued, care must be taken not to translate equally the number of years of schooling.

3. *Acculturation.* Though sometimes understood in general counseling and some testing situations, this is rarely appreciated by neuropsychologists. Whereas one might be able to use acculturation measures (see Magana et al., 1996), number of years in U.S. culture, knowledge of English, employment records, and language spoken at home are some of the variables that could be easily obtained in an interview.

The aforementioned information provides the clinician with a working hypothesis of neuropsychological impairment. This hypothesis helps the clinician identify the types of tests that are necessary and most appropriate. For example, if a person does not speak English (e.g., Vietnamese), the use of some portions of the Halstead-Reitan Neuropsychological Battery (e.g., Speech-sounds Perception Test) would be totally inappropriate, because some items are nothing more than tests for phonetic understanding.

3. Neuropsychological Testing

The lengthiest portion of any neuropsychological evaluation is the testing. Indeed, it is common clinical knowledge that neuropsychological evaluations take twice as long as standard clinical ones, in large part because of the extensive set of labor-intensive tests. In this section we address the different concerns as well as tests that could be used with culturally dissimilar patients. We begin with specific suggestions for the selection of appropriate neuropsychological tests:

1. Address the variables that need to be measured, then select the tests that measure that variable. Sometimes the abilities that need to be measured do not have a cultural equivalence (Helms, 1992). For example, time is often an important variable in determining intelligence in North American cultures. If intelligence is the issue, time might not be that valuable a measure in certain ethnic groups.

2. Select measures that have been adequately translated. By this we mean that the cognitive equivalence and not the literal one is being measured. This should include an understanding of the underlying factors that the test measures and a point-to-point correspondence with the translation. For example, the recall of digits is an integral part of several tests of attention, memory, and intelligence. However, if the issue is memory, then the number "eight" is a monosyllabic memory, whereas "*ocho*" (Spanish for eight) is two syllables. This becomes even more complex when going between American and Asian cultures and languages.

3. Use tests that have appropriate norms. For example, a recent study by Camara, Nathan, and Puente (in press) revealed that the most common test used by neuropsychologists is the MMPI. The MMPI has been translated into various languages but no formal norms are available in most instances for groups other than the mainstream United States population.

4. Use tests that have specific instructions and protocols. It is our contention that greater errors are made when the degrees of freedom are larger in circumstances where culture and language become intervening variables.

5. Select tests that reflect the language ability and culture of the patient. Tests such as the Mini-Mental Status Exam (MMSE) is relatively easy and brief. However, even with such a test, education can have significant effects. Bertolucci, Brucki, Campacci, and Juliano (1994) have reported that in illiterate patients, a cutoff of 13 should be used to detect pathology. Of particular concern is the use of intellectual tests, especially in educational settings. Since the likelihood of a false-positive is greater with ethnic minorities, care must be taken not to make educational placement decisions in specific programs (e.g., brain-injury programs) using these tests alone (Puente & Salazar, 1998). Another example comes from the work of Loewenstein and Rubert (1992), who discovered that differences between elderly Hispanic and white European-American individuals on dementia screening was due to performance on tests involving fluency with the letters F, A, and S. These letters occur with greater frequency in the English than in the Spanish language.

6. Be careful not to assume that nonverbal tests mean nonculturally biased tests. As Mahurin et al. (1992) have found, some nonverbal tests yield differences in different cultural groups. If possible, use nonverbal tests that appear to be culture-free. Cuevas and Osterich (1990) reported that the original booklet version of the Category test appears to have cultural equivalence, especially for men.

7. If available, use ecologically valid, tests of function, especially of activities of daily living. One example of this is the Direct Assessment of Continual Status by Loewenstein et al. (1989). Of course, one must be also concerned about the lack of reliability that such tests often provide.

4. Interpretation of Neuropsychological Test Results

Once the testing is complete, then comes the most difficult part of an evaluation—the integration of record, clinical, and testing information. This task is difficult in and of itself without adding cultural and educational confounds. Considering that it is almost impossible to find a perfect evaluation situation (i.e., similar culture and language between tester and patient, adequate tests, and norms, etc.), it is imperative to be extremely careful with the integration of a variety of data to address the presence and impact of a brain injury. We offer several suggestions in attempting this difficult task;

1. Interpret the results in a biopsychosocial context. Whenever possible, understand the biological, psychological, and social context of the patient, including, but not limited to, language and culture.

2. Appreciate what the criterion variable is. This is a difficult issue. If the question is whether a patient is brain-injured, extremely careful attention must

be paid to all the issues addressed in this chapter. If the question is whether the patient has the capacity to adapt to the culture where the patient is residing, then it might be reasonable not to accommodate accordingly. In other words, the question might be more of acculturation than brain function. Of course, it could very well be that both questions bear being asked, and the evaluation strategies might actually be mutually exclusive. Here is where clinical acumen, including understanding of the referral question, would be valuable.

3. Use a variety of sources of information. Traditionally, neuropsychologists rely heavily on test results, interview, and, typically, existing records. Such sources of information, while valuable, may be insufficient. The clinician might consider alternative strategies, including collateral interviews, thorough histories, assessment of social abilities, and so on. Although immigrants often score poorer on standardized neuropsychological tests, sometimes they are successful in adapting to the immeasurable demands placed on them by a foreign culture and language.

4. Avoid stereotypical interpretations. Although it is imperative to guide interpretation with existing literature, as Velasquez et al. (1997) has underscored, most of that literature does not exist for culturally dissimilar patients. Although intuition would suggest something to be true (e.g., whenever possible, use nonverbal tests), existing studies sometimes provide differing conclusions. An interesting example comes from the study by Karno and Jenkins (1993) that reports that schizophrenia has a better prognosis in less developed countries than in more developed ones.

5. If follow-up with the patient is possible, explain the results in a manner that could be understood by the patient and their family. Avoidance of technical and medical terms and explaining the results in practical, day-to-day, colloquial language will increase an understanding of the situation. One must realize that these individuals may not only have educational and cultural differences, but these are superimposed on neuropsychological deficits. The combination makes for a unique and challenging task of information dissemination.

III. FUTURE PERSPECTIVES IN THE ASSESSMENT OF CULTURALLY DISSIMILAR PATIENTS

In the first section we presented the more theoretical aspects of the neuropsychological assessment of culturally and educationally dissimilar patients. In the second section, our intent was to focus more on the pragmatic aspects of the assessment. In this third, and final section, we address the issues of future directions for both theory and practice. Relative to theoretical issues, we purport to address the potential areas for research as well as to what this research might mean in the development of comprehensive theories of human brain function and dysfunction. In the second portion, we address specific directions we believe practitioners in the field will eventually have to take into consideration.

The investigation of the existence of a neuropsychological "g" is at the foundation of what could be called cross-cultural or even cultural neuropsychology. The assumption is that, at birth, all humans possess roughly the same cognitive capacity at least across cultures. In other words, there are no major cognitive capacity differences across cultures, at least at birth. Evidence for this type of thinking has been found in studies on language. Furthermore, as cognitive, emotional, and personality capacity expands, it becomes more susceptible to environmental effects. In such a manner, the existing g becomes slowly molded to adapt to the specific tasks, cognitive or otherwise, that are demanded from the environmental cultural situation. As Ardila (1995) has suggested, we appear to have the same cognitive capacity to avoid danger, especially physical. However, a more neo-Darwinian or sociobiological perspective might provide a theoretical perspective on how a common neuropsychological g becomes culturally sensitive and globally fragmented. Thus, issues of what is good cognitively, such as faster is better, becomes incorrectly synonymous with a majority culture— as in the case of American culture where everything fast, from food to thinking, is desirable. Thus, an individual that does not understand and possess this important grain of knowledge is then considered as brain-impaired. Whereas some minority group members are certain to be brain-injured, if nothing else due to statistical probabilities, not all culturally dissimilar or educational disadvantaged individuals possess dysfunctional brains. It almost seems as in attempting to avoid Type I error in measurement, neuropsychologists are willing, maybe unknowingly, to make just as serious Type II errors. The end result is both mistaken identity and diagnosing in the short run and nongeneralized theories about brain function and dysfunction in the long run.

In addition, this approach to clinical neuropsychology can provide fruitful information to questions posed in related disciplines. For example, Neiser (1982) suggested that memory should be studied in a multidisciplinary perspective. Many of the cognitive studies of memory have been formulated for both developed and nondeveloped countries. Although not as of yet pursued, as these studies accrue comparisons between the cognitive underpinnings of memory across different cultures could be realized.

In terms of the application of cultural concerns to clinical neuropsychology, several issues should be considered. Few training programs contain courses on cross-cultural psychology, though a larger number purport to address ethnic-minority issues. In neuropsychology, one study (Echemendia, Harris, Congett, Diaz, & Puente, 1997) found that neuropsychologists are indeed concerned with these issues in an increasing fashion. However, the authors indicate that most neuropsychologists not only have limited training in dealing with these concerns, but similarly have not changed practice parameters to address these concerns. This paradoxical situation, of concern but warranting no action, provides an avenue from which to pursue a minimizing of the reported gap.

The following are proposed as potential solutions to this problem:

1. Increase the number of ethnic minorities in neuropsychology. Puente and Marcotte (in press) have reported that in Division 40—clinical neuropsychology—of the American Psychological Association, ethnic minorities represent a disproportionately smaller number of members, fellows, and officers of the division relative to other divisions. This is particularly problematic in light of the relative small number of ethnic minorities within APA.

2. Increase the number of tests and norms currently available. Using Hispanics as an example, a plethora of tests are reported to be available here and there. Only a very small number have been scientifically translated and normed. Even then, what is available is at best but a small step. For example, Ardila, et al. (1994) contains norms of literate and illiterate individuals, but the aged are disproportionately represented.

3. Encourage publishing companies to support these efforts. The senior author was involved in a 10-year project involving the translation and standardization of the Weschler scales into Spanish. Due to economic and related concerns (including sampling problems in the trial phases), the project was placed on what appears a relatively permanent hold.

4. Support research that provides the foundation for the development of these tests. An analysis of convention and published papers in neuropsychology over the last 20 years (Puente & Perez-Garcia, in press) does not provide much hope for this to be resolved. Indeed, ethnic-minority concerns represent no more than about 1% of convention presentations and published reports in the neuropsychological literature.

5. Teach students, both undergraduate and graduate, about the importance of cultural and educational issues in understanding brain function and dysfunction. In most neuropsychological textbooks, education though not illiteracy—is given serious concern. Culture, in contrast, is rarely, if ever, mentioned.

6. Make practitioners aware that being "aware" is simply not enough. Increasing the understanding of these variables, as APA has done in its current rewrite of both the ethics as well as the testing standards would appear an excellent start. However, neuropsychologists have traditionally been isolated from APA and from the impact of culture on neuropsychological performance.

IV. CONCLUSION

The involvement of understanding the role of educationally and culturally dissimilar individuals is a relatively new enterprise within clinical neuropsychology.

Although education has often been factored into the equation of neuropsychological knowledge, illiteracy has not. Furthermore, ethnic minorities and culturally dissimilar groups have not been well understood despite the unprecedented growth within the field. This chapter has presented both theoretical and pragmatic issues. Although clearly these efforts should be considered as a "work-in-progress," we hope that the eventual inclusion of these concerns will increase not only the understanding of all people with brain injury but will expand the horizons of our understanding of brain function and dysfunction as well.

REFERENCES

Ardila, A. (1993a). Historical evolution of spatial abilities. *Behavioral Neurology, 6,* 83–87.

Ardila, A. (1993b). People recognition: A historical/anthropological perspective. *Behavioral Neurology, 6,* 99–106.

Ardila, A. (1995). Directions of research in cross-cultural neuropsychology. *Journal of Clinical and Experimental Neuropsychology, 17,* 143–150.

Ardila, A., Rosselli, M., & Puente, A. E. (1994). *Neuropsychological assessment of the Spanish speaker.* New York: Plenum Press.

Berry, J. W. (1990). *Psychology of acculturation.* Nebraska Symposium of Motivation, 1989, 201–234.

Bertolluci, P. H. F., Brucki, S. M. D., Campacci, S. R., & Juliano, Y. (1994). *O Mini-Examen do Estado Mental en uma populacao geral. Arquives do Neuropsiquatria, 52,* 1–7.

Betancourt, H., & Lopez, S. R. (1993). The study of culture, ethnicity, and race in American psychology. *American Psychologist, 48,* 629–639.

Brislin, R. W. (1980). Translation and content analysis of oral and written material. In H. C. Triandis & J. W. Berry (Eds.), *Handbook of cross-cultural psychology.* Vol. 2: Methodology (pp. 389–444). Boston: Allyn & Bacon.

Camara, W., Nathan, J. & Puente, A. E. (in press). Psychological test usage in professional psychology. *Professional Psychology.*

Campbell, P. R. (1994). *Current population report: Population projections for states, by age, sex, race, and Hispanic origin: 1993 to 2020.* Washington, DC: U.S. Department of Commerce.

Chen, E. Y. H., Lam, L. C. W., Chen, R. Y. L., & Nguyen, D. G. H. (1996). Negative symptoms, neurological signs and neuropsychological impairments in 204 Hong Kong Chinese patients with schizophrenia. *British Journal of Psychiatry, 168,* 227–233.

Cuellar, J. B. (1990). Hispanic-American aging: Geriatric education curriculum developed for selected health professionals. In M. S. Harper (Ed.), *Minority aging: Essential curricula content for selected health and allied health professionals.* [DHHS Pub. No. HRS P-DV-90-4]. (pp. 365–413) Washington, DC: U.S. Government Printing Office.

Cuevas, J. L., & Osterich, H. (1990). Cross-cultural evaluation of the Booklet version of the Category Test. *International Journal of Clinical Neuropsychology, 12,* 187–190.

Echemendia, R., Harris, J. G., Congett, S., Diaz, M. L., & Puente, A. E. (1997). Neuropsychological training and practice with Hispanics: A bational survey. *The Clinical Neuropsychologist, 11,* 229–248.

Fowers, B. J., & Richardson, F. C. (1996). Why is multiculturalism good? *American Psychologist, 51,* 609–621.

Glosser, G., Wolfe, N., Albert, M. L., Lavine, L., Steele, J. C., Calne, D. B., & Schoenberg, B. S. (1993). Cross-cultural Cognitive Examination: Validation of a dementia screening instrument for neuroepidemiological research. *Journal of the American Geriatric Society, 41,* 931–939.

Greenfield, P. M. (1997). You can't take it with you. Why ability assessments don't cross cultures. *American Psychologist, 52,* 1115–1124.

Hall, C. C. I. (1997). Cultural malpractice: The growing obsolescence of psychology. *American Psychologist, 52,* 642–651.

Helms, J. E. (1992). Why is there no study of cultural equivalence in standardized cognitive ability testing? *American Psychologist, 47,* 1083–1101.

Jacobs, D. M., Sano, M., Albert, S., Schofield, P., Dooneief, G., & Stern, Y. (1997). Cross-cultural neuropsychological assessment: A comparison of randomly selected, demographically matched cohorts of English- and Spanish-speaking older adults. *Journal of Clinical and Experimental Neuropsychology, 19,* 331–339.

Jensen, A. R. (1980). *Bias in the mental testing.* New York: Free Press.

Karno, M., & Jenkins, H. (1993). Cross-cultural issues in the course and treatment of schizophrenia. *Psychiatric Clinics of North America, 16,* 339–350.

Loewenstein, D. A., Amigo, E., Duara, R. et al. (1989). A new scale for the assessment of functional status in Alzheimer's disease and related disorders. *The Journal of Gerontology, 4,* 114–121.

Loewenstein, D. A., Ardila, A., Rosselli, M., Hayden, S., & Eisdorfer, C. (1992). A comparative analysis of functional status among Spanish- and English-speaking patients with dementia. *Gerontologist, 47,* 389–394.

Loewenstein, D. A., Arguelles, T., Arguelles, S., & Linn-Fuentes, P. (1994). Potential cultural bias in neuropsychological assessment of the older adult. *Journal of Clinical and Experimental Neuropsychology, 16,* 623–629.

Loewenstein, D. A., Arguelles, T., Barker, W. W. & Duara, R. (1993). A comparative analysis of neuropsychological test performance of Spanish-speaking and English-speaking patients with dementia. *Journal of Gerontology, 48,* 142–149.

Loewenstein, D. A., & Rubert, M. P. (1992). The NINCDS-ADRDA neuropsychological criteria for the assessment of dementia: Limitations of current diagnostic guidelines. *Behavior, Health and Aging, 2,* 113–121.

Loewenstein, D. A., Rubert, M. P., Arguelles, T., & Duara, R. (1995). Neuropsychological test performance and prediction of functional capacities among Spanish-speaking and English-speaking patients with dementia. *Archives of Clinical Neuropsychology, 10,* 75–88.

Magana, J. R., de la Rocha, O., Amsel, J., Magana, H. A., Fernandez, M. I., & Rulnick, S. (1996). Revisiting the dimensions of acculturation: Cultural theory and psychometric practice. *Hispanic Journal of Behavior Sciences, 18,* 444–468.

Mahurin, R. K., Espino, D., & Holifield, E. B. (1992). Mental status testing in elderly Hispanic population: Special concerns. *Psychopharmacology Bulletin, 28,* 391–399.

Maj, M. (1993). Mild cognitive disfunction in physically asymptotic HIV infection: Recent research evidence and professional implications. *European Psychiatry, 8,* 173–177.

Maj, M., Janssen, R., Satz, P., Zaudig, M., Starace, F., Boor, D., Sughondhabirom, B., Bing, E. G., Luabeya, B. M., Ndetei, D., Riedel, the older adult. *Journal of Clinical and Experimental Neuropsychology, 16,* 623–629.

Maj. M., DiElia, L., Satz, P., Janssen, R., Zauding, M., Uchiyama, C., Starace, F., Galderisi, S., & Chervinsky, A. (1993). Evaluation of two new neuropsychological tests designed to minimize cultural bias in the assessment of HIV-1 seropositive persons: A WHO study. *Archives of Clinical Neuropsychology, 8,* 123–135.

Maj, M., Janssen, R., Starace, F., Zauding, M., Satz, P., Sughondhabirom, B., Luabeya, M., Riedel, R., Ndetei, D., Calil, H. M., Bing, E. C., Louis, M., & Sartorius, N. (1994a). WHO neuropsychiatric AIDS study, cross-sectional phase I. *Archives of General Psychiatry, 51,* 39–49.

Maj, M., Satz, P., Janssen, R., Zauding, M., Starace, F., DiElia, L., Sughondhabirom, B., Mussa, M., Naber, D., Ndetei, D., Schulte, G., & Sartorius, N. (1994b). WHO neuropsychiatric AIDS study, cross-sectional phase I. *Archives of General Psychiatry, 51,* 51–61.

Neisser, U. (1982). *Memory observed. Remembering in natural contexts.* New York: Freeman.

Ostrovski-Solis, F., Ardila, A., Rosselli, M., Lopez-Arango, G., & Uriel-Mendoza, V. (1998). Neuropsychological test performance in illiterate subjects. *Archives of Clinical Neuropsychology, 13,* 645–660.

Phinney, J. S. (1996). When we talk about American ethnic groups, what do we mean? *American Psychologist, 51,* 918–927.

Pontius, A. A. (1993) Spatial representation, modified by ecology. From hunter-gatherers to city dwellers in Indonesia. *Journal of Cross-cultural Psychology, 24,* 399–413.

Puente, A. E. (1992). Historical perspectives in the development of neuropsychology as a professional psychological specialty. In C. R. Reynolds & E. Fletcher-Janzen (Eds.), *Handbook of clinical child neuropsychology* (pp. 3–16). New York: Plenum.

Puente, A. E., & Marcotte, A. (in press). History of the Division 40- Clinical Neuropsychology. In D. Dewsbury (Ed.), *History of the divisions of the American Psychological Association.* Washington, DC: American Psychological Association.

Puente, A. E., & McCaffrey, R. M. (1992). *Handbook of clinical neuropsychological assessment: A biopsychosocial perspective.* New York: Plenum.

Puente, A. E., & Perez, M. (in press). Psychological assessment of ethnic-minorities. In G. Goldstein & M. Hersen (Eds.), *Handbook of psychological assessment* (3rd ed.). Boston: Allyn & Bacon.

Puente, A. E., & Perez-Garcia, M. (in press). Clinical neuropsychology: History, trends, and prospects. *Brazilian Journal of Psychology.*

Puente, A. E., & Salazar, G. D. (1998). *Assessment of minority and culturally diverse children.* In A. Prifitera & D. Saklofske (Eds.), *WISC-III: Clinical use and interpretation,* (pp. 227–248). San Diego: Academic Press.

Roselli, M. (1993). Neuropsychology of illiteracy. *Behavioral Neurology, 6,* 107–112.

Roselli, M., & Ardila, A. (1991). Effects of age, education and gender on the Rey-Osterrieth Complex Figure. *The Clinical Neuropsychologist, 5,* 370–376.

Roselli, M., & Ardila, A. (1993). Effects of age, gender and socioeconomical level on the Wisconsin Card Sorting Test. *The Clinical Neuropsychologist, 7,* 145–154.

Roselli, M., Ardila, A., & Rosas, P. (1990). Neuropsychological assessment in illiterates II: Language and praxic abilities. *Brain and Cognition, 12,* 281–296.

Taussig, I. M., Henderson, V. W., & Mack, W. (1992). Spanish translation and validation of a neuropsychological battery: Performance of Spanish- and English-speaking Alzheimer's disease patients and normal comparison subjects. *Clinical Gerontologist, 2,* 95–108.

Velasquez, R. J., Gonzales, M., Butcher, J. N., Castillo-Canez, I., Apodaca, J. X., & Chavira, D. (1997). Use of MMPI-2 with Chicanos: Strategies for counselors. *Journal of Multicultural Counseling and Development, 25,* 107–120.

Willey, M. M., & Herskovits, M. J., (1927). Psychology and culture. *Psychological Bulletin, 24,* 253–283.

PART IV

Training in Cultural Competence

Limitations of the Multicultural Approach to Psychotherapy with Diverse Clients

CHARLES NEGY

Department of Psychology
University of Central Florida
Orlando, Florida

Within the field of psychology, the study of culture and how it influences behavior has blossomed tremendously within the last decade. There appears to be a steady and growing appreciation among psychologists that humans are, in various and in complex ways, influenced by their sociocultural environment. Concomitantly, there is greater awareness of the fact that behaviors considered pathological in one culture may be quite acceptable or even promoted in other cultures (Vacc, Wittmer, & DeVaney, 1988). The recognition that humans are influenced by their sociocultural milieu is not particularly new to the field of psychology (Klineberg, 1980). As early as the 1920s, psychologists were acknowledging that sometimes a person's culture may explain his or her behaviors, values, and even feelings rather than intrapsychic determinants per se (Betancourt & Lopez, 1993).

In the context of therapy, the notions about the influence of culture increasingly are becoming incorporated into clinical and counseling psychology (Arredondo, 1994). Today, many clinicians and counselors no longer assume that behaviors manifested by a client—who is of a dissimilar race or ethnicity than that

Handbook of Multicultural Mental Health: Assessment and Treatment of Diverse Populations
439

of the therapist—is pathological solely because the behavior in question is considered pathological from the therapist's cultural standpoint (Vacc et al., 1988).

The fact that psychologists in the United States are increasingly recognizing that one's cultural upbringing may be as much of a contributing determinant to a person's "worldview" as are noncultural or intrapsychic factors is a step forward for psychology and is to be applauded. This growing awareness and appreciation for the importance of culture in understanding human behavior accounts for the current explosion of literature available on this topic.

Nevertheless, as books and publications on multicultural therapy and psychology continue to proliferate, certain assumptions or perspectives appear to have become fundamental to this subfield of psychology. As an educator training graduate students to be therapists for the past four years at a predominantly Hispanic university, and as a clinician providing services to mostly low-income minority children and families for almost a decade, I have found these assumptions to be incongruous with the professional experiences I have had with minority students and clients. These assumptions or perspectives are the focus of this chapter, in which I delve into controversy on occasion. However, my purpose is to critically examine some of these perspectives and to offer suggestions when appropriate on ways to enhance multicultural psychology's scientific basis and clinical utility.

These perspectives overlap to some extent but are treated separately. Further, although the perspectives can be discussed in the broader context of psychology and education, I will limit my discussion on these issues to the domain of psychotherapy, primarily because it is within this context where genuine disservice to clients can occur because of therapists' misguided adherence to wrongful assumptions and ideas. Also, because these ideas and perspectives are commonly found in literature utilized in multicultural therapy and counseling courses—courses that are customarily offered and sometimes required of students pursuing doctoral degrees in clinical and counseling psychology programs (Bernal & Castro, 1994)—the ideas warrant additional scrutiny.

I. MINORITY CLIENTS' RACE OR ETHNICITY IS NECESSARILY RELATED TO THE PRESENTING PROBLEM

In multicultural literature, it has been suggested that clinicians and counselors be cognizant of how being a racial or ethnic minority in the United States has influenced the psychosocial development of members of minority groups (e.g., Jackson, 1987). Some models of multicultural psychology share the assumption that "Minority groups develop modal personality patterns in response to white racism" (Helms, 1987, p. 241). Clinicians are expected to "be aware of the sociopolitical forces that have impacted the minority client" (Sue & Sue, 1990, p. 160) and be "comfortable with differences that exist between themselves and their clients in terms of race and beliefs" (Sue & Sue, 1990, p. 167). For therapy with diverse families, therapists should "work to help clients clarify the various facets of their identity to increase their flexibility to adapt to America's multi-cultural society" (McGoldrick & Giordano, 1996, p. 6).

These suggestions have validity and may be appropriate in some cases. However, with such emphases being made to attend to minority clients' racial or ethnic status in a therapy context, caution seems warranted. To what extent should therapists focus on the racial or ethnic background of diverse clients and bring their clients' ethnicity to the forefront of the therapist–client dialogue? Is it not conceivable that some minority clients' presenting problems are similar to majority clients' problems in the sense that the problems have no relationship to culture or ethnicity?

For example, in the above statement by McGoldrick and Giordano (1996) about ethnically diverse families in therapy, their advocacy to work on diverse clients' identities seems to ignore the fact that therapists must first determine what the clients' presenting problems are as the clients *themselves* define them. After obtainment of a greater understanding of why the clients have sought therapy, therapists then are in a better position to determine if focusing on racial or identity issues is warranted.

Essentially, when therapists approach clients as "ethnic entities" rather than as unique individuals with their own set of problems, therapists risk imposing their own issues or concerns onto the clients (one might even argue that making assumptions about clients' issues *a priori* based on our knowledge of clients' race or ethnicity is in itself a form of racism and therefore, inappropriate). The point here is that, just as it would be a mistake to ignore the possibility that clients' minority status is related to their presenting problems, it also would be a mistake for therapists—even having the best of intentions to be sensitive to minority concerns—to make assumptions about the role clients' race or ethnicity plays with respect to their concerns. The challenge it seems for therapists is to be open and sensitive to cultural concerns, especially those presented by clients, while being careful not to make cultural overgeneralizations based on stereotypes (Casas, 1984; Ho, 1995).

II. NON-WHITE CULTURES ARE INFALLIBLE

Social scientists wishing to learn about people of different cultures or racial groups should be exposed to negative as well as to positive aspects of the culture of focus (Eisenman, 1998). In all probability, all cultures have imperfections, and social scientists should feel free to discuss the shortcomings of any culture in a dispassionate way. Yet, ethnic and racial groups are often characterized in multicultural textbooks in almost exclusively positive terms even when explaining characteristics that probably have fallible causes. A case in point is Christensen's (1989) discussion of illegitimate Puerto Rican children being reared by their father's lawful wife (instead of by their mother who was their father's mistress). Christensen attributed this to Puerto Ricans' "love for children" and indifference to illegitimacy. This explanation ignores the more likely reason, which is to minimize the negative social consequences of the illegitimate birth to both the child and the mistress due to the general lack of acceptance of Latin American women having sexual relations outside of marriage (Falicov, 1982; Stevens, 1973).

Another example is Nwadiora's (1996) portrayal of Nigerian families living in the United States. Regarding Nigerians' respect and appreciation for children, Nwadiora reported that Nigerian families are quite democratic when solving family problems and "sometimes invite younger family members to express their views" (p. 129). Later, Nwadiora writes that "children are extremely important, because they ensure the longevity and continuity of several generations," (p. 136). Yet, in the same passage, Nwadiora states, "Girls are perceived as sources of potential wealth to families because of the anticipated dowry the bridesgroom will pay." In other words, children—particularly girls—are commodities to be traded as wives in exchange for money. Nwadiora also denies the extent to which female circumcision is a problem among Nigerian girls by claiming that the practice is "extremely rare" in Nigerian society and that the "much ado in the media about clitorectomy" is the result of institutional racism on the part of United States media.

How are therapists supposed to fully understand diverse clients' problems within a cultural context if the social science literature that provides them with information on other cultures is replete with defensive and romanticized cultural characterizations? It seems that one of the greatest challenges multicultural psychology poses to contemporary United States psychotherapists is for therapists to respect and appreciate diverse cultures while simultaneously having to acknowledge (and occasionally deal with in therapy) the fact that many specific practices in various cultures clearly violate fundamental human ethics and sometimes United States law (cf. Fowers & Richardson, 1996).

In my practice with low-income Mexican Americans in the southern portion of Texas, I commonly encountered parents reporting that as a form of punishment, they required their children to kneel down, often on bottle-caps (fichas) turned upside down, for a specified period of time. Not every low-income Mexican American parent utilized this form of punishment, but this version of "time-out" used by many residents in that region of Texas was common enough that virtually all practitioners who resided in that area were aware of this form of punishment. Because that practice was unique to this subgroup of minorities in the United States, should I have adopted, as a therapist, a relativistic stance and condoned it? In order to sensitize both the parents who engaged in that practice and the Mexican American graduate students I trained as therapists to the unacceptability of that behavior, I would invite them to imagine the supervisor at their place of employment mandating them to roll up their pants and to kneel on bottle-caps whenever the supervisor became angry at them. In this example, my commitment to treating children humanely took precedence over respecting a specific behavior commonly practiced by members of a diverse culture.

As Sue and Sue (1990) have indicated, researchers should not be tempted to "selectively publish findings that perpetuate 'good' characteristics of minority groups and that censure 'bad' ones" (p. 26). Not all cultural practices are ethical (McGoldrick & Giordano, 1996), and therapists will need to balance their commitment toward not imposing their cultural values onto clients with not ignoring specific cultural practices that most thoughtful individuals would find unacceptable.

III. RACE AND ETHNICITY ARE STRONGER PREDICTORS OF BEHAVIOR THAN SOCIAL CLASS

With so many multicultural articles and books focusing on ethnicity and culture, and literally only a handful of articles focusing exclusively on social class, it is easy to conclude that race and culture are more meaningful and predictive as variables explaining human behavior than is the variable of social class. In fact, many empirical studies examining correlates of race and culture fail to even measure socioeconomic status (SES) and to include it in the analyses (Negy & Woods, 1992). Studies that have often have found SES to correlate more strongly with the variables of interest than ethnicity or culture (e.g., Buriel & Saenz, 1980; Cashmore & Goodnow, 1986; Cuellar, & Roberts, 1997; Griffith & Villavicencio, 1985; Gutierrez, Sameroff, & Karrer, 1988; Lambert, 1987; Negy & Snyder, 1997; Soto, 1983). Moreover, studies on ethnic minorities frequently are studies on low-SES ethnic minorities in actuality, thereby not adequately disentangling ethnicity from social class. When this occurs, the results potentially can lead to distorted portrayals of ethnic minority groups (for more discussion of this, see Arbona, 1994; Casavantes, 1976; Massaquoio, 1993).

The question of which variable—ethnicity or social class—is a more powerful variable shaping people's lives rarely is fully examined in the literature beyond a few statements. Yet, overfocusing on diverse clients' ethnic culture while overlooking important aspects of clients' socioeconomic background conceivably could lead to erroneous diagnostic conceptualizations. Specifically, clinicians might make cultural misattributions for problematic behaviors that in reality have socioeconomic origins. As a result, therapists might elect to ignore the problematic behaviors in question, having explained them away as "cultural" or because of their commitment to being culturally nonjudgmental. In the previously discussed example of low-SES Mexican Americans in southern Texas who punish children using an inappropriate form of time-out, clinicians should not assume that that practice is common among Mexican Americans in the United States or even among Mexicans in Mexico. In all likelihood, the use of such punishment reflects those parents' relative lack of formal education, and clinicians should not avoid addressing such an issue solely because of their desire to be culturally sensitive.

Given the enormous *intra*racial variation that exists within each racial and ethnic group that is unexplained by race or culture, multicultural psychology may overestimate the impact culture or race has on behavior while underestimating the impact SES has on behavior. This imbalanced view may reflect our society's contemporary preoccupation with race and ethnicity and our de-emphasis on social class (Wilson, 1980). Ho (1995) is one of the few multicultural authors who discusses this issue at length. Ho states that knowing clients' cultural group membership often is of little help in understanding diverse clients' problems. However, focusing on diverse clients' "internalized culture" (the degree to which they adhere to prevailing cultural norms) may "enable us to deal with findings that there may be more similarity among members of comparable socioeconomic statuses across groups than among members of different socioeconomic statuses within the same group" (Ho, 1995, p. 6).

In summary, multicultural authors and clinicians providing therapy to diverse clients should not neglect to consider socioeconomic issues, especially in light of the fact that a disproportionate number of minorities in the United States occupy the lower echelons of society. Viewing behaviors from multiple angles (e.g., from a universal perspective, from majority- and minority-cultural perspectives, and from social class perspectives, etc.), the clinician should be in a better position to discern pathology from nonpathology and obtain a more comprehensive understanding of the nature of diverse clients' problems.

IV. IN A MULTICULTURAL THERAPY SITUATION, THERAPISTS ARE WHITE AND CLIENTS ARE NON-WHITE MINORITIES

Currently, there is a plethora of articles and books written on multicultural psychology and many are written within a framework in which therapists (or therapists in training) are assumed to be White and clients are assumed to be non-White (e.g., Arroyo, 1996; Casas, 1987; Corvin & Wiggins, 1989; Helms, 1987; Ponterotto & Pedersen, 1993; Sue, 1993). Although it is accurate that the majority of therapists and graduate students in clinical and counseling programs are White, there is usually a respectable percentage of graduate students who belong to ethnic and racial minority groups who will eventually work in settings where they will likely have to provide services to clients whose ethnicities differ from their own (Russo, Olmedo, Stapp, & Fulcher, 1981). Given that many articles on multicultural psychology are written with the assumption that therapists are White and clients are ethnic minorities, this raises questions regarding the multicultural training non-White minority psychologists are receiving. For example, are African-American graduate students being adequately trained to provide psychological services to Spanish-speaking Hispanic clients? Likewise, are Asian Americans receiving training on how to work effectively with White low-SES clients? Being a minority or majority member in the United States does not ensure that the person is well versed on the White-American culture, on his or her own racial culture, or on the cultures of other ethnic minority groups (Hall, 1997).

In light of the complexity of culture, perhaps authors of multicultural textbooks should consider including a chapter on White Americans. At the very least, it is suggested here that it is time for authors writing on this topic to approach it without making assumptions about the ethnicity of either the therapist or the client except for their cultural dissimilarity. This would increase the pedagogical usefulness of much of the literature used in multicultural courses so that multiethnic students enrolled in such courses might view the material as having increased relevance to them as budding therapists in an increasingly multiethnic society.

V. RACISM AND PREJUDICE ARE UNIQUE CHARACTERISTICS OF WHITE THERAPISTS

Some multicultural authors (e.g., Corvin & Wiggins, 1989; Sue, 1993) demand openly that White therapists acknowledge and resolve their ethnic prejudices in order to better serve non-White clients, yet minority therapists are left unchallenged to confront their prejudices—prejudices that equally can jeopardize the quality of services they provide to White clients and to dissimilar minority clients.

Ethnic prejudice exists throughout the world as evidenced by the number of ethnic and tribal clashes that have occurred throughout history and that currently occur worldwide (Ponterotto & Pedersen, 1993). Within the United

States, in addition to examples of past racism committed by some Whites towards some non-Whites (e.g., slavery, exploitation of Chinese for labor, etc.), as well as more current examples (e.g., the recent burnings of Black churches, etc.), racism and prejudice also exist within non-White groups. Some examples include the African Americans in south central Los Angeles who specifically targeted non-Blacks for violent attacks during the Los Angeles riots over the Rodney King verdict; an African American employee shooting and killing five White co-workers in order to "punish some of the cowardly, racist, devils" he held responsible for his being fired ("Racial Slayings," 1996); clashes between Cuban and African Americans in Miami during the 1980s; and clashes between Jewish and African Americans in New York City ("The Rift between Blacks and Jews," 1994). Even in the social science literature, there are subtle examples of prejudice displayed by some authors of minority membership. For example, the term *White racism,* which can be observed in some multicultural literature (Grier & Cobbs, 1968; Helms, 1987; Hodge, Struckmann, & Trost, 1975; Jackson, 1987; Kovel, 1970; Sue & Sue, 1990), is itself a racial stereotype of Whites implying that all Whites are overt racists. To illustrate this point, currently over half of all violent crimes committed in the United States are committed by African Americans (Kennedy, 1997), yet no one casually uses the term *Black aggression* in a way that implies that aggression is a predominant characteristic of African Americans. The point is, racism and prejudice are human characteristics (Comaz-Diaz, Lykes, & Alarcon, 1998; Mays, Bullock, Rosenzweig, & Wessels, 1998; Rogers, Spencer, & Uyangoda, 1998; Smith, 1998; Yee, 1996), and multicultural psychologists should bear this in mind in their treatment of cross-ethnic issues (for a rare and interesting discussion of *ethnicism*—prejudice ethnic minorities can have towards other ethnic minorities—see Yaffe, 1994).

Returning to the focus of multicultural therapy, a minority therapist can harbor negative attitudes towards White clients and towards other minority clients that can interfere theoretically with the therapeutic process. Regarding minority clients, if White therapists fail to develop rapport with them, some suggest (e.g., Sue & Sue, 1990) it is due to the therapists' ineffectiveness at working with minorities. But the therapist–client relationship is a relationship involving at least two people. Each person brings to the relationship his or her own ideas, feelings, and biases. If a minority client does not trust a White therapist solely because of the therapist's race, this is *the client's* prejudicial attitude that may interfere with the development of a therapeutic relationship. For such a situation, it has been stated that "the onus of responsibility for proving trustworthiness falls on the counselor" (Sue & Sue, 1990; p. 90) because "White people are perceived as potential enemies unless proved otherwise" (Sue & Sue, 1990; p. 79). But this is tantamount to informing an African American that he needs to demonstrate to Whites that he is trustworthy before he will be accepted by Whites. The African American's likely (and justifiable) response would be anger at the thought of having to prove himself to Whites before he could be trusted.

In reality, when a mixed-ethnic therapist–client relationship goes awry, it is difficult to pinpoint the reason(s) for the failed relationship if the client never returns. Although debatable, in the absence of information from interviewing both therapist and client to obtain their points of view on why the relationship failed (or having access to videotaped sessions), it may be paternalistic to place the blame for the failed relationship on the therapist. Consistent with humanistic psychology (as well as feminist psychology), perhaps therapists should not treat the therapist–client dyad similar to an adult–child relationship (e.g., one in which the adult [therapist] needs to accept responsibility for a problematic relationship more so than the child [client]).

It is suggested that multicultural psychology acknowledge that both therapists and clients can hold prejudiced attitudes *irrespective* of their race or ethnicity, and regardless of either one's race or ethnicity, this can jeopardize the therapeutic relationship and treatment outcome. Suggestions such as, "it is essential that White trainees explore . . . how racism is demonstrated in their personal and professional life" (Corvin & Wiggins, 1989, p. 113) and that Whites "need to begin admitting that they are not immune from inheriting the racial/cultural biases of their forebears" (Sue, 1993; p. 245) are valid suggestions, but should be suggested to all therapists regardless of their ethnic group membership.

VI. PSYCHOLOGY IS IRRELEVANT TO "MINORITIES"

Some social scientists interested in multicultural issues assert that, because much of psychology's notions about human behavior were developed based on the behavior of White Americans and Europeans, psychology's principles are irrelevant and nonapplicable to non-White minorities (Bell, 1971; Graham, 1992; Gunnings, 1971; Guthrie, 1976; Hall, 1997; Katz, 1985; Mitchell, 1971; Sue & Sue, 1990). More specific to therapy, "Minority intellectuals have criticized contemporary counseling approaches which they contend have been developed by and for the White, middle-class person" (Atkinson, Morten, & Sue, 1989; p. 16). In addition to the charges of irrelevance, Sue and Sue (1990) state that "traditional counseling theory and practice have done great harm to the culturally different" (p. v). Hall (1997) offers the grim warning that if the practice of psychology does not respond to the changing ethnic demographics occurring in the United States, the field will "lose its relevance as a profession" (p. 649).

The question of whether or not psychological principles and therapeutic techniques are effective with culturally diverse populations is an important question that needs to be examined extensively. In fact, cross-validation studies perhaps are in order to determine the effectiveness of specific therapies with minority group members just as cross-validation studies have been conducted using intelligence and other psychological tests with non-White populations. Amid the clamor over psychotherapy's utility and appropriateness with diverse clients, one might conclude that psychology—and by implication psychotherapy—are irrelevant and ineffective for minority populations. Are behavior management techniques less effective for Hispanic children than for White children? Do African American couples benefit from marital therapy as much as White couples? Regarding diagnostic conceptualizations, is the array of life problems encountered by minority clients and presented in therapy vastly different than the problems presented by White clients? Ordinarily, one might consult with the empirical literature to answer such questions, yet, the available data on these topics are somewhat limited (S. Sue, 1988). Nonetheless, various reviews have been made on research comparing treatment outcomes between mostly, although not exclusively, African American and White clients (e.g., Abramowitz & Murray, 1983; Atkinson, 1985; Sattler, 1977). The general consensus among the reviewers is that minority clients appear to benefit equally from traditional forms of therapy as do White clients. In fact, S. Sue (1988) reviewed the research findings and cautiously concluded that "Despite the strongly held opinions over the problems ethnic clients encounter in receiving effective services, empirical evidence has failed to consistently demonstrate differential outcomes for ethnic and White clients" (p. 301). S. Sue also stated that "many ethnic psychotherapists have strongly endorsed the value of psychotherapy with ethnic individuals" (p. 305). Sue quoted Evans, an African American, as having stated "many more black and poor people are helped by the psychotherapies than is acknowledged" (Evans, 1985, p. 457).

In essence, the assertion that psychological principles and therapeutic techniques apply to White Americans but not to ethnic minorities appears to be unsubstantiated. To the contrary, the data that exist tend to support the view that psychology has much to offer diverse ethnic clients, especially when psychotherapists take clients' cultural experiences and commitment to their ethnic heritage into consideration.

VII. CONCLUSION

An attempt has been made in this chapter to delineate and discuss selected assumptions or perspectives within multicultural therapy that may be problematic and impede the advancement of therapy with diverse ethnic and racial clients. The extent to which multicultural psychology and therapy become sociopolitical endeavors rather than academic endeavors may prevent multicultural psychology from having the scientific credibility and clinical utility that it might have otherwise. Naturally, multicultural research cannot be separated completely from the confluence of social issues often associated with multicultural topics. Nonetheless, the politicized aspects of multicultural psychology might be attenuated with collective commitments by researchers towards grounding multicultural psychology in empiricism, including empirically derived theories and therapeutic techniques.

A distinction often made in multicultural literature is between *etic* and *emic* perspectives regarding behavior. An etic perspective refers to viewing behavior in light of some set of universal standards for behavior, whereas, an emic perspective is viewing behavior within the unique standards of a particular culture (Draguns, 1981). A valid concern of multicultural psychologists is that mainstream U.S. psychologists often perceive diverse clients' behaviors and formulate subsequent treatment plans all from a U.S. emic perspective with little if any reservation because the therapists assume that their values more or less reflect universal values. To whatever extent this occurs would be tantamount to therapists imposing their cultural values onto clients whose worldviews and beliefs may differ vastly from those of the therapists.

An example of this comes from a colleague of mine who had a single therapy session with a young Salvadorean woman who had come to the United States 10 years ago and lived alone with her mother. One of the client's presenting problems was that she increasingly found herself wanting to go out and do things, such as date, but was distressed over what might become of her mother if she were to become seriously involved with a man and marry and leave her mother behind. My colleague's counsel was to inform the client that her mother was an adult and could fend for herself; the client had every "right" to pursue her own life and should not feel guilty for disconcerning herself over her mother's welfare.

Although my colleague's advice might have been valid for clients who are highly acculturated to mainstream United States culture, the advice probably was incongruent with the client's cultural values and illustrates a case in which U.S. emic values were promoted as if they were etic values. The Salvadorean client likely perceived the advice to disconcern herself with her mother in order to pursue her own goals as a recommendation to abandon her mother because feeling responsible for aging parents generally is more pervasive among Latin Americans than among North Americans (Falicov, 1982).

The point here is that both etic and emic perspectives have merit when conceptualizing psychopathology but must be applied judiciously to the specific problems presented by diverse clients. There are situations in which the culture of diverse clients is relevant to their problems and occasions when culture is irrelevant. Also, there are times when treatment should be congruous with clients' cultural norms, and times when "the objective of treatment is to change culturally prescribed behaviors' (Rogler, Malgady, Costantino, & Blumenthal), 1987, p. 568). Therapy is a collaborative venture between therapists and clients with both parties making informed decisions in the mutual pursuit of making clients' lives better. Culturally sensitive therapists must be willing to entertain multiple explanations for diverse clients' behaviors, be culturally empathic, and question their assumptions about the nature of human behavior in all of its vicissitudes (Lopez, et al., 1989; Rogler, Malgady, Costantino, & Blumenthal, 1987).

In closing, the fact that race, ethnicity, and culture have become a pivotal contemporary focus in psychology is belated but commendable. Multicultural psychology reminds us that people are, in varying degrees, influenced by their racial or cultural heritage and that psychologists and social scientists should be cognizant of this when studying human behavior and when providing psychological services to diverse populations. Moreover, multicultural psychology has greatly contributed to increasing clinicians' and counselors' sensitivities to potential cultural concerns of minority clients. It is hoped that this chapter will generate further discussion on the topics presented herein and that clinicians and researchers interested in multicultural issues will pursue empirical research more vigorously in order to shed more light on some of the questions raised throughout this chapter.

REFERENCES

Abramowitz, S. I., & Murray, J. (1983). Race effects in psychotherapy. In J. Murray & P. Abramson (Eds.), *Bias in psychotherapy* (pp. 215–255). New York: Praeger.

Arbona, C. [Discussant]. (1994). In W. B. Walsh (Chair), *Career assessment with racial ethnic minorities*. Symposium conducted at the annual convention of the American Psychological Association, Los Angeles.

Arredondo, P. (1994). Multicultural training: A response. *The Counseling Psychologist, 22,* 308–314.

Arroyo, J. A. (1996). Psychotherapist bias with Hispanics: An analog study. *Hispanic Journal of Behavioral Sciences, 18,* 21–28.

Atkinson, D. R. (1985). A meta-review of research on cross-cultural counseling and psychotherapy. *Journal of Multicultural Counseling and Development, 1,* 138–153.

Atkinson, D. R., Morten, G., & Sue, D. W. (1989). *Counseling american minorities: A cross-cultural perspective* (3rd Ed.). Wm. C. Brown Publishers: Dubuque, IA.

Bell, R. L. (1971). The culturally deprived psychologist. *The Counseling Psychologist, 2,* 104–107.

Bernal, M. E., & Castro, F. G. (1994). Are clinical psychologists prepared for service and research with ethnic minorities? *American Psychologist, 49,* 797–802.

Betancourt, H., & Lopez, S. R. (1993). The study of culture, ethnicity, and race in American Psychology. *American Psychologist, 48,* 629–637.

Buriel, R., & Saenz, E. (1980). Psychocultural characteristics of college-bound and noncollege-bound Chicanas. *Journal of Social Psychology, 110,* 245–251.

Casas, M. (1984). Policy, training and research in counseling psychology: The racial/ethnic minority perspective. In S. Brown & R. Lend (Eds.), *Handbook of counseling psychology* (pp. 785–831). New York: Wiley.

Casas, J. M. (1987). The status of racial- and ethnic-minority counseling: A training perspective. In P. Pedersen (Ed.). *Handbook of cross-cultural counseling and therapy*, (pp. 267–274). New York: Praeger.

Casavantes, E. (1976). Pride and prejudice: A Mexican-American dilemma. In C. A. Hernandez, M. J. Haug, & N. N. Wagner (Eds.), *Chicanos: Social and psychological perspectives* (pp. 9–14). Saint Louis, MO.: The C. V. Mosby Company.

Cashmore, J. A., & Goodnow, J. J. (1986). Influences on Australian parents' values: Ethnicity versus socioeconomic status. *Journal of Cross-Cultural Psychology, 17,* 441–454.

Christensen, E. W. (1989). Counseling Puerto Ricans: Some cultural considerations. In D. R. Atkinson, G. Morten, & D. W. Sue (Eds.) *Counseling American Minorities: A cross-cultural perspective* (3rd ed.), (pp. 256–270). Dubuque, IA: Wm. C. Brown Publishers.

Comaz-Diaz, L., Lykes, M. B., & Alarcon, R. D. (1998). Ethnic conflict and the Psychology of Liberation in Guatemala, Peru, and Puerto Rico. *American Psychologist, 53,* 778–792.

Corvin, S., & Wiggins, F. (1989). An antiracism training model for white professionals. *Journal of Multicultural Counseling and Development, 17,* 105–114.

Cuellar, I., & Roberts, R. E. (1997). Relations of depression, acculturation, and socioeconomic status in a Latino sample. *Hispanic Journal of Behavioral Sciences, 19,* 230–238.

Draguns, J. G. (1981). Counseling across cultures: Common themes and distinct approaches. In P. B. Pedersen, J. G. Draguns, W. J. Lonner, & S. E. Trimble (Eds.), *Counseling across cultures* (2nd ed., pp. 3–21). Honolulu: University of Hawaii Press.

Eisenman, R. (1998). The taboo on negative information about African Americans. *Journal of Information Ethics, 7* (1), 10–14.

Evans, D. A. (1985). Psychotherapy and black patients: Problems of training, trainees, and trainers. *Psychotherapy, 22,* 457–460.

Falicov, C. J. (1982). Mexican families. In M. McGoldrick, J. K. Pearce, & J. Giordano (Eds.), *Ethnicity and family therapy* (pp. 134–163). New York: The Guilford Press.

Fowers, B. J., & Richardson, F. C. (1996). Why is multiculturalism good? *American Psychologist, 51,* 609–621.

Graham, S. (1992). "Most of the subjects were White and middle-class": Trends in published research on African Americans in selected APA journals, 1970–1989. *American Psychologist, 47,* 629–639.

Grier, W., & Cobbs, P. (1968). *Black rage.* New York: Basic Books.

Griffith, J., & Villavicencio, S. (1985). Relationships among acculturation, sociodemographic characteristics and social supports in Mexican-American adults. *Hispanic Journal of Behavioral Sciences, 7,* 75–92.

Gunnings, T. S. (1971). Preparing the new counselor. *The Counseling Psychologist, 2* (4), 100–101.

Guthrie, R. (1976). *Even the rats were white.* Boston: Little Brown.

Gutierrez, J., Sameroff, A. J., & Karrer, B. M. (1988). Acculturation and SES effects on Mexican-American parents' concepts of development. *Child Development, 59* (1), 250–255.

Hall, C. (1997). Cultural malpractice: The growing obsolescence of Psychology with the changing U.S. population. *American Psychologist, 52,* 642–651.

Helms, J. E. (1987). Cultural identity in the treatment process. In P. Pedersen (Ed.) *Handbook of cross-cultural counseling and therapy* (pp. 239–246). New York: Praeger.

Ho, D. Y. F. (1995). Internalized culture, culturocentrism, and transcendence. *The Counseling Psychologist, 23,* 4–24.

Hodge, J., Struckmann, D., & Trost, L. (Eds.) (1975). *Cultural bases of racism and group oppression.* Chestnut Hill, MA: Two Riders.

Jackson, G. G. (1987). Cross-cultural counseling with Afro-Americans. In P. Pedersen (Ed.). *Handbook of cross-cultural counseling and therapy* (pp. 231–237). New York: Praeger.

Katz, J. H. (1985). The sociopolitical nature of counseling. *The Counseling Psychologist, 13,* 615–624.

Kennedy, R. (1997). *Race, crime, and the law.* Pantheon Books, New York.

Klineberg, O. (1980). Historical perspectives: Cross-cultural psychology before 1960. In Triandis, H. C., & Lambert, W. W. (Eds.), *Handbook of Cross-Cultural Psychology.* Vol 1, Boston: Allyn & Bacon.

Kovel, J. (1970). *White racism: A psychohistory.* New York: Vintage.

Lambert, W. (1987). The fate of old country values in a new land: A cross-national study of child rearing. *Canadian Journal of Psychology, 28,* 9–20.

Lopez, S. R., Grover, K. P., Holland, D., Johnson, M. J., Kain, C, D., Kanel, K., Mellins, C. A., & Rhyne, M. C. (1989). Development of culturally sensitive psychotherapists. *Professional Psychology: Research and Practice, 20,* 369–376.

Massaquoio, H. J. (1993, August). The black family nobody knows. *Ebony,* pp. 28–31.

Mays, V. M., Bullock, M., Rosenzweig, M. R., & Wessells, M. (1998). Ethnic conflict: Global challenges and psychological perspectives. *American Psychologist, 53,* 737–742.

McGoldrick, M., & Giordano, J. (1996). Overview: Ethnicity and family therapy. In M. McGoldrick, J. Giordano, and J. K. Pearce (Eds.), *Ethnicity and family therapy* (2nd ed., pp. 1–27). New York: The Guilford Press.

Mitchell, H. (1971). Counseling black students: A model in response to the need for relevant counselor training programs. *The Counseling Psychologist, 2* (4), 117–122.

Negy, C., & Snyder, D. K. (1997). Ethnicity and acculturation: Assessing Mexican American couples' relationships using the Marital Satisfaction Inventory-Revised. *Psychological Assessment, 9,* 414–421.

Negy, C., & Woods, D. J. (1992). A note on the relationship between acculturation and socioeconomic status. *Hispanic Journal of Behavioral Sciences, 14,* 248–251.

Nwadiora, E. (1996). Nigerian families. In M. McGoldrick, J. Giordano, & J. K. Pearce (Eds.) *Ethnicity and family therapy* (2nd ed., pp. 129–140), New York: The Guilford Press.

Ponterotto, J. G., & Pedersen, P. B. (1993). *Preventing prejudice: A guide for counselors and educators.* Sage Publications, Newbury Park, CA.

Racial Slayings. (1996, February 12). *USA Today,* p. 3A.

Rogers, J. D., Spencer, J., & Uyangoda, J. (1998). Sri Lanka: Political violence and ethnic conflict. *American Psychologist, 53,* 771–777.

Rogler, L. H., Malgady, R. G., Costantino, G., & Blumenthal, R. (1987). What do culturally sensitive mental health services mean? *American Psychologist, 42,* 565–570.

Russo, N. F., Olmedo, E. L., Stapp, J., & Fulcher, R. (1981). Women and minorities in psychology. *American Psychologist, 36,* 1315–1363.

Sattler, J. M. (1977). The effects of therapist-client racial similarity. In A. S. Gurman & A. M. Razin (Eds.), *Effective psychotherapy: A handbook of research* (pp. 252–290). Elmsford, NY: Pergamon.

Smith, D. N. (1998). The psychological roots of genocide: Legitimacy and crisis in Rwanda. *American Psychologist, 53,* 743–753.

Soto, E. (1983). Sex-role traditionalism and assertiveness in Puerto Rican women living in the United States. *Journal of Community Psychology, 11,* 346–354.

Stevens, E. P. (1973). Machismo and marianismo. *Society, 10,* 57–63.

Sue, D. W. (1993). Confronting ourselves: The white and racial/ethnic-minority researcher. *The Counseling Psychologist, 21,* 244–249.

Sue, D. W., & Sue, D. (1990). *Counseling the culturally different: Theory and practice* (2nd Ed.). John Wiley & Sons: New York.

Sue, S. (1988). Psychotherapeutic services for ethnic minorities: Two decades of research findings. *American Psychologist, 43,* 301–308.

"The Rift between Blacks and Jews." (1994, February 28). *Time,* pp. 28–34.

Vacc, N. A., Wittmer, J., & DeVaney, S. B. (1988). Introduction. In N. A. Vacc, J. Wittmer, & S. B. DeVaney (Eds.) *Experiencing and counseling multicultural and diverse populations* (pp. 3–9). Muncie, IN: Accelerated Development Inc.

Wilson, J. W. (1980). *The declining significance of race: Blacks and changing American Institutions.* Chicago: The University of Chicago Press.

Yaffe, J. (1994). Institutional and racial barriers to employment equity for Hispanics. *Hispanic Journal of Behavioral Sciences, 16,* 211–229.

Yee, Y. T. (1996). Difference, not prejudice, engenders intergroup tension. *American Psychologist, 51,* 267–268.

CHAPTER 22

Responding to the Challenge: Preparing Mental Health Professionals for the New Millennium

GEORGE K. HONG
MARGARET GARCIA
MARCEL SORIANO
Division of Administration and Counseling
California State University, Los Angeles
Los Angeles, California

A major challenge for mental health professionals who seek to practice effectively in the new millennium is the increasing cultural diversity of the United States population. This issue must be addressed by training programs in their curriculum, as well as by individual clinicians in their personal and professional development. This chapter examines the competencies required for effective mental health practice with culturally and linguistically diverse clients. It also explores curriculum development and training strategies for implementing these competencies, which are crucial for preparing graduate students as well as professionals to respond to the challenges posed by the demographics of the new millennium. It is written for both trainers and trainees.

I. DEMOGRAPHIC TRENDS OF THE UNITED STATES

Demographic patterns in the United States have dramatically changed throughout the 20th century and are projected to continue shifting in the next millennium. From the late 19th century to the middle of the 20th century, three-fourths

Handbook of Multicultural Mental Health: Assessment and Treatment of Diverse Populations

of all immigrants to the United States were from European countries (Fuchs, 1993). This pattern of immigration was partly a result of the geopolitics of the world at that time, especially of Europe. It was also a consequence of discriminatory immigration policies and legislation that were reflective of the blatant racism present in the social and political climate of the United States for most of that period. A cogent example was the infamous Chinese Exclusion Act passed by Congress in 1882. This act essentially prohibited all immigration from China, and was subsequently extended to other Asian groups (Uba, 1994; Wong, 1988). The pattern of immigration changed in the 1960s with the enactment of the 1965 Immigration and Nationalization Act, which established a less biased system for immigrants of all countries, regardless of race or ethnicity (Wong, 1988). Since then, about 62% of the immigrants have been from Asia and Latin America (Fuchs, 1993). In 1980, 85% of all immigrants were Asian and Hispanic, whereas less than 6% were European.

The Hispanic population has demonstrated to be the fastest growing community in terms of numbers, with 9 million in 1970, 14.6 million in 1980, and 22.4 million in 1990. The Asian/Pacific Islander American population was the fastest growing group in terms of rate of increase. It has slightly more than doubled from 1.4 million in 1970, to 3.5 million in 1980, and again more than doubled to 7.3 million in 1990 (U.S. Bureau of the Census, 1993). Americans of Hispanic origin are projected to replace African Americans as the largest minority by the first two decades of the 21st century (U.S. Bureau of the Census, 1997).

The projections for the major racial groups in the United States Census are shown in Table I. In reading this table, it should be noted that Americans of "Hispanic origin" may include people of any race identified in the Census, such as White, Black, American Indian, Eskimo and Aleutian, and Asian and Pacific Islanders. In other words, the numbers in the "Hispanic origin" category overlap with those in the other racial categories. For example, in the year 2050, the projected number of White Americans is 294.6 million. However, this number is actually composed of 86.7 million White Americans who are of Hispanic origin, and 207.9 million White Americans who are not of Hispanic origin. This means that in the year 2050, White Americans who are not of Hispanic origin will make up only about 52.8% of the projected total United States population, whereas people of Hispanic origin and people in the other Census racial categories will make up the remaining 47.2%. If this predicted demographic trend continues, the current ethnic minorities, that is, Hispanics, African Americans, Asian and Pacific Islanders, and American Indian, Eskimo and Aleutian, will collectively become the numerical majority of the United States population sometime in the second half of the 21st century.

Given the cultural diversity of the United States population in the coming decades, it is increasingly likely that mental health professionals will be providing services to clients whose cultural backgrounds are different from theirs. This

TABLE 1 Projected United States Population by Race for 2000–2050[a]

Year	Total U.S. population	White	Black	American Indian, Eskimo, Aleut	Asian/Pacific Islander	Hispanic origin[b]
2000	274,634	225,532 (82.1%)	35,454 (12.9%)	2,402 (0.9%)	11,245 (4.1%)	31,366 (11.4%)
2010	297,716	239,588 (80.4%)	40,109 (13.5%)	2,754 (0.9%)	15,265 (5.1%)	41,139 (13.8%)
2020	322,742	254,887 (78.9%)	45,075 (14.0%)	3,129 (1.0%)	19,651 (6.1%)	52,652 (16.3%)
2030	346,899	269,046 (77.6%)	50,001 (14.4%)	3,515 (1.0%)	24,337 (7.0%)	65,570 (18.9%)
2040	369,980	281,720 (76.1%)	55,094 (14.9%)	3,932 (1.1%)	29,235 (7.9%)	80,164 (21.7%)
2050	393,931	294,615 (74.8%)	60,592 (15.4%)	4,371 (1.1%)	34,352 (8.7%)	96,508 (24.5%)

[a] In thousands and as percentage of total population.

[b] Persons of Hispanic origin may be of any race; numbers overlap with counts in the other four racial categories.

Source: U.S. Bureau of the Census, 1997, middle series projections.

issue goes beyond the differences between ethnic majority and ethnic minority populations. Rather, it involves mental health professionals of any cultural background who may be called on to provide mental health services to clients of other cultural backgrounds. As such, cultural proficiency is an imperative in the training of all mental health professionals regardless of their cultural heritage.

II. ETIC AND EMIC APPROACHES TO MULTICULTURAL CLINICAL SERVICES

Although there is general consensus among the major mental health disciplines concerning the importance of cultural sensitivity in clinical services, the actual application of cultural considerations into psychological theory and practice has been the focus of debate.

A. THE ETIC VERSUS EMIC DEBATE

Until recently, most training institutions prepared mental health professionals to apply universal methods of assessment, therapy and counseling to clients from diverse cultural backgrounds. Theories of personality development have been thought to be universal in nature, and therefore therapeutic approaches stemming from such theories should have wide applications. Generally, this is known as the etic approach to multicultural psychotherapy and counseling (Fukuyama, 1990). The etic approach does not disregard differences across cultures, it simply focuses on the common themes as they relate to counseling and psychotherapy. Culture or worldview is regarded as just one among many factors to consider in providing mental health services to a client. Proponents of this approach assert that minor modifications are sufficient to account for cultural differences in clients. In contrast, the emic approach asserts that psychotherapy and counseling must be practiced within the context of a particular culture (Locke, 1990). This approach seeks to make major adjustments in theories and techniques in therapeutic practices across cultural groups, or even seeks to develop culturally specific theories and techniques. Although it may be interesting to go deeper into the theoretical issues fueling the debate between the proponents of the etic versus emic approaches, we think it is more practical for us to examine their merits in terms of their actual impact on clinical training and practice.

B. LIMITATIONS OF ETIC AND EMIC APPROACHES

As most mental health professionals experienced in working with ethnic minorities would know, methods based on the extreme position that the Western mainstream model of psychotherapy is universal are simply too general to be practical. In addition, when translated into practice, the etic approach runs the risk of underestimating the overarching effect cultural frameworks have on every aspect of mental health services (Hong & Ham, 1994). These include conceptualization of mental health and illness, perception and expectation of mental health agencies and professionals, symptom manifestation, help-seeking behavior, therapist–client relationship, therapeutic goals, strategies, and process, among others. By treating culture simply as one among many other factors to consider, mental health professionals utilizing the etic approach could overlook the salience of culture in many of these critical areas. Indeed, as reflected in the curricula of some training programs, this approach may result in minimum attention being given to cultural competence. For example, cultural issues in mental health services are covered in a single "multicultural" course, and the content is seldom, if ever, emphasized or given further elaboration in other clinical courses. This, in actuality, perpetuates the status quo, and proves to be inadequate in preparing mental health professionals to meet the needs reflected in the new demographics of the United States in the coming years.

In contrast, emphasizing that all therapeutic transactions, and in fact all human perceptions and social interactions, occur within the context of culture, the emic approach alerts the clinician to the impact of culture in all aspects of mental health services. In particular, it highlights the importance for the clinician to be aware of his or her own culture and worldview, and to take the client's culture and worldview into objective consideration, in defining the presenting problem as well as the intervention strategies. This is especially crucial when clinicians are providing service to clients from cultural backgrounds different from themselves. For example, clinicians must make every effort to "see" how the client might behave and reason in certain ways as related to the identified problem. Unless the clinician tries to "walk" in the client's shoes and perceive the situation through the client's lenses, the emic perspective would indicate that one is not professionally able to really understand the client's problems or come up with the best or most appropriate interventions. The emic approach challenges one to *think ethnic* in order to fully appreciate a client's frame of reference.

Yet, when taken to the extreme, the emic position also raises practical concerns. The generic labels Hispanic Americans, Asian Pacific Americans, Native Americans, African Americans, as well as White Americans actually cover many different ethnic groups from numerous cultures and subcultures all over the world. For example, in Los Angeles county, there are 90 major languages, or 240 languages and dialects, spoken by the students in the public schools (Los Angeles County Office of Education, 1994). This is reflective of the cultural and ethnic diversity of the region. If the emic approach is taken to mean culture-specific mental health services for each ethnic group, it will basically be impossible to provide culturally responsive services for such diverse populations. The potential list of cultures to study will also become an insurmountable hurdle for professionals and students. It may even lead to the erroneous belief that because in-depth understanding of specific cultures is essential for cultural proficiency, then one might be better off by solely focusing on serving clients from one's own cultural heritage, as there are too many cultures to learn and too much complexity within each culture to master. Instead of promoting cultural competence, this position can actually result in a form of ethnic segregation in the profession, with clinicians from each ethnic group working primarily within their own group. For example, only Asian Americans might feel confident enough to study mental health services for the Asian American groups, only Hispanic Americans might feel confident enough to study Hispanic groups, and the same for African Americans, Native Americans, White Americans, and so on. In fact, we have already noticed this tendency in the field from some students and professionals of both ethnic minority and majority backgrounds. They feel too intimidated by the challenges of multiculturalism, and prefer to retreat to their own ethnic communities. Indeed, overemphasizing cultural diversity and uniqueness can become an insurmountable barrier and a disservice to the cause of multiculturalism in mental health services. It may discourage professionals and students from truly developing the cultural proficiency required for effective practice in a multicultural society, where they will be expected to serve clients from diverse ethnic backgrounds, rather than treating clients exclusively from their own ethnic communities.

C. AN INTEGRATED ETIC–EMIC APPROACH

Actually, the etic and emic approaches are not necessarily mutually exclusive, especially from an applied perspective. One can combine the most practical elements of each approach to formulate a training model that includes general, universal techniques as well as specific skills relevant to specific cultural groups that the particular mental health professionals are likely to encounter. This integrated approach includes skills for communicating across cultures and efforts to sensitize clinicians to be aware of differences in worldviews, values, norms, styles of communication and social interaction, and group experiences, among others. Furthermore, while acknowledging the diversity of the many ethnic groups constituting the population of the United States, we also need to recognize that there are commonalities that justify discussing certain groups under a more general framework. This makes the task of cultural proficiency development more manageable for both trainers and trainees. We will elaborate on this issue at a later point.

Integration of the etic and emic approaches involves learning about the general clinical principles but, at the same time, viewing the clinical method as fundamentally personal. Any relevant information is applied with regard to the uniqueness of the cultural context and the personal situation of the client. There are at least two aspects of the clinical issue that need to be considered. First, the issues presented by a client are fundamentally personal to the client, irrespective of whomever else may share the problem. For example, an adolescent girl suffering from anorexia nervosa will grapple with issues surrounding weight gain and body image. Despite the fact that many other young women may be facing these same issues, the problem is unique within this adolescent's own personal experiences. The second aspect concerns the client's specific life context or situation. How does the clinician define the context or gain understanding of the situation from the client's perspective? In the example of the anorexic adolescent, the clinician will need to have an understanding of her sociocultural context, investigate her support system, obstacles, assets, and skills. Yet, recognizing a support system across cultures is challenging. A naive clinician may fail to acknowledge the opportunities for support within a particular culture, and may unintentionally misdirect the adolescent in coping with her own self-image, her physical health, and her family's values and norms regarding eating habits and thin-body ideals. Mental health professionals require skills in the applications of science to the cultural context, and a thorough understanding of science and scientific values (Trierweiler & Stricker, 1998). Thus, in working with this adolescent, a mental health professional needs to understand the general psychological and health issues concering anorexia nervosa, a subject matter on the etic level. At the same time, on the emic level, the clinician also needs to understand the adolescent's problem in her own cultural context, and from her own personal perspective. The effective mental health professional will develop situation- and context-specific hypotheses, collect data based on observations and interactions with the client in the client's social environmental context, and employ techniques derived from general clinical principles and adapted to the client's specific cultural context. This, in essence, is what we advocate as the integrated approach utilizing both the etic and emic perspectives. This balanced approach presents the subject matter of multicultural mental health services in a more attainable and practical format. It serves as a viable method for cultural proficiency training, which both trainers and trainees find effective.

III. COMMONALITIES AMONG DIVERSITIES

In the United States, a growing challenge to the provision of culturally appropriate mental health services is the fast growing cultural and ethnic diversity documented and projected in the Census data. Indeed, many cultures and subcultures exist within the general labels Asian American, Hispanic American, African American, Native American, as well as White and other American populations. This is further complicated by socioeconomic differences within ethnic groups, and the mixture of particular ethnic cultures with mainstream United States culture over time. As such, determining which cultures and cultural elements to include in training is an ambitious endeavor in itself. Again, our integrated etic–emic approach can be applied to address this situation concerning within-group differences by identifying ethnic groups that share sufficient cultural commonalities to be discussed under a general label, while at the same time, alerting students and clinicians to the possible differences within each general grouping. We will illustrate this with examples from the Asian American and Hispanic American populations.

A. Asian Americans

The term Asian/Pacific Islander Americans is used by the U.S. Census Bureau to denote over 51 groups of people. Among these, 30 are Asians and 21 are Pacific Islanders. The ten largest Asian groups are identified in the Census. They include, in descending order by size, Chinese, Filipino, Japanese, Indian, Korean, Vietnamese, Cambodian, Hmong, Laotian, and Thai. Twenty other smaller Asian groups are usually listed as "other Asians," including an "Asian-not specified" category. The Pacific Islander groups identified in the Census include Hawaiian, Samoan, and Guamian, whereas eight other groups are typically listed as "Other Pacific Islanders." In a cultural competence training program, the first step is to recognize that Asian Americans and Pacific Islander Americans need to be discussed as separate groups due to the differences in their cultural heritage. Their combination under a general label is simply a matter of bureaucratic convenience.

Looking at Asian Americans alone, one has to recognize that many of the countries in Asia share common cultural traditions. Historically, China in the East and India in the South were the two centers of civilization in the region. Their cultures strongly influenced those of their neighbors and other countries in Asia. As such, instead of discussing the cultures of each individual Asian American group, it is reasonable to discuss them under the general labels East Asian, South Asian, and Southeast Asian, the latter group often reflecting differing degrees of East and South Asian cultural heritage. It should be emphasized that we are talking of cultural traditions rather than political entities or nations. For example, no researcher or scholar will deny the fact that the cultures of China, Korea, and Japan all share the core influence of Confucianism, Buddhism, and Taoism. However, this is very different from saying that a Chinese is "just the same" as a Japanese or a Korean, or vice versa. Countries belonging to the same cultural heritage still have their individual national pride, as well as a history of wars, conflicts, or rivalries. Many people from these countries will likely find it to be offensive to be considered a national of another country, if done deliberately. Herein lies the sensitivity of cultural competence training. On one hand, we can discuss common cultural elements shared by different groups. On the other hand, we need to be sensitive to national and ethnic pride, especially as professed by immigrants and their descendants in the United States. Sometimes, the insistence in being identified as distinct groups rather than being given general labels is a result of a common desire for ethnic recognition rather than an indication of major cultural differences.

Until recently, the term Asian American, especially in the mental health literature, referred mainly to East Asians, such as Chinese Americans, Japanese Americans, and Korean Americans. These three were among the largest "visible" Asian groups with a long history of presence in the United States. Asian Indian Americans were not included as "Asian" in the Census until 1980, and Southeast Asians did not arrive in large numbers until the 1980s. The number of Filipino Americans also increased significantly during this period. Being the more "Americanized" group of all Asian immigrants, Filipino Americans were historically not given much attention in the discussion of cultural adaptation in mental health services for Asian Americans. Although overall, the East Asian groups still represent the vast majority of Asian Americans, it is now crucial to include a discussion of the South Asian groups, as well as that of Southeast Asian groups. It is also important to identify the cultural heritage of the Philippines as the most westernized of the Asian countries, sharing the influence of Spanish and American cultures, and those of neighboring Asian countries.

In addition to the major cultural traditions of Asia, it is necessary to examine the issue of traditional Asian cultures versus contemporary Asian cultures as practiced there today (Hong & Ham, 1994). This should also include regional differences, especially between the metropolitan or major urban centers, which are usually more westernized, versus the rural areas, which are usually more traditional. It is also important to discuss Asian cultures versus Asian American cultures, with the latter often reflecting a mixture of Asian and mainstream cultures.

As applied to actual training, we can introduce the subject matter of Asian American mental health issues by identifying the major groups covered by the generic label Asian Americans, and discuss the usefulness of this label as used in different contexts. The major cultural traditions, namely East Asian, South Asian, and Southeast Asian can then be discussed in general, along with the precautions on regional differences or adaptation to United States society. This will give students and trainees the foundation to go deeper into specific groups as warranted by their professional work. Depending on the nature or purpose of the training program, the presentations and discussions can cover details on specific groups that the trainees are more likely to encounter, for instance, due to the demographics of the geographical region where they will be practicing. Trainees can also be instructed to read or research further on issues relating to particular Asian American groups in which they are personally interested, or with which they anticipate working. In this manner, rather than being over-whelmed by the diversity among Asian Americans, trainees will find the subject matter more palatable and useful.

B. HISPANIC AMERICANS

As used in the U.S. Census, Americans of "Hispanic origin" can be of any race. For example, the 22.4 million Americans of Hispanic origin reported in the 1990 Census includes 20.4 million Whites, 1.2 million Blacks, 0.3 million American Indian, Eskimo, or Aleutian, 0.5 million Asians and Pacific Islanders (U.S. Bureau of the Census, 1997). The three major groups of Americans of Hispanic origin identified in the Census are Mexican, Puerto Rican, and Cuban, with Mexican Americans being by far the largest, making up about 64% of the Hispanic American population (Paniagua, 1998). The term "Other Hispanic" encompasses 13 other groups under the subcategories of Dominican, Central American, and South American, plus an additional "all other Hispanic origin." Outside of Census definitions, language, family name, or ancestry are usually the determinants for the label of Hispanic (Paniagua, 1998). In the literature and mass media, the term Hispanic is often used interchangeably with Latino. However, there are some who prefer the term Latino, feeling that Hispanic carries colonial connotations. While acknowledging their preference, the term Hispanic is used here in order to be consistent with the language used in the Census data.

Approaching the issue from the perspective of culture rather than races or countries of origin, Robinson (1998) identified 17 major Hispanic subcultures among Hispanics residing in the United States. In California, four major groups are immigrant Mexicans, middle-class Mexicans, barrio dwellers, and Central Americans of Pico Union. In Texas, Mexican Americans distinguish themselves from the California Mexicans, with the largest Latino population living in South Texas. In Houston, Mexican and Central Americans make up 28% of the pop-ulation, and Mayan Indians of Guatemala stand out as a separate subculture. Robinson (1998) indicates that Chicago Hispanics are more diverse in represen-tation than in New York or Los Angeles, with the largest groups being Mexican and Puerto Rican followed by Ecuadorans, Guatemalans, and Cubans. In Mi-ami, Cubans, Nicaraguans, and other South Americans make up about 60% of the population and carry strong political and economic influence. "Neoyorquinos" are the Puerto Rican, Dominican, and Columbian groups that form the majority of the Latino population in New York. Finally, Robinson (1998) identifies the descendants of the original Spanish conquistadors living in New Mexico and the migrant workers in United States farming communities as distinct subcultures among Hispanic Americans.

In addition to the above differentiation in cultures and subcultures among Hispanics in the United States, mental health professionals who want to be culturally competent with Hispanic American clients must also recognize the importance of age, gender, socioeconomic class, religion, generational status, immigration, and acculturation. In particular, skin color is a significant factor, as darker skinned Hispanics are more likely to experience racism than lighter skinned Hispanics within mainstream White American, as well as within Hispanic American settings (Comas-Diaz, 1998).

The extensive heterogeneity coupled with the definite apparent commonalities within the Hispanic population again highlight the need of our integrated approach utilizing both the etic and emic perspectives. In introducing the topic of Hispanic American mental health services, we can start by identifying the major groups covered by the generic label Hispanic Americans, and discuss their distribution in various parts of the United States. While acknowledging and reviewing the diversity among the Hispanic American population, the discussion can focus more on the larger groups such as Mexican, Puerto Rican, and Cuban Americans, along with groups that students and trainees are most likely to encounter in their geographical region. The major cultural elements common to many Hispanic groups can then be discussed in general, along with the precautions on differences based on countries of origin, socioeconomic considerations, and degree of acculturation to mainstream United States society, among others. In general, there are a number of sociocultural factors concerning Hispanic American clients that we can discuss with students and trainees. Some of these factors are common for working with any ethnic group where diversity exists in English language acquisition and level of acculturation into mainstream U.S. society. Within Hispanic groups, it is also important for clinicians to be prepared to work with the clients' religious and folk beliefs. The clinician who dismisses the role of the folk healer presents an example of the limitations of insight into the emic perspective, and therefore fails to understand the client's support system.

Students and trainees are not expected to understand the total belief systems within the Mexican, Puerto Rican, Cuban, or Dominican cultures. What is important, however, is to recognize that clients will have personal backgrounds enriched with a wide variety of spiritual beliefs that should not be severed from the clinical protocol. Likewise, students and trainees should be informed of culturally embedded concepts such as machismo (physical strength, masculinity, aggressiveness), *familismo* (family), and *ataques de nervios* (nervous attacks) versus being *loco* (crazy) (Paniagua, 1998). Furthermore, they need to be prepared to face the dilemma they will encounter when dealing with specific clinical issues in the context of cultural values. For example, suppose a man who has migrated to the United States from a Latin American country experiences symptoms associated with posttraumatic stress disorder. Suppose further that the client was a victim of natural disaster such as severe flooding. The clinician must take into account the personal and cultural belief systems held by the client and avoid addressing the problem solely as a reaction to flooding. It is quite possible the client may not view the natural disaster as random and unprovoked by his own behavior. In this case, a clinician who is open and willing to address the client's recurrent feelings of distress in the context of a spiritual belief system will likely be more effective in helping the client. Furthermore, the client might also be blaming himself for failing to take care of his family in this disaster. Such feelings must also be understood and addressed within his cultural context.

Understanding the general sociocultural factors common to many Hispanic American groups will give students and trainees the foundation to go deeper into specific groups as warranted by their professional work. Again, they can be instructed to read or research further on issues relating to particular Hispanic American groups in which they are personally interested, or with whom they anticipate working. The training can also cover specific groups in greater detail, depending on the needs of the trainees or the nature or purpose of the training program. In this manner, the combined etic and emic approach will help to make the subject matter more attainable and less overwhelming for students and trainees.

C. GENERAL CONSIDERATIONS

In approaching the subject of cultural proficiency training, it is important to bear in mind that the general ethnic/racial labels used in the U.S. Census as well as in many textbooks typically include groups that share commonalities as well as diversities. The previous discussion is simply an illustration of the issues using the Asian American groups and the Hispanic American groups as examples. The same observations can be made of other ethnic/cultural groups. For instance, in mental health services for African Americans, clinicians need to be aware of the differences in values, norms, and expectations due to socioeconomic group differences, as well as the differences among new immigrants versus those who have been in the United States for generations, in addition to regional differences and other considerations. The same is true for Native Americans, which, far from being a single cultural group, is a general label referring to about 550 federally recognized nations, tribes, bands, clans, or communities, speaking a variety of tribal languages, with a number of different cultural traditions (Axelson, 1999).

The White American population is also composed of diverse ethnicities. In addition to people from Western Europe, this term also includes people from other areas, cultures, or ethnic backgrounds. Some of the White American subgroups frequently mentioned in the literature are Jewish Americans, Italian Americans, Polish Americans, and Appalachian Americans. Besides these groups, the term White Americans also includes, among others, people from other Eastern European countries, the Middle East, and the former U.S.S.R. Immigrants from these regions constitute a growing presence in some areas of the United States. As such, mental health professionals need to understand the differences among the various White American subgroups, as well as the general mainstream White population. In addition, socioeconomic issues and regional subcultures within the United States are important considerations.

In view of such diversities among the U.S. population, the integrated etic–emic approach offers a practical strategy for cultural proficiency training. This approach presents the commonalities in the cultural orientation of the groups encompassed by the general ethnic categories, while at the same time, alerting the mental health professional to the possible diversities among them, and focusing more on the specific groups with which one is most likely to work.

As applied to actual clinical practice, etic principles help mental health professionals find a common ground from which to begin a professional journey into the lives of their clients as fellow human beings and cultural beings. However, it is important for the clinician to move from a general approach to a more specific, emic approach that recognizes the client's specific cultural experiences. Similarly, in the context of professional training, starting from an etic perspective can help students and trainees develop a firm grasp of general clinical principles that they will subsequently learn to adapt to particular cultures through an emic perspective. Emphasizing an exclusive emic approach too early in a training program may simply force students and trainees to narrow their scope of competence to one or two specific groups within a general ethnic/ cultural category. This will not permit them to take full advantage of cultural commonalities that make it possible for them to generalize their knowledge to other groups sharing a similar cultural heritage. The integrated etic–emic approach starts with the general principles of counseling and therapy as well as human development; but at the same time, alerts students and trainees that each of these principles must be considered and applied within the context of the client's culture. As each principle is introduced, the trainer uses examples from one or two cultures other than mainstream White culture to illustrate its relevance or application in different sociocultural contexts. However, the more detailed discussion of applying these principles to specific ethnic/cultural groups is held off until students and trainees have a firm understanding of the general principles. In sum, the integrated etic–emic perspective is a practical approach that provides students, trainees, and clinicians a general view of human similarities and the sociocultural issues of the major ethnic/cultural groups, while helping them to understand the nuances of both between-group and within-group differences as well as similarities.

IV. SPECIFIC MULTICULTURAL CURRICULUM AND TRAINING ISSUES

Having examined the strategy for addressing general cultural characteristics and specific group differences, we will now consider particular issues relating to curriculum and training cultural proficiency. Although this discussion is focused more on preservice training in university programs, many of the issues discussed here are also applicable to in-service training or professional development of clinicians who are practicing in the field.

Cultural proficiency is a continuum rather than a dichotomous "all-or-nothing" professional skill or personal quality. One important consideration in training is that course work must be designed to meet the level of competence from which the students or trainees are starting. It must also be geared towards a level that they can be realistically expected to achieve at the conclusion of training. There are two very useful paradigms in the literature for conceptualizing the levels of cultural competence: (a) the cultural competence continuum, and (b) the three domains of multicultural competence. From our perspective, these paradigms can be used to complement each other in curriculum and training.

A. THE CULTURAL COMPETENCE CONTINUUM

Among the most useful tools developed to help one understand and assess cultural proficiency is the cultural competence continuum by Terry Cross (Cross, Bazron, Dennis, & Issacs, 1989), which can be applied to institutions as well as individuals. This paradigm defines six positions along a continuum, ranging from cultural destructiveness on the negative end, to cultural incapacity, cultural blindness, cultural precompetence, cultural competence, and finally cultural proficiency on the positive end. It should be noted that these six levels are not discrete steps. Each level can have many substeps that comprise numerous positions along the continuum. The six levels are just convenient labels describing the major positions along this continuum. Here we will discuss the application of this model to individuals.

Cultural destructiveness is on the most negative end of this scale. It is represented by attitudes, beliefs, and behaviors that are inherently damaging to targeted cultures and to the individuals within those cultures. Individuals in this position are typically those espousing racism, believing that a dominant race and culture is superior and seeking to suppress or eradicate other "lesser" cultures. They act to favor the dominant group while denigrating and discriminating against others. Although individuals who consciously and blatantly endorse racism are unlikely to enroll in a cultural proficiency course, there may be some who enter a mental health training program without realizing that cultural proficiency is an integral component of clinical skills. The more common situation, though, are individuals who are not consciously aware of the cultural destructive implications of their views and attitudes. Indeed, we often come across students who acknowledged that they did not realize they were on this end of the scale until they applied the continuum to themselves. In this regard, the cultural competence continuum is a valuable tool for self-examination in a training program.

Cultural incapacity is the next position on the continuum. It is manifested by individuals who do not intentionally seek to be culturally destructive, but still demonstrate an extremely biased position, believing in the inherent superiority of the dominant group, and often holding a paternalistic or patronizing attitude over minority groups. For example, they may uphold discriminatory policies and practices or communicate subtle messages to minority people that they are not valued or welcomed. They commonly hold lower expectations for people from minority backgrounds. Occasionally, these individuals may consider themselves "open-minded" and "ready" to work with minority clients, without realizing their patronizing attitude. In this regard, it is sometimes quite difficult for an individual to realize that one is on the cultural incapacity level of the cultural competence continuum. Careful self-reflection along with constructive and supportive feedback from others, will be helpful for individuals at this level to recognize their position.

Cultural blindness is the level most often submitted as the socially desirable position by well-intentioned but uninformed individuals who profess that "people are the same" and should therefore just be treated equally. What is significant here is the lack of knowledge displayed by culturally blind individuals who know little or nothing about the importance of culture, ethnicity, language, and traditions as significant elements in one's personal and social development. Often couched with humanistic terms like "human being," "person," or similar words, the culturally blind position advises one to ignore color and ethnicity, and merely see "people as people." Also important is the ethnocentric perception that values and behaviors of the dominant culture are universal and shared by all. This leads to clinical practices in which the traditional approaches designed for the mainstream cultural group are assumed to be applicable across the board to all other cultural and socioeconomic groups. Based on our own experience, cultural blindness and cultural precompetence, the next level on the continuum, are commonly found among students and trainees in mental health training programs.

Cultural precompetence is significant in that, at this level, individuals become aware of their own personal limitations in cross-cultural communication and relationships. These individuals desire to provide fair and equitable treatment to everyone, but find themselves frustrated at not knowing exactly what is possible or how to proceed. Individuals at this level sometimes may engage in a single act of cultural responsiveness, and assuming this to be sufficient, develop a false sense of accomplishment. Conversely, they may be discouraged by a single failed attempt to reach out to clients of other ethnic backgrounds and feel reluctant to try again. In working with students and trainees at this level, the faculty or trainers should be sensitive to their good intentions and be supportive both in directing them to take a more comprehensive view of cultural responsiveness and in encouraging those who have experienced failures in their past attempts to be culturally responsive. Care should be taken to approach their concerns in a positive and constructive manner, ensuring that they do not feel belittled or criticized for what they have achieved or failed to achieve so far in their attempts.

Cultural competence is exemplified by individuals who value cultural diversity and whose acceptance and respect of differences propel them to continue their own personal self-assessment and self-development regarding cultural knowledge. The level of sophistication and awareness of the dynamics of difference are continuously developing, with the individual beginning to accumulate a critical mass of rewarding cross-cultural encounters where he or she successfully managed the dynamics of difference. Culturally competent mental health professionals are cognizant of the need for cultural adaptations in their beliefs, attitudes, policies, and practices in order to provide effective service to diverse communities. They are sensitive to the needs of culturally diverse clients and continuously seek to expand their cultural knowledge and skills. This is the level for which mental health training programs should aim, in preparing their students and trainees to work in the multicultural society of the United States.

Cultural proficiency is the most positive end of the scale and the most advanced stage of competence. This level is demonstrated by persons who hold culture in high esteem and are committed to continue to learn and contribute to the knowledge base of culturally competent practice. Mental health professionals at this level are knowledgeable about cultural issues and seek to conduct research, develop new approaches based on diverse cultures, and disseminate new information on culturally responsive services. They engage in, and also seek to promote, culturally appropriate services to clients. For them, cultural proficiency is not an end point. Rather, it is a lifelong journey of professional and personal development. Cultural proficiency involves valuing lifelong learning, and training programs should inspire in their graduates.

In sum, the cultural competence continuum is a useful framework for training programs to gauge the needs of their students and trainees and to define realistic learning goals, guiding and encouraging students and trainees to move forward onto the more advanced levels. A training program can also apply this framework for self-evaluation to determine to what extent it is culturally responsive on the institutional level. Finally, we also want to encourage students and trainees to utilize this model as a means of self-exploration and development. It is important to remember that cultural proficiency does not stop with graduation from a training program or with the attainment of professional licensure. It is a lifelong learning process that a responsible mental health professional will pursue.

B. THREE DOMAINS OF MULTICULTURAL COMPETENCE

The second useful paradigm for cultural competence is presented by a number of authors in the field of multicultural counseling and psychotherapy (Arredondo et al., 1996; Pedersen, 1988; Sue, Arredondo, & McDavis, 1992; Sue et al., 1982), often referred to as "Pedersen's Model of Training." This approach identifies three domains in cultural competence: awareness, knowledge, and skills. These three domains or dimensions can be conceptualized as developmental levels with trainees progressing from one stage to another. They can also be operationalized into specific goals and objectives for a multicultural training curriculum (Arredondo et al., 1996; Sue et al., 1992). We will examine their applications here.

1. Awareness Level

The first stage or domain is *awareness,* which is also called the beliefs and attitudes dimension. Here, students and trainees develop awareness of their own cultural heritage and values, as well as their negative emotional reactions, preconceived notions, biases, and stereotypes about other ethnic groups. They also learn to respect their clients' beliefs, values, and culturally based helping practices (Arredondo et al., 1996; Sue et al., 1992).

In our experience, most of the students in graduate programs have some ideas about cultural beliefs and values, especially about biases, stereotypes, and discriminatory practices in the United States. What they often need here is to approach these issues explicitly and subjectively to examine how their culture is affecting their perceptions of other cultures, as well as the extent to which they are aware of the values, beliefs, and practices of other ethnic groups. This applies to students of all ethnic groups, majority as well as minorities. Thus, in a multicultural course, one needs to address issues on the awareness level before moving on to the knowledge stage.

One useful activity for the development of awareness is to have students examine themselves via the cultural competence continuum (Cross et al., 1989) discussed in the previous section. This can be done privately and anonymously so that an individual will not feel embarrassed or defensive in exploring and identifying one's position on the scale. We have been impressed by the number of students who frankly admitted that this exercise was instrumental in helping them realize their positions on the negative levels of the scale. They found the continuum very helpful in identifying their blind spots and helping them set new goals for their cultural competency development. Another useful exercise is to have students research and discuss their families and cultures of origin (Hong & Ham, 1994). Besides awareness of one's own cultural heritage, the class discussions can also help students become aware of the differences in values, beliefs, and practices of diverse cultures.

2. Knowledge Level

The second stage or dimension is knowledge. Here, students and trainees acquire specific knowledge of their own cultures, as well as the cultures and life experiences of their clientele, including community issues concerning specific ethnic minority groups. They develop knowledge about cross-cultural communication, as well as cultural issues in assessment, clinical intervention, and the institutional barriers to mental health services (Arredondo et al., 1996; Sue et al., 1992).

Typically, the syllabus of a multicultural course at the graduate level is focused on the awareness and knowledge levels and covers issues concerning the major ethnic minority groups in the United States, namely, African Americans, Hispanic Americans, Native Americans, and Asian/Pacific Islander Americans, sometimes including the ethnic minority groups within the White population. Given the amount of information, there is usually insufficient class time to discuss all the topics in one semester or quarter. As a result, many issues are often left as literature research and reading assignments. This is not a preferable way to approach this domain, as class discussions have an important role in clarifying issues and exposing students to first-hand information provided by students of diverse ethnic backgrounds. In order to prepare mental health professionals to practice effectively in the culturally diverse United States of the new millennium, we want to encourage training programs to extend their multicultural course to at least two semesters and maybe more. This would allow sufficient class time to address all the essential topics concerning the different minority groups, using the integrated etic–emic approach discussed earlier. This extension is justifiable in light of the new demographics.

In addition to reading the literature, direct exposure to minority cultures and communities is also a crucial part of training on the knowledge level. This can be done by organizing visits to community agencies, especially mental health clinics. Students can also be assigned to visit and observe specific ethnic communities or neighborhoods, relating their observations to reading assignments (Hong & Ham, 1994). Guest lectures by individuals from different ethnic backgrounds and films depicting life experiences of ethnic minorities can be also used as supplements or alternatives. These alternatives may be necessary for training programs located in geographical areas where one or more of the major minority groups do not have community agencies for students to visit.

3. Skills Level

The third stage or dimension is skills. Here, students and trainees develop specific clinical skills for assessment, counseling, and psychotherapy with clients from minority cultures. Students find appropriate resources for consultation and referrals for their clients. They also learn to provide intervention at the institutional level (Arredondo et al., 1996; Sue et al., 1992).

Although the awareness and knowledge domains can be covered in the context of a multicultural course, competence at the skills level can be addressed later in a practicum or internship. To be proficient at this level, students need to integrate information from multicultural courses with their other clinical courses, which, ideally, have also covered specific subject matters in a multicultural context. At this stage, the students are ready for "hands-on" experience. Community agencies are ideal placement sites, as students will have the opportunity to acquire clinical experience while having further exposure to the community (Hong & Ham, 1994). For students and trainees who have difficulty working in certain community agencies due to language barriers, placement in mainstream institutions, such as public schools and college counseling centers, can be an alternative. However, we do encourage students, regardless of their ethnicities, to develop the language skills required for serving the client population they are to work with, as this is one of the competencies at the skills level (Arredondo et al., 1996; Sue et al., 1992).

At the skills level, reflective thinking is a crucial component of the training experience. This is a process that requires deliberate and focused attention on one's thoughts, words, and behaviors as well as their effects in the clinical setting. A number of activities can help students develop skills in reflective thinking, including journal writing, group discussions, case studies, and coaching. Coaching is different from supervision in that the student is guided, but not evaluated. As such, the student is more likely to take risks in sharing sensitive thoughts about a case and one's personal reactions. Students with reflective skills are more likely to develop the cognitive complexity to gain knowledge through investigating different assumptions stemming from different cultural experiences (King & Shuford, 1996). In training students at the skills level, it is important for faculty to recognize that reflectivity is not a spontaneous process. Consequently, instructions and opportunities for students to reflect should be clearly designated as activities in training programs.

In addition to reflective thinking, many practical skills have been identified to be crucial for multicultural mental health services. The following are some of the major ones discussed in the literature (Arredondo et al., 1996; Pedersen, 1988; Sue et al., 1982; Sue et al., 1992):

1. Cross-cultural communication skills, both verbal and nonverbal, including language, idioms, etiquette, customs, and the like

2. Skills in assessment, including recognition of culture-bound syndromes and cultural variations of diagnostic categories in the *DSM*, and for professionals who provide psychological testing, skills in the selection, administration, and interpretation of tests for a client of a given ethnicity

3. Skills in identifying and integrating specific cultural issues in both diagnostic and treatment formulation

4. Skills in identifying and consulting with traditional helpers in the client's ethnic community

5. Skills in applying emic approaches in assessment and treatment

6. Skills in advocating for a specific client or a client population and for interventions on the institutional level to ensure the availability of services as well as to eliminate societal or institutional conditions that are detrimental to the mental health of a specific cultural/ethnic group

7. Skills in accessing the literature, prevalence data, and other clinical information on specific racial/ethnic groups living within a given community

8. Reflective skills in monitoring one's performance and effectiveness within specific cultural contexts.

Again, these skills are best learned when there is a balance of real-life experience from fieldwork or internships, and solid theoretical background from course instructions.

C. LIFELONG PROFESSIONAL DEVELOPMENT

Cultural proficiency is a goal for lifelong professional development. Mental health professionals should continuously refine and develop their multicultural skills in order to maintain their relevance in the field. In this regard, in-service training and professional development workshops are crucial activities. The cultural competence continuum (Cross et al., 1989) and the cultural competence domains (Arredondo et al., 1996; Sue et al., 1992) are both very useful frameworks for workshop faculty and mental health professionals to evaluate their needs and to plan the curriculum. For example, we have sometimes encountered occasions where professionals may want to learn specific skills in working with a particular ethnic group, but they actually do not have sufficient knowledge concerning the group's culture or life experience. In this situation, it is necessary to step back and clarify the knowledge issues, such as the particular ethnic group's family structure and values, or their premigration, migration, and postmigration experience, before discussing specific clinical intervention skills. Indeed, trainers need to be flexible and creative in the presentation of professional development workshops so that participants can truly learn from them, rather than mechanically adopting a set of techniques without really understanding their rationale or basis.

V. CONCLUDING REMARKS

In order to provide effective services to the culturally diverse society of the United States in the new millennium, mental health professionals need to continuously assess their cultural proficiency. Although there are diversities in the many ethnic groups constituting the U.S. population, there are also commonalities among the cultural heritage of various groups. In approaching the issue of cultural competence, one should not overemphasize differences and ignore commonalties. This will lead to divisiveness, as well as a de facto ethnic segregation within the profession. As an alternative, this chapter presented an integrated etic–emic approach that acknowledges the right and the need for individual ethnic groups to be recognized, but at the same time, discusses their issues in conjunction with other groups who share a common cultural heritage. The subject matter is presented in a practical format that helps a clinician to master the general skills of working with various groups sharing common cultural elements, while learning the specific issues pertaining to particular groups with which one is most likely to work. In addition, we recommend using the cultural competence continuum and the three domains of cultural proficiency as tools for planning university course work, as well as in-service training and professional development workshops. We hope the ideas presented here will help mental health professionals face the exciting challenges posed by the demographics of the new millennium.

REFERENCES

Arredondo, P., Toporek, R., Brown, S. P., Jones, J., Locke, D. C., Sanchez, J., & Stadler, H. (1996). Operationalization of the multicultural counseling competencies. *Journal of Multicultural Counseling and Development, 24,* 42–78.

Axelson, J. A. (1999). *Counseling and development in a multicultural society* (3rd ed.). Pacific Grove, CA: Brooks/Cole.

Comas-Diaz, L. (1998). Mental health needs of Latinos with professional status. In J. G. Garcia & M. C. Zea (Eds.), *Psychological interventions and research with Latino populations* (pp. 142–165). Boston, MA: Allyn & Bacon.

Cross, T. L., Bazron, B. J., Dennis, K. W., & Issacs, M. R. (1989). *Towards a culturally competent system of care: A monograph on effective services for minority children who are severely emotionally disturbed.* Washington, DC: CASSP Technical Assistance Center, Georgetown University Child Development Center.

Fuchs, L. H. (1993). Immigration. In *New Grolier Multimedia Encyclopedia* (Version 6.03) [CD]. Danbury, CT: Grolier, Inc.

Fukuyama, M. A. (1990). Taking a universal approach to multicultural counseling. *Counselor Education and Supervision, 30,* 6–17.

Hong, G. K., & Ham, M. D. (1994). Psychotherapy and counseling for Chinese Americans: Curriculum and training issues. *Bulletin of the Hong Kong Psychological Society, 32/33,* 5–19.

King, P. M., & Shuford, B. C. (1996). A multicultural view is a more cognitively complex view: Cognitive development and multicultural education. *American Behavioral Scientist, 40*(2), 153–164.

Locke, D. C. (1990). A not so provincial view of multicultural counseling. *Counselor Education and Supervision, 30,* 18–25.

Los Angeles County Office of Education (1994). *Facts.* Los Angeles: Author.

Paniagua, F. A. (1998). *Assessing and treating culturally diverse clients: A practical guide* (2nd ed.). Thousand Oaks, CA: Sage Publications.

Pedersen, P. (1988). *A handbook for developing multicultural awareness.* Alexandria, VA: American Association for Counseling and Development.

Robinson, L. (1998, May 11). 'Hispanics' don't exist. *U.S. News and World Report, 124*(18), 26–32.

Sue, D. W., Arredondo, P., & McDavis, R. J. (1992). Multicultural competencies/standards: A pressing need. *Journal of Counseling and Development, 70*(4), 477–486.

Sue, D. W., Bernier, Y., Durran, A., Feinberg, L., Pedersen, P., Smith, E. J., & Vasquez-Nuttal, E. (1982). Position paper: Cross-cultural counseling competencies. *The Counseling Psychologist, 10,* 45–52.

Trierweiler, S. J., & Stricker, G. (1998). *The scientific practice of professional psychology.* New York: Plenum Press.

Uba, L. (1994). *Asian Americans: Personality patterns, identity, and mental health.* New York: The Guilford Press.

U.S. Bureau of the Census (1993). *Statistical abstract of the United States.* Washington, DC: Government Printing Office.

U.S. Bureau of the Census (1997). *Statistical abstract of the United States.* Washington, DC: Government Printing Office.

Wong, M. G. (1988). The Chinese American family. In C. H. Mindel, R. W. Harbenstein, & R. Wright (Eds.), *Ethnic families in America: Patterns and variations* (pp. 230–257). New York: Elsevier Scientific Publishing Co.

INDEX